ONE MORE GOOD FLIGHT

ONE MORE GOOD FLIGHT

THE AMELIA EARHART TRAGEDY

Ric Gillespie

NAVAL INSTITUTE PRESS
Annapolis, MD

Naval Institute Press
291 Wood Road
Annapolis, MD 21402

Library of Congress Cataloging-in-Publication Data

Names: Gillespie, Ric, 1947- author. | International Group for Historic
    Aircraft Recovery. Earhart Project.
Title: One more good flight : the Amelia Earhart tragedy / by Ric
    Gillespie.
Description: Annapolis, MD : Naval Institute Press, [2024] | Includes
    bibliographical references and index.
Identifiers: LCCN 2024004533 (print) | LCCN 2024004534 (ebook) | ISBN
    9781682479384 (hardcover) | ISBN 9781682479391 (ebook)
Subjects: LCSH: Earhart, Amelia, 1897-1937. | Women air pilots--United
    States--Biography. | Search and rescue operations--Pacific Area. |
    United States. Navy--Search and rescue operations. | United States.
    Coast Guard--Search and rescue operations. | BISAC: HISTORY / Modern /
    20th Century / General | BIOGRAPHY & AUTOBIOGRAPHY / Women
Classification: LCC TL540.E3 G553 2024 (print) | LCC TL540.E3 (ebook) |
    DDC 629.13092--dc23/eng/20240718
LC record available at https://lccn.loc.gov/2024004533
LC ebook record available at https://lccn.loc.gov/2024004534

♾ Print editions meet the requirements of ANSI/NISO z39.48-1992 (Permanence of Paper).
Printed in the United States of America.

32 31 30 29 28 27 26 25 24   9 8 7 6 5 4 3 2 1
First printing

All maps created by Pat Thrasher

Contents

PART ONE
The Real Amelia Earhart

PART TWO
1937: The Final Flight, the Failed Search, and Earhart's True Fate

PART THREE
Changing Mystery to History

Illustrations

Preface

Shortly before embarking on her attempt to circumnavigate the globe, Amelia Earhart confided to *Herald Tribune* aviation editor and longtime friend C. B. Allen, "I have a feeling there is just about one more good flight left in my system and I hope this trip around the world is it." Earhart's "one more good flight" ended in what would become one of history's greatest mysteries, and over the decades, dozens of books have argued for a cavalcade of solutions. None have presented proof.

Neither does this one. Proof, as a scientific principle, exists only in mathematics and logic. The validity of a proposed solution to a mystery is always a question of probability. One hundred percent is unachievable but, with sufficient supporting evidence, the probability that the answer is true can be high enough for the solution to be accepted as fact. I believe the evidence presented in this book meets that standard.

This book is the product of the Earhart Project, a thirty-four-year investigation of the Earhart tragedy by The International Group for Historic Aircraft Recovery (TIGHAR), the nonprofit foundation it is my privilege to lead. TIGHAR's inquiry differed from others in that we had no agenda. We were not out to advocate, excuse, honor, or impugn. We saw the Earhart disappearance as an aviation accident, and we reasoned the answer to its cause and outcome should be discoverable if we could find, assemble, and analyze the relevant data.

An essential part of any aviation accident investigation is the consideration of human factors, and the cultural status of the human in this case made that assessment especially difficult. Filmmaker Ken Burns has observed that iconic historical figures are often "smothered in mythology," and it is the task of the historian to liberate them from "the barnacles of sentimentality that attach." Barnacles might not be the most apt metaphor for the legends surrounding the life and loss of aviator Amelia Earhart, but no American icon has been more smothered in mythology since George Washington chopped down the cherry tree. To understand why she died, it is necessary to strip away the myths and sentimentality that have grown up over the years and examine the hard truths behind Earhart's aviation career, how her trip around the world came about, and why it went so terribly wrong.

My own professional background in aviation provided some important insights when addressing events that occurred in the context of golden age aviation. My five-thousand-plus hours of pilot-in-command time in an array of piston-powered aircraft—from open-cockpit biplanes to large, twin-radial engine aircraft similar to Earhart's Lockheed Electra—gave me a seat-of-the-pants feel for flying in the 1930s. I also had the advantage of a twelve-year career as an underwriter and accident investigator in the aviation insurance business, but uncovering the truths behind the Amelia Earhart tragedy was far beyond the capabilities of any one person.

Determining the cause and consequences of the events of July 2, 1937, was a group accomplishment by dozens of professionals from a dizzying array of scientific disciplines and volunteer researchers who dedicated untold thousands of hours, and sometimes literally risked their lives, to find and assemble the pieces of an impossibly complex jigsaw puzzle. I am immensely proud of their achievement. Each piece of the puzzle was, itself, a mystery to be solved, usually by old-fashioned detective work and forensics, but sometimes through pure dumb luck. The puzzle is not, and never will be, finished, but the picture is more than sufficiently complete to know what happened.

I received no compensation for writing this book beyond my regular remuneration as the executive director of TIGHAR. The organization holds the copyright and will receive any royalties, but the words in this narrative are mine and mine alone, as are any errors.

Acknowledgments

When a large group of people from disparate backgrounds and disciplines join together to address a project of great complexity, whether it be putting astronauts on the moon, developing a vaccine for a deadly virus, or solving a historical mystery, the total effect can be greater than the sum of its parts.

I saw this "hive mind" phenomenon demonstrated repeatedly during the Earhart Project. Many researchers had strong academic credentials, while others did not. Some spent weeks, months, or years collecting and analyzing data; others provided the skepticism and argument so crucial to unbiased investigation. Acknowledging the specific contributions of nearly two hundred individuals would take a separate volume, but a few names require special thanks and recognition.

First and foremost is my wife and cofounder of TIGHAR, Pat Thrasher. She is the first editor of everything I write. The investigation could not function without her tireless administrative attention, and the book's illustrations are a testament to her artistic skill.

Randy Jacobson's compilation and chronological databasing of U.S. government correspondence, radio messages, ships' logs, and weather reports exposed the fallacies in the official after-action reports upon which all previous theories about Earhart's fate had been based and provided us with a day-by-day, and in many cases minute-by-minute, record of what really happened.

Dan Brown and Bill Davenport worked tirelessly to gather and compare correspondence, Bureau of Air Commerce records, press reports, and photographs to track the changes and modifications to the Earhart Electra from delivery to disappearance.

Jeff Glickman's cutting-edge forensic imaging expertise coaxed crucial evidence from obscure historical photos.

Bob Brandenburg's genius in electromagnetic forensics and his encyclopedic knowledge of all things nautical turned historical records into smoking gun data.

Kenton Spading's dogged pursuit of long-lost British documents resulted in the discovery of Western Pacific High Commission File 4439, "Skeleton, human, Finding of on Gardner Island."

Karen Burns conducted forensic decomposition experiments on Nikumaroro that replaced speculation about indigenous scavengers with hard data.

Richard Jantz applied his internationally renowned expertise in forensic anthropology to the bone measurements in File 4439 and found them to be a better than 99 percent match to Earhart.

Special thanks must also go to the many organizations and agencies that performed essential analyses and services for TIGHAR.

Museums
Air Mobility Command Museum, Dover Air Force Base, Dover, DE
Military Aviation Museum, Virginia Beach, VA
National Museum of Naval Aviation, Pensacola Naval Air Station, Pensacola, FL
National Museum of the Pacific War, Fredericksburg, TX
New England Air Museum, Windsor Locks, CT
Oakland Aviation Museum, Oakland, CA
Royal New Zealand Air Force Museum, Christchurch, NZ
Smithsonian Institution National Air and Space Museum, Washington, DC
Smithsonian Institution Natural History Museum, Washington, DC
Umwanibong Cultural Centre & Museum, Tarawa, Republic of Kiribati

Laboratories
Armed Forces DNA Identification Laboratory, Frederick, MD
Federal Bureau of Investigation Laboratory, Washington, DC
Lehigh Testing Laboratories, Wilmington, DE
Massachusetts Institute of Technology, Cambridge
Massachusetts Materials Research, Inc., West Boylston
National Geospatial-Intelligence Agency, Washington, DC
National Transportation Safety Board Laboratory, Washington, DC
Pennsylvania State University, Radiation Science and Engineering Center, State College
University of Oklahoma, Ancient DNA Laboratories, Norman
University of Tennessee, Anthropology Department, Knoxville

Archives and Libraries
Davis-Monthan Aviation Field Register, Tucson, AZ
Experimental Aircraft Association Library, Oshkosh, WI
Kiribati National Archives, Tarawa, Republic of Kiribati
Library of Congress, Washington, DC
National Archives and Records Administration, College Park, MD, and San Bruno, CA
Oxford University, Rhodes House Library, Oxford, England
Public Records Office, Kew, England
Purdue University Archives and Special Collections, West Lafayette, IN
Tuvalu National Archives, Funafuti, Tuvalu
United States Air Force Historical Research Agency, Maxwell Air Force Base, AL
University of Adelaide, Adelaide, South Australia, Australia
University of Auckland, Auckland, NZ
University of California Los Angeles Film and TV Archive
University of Sydney, New South Wales, Australia

Finally, Auburn University history professor William Trimble's critique and copy editor Lisa Yambrick's edits and recommendations were of immeasurable value in making this wide-ranging work both academically sound and reader-friendly.

PART ONE

THE REAL
AMELIA EARHART

1

Plane Crazy

1927–31

In reflecting upon the life and death of her friend and fellow pilot Amelia Earhart, Florence "Pancho" Barnes wrote: "There were at that time, dozens of more competent women pilots than Amelia but because of her disappearance and all of the publicity that surrounded her last flight, she achieved her great aim, to be the most famous woman pilot. She will undoubtedly continue to hold this position—and I hope she does."[1] Barnes' prediction, and selfless wish, came true to a degree she could never have imagined.

Lost in the glare of Earhart's posthumous elevation to aviation sainthood are the other women pilots of aviation's golden age who, as much as Earhart, defied the era's systemic misogyny to prove a woman's place was in the cockpit. Forgotten is how Earhart substituted courage for competence to achieve fame, and missing is an appreciation of the unique socioeconomic environment that made it possible.

In the 1920s American women were throwing off the corsets and conventions of Victorian expectations. The Great War had taken many of them out of the kitchen and into the workplace, where they found a new sense of worth and purpose they were loath to relinquish when the boys came back from over there. In 1920 the Nineteenth Amendment gave them the right to vote, but women were still prohibited from serving on juries, driving taxicabs, and working night shifts.[2]

In 1919 Prohibition gave everyone a law to break and, beginning in 1921, Margaret Sanger's American Birth Control League made information about contraceptive techniques widely available. Speakeasies catered to "flappers" in daring fashions who smoked cigarettes, loved jazz, and popularized sexually scandalous dances like the Charleston and the Shimmy. While the 1920s roared, women demanded admission to career opportunities in traditionally male-only pursuits and professions but with little success—until a seminal event in 1927 sparked a paradigm shift in American popular culture.

America invented the flying machine in 1903 and then dropped the ball. Frustrated by government indifference and bureaucratic stonewalling by the U.S. Patent Office, in 1909 the Wright

brothers turned to France, where Wilbur Wright's flying demonstrations became a national phenomenon and inspired an explosion in aeronautical innovation. Historians have acknowledged
the Gallic dominance of aviation's infancy: "[D]uring the years before 1914 the French identified
themselves and were identified by others as the 'winged nation' par excellence. It was a Frenchman,
Louis Blériot, who was the first to fly the English Channel; and it was the French who organized the
first successful aviation competition, staged the first exhibition of aircraft, operated the first flight
training schools, and led the world before 1914 in the manufacture of airplanes."[3]

At home, aviation development stagnated. When the country entered World War I in 1917,
American pilots flew French and British aircraft. After the war, "barnstormers" flew obsolete surplus
trainers from town to town selling rides. Air circuses featured death-defying stunts and intentional
crashes. Airlines flew mostly empty airplanes, surviving entirely on government airmail contracts.

On May 20, 1927, a young, publicity-shy airmail pilot named Charles Lindbergh coaxed his
overloaded single-engine monoplane off a muddy runway on Long Island in the latest attempt to
win the $25,000 Orteig Prize for the first nonstop flight connecting New York to Paris. So far, four
Americans had died in attempts to get large, tri-motored machines off the ground with sufficient
fuel to make the flight. Twelve days earlier, French wartime aces Charles Nungesser and François
Coli had taken off from Paris with enough gas to reach New York. If the famous fliers succeeded, as
everyone (including Lindbergh) fully expected, it would further cement France's place as the world
leader in aviation, but their giant white biplane did not arrive.

As Lindbergh later wrote, "Step by step, newspaper headlines have followed Nungesser and Coli
. . . only to have them vanish like midnight ghosts."[4] A fruitless international search dominated the
headlines until Lindbergh, dubbed the Flying Fool by a skeptical press, was on his way. Millions on
both sides of the Atlantic held their breath. Thirty-three-and-a-half hours later, the *Spirit of St. Louis*
landed in Paris, and the world changed.

For Americans, Lindbergh's accomplishment was affirmation of their own exceptionalism. His
achievement was a national achievement. As proclaimed in a song that hit the airwaves two days
later, he was "Lucky, Plucky, Lindbergh, the Eagle of the U.S.A.,"[5] and the nation was suddenly
plane-crazy. In quintessentially American style, Lindbergh's fame inspired a flood of glory-hunting
would-be trans-Atlantic fliers. Some sought to (and did) beat his distance record, while others tried
to be the first to cross east to west against the prevailing winds. Another obvious prize was the dis-
tinction of being the first female to make the crossing. The woman wouldn't need to be the pilot. Just
being aboard was seen to be an incredible act of bravery; and so it was. By June 1928 five women had
tried; one was rescued at sea, one crashed on takeoff, and three had disappeared.

The sixth aspirant was Amy Guest, a fifty-five-year-old heiress who bought a tri-motored Fokker F-VII on floats and hired two experienced male aviators to fly her across the Atlantic. When her
family vetoed her participation in the flight, Guest sought a replacement who met specific qualifications. Although she was expected to do no flying, for appearance's sake, she should be a licensed
pilot. She must be good looking, be of the right type to meet with approval among polite society, and
have a good education. The unstated but most important trait was the courage to undertake such a
hazardous venture.

Publisher George Palmer Putnam found a thirty-year-old social worker who filled the bill. Her name was Amelia Earhart, and she had been an off-and-on recreational pilot since 1921. For Putnam, that she was attractive but not glamorous was a plus, and she bore an astonishing resemblance to Charles Lindbergh. She had never completed a course in higher education, but she was well-read, articulate, and scandal-free. When asked by Guest's attorney, "Why do you want to fly the Atlantic?" she answered with a question: "Why does a man ride a horse?" Nonplussed, the lawyer said, "Because he wants to, I guess." Her response: "Well, then." Asked if she wanted to be paid, she said, "No, thank you."[6] Putnam was put in charge of organizing the flight, and his shrewdness was quickly evident.

To accomplish its purpose, the Fokker need not duplicate Lindbergh's New York to Paris feat; it need only carry a female across the Atlantic Ocean. A landing anywhere in the British Isles would do the job, so the departure would be from Newfoundland, the most easterly point in North America. From there to Ireland was two thousand miles, just over half the distance flown by Lindbergh. Putnam negotiated a $10,000 agreement with the *New York Times* for the exclusive rights to Earhart's story, and he staged photo sessions in New York carefully posed to maximize her resemblance to Lindbergh, prompting the press to dub her Lady Lindy. Another deal gave Paramount News exclusive rights to newsreel coverage.[7]

The Fokker's departure from Trepassey Bay, Newfoundland, was delayed for weeks by mechanical trouble and contrary winds. When the two male fliers became discouraged and turned to drink, it was Earhart who held the project together. On June 17, 1928, pilot Wilmer Stultz finally succeeded in coaxing the overloaded tri-motor into the air. Twenty hours and forty minutes later, he, mechanic Louis Gordon, and passenger Amelia Earhart touched down in Burry Port, Wales.

Public reaction to the flight was phenomenal, with ticker-tape parades in New York and Chicago, but the lion's share of the attention was on Earhart. Both she and Putnam, each for their own reasons, saw promise in a continued relationship. For Earhart, her newfound fame and Putnam's promotional support might make aviation a profession instead of a social worker's hobby. For his part, Putnam saw a property with tremendous potential for further development.

America's sudden obsession with all things aeronautical meant opportunities for women, not just as baggage, but as pilots. A few airplane manufacturers, eager to show that flying was safe and easy, hired women as sales demonstration pilots. After all, if a girl could learn to fly, anyone could. Louise Thaden sold airplanes for Travel Air in Wichita, Kansas; Elinor Smith flew for

Photo 1. Amelia Earhart poses for preflight publicity photos, June 1928. TIGHAR Collection

Bellanca Aircraft in New Castle, Delaware; and Ruth Nichols was a "flying salesgirl" for Fairchild Aircraft in Baltimore, Maryland.[8] In search of publicity, companies loaned airplanes to women for attempts to win races or set altitude, endurance, and speed records, but the machines were rarely top-of-the-line, high-performance types, and the records were "women's records," not to be confused with real records set by men like Jimmy Doolittle and Col. Roscoe Turner.

Nonetheless, Ruth Elder, Blanche Noyes, Ruth Nichols, and others made headlines in a country hungry for aviation heroes. They were young, many were beautiful, and all were skilled aviators and extraordinarily brave. They knew they were being exploited, but they accepted it as the price they had to pay to fly, and nothing mattered more than flying.

With the Atlantic flight, Amelia Earhart joined the ranks of famous women aviators without having to prove her piloting ability; all she had to prove was her courage. But even with Putnam's talent for monetizing her accomplishment, if Earhart was going to make a living as a flier, she would have to do some newsworthy flying. While in London in May 1928, she bought the 85-horsepower (hp) Avro Avian biplane in which Mary, Lady Heath, had recently completed a twelve-thousand-mile solo round-trip flight from England to South Africa. But within weeks of the little airplane's arrival in the United States, Earhart had ripped off the landing gear, shattered the propeller, and cracked one wing in a landing accident. This was not the newsworthy kind of flying she needed.

Putnam quickly covered for her in a statement to reporters: "Miss Earhart made a perfect landing and was taxiing to a stop when the plane hit an unmarked ditch. The plane made what is called a ground loop and nearly turned over. Miss Earhart feels it is unfortunate that the accident should have happened, particularly as it occurred through no fault of hers."[9]

The best opportunity for Earhart to establish her credentials as a pilot was at the following year's National Air Races in Cleveland, Ohio, featuring ten days of military aviation demonstrations, stunt flying, wing-walking, and parachute jumping. The closed course and cross-country races would draw thousands of paying spectators, and the world's premier aviators (male, of course) would vie for top honors and purses in the hottest ships commercial manufacturers and private designers could devise.

To an even greater degree than motor racing, air racing offered the public cutting-edge technology, record-setting speed, and, all too often, accidents and death. Female participation was traditionally limited to parachute jumps, but for the 1929 National Air Races in August, there would be a women's air derby. Derisively labeled the "Powder Puff Derby" by humorist Will Rogers, the race was to be a grueling nine-day, 2,800-mile transcontinental marathon from Santa Monica, California, to Cleveland. Earhart would be up against some of the best women pilots, but they were perpetually cash-strapped and would be flying whatever craft they could beg, borrow, or steal.

Thanks to Putnam's adroit, if ruthless, management, Earhart was in a better financial position to pick a mount. In March 1929 she went to the Bellanca Aircraft factory intending to buy one of the company's new CH Skyrocket monoplanes. Elinor Smith later described what happened:

> George Haldeman [Bellanca's chief engineer] invited her to go up for a trial spin, and the three of us took off. She sat up front with him, and I stayed down in the last of the cabin's six seats. We had climbed to about 1,000 feet when George leveled off and motioned Amelia

Photo 2. Amelia Earhart, Ruth Nichols, and Louise Thaden in 1929. George Putnam taught Earhart to always stand on the left in group photos so her name would appear first in the caption. TIGHAR Collection

to take over the controls. Our big calm bird suddenly lurched out of control and wobbled all over the sky. Amelia was embarrassed and motioned George to take over. He landed, and we disembarked in silence.

She pulled me aside and asked if we could go up again by ourselves. . . . We were quickly airborne. I flew about 15 miles north of the field. When I climbed to 2,000 feet I guided Amelia through some gentle, banking turns, carefully explaining the ship's normal flight positions. . . . Again we slipped and skidded all over the sky. I was baffled, for once the ship's flying position was established, the rest of it should have been exactly like flying a small biplane.

I pointed to the fuel gauge, and Amelia understood we would have to go back. I set down at the far end of the field to give her time to compose herself and me time to think of something to say. I have yet to live through a more awkward moment. Either Lady Lindy had never flown at all, or she had flown only briefly.[10]

Giuseppe Bellanca was protective of his firm's reputation and was notoriously discriminating about who was allowed to buy his designs. After hearing Smith's account of the trial flights, he decided not to sell the airplane to Earhart.

Undaunted, Earhart doubled down on her desire for a high-performance ship and, in July 1929, bought a Lockheed Vega. The Vega 1, introduced by the newly incorporated Lockheed Aircraft Company in 1927, was a snub-nosed bullet. In a world of angular frame-and-fabric biplanes with strut- and wire-braced wings, the Vega was a high-wing cantilevered (strutless) monoplane with a smooth, cylindrical molded plywood fuselage and a 220 hp Wright Whirlwind engine.[11] With a maximum speed of 135 miles per hour (mph), it was faster than most of its contemporaries, but swiftness came at a price. The Vega's high center of gravity and narrow landing gear made it a bear to land.

As Earhart later told it, she bought a "third-hand clunk" Vega and flew it from New York to the Lockheed factory in California for "a few adjustments." Upon evaluating the airplane, Lockheed was appalled at its handling characteristics. "The fact that [Earhart] should have been able to herd such a hopeless piece of mechanism across the continent successfully" so impressed Lockheed management that they swapped it for a brand-new Vega at no charge. The "clunk" never flew again.[12]

What Earhart neglected to mention was that Army Air Corps Lt. Orville Stevens had been flying the airplane for her since its purchase, and he accompanied her on the cross-country trip. The Vega cockpit had only one seat, so unless Lieutenant Stevens was just hitchhiking a ride to California in a "third-hand clunk" with a pilot who had never before flown a hot ship, it was the Army pilot who herded the "hopeless mechanism" across the continent.[13]

Flying with a man in the Women's Air Derby was out of the question, so Putnam approached Elinor Smith with a proposition. He would pay her seventy-five dollars a week to pilot Amelia's plane in the race and, afterward, in a nationwide speaking tour. Smith turned down Putnam's offer, so Earhart would be flying the Vega herself.

Meanwhile, the race organizers were having second thoughts about the Women's Air Derby. In June the officials decided it was "too much of a task on the ladies." The course would be dramatically shortened, and each woman would be required to fly with a man. Louise Thaden was livid and met with Earhart to discuss what could be done. Earhart proposed a boycott, Thaden agreed, and the other entrants signed on. In a public announcement, Earhart said, "None of us will enter, unless it's going to be a real sporting contest. How is a fellow going to earn his spurs without at least trying to ride?"[14]

Press coverage of the revolt was disastrous for the race organizers, and they scrapped the proposed changes. Under Earhart and Thaden's leadership, the women pilots had banded together in opposition to sexist inequality and won. A sisterhood had been forged that would, later that year, flower into a quasi-union for women pilots. All licensed female fliers were invited to join. Eighty-five percent (ninety-nine women) responded, and the organization was dubbed the Ninety-Nines.

With 600,000 paying spectators, the 1929 National Air Races dwarfed the World Series, Kentucky Derby, and Indianapolis 500 combined. On August 27 Louise Thaden, the "World's Leading Woman Flier,"[15] made a perfect landing before a cheering crowd in Cleveland, winning the Women's Air Derby, but her victory was tempered by the death of Marvel Crosson, who had crashed shortly after leaving Yuma, Arizona, the day before.[16]

Elinor Smith was standing at the finish line in Cleveland as the racers came in:

A shout went up as Earhart's Lockheed hove into view, but when the elapsed times were announced, she finished a full two hours behind Thaden, a disappointing third. Because she was flying the fastest ship in the race, her lack of expertise in both navigation and flying was pitilessly exposed. Her landing in Cleveland was amateurish as she bounced the big monoplane completely across the vast airport. There were snide remarks from onlookers as she frantically braked the ship out of a ground loop before rolling to a stop.

But at that moment I was filled with admiration for her. Had her detractors known what they were looking at, they would have been cheering.

It was barely five months since the New Castle incident. . . . There was absolutely no way she could have built enough air time to be at ease behind the controls of the fastest heavy monoplane in the air. The landing speed of the Lockheed was at least a third faster than any other plane in the race, and some of the airports along the way were little more than cow pastures. Her difficulties were compounded by the extreme heat. When she failed to realize that this would thin the air, making it less resistant, thereby decreasing its lift and increasing her landing speed, she nosed over in Yuma, Arizona, and a new propeller had to be flown in to enable her to stay in the race. Despite this delay, she flew on to overtake the others but used up precious time when she lost her way on several laps. From Putnam's standpoint this competition was a disaster. But from hers, it was a challenge that she met head-on. . . . This was gut courage that transcended the sanity of reason. [17]

Earhart needed to find another way to bolster her flying credentials. Navigation errors had cost her the Women's Air Derby despite having the fastest aircraft, so solo cross-country races were out. If she could get access to faster aircraft than other women, setting women's speed records would be a sure bet. In November Earhart set a women's speed record in a borrowed Vega 2 with a 300 hp engine, and the following year she set three more records in a 450 hp Vega DL-1.

Earhart's professional collaboration with George Putnam was working well, but Putnam wanted more and peppered a reluctant Earhart with marriage proposals. In February 1931 Earhart relented, with a written caveat that "I shall not hold you to any midaevil [sic] code of faithfullness to me nor shall I consider myself bound to you similarly."[18] The extent to which she availed herself of the sexual freedom she insisted upon has never been reliably established.

In April 1931 Earhart set an unofficial altitude record in a Pitcairn autogyro (a rotary-wing, short-takeoff-and-landing predecessor of the helicopter) and that summer made a round-trip coast-to-coast flight sponsored by Beechnut, destroying two autogyros in the process. If she was going to maintain and grow her fame, she needed something more; the something more she had in mind was to reprise her 1928 Atlantic crossing, but this time as pilot, and she would do it alone. Being not just the first woman, but the first person, to solo the ocean since Lindbergh would be sure to put her on top as the nation's most famous female flier.

She had upgraded from the Vega 1 to a Vega 5 with more than twice the horsepower, higher speed, and greater payload. Modified with long-range fuel tanks, it would be the perfect airplane to carry the first woman to fly solo from Newfoundland to Paris.

Ruth Nichols thought so too. She had set women's speed and altitude records with her Vega 5, and on June 22, 1931, while Earhart dreamed, Nichols took off from Brooklyn, headed north, in a much-heralded attempt to become the first woman to solo the Atlantic.

2

Fame and More Fame

1932–35

Before setting off, Ruth Nichols had assured her investors, "There is no possibility of failure except the usual law of Fate, which we meet every day of our lives."[1] It took fate a little over three hours. The runway at her first stop, Saint John, New Brunswick, was short and surrounded by trees. Nichols landed long and tried to go around but hit a rocky embankment, wrecking the Vega and breaking two vertebrae in her back.

A year later, Earhart was ready to make her bid. Putnam had savvily timed her departure for the fifth anniversary of Lindbergh's flight, May 20, 1932. Earhart would follow the same route Nichols had planned to take, but she would not try to deal with the treacherous airfield that defeated her friend. Veteran Atlantic flier Bernt Balchen would fly the Vega from New York to New Brunswick and on to Newfoundland, while Earhart rode in the cabin behind a fuel tank with her mechanic, Eddie Gorski. After a short stop in Saint John, they arrived in Harbour Grace at 2:15 p.m., where Earhart "found a friendly bed and restful nap" while Balchen and Gorski serviced the ship. At 7:12 p.m. she took off and set out across the Atlantic for the second time.[2]

During the night, ice nearly brought Earhart down, the engine's exhaust manifold cracked, and she landed far off course in County Derry, Ireland, six hundred miles short of her intended destination of Paris, but no matter. She had soloed the Atlantic, and the triumph had the desired effect. With another Manhattan ticker-tape parade, a gold medal from the National Geographic Society, and a Congressional Distinguished Flying Cross (the first and only such medal awarded to a civilian), she was the world's most famous woman pilot.

A congratulatory telegram from Eleanor Roosevelt, the wife of the governor of New York, took on special significance when the presidential election on November 8 made Mrs. Roosevelt first lady of the United States. Less than two weeks later, Earhart and Putnam were invited to dinner at the Roosevelts' home at Hyde Park, New York. Earhart and Mrs. Roosevelt struck up a friendship, adding a White House connection to Earhart's fame and influence.

Other aviators set records and made headlines, but it was Earhart who was constantly in the news, speaking out for aviation and women's rights in magazine articles, books, and hundreds of paid speaking engagements that also raised money for her next adventure. Branding also maintained name recognition and generated income through a line of lightweight "Amelia Earhart Luggage," women's fashions "designed by Amelia Earhart," and innumerable product endorsements from chewing gum to candy, automobiles, and airplane engines.

In late 1934, having twice conquered the Atlantic, Earhart set her sights on the Pacific, but with a carefully selected record in mind. Flying from California to the territory of Hawaii meant finding the islands after a 2,400-mile trek over trackless ocean. Many had tried, some had succeeded, and others had died—most recently Australian aviator Charles Ulm. On December 3, 1934, Ulm and his two-man crew missed Hawaii, ditched at sea, and were never found despite a month-long search by U.S. Coast Guard ships. For one cutter, USCGC *Itasca*, it would not be the last failed search for a missing airplane.

Finding a continent is easier than finding islands, but most pilots could not afford to ship their aircraft to Hawaii, so no one, male or female, had made the trip in the opposite direction. When Earhart announced she would fly her Vega from Honolulu to Oakland, the proposed flight came under criticism from the *Honolulu Star-Bulletin* for being a pointless publicity stunt. The British weekly *The Aeroplane* called it a "useless adventure."[3] If Earhart should suffer a similar fate as Ulm, the taxpayers would pay the price for her folly—an unwittingly prescient prediction.

Folly or no, the prospect of another first-ever solo transoceanic record was irresistible. To help prepare for the Honolulu to Oakland flight, she hired Hollywood stunt pilot Paul Mantz to be her technical adviser. His company, United Air Services, Ltd., was based at the Union Air Terminal in Burbank, California, about a mile from the Lockheed factory. For convenience, Earhart rented a house in nearby North Hollywood. She loved California—the warm climate, good flying weather, vibrant aviation community—and she enjoyed rubbing elbows with the constellation of Hollywood stars in Mantz's circle of friends.

Having no experience in long-distance flying, Paul Mantz might seem an odd choice, but in some important respects he was perfect. As an aerial stuntman, his expertise in piloting technique was unparalleled and, as a creature of the motion picture industry, he understood show business—and show business was the essence of Earhart's quest for fame. Mantz, like Earhart's friends and competitors, knew her public persona was carefully crafted. As Elinor Smith put it in her 1981 autobiography *Aviatrix*, "The image of a shy and retiring individual thrust against her will into the public eye was a figment of Putnam's lively imagination. Amelia was about as shy as Muhammad Ali."[4]

Earhart, Putnam, and Mantz took the Vega to Oahu aboard the Matson liner *Lurline*, but preflight press coverage turned sour. Word had leaked that Earhart would be paid $10,000 by the Hawaiian Sugar Planters' Association to make the flight as a way of promoting closer ties between Washington and the territory of Hawaii. Earhart was accused of being a shill for lobbyists seeking more favorable tariffs.[5]

Spooked by the negative press, the businessmen threatened to back out of the deal until Earhart confronted them during a meeting at the Royal Hawaiian Hotel four days before her planned departure: "Gentlemen, there is an aroma of cowardice in this air. You know as well as I do that the rumor is trash, but if you can be intimidated, it might as well be true. Whether you live in fear or defend your integrity is your decision. I have made mine. I intend to fly to California within this next week, with or without your support."[6]

The threat was withdrawn, and Earhart made the flight, landing in Oakland before an adoring crowd, a forest of newsreel cameras, and one exasperated Cassandra. When the tumult subsided, Louise Thaden took Earhart aside: "Maybe I'm getting old, but darn your hide, I could spank your pants! Would you mind telling me sometime in strict confidence why the heck you DO things like that? Dimmit, you're worth more alive than dead, and what profit fame when you are not here to reap the benefits, presupposing there are benefits. I wish you would rest on your laurel. When it comes down to brass tacks, I don't know you at all. I doubt anyone does."[7]

That spring, the government of Mexico, seeking to bolster tourism, invited Earhart to make a flying visit to Mexico City, the cost to be covered by a deal to give her two hundred special commemorative postage stamps she could sell. From there she would set another record by flying nonstop to Newark, New Jersey.

On May 8, 1935, during the seven-hundred-mile flight across the Gulf of Mexico, Earhart reflected on her past ocean crossings and had something of an epiphany:

> All three voyages were flown chiefly at night, with heavy clouds during most of the daylight hours. So in the combined six thousand miles or more of previous over-ocean flying it happened I had seen next to nothing of ocean.
>
> Given daylight and good visibility, the Gulf of Mexico looked large. And wet. One's imagination toyed with the thought of what would happen if the single engine of the Lockheed Vega should conk.
>
> So, on that sunny morning out of sight of land, I promised my lovely red Vega I'd fly her across no more water. And I promised myself that any further over-ocean flying would be attempted in a plane with more than one motor, capable of keeping aloft with a single engine. Just in case.
>
> Where to find the tree on which costly airplanes grow, I did not know. But I did know the kind I wanted—an Electra Lockheed.[8]

Earhart's enthusiasm is not hard to understand. To a degree matched by few other aircraft of aviation's golden age, the Lockheed Model 10 Electra had what can only be called charisma. The perfectly proportioned nose pointed skyward with an air of self-assurance and even arrogance. To either side, the hulking engines spoke of muscularity and the ability to pull the gracefully tapering silver fuselage through the sky with ease and speed.

Although the Model 10 served with many airlines in the United States and overseas, the design will always be emblematic of Earhart's ill-fated world flight, but traditional accounts of how she acquired her Electra are largely myth. According to legend, the money came from Purdue University, and that is true, but it didn't happen the way Earhart and her husband George Palmer Putnam described the process—not even close. As Earhart told it in *Last Flight*, published posthumously in

Photo 3. The Lockheed Model 10 Electra prototype. Its first flight was on February 23, 1934. James Borden Photography Collection

1937: "One day last summer President Edward C. Elliott of Purdue asked my husband what most interested me beyond academic matters. . . . [H]e divulged my suppressed pilot's yearnings for a bigger and better airplane."[9]

George Putnam repeated the fable in his 1939 book *Soaring Wings*: "In the summer of 1936 President Elliott of Purdue asked me what I thought there was in the field of research and education that interested [Amelia Earhart] most beyond academic matters. I told him she was hankering for a bigger and better plane."[10] By the summer of 1936 Earhart's Electra had already been built and delivered. The suggestion that Purdue University satisfy his wife's hankering for a bigger and better plane dates from November 1935.

Earhart's association with Purdue grew out of a September 1934 conference in the Grand Ballroom of the Waldorf Astoria in Manhattan. Three thousand attendees heard First Lady Eleanor Roosevelt, New York mayor Fiorello LaGuardia, Purdue University president Edward C. Elliott, Amelia Earhart, and other influential public figures speak about the changing world and nation. Elliott felt that the country's economic recovery from the Great Depression relied upon harnessing the energy of young people, especially women. The head of the Girl Scouts of America spoke of the need to prepare young women to be competent household managers and good wives. Amelia Earhart had a message more in tune with Elliott's: women were being unfairly denied professional positions in aviation. The education of young women in technical fields was essential to the future of the industry.

Elliott was impressed with Earhart and began trying to figure out a way to use her to boost the university's appeal to women. By the following spring he was ready to make her a formal proposal. On May 18, 1935, he asked that she accept a position as "Department Head, or nonresident professor, or lecturer on careers for women" in a new department that would provide professional advice to female students. She would be paid $2,000 per year but would need to spend only two weeks out of each semester at the university giving addresses, classes, or conferences. She would also be chief consultant for the university's work in aeronautical engineering.[11]

Earhart eagerly accepted the offer. Working with young women to bring them out of the kitchen and into the cockpit would put her hard-won fame to use in the most productive way possible. Besides, being chief consultant in aeronautical engineering was irresistibly flattering to the woman who had never completed a course in higher education beyond high school and who had said her flights had meant nothing toward scientific advancement in aviation.[12]

Elliott's gambit worked. The announcement on June 3, 1935, that Amelia Earhart Putnam would join the Purdue University faculty as a woman's career adviser prompted a fifty-percent increase in the enrollment of freshman women before Earhart ever set foot on campus.[13]

For Earhart, the timing of this new career opportunity was perfect. By the summer of 1935 she had accepted that her long-distance flying career was probably over. Entrepreneurial aviation record-setting in single-engine wooden airplanes, so popular throughout the late 1920s and early 1930s, was a dying profession. The boundaries of flight were now being pushed back by a new generation of all-metal commercial designs whose cost was far beyond the reach of even a well-sponsored individual. The 1934 MacRobertson Race from England to Australia had been won by a small, purpose-built de Havilland Comet, but second and third place went to a Douglas DC-2 and a Boeing 247, large, off-the-shelf, multi-engine commercial airliners. In April 1935 Pan American's Pacific Division, under the guidance of senior navigator Fred Noonan, began surveying airmail and passenger routes across the northern Pacific with four-engine Sikorsky flying boats. Aviation was emerging from its reckless adolescence and starting to find its way as a viable transportation industry.

Not only were new airplanes becoming too expensive, but some in the press also had begun to see "individually sponsored trans-oceanic flying" as the "the worst racket" in aviation.[14] As *Newsweek* put it, "Every so often Miss Earhart, like other prominent flyers, pulls a spectacular stunt to hit the front pages. This enhances a flyer's value as a cigarette endorser, helps finance new planes, sometimes publicizes a book."[15] Only once, at the beginning of her career, did Earhart endorse a brand of cigarettes, but it was true that her primary sources of income were product endorsements, book sales, and the lecture circuit. It was a business model managed and honed to perfection by Putnam.

After the Mexico City to Newark flight in May 1935, with no further records to set in the obsolete Vega, Earhart was ready to move on. In June she accepted the part-time consulting job at Purdue and, in July, ordered the long-range fuel tanks removed from her Vega and had the cabin converted to passenger configuration for use in a charter and flight school business she was planning to start in partnership with Mantz. The future that lay before her, while less exciting than spanning oceans, promised a rewarding, more stable, and certainly much safer lifestyle. As if to put an exclamation point on the latter consideration, on August 15, 1935, Earhart's friend Wiley Post and humorist Will Rogers were killed when their Lockheed Orion crashed shortly after takeoff near Point Barrow, Alaska.

It is tempting to imagine what Amelia Earhart's legacy might have been had the trajectory of her life continued on this new and tamer course. She actively campaigned for Franklin D. Roosevelt and down-ballot Democrats in the 1936 election, but her ideology went far beyond democratic

Photo 4. Partners in business and marriage: Amelia Earhart and George Putnam, 1935.
Courtesy of Remember Amelia, the Larry C. Inman Historical Collection on Amelia Earhart

socialism. In a May 22, 1936, letter to her mother, she wrote: "Please don't down the Roosevelt administration. It's all right to be reactionary inside but it is out of step with the times to sound off about the chosen people who have inherited or grabbed the earth. You must think of me when you converse and I believe the experiments carried on today point the way to a new social order when governments will be the voice of the proletariat far more than democracy can ever be."[16]

Charles Lindbergh's opposition to U.S. support for Britain in the three years before Pearl Harbor and American entry into World War II toppled him from his pedestal of fame. Had she not joined the ranks of American icons who died young, the Cold War might have brought down a fifty-year-old Earhart.

George Putnam recognized Edward Elliott's enthusiasm for his wife's association with the university as an opening that, if properly exploited, could put Earhart back in the lucrative long-distance flying game. The die was cast at a meeting in Washington, DC, on November 11, 1935, at which Putnam presented Elliott with a proposal he called the Amelia Earhart Project. Earhart was not present, having arrived in Lafayette, Indiana, five days earlier to start her work at Purdue. Throughout the fall of 1935 she had been occupied with a brutal schedule of 136 speaking engagements to audiences totaling 80,000 people—driving, not flying, from town to town across the Midwest. For $250 she gave what Putnam called "a straight, flying-is-safe and pleasant sermon" to women's clubs and civic groups.[17] In her surviving letters and telegrams from that time, there is nothing relating to the proposal her husband presented to Elliott on November 11.

In a typed memorandum describing the project, Putnam came right to the point: "The widespread attention given Amelia Earhart's association with Purdue has identified her with the University. A further focusing of interest on this alliance can be of increasing importance from the standpoint of external institutional propaganda and internal inspiration."[18] In fairness, the term "propaganda" did not carry the pejorative connotation it has acquired since then.

According to Putnam, Earhart wanted to continue her "pioneering flying," set new records, and conduct "certain flights as laboratory tests involving various scientific aspects of modern aviation." However, her current airplane "is no longer sufficiently speedy or modern to hold its place in competition." And, for further overwater flying, she wanted "a two-motor plane."[19]

Without mentioning the make or model, Putnam said there was an airplane available that fit the bill: "It embraces refinements and improvements whose practical demonstration can be important factors in commercial aeronautical progress." It was a multi-engine aircraft capable of sustained flight on one motor. It had a maximum cruising speed of over 225 mph and a cruising range, with full load, of more than six thousand miles. Equipped with "special tanks, instruments, and other devices," this marvelous machine was not an experimental ship but rather a "development of proved design." It could be had as a stock model or a "custom-built job" for a base price of $30,000: "The maximum total cost, including special equipment, preparation, flight outlays, etc., would be $40,000. That figure would be the guaranteed top."[20]

After becoming "intimately familiar with the ship under all conditions," Earhart would establish some new transcontinental records, make a flight to Panama or Cuba, and undertake "detailed experimental work at various altitudes, including oxygen flight."[21] These preliminary flights would be followed by "the ultimate big flight, to be attempted only if and when everything proves out satisfactorily, to be *around-the-world* [emphasis in the original], starting at the Purdue airport and ending at Purdue. The plane could carry the name 'Purdue.'"[22]

If the university would put up the money, Putnam was willing to share the net financial returns from the world flight. Finally, "at the end of its career of usefulness the plane itself could be installed as a permanent exhibit at Purdue. Meanwhile it would be usable by Miss Earhart—to be maintained and operated at her expense."[23]

The airplane he described did not exist. It is clear from later correspondence that the airplane Putnam had in mind was to be either a modified or custom-built Lockheed Electra, but the capabilities Putnam claimed were pure fantasy. In November 1935 the Model 10 Electra had been in production for a year and a half. Lockheed had delivered thirty-six Model 10As powered by Pratt & Whitney 450 hp Wasp Jr. engines, and five Model 10Bs with Wright 450 hp Whirlwinds.[24] Neither version was capable of anything near the performance described by Putnam. Even the more powerful Model 10E with Pratt & Whitney 550 hp Wasp engines (planned but not yet in production) would fail to meet Putnam's claims.

President Elliott's reaction to Putnam's proposal was enthusiastic. Upon his return to Purdue on November 14, he wrote: "Since our thrilling conversation Monday, I have accumulated some ideas which I hope to be able to discuss with you when I am in New York during the week of the twenty-fifth. I have just come from a conference here in connection with the aeronautical meeting in progress on the campus today and tomorrow. A.E. is performing in noble fashion. She has the entire campus on its toes."[25]

While performing in noble fashion, Earhart was not involved in the discussions that would so profoundly affect her life. The legend that has grown up around Earhart would have it otherwise. An oft-repeated story is that "in the autumn of 1935, at a dinner party at Elliott's home, Amelia outlined her dreams for women and aviation and spoke of her desire to conduct studies on how long-distance flying affected pilots. Before the evening was over, guest David Ross offered to donate $50,000 as a gift toward the cost of providing a machine suitable for the flying laboratory."[26]

Versions of the story in several Earhart biographies vary as to exactly who was present and how much was pledged, but none of the accounts give a specific date for the dinner. The event is not mentioned in Earhart, Putnam, or Elliott correspondence nor in any other contemporary source. The only time Earhart was at Purdue in the autumn of 1935 was from November 6 to November 26. On December 7, 1935, by which time Earhart was gone from Purdue, Elliott wrote to Putnam saying only that he had "been able to do some preliminary work with reference to the proposal presented in your memorandum."[27] The apocryphal dinner party story is charming, but it is not how Purdue University came to fund the purchase of the aircraft in which Amelia Earhart met her fate.

On December 9 Putnam thanked Elliott for his "pleasant note of the 7th" and mentioned that he had taken some initial steps toward soliciting the involvement and support of the National Geographic Society: "This would lend a further dignity and international importance to the whole project. Also, of course, it would be a great financial aid. As I hear further from them I will report to you."[28] Elliott did not share Putnam's enthusiasm for courting National Geographic's participation and made no response to the suggestion.

Exactly when Putnam told his wife he may have found the tree upon which costly airplanes grow is not clear, but Earhart was delighted. Contrary to legend, it was not the prospect of a trip around the world that excited her so much as the opportunity to make genuine contributions toward aeronautical progress through "certain flights as laboratory tests" in a state-of-the-art aircraft.

Elliott visited Putnam and Amelia in New York over the Christmas holidays to discuss "important and encouraging new developments in the new project."[29] Possible donors had made no firm commitments, but they were reacting favorably to Elliott's advocacy for the Amelia Earhart Project. Earhart seems to have been as unaware as Elliott that Putnam's promise of scientific tests was a ruse to acquire an airplane for a lucrative record-setting world flight in the same pattern as her previous ocean flights.

3

Bait and Switch

JANUARY–FEBRUARY 1936

As the new year dawned, Purdue was taking the bait. Putnam's proposal for a program of scientific test flights, although based on a fictional airplane and lowball costs, was viewed favorably by possible donors. Despite his characterization of a flight around the world as a possible crowning achievement to be attempted only "if and when everything proves out satisfactorily," Putnam planned to move the world flight to the front of the agenda—but first he needed hard numbers on a real airplane capable of doing the job.

In Western Union overnight telegrams sent a few days before January 4, Putnam asked Paul Mantz to get the "bottom price on small twin-engine Lockheed and delivery likelihoods without engines or instruments of plane we've discussed."[1] The small twin-engine Lockheed they had discussed was a new six-passenger model the company had begun designing in response to a Bureau of Air Commerce invitation for a "feeder-liner" to serve small commercial markets.[2] One-third lighter than the 10A but sporting the same 450 hp Pratt & Whitney Wasp Jr. engines as its big sister, the Lockheed Model 12 Electra Junior would be cheaper and faster and would have greater range than the full-size Electras. Putnam felt confident he could get the engines and instruments donated regardless of which model was chosen. He also advised Mantz that he was "obtaining data here on floats."[3]

There is no surviving record of whose idea it was for Earhart to fly around the world on floats, and it is difficult to understand the rationale behind such a proposal. The overarching challenge to a trip around the world was spanning the vast expanse of the Pacific. Floats would provide a measure of safety in the event of a forced landing at sea but, for the rest of the trip, they would be a liability, denying the flight the use of virtually all of the world's airports.

On January 2, Putnam sent Elliott an update on the selection of an airplane. They were making "interesting progress . . . as to cost, delivery date, performance, etc."[4] He estimated that they would decide within ten days or so which of two models was preferable. Putnam also informed Elliott that "we are also getting full data concerning floats. This will be the first flight of the kind on pontoons."[5]

With his news about the plane, Putnam also sent Elliott a copy of a letter he had just written to Jack LaGorce, vice president at the National Geographic Society, soliciting financial support for a flight *around the world.* Putnam justified seeking supplemental funding from the society as "the removal of necessity for any commercialization. . . . No product endorsements or media deals, just 'straight pioneering.'"[6] Earhart and Putnam made their money from postflight books and speaking engagements. Getting the money to do the flight from National Geographic rather than through media deals and product endorsements would be easier and look better without inhibiting their ability to capitalize afterward.

Two days later, January 4, Putnam received an encouraging letter from Elliott: "This is being written to say confidentially that, providing a proper scientific research foundation can be established, there is no doubt now as to the availability of the money."[7] Exactly who gave Elliott the assurances he communicated confidentially to Putnam is not known. The donors wished to remain anonymous and apparently succeeded. Their identities and the amounts they donated are nowhere to be found in Purdue records. The David Ross mentioned in the apocryphal dinner story may well have been the initial guarantor. Ross was a prominent Indiana industrialist and president of Purdue's board of trustees. It had been at his suggestion the university set up the Purdue Research Foundation. Indiana businesses run by successful Purdue alumni would make financial contributions to the university to fund research that would, in turn, benefit Indiana-based industry—a win-win for the school and Indiana business. The research foundation was the obvious context within which to create a special fund for aeronautical research.

Putnam immediately replied: "Thanks for your note of the 2nd. That's good news." The bad news was that support from the Purdue Research Foundation would be conditional upon a proper foundation of scientific research. Putnam worried that his letter to National Geographic, which had jumped the gun and focused exclusively on the world flight, might not "supply sufficient information concerning the research characteristics of the project."[8] It also occurred to him that putting the airplane on floats might create a problem for a key element in the plan: having the world flight begin and end at Purdue. "Is there any sizeable lake conveniently near to Lafayette?"[9]

It was becoming increasingly urgent to settle on an airplane, but Mantz had not answered his telegrams, and Putnam was furious: "Please let me have immediately the data requested in my night letter of some days ago regarding the Junior Electra—the new smaller ship. . . . If you are sunk in your troubles so that you cannot attend to these matters, let me know at once, as matters are reaching a crisis here and I cannot afford delays. If necessary I will have to deal directly with Lockheed, but of course it is much better to handle it through you—if you can attend to the job."[10]

The troubles Mantz was sunk in were divorce proceedings. His wife Myrtle wanted out and was threatening to go public with her accusations that Mantz had been having an affair with Putnam's wife. Given Earhart's views on marital fidelity, such a liaison would not have been out of character, but there is no known evidence the accusation was true. Earhart, meanwhile, was on the road doing public appearances and seems to have been uninvolved in these discussions.

In considering the full-size Electra, Putnam was trying to decide between the Model 10A and the Model 10B, but neither version offered the performance he had promised Purdue. He asked Mantz, "Is it possible to use straight Wasps in the Electra?"[11]

Putnam's question is a measure of the extent to which he was out of touch with Lockheed. The company was, in fact, already using straight Wasps in the Electra. The Model 10E with 550 hp Wasp engines had been in production since early December.[12] It had been developed at the request of Pan American Airways, which wanted a more powerful Electra for its subsidiary airline Aerovias Centrales operating out of high-altitude airports in Central America. The R-1340 Wasp was a physically larger, heavier, and thirstier engine than either the 450 hp R-985 Wasp Junior of the Model 10A or the Model 10B's Wright R-975 Whirlwind, but it delivered superior load-carrying ability and takeoff performance and a small increase in speed. With the big Wasps, the Model 10E was something of a brute: louder, heavier, and less forgiving than its little sisters.

Meanwhile, the switch in Putnam's bait-and-switch had hit a snag. A January 6, 1936, letter from Elliott confirmed Putnam's concerns that the change in focus from test flying to world flying was not going well: "I do not think that the outline of the scientific and research features of the flight, as presented in your memorandum to LaGorce [at National Geographic], contains sufficient detail that would be convincing to the donor representatives of the University." Elliott insisted that before any final understanding could be reached, another in-person conference would be necessary. If National Geographic was going to be involved, their representative should also be there.[13]

Putnam had reached out to LaGorce without first checking with Elliott or Earhart, and now he had to backtrack. Later that same day, Putnam wrote to Elliott explaining that, after talking it over with his wife, he could see "some debits"[14] in National Geographic's possible participation. It is not hard to see why Earhart did not think that bringing National Geographic on board was such a great idea. The society was a publicity juggernaut; adding National Geographic to the world flight would dilute the Earhart brand. He included a copy of a second letter to LaGorce tamping down the tone of his original pitch and assuring him "the Society's maximum participation and sponsorship along the lines discussed is not essential to the project's inception."[15]

The next day, January 7, Mantz finally replied to Putnam with a telegram that seemed to change everything. He reported it would take a year for Lockheed to deliver an Electra Junior on pontoons, and putting floats on a full-size Electra would cost $30,000, effectively doubling the price of the basic airplane. "For your requirements feel Sikorsky S43 ideal for distance required in addition to a good hundred and seventy mph cruising. Advise next steps."[16]

In Mantz's view, Lockheed was out of the picture. The perfect machine for a circumnavigation of the globe was the new Sikorsky S-43 Baby Clipper. The S-43 was a smaller amphibious version of the S-42 four-engine flying boats used by Pan American to survey routes across the Pacific. Powered by two 750 hp Pratt & Whitney Hornet engines, the Baby Clipper was fast and capable of lifting a heavy fuel load. Most important, because it was equipped with retractable landing gear in a flying boat hull, the aircraft was equally at home on water or land. Earhart would therefore be able to use Pan Am facilities at Midway and Wake islands to get across the Pacific.

In his reply to Mantz, Putnam agreed that the Sikorsky amphibian would be the safest choice, but Earhart would not hear of it. Her priority was the scientific work and, to her mind, a Lockheed Electra was the only choice. She was resigned to the idea that the world flight would have to come first, but the airplane would have to be an Electra. Faced with Earhart's veto, Putnam made the best of it. The price of an S-43 was $110,000, "but the finances presumably will boil down into us spending nearly as much as we would on an Electra, and in the end having nothing to show for it."[17] They would have to work something out with Lockheed.

Putnam could not understand Lockheed's quotation of $30,000 for pontoons: "There is something funny here. Of course, if they don't want to do business with us let them say so at once."[18] He was "in lengthy conversations" with the Edo Company, the leading manufacturer of pontoons for aircraft.[19] "What we want is an Electra. If we can get the bare ship for $32,000 and Edo is right that they can get the floats on within $15,000 and Lockheed will give us a square deal (at cost) for tanks, etc. I would be able to close immediately."[20] Close immediately? The funding from Purdue was not yet confirmed and relied upon a program of scientific research that had not yet been adequately described.

Putnam suggested that Mantz sit down with Allen Lockheed, founder and former owner of Lockheed Aircraft Corporation, to see if he would design a "a special ship built to order. Of course, it is pretty dangerous because there are apt to be bugs." Nonetheless, if Lockheed was not going to be "halfway decent," he would rather spend $30,000 on an "experimental job."[21]

To put pressure on Lockheed, he included a second letter: "The enclosed letter is written so that you may show it to the Lockheed people. I think that would be smart. It would sort of indicate that you are taking them into your confidence. The implication might be that I did not know that you were showing it."[22]

The letter Mantz was instructed to leak to the Lockheed people was a (supposedly) private communication between Putnam and Mantz. He understated the quote for floats from Edo as being "less than $10,000." He also claimed "the whole matter is moving into focus fast. The funds are available. We are considering several alternate ships."[23]

In the bogus letter, Putnam wrote that Lockheed should do all special modifications to an Electra at actual out-of-pocket cost for labor and materials: "I don't believe Lockheed would insist on making money out of A.E. on a project of this kind. For an Electra on floats to make the first round-the-world flight is a uniquely valuable exploitation bull's-eye."[24] And he added a manipulative postscript: "I am having conversations with the Sikorsky crowd now. It looks interesting. From the safety standpoint that is probably the best bet. I think the economics can be arranged. The primary unsatisfaction [sic] is that of course we wouldn't want a Sikorsky after the flight."[25]

Putnam ended his letter to Mantz with an admonition to "roll up your sleeves" and "iron this thing out as quickly as you can."[26] Earhart and her husband were together in New York at this time and presumably communicating with each other. To what degree Earhart was complicit in her husband's duplicitousness is not recorded.

Earhart departed to begin a new lecture tour the next day, January 8, and Putnam wrote to Elliott with the news that Pratt & Whitney had gladly agreed to contribute the engines for the still-theoretical airplane. To justify moving the world flight to the top of the project's agenda, Putnam stressed that the flight itself would constitute important aeronautical research. He promised to "prepare an exposition of the research features of the flight, in preliminary form, to expand as you advise."[27] There is no record of any such exposition ever being drafted.

Two days later, on January 10, Putnam wired Elliott that National Geographic had decided against being associated with the project and added a positive spin: "While disappointing [it] has advantages [and] simplifications especially regarding Purdue, our exclusive responsibility to which [is] naturally primary. [In] some ways [it] makes my job easier."[28]

With the question of National Geographic's participation settled, Elliott decided that the best way to find out how the Purdue Research Foundation felt about the world flight project was to ask its director, G. Stanley Meikle. That the project had come this far without the all-important research foundation being in the loop is more than a bit surprising. Meikle took the matter seriously and by January 18 had written an eight-page treatise titled "Notes Pertaining to the Development of Purdue Educational and Research Program in Aeronautics." He sent his notes, "which have been prepared as a result of our recent conversation concerning the possibilities of aerial expeditions," to Elliott on January 23.[29]

The document begins with a detailed review of Purdue's six years of "continuous and persistent effort"[30] devoted to aeronautical research and the university's specific desire to explore the mysteries of high-altitude flight, especially the stratosphere's "strong, undisturbed, unidirectional winds or drifts which are much more favorable to flight than the violent disturbances which haunt the heavier strata enveloping the earth."[31] Meikle noted that "the real task of exploring the possibilities of flight in the stratosphere is yet to be undertaken. The craft which will successfully penetrate it and maintain prolonged flight in comfort and safety has yet to be designed."[32] Meikle did not know Lockheed and the Army Air Corps were, at that moment, designing the XC-35, a pressurized Electra with turbocharged engines for flight in the stratosphere to investigate what would one day become known as the jet stream. First flown in June 1936, the XC-35 won the 1937 Collier Trophy for the year's most valuable contribution to aircraft development.

Meikle hoped such an aircraft could be developed under the auspices of the Purdue Research Foundation, but he lamented that "the Foundation at present has no funds with which to finance such a worthy scientific venture."[33] As a way to attract funding, he suggested that "well planned explorations into the stratosphere, or into other uncharted realms of space, in the interest of science and aviation might stimulate donations devoted to aeronautical research."[34]

Nowhere did Meikle make specific reference to Amelia Earhart or to a flight around the world, but in a note of caution, he warned that it would be unwise for the university to become associated with any venture that was "not based upon a serious intent to collect scientific and engineering data." Publicity was only beneficial if the scientific and engineering objectives could "withstand the scrutiny of public opinion."[35]

In an eerily prophetic comment, Meikle also recognized the element of risk. "Sometimes man's skill and knowledge are insufficient to conquer the elements which confront him," and he "passes into oblivion," leaving only "fragmentary bits of mute evidence of disaster of unknown origin."[36] Nonetheless, as long as the venture was a well-planned and worthy scientific expedition, "the University and Foundation might properly agree to provide for the expenses from funds made available for the purpose."[37]

With Meikle's agreement-in-principle in hand, Elliott wrote to Putnam on January 27 to say that the university's lawyer was drafting a tentative memorandum of agreement. Once Putnam had reviewed it, there would need to be a meeting of the directors of the foundation, but "in so far as the Purdue Research Foundation is concerned, its minimum share of the funds is already guaranteed. The important question is to determine a proper scientific program which can be approved."[38]

For Putnam, things were moving in the right direction, but there was still the problem of articulating a proper scientific program, and the all-important world flight was not yet on the table. Severe winter weather prevented further progress for the next two weeks, but on February 10 Elliott wrote to Putnam with the news that Meikle had made preliminary contact with Vincent Bendix in New York, and his reaction was "favorable."[39] Support from Bendix was seen as key to the project. Since 1931, Bendix Aviation Corporation, a leading manufacturer of aircraft parts, had maintained a high profile through its sponsorship of the Bendix Trophy transcontinental air race. In 1936 Vince Bendix was beginning to expand his holdings into the field of aircraft radio, and the opportunity to test Bendix innovations in radio navigation equipment was exactly the kind of research the foundation had in mind.

Putnam caught up with Earhart on her lecture tour in Tennessee and drove with her to California, arriving in Burbank around February 1 to try to sort out the airplane.[40] The problem they laid out for Lockheed was the need for a ship capable of crossing the Pacific. Floats would allow Earhart to island-hop across, using the Pan American flying boat facilities at Midway, Wake, and Manila, but the costs in time and money to put an Electra on floats made the prospect impractical. What was needed was an Electra that could cross the Pacific nonstop.

On February 12 Putnam wrote to Elliott with some good news: "It begins to look as if we might be able to get a ship of sufficient cruising range, perhaps, to negotiate the hop from Honolulu to Suva, or to Japan. . . . If this should work out, our financial and mechanical problems will be very greatly simplified."[41]

Lockheed engineers calculated that, theoretically, a Model 10E could be modified with additional fuel tanks to deliver a range of 4,500 miles, enough to fly the 3,200 miles from Honolulu to Suva, Fiji, or 3,900 miles from Honolulu to Tokyo, Japan, with adequate reserves. In 1928, the same year Earhart crossed the Atlantic as a passenger in a tri-motored Fokker F-VII on floats, Australian Charles Kingsford-Smith flew the same type, on wheels, from Honolulu to Suva, landing in a soccer stadium. The field was too short, and he had to intentionally ground-loop the big Fokker to avoid hitting an embankment. Honolulu to Japan is 3,900 miles, a greater distance, but Tokyo had a real airport. A modified Model 10E might be the answer.

Putnam told Elliott he expected to be flying back to New York about February 20. By that time he expected to be ready to place an order for the aircraft: "Will it be necessary or helpful for me to plan to stop at Lafayette enroute east?"[42]

Indeed it was. Putnam's presence at Purdue to discuss the proposal being drafted by Meikle and the university's lawyer was essential, but on February 15, Putnam wrote that his departure from California would be delayed at least another week. He was "greatly pleased" with the progress being made toward selection of an aircraft and expected to have a tentative contract with the manufacturer in a few days. Doing away with the pontoons not only reduced the cost but also restored the "ideal procedure" of starting and finishing the world flight at Purdue.[43]

Meanwhile, at the Purdue Research Foundation, director Stanley Meikle was coming around. His concerns about the lack of a detailed program of scientific test flights were overshadowed by the potential financial rewards to be had from the university's support of the proposed world flight. In "General Notes Pertaining to the A.E. World Flight," Meikle expressed his opinion that "any scientific body actively interested in the science of flight might properly be prompted to donate substantial funds to an A.E. World Flight."[44] It was essential that the money go to a permanent fund established by the foundation for scientific research in aeronautics. Otherwise, "There is danger that the enterprise will be looked upon as an ingenious scheme devised primarily for the purpose of raising funds."[45] For George Putnam at least, that is exactly what it was. His bait-and-switch had morphed the proposed "detailed experimental work at various altitudes, including oxygen flight"[46] into Purdue's enabling of Earhart's return to record-setting ocean flying.

Meikle proposed that the foundation establish a research fund to be known as the Amelia Earhart Putnam Research Fund for Aeronautics.[47] The fund would accept donations made to the project and serve as a repository for the scientific data resulting from the world flight. His original plan had been for the airplane to be owned by Purdue and deeded to Earhart after the flight was concluded, but he now suggested a more arm's-length relationship. He drafted a tentative proposal that specified that the foundation's support would be in the form of "an unconditional donation in the interests of science to be used toward the purposes of this project."[48]

The unconditional donation would be anything but unconditional. In a tour de force of double-speak, Meikle wrote: "Obviously, it will be necessary for the Flight Commander and the Flight Manager to accept this tentative proposal. It would seem to me that such acceptance should include a definite statement of plans put in language which will in no manner vary the intentions of the donor to make an unconditional donation."[49]

Meikle went on to list fourteen conditions, including guarantees that Amelia Earhart would be the pilot; George Putnam would arrange for and manage the world flight; the flight would be made in an Electra; the flight would start and end at the Purdue airport; the flight would leave the shores of the United States at Washington "carrying messages of good will from members of the official family"; and all money generated by the flight, the sale of news items during the flight, and the first story at the end of the flight would go to defray the expenses of the flight and "provide for the permanent A.E.P. Research Fund for Aeronautics."[50] Meikle's list did not include a requirement to gather scientific data.

The conditions listed in Meikle's general notes were not included in the tentative proposal. He explained, "I feel certain that the integrity of both A.E. and G.P.P. is sufficiently well known so that a positive statement of what they intend to do will be an adequate guarantee of fulfillment."[51]

On February 27, 1936, Meikle sent his tentative proposal and accompanying general notes to Elliott to be presented to, and presumably approved by, Putnam when he arrived in Lafayette en route to New York, but as the month ended, Putnam had still not appeared.

4

The Realization
of a Dream

MARCH–JULY 1936

Putnam did not stop in Indiana on his way to New York and so was not aware of Meikle's embrace of the world flight, nor of the tentative proposal he had drafted or the conditions Putnam and Earhart would have to agree to. Still in sales mode, on March 2 Putnam sent a letter to President Elliott detailing the plan for "another world flight."[1]

Circumnavigation of the globe by air was nothing new. The U.S. Army had been the first in 1924. The *Graf Zeppelin* was next in 1929. Wiley Post had done it twice, with navigator Harold Gatty in 1930 and again solo in 1933. In 1935 Pan American Airways inaugurated airmail service across the Pacific and added scheduled passenger service in September 1936, making it possible for anyone to make the entire journey around the world as a commercial airline passenger.[2]

Nonetheless, Putnam wrote that a world flight by Earhart would be of great value: "Those concerned with the development of aviation are convinced that such a world flight is of prime importance in stimulating greater interest in pure and applied research in aeronautics."[3] There seems to be no contemporary record of an aviation authority expressing this opinion.

Putnam expected Earhart's world flight would take place in late 1936 or early 1937. She would begin with a send-off in Washington, DC, after which she would fly to Purdue for the official beginning of the world flight. Her route would be from Lafayette, Indiana, to San Francisco; Honolulu; Tokyo, Japan; Hong Kong, China; Rangoon, Burma; Karachi, India; Cairo, Egypt; Dakar, French West Africa; Natal, Brazil; Havana, Cuba; New York; and back to Purdue.

Abandoning the idea of possibly crossing the Pacific via Fiji, Putnam told Elliott the trip would include "the unprecedented exploit of bridging the 3,900 miles of Pacific between Honolulu and Japan."[4] Putnam saw the flight's importance to aviation "in its utilization of a twin-engine plane and the latest in all branches of scientific aeronautical equipment." All previous circumnavigations had been in single-engine aircraft, but the advantages of multi-engine, all-metal aircraft in long-distance flying were not in question. Two of the top three finishers in the 1934 MacRobertson Trophy Air Race from England to Australia had been twin-engined American airliners, a Douglas DC-2 and a

Boeing 247. In 1935 Pan American Airways had begun scheduled airmail service across the Pacific in four-engined Martin M-130 flying boats.

Putnam believed the most important aspect of the world flight would be Earhart's star power: "Above all, its public interest lies in the record and personality of its pilot."[5] Earhart's airplane would be "a two-motor Electra all-metal monoplane" with "an assured 4,500-mile cruising radius." Putnam promised Elliott that "there is nothing new or experimental about the Electra plane." Although it was true the Model 10 was a well-established design with some fifty examples in service, the proposed long-distance modification of the Model 10E was an entirely experimental concept. Only three of the big-engined Electras had been built, and all had the standard 830-mile maximum cruising range. Lockheed's guarantee that an Electra could get off the ground with enough fuel to achieve a 4,500-mile range was sales talk based on theoretical calculations.

Putnam's description of the pricing was worded to make it sound like Lockheed was offering a bargain: "The normal price of the Electra to the airlines ranges from $50,000 to $55,000. The price we are to pay (still subject to some revision) is $42,000, which price includes about $8,000 worth of extra work, primarily in the installation of the necessary fuel tanks."[6] Putnam's implication that Lockheed was offering a 16 to 24 percent discount was more than a little misleading. In fact, the manufacturer's discount was less than 7 percent. Lockheed quoted Putnam the standard price for a 10E—$55,910—plus $8,500 for "gasoline capacity to provide range of 4,500 miles" for a total purchase price of $64,410. Putnam had succeeded in getting Pratt & Whitney and Hamilton Standard to donate engines and propellers worth $19,263.90, thus reducing Lockheed's price to $45,146.10. For its part, Lockheed offered a "special rebate" of $3,136.10, bringing the final cash price to $42,010. Putnam acknowledged that acquiring the airplane was just the first step: "The problem of raising sufficient funds for the flight is one yet to be solved."[7]

Elliott shared Putnam's letter with Purdue Research Foundation director Stanley Meikle who, in turn, sent it on to the university's lawyers with a copy of the tentative proposal to be sent to Earhart outlining Purdue's sponsorship of the project. Attorney Allison Stuart did not like it. He was concerned the proposal could be construed as Purdue offering a contract for Earhart to make the world flight. On March 11 he told Meikle, "If it is deemed necessary to have a statement of this kind we suggest that the order of things be reversed."[8] Earhart, or Putnam on her behalf, should make a proposal to the university.

This was a problem. Meikle was running out of time. In three days the research foundation board of trustees would meet to consider funding the world flight project. For more than a month he had been struggling to put together an acceptable way for Purdue to be involved, but the board would not approve a deal that had not been cleared by the lawyers. It was too late to get a new letter from Putnam, so Meikle reworded Putnam's letter. He asked the board to grant the funding on the condition that Earhart/Putnam would give the research foundation a letter like this. The foundation would respond with an agreement for Earhart to sign. Upon her acceptance of the agreement, the foundation would make an unconditional grant to Earhart and create a special Amelia Earhart Putnam Research Fund for Aeronautics to accept further donations. (The Putnam name was later dropped.)

On March 14 the board of trustees approved the plan, and Elliott wrote to Putnam with the good news: "The Directors of the Foundation have approved the utilization of $40,000 of Foundation funds for the purpose of promoting the flight." There were two enclosures. All Putnam needed to do was give him a letter like the enclosed exhibit A: "This, as you will see, has been prepared on the basis of your letter of March 2 . . . upon the receipt of which I would respond as per Exhibit B. . . . Your response to the proposal of Exhibit B would then complete the necessary preliminary negotiations."[9] Elliott hand-delivered the documents to Putnam in New York on March 15, and the next day Putnam sent Meikle the required reworded proposal.

Earhart's dream of a Lockheed Electra for "pioneering flying" and "certain flights as laboratory tests involving various scientific aspects of modern aviation" was coming true. To what extent a flight around the world was ever part of that dream is not clear, but it was the cornerstone of the deal her husband had brokered. The money for the basic airplane was now assured, and the list of in-kind contributors to complete the machine was impressive. Engines, spark plugs, propellers, and some instruments were already being donated. Standard Oil's aviation arm STANAVO had agreed to provide the gas and oil. But if there was going to be a world flight, there would need to be more cash—lots of it. Her husband had roughed out some preliminary estimates:

- $5,000 for the purchase and installation of extra equipment
- $4,000 for test flying
- $3,000 for administration
- $3,000 for advance flight arrangements
- $2,000 for expenses en route
- $3,000 for copilot and technical advisor
- $2,000 for insurance
- $5,000 for "unexpected" costs.[10]

The $27,000 in cash costs added to the $42,000 purchase price brought the estimated total to $69,000, against which they had $40,000 pledged by Purdue. Finding sponsors to fill the $29,000 gap would be critical.

A key potential contributor was fifty-five-year-old Vincent Bendix, founder and chief executive officer of Bendix Corporation. In 1910 Bendix had invented and patented the Bendix drive that made electric starters for gasoline engines practical. He founded the Bendix Brake Company in 1923 after acquiring patents for brake drum/shoe design and, the next year, established the Bendix Corporation in South Bend, Indiana. Bendix Aviation was founded in 1929, and in 1931 it established the Bendix Transcontinental Air Race as part of the National Air Races.

As an Indiana-based giant in the aviation industry, Bendix was a natural target for support of the world flight project. By the time the Purdue deal was finalized, Putnam had succeeded in getting an "informal" promise from Vincent Bendix to provide some of the instruments for Earhart's nascent Electra, but there had been no discussion of a financial contribution. With Purdue's participation finally settled, how best to approach Bendix for cash and who should make the pitch became the subject of much anxious correspondence among Putnam, Elliott, and Meikle. As usual, Earhart was not in the loop.

At the same time, Putnam was impatient to close the deal with Lockheed and get them started building the airplane. Earhart had not yet received, let alone signed, the agreement with Purdue when, on March 16, her husband fired off a wire to Lockheed president Robert Gross:

Financial arrangements just completed. Sending this wire so no time lost. This week can send initial payment based on price performance guarantees quoted in your letter. However, hope as we proceed some price reduction can be arranged, feeling of those associated with project being that under circumstances all concerned would be willing deliver products at actual cost without profit. For instance, engine, props, instruments, fuel, all being contributed outright. For your confidential information AE and myself receiving no financial compensation. Remaining money resulting from flight proceed[s] to go to permanent fund for aeronautical research at Purdue University. Subject further discussion please wire what amount needed now and whether can meet June fifteenth delivery date. Am requesting engine delivery by May twentieth. Please step on it. Regards.[11]

March 16 was a Monday, and it was Friday before Gross responded with a completed "order blank" for Earhart to sign for one Lockheed Electra 10E airplane "gasoline capacity to provide range of 4500 miles." The delivery date was to be on or about July 1, 1936. The order was mailed to New York on March 20. That same day, Meikle sent Earhart a letter for her to sign and return, officially accepting Purdue's terms for supporting the world flight.

Things were moving quickly. Earhart received and signed both the Purdue letter and the Lockheed order form on Monday, March 23. Lockheed required a deposit of $10,000—money Earhart and Putnam did not have. Earhart returned the Lockheed order with a check dated March 24 for the required $10,000. To cover the check, Elliott sent a check for $12,000 to Putnam that same day.[12]

In California, Paul Mantz was doing all he could to move the project forward. One problem was getting an airplane built any time soon. The Model 10 was proving to be a winner for Lockheed. Some fifty Electras were in service; thirty-nine flew for domestic carriers Northwest, Pan American, Braniff, Eastern, and Delta, plus four with LOT in Poland. Five served as corporate aircraft, including one in the Soviet Union. The U.S. Navy had an Electra, as did the Japanese Imperial Government.[13]

There were more orders to fill, and the factory floor at the Lockheed plant was crowded with airplanes under construction. To accommodate Earhart, Lockheed management allowed her to jump the queue. On March 23 Mantz wrote to Putnam, "I talked to Cyril Chappellett [sic] [Lockheed secretary] the other day, and he stated they had a fuselage practically finished and the ship pretty well under way, which they intend to assign to you in order to get it out around July, otherwise, heaven knows when you'll get delivery."

The airplane Lockheed appropriated to be completed as Earhart's 10E Special was c/n (constructor's number) 1055, the fifty-fifth Model 10 built. It is unlikely that the originally intended owner of c/n 1055 knew why or by whom his place in the production line had been usurped. Putnam insisted that "the whole matter be held confidentially" until the time was right for an official announcement, which he expected would be around the middle of April.[14] In the meantime, even internal Lockheed memos referred to the customer for the "special 10E" as "Livingston."[15]

Mantz dove into the details of how the ship should be equipped. In a March 24 letter to Putnam, he cautioned that Pratt & Whitney should not send engines equipped with automatic mixture control; instead, Putnam should buy a Cambridge double-dial mixture control. Earhart would need to manually control the fuel/air mixture to achieve maximum range.[16] In Mantz's view, another purchase of critical importance was a Sperry robot pilot. "The task AE has ahead of her, regardless of whether she takes someone with her or not, I can not see how the job can be done properly without this instrument, as it would most certainly eliminate 50% of the fatigue."[17]

And then there was "the radio situation." There must be an "all wave receiver capable of listening on all marine bands and bands used by major airlines in Europe and Asia." The transmitter should have crystals to cover all of the various wavelengths that would be needed. He preferred that the radios be Western Electric because parts were available worldwide.[18]

While Mantz and Putnam worked on technical issues, Earhart was back on the road doing speaking engagements. Despite efforts to keep the whole matter confidential, rumors began to circulate that she was planning to fly around the world. In an April 1 letter to her friend and fellow famous female aviator Ruth Nichols, Earhart wrote: "As to world flights, etc. The nearest I am to one of those is, confidentially, to have use of some new equipment. However, that is for technical problems, at least for the present. I am tied up with lectures until May first, so reports of my going round the world in June are slightly incoherent."[19]

But the rumors persisted, and Putnam and Purdue were eager to take control of the narrative with an official statement. Purdue Research Foundation director Stanley Meikle crafted a press release he sent to Putnam on April 3. Three days later, Putnam returned it with a few minor changes. Putnam said he would make the release on either Sunday, April 19, or Monday, April 20.[20] President Elliott was afraid they were moving too fast. On April 9 Meikle sent a telegram to Putnam saying President Elliott felt "it might be very inadvisable to make announcement before meeting of Trustees on Wednesday [April 22]" unless the delay would create "positive hazards."[21]

Two days later, all hell broke loose. On the morning of April 11, Putnam was in Chicago when he received a wire from his secretary in New York saying the afternoon edition of the *New York Sun* carried an announcement that Amelia Earhart intended to fly around the world. Purdue's involvement was nowhere mentioned. This was potentially catastrophic. Without the Purdue connection, a world flight would appear to be just another publicity stunt. Solicitations of cash, equipment, and services would be compromised. Regaining control of the narrative was essential.

Putnam immediately got on the phone to Meikle and urged that the Purdue announcement be released the next day, April 12, as originally planned. Meikle passed the news to Elliott, who remained adamant that they wait until after the trustees' meeting on April 22. Shortly after noon, Meikle called Putnam back with Elliott's decision. Later that afternoon, Putnam called again to say that he was getting phone calls at home from *New York Herald* and *Tribune* reporters asking for information about the world flight. Putnam put them off. He and his wife were prepared to come to West Lafayette immediately to discuss the situation.

In a letter to Elliott memorializing the day's frantic events, Meikle wrote: "It is not surprising that with all the efforts which have been made to interest manufacturers in furnishing funds and equipment, this leak should have occurred. Both Miss Earhart and Mr. Putnam seem to be very much concerned. The fact that the press is not controllable and that the story threatened to 'break' without reference to Purdue or the Foundation seemed to cause them a great deal deeper concern."[22] Meikle ended his letter to Elliott with his assurance that "I have maintained gently but firmly that the prepared news item originating from your office must not be released until the Trustees have considered the whole matter."[23]

Photo 5. Amelia Earhart and Purdue University president Edward C. Elliott hold a model of a Lockheed Model 10 Electra. TIGHAR Collection

Three days later, on April 14, Earhart and Putnam arrived at Purdue. After five days of discussions, Putnam prevailed, and the Purdue announcement was released on Sunday, April 19. The three-and-a-half-page press release made no mention of a world flight: "Amelia Earhart today announced her purchase of a 'flying laboratory.' Through the individual generosity of several of the members (who desire to remain anonymous) of the Purdue Research Foundation. . . Miss Earhart's purchase of a fast Electra airplane has been made possible."

Although Earhart would own the plane and be entirely responsible for its use, she would cooperate with the university in "the expansion of research and education in the field of aeronautics." At the same time, the Purdue Research Foundation announced the establishment of the "Amelia Earhart Fund for Aeronautical Research" to provide "a more aggressive aeronautical research program in the field of pure and applied science."

Earhart's quoted statement had a characteristically feminist tone: "I am sincerely grateful to President Elliott and the friends of Purdue who are making possible my new airplane. I hope its use may result in constructive accomplishment—both for Purdue and for women in general. For it is not often we of the feminine persuasion are given such opportunities to pioneer in our chosen fields."

Delivery of the Electra was expected in July, after which there would be a series of trial flights in southern California and at Purdue: "The many possibilities to be checked as opportunity offers include speed and fuel consumption under varying conditions; television experimentation; the use of oxygen; radio communication and navigation instruments and methods; the human equasion [*sic*] of fatigue and endurance in relation to altitude, sleep, eyestrain, etc. Periodic 'field tests' on actual flights are planned later. Such flights will probably include continental crossings and possibly a South American journey."[24]

The media response to the news was underwhelming. The Associated Press and United Press both put the story on the wire, but none of the major newspapers picked it up. The *Salt Lake Tribune* gave the news a few column inches on page two under the cryptic headline "Purdue Given Financing for Amelia Earhart Hop": "Announcement of the establishment of a fund for purchase of a 'flying laboratory' in which Amelia Earhart, first woman to fly the Atlantic, will hop here and there around the world was announced today by Purdue University."[25] The headline for the brief story on page three of the April 20 evening edition of the *Berkeley Daily Gazette* could have benefited from some proofreading: "Plant Bought as 'Air Laboratory.'"[26] The impact of the press release may have been disappointing, but at least the world flight cat was back in the bag.

In Burbank, Lockheed engineers Clarence "Kelly" Johnson and W. C. Nelson were preparing Lockheed Report 487, "Range Study of Lockheed Electra Bimotor Airplane," to reassure management, and the customer, that they could deliver on the promise of producing an Electra with an unrefueled range of 4,500 miles. Lockheed had made Putnam that assurance in early February in trying to close the sale. Now that the deal was sealed, somebody apparently decided it would be a good idea to have a technical study to back up the sales promise.

The range study was said to be "a complete study of the factors determining the maximum practical range of the Lockheed Electra Model 10E bimotor airplane. . . . The complete performance has been computed conservatively based on actual flight tests results on a Model 10E."[27] Which 10E was used in the tests is not mentioned in the report, but it was probably the prototype, c/n 1041, registered to Lockheed Aircraft Corporation as NX14971 in February 1936. How much of the data in the report were derived from actual flight tests versus hypothetical calculations is not clear.

The report contradicts itself. On page one, it asserts that "fuel consumption data is based on results which have been obtained in flight with careful mixture control." But on page twenty in the "Appendix and Computations" section, the report admits that "complete data on the fuel consumption of the engine was not available so generalized data on air-cooled engines was used."[28] The study concludes, "It is possible to fly a Lockheed Electra Model 10E non-stop for a distance between 4,100 to 4,500 miles starting out with 1,200 gallons of gasoline and the proper amount of oil."

The key was precise mixture control using a Cambridge exhaust gas analyzer. A series of graphical curves specified optimum power and mixture settings for various weights. To get the maximum range, the pilot would have to follow a constantly changing power/speed/mixture profile as fuel was burned and weight decreased. With 1,200 gallons of gas, the Electra would weigh 16,500 pounds, an increase of 6,000 pounds (57 percent) over the normal maximum gross weight of 10,500 pounds. At that weight, takeoff from a good hard-surface runway at sea level and standard temperature, using 30 degrees of flaps, was calculated to require just under 2,100 feet.[29] Report 487 was not completed until June 4, 1936, but it showed that, in theory, a Model 10E could perform as promised if it was properly equipped and flown to exacting standards.

On May 26 Earhart paid a visit to the Lockheed plant to see her Electra under construction. Publicity photos taken that day show the fuselage framed up and skinned but still lacking engines, landing gear, and outer wings. The plywood flooring was installed, but otherwise the interior of the aircraft was a bare shell.

The Lockheed Model 10, like most all-metal aircraft, is of semi-monocoque construction. Aluminum skins are riveted to circumferential formers and longitudinal stringers that distribute the aerodynamic loads. Designed as an airliner, the Electra's cabin featured a window for each of its ten passengers, but windows are holes in the aluminum shell that weaken the integrity of the structure. Faced with the need to deliver an aircraft able to withstand the forces generated by much greater weight, and free of the need to accommodate passengers, Lockheed engineers strengthened the fuselage of c/n 1055 by eliminating all but the rearmost cabin window on each side. In the two surviving windows, the stringer that would normally be cut out to provide an unobstructed view was left in place. The result was an immensely strong fuselage framework uninterrupted except for the solid cabin door standard on all Electras.

A June 2 internal Lockheed memo describes the initial plan for how the 10E Special was to be completed to meet the 1,200-gallon fuel capacity and 16,500-pound gross weight anticipated by Report 487. Luxuries such as soundproofing and the cabin ventilating system were to be sacrificed to save weight. The 200 gallons of gas in the standard wing tanks would be supplemented by installing 102-gallon fuel tanks in the two wing root baggage lockers. Another eight hundred gallons of fuel would be carried in an unspecified number of tanks mounted in the cabin. Total weight was expected to come in at 16,141 pounds with 1,204 gallons of fuel.[30]

Due to unspecified delays, Lockheed missed the promised July 1 delivery by almost three weeks. On July 19 the aircraft was finally ready for inspection; Bureau of Air Commerce inspector L. H. Steward approved the "Electra 10E Special" for owner Lockheed Aircraft Corporation. The empty weight of the aircraft was 7,340 pounds. No gross weight or maximum payload was listed, but the fuel setup was a bit different than anticipated in June. The total capacity was 1,198 gallons, distributed in thirteen tanks.[31]

With the inspection completed and approved, Lockheed applied for the airplane to be licensed in the experimental category. Whoever typed the application jumped the gun and described the "purpose for which the aircraft will be used" as "Long distance flights and research." Those words were crossed out and "for factory test work" was hand-printed on the form.[32]

The application was not notarized and submitted until July 22. Contrary to the paperwork, and possibly in deference to a press event Putnam had planned for July 21, the airplane was marked NR16020, falsely implying that it was registered in the restricted category and had been approved for international flight.

The next day, July 20, was a busy one. At Lockheed, test pilot Elmer McLeod took the ship up for its first flight. His logbook entry reads, "X16020 First Test. A & E [Airframe and Engine], Lockheed to Lockheed." The duration of the flight was one hour and fifty minutes, covering 280 miles for an average speed of 153 mph.[33]

In New York, George Putnam was sorting out an important detail in the deal with Purdue. Lockheed was ready to deliver the airplane and they wanted to be paid, but before the university disbursed further funds to Earhart, Putnam needed to be sure that the money would not be subject to tax. The agreement with Purdue was that Earhart would use the funds to purchase the Electra for a world flight and subsequent aeronautical research. The problem was, any perception that she would be fulfilling a contract with Purdue would make the funds taxable as income.

In 1936 gifts of less than $50,000 were exempt from tax. In a letter to Stanley Meikle, Putnam asked for a letter from the Purdue Research Foundation specifying that "the gifts to Miss Earhart are outright and without obligation of performance on her part." He pointed out that this would also protect the foundation by "showing it was in no wise responsible for any possible mishap resulting from the project." To make it easy, Putnam's lawyer provided the wording for the desired letter. Putnam said he was taking steps to secure similar letters from other contributors.[34]

In a separate letter that same day, Putnam pressured Meikle to act without delay. Noting that the ship had today "presumably" made its first flight, he said delivery of the aircraft would be made sometime during the coming week: "I am, therefore, equipping Miss Earhart with a check for $34,000, instructing her however not to turn it over to Lockheed until I have wired her that covering funds have been deposited here."[35]

Putnam went on to outline an ambitious plan for the rest of the year. For the next thirty days, Earhart would work closely with Lockheed to "make the many physical adjustments in the ship that will inevitably be required." Purdue president Elliott was scheduled to be in Los Angeles in early August, and Earhart was looking forward to taking him for a ride in what Putnam referred to as "the University's 'flying laboratory,'" which, he said, would be painted in Purdue colors (even though everyone had just gone to great lengths to make sure the airplane, in no respect, belonged to the university).

In late August Earhart flew the Electra to New York for the start of the transcontinental Bendix Trophy race on September 4. On the way she made a brief stop at Purdue. After the New York to Los Angeles race, the ship remained in California for the rest of September so that "further adjustments" could be made following the "trans-continental shake-down flight."

In October Earhart would be on the road again with a series of scheduled appearances in the Midwest, ending up in West Lafayette, "if appropriate," at the end of the month. She had nothing scheduled for November and might bring the ship to Purdue for "a considerable visit" to work out "other various matters preliminary to contemplated flights."

Finally, Putnam revealed plans for a "fairly spectacular shake-down flight to the south," possibly from Los Angeles to Mexico City, to Panama, Venezuela, Havana, New York, Purdue, and back to Los Angeles. Preparations for the world flight were "beginning to take form," but he did not expect the circumnavigation to "take shape" until February.[36]

On July 21 Amelia Earhart presented her new "flying laboratory" to the press. The airplane had been moved from Lockheed's Turkey Crossing factory and airstrip a short distance up the road to Union Air Terminal on the Burbank airport, where Earhart posed for photos and recited a rehearsed statement for the newsreel cameras: "This new Lockheed is the realization of a dream. It comes to me through Purdue University and is a real flying laboratory equipped with all the latest instruments. With it, I hope to accomplish something really scientifically worthwhile for aviation. I myself am particularly interested in the reaction of the human being toward all aspects of flying."[37]

Photo 6. Electra as delivered, July 21, 1936. When first presented at a press event prior to its formal sale to Earhart three days later, the Model 10E Special was registered by Lockheed in the Experimental Category as X16020 but bore the bogus markings NR16020, indicating approval for international flight in the restricted category. The cabin's two windows (one on each side) were bisected by longerons that strengthened the fuselage. A belly wire receiving antenna ran from the starboard pitot tube under the nose to a mast just forward of the cabin door. A trailing wire transmitting antenna deployed from the extreme tip of the tail. TIGHAR Collection

Answering a question from a reporter, she said, "Well yes, I am a member of the faculty of Purdue but I have a leave of absence while I work on this particular project." Responding to another question: "I hope the experiments will include altitude flying and (with a slight pause and smile) also long distance work." A photo of Earhart in the cabin shows the initial fueling system for the fuselage tanks. The two forward tanks were serviced via a single filler neck above the port-side tank. The remaining five fuselage tanks were filled by means of two fueling stations in the port side of the fuselage where windows were located on the passenger version of the 10E.

Press reports described the flying laboratory as being equipped with "a Sperry auto-gyro robot pilot, a fuel minimizer, wind [*sic*] deicers, radio homing and two-way sending devices."[38] In actuality, the airplane still belonged to Lockheed, was incorrectly marked, and was not completed. The Sperry gyro pilot was not present; there was not, nor would there be, deicing equipment; there was no homing device; and the Western Electric radios were yet to be installed.

Elmer McLeod gave Earhart her first ride in the new ship. The two-hour-and-ten-minute flight included several takeoffs and landings and covered some four hundred miles.[39] The Electra was an enormous step up from the single-engined Lockheed Vega in which she had built her career. She would need a great deal of instruction and practice before she was ready to fly the machine alone. Nonetheless, the *Los Angeles Times* headline read "Flying Laboratory Put Through Its Initial Experiment by Famed Aviatrix."[40]

That same day, Earhart gave Lockheed a letter authorizing the company "to deliver when completed Electra airplane No. 1055, which you are now constructing for me, to my agent, Paul Mantz, at Las Vegas, Nevada."[41] Lockheed routinely made deliveries of new aircraft in Nevada to avoid California sales tax. Earhart probably delegated acceptance of the airplane to her technical adviser as the person best qualified to judge whether the machine was satisfactory.

McLeod logged test flights in X16020 on July 22 and 23 before delivering the airplane in Las Vegas, where ownership was transferred to Earhart "in consideration of the sum of TEN & no/100 dollars" on July 24—her thirty-ninth birthday. On the typed bill of sale, the *NR* of NR16020 is written over with an *X*.[42]

A series of undated photos taken near the Lockheed plant appear to show Earhart and Mantz upon his return from Las Vegas. Earhart is beaming. It is her birthday, and the Electra, the realization of a dream, is finally hers. The starboard-side belly antenna wire (absent in the Burbank press event photos) suggests that the radios had been installed. The plane is still incorrectly marked NR16020.

On Saturday, July 25, McLeod logged a one-hour test flight from "Burbank to Burbank" with three takeoffs and landings. The airplane was now based with Mantz Flying Service at Burbank, and this was probably an instructional flight for either Earhart or Mantz.

On July 27 Lockheed notified the Bureau of Air Commerce that serial number 1055 had been sold to Amelia Earhart and enclosed Earhart's application for a license in the restricted category.[43]

5

Teething Troubles

AUGUST–SEPTEMBER 1936

Shortly after Earhart filled out the paperwork to register her new airplane in the restricted category, a problem was discovered in the long-range fuel system, and the application was canceled. The seven fuselage tanks were removed from the aircraft, leaving only the three fuel tanks in each wing. With the airplane stuck in the experimental category until a new license application could be submitted and approved, the *NR* markings on the wings and tail were changed to *X*.

While the fuel system problems were being addressed, Earhart continued to promote her new airplane. On Sunday, August 2, McLeod and Earhart flew X16020 to Mills Field, San Francisco (now the site of San Francisco International Airport), making the 325-mile flight in one hour and fifty-five minutes for an average speed of 169 mph. McLeod didn't log the flight, so he was apparently acting as instructor with Earhart as pilot in command.[1] They arrived unannounced and stayed overnight "incognito" before hopping the seven miles to San Francisco Bay Airdrome in Alameda to show off the 10E Special and see inventor Elmer Dimity demonstrate a ninety-foot "plane parachute" before returning to Burbank that afternoon.[2]

A photo taken on that occasion shows the cabin interior minus the fuselage tanks and reveals some of the changes made since the July 21 press event. Crumpled aluminum foil now covered the cabin walls. (Electra cabins were soundproofed with kapok covered with crumpled aluminum foil.) To save weight, Earhart's airplane was delivered without insulation, but the big-engined Model 10E was notoriously loud. After a few flights, Earhart apparently changed her mind.

No record has survived to document the nature of the fuel system problem, but some of the steps to correct it are evident. The photograph shows that a false floor of plywood with cradles to stabilize the fuselage tanks had been laid over the standard flooring, and a narrow wooden strip had been fastened along the edge next to the metal ductwork of the cabin heating system. Excessive heat in fuel lines can cause vapor lock. The wooden strip might have been installed to support insulated barriers to shield the fuselage tanks from the heating ducts. (A single supplemental fuselage tank in a later Electra was insulated from the cabin heating ducts with thick asbestos padding.[3])

Photo 7. Electra's cabin without tanks, August 3, 1936. The special fuselage fuel tanks were removed due to an unspecified problem—probably vapor lock in the fuel lines. TIGHAR Collection

The tanks were still out when Earhart submitted a new application to license the aircraft in the restricted category on August 6. The aircraft, without the long-range system, was approved the next day, and the wings and tail were marked R16020.[4] Exactly when the fuselage tanks were reinstalled is not recorded, but among the changes made was the addition of two more fueling ports on the left side of the fuselage. The original manifold system of two ports serving five tanks in the cabin and one port serving both forward tanks was changed. The new configuration had four tanks in the cabin and two forward tanks, each with its own fueling port.

In preparation for a visit from Edward C. Elliott scheduled for August 20, the engine cowlings were painted in Purdue's gold and black colors. Elliott was suitably impressed but admitted, "I have flown thousands of miles on air lines, but as far as the ships themselves are concerned, I'm pretty uninformed."[5] The Purdue president was also probably not informed that Paul Mantz had arranged to borrow the new plane for some stunt work in an MGM romantic comedy then in production.

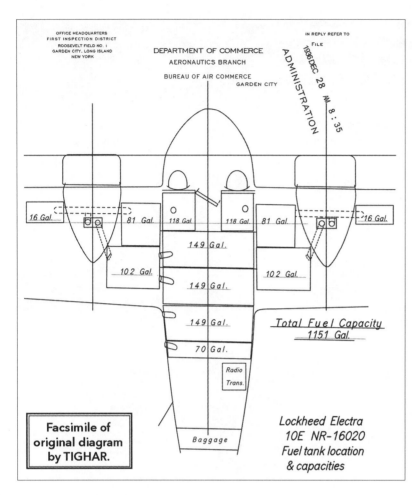

Photo 8. Schematic of fuel tank configuration of Earhart's Electra
Bureau of Air Commerce

Shortly after Elliott left Burbank for alumni meetings in San Francisco, the Electra's registration markings were altered for a disguised appearance in *Love on the Run* starring Joan Crawford and Clark Gable. In the film, Gable's character steals an airplane, frightens a crowd with wild taxiing, and makes a barely controlled takeoff. The Electra's brief movie career was not filmed at Burbank and went unnoticed by the press. How much MGM paid for the undignified and unpublicized use of the airplane is not recorded.

On August 14 Putnam had announced his wife would enter the Bendix Trophy Transcontinental Speed Classic to be held September 4.[6] The cross-country contest, sponsored by industrialist Vincent Bendix, was the nation's premier long-distance air race and a rare opportunity for men and women to compete head to head, but men invariably took top honors. They were not necessarily better pilots, but they always had the fastest airplanes. In the July 1933 Bendix race, the first four places went to men flying custom-built ships. Amelia Earhart in her Lockheed Vega 5 and Ruth Nichols in a Lockheed Orion were the only females in a field of ten. Earhart came in fifth, and Nichols placed sixth.

Two months later, popular racing pilot Florence Klingensmith was killed in a spectacular crash while competing with men in a pylon race. An inquest found the cause to be structural failure of the right wing, but soon speculation began to circulate in the press of another explanation: pilot error. Bureau of Air of Commerce licensing requirements stipulated "All women should be cautioned that it is dangerous for them to fly within a period extending from 3 days prior, to 3 days after, the menstrual period."[7] The *Chicago Daily News*, primary sponsor of the National Air Races, reported without evidence that Klingensmith had been unable to deal with the emergency because she was in a "weakened condition" due to menstruation.[8] Erasing the progress made since the rebellion of 1929, race organizers banned women from air racing: "There is no more place for women pilots in the high speed, free-for-all air race game than there is a place for women drivers on the speedway at Indianapolis."[9]

The women hit the roof. Ruth Nichols argued, "Women have the same inherent right to be killed in airplane races as men have." Earhart was equally vocal: "When a man cracks up, no one pays any special attention. But oh, when a girl does."[10] For their part, the men sided with the women. New York *Herald Tribune* reporter C. B. Allen wrote, "More and more veteran patrons of the National Air Races are swinging to the belief that if a little of the energy expended on eliminating women were devoted to tightening up restrictions on the air-worthiness of participating planes American air meets would be attended by fewer fatalities."[11]

The ban held for 1934, but under increasing pressure from aviation editors, race organizers permitted women to compete with men in the 1935 Bendix Trophy race. Two women picked up the gauntlet: newcomer Jacqueline Cochran, and Earhart, fresh from her Honolulu to Oakland and Los Angeles to Mexico City to Newark record flights. To help with navigation, she brought along Paul Mantz and engine manufacturer Albert Menasco. Cochran quit after three hundred miles. Earhart and company finished a disappointing fifth.

The blinding pace of aeronautical development had left Earhart behind. Her beloved Vega could no longer compete, and it looked like her record-setting days were over, until the Electra changed everything. Due to airport expansion under way in Cleveland, the 1936 National Air Races were to be held at Mines Field in Los Angeles. The cross-country Bendix race would launch from Floyd Bennett Field in Brooklyn, New York. The entrant with the shortest total elapsed time between takeoff and landing would take away $6,750 in prize money (40 percent of the $15,000 total purse). The Electra would not be the fastest aircraft entered in the race, but, if all went well, it was a sure winner. The 10E Special's long-range capability should enable Earhart to make the 2,400-mile flight nonstop. Everyone else would have to make a refueling stop in Kansas City, Missouri.

But if Earhart was going to take on the Bendix, she was going to need help. At more than double the weight and horsepower of her old Vega 5C, the 10E Special was a giant step up in performance and complexity. Earhart had no experience with retractable landing gear, wing flaps, and propellers whose pitch had to be adjusted to match throttle settings.

Most important, two engines meant learning how to fly the airplane in the event of an engine failure. In a single-engine airplane, the procedure is simple—find a place to land. A twin-engine aircraft offers the ability to continue the flight, but the pilot must deal with all the thrust coming from one side—a critical skill set made more difficult in those days by the absence of full-feathering propellers. In 1936 the ability to turn propeller blades knife-edge to the wind had not yet been developed so, unless carefully managed, the propeller on a dead engine would "windmill," creating enormous aerodynamic drag and almost certain loss of control. Getting the procedure for dealing with an engine failure exactly right was a matter of life and death.

For the Bendix race, Earhart needed someone to accompany her who had experience in large multi-engine aircraft. The perfect choice was her friend Helen Richey. At age twenty-seven, Richey had won a major air race, set endurance and altitude records, and, although new to the Lockheed Model 10, had many hours in Ford and Stinson tri-motors during her career as an airline pilot.

Richey brought the piloting and navigation skills needed to make the Electra a viable competitor in the Bendix race, and she owed a debt of gratitude to Amelia Earhart. In 1934 Richey was hired by Pennsylvania Central Airlines, becoming the first woman to fly for a regularly scheduled commercial airline, but the male pilots denied her membership in the Airline Pilots Association. Earhart led a public protest against the pilot's union, but to no avail, and Richey resigned after less than a year on the line.

The 1936 Bendix race drew a flock of female entries. In addition to Earhart and Richey in the 10E Special, Laura Ingalls was entered in a Lockheed Orion, Jacqueline Cochran signed up with a Northrop Gamma, and Martie Bowman entered her WACO INF. Louise Thaden and Blanche Noyes would compete in a Beechcraft C17R Staggerwing.

The male competition was also stiff. The 1935 Bendix winner Benny Howard was back with his DGA (damned good airplane) "Mr. Mulligan," this time accompanied by his wife Maxine. Joe Jacobson would fly a Northrop Gamma, while William Gulick, William Warner, and a mechanic raced a big Vultee. Col. Roscoe Turner entered his Wedell-Williams racer, and a stock Douglas DC-2 flown by George Pomeroy and Louis Brewer, with mechanic Irving Picker aboard, rounded out the field.

On August 29 Earhart, with Paul Mantz and mechanic Ruckins D. "Bo" McKneely aboard, left Burbank for New York. An eight-hour flight to Kansas City provided an opportunity for Mantz to give Earhart more instruction before leaving the flight to return to California. Earhart told the Associated Press she had not yet decided whether to enter the race and the trip to New York was solely to "find out what the ship could do."[12]

One thing the ship could do was leak oil. The Electra arrived in Kansas City streaming oil from both engines. McKneely thought the problem was solved when they left the next morning, but on the way to New York, the engine nacelles again became streaked with black. Earhart diverted to Cleveland, where McKneely again addressed the problem. The next morning they continued on and became the first of the competitors to arrive at Floyd Bennett Field.

In the days before the race, Earhart and McKneely were joined by George Putnam, who watched anxiously while a team of mechanics, probably from Pratt & Whitney in Connecticut, worked on the oil leak problem. Helen Richey arrived from her home in McKeesport, Pennsylvania, but her participation in the flight was largely ignored by the press.

Among the prerace festivities at Floyd Bennett Field was the departure on September 2 of a highly publicized attempt at the first over-and-back double crossing of the Atlantic. Celebrated Eastern Airlines captain Henry T. "Dick" Merrill and popular entertainer Harry Richman would fly Richman's new Vultee V-1A nonstop to London, refuel, and return to New York. Powered by a single 1,000 hp Wright Cyclone engine, the aircraft was christened "Lady Peace" as a hopeful gesture in the

Photo 9. Prior to the start of the Bendix Trophy Race, Earhart poses for a promotional photo shoot surrounded by Amelia Earhart luggage, September 1936. Helen Richey sits in the door of the unfinished cabin.
Purdue University Archives and Special Collections

deteriorating European political climate. To enhance buoyancy in the event of a ditching, the wings were packed with 41,000 ping pong balls. Of most interest to Amelia Earhart was the ship's radio navigation equipment. Her aircraft was not yet equipped with a radio direction finder. A prototype Bendix radio compass installed in the Vultee was more advanced and user-friendly than conventional radio direction finders. The historic round-trip would be completed without a hitch and, within a few weeks, Earhart would have the new system installed in the Electra.

On September 4, at their appointed takeoff time of 1:47 a.m., Earhart and Richey pointed the Lockheed's nose westward and immediately faced a crisis. Shortly after takeoff, the emergency hatch over the pilot's seat blew open and, according to Earhart, "almost pulled us right out of the cockpit." Hyperbole aside, the noise, wind, and confusion in the darkness were terrifying. The hatch was a standard feature on all Electras but was seldom used; crews boarded through the cabin door. In the 10E Special, entering the cockpit from the cabin meant an undignified belly-crawl over the fuselage fuel tanks. Earhart routinely climbed up on the wing and hoisted herself into the front office via the emergency hatch—an athletic and awkward maneuver, especially since the hatch opened outward over the wing. Although newspapers reported the door "broke" open, the mishap was more likely due to the hatch being improperly latched before takeoff. Once open in flight, retrieving it required standing or kneeling on the pilot's seat, reaching out, and wrestling the aluminum panel against a one-hundred-plus mile-per-hour breeze. The women eventually got the hatch back in place and, according to press accounts, tied it down with a "rag" (Earhart's trademark scarf, perhaps). The need to get the wayward hatch securely wired shut and an unspecified problem with the new fuel system meant a stop in Kansas City. The entire affair cost the flight an estimated forty minutes and any chance of placing well in the race.

Some of the other competitors had more serious trouble. Roscoe Turner crashed on his way to New York and did not compete. During the race, Joe Jacobson's Northrop Gamma blew up in flight over Kansas. Jacobson was thrown clear, and after some initial fouling, his parachute opened, and he landed without injury. Howard's "Mister Mulligan" threw a propeller blade over New Mexico. The imbalance made the machine uncontrollable, and the resulting crash severely injured Howard and his wife.

In a startling upset, women took both first and second place. Louise Thaden and Blanche Noyes in their Staggerwing Beechcraft won the race with a total elapsed time of fourteen hours and fifty-four minutes. Laura Ingalls' Lockheed Orion was second at fifteen hours and forty-five minutes. Bill Gulick's Vultee was third, and George Pomeroy's DC-2 got stuck in the mud during its refueling stop, causing him to finish fourth. Earhart and Richey finished fifth and last with a time of sixteen hours and thirty-five minutes. Their 5 percent of the purse came to $750. Whether or how it was split between Earhart and Richey is not recorded.

Following the Bendix race, the plan was for the plane to remain in California through October, where Mantz would oversee more work on the fuel system. By way of remuneration for his services, he would also be able to use the Electra for more film work. The cooperation and support of the Roosevelt administration State Department would be essential in getting the many diplomatic clearances needed for a world flight, so Earhart would spend October on the East Coast campaigning for Roosevelt's reelection. In November, she would take the Electra to Purdue for a visit before embarking on the "fairly spectacular shake-down flight to the south" that Putnam had promised.[13] The world flight that would "put us all on easy street"[14] was supposed to "take shape"[15] in February. It was an ambitious program, but the best laid plans of mice, men, and aviators "gang aft agley."

The Bendix race had been an inauspicious debut for the "Flying Laboratory," and funding for the still-secret world flight was $10,000 short. To get the project back on track, Putnam needed to shuffle the deck. The first step was to create some positive buzz. After months of deflecting rumors about a possible circumnavigation, on September 16 in an interview with the Associated Press, Earhart let drop she was "nearly sold" on the prospect of a world flight, "but I'm not sure. . . . I have no definite plans yet."[16] Dozens of newspapers around the country picked up the story.

Two days later, without telling Paul Mantz, Earhart and Putnam, accompanied by mechanic Bo McKneely, departed in the Electra for West Lafayette, Indiana, arriving at Purdue on September 19 where, according to press reports, Earhart would "stay at the school for six weeks to continue her experiments with the new airplane."[17] In truth, she stayed just long enough for a few photos with students before driving to Pennsylvania and New York, arriving at the New York Democratic Party state convention in Syracuse on September 29.[18] McKneely stayed at Purdue with the airplane to do the needed work.

Paul Mantz was not happy. Moving the ship to Indiana had cut the legs out from under his deal for some lucrative Hollywood film work. Back in Manhattan the day after the convention, Putnam wrote Mantz a letter explaining the primary reason for putting the airplane at Purdue: "Call it political. They have been wonderfully good to us and of course we want to cooperate in every way. It means much to them to have the airplane there. Also, frankly, we need $10,000 more and that's what I'm working on. . . . As regards the Purdue people, we made a number of commitments about the plane. One with an advertising agency which may lead to some fat returns."[19]

The addition of a Bendix radio compass prototype like the one "Lady Peace" had used on its round-trip Atlantic crossing was another reason for the Electra to be at Purdue. The system's inventor, Fred Hooven, was based not far away at Wright Field in Dayton, Ohio, and would come to Purdue to do the installation.

Putnam told Mantz it looked like the airplane would return to California in mid-November, but first it would go to Bell Laboratories and Western Electric in New Jersey "to get the radio stuff absolutely right. Perhaps you can work out some way of making some motion picture money with it in late November or December."[20]

Putnam added a confidential note about progress in solving the world flight's biggest logistical challenge: getting the Electra across the Pacific Ocean. By 1936 commercial air routes had been established across most of the globe. Aeropostale provided weekly airmail service across the south Atlantic with landplanes. Imperial Airways flew regular passenger schedules from London to South Africa, India, and Australia. KNILM (Royal Dutch East India Airlines) serviced southeast Asia. Pan American Airways was island-hopping from California to China with flying boats but, with no airports in the middle of the ocean, getting across the Pacific in a land plane was problematic. The broad expanse of the central Pacific had been spanned only twice. In 1928, the same year Earhart came to fame for crossing the Atlantic as a passenger aboard a Fokker F-VII tri-motor, Australian Charles Kingsford-Smith flew a similar Fokker F-VII, 3,144 miles nonstop from Hawaii to Fiji.

In 1931 the Japanese newspaper *Asahi Shimbun* offered $25,000 for the first nonstop flight from Japan to North America. Americans Clyde Pangborn and Hugh Herndon won the prize in "Miss Veedol," a single-engined Bellanca Skyrocket J-300 Long Distance Special. Loaded with 915 gallons of fuel, the flight took off from a beach in northern Honshu and flew an astonishing forty-one hours and thirteen minutes to a crash landing near Wenatchee, Washington, a distance of 5,500 miles.

Putnam's plan was for Earhart to fly nonstop from Honolulu to Tokyo. To make the jump with a 15 percent reserve required a range of 4,500 miles, and Lockheed Report 487 had suggested that a Model 10E Electra with 1,200 gallons of gas could do the job. Earhart's 10E Special was delivered with a total fuel capacity of 1,198 gallons, but the prospect of an unrefueled flight to Japan was soon abandoned. Fixing problems with the original fuel system had reduced the total to 1,151 gallons, and everyone—Putnam, Mantz, and Earhart—had concerns about her ability to control the airplane in a heavily overloaded takeoff. By late September 1936, someone—there is no record who—had come up with the idea of taking off from Hawaii with a partial load and refueling in flight 1,300 miles later from a U.S. Navy flying boat over Midway Island.

In 1936 air-to-air refueling meant dangling a hose from the aircraft acting as tanker to the aircraft to be fueled. Someone in the receiving ship had to get hold of the hose and guide it into a tank. The U.S. Navy had conducted experiments in air-to-air refueling in 1930 using a Martin T4M torpedo bomber as the tanker to deliver fuel to a Douglas PD-1 patrol bomber. They found the procedure "entirely practicable" but had gone no further.[21] In 1932 Louise Thaden and Frances Marsalis had set a women's endurance record of 196 hours aloft (nearly nine days) with a total of seventy-eight aerial refueling contacts. The following year, Helen Richey and Marsalis pushed the record to 237 hours. Both records were set in small, slow, single-engine Curtiss Thrush aircraft. No one had ever attempted in-flight refueling in a fast, multi-engine ship like the Electra.

Putnam pitched the idea to Rear Adm. Arthur B. Cook, chief of the Navy's Bureau of Aeronautics, and got a favorable response. At the end of a September 30, 1936, letter to Paul Mantz, Putnam wrote, "Confidentially, we are very encouraged with the attitude of the Navy about refueling. If this comes through there would be practice in San Diego. This would also mean a hatch in the top of the fuselage for refueling. You might give this some consideration."[22]

Earhart would need someone to handle the fueling hose, but she had already realized she would need a navigator for the trans-Pacific portion of the world flight. Although far from a done deal, the prospect of Navy support made air-to-air refueling look like a viable plan for getting the world flight across the Pacific.

6

Delay, Desperation, and Deliverance

OCTOBER–DECEMBER 1936

October 1936 got off to a promising start. At Purdue, inventor Fred Hooven, vice president and chief engineer of Bendix Radio Products, arrived from Dayton to install a prototype of his new radio compass direction finder in the Electra. Conventional loop antenna systems required the operator to rotate the loop until the quietest signal was heard in the headphones (known as "getting a minimum"). The bearing thus obtained ran in two opposite directions, so the operator had to resolve the "180° ambiguity" to determine which direction led to the station. Hooven's system did all that automatically: the operator dialed in the frequency, and a needle on a compass pointed to the station. Hooven's invention is still in use today as the automatic direction finder.

The equipment Hooven installed included a dedicated receiver situated atop one of the fuel tanks in the cabin. The loop antenna for the radio compass was encased in a translucent fairing on the top of the cabin. A wire "sense antenna" ran along the port side of the belly. Earhart was on the road, so she was not there to oversee the installation or receive instruction on how to operate the new system. As she toured from Massachusetts to Michigan and beyond in her Cord automobile, attending conferences and giving speeches, her husband was in New York trying to confirm Navy cooperation for the aerial refueling plan. Having received encouragement from Rear Admiral Cook, on October 16, Putnam wrote directly to Secretary of the Navy Claude A. Swanson.

After outlining Earhart's world flight plans and her intention to fly from Hawaii to Japan, Putnam explained the Electra had a total fuel capacity of 1,250 gallons (the actual capacity was 1,151 gallons), but "our desire is to avoid the hazard of the takeoff at Honolulu with the full load. . . . We would like to work out arrangements under which an aerial refueling operation can be conducted over Midway Island."

Putnam had it all planned out. Earhart would take off from Hawaii with one thousand gallons of gas and rendezvous with a Navy aircraft over Midway, having by then burned off about three hundred gallons. She would take on about five hundred gallons, bringing her fuel load "to the approximate maximum capacity, supplying ample for the remaining 2800 miles to Tokio [sic], or possibly a route via Guam to Manila." Putnam assured Swanson that the Electra "is an extremely stable ship, and with its flaps is able to remain aloft under full control at a very low speed . . . a comparatively easy ship to contact and work with on a refueling operation."

A special top fuselage hatch and equipment leading to the fuselage tanks would be installed in close cooperation with Navy authorities. The installation could be done at Los Angeles or San Diego, and Earhart and her navigator would be available "for some actual practice in refueling work at the convenience of the Navy in December and/or January." Specifically, "It is our understanding that some new Navy boats now reaching completion in San Diego will after the first of the year be ferried out to Honolulu." Putnam suggested an ideal situation would be for Earhart to practice in San Diego with the flying boat and crew who would do the refueling over Midway. The "new Navy boats" he was referring to were twelve Consolidated PBY-1 patrol bombers just entering service with Squadron VP-6F and scheduled to fly from San Diego to Pearl Harbor in late January. Putnam ended his letter with a request the entire project "be held in strictest confidence."[1]

While waiting for a response, Putnam had to sort out a paperwork foul-up. The Bureau of Air Commerce had gotten around to sending him the new aircraft license for posting in the Electra's cockpit.[2] Putnam forwarded it to mechanic Bo McKneely at Purdue, who noticed the license authorized only 394 gallons of fuel instead of the 1,148 gallons of the previous license. On October 24 Putnam wrote to J. Carroll Cone, assistant director at the Bureau of Air Commerce, expressing his puzzlement: "Evidently there was some error in issuing the new license."[3] The error, it turned out, was Earhart's. The license conformed to the application signed by Earhart on August 6, 1936, during the time the fuselage tanks were removed. There would be no new license until an application was "properly executed by A. E. and submitted to the local inspector and the aircraft presented for inspection."[4]

Getting a new inspection would have to wait. The more pressing problem was finding a way to get his wife across the Pacific without forcing her to make a takeoff that everyone, including Earhart, feared was beyond her skill level; but if Putnam thought going directly to the Secretary of the Navy would fast-track approval for his aerial refueling scheme, he was mistaken.

Swanson did not reply to Putnam's letter but sent it down through channels to Adm. William H. Standley, Chief of Naval Operations (CNO), who sent it, in turn, to Rear Admiral Cook at the Bureau of Aeronautics. It was Cook who had encouraged Putnam to seek Navy support. He now wrote he believed "the attitude of the [Navy] Department toward pioneering aeronautical ventures should, in general, be cooperative."[5] By assisting Earhart, "some benefit might accrue to the Navy in the line of development of fueling from the air," but he cautioned "many matters would have to be considered before rendering [a] definite decision to participate in the suggested program." Cook suggested Putnam's letter be sent to Arthur J. Hepburn, commander-in-chief, U.S. Fleet, for endorsement by "the forces afloat."[6]

On October 30, the CNO wrote to Putnam, "Inasmuch as this matter is one which involves questions of precedent and policy, as well as numerous other considerations, it is not practicable to reply definitely at this time. The matter is under consideration and you will be informed later of the Department's decision."[7] This was not good, and Putnam was worried. The Navy's tone had cooled since Cook's initial enthusiasm. If the aerial refueling deal fell through, Earhart would be faced with a maximum-load takeoff from Hawaii—something nobody wanted. Election day came and went, Franklin Roosevelt was reelected in a landslide, but a week went by with no further word from the Navy.

On November 9 Putnam wrote to Paul Mantz with another idea: "What we have in mind is the remote possibility of sending a land plane and pilot, by steamer, to Suva." (Putnam's use of "we" suggests Earhart had endorsed the plan.) Suva was 3,100 miles from Honolulu, 800 miles closer than Tokyo, so she wouldn't need to take off with a full load. The trouble with Suva, and the reason they had dismissed going that way before, was the absence of an airport in Fiji. There was nowhere the Electra could land, refuel, and take off. Mantz owned a Stearman Speedmail, a large, single-engine biplane designed as a mail plane and capable of carrying a heavy cargo load. Maybe Mantz could outfit the Stearman as a tanker and ship it to Fiji with a skilled pilot. The Stearman could take off from a beach or golf links to meet the Electra and refuel it over Suva, thus eliminating the need for a hazardous landing and takeoff. After refueling in midair, Earhart would continue another 1,700 miles to Brisbane, Australia.[8]

Mantz thought it might work, but his Stearman would be able to carry only about one hundred gallons of gas for refueling, "which would necessitate taking off, refueling, coming back, and filling up again five or six times to give her sufficient gasoline. This would take three hours or more, which I don't think would be so good." Mantz felt Putnam would be better off "buying one of those old 40Bs [Boeing Model 40B mail plane], such as United Air Lines used to have." He thought Putnam could get and equip one for about $2,000 and sell it afterward for $1,000. Handwritten notes on the letter, presumably by Putnam, suggest he figured the entire operation would cost about $26,000.[9] Nobody mentioned that the proposed 4,800-mile nonstop flight from Honolulu to Brisbane would put Earhart at the controls for at least thirty-two hours plus whatever time it took to refuel over Suva. Born of desperation, the plan was patently hare-brained. They really needed the Navy.

Pulling out all the stops, Earhart went to the top. On November 10 she wrote a three-page plea to President Roosevelt. After outlining her world flight plans, she wrote, "The chief problem is the jump west from Honolulu. The distance thence to Tokio [sic] is 3900 miles. I want to reduce as much as possible excessive over-load. With that in view, I am discussing with the Navy a possible *refueling in the air over Midway Island*" (emphasis in original). She explained the proposal was now on the desk of Admiral Standley. This was no time to play fair, and Earhart turned on the charm: "In the past the Navy has been so progressive in its pioneering, and so broad-minded in what we might call its 'public relations,' that I think a project such as this (even involving a mere woman!) may appeal to Navy personnel. Its successful attainment might, I think, win for the Service further popular friendship. . . . Knowing your own enthusiasm for voyaging, and your affectionate interest in Navy matters, I am asking you to help me secure Navy cooperation—that is, if you think well of the project." FDR scrawled across the top of the letter, "Do what we can and contact Mr. Putnam."[10] Six days later, naval aide to the president Paul Bastedo passed the letter to Chief of Naval Operations Standley,[11] noting that Mr. Putnam had already been in touch with the Navy Department about Miss Earhart's proposed flight. "I feel confident everything will be done to assist her."[12]

Regardless of how CNO Standley may have felt about the project, he now had a direct order from the commander-in-chief to "do what we can." On November 19 he wrote to George Putnam with the good news: "I am pleased to inform you that, after much investigation, the Department is willing to render the assistance requested, subject however to the successful completion of preliminary preparations and trials." Earhart would have to buy the gas for her own plane and cover any unusual expenses incurred by personnel engaged in the work. Putnam was to now coordinate with the commander-in-chief, U.S. Fleet, who was tasked with working out all the details concerning the preparation, preliminary tests, and actual refueling operations.[13] Putnam replied the very next day, expressing "the very deep appreciation of Miss Earhart and myself."[14] Navy cooperation for the aerial refueling plan now seemed assured, but the possibility of a better solution to the problem was already in the works.

Five days earlier, on November 14, Putnam in New York wrote to Paul Mantz in Burbank with good news and bad news. He began with the good news: "Apparently the Department of Commerce is about to make a landing field on an island far west of Honolulu, which is almost ideally situated for our purposes."[15] Refueling at a mid-Pacific airfield would eliminate the need for a complicated aerial refueling operation or a maximum-load takeoff from Hawaii. Where he got the confidential information is not recorded, but it probably came in a phone call from Earhart's close friend Eugene Vidal, director of the Commerce Department's Bureau of Air Commerce.

Vidal had a problem. His job was to regulate and promote the growth of commercial air travel, but dwindling budgets forced cuts in navigation services at the same time the public and the press were decrying a rash of domestic airline accidents. The nation's premier international airline, Pan American Airways, enjoyed a better safety record, but the "chosen instrument" for the projection of American aviation commerce was encountering obstacles to the expansion of its overseas routes.

International service required the development of terminal and refueling facilities in destination countries. To the frustration of Pan American and the U.S. State Department, the potentially lucrative routes across the north Atlantic to Europe were stymied by Britain's refusal to grant landing rights in Newfoundland and England despite the U.S. offer of reciprocal accommodations. The British did not yet have an aircraft that could profitably carry passengers and mail on such a long trip and had no desire to award a north Atlantic monopoly to the Americans. With the Atlantic blocked for the moment, Pan American formed a Pacific Division and, in 1935, established routes across the north Pacific using American possessions as stepping-stones to Manila and Hong Kong. The southern routes to New Zealand and Australia hit another British roadblock.

Transoceanic air commerce depended on aircraft that could safely carry large payloads over great distances. Large payloads meant large aircraft and, in the 1930s, the state of aircraft engine development dictated that large aircraft required very long takeoff runs to get airborne. Suitable runways were nonexistent. The answer was the flying boat, a compromise creature with the wings of an aircraft and the body of a boat. Neither fish nor fowl, flying boats were awkward on the water and slow in the air. Their redeeming virtue was that they could carry a profitable load of passengers and mail, and they could turn any stretch of water into an airport, so long as the water was relatively calm.

The refueling stops along Pan Am's north Pacific route—Hawaii, Midway, Wake, and Guam—featured harbors or lagoons that provided sheltered water for the airline's four-engine flying boats. On the projected route to New Zealand and Australia, most of the south Pacific atolls known to feature usable lagoons already belonged to His Majesty King Edward VIII, or, at least, such was the opinion of His Majesty's government.

Vidal believed that large land planes with powerful, reliable engines would soon tuck up their wheels and span the oceans with greater speed and fewer refueling stops than the ponderous flying boats. In 1935 Boeing had produced the B-15, a giant bomber with a five-thousand-mile range. Vidal was sure similarly long-legged commercial land planes were soon to follow and airline/airmail service from the United States to Australia would be possible if there was an American mid-Pacific refueling stop.

Employing obscure nineteenth-century legislation, Vidal engineered the U.S. annexation of three barren, uninhabited islands—Jarvis, Baker, and Howland—and "colonized" them with a handful of Hawaiian youths. A year later, no long-range airliner had been developed, no island airfield had been built, and Congress was chafing at the cost of Coast Guard expeditions to resupply the colonists. The American Equatorial Islands were beginning to look like the American Equatorial White Elephants.

Vidal was aware of Earhart's still-secret plan to fly around the world early the next year and the difficulties she was having figuring out a way to get across the Pacific. Sometime in early November 1935, it struck him he could solve his problem by solving hers. Earhart's use of one of the islands during her world flight would demonstrate their value to trans-Pacific commercial aviation.

The possibility of an airport in the ocean was a godsend, but Putnam's November 14 letter to Mantz also broke the bad news that "apparently Bo has accomplished just nothing at Purdue." Putnam wasn't sure whether the problem was the "non-arrival of material" or "lack of headwork on McKneely's part," but it would fall to Mantz to get the needed work done once the plane was back in California. A month had been wasted, but there was "no use crying over spilled time."[16]

Meanwhile, unaware of the Bureau of Air Commerce plan, the Navy was working on the details of the aerial refueling proposal. Commander-in-chief, U.S. Fleet Adm. William Leahy delegated the job to Commander, Aircraft Base Force, Rear Adm. Ernest J. King. He had earned his wings in 1927 and served as captain of the aircraft carrier USS *Lexington* from 1930 to 1932. For the first time, the aerial refueling project was in front of a hard-nosed, experienced naval aviator who did not confuse celebrity with ability. He looked at Putnam's outline and, on November 29, gave Admiral Leahy his opinion.

King felt the PBY-1 was a good choice and could fulfill the role of tanker with minimal modification. His principal area of concern was the same one that had prompted the aerial refueling idea in the first place—Earhart's piloting ability: "The chief factor attending the feasibility of the proposed plan is airmanship." He explained the task of the refueling plane "is simply to fly a straight course, at steady speed, in a shallow glide. However, the plane being refueled must fly a very precise formation underneath the refueling plane during the entire period of contact and must follow special procedures for approach and departure to avoid fouling of the hose in the propeller or any other part of the lower plane."[17]

King had no concerns about the ability of the Navy crew to handle the tanker, but "the ability of the pilot of the receiving plane has not been demonstrated and, since this phase of flying is not ordinarily practiced by, or included in the training of, civilian or commercial aviators it is reasonable to assume that considerable special training will be required to assure the success of the undertaking." King felt that such special training should not take up Navy time and expense but should be "obtained commercially." Only then would there be rehearsals with a Navy crew and plane. He also pointed out that the cost of sending a seaplane tender and two PBYs from Hawaii to Midway would require "special allotments" to the tune of $1,000 to cover gasoline and oil for the Navy planes, and 900 barrels of fuel oil for the tender.[18]

King had to know his review would kill the project. The cost in time and money for Earhart to become competent at aerial refueling through instruction "obtained commercially," presuming such instruction was even available, would be prohibitive. King's recommendations were forwarded up the chain of command and were on the CNO's desk on December 2, 1936, but they were never communicated to Putnam. Two days later, the CNO sent a message down the chain: "Arrangements for refueling no longer required."[19]

Before Putnam and Earhart knew the aerial refueling door had closed, a door to deliverance had opened. On November 17 Earhart was with her husband at their Manhattan Seymour Hotel residence when the phone rang. Gene Vidal was calling from Washington to say the island airport project was moving forward. The day before, Richard Black, the Department of Interior official responsible for the islands, had received a telegram from his superiors directing him to "Please ascertain availability tractor equipment in Hawaii for January expedition to Equatorial Islands. Desire to have landing field prepared on Jarvis Island earliest date practicable."[20] Black was puzzled. Jarvis had previously been determined to be the most suitable for an airfield, but the push to begin construction came out of the blue with no explanation for the urgency.

Earhart told Vidal she and her husband were scheduled to travel to Purdue the next day where they would pick up McKneely and fly the Electra to South Bend, Indiana, to spend a few days with sponsor Vince Bendix before flying the ship back to New Jersey for radio work by Western Electric and Bell Labs. Vidal said he would get more information to her while she was in South Bend.

That afternoon, Vidal telegrammed his assistant William Miller in Cincinnati: "Meet Amelia Earhart at South Bend Indiana Airport Saturday with information as to three Pacific islands. She can now be reached at Seymour Hotel, New York."[21] Miller immediately wired Earhart, "In accordance with conversation with Vidal this date, I will meet you at South Bend Airport this Saturday with information relative to Pacific Islands."[22]

Earhart, Putnam, and McKneely arrived in South Bend from Purdue on Thursday, November 19, to discuss a new homing device for the Electra. The radio compass recently installed in the ship was a Bendix product, but Vincent Bendix had another Bendix direction finder he wanted Earhart to use instead and reportedly offered a $5,000 contribution as an incentive.[23] On Saturday, November 21, Earhart and Putnam were Bendix's guests at the Northwestern–Notre Dame football game. Whether they connected with Miller as arranged is not recorded. The next day they flew the Electra to New York.

Over the next few days, Western Electric technicians installed a vertical mast on the top of the cabin aft of the radio compass antenna. Wires from the mast connected to the tips of the aircraft's two vertical stabilizers forming a "dorsal vee" antenna linked to the Western Electric 13-C transmitter on the cabin floor behind the fuselage fuel tanks. As originally installed, the Electra's transmitting antenna was a long wire that was played out after takeoff to trail behind the aircraft. Earhart could now transmit without laboriously extending and then retracting the trailing wire before landing.

To address the licensing problem, Earhart had the Electra inspected by the Bureau of Air Commerce at its facility on Roosevelt Field in Garden City, New York, and signed a new license application for NR16020 requesting approval "for scientific research and special flights." Although still marked R16020, the addition of the international N had been approved September 21 "subject to the provision that you will not engage in international flight without having obtained prior permission."[24]

The Bureau of Air Commerce inspection found the aircraft to have twelve fuel tanks with a total capacity of 1,151 gallons. A diagram of the fuel tank layout was included in the report. The inspection form noted there was a Western Electric transmitter in the rear of the cabin, a Western Electric receiver under the copilot seat, and a Bendix radio compass in the cabin behind the copilot seat. The inspection form noted the total flight time on the aircraft as seventy-four hours.[25] The application form dated the same day, November 27, had the time as seventy-four hours and twenty-two minutes.[26]

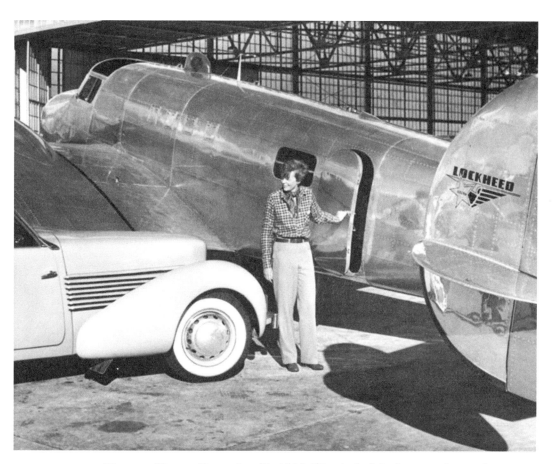

Photo 10. Electra, December 21, 1936. The dark globe in a translucent dome on the top of the fuselage is the antenna for the Bendix radio compass installed in October 1936. A dorsal vee wire antenna, added while the airplane was at Western Electric/Bell Labs in New Jersey in November, runs from the mast on top of the cabin to the tip of each vertical fin. TIGHAR Collection

Earhart's pilot logbook has not survived, so how many of the seventy-four hours represented pilot-in-command time by Earhart is not known, but Lockheed testing, Mantz's work for the film *Love on the Run*, and instructional flights for Earhart can be reasonably estimated to amount to at least twenty-four hours. So far, four months after delivery, Earhart had very little time-in-type.

The Electra remained at Roosevelt Field while Earhart joined Gene Vidal and his son Gore the next day for the Army-Navy football game in Philadelphia. Vidal and Earhart probably discussed the developing plan for the world flight to refuel at an airfield to be built on Jarvis Island. It may have been at this time that they realized Howland Island, although slightly farther from Hawaii, was better situated for Earhart's route.

Six days later, on December 4, Putnam phoned the State Department to inform them the route for Earhart's world flight had changed. She would now cross the Pacific via the Hawaiian Islands to Howland Island, then Brisbane and Port Darwin, Australia, or possibly from Howland Island to Port Moresby or Lae, New Guinea, and thence to Port Darwin.[27]

The next day, Earhart, accompanied by her friend Jacqueline Cochran and mechanic McKneely, took off from Roosevelt Field for what was billed as a leisurely trip back to Burbank. Their first stop was Wright Field in Dayton, Ohio, to have the Bendix radio compass checked.[28] Earhart had not been present when Fred Hooven installed the device at Purdue in October so some instruction and adjustments were needed. They remained in Dayton while "workmen tinkered with the radio homing device"[29] before continuing westward on December 8. Two days later they arrived in Burbank, where Mantz's shop went to work making the changes McKneely had been unable to accomplish at Purdue, including reversing the troublesome hatch so that it opened inward over the cockpit.

As 1936 came to an end, the lost month at Purdue had erased any chance of a "fairly spectacular shake-down flight to the south,"[30] but prospects for the world flight were looking up. The problems with the fuel system seemed to be resolved, there was an offer on the table for more sponsorship from Bendix, and a way had been found to get Earhart across the Pacific without aerial refueling or asking her to make a maximum-load takeoff.

7

House of Cards

JANUARY–FEBRUARY 1937

The new year started with a frightening incident that could have destroyed the airplane, but exactly what happened is not clear. Earhart never wrote about it, and the four published newspaper accounts contradict each other.[1] As best as it can be pieced together, on January 3 Earhart and Mantz flew the Electra to Mills Field in San Francisco. The purpose of the trip is unknown. The next day, in attempting to warm the engines for the return flight, a backfire started a fire in one engine that was extinguished with the automatic fire suppression system. An attempt to start the second engine resulted in a larger fire that was put out by airport personnel with hand-held fire extinguishers. Both fires were put out before there was any significant damage, and the plane departed for Burbank a short time later.

Engine fires at start-up are usually caused by improper starting procedure. Successive fires in separate engines suggest a serious lack of knowledge or attention. One newspaper story has Earhart at the controls; another says Mantz was responsible. The other two accounts lay the blame on an unnamed mechanic who was trying to be helpful.

In New York, George Putnam was coordinating with Standard Oil to deliver drums of donated fuel to key destinations on the world flight, working with the Department of State to secure permits and clearances from the many nations the flight would pass through, and, as always, struggling to raise money. In Honolulu, the cutter USCGC *Duane* was preparing to depart on its January cruise to resupply the three American Equatorial Islands. Aboard would be two borrowed Army tractors, a truck, a road grader, and a civilian construction crew tasked with building an airfield on Howland.[2] Timing was tight. The runway project was expected to take three months and had to be completed in time for the March cruise that would support Earhart's world flight, now scheduled to leave California in early March. *Duane* was scheduled to sail on January 6 but, on January 5, there was a hitch that threatened to scuttle the whole project.

Before they could be loaded aboard ship, the borrowed vehicles needed repairs that were expected to take three days, but the Works Progress Administration (WPA) funds needed to cover the repairs, purchase gasoline for the vehicles, buy necessary tools, and pay the wages for the airfield construction personnel were held up.[3] The cash needed was only about $3,000,[4] but the Treasury Department required authorization from the president to release the money. The White House had received the request, but there was no urgency because the Bureau of Air Commerce had presented construction of an airfield on Howland as a step toward the eventual establishment of commercial air service to Australia and New Zealand. Out of respect for Putnam's request to keep the world flight strictly confidential, there was no mention of Earhart's use of the island. President Roosevelt knew Earhart was planning a circumnavigation, but the last he knew, she intended to cross the Pacific via Midway and Japan. Unless the cutter's departure could be postponed and there was immediate executive action to free up the money, USCGC *Duane* would sail without the construction party, and there would be no airfield on Howland—and no world flight for the foreseeable future.

The Bureau of Air Commerce was successful in convincing the Coast Guard to push the sailing date to January 12, but there was only one person who might convince the president to fast-track the money. On January 7 Earhart sent a desperate telegram to Roosevelt, bringing him up to date on her plans, explaining the crisis, asking him to expedite his executive approval of the money, and begging him to "forgive this troublesome female flyer for whom this Howland Island project is key to [her] world flight attempt."[5] The president quickly authorized the disbursement, disaster was averted, and the cutter sailed for Howland on January 12 with the equipment, tools, and personnel needed to build the airfield.

Two days later, the *Honolulu Star-Bulletin* ran an Associated Press story datelined Washington, DC, reporting, "WPA officials announced today that $3,061 has been allocated and $36,000 earmarked for immediate construction of an airport on Howland Island to provide an air base between the United States and Australia and New Zealand. President Roosevelt approved the project last week, setting machinery in motion for immediate construction. WPA employes [*sic*] with tractors and other equipment left Honolulu yesterday for Howland aboard the coast guard cutter Duane."[6] There was no mention of Amelia Earhart.

The same day, the United States Lines ship SS *American Banker* made port in New York and its master, Capt. Harry Manning, disembarked to begin a three-month leave of absence to be Earhart's navigator for the Pacific portion of her world flight.

Amelia Earhart and Harry Manning were both thirty-one when they met in 1928. The suddenly famous flier was on her way home from England aboard the United States Lines SS *President Roosevelt* to be feted with a New York City ticker-tape parade for being the first woman passenger to cross the Atlantic by air. To give her a respite from press attention aboard ship, the vessel's young captain invited her to spend time with him on the bridge. The two struck up a friendship that continued after the ship made port. The next year, Manning himself was honored with a ticker-tape parade for his role in a dramatic rescue at sea, and in 1930, perhaps inspired by his friendship with Earhart, Manning earned his pilot's license.

In 1936, as a personal friend, minor celebrity in his own right, master mariner, experienced navigator, licensed pilot, and amateur radio enthusiast, Harry Manning was Earhart's choice to accompany her on the Pacific portion of the world flight. Exactly when he was recruited is not clear, but his name first appears as navigator for the world flight in a letter George Putnam wrote to the Bureau of Air Commerce on October 15, 1936, asking for help from the Department of State in securing the necessary permits from various countries.[7] At that time, the anticipated route across the

Pacific was from San Francisco to Honolulu and from there to either Manila or Tokyo. The tentative departure date was February or March 1937. Manning's duties as a sea captain likely prevented him from participating in much of the planning for the world flight until his three-month leave of absence began, and by then, the route across the Pacific had evolved in ways that greatly increased the difficulty of his task.

Although relieving Earhart from the need to make a maximum-weight takeoff or perform aerial refueling, crossing the Pacific via Howland Island meant the absolute necessity of finding a tiny speck of land in a vast expanse of ocean. Pan American Airways regularly met that challenge in hopscotching from Oahu to Midway to Wake Island by a combination of dead reckoning and celestial and radio navigation. A radio operator aboard the clipper sent signals to direction-finding stations at the departure and destination points. The ground station determined the aircraft's relative bearing from or to the station and transmitted that information in Morse code to the plane's radio operator, who passed the information to the navigator. Radio bearings provide directional information but not distance, so the navigator used dead reckoning and celestial observations to estimate the flight's position, winds, and ground speed. The navigator was then able to give the pilot a compass heading to fly and an estimated time of arrival at the destination. It was a good system that reliably guided the Pan Am flying boats from island to island.

Manning planned to use an adaptation of the Pan Am system to find Howland. There would be no direction-finding facility on the island, so the Pan Am system would be reversed. Instead of receiving guidance from the ground, a radio direction finder on the plane would be used to home in on signals transmitted from a Coast Guard cutter standing off Howland. Aboard the Electra, Manning would serve as both radio operator and navigator, tracking and guiding the flight's progress with celestial observations until the plane was close enough to take bearings on signals sent by the cutter. The plan was for him to accompany Earhart as far as Australia and then return home, leaving her to complete the circumnavigation solo.

Navigating a ship is different from guiding an airplane. Although the principles and tools are the same, everything in aviation happens faster, fuel is far more limited, and margins for error are smaller. On a ship, celestial observations—establishing position using a sextant to take sightings of the sun and stars by measuring their height above the horizon—use the natural line between sea and sky. Observations from an aircraft at altitude require an instrument that uses a bubble to create an artificial horizon.

Harry Manning had never done celestial navigation from an airplane, so his requirements for a navigator's station in the rear cabin of the Electra were based on anticipation rather than experience. He considered good visibility from both sides of the cabin essential, but accommodating him came at a price. Lockheed engineers designed the 10E Special to carry 1,200 gallons of gasoline, enough to fly nonstop from Hawaii to Japan. To withstand the stresses of a full-fuel takeoff, they had delivered an Electra with an immensely strong fuselage by eliminating most of the windows. Even the two remaining cabin windows were bisected by a stringer to create an unbroken framework. In late January 1937, to accommodate Manning's desire for improved visibility, the stringers in the cabin windows were cut out, a window was added to the cabin door, and a large hole was cut in the starboard side of the aircraft for the installation of a special window in the lavatory compartment at the rear of the cabin. A cardboard mailing tube is strongly resistant to bending until you start cutting holes in it. Manning's windows significantly weakened the fuselage, but changes to the fuel system had reduced maximum capacity to 1,151 gallons and the Howland Island route had eliminated the need for a full-fuel takeoff, so the compromised structural integrity seemed permissible.

There is no mention of the modifications in private correspondence, Lockheed memoranda, or Bureau of Air Commerce records, so where the work was done is not recorded. But during this same period, the registration numbers on the wings and tail were changed from R16020 to NR16020, reflecting the approval for international flight granted the previous September.[8] The repainting was reportedly mentioned in a Lockheed repair order dated January 26, 1937,[9] so the airplane was in the Lockheed shop around the time the structural work was done. More changes were also made to the fueling ports on the left side of the fuselage. The third port was skinned over and a new one added farther forward.

Around this time, the decision was made to give the aircraft the ability to communicate with ships at sea. All radio-equipped oceangoing vessels monitored 500 kilocycles as a "calling" and emergency frequency but, as delivered, the Electra's Western Electric transmitter could broadcast on only two frequencies, 3105 kilocycles and 6210 kilocycles. The Western Electric receiver could operate on a wide range of frequencies, but not on 500 kilocycles. Correspondence from Western Electric's Los Angeles office dated January 25, 1937, shows plans to add the frequency to the transmitter were under way at that time. Adding the frequency, like adding the windows, was probably at the suggestion of sea captain Harry Manning. The radio work was to be done by Western Electric in New Jersey while Earhart was on the East Coast to officially announce the world flight at a special press event in New York in early February.

For maximum impact, it was important to keep a lid on the news until then, but someone in Central America leaked confidential, but out-of-date, State Department correspondence to an Associated Press reporter, and a story appeared in the *Bakersfield Californian* headlined "Earhart Planning Round World Hop." The article, datelined Georgetown, British Guiana, said, "The aviatrix will leave San Francisco to fly via China, French Indo-China, India, Arabia, East Africa, Brazil, British Guiana, Venezuela, and complete the trip in Miami. . . . [S]he will be accompanied by Harry Manning, navigator."[10] Earhart quickly demurred: "If the newspapers keep on planning for me to circumnavigate the globe, it might give me an idea, however." She declared she was leaving about February 1 for New York to bring her husband, George Palmer Putnam, back to their North Hollywood home.[11] Nonetheless, the world flight cat was out of the bag again. The January 31, 1937, *New York Times* carried a story headlined "Captain Manning to Serve with Amelia Earhart on Her Round-World Flight." The article said, "He has left for California to train for the post."[12]

Exactly when Harry Manning arrived in Burbank is not recorded, but on February 9 he headed back to the East Coast aboard the Electra with Earhart and mechanic Bo McKneely. Accompanying them as far as St. Louis were Paul Mantz and Hollywood special effects expert Fred Jackman. Why Mantz and Jackman were traveling to St. Louis is not clear, but the latter's presence aboard the Electra was in violation of the aircraft's restricted license, which limited passengers to "bona-fide members of the crew."[13]

Mantz saw the trip as an opportunity to give Earhart more instruction in her twin-engine piloting skills, which he described as "rough."[14] He was especially concerned about her habit of maintaining directional control on takeoff with the throttles.

In a multi-engine tail-wheel aircraft, it is common practice to use differential power to assist with steering while taxiing but, during the takeoff, the correct technique is for the throttles to stay full forward while the pilot performs a delicate dance on the rudder pedals to keep the tail where it belongs. Course corrections made by retarding one of the throttles are imprecise and can quickly get out of hand, especially at high takeoff weights. Earhart's flawed technique was asking for trouble.

The journey got off to a rocky start. More problems with the fuel system meant a visit to the Lockheed plant and a delayed departure; then "a slight oil spray" prompted an unscheduled overnight stay in Albuquerque.[15] Arriving in St. Louis the next day, Earhart changed her story again. She was on her way to New York for a belated wedding anniversary celebration with her husband.[16]

On February 11 Earhart, Manning, and McKneely landed at Newark Airport in New Jersey and proceeded to a press conference at the Barclay Hotel in Manhattan where Earhart finally confirmed the rumors and officially announced her world flight. Harry Manning would be her navigator for the Pacific portion of the trip. The circumnavigation would start from Oakland, California, and cross the Pacific via Honolulu; Howland Island; Lae, New Guinea; and Darwin, Australia, where Manning would leave the flight. Earhart would continue around the world alone. The airplane was expected to be ready by March 1, but Earhart said she would not "be stampeded into making too early a start." Press coverage of the news was widespread, with Associated Press and United Press wire stories making the front page of many newspapers, although the *New York Times* relegated the story to page twenty-five.[17]

At Newark, Western Electric technicians made the necessary changes to the transmitter and receiver to give the airplane 500 kilocycle capability. Communication on that frequency would have to be done in Morse code because radiotelephone traffic on 500 kilocycles was prohibited by international agreement, but Manning was adept at code, and the navigator's station would be equipped with a telegraph sending key.[18]

On February 14, while the aircraft was in Newark, Earhart sent a telegram to Paul Mantz informing him she had changed her mind about a crucial piece of navigation gear.[19] Bendix representative Cyril Remmlein had visited Earhart and Manning to show them the receiver and direction finder Vince Bendix wanted them to use. Then in service with the Navy, the RA-1 receiver and compatible direction finder was about to be marketed to the airlines, and Earhart's use of the system on her world flight would generate valuable publicity, but accepting Bendix's offer meant removing the more user-friendly Bendix radio compass. Both systems used a fixed "sense antenna" to resolve 180-degree ambiguity, but the radio compass automatically determined the bearing to the selected station. To get a bearing using the RA-1 system, the pilot had to rotate a circular loop antenna until a minimum signal was heard in the headphones—a difficult task in heavy static.

Why Earhart decided to downgrade the airplane's radio direction-finding capability is not clear. Bendix was reportedly offering a $5,000 contribution as an incentive, and the world flight certainly needed the money, but there may have been another reason to make the switch. Western Electric had modified its transmitter and receiver so that Manning could communicate with ships, but he also wanted to be able to check his position by taking bearings on ships. The frequency range of the prototype radio compass installed in the Electra is not recorded, but if it did not cover 500 kilocycles, Manning would want a system that did. On February 16 Mantz replied to Earhart's telegram to tell her installing a rotating loop antenna over the cockpit would be "a fairly simple job."[20]

Photo 11. February 26, 1937: Earhart poses with the loop antenna for the Bendix radio direction finder that will replace the user-friendly radio compass installed the previous October by inventor Frederick J. Hooven. Purdue University Archives and Special Collections

The next day Earhart, Harry Manning, George Putnam, and Bo McKneely began the journey back to California with a two-and-a-half-hour flight to Cleveland, Ohio. Upon arrival she said, "We just loafed along. There was no hurry and I like to coddle my engines."[21] A snowstorm kept them on the ground and prevented a planned stop at Purdue the following day, but on February 19 they continued westward. Manning used the opportunity to practice his aerial navigation skills, and it did not go well. He passed a note to Earhart giving their position as over southern Kansas when they were, in fact, over northern Oklahoma.[22] There was also trouble with the airplane. One of the propellers refused to change pitch, prompting an unscheduled stop in Blackwell, Oklahoma.[23] McKneely was able to get the prop working again, but when the flight continued on to Burbank the next day, Earhart was unable to hear anything on the newly modified Western Electric receiver. Inspection by local radio technician Joseph Gurr identified the problem: the antenna wire was not plugged in to the receiver.[24]

Cyril Remmlein arrived from Washington to install the new Bendix receiver and direction finder on February 25, 1937. The next day Earhart posed with the loop antenna for a publicity photo shoot and announced the world flight would depart on March 15.[25]

When first proposed by Putnam fifteen months earlier, a world flight would be attempted when Earhart was "intimately familiar with the ship under all conditions" and "only if and when everything proves out satisfactorily."[26] At the end of February, with two weeks left before the scheduled departure, the airplane still had frequent mechanical issues; a new direction-finding system had yet to be tested; the plan for the crucial Pacific portion of the trip had been designed by a navigator who had never navigated an ocean flight; and Earhart's ability to control the aircraft in a heavily loaded takeoff was in doubt.

8

The Weakest Link

MARCH 1937

Harry Manning's navigational error during the trip from Newark to Burbank bothered George Putnam. If the navigator couldn't keep track of which state he was in, how could he hope to find a tiny island in the middle of a trackless ocean? Putnam's Bureau of Air Commerce contact Bill Miller was scheduled to meet with Manning in Oakland to coordinate Pan American Airways radio direction-finding (RDF) support for the upcoming flight to Honolulu.[1] On March 1 Putnam asked Miller to do him a favor:

> Confidentially, I'd like to establish close contact with one of the best of the practicing nav-igators of Pan Am on the Pacific run. Perhaps we could induce him to run down here as my guest for a talk with Manning. Or if that doesn't work out, we will send Manning up for a visit with you—and them. Strictly between ourselves, there doubtless is much that Manning can go over with them to advantage. Naturally, his experience is limited in a job like this—and they might be able to help.[2]

The next day, Manning and Miller met with Pan Am representatives in Oakland to work out radio protocols, but whether Manning also received the navigational advice Putnam recommended is not recorded.

On March 3 Manning returned to Burbank where final modifications to the airplane were being completed. The loop antenna for the new Bendix RDF system was installed above the cockpit, and the trailing wire antenna was relocated. The aircraft had been delivered with a wire that was manu-ally fed out from the extreme tip of the tail. Cranking the wire out after the plane was airborne and reeling it back in before landing was laborious so, to reduce the workload, an electrically driven reel was installed in the cabin with the antenna wire deploying from a short mast under the navigator's station. It was also at this time that orange markings were added to the wings and tail of NR16020 to enhance visibility in the event the plane was forced down.[3] During the world flight, the Electra would be refueled many times in remote locales. To facilitate communication with servicing per-sonnel, an illustrated fueling form was drawn up and printed.

On March 4 and for the next three days, the Electra sported drag-reducing "spinners" (domed aluminum cones) on the propeller hubs, but they were apparently judged to not be worth the added difficulty in servicing the props and were gone by March 7. During that time, the preparations for the world flight were getting a great deal of attention from photographers and newsreel cameramen, so there are many pictures of the airplane with spinners on the propeller hubs, but they all date from those few days.

Lockheed's Kelly Johnson flew with Earhart on March 5 to determine the best power, propeller revolutions per minute (RPM), and mixture settings for various altitudes to achieve optimum fuel economy.[4] From the data he collected, Johnson provided Earhart with an hour-by-hour guide for conducting long-distance flights in the Electra.[5]

Harry Manning did not participate in the research flight, but he did make refinements to his navigator's station. A low plywood platform had been built in the cabin over the Western Electric transmitter just behind the fuselage fuel tanks so that the navigator could sit on the platform and take visual bearings on ground objects through the two standard cabin windows using a pelorus—a telescopic sight mounted on a compass rose. Three instruments needed to determine true airspeed—an altimeter, an airspeed indicator, and an outside air temperature gauge—had been mounted on the cabin wall beside the starboard-side window, but photos show that by March 6 only the altimeter was on the wall, and the other instruments had been mounted in the plywood platform.

Putnam was still worried about Manning's aerial navigation skills and, after discussing the matter with Bill Miller and Paul Mantz, he decided to conduct a test. On March 10 the Electra made a predawn takeoff from Burbank with Mantz at the controls and radio technician Joe Gurr in the right seat. Putnam rode in the back with Harry Manning. Flying westward out over the ocean for an hour, Gurr ran checks on the radios, and Manning was given the task of guiding the flight back to Burbank using only celestial and dead reckoning techniques. He was off by twenty miles. Had the

Photo 12. Amelia Earhart and Harry Manning in the navigator's station of NR16020, March 6, 1937
Purdue University Archives and Special Collections

target been Howland Island, they would have missed it. To Manning it was verification that the key to finding Howland was RDF, which had always been his plan, but for Putnam it was confirmation that Manning's navigational skills were not up to the task.

Upon their return Putnam phoned Miller in Oakland. It was five days until the world flight's scheduled departure on March 15, and they had a navigator who could not navigate. Something had to be done. Miller said Pan Am's senior navigator Fred Noonan had recently left the company and was living in Oakland; he might be available. Putnam asked him to set up an appointment.[6] Presumably Earhart was party to these discussions, but it was clearly Putnam and Mantz who were running the show.

Miller also had some good news. He had received word from the State Department that all diplomatic permissions and clearances for the world flight had been obtained, so he had cabled the Department of Commerce to send Earhart the necessary official letter authorizing her to depart. That afternoon, the airplane and the entire world flight team relocated to the Naval Reserve Air Base in Oakland for final preparations.

The authorization letter was supposed to arrive the next day, March 11, via airmail special delivery. Instead, there was a cable from Robert Reining, chief of the Bureau of Air Commerce registration section: "Earhart letter authority withheld pending receipt inspector's report flight check approving instrument rating."[7]

Earhart had been advised of the requirement that she get an instrument rating added to her pilot's certificate five months earlier, but she had not complied. An instrument rating involved a written test, a blind-flying demonstration, and a flight test to show proficiency in radio navigation. The blind-flying test would be no problem, but the aircraft's RDF equipment had been in flux until just a few days ago, and the plan was for Manning, not Earhart, to operate it. She could hardly admit she was unable to pass the test, so she claimed the flight check would put too much time on her engines and force her to overhaul them during the world flight.

The argument was entirely specious. Her R-1340 S3H1 engines were virtually new with less than 170 hours of operation against a recommended time between overhauls of 1,200 hours.[8] The entire world flight could be projected to take well under three hundred hours. Nonetheless, Reining relented and gave Earhart a way out. The Bureau of Air Commerce would settle for "a nonscheduled instrument rating or flight check ability to fly entirely by instruments." She could skip the written exam and radio navigation flight test. Earhart immediately seized upon the easier option and made arrangements to take a blind-flying flight check that same day. That evening, Reining received a cable from R. D. Bedinger, chief of the bureau's general inspection services in Oakland: "Flight check Earhart instrument flying satisfactory. Written and Radio flying not given account of her desire to expedite and save engines."[9] The Bureau of Air Commerce had cut her a break. In the long run, it was the worst thing they could have done.

The authorization letter arrived the next day, Friday, March 12, but so did wet weather. Earhart announced she would be making some local test flights despite the rain and planned to depart for Hawaii on Monday, March 15, or possibly Sunday if the weather was favorable.[10]

Later on Friday Putnam, Earhart, and Manning met with Noonan. Fred agreed to help, but there was no time to get him a visa for Australia, so he could accompany the world flight only as far as Howland. He would hitch a ride home from the island with the Coast Guard.

Saturday, March 13, brought good news. Despite bureaucratic foul-ups and equipment break-downs, the runways on Howland would be completed in the nick of time, and the Coast Guard was standing by, ready to support Earhart's expected arrival. The Pacific weather forecast called for strong headwinds along the first 1,500 miles of the route to Hawaii. Undeterred, Earhart announced she would begin her world flight the following day.

Meanwhile she took advantage of gaps in the rain showers to do an air-to-air publicity photo shoot over the nearly completed Golden Gate Bridge. Afterward, the Electra was loaded to "near capacity" (the exact load is not recorded), and Earhart, Mantz, Manning, and Noonan took NR16020 out for a final test to check the equipment and familiarize Noonan with the aircraft.

Earhart had made no announcement about adding a new crew member, and Noonan's sudden appearance puzzled the reporters covering the world flight preparations: "The only indication of the change in plans came from Captain Manning who said 'Noonan's going along with us as far as Howland.'"[11] Pressed for comment, Putnam was equivocal, saying the famous navigator's participation in the world flight had not been finally decided.[12]

The two-hour test flight found no discrepancies with the aircraft, but it did nothing for Mantz and Putnam's confidence in Manning. Noonan found Manning's Bausch & Lomb bubble sextant inadequate. He preferred a Pioneer bubble octant like the one he had used at Pan Am, but he did not know where they could scrounge one on short notice. For Putnam it was one more indication Manning did not know what he was doing. There would be no more waffling about Noonan's addition to the team.

Mantz was still not happy with Earhart's takeoff technique. It was a concern that had haunted the project from the beginning. The 10E Special could deliver a range of 4,500 miles with a full fuel load, but all of the planning for crossing the Pacific had been built around avoiding the need for Earhart to make a heavy-weight takeoff. Her longest flight and heaviest load to date had been for the 1,400-mile leg from Kansas City to Los Angeles in the Bendix race the previous September, but she had had Helen Richey aboard to help. The trip to Honolulu would be 1,000 miles longer and the 900-gallon fuel load would mean a gross weight of 14,000 pounds, far greater than any load the ship had previously been asked to carry. Mantz made a last-minute decision to go along. They had iden-tified and corrected the deficiency in the flight's navigational capability. Earhart was now the weakest link in the Pacific plan. The departure from Oakland would give Mantz one last chance to impress upon her the importance of not trying to control the takeoff run with differential engine power.

The turf surface at Oakland was another concern. The rain had left it a pox of puddles and unac-ceptable for the following day's takeoff unless work crews could complete a special runway extension. Failing that, the announced alternative plan was for the ship to leave Oakland with a partial load and fly across the bay to Mills Field in San Francisco, which had a three-thousand-foot paved runway. Fueling would then be completed and the flight would continue from there.[13]

The Mills Field airport manager did not like the idea. Wind conditions meant the takeoff from San Francisco would have to be made toward construction off the end of the runway and, given the heavily overloaded condition of the Electra, he judged the proposed takeoff too hazardous.[14] Con-fident Washington would once more come to her rescue, Earhart appealed directly to the Bureau of Air Commerce to override the local authority and approve her plan.

Photo 13. Electra in Oakland, California, March 14, 1937. It stands ready for Earhart's first world flight attempt. The loop antenna for the Bendix radio direction finder is in place over the cockpit, and the trailing wire antenna has been moved from the tail to deploy from a mast visible on the belly just forward of the man's legs (*center left*). Photo courtesy of William T. Larkins

The next morning, page one of Sunday newspapers across the country reported Earhart would begin her world flight that afternoon and revealed yet another surprise addition to the crew. Paul Mantz would be in the copilot's seat for the trip to Honolulu. Earhart explained Noonan and Mantz wanted to come along, and she was glad to have their help. "Paul Mantz will be relief pilot as far as Honolulu. That will cut down the fatigue factor for me. And Noonan will be relief for Captain Manning who actually has almost too much to do without help."[15] It would also be handy to have Mantz in Hawaii to oversee servicing the Electra for the flight to Howland.

By shortly after noon it became apparent there would be no departure that day. Storm conditions over the Pacific had caused a scheduled Pan American flight to Hawaii to abort, the Oakland runway was still a mess, and the Bureau of Air Commerce declined to countermand the San Francisco airport manager's refusal to allow Earhart to use Mills Field.[16] Earhart's close friend Gene Vidal had stepped down as bureau director in February, and the new boss, Fred Fagg, was less inclined to intercede on her behalf.

Monday, March 15, found the world flight still stuck on the ground. The Oakland runway was too muddy, the storm over the Pacific continued, and they needed to find Fred an octant. The Navy commander at Oakland thought of a possible solution. The Naval Air Station at North Island, San Diego, had bubble octants, and Harry Manning held a commission as a lieutenant commander in the Naval Reserve. A call to the commanding officer in San Diego prompted an official message to the Secretary of the Navy asking permission to lend Manning an octant.[17]

The next morning, word arrived that the request had been granted. Pioneer bubble octant number 12–36 would be sent via Air Express on a United Air Lines flight due to arrive in Oakland at 2:50 p.m.[18] The timing was too tight for a world flight departure that day, so the decision was made to let the runway dry and the Pacific weather improve for another day. Earhart announced the trip would begin the next afternoon.

At four o'clock on the afternoon of March 17, 1937, the Electra taxied out for takeoff with Earhart in the left seat, Paul Mantz beside her in the copilot seat, and the two navigators in the rear cabin. At the end of the runway Earhart swung the airplane into position for takeoff. Mantz eased

Photo 14. Paul Mantz, Amelia Earhart, Harry Manning, and Fred Noonan pose for the cameras before departing for Honolulu, March 17, 1937.
Courtesy of Remember Amelia, the Larry C. Inman Historical Collection on Amelia Earhart

the throttles forward and shouted over the rising roar, "Never jockey the throttles. Hold her straight with the rudder and push everything to the firewall, smoothly!"[19] With Earhart dancing on the rudder pedals and Mantz holding the throttles firmly against the stops, NR16020 splashed through the remaining puddles and was off the ground in less than two thousand feet.

The flight went well until the same problem arose that had prompted an unscheduled stop in Oklahoma on the way home from New Jersey a month earlier: the right-side propeller refused to change pitch. NR16020 was equipped with the new Hamilton Standard "constant speed" propellers, which automatically adjusted blade pitch to maintain the RPM set by the pilot. About halfway from Oakland to Honolulu, the starboard-side prop stopped responding and froze in fixed pitch. Kelly Johnson's recommended power management schedule called for only minor periodic adjustments to the RPM, so the malfunction did not seriously affect the progress of the flight.

As the aircraft neared its destination, a potentially more serious problem went undetected. Noonan's error in plotting a celestial fix taken when the flight was about two hours out, apparently due to a mistake in reading the octant index drum when transcribing the sight data, put the flight fifty-five nautical miles northwest of its actual location. Noonan would have missed Oahu had not Manning discovered the mistake when a direction-finding bearing from Pan Am revealed the discrepancy. A new star shot by Noonan corrected the plot of the plane's position. Guided by further direction-finding bearings, the flight continued to a successful arrival over Wheeler Army Airfield shortly after dawn.

Earhart had grown fatigued during the night, and Mantz had been flying the crippled Electra from the pilot's seat for the past several hours. With the prop stuck in cruise pitch, the right-hand engine would not accept full power, so the approach and landing would have to be done right the first time. Once the landing gear and wing flaps were lowered, the ship would be committed to land—a go-around was out of the question—so it was Mantz who flew the approach and landing.[20]

The Electra had been in the air for fifteen hours and forty-eight minutes when it touched down in Oahu, beating the times set by Pan Am's flying boats by more than an hour, but the comparison is apples and oranges. Although slower than the Electra, the airline's four-engine Martin M-130s could carry profitable payloads over greater distances than any land plane.

Reporters who greeted the Lockheed when it taxied in and shut down in front of the Army hangar noticed it was Mantz who emerged from the cockpit first and that Earhart looked tired, but she insisted she was feeling fine and that the trip "was very nice."[21] There was no public mention of the propeller problem, but Mantz did bring it to the attention of the Army engineering officer who was to service the plane for the next morning's expected departure for Howland Island. The Army changed the oil, cleaned and gapped the spark plugs, and performed a number of other routine checks. In servicing the propellers they found the hubs took a surprising amount of grease, although there was no sign of a leak. Mantz returned to the field that afternoon to run up the engines and make sure the problem had been fixed, but the right-hand prop would still not respond. Army mechanics dismantled the hub and found the propeller blades to be "very badly galled and the blades frozen solidly in the hub."[22] Both propellers were sent to the Air Corps Hawaiian Air Depot at Pearl Harbor for overhaul, where engineers found the cause of the problem to have been the use of an improper grease that had turned to a soft putty-like compound during the flight, making it useless as a lubricant. The same was true of the left-hand propeller, but the damage was not as serious. The props and hubs were rebuilt and lubricated with the correct grease. Mantz had told the Army mechanics Earhart might want to depart for Howland as early as eight o'clock the next morning, so they worked all night to have the plane ready on time, but Earhart stood them up. Instead, Mantz arrived at eleven o'clock and ran up the engines to confirm the props were working correctly.[23] Everything checked out, but there would be no departure for Howland that day.

Wheeler Army Airfield, like Oakland, was unpaved, and the weather forecast called for the possibility of rain showers. Seeking to avoid the kind of delays that had plagued the departure from California, Mantz moved the airplane across town to the three-thousand-foot paved runway at Luke Field, the joint Army/Navy air base on Ford Island in Pearl Harbor. That afternoon, in fueling the Electra for the flight to Howland, it was discovered the gasoline Standard Oil had provided for Earhart was contaminated with sediment. After "considerable arguing and wrangling,"[24] fueling was completed with gas provided by the Army Air Corps.

At 5:40 a.m. on March 20, 1937, NR16020 taxied out loaded with nine hundred gallons of fuel—the same load carried for the Oakland/Honolulu flight—but this time with Earhart alone at the controls. Whether either of her companions was in the copilot seat is unclear. The official record says only that Manning and Noonan "took their places" before Earhart taxied out to take off.[25]

When in position for takeoff, Earhart pushed both throttles to full power. As the plane gathered speed, she eased the control wheel forward to raise the tail. Gerald Berger, the Navy aircraft mechanic who was driving the crash truck assigned to follow the aircraft, was in the best position to see what happened next: "Looked to me like she tried to pull it off too soon and it settled back down crooked."[26] The aircraft began to veer to the right.

Amelia Earhart's defining trait and greatest virtue was her determination to live by her own rules, but airplanes obey only the laws of physics. In that crucial moment, Earhart did exactly what Mantz had repeatedly told her never to do: "I reduced power on the opposite engine and succeeded in swinging from the right to the left. For a moment I thought I would be able to gain control and straighten out the course. But, alas, the load was so heavy, once it started an arc there was nothing to do but let the plane ground loop as easily as possible."[27]

There was nothing easy about the ground loop. The Electra spun to the left like a dog chasing its tail. As the rotation accelerated, centrifugal force flung all the weight to the outside of the arc. The right wing lowered, the plane tipped up, the left wheel came off the ground, and the mass of the plane bore down as a side load on the right-hand landing gear. The entire assembly was torn loose and was left behind on the pavement. The right wing smashed to the ground, and the left-side gear folded outward as the Electra continued its rotation, sliding on its belly, sparks flying, gasoline streaming from ruptured fuel drains, until finally coming to rest facing backward. There was no fire. Berger's crash truck was on the scene within seconds.

The United Press reporter described Earhart as "calm and collected" after the crash. Manning was quoted as saying, "I was sitting beside Miss Earhart. She was absolutely cool. She is the nerviest pilot I ever saw." Noonan said, "Miss Earhart's extremely good judgement and expert handling of the controls saved us from a bad smash."[28] Indeed, the traditional view among Earhart biographers is that Earhart's calm and deliberate action in shutting down the engines prevented a catastrophic conflagration, but as is so often the case with Earhart, the traditional version of events is not supported by the available evidence.

Earhart never said she killed the switches, and the forward curl of the wrecked propeller tips is a classic indication the engines were still pulling power when the props contacted the runway. Witnesses saw sparks as the plane slid on its belly, and there was a puddle of fuel around the wreck when the first responders arrived, but there was no fire because the area was immediately washed down with the fire hose from the crash truck.

Manning's claim that he was sitting beside Earhart is contradicted by crash truck driver Gerald Berger, who was first on the scene. With a possible fire imminent, Berger's first thought was to extricate the crew. While the crash crew hosed down the spilled fuel, he scrambled up on the right wing and leaned across to open the cockpit hatch. He rotated the loop antenna to get it out of the way but the hatch could only be opened from the inside. According to Berger, it was Fred Noonan who reached across from the copilot position to unlatch the hatch. "There was another fella in the back. They had a bunch of extra fuel tanks in the cabin and he was back behind them. I don't think I talked to him at all."[29]

When the hatch was open, Berger and a few bystanders who had rushed to the wreck saw that Earhart was unconscious: "She was slumped over sort of down to the right. . . . He was fine but she was real groggy. We got her up and out of there and standing on the wing and she came around."[30] Among the men present was Thomas Abrams, whose 1962 obituary noted that, in addition to being the first Black police officer in Spartanburg, South Carolina, Abrams had served in the U.S. Navy as a naval mess attendant and was at Fleet Air Base, Pearl Harbor, at the time of Earhart's accident. He was credited with being "the first man on the scene pulling her from the mangled plane."[31] Photos

Photo 15. March 20, 1937. In the immediate aftermath of the ground loop, Earhart and Noonan stand on the wing as Paul Mantz makes sure all systems are shut down. The forward curl of the propeller tips indicates Earhart did not cut the power before the landing gear collapsed. TIGHAR Collection

taken soon afterward confirm Abrams' presence and show Earhart and Noonan standing on the left wing. None of the first responders were interviewed by the press or for the Army's crash report, so their heroism has gone unsung, and the true nature of the accident's immediate aftermath remains unknown.

Once she had recovered her composure, Earhart was upbeat: "Only our spirits were bruised. The flight is not abandoned. It will be merely delayed."[32] But Harry Manning's spirit was more than bruised. His statements to the press at the time notwithstanding, years later he described the experience: "One second I was looking at the hangars, the next second the water. I was ready to die. It was phenomenal that none of us was injured. She simply lost it. That's all. I decided then and there that was it for me. I'd been ready to leave anyway because of Putnam."[33]

Leaving the aircraft for the Army to secure and ship back to Lockheed for repair, Earhart, Manning, and Noonan sailed for Los Angeles that afternoon aboard the Matson Line's SS *Malolo*. Noonan agreed to stay on as the sole navigator and gave Manning a signed receipt for the borrowed Navy octant that same day, but Earhart did not announce Manning's departure from the team until three days after they were back in California. She told the press he was forced to drop out because his leave of absence from United States Lines was expiring.[34]

The weakest link had failed and, as a consequence, Manning was gone. The plan for finding Howland Island had been built by and around Harry Manning: the elaborate navigator's station with special windows, the 500 kilocycle frequency capability, the reliance upon Morse code communication, the Bendix Navy-type receiver and radio direction finder, and all the procedures and protocols arranged with Pan American and the Coast Guard.

Repairing the Electra would take time and money, but more than the airplane was broken.

9

Aftermath

APRIL 1937

The only person to benefit from the debacle in Hawaii was Fred Noonan. The night before the ill-fated takeoff for Howland, Noonan had sent a telegram to his fiancée, Mary Beatrice "Bea" Martinelli, who ran a hairdressing salon out of her home in Oakland: "Leaving 1:30 a.m. your time. Amelia has asked me to continue with her at least as far as Darwin, Australia and possibly around the world. Will keep you advised. Trip around world will be completed before I can return from Australia. I love you, Fred."[1] In his message to his bride-to-be, Noonan did not appear to be concerned about the cost of a steamer ticket if he left the flight in Darwin, nor did he mention anything about increased compensation for his services if he were to continue on as Earhart's navigator. His sole concern seemed to be the length of time it would take him to get home. He assured Bea that flying around the world with Earhart would be faster than sailing back across the Pacific from Australia. The content of Noonan's telegram is consistent with an agreement by which Earhart and Putnam covered his expenses but left it up to him to turn fame into fortune.

The wreck at Luke Field the next morning did not enhance anyone's fame or fortune, but Manning's resignation cemented Noonan's position as the sole navigator for a second world flight attempt, and he got back to his sweetheart sooner than expected. On March 25, five days after the accident, Earhart and company arrived back in California. Two days later, Noonan and Martinelli were married in Yuma, Arizona. According to newspaper accounts, the couple planned to settle in Oakland but would "spend a brief honeymoon in Hollywood as Noonan is now engaged with Miss Earhart in preparing plans for the re-start of the world flight."[2]

Eight days later, Fred Noonan found himself in yet another wreck. April 4, 1937, was his forty-fourth birthday, and that night, as he and his bride drove through Fresno on their way back to Oakland along the Golden State Highway, they hit another car head-on. Noonan escaped with minor bruises, but his wife was hospitalized with "an extensive laceration on the knee and other injuries." The other driver was not injured, but the man's wife and infant daughter were treated for bruises at Fresno Emergency Hospital and released. Noonan was cited for driving in the wrong lane.[3]

For Earhart and Putnam, the crash in Hawaii was a public relations disaster. The March 29 issue of *TIME* magazine drew on the title of a popular Eugene O'Neill play for a piece titled "Mourning

Becomes Electra." After pointing out that several people had flown around the world on commercial airlines, the article said, "Last week Aviatrix Amelia Earhart Putnam took off from Oakland 'to establish the feasibility of circling the globe by commercial air travel.' . . . With her as navigators she took three men, but not her publicity-wise husband, who stayed at Oakland to sell her autographs at $6 each." *TIME*'s description of the accident was no less sarcastic: "Down the long concrete runway of Luke Field the ship shot at 60 m.p.h. Suddenly the left tire blew out. Lurching, the plane crumpled its landing gear, careened 1,000 feet on its bottom in a spray of sparks while the propellers knotted like pretzels. With sirens screaming, ambulances dashed to the wreck just as Flyer Amelia stepped out white-faced. Said she, 'Something must have gone wrong.'"[4]

The unkindest cut came from aviation expert Maj. Alford Williams in his March 31 weekly column on aeronautical matters syndicated in newspapers across the United States. Williams excoriated "individually sponsored trans-oceanic flying" as "the worst racket" in aviation and charged that "the personal profit angle in dollars and cents, and the struggle for personal fame, have been carefully camouflaged and presented under the banner of 'scientific progress.'"

The major was not bashful about naming names: "Amelia Earhart's 'Flying Laboratory' is the latest and most distressing racket that has been given to a trusting and enthusiastic public. There's nothing in that 'Flying Laboratory' beyond duplicates of the controls and apparatus to be found on board every major airline transport. And no one ever sat at the controls of her 'Flying Laboratory' who knew enough about the technical side of aviation to obtain a job on a first-class airline." Williams did not buy the blown tire story either: "She lost control of the airplane during a takeoff on the concrete runway of a standard Army airdrome and wrecked the 'Flying Laboratory.' . . . That ship got away from her—that's the low down." Most ominously for Earhart, Williams called for government action to stop her: "It's time the Bureau of Air Commerce took a hand in this business and it's my guess that the bureau will not grant Mrs. Amelia Earhart permission to make another attempt."[5]

The day of the accident, Putnam sent a telegram to Secretary of Commerce Daniel C. Roper conveying Earhart's "deepest appreciation for the generous cooperation given her by the Department of Commerce." She was "sorry for all the trouble" and wanted the secretary to know that she "intends to try again when repairs are completed and next time hopes to be less of a nuisance to all concerned." The telegram ended with a special plea: "Especially I want to add that Bill Miller has been of invaluable help and our greatest hope is that he may be on deck with us when we try it again."[6] Earhart and Putnam were sincere in their desire to retain Miller's services. As the bureau's point man in the colonization of the Equatorial Islands, Miller knew the ground and knew the people. Since his first wire to Earhart in November 1936, Miller had sent well over a hundred telegrams and cables coordinating every aspect of Earhart's projected flight across the Pacific with dozens of agencies and individuals in the United States and abroad.

Putnam sent several other telegrams that day to various government agencies; all of them passed along Earhart's thanks, announced her intention to try again, and expressed her hope to be less of a nuisance next time. There is no record of a telegram to Fred Fagg, William Miller's boss and Gene Vidal's successor as director of the Bureau of Air Commerce. Fagg's bureau had already demonstrated that the days of special treatment for Earhart were over. Putnam may have thought that he had a better chance of hanging on to Miller by going over Fagg's head and appealing directly to the secretary of commerce, but Roper's reply was not encouraging: "Please express to Miss Earhart my thanks for her cordial message to the Department of Commerce for its cooperation. Also my congratulations on her splendid feat and my most sincere regret that a disappointing mishap has delayed her effort. You may be sure that the Department of Commerce is proud to have had a part in this achievement."[7] For all its kind sentiments, the message made no mention of Miller, who was on his way to Australia on another assignment.

Losing Miller was a serious blow. He and Manning had set up all the radio protocols and Coast Guard coordination essential to the Pacific portion of the world flight. All of that would have to be done again for a second attempt, and now Miller and Manning were both gone. The house of cards was collapsing.

If Roper's letter implied a cooling of enthusiasm in Washington, there was nothing subtle about the sudden chill in Hawaii. Prior to the accident, the Army had extended every courtesy to accommodate Earhart, and the Air Corps Hawaiian Air Depot had worked all night to rebuild the Electra's propeller hubs at no charge. After the accident, the work of preparing the wrecked plane for shipment was billed according to regulations. When Earhart requested that the Electra be shipped to California on an Army transport ship, the answer was no.[8] Forced to buy space aboard a commercial vessel, she requested the use of a Navy barge to move the plane from Pearl Harbor to Honolulu. Again, the answer was no.[9] The plane made the trip to the dock on a commercial barge and returned to California aboard the Matson liner SS *Lurline*. The price tag for the prep work and transportation came to more than $4,000.

To make sure the problems she was having with the Commerce Department did not spread to other agencies, Earhart took matters in hand to make sure that she could continue to count on support from the Coast Guard, the U.S. Navy, and the Department of the Interior. On April 27 Earhart sent a telegram to Rear Adm. Russell R. Waesche, commandant of the Coast Guard, asking to see him the next day, preferably in the morning.[10] Waesche replied that he would be "delighted to see you anytime tomorrow morning, Wednesday, any time convenient yourself."[11] She also visited the Chief of Naval Operations. Apparently the visit was a success; later that day, the CNO advised the U.S. naval station in Samoa that "Amelia Earhart second flight starting within two or three weeks. Please have *Ontario* ready to render same service as on previous attempt. Will advise time plane departure Oakland."[12] (The oceangoing tug USS *Ontario* had been positioned halfway between Howland and New Guinea in March.)

Earhart also paid a call on Richard Black's superiors at the Interior Department's division of territories and island possessions. After the meeting, Black was notified that Earhart had said she would be departing for Hawaii at the end of May and, after a short layover, would proceed to Howland. Although the letter to Black mentioned how charming Earhart had been, it also instructed him to work with other agencies to arrange for the island to receive a precautionary visit by a military aircraft before the date of Earhart's anticipated arrival.[13]

The directive did not surprise Black. He was being ordered to implement his own idea. A week earlier, Black had advised Washington that he had, on his own initiative, written a memorandum to the local Navy intelligence officer offering the use of "Howland Island emergency landing fields in projected fleet operations." Black told his bosses that "best interest of government served if service plane were first to use fields. This recommendation made as result of recent happenings."[14]

The division's acting director, Ruth Hampton, replied to Black's cable and authorized him, after the fact, to "inform Army and Navy that all facilities JHB [Jarvis, Howland, Baker] islands available to them for flight operations or otherwise as may be required." She also asked Black what he meant by "recent happenings." Black explained that the term referred to "Army, Navy and Commerce unofficial attitude toward Earhart accident Luke Field. Campbell [the Commerce Department engineer who had built the Howland runways] and I feel that in view of such uncertainty better for service plane to make first use Howland fields."[15]

Hampton responded with a short encrypted message.[16] Messages that were originally sent in cipher are not at all unusual among the archived official government communications relating to the Earhart flights. All have been decoded, except one: Hampton's message is the only undecoded message among the thousands in the Earhart archives. The cipher Hampton used is no longer available, so the telegram's content remains a mystery. Black replied with an unencrypted telegram saying that he was sending a letter with "full explanation . . . on Clipper flying Tuesday."[17] It seems clear that the acting director wanted more information about the "unofficial attitude" toward Earhart's accident and the "uncertainty" it caused.

Although subsequent correspondence confirms that Black's "full explanation" letter arrived in Washington, it has not been found. Neither Hampton's encrypted query nor Black's missing letter was designated classified, so any information they contained was not officially secret. The context of the discussion in which the two communications occur, and the documented disparity between Earhart's popular image and her performance in Hawaii, leave little doubt about the nature of Black's concerns. The missing files suggest a politically motivated purge of correspondence derogatory toward the Roosevelt administration's darling.

As head of the Equatorial Islands project, Black's primary interest was in the islands' continued development, and Earhart's landing on Howland would serve that purpose. A Pan American Airways flying boat had just completed the first survey flight from Hawaii to New Zealand, landing and refueling in the lagoon at Kingman Reef.[18] There was much discussion in the press about the prospect of commercial air service to the south Pacific, but Howland was not part of the equation.[19] If Earhart successfully crossed the Pacific Ocean in a land plane, the usefulness of Howland's airport—and the value of the American Equatorial Islands—would be dramatically demonstrated. But the portents were not promising.

Despite setting a speed record from California, Earhart had arrived in Hawaii in an airplane crippled by shoddy maintenance. Regardless of whether the accident that ended her first attempt to fly to Howland Island was the result of a mechanical failure, as she claimed, or simply poor piloting, it did nothing to inspire confidence that another try would have a happier result. If Earhart's second world flight attempt ended in failure, perhaps this time with a crash at Howland Island, it could be very difficult for the division of territories and island possessions to argue for further development of the islands. There might also be some politically embarrassing questions asked about how the airport came to be built.

Black felt that the best protection against such eventualities was to validate the utility of the island airfield before Earhart had a chance to try again—hence his attempt to interest the Navy in making some use of the island during upcoming fleet maneuvers. All that was needed was for a plane

Photo 16. Electra's
ignominious return
to California
Courtesy of Remember
Amelia, the Larry C. Inman
Historical Collection on
Amelia Earhart

from an aircraft carrier to land and take off as a demonstration that the island could be used as an emergency landing facility. In the end, the Navy was not interested, and the projected fleet operations took place without using Howland.

On April 2, 1937, looking forlorn and filthy, the once-proud 10E Special was off-loaded in San Pedro, California, and trucked to the Lockheed plant near Burbank where engineers began assessing the wreck and writing repair orders. The damage was extensive. The starboard-side outer wing was a total loss. Both landing gear assemblies had failed where they attached to the aircraft, so the repair orders called for those structures to be reinforced.

The engine cowlings were a write-off but, despite the badly curled propeller blades, the hubs were okay and the engine crankshafts were not bent. The long slide on the belly had wiped out the antennas and the trailing wire mast on the underside of the aircraft. Many of the belly skins would need to be replaced, and the tail surfaces would need considerable repair. Returning NR16020 to service was estimated to take five weeks and cost $12,500.[20]

More consequential than the damage to the plane were the decisions Earhart made about how to proceed with preparations for a second world flight attempt. Manning's departure was also the departure of any competence in radio communication or RDF navigation, but she made no attempt to replace him. Fred Noonan, whom she hailed as "tops among aerial navigators,"[21] would now accompany her for the entire world flight. Down through the decades, that appellation has been an accepted truth but, like so much of the Earhart legend, it is based upon publicity and presumption rather than fact.

Noonan had enjoyed a long and successful nautical career. Although he held a license for "master–any ocean," he never captained a vessel but served mostly as chief mate aboard freighters sailing out of New Orleans and Galveston to ports in South America. His experience in aerial navigation was entirely in the context of his employment at Pan American Airways. He started with the airline in 1930 working in the Caribbean division as an airport manager, but he was not hired for his managerial skills. Pan Am aspired to establishing transoceanic routes to Europe and the Orient. Plans for a lucrative trans-Atlantic route were thwarted by Britain's refusal to grant landing rights, so Pan Am turned its ambition westward and began the daunting task of establishing airmail and passenger service to the Philippines and China.

Navigating across the world's largest ocean would mean island-hopping from a home terminal at Alameda on San Francisco Bay to bases in American territories on Oahu, Midway, Wake Island, Guam, Manila, and ultimately to Hong Kong. Safe arrival at small, isolated atolls after thousands of miles over featureless seas would be guaranteed by RDF facilities at each destination staffed by skilled operators. Early in 1935 Pan Am construction crews from the chartered freighter SS *North Haven* began building antenna arrays, offices, and hotels for passengers on Midway and Wake.[22] Meanwhile, Noonan trained navigators and developed navigational techniques in long Atlantic research flights out of Miami.

On April 16–17, 1935, Pan American's new Pacific Division tested its aircraft and navigation system in a survey flight from California to Hawaii with a Sikorsky S-42B christened Pan Am Clipper. The six-man crew consisted of chief pilot Ed Musick in the left seat, first officer R. O. D. Sullivan, junior flight officer Harry Canaday, radio operator W. T. Jarboe, engineering officer Victor Wright, and navigation officer Fred Noonan.[23]

It was the navigator's job to keep track of the flight's progress through celestial observations. Noonan used successive sun shots during the day and star sights at night to assess and correct for the effect of headwinds, tailwinds, or crosswinds, but he did not attempt to keep the flight precisely on track and habitually relied on two-star, rather than more precise three-star, fixes.

As Noonan explained in an internal company memo immediately after the first survey flight:

> The factors which contribute to inaccuracies in surface navigation—currents other than anticipated or estimated, lack of sights, inaccurate radio bearings, etc.—are all encountered in aerial navigation and commonly in intensified form. Hence is it impossible on an extended flight to obtain consistently accurate "fixes" by any single method, or by any combination of methods. But by an understanding of the weaknesses of each method, it should be possible to greatly minimize the errors inherent in all of them.[24]

He went on to caution that "the inaccuracies of direction finding bearings can be very definitely cataloged: twilight effects, faint signals, wide splits of minima, and inaccurate calibration."[25]

Noonan saw radio direction finding as a useful but less-than-perfect check on traditional navigation. His confidence in his own accuracy, however, was legendary. In a 1974 letter, Pan Am's first publicity director, William Van Dusen, wrote: "He was a cool one, never got excited. On the first return survey flight from Hawaii (the schedule called for 12½ hours) the *China Clipper* was out 22 hours. Everyone thought they might be lost. We radioed Noonan through Musick. Fred was reading a mystery story. 'Tell 'em not to worry,' he told Musick. "My navigation's alright, the wind's just bad. Tell 'em we'll be there in another hour and thirty-five minutes.' And they were right on the dot!"[26]

The first official airmail flight to Manila in November 1935 was a national event that conferred celebrity status on the crew of the Martin M-130 China Clipper. Fred Noonan was hailed as the ship's navigator, and chief pilot Musick made the cover of *TIME* magazine.

Pan Am inaugurated passenger service from San Francisco to Manila with the Hawaii Clipper on October 21, 1936. Demand was heavy and, with the two other M-130s, China Clipper and Philippine Clipper, in service, the airline began scheduling weekly flights to Manila. For the crews, each round-trip involved 16,000 miles of flying over a period of twelve days. The hiring and training of new personnel had not kept pace with the expansion of service, so there were no relief crews along the route. Pilots, navigators, radio operators, and flight engineers were averaging 125 hours a month in the air—far in excess of Department of Commerce regulations.

Noonan did not handle the pressure well. In a 1975 interview, Pan Am pilot Harry Canaday recalled the anxiety Noonan's behavior caused for chief pilot Ed Musick:

> Ed was extremely interested in the navigation and who wouldn't be? Responsible for an airplane out over the waste of the Pacific? And Noonan was the best navigator we could find and he knew it. However, Fred, shall we say, liked to have a good time. Nobody in the crew liked a good time better than Fred. And he was always the first one out, the first one ashore and on his way to find a good time. You never ran into Musick but that he would say, "Have you seen Fred?" Or, if there was a group of us sitting around, he would walk up: "Has anyone seen Fred?" You could just be certain that that was going to be the greeting. He was always concerned whether Fred would make it. It was a variable. There are all kinds of stories you could tell about Fred. You wouldn't want to put it in your book, of course.[27]

In a 1936 letter written to a friend, Noonan's first wife Josephine expressed her growing distress that her husband had started drinking heavily.[28] Honolulu-based Associated Press correspondent Russell Brines remembered Noonan as "one of the country's best aerial navigators and one of its most accomplished six-bottle men."[29]

Noonan's performance began to suffer, as described by senior radio engineer Hugo Leuteritz in an unpublished autobiography:

> A flight took place—Musick was Captain and Nunan [*sic*] was navigator. Nunan had no use for the DFs. However, in this particular case, Musick was making the flight from Midway to Wake and the DF at Wake showed that he wasn't on his course. Based on celestial navigation, [Nunan], they filed an ETA [estimated time of arrival] of X hours, and they flew for X hours. The DF showed that he was 200 miles south of Wake. But celestial showed him on-course. At X hours, there was no Wake. The DF operator advised the airport manager that according to the DF the airplane was approximately 200 miles off and would pass Wake to the south—and he wanted instructions as to what to do. The airport manager didn't know whether to take the operator's word for it or the ETA. He waited ten minutes and the DF definitely showed that Musick was passing Wake to the south. The airport manager then took it upon himself to send a message to Musick saying the DF says you are passing 200 miles south of Wake and the angle; please verify. (I verified this story from the

log and from Musick.) When Musick got the report, he asked Nunan: "Are you *sure* of your navigation?" Nunan said yes. Musick said: "What is our ETA now?" Nunan said, "We must be hitting a headwind." This was in the daytime when they could see [apparently a reference to drift sightings]. Nunan said, "We'd better check for another twenty minutes and then I am sure we will sight it." Musick said, "We are not going to fly another 20 minutes. The DF says we are 200 miles south of Wake. I am heading north." At Wake, they got the message that the airplane was turning north and pretty soon they got the "sighting message." When Musick landed, he went up and verified the report and thanked the operator. He said to Nunan, "You had better bone up on your navigation."

Nunan was called on the carpet for it because it got to Priester's [Pan Am vice president and chief engineer Andre A. Priester] attention—this navigation error. And it was shortly after that that Nunan went with Amelia Erhart [*sic*].[30]

In his 1939 book *Crate to Clipper*, Pan Am pilot William Grooch described the circumstances leading to Noonan's departure from the airline:

There was growing unrest among the junior pilots. They contended that the work was far more difficult than that of other airlines; compensation was inadequate and the order of promotion vague. Ed [chief pilot Ed Musick] felt they had a just grievance. He championed their cause with company officials, pointing out that his own promised raise in salary had not materialized. They shrugged and passed the buck to the New York office. The matter was pigeonholed. Ed strove to convince the pilots that the delay was due to the press of more urgent business.

"They're snowed under," he argued. "We'll just have to be patient until they straighten out a few things in Alaska, China and South America."

Fred Noonan said, "We've lived on promises for a year. I'm through." He resigned immediately. The others grumbled but carried on.[31]

Disenchanted, unemployed, his reputation in tatters, the forty-three-year-old Noonan was trying to put his life back together. His ten-year marriage to Josephine Sullivan ended in a Mexican divorce on March 3, 1937, by which time he was already engaged to Bea Martinelli. Nine days later, Amelia Earhart, George Putnam, and Harry Manning paid him a visit. Earhart's much-heralded circumnavigation was scheduled to depart from Oakland in three days, and they needed his help to get the flight as far as Howland Island. Noonan accepted the gig. He hoped to eventually open a school for navigators, so name association with Amelia Earhart was a welcome opportunity to rebuild his image and launch a new career. There is no record of a compensation agreement.

After the accident in Hawaii, Noonan agreed to stay on as the sole navigator for the entire circumnavigation. Neither he nor Earhart appears to have given any thought to filling the gap in radio expertise left by Manning's resignation. Aboard the Pan Am Clippers, a dedicated radio operator handled all communications, so there was no need for Noonan to know Morse code. He was famously skeptical of RDF and had absolute confidence in his own navigational precision. Like his partner aboard the Electra, whatever he lacked in ability, he made up for in ego.

10

Formula for Failure

MAY 1937

Rather than replace the lost radio expertise, Earhart elected to remove the equipment she didn't know how to use. Low frequencies require long antennas—hence the Electra's trailing wire. It had been intended primarily for transmitting on the international nautical calling and emergency frequency, 500 kilocycles. That wavelength was restricted to Morse code transmissions, and neither Earhart nor Noonan knew Morse, so Earhart directed the repair shop to not reinstall the trailing wire. Eliminating the reel of wire saved weight but, because most radio direction finders could only respond to low-frequency signals, she was removing her ability to get navigational help; a ground station could not get a bearing on her because she could no longer transmit on a frequency they could use. It would now be up to her to take a bearing on a signal sent by the ground station using her Bendix loop antenna.

With the trailing wire gone, Earhart's radio consultant Joe Gurr felt he could give the plane at least some capability on 500 kcs. He added a loading coil to the transmitter and made the dorsal vee wire antenna longer by moving the supporting mast forward about four feet. He succeeded only in making an already marginal system worse.

The rationale for installing the Bendix RA-1 receiver on top of a fuel tank in the cabin had been for Harry Manning to be able to communicate in code with ships at sea and take bearings on them to establish his position, but with Manning gone, that was no longer an option. The Bendix radio direction finder coupled to the Bendix receiver could alternatively be coupled to the Western Electric receiver under the copilot's seat, so Earhart decided to save weight by getting rid of the Bendix receiver and its sense antenna on the belly. By eliminating one crew member, the trailing wire, and the Bendix receiver, Earhart had made the Electra a bit lighter at the expense of seriously degrading the world flight's chances of finding Howland Island.

Little is known about Noonan's activities during the time the Electra was in the shop, but there is no indication he was involved in decisions about changes to the aircraft. He maintained a post office box address in Hollywood, and a business directory published later that year lists a residence address in Los Angeles. During that time, Earhart and Putnam traveled back and forth between the two coasts, fundraising and fence-mending on the East Coast and monitoring the progress of repairs to the airplane in Burbank. Noonan did not attend the meetings in Washington, and he does not appear in the photos and newsreels of Earhart inspecting the Electra in the repair shop.

Putnam scrambled to raise the money to pay for the repairs and the costs associated with organizing a second try. In an April 12, 1937, letter to Purdue's Stanley Meikle, he laid out the financial situation. To that point, the world flight project had raised $69,500. Expenditures up to the time of the accident came to $63,000, of which $60,000 was for the purchase of the airplane (engines, propellers, instruments, and radios had been donated) and the rest for preparations, test flying, administration, and so forth. The remaining $6,500, plus another $5,000 to be paid by the *New York Herald Tribune* upon completion of the flight, had been expected to cover the cost of flying around the world. The accident changed all that.

Repairing the Electra and reorganizing the circumnavigation was expected to cost in the neighborhood of $50,000. Putnam thought the autographed commemorative postal covers being sold through Gimbels department stores would bring in about $5,000. He and Earhart were personally kicking in $10,000 and felt they could raise a similar amount from friends, but that would still leave the world flight between $5,000 and $10,000 short. It was Putnam's hope that Purdue's donors would make up the difference.[1]

The world flight was shaping up to be, at best, a break-even proposition, but, as with Earhart's previous record-setting flights, financial reward would come from capitalizing on the resulting fame through speaking engagements and book sales. Toward that end, Putnam negotiated a deal with publisher Harcourt Brace for a book to be titled *World Flight*. The daily travelogue articles Earhart was to file with the *New York Herald Tribune* syndicate would make up the bulk of the narrative. Before leaving on the world flight, Earhart would write the introductory chapters describing the acquisition of the Electra, the preparations for the first world flight attempt, the accident in Hawaii, and the launch of the second attempt. For the book to be finished by September in time for the all-important Christmas market, it was essential that the flight get under way as soon as possible.

Getting the writing done put an additional burden on Earhart as she monitored the repair of the airplane, helped Putnam with the fundraising, and dealt with two complications created by the projected departure date. The first was weather-related. Adhering to the original east to west route had the advantage of putting the challenging Pacific legs at the start of the trip when the crew was fresh, but a westward departure in late May would mean facing the south Atlantic roughly a month later when strong adverse winds and storms were likely.

The other obstacle was political. The Department of Commerce was getting fed up. On May 9, as repairs at Lockheed neared completion, Eastern Airlines star pilot Dick Merrill took off from New York in a duplicate of Earhart's Model 10E Special bound nonstop for England to bring home photos of the coronation of King George VI for the Hearst syndicate. There were also plans for a trans-Atlantic race to commemorate the tenth anniversary of Lindbergh's epic flight to Paris. Two days later, the department announced it was "seriously considering" a ban on what Maj. Al Williams had called "the worst racket in aviation." The Bureau of Air Commerce was thinking of changing the regulations for aircraft licensed in the restricted category, such as NR16020. A *Washington Post* article titled "U.S. Proposes Curb on Freak Ocean Flights" quoted Col. J. Monroe Johnson, assistant secretary of commerce: "At an early date, a study will be made looking toward the revision of licenses for what might be termed 'freak flights.'" The *Post* wondered "whether the department will issue another license to Earhart for a second try to circle the globe."[2]

So did Earhart. Given her aircraft's mechanical trouble on the trip from Oakland to Honolulu, not to mention the crash at Luke Field, the chances of the bureau allowing her to immediately set off across the Pacific in an aircraft fresh out of a major rebuild were slim. Earhart acknowledged as much in the writing she did for the forthcoming book. "It is only fair to record that the Bureau of Aeronautics [*sic*] probably would have preferred that I abandon the effort."[3]

In an attempt to solve both problems, Earhart reversed the direction of the world flight. Her decision surprised almost everyone. The surviving correspondence indicates Earhart did not mention it during her fence-mending visits to the Coast Guard, Navy, and Interior Department in late April. She could hardly admit the political motivation for the change, so she focused on the weather. The plan was first revealed in a May 5 letter from George Putnam to Richard Southgate, his State Department contact:

> For your information it now appears that Miss Earhart will be able to renew her world flight attempt the latter part of May.
>
> The original plan contemplated proceeding from Venezuela to Los Angeles via Central America and Mexico. Confidentially, because of increasing rains in that region it is now likely that she will attempt to fly from California, via a point in Texas, to Miami, and thence to Venezuela and on to Natal, via Porto [*sic*] Rico. That is, going West–East. . . . Because of changed weather conditions it is now possible that the route in Africa may also be changed.[4]

Three days later, on May 8, Putnam revealed the new plan to the Chief of Naval Operations:

> This note is to lay before you the exact situation. It is for the moment very confidential. Aside from Miss Earhart and myself only two people know the revised plan.
>
> The delay from the chosen mid-March date has resulted in changed weather conditions on several stretches of the proposed route. In a couple of instances these are drastic. Specifically, the weather probabilities in the stretch from Natal north are increasingly bad as June advances. The same is true of the Dakar-Aden-Karachi route. Obviously it is therefore desirable to get to Natal and across the South Atlantic and Africa as promptly as possible. So Miss Earhart has decided to reverse the route and to proceed from west to east.[5]

Putnam went on to explain that there would be "no announcement." The takeoff from Oakland would "be simply the commencement of another 'trial flight.' . . . As matters stand, this 'sneak' takeoff from Oakland will occur probably between May 18th and May 24th."[6]

Putnam said his best estimation was that his wife would reach Howland Island "somewhere between twenty-five and thirty days from the date of takeoff" and expected to be able to provide the Navy with more specific information "about a fortnight in advance" of the Lae–Howland flight.[7] Neither the Coast Guard nor the Interior Department was notified of the change.

Southgate replied to Putnam that same day. Not only would new clearances be needed from the various countries to be visited, but Southgate, on his own initiative, had discussed the matter "informally with an officer of the Department of Commerce, who stated in view of the changed circumstances it would be necessary to issue a new letter of authority for the flight. He suggested that you be advised to communicate directly with the Department of Commerce, furnishing the latest information concerning Miss Earhart's plane."[8] The news that Commerce was going to require a new letter of authority for the flight was not welcome, but neither was it unexpected. Ever since Eugene Vidal's departure, the Bureau of Air Commerce had been more hindrance than help to Earhart.

The gambit of reversing the direction so that there would now be a shake-down flight from California to Florida before committing to the world flight worked. On May 14, 1937, the Department of Commerce sent Earhart a new letter of authority and asked the Department of State to "go ahead with the matter of notifying the various foreign Governments involved."[9]

Bringing foreign governments up to speed and reaffirming permissions was a straightforward process, and the drums of fuel donated by Standard Oil were already in place at the appointed airfields. However, Earhart's decision to eliminate the trailing wire antenna, forgo the ability to transmit on 500 kcs, and abandon Morse code made updating the plan for finding Howland Island vital. But now, with Manning and Miller gone, there was no one in Earhart's circle with the expertise to do it—so it did not get done.

Paul Mantz had continued to provide technical assistance while the Electra was being repaired. Knowing that fuel management would be critical on the world flight, he had the Cambridge exhaust gas analyzer and Eclipse fuel flow meter recalibrated. He also knew that, with Manning gone, Earhart needed instruction in how to use the Bendix radio direction finder. By no means should she set off around the world until she was comfortable with the system she would be relying upon to find Howland Island.

On May 19 the repaired Electra passed government inspection, and the next day Earhart flew the ship to Oakland, staying just long enough to pick up the "world flight—second take off" commemorative postal covers that had been sold to help finance the flight. Her takeoff for the hop back to Burbank was the official, albeit unannounced, beginning of the second world flight. The aircraft performed to her satisfaction, and the following day, May 21, 1937, Earhart and Noonan loaded NR16020 and, with George Putnam and mechanic Bo McKneely as passengers, set off for Miami. If the cross-country shake-down flight and any necessary subsequent corrective work went well, she would go public before she and Noonan continued on to Puerto Rico and the world.

The first leg of the trip to Miami was supposed to be seven hundred miles, about five hours, from Burbank to El Paso, Texas, but it was after two o'clock in the afternoon before they were ready to depart. Rather than arrive after dark, Earhart changed the destination to Tucson, Arizona, 450 miles—about three and a half hours—away.

Arriving in Tucson, she parked the plane on the ramp while she arranged for overnight hangar space. When she restarted the engines to move the ship, she apparently overprimed the left engine. It backfired and burst into flame, as it had done in San Francisco in January. Earhart immediately killed the engine and triggered the fire bottle. The fire was extinguished with no damage to the airplane. That night, McKneely recharged the fire suppression system and cleaned up the mess.

Stopping in Tucson put them behind schedule, so Earhart decided to make the eight-and-a-half-hour flight directly to New Orleans, but skipping the refueling stop in El Paso meant a bigger fuel

Photo 17. May 21, 1937. On the ramp at Burbank's Union Air Terminal, Earhart and Noonan load the Electra for the shake-down cross-country flight to Miami and the secret start of the second world flight attempt. In the rebuild after the Hawaii accident, the Bendix RA-1 receiver and the trailing wire antenna were removed, and the mast for the dorsal antenna was moved forward four feet. The repairs passed Bureau of Air Commerce inspection two days prior. In the photo, Earhart is conferring with a mechanic near the tail. Noonan's wife Mary Bea watches as Noonan carries bags from the trunk of his Terraplane convertible. TIGHAR, Dusty Carter Collection

load and a heavier takeoff. Cool air is denser than warm air, and daytime temperatures in Tucson could easily reach 100°F, thinning the air and lengthening the takeoff. To keep the run as short as possible and also assure a daylight arrival in New Orleans, the Earhart party left Tucson at 7:30 a.m. the next morning.

The flight to New Orleans was uneventful, but when Earhart tried to use the automatic pilot, it "hunted" back and forth fifteen degrees to either side of the desired heading. She made no attempt to use the Bendix radio direction finder now coupled to the Western Electric receiver.

The next day, to test Fred Noonan's overwater skills, Earhart took a straight shot from New Orleans 450 miles across the Gulf of Mexico to Florida. Noonan, navigating solely by dead reckoning, hit the coast at Tampa under one minute and less than three miles from his predicted landfall. It was an impressive feat, especially given the erratic autopilot. The performance of the newly modified radio transmitter and antenna, on the other hand, was less than impressive. While out over the gulf, Earhart was unable to make contact with any station.

The Electra arrived in the Miami area at three o'clock that afternoon. Earhart's reversal of her route around the world had not been announced and, publicly, the cross-country trip was only a test flight to "tune up" the newly repaired plane. Nonetheless, the press was eagerly awaiting her arrival at Miami Municipal Airport, but she landed at the wrong airport. Earhart mistook Eastern Airlines' Thirty-Sixth Street Airport for her intended destination. Upon touching down, she immediately realized her mistake and took off again. A few minutes later, embarrassed and flustered, she botched the landing at the correct airport, dropping the Electra in so hard "the creak of metal could be heard all over the airport."[10] McKneely put the airplane in the hangar to inspect the landing gear. He found no damage from the hard landing, but he did discover someone had scratched their initials in one of the struts. There was a worried call to Lockheed, but the engineers said that if the scratches could be polished out, there was no need for concern. The marks polished out, and the undercarriage was pronounced okay.

Over the next week, Pan American technicians from the airline's Dinner Key facility tried to sort out the wandering autopilot and fix the mess Joe Gurr had made of the aircraft's transmitter. On Saturday, May 29, although neither problem had been resolved, Earhart publicly announced she had reversed her route and the second world flight had begun. She would depart for Puerto Rico either the next day or possibly Monday or Tuesday.

Herald Tribune reporter Carl B. Allen knew Earhart well and had been covering her flights for years. Before her first world flight attempt, he had made a detailed list of all the plane's equipment. Upon inspecting NR16020 in Miami, he queried Earhart about the absence of the "marine frequency radio [the Bendix RA-1 receiver] for obtaining position fixes from ships at sea and shore stations operating on that band." She replied:

> Oh, that was left off when Manning had to drop out of the flight. Both Fred Noonan and I know Morse code but we're rank amateurs and probably would never be able to send and receive more than 10 words a minute; and the professionals just can't be bothered with "ham" operators who can't match their own speed. ["Ham" operators are licensed amateurs who have passed a test on radio theory, regulations, and operating practices. Earhart and Noonan were not hams.] So the marine frequency radio would have been just that much more dead weight to carry and we decided to leave it in California.[11]

About this time, there was another change made to the airplane, obvious in photographs but unnoticed by the press and unmentioned in any known document. The large navigator's window on the starboard side of the lavatory compartment was removed and replaced with a plain aluminum patch. The most plausible explanation for the need to remove the window is Earhart's hard landing upon arrival in Miami six days earlier. Installing the special window the previous January involved cutting a hole and removing sections of two longitudinal stringers, significantly weakening the rear part of the fuselage. Smacking the airplane down on the runway imparted a vertical load that could have flexed the structure enough to crack the window. Whatever the cause, Fred Noonan considered many of the modifications made at Harry Manning's suggestion to be unnecessary, so the window and surrounding coaming were removed and the hole patched over with aluminum sheet.[12] Why the work was not done sooner is not known. (Photos show the window still in place as late as Saturday afternoon, May 29.) It may be that the right size and gauge of aluminum sheet was not available locally and had to be ordered from Alcoa. In any case, photos taken on Monday, May 31, show a shiny new patch where the window had been.

On Saturday, Pan American technicians were still struggling with the autopilot and the transmitter. They thought an adjustment to the Sperry gyro pilot's rudder control unit would correct the wandering. As for the Western Electric 13C, a bench check showed nothing wrong with the transmitter. The problem was the antenna; it was too long. The original length had been set when Western Electric installed the dorsal antenna during Earhart's visit to New Jersey in November 1936. After her decision to eliminate the trailing wire, Joe Gurr, in an attempt to give the airplane some degree of ability on 500 kcs, had significantly lengthened the antenna by moving the supporting mast forward. Pan American found the plane's output on the low frequency too poor to be of any use. All Gurr had accomplished was to greatly compromise performance on the two high frequencies, 3105 and 6210 kilocycles.

Returning the mast to its former position and rewiring the entire dorsal antenna was not an option in the time available, so they tried removing the loading coil Gurr had added and shortening the total antenna length by changing the route of the wire connecting the antenna to the transmitter. During a one-and-a-half-hour test flight the next morning, Sunday, May 30, the autopilot still wandered, and Earhart was unable to contact anyone on the radio. She did not try to use the radio direction finder. Pan American techs had checked it out on the ground earlier and found it to be working correctly.

The media were expecting Earhart's departure for Puerto Rico Monday or Tuesday at the latest, but the airplane still had unresolved equipment issues. Earhart, at least outwardly, was unconcerned. That afternoon she and Fred accepted an invitation from a local businessman to go deep-sea fishing. The next morning they visited the Pan American seaplane base at Dinner Key to thank everyone for their help. Technicians said they were sure that further adjustments to the autopilot had now fixed the wandering problem. They had also further shortened the length of the transmitting antenna by again changing the route of the lead-in wire, and they were sure the transmitter would now function normally. Earhart decided another test flight was unnecessary. She would have the Electra fueled with six hundred gallons that afternoon and leave for San Juan early Tuesday morning. If problems persisted, she would return to Miami, but if everything checked out as predicted, the world flight would be under way.[13]

Earhart told the Miami Coast Guard station she would not try to communicate with any radio station but would broadcast her position at fifteen and forty-five minutes past each hour on 6210 kilocycles and would also transmit on 3105 kcs. She said she would use her receiver most of the time to take radio bearings.[14]

Not try to communicate with any station? How could she know whether her transmitter was working correctly and her position reports were being heard if she didn't get confirmation from the receiving station? Use her receiver most of the time to take radio bearings? She had never used her direction finder to take a bearing by herself. Gone was any pretense of the lofty purpose Putnam had sold Purdue. To a reporter's question, Earhart answered, "Do I expect this trip around the world to

Photo 18. Often represented as George Putnam's final goodbye to his wife before her departure from Miami on June 1, 1937, this photo was staged the previous day. Purdue University Archives and Special Collections

Photo 19. George Putnam bids farewell to Earhart in the predawn light, June 1, 1937. Photo by Lloyd "Bud" Harvey, used by permission

be of any scientific value? No, not much. I'm going for the trip. I'm going for fun. Can you think of a better reason?"[15]

On Tuesday, June 1, 1937, dawn was just a promising blush on the horizon when Earhart and Noonan climbed through the cockpit hatch and settled into their seats for the trip to San Juan, Puerto Rico. George Putnam clambered up the wing and stood beside the open hatch to wish them well and say goodbye. Ever the savvy publicist, he had staged a touching, well-lit farewell photo the day before with a smiling Earhart crouching at the trailing edge of the wing while he stood on the ground, gently holding her hand. At 5:56 a.m., as the sun came up, Amelia Earhart and Fred Noonan set off to circle the globe.

Paul Mantz was in St. Louis for an aerobatic competition when he learned of Earhart's departure from a radio news program. He was furious. Her first world flight attempt had ended in ignominy because she had ignored his advice. Now she had done it again. Despite his urging, she had not taken the time to let him show her how to take bearings with the radio direction finder. Mantz smelled disaster.[16]

Richard Black, the Department of Interior administrator responsible for supporting Earhart's use of Howland Island, was also blindsided. He queried his superior: "In view of recent press notices that Earhart flight reversed . . . that Bureau of Air Commerce might ban flight as unnecessary, request information concerning these matters."[17] The reply was not reassuring: "We have no further information than contained in press. No requests have been received from Miss Earhart or Mr. Putnam. Suggest you contact Navy, Coast Guard, and Putnam's representative Honolulu and endeavor secure information."[18]

There was no Putnam representative in Honolulu, and the Navy and Coast Guard were just as much in the dark as the Department of the Interior. Earhart and Noonan were on their way without having made an attempt to notify, let alone coordinate with, the people upon whose assistance their ability to find Howland Island, and therefore their very lives, depended.

11

Barging Through

JUNE 1–8, 1937

The Electra headed out across the Caribbean bucking a 25 mph headwind, but for the first time since leaving California, the airplane was behaving. The Sperry gyro pilot was finally holding a straight course, and, soon after her departure, Earhart used her receiver to hear a news report of her takeoff on Miami commercial station WQAM. She also successfully used her transmitter to make position reports to the Department of Commerce radio station in Miami at quarter to and quarter past each hour on her daytime frequency, 6210 kcs. They were able to hear her until she was about four hundred miles away. Whether she attempted to use her radio direction finder is unknown.

As Noonan tracked the Electra's progress southward using dead reckoning and landmarks, Earhart let the autopilot do much of the flying while she made notes about the "opalescent sea" and islands where "small streams look like green snakes." The seven-and-a-half-hour trip to San Juan was the first time she and Noonan worked alone together. Her jotted comments about the navigator speak of "Freddie looking for lighthouse" and "Freddie points out a partly submerged wreck off shore." But there is a growing admiration in notations such as, "6:35. We sight a reef. Freddie said we'd pass one at 6:40. Pretty good," and, "Freddie says San Juan at 1:10 EST from white hankies of foam?" (an allusion to Noonan's ability to judge surface wind speed and direction from the appearance of the sea). Familiarity, in this case, seems to have bred respect, and Earhart's notes written later in the world flight refer to Noonan as "Fred" or "F.N.," never "Freddie."[1]

The flight to San Juan went without incident, and Noonan hit his estimated arrival time on the nose. Earhart described the journey in her posthumously published book, commenting, "What with such expert navigational help and the assistance of the Sperry gyro-pilot, I began to feel that my long-range flying was becoming pretty sissy. The ease and casualness were further accentuated by the marvelous help of radio."[2] And yet she made no mention of using her RDF during the flight from Miami. All of the navigation was done by Noonan using dead reckoning verified by occasional landmarks. The same was true of the legs flown over the next five days down through South America to Natal, Brazil, the departure point for their crossing of the south Atlantic.

In a letter to a young female acquaintance written from Fortaleza, Brazil, on June 5, Noonan described crossing "hundreds of miles of unexplored dense virgin jungle. . . . It was interesting because of the lack of recognizable landmarks—a jungle is equally as devoid of distinguishable landmarks as an ocean. In consequence, at several times we had to rely upon celestial navigation to ascertain our position." But their route from Caripito, Venezuela, to Paramaribo, Dutch Guiana, to Fortaleza ran along the coast and at no time crossed "hundreds of miles of unexplored dense virgin jungle."[3]

From Fortaleza, Earhart and Noonan made the short hop to Natal on the easternmost tip of Brazil. In the predawn darkness of June 7 they set off across the south Atlantic for Africa. The 3:15 a.m. takeoff was intended to allow the flight to reach its destination—Dakar, French Senegal—before nightfall, but thirteen hours and twenty-two minutes later, at 7:35 p.m. local time, three minutes before sunset, the Electra touched down unannounced at Saint-Louis, 163 miles beyond Dakar. That same evening, Earhart sent a press release to the *Herald Tribune* explaining what had happened:

> Here at St. Louis are the headquarters of Air France for the trans-Atlantic service and I am grateful for the field's excellent facilities, which have generously been placed at my disposal. But it is only fair to say that I had really intended to land at Dakar 163 miles south of St. Louis. The fault is entirely mine.
>
> When we first sighted the African coast, thick haze prevailed. My navigator, Captain Fred Noonan, indicated that we should turn south. Had we done so, a few minutes would have brought us to Dakar. But a left turn seemed to me more attractive and fifty miles of flying along the coast brought us here.
>
> Once arrived over the airport and having definitely located ourselves, it seemed better to sit down rather than retrace our track along a strange coast with darkness imminent.[4]

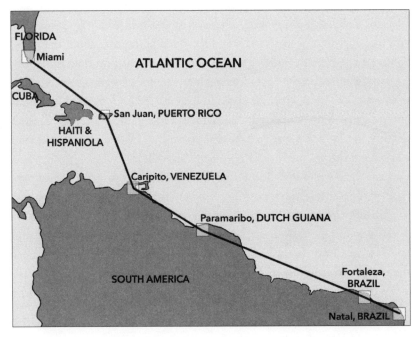

Map 1.
Miami
to Natal

It was a good story, but it was not true. The chart Noonan used to track the flight's progress was sent home later in the trip and is now in the Amelia Earhart Collection at Purdue University.[5] Noonan's hand-drawn course lines and notations, and two notes he passed to Earhart during the flight, support his own description of events in a private letter he sent to actor Eugene Pallette from Dakar two days later. In the letter, Noonan described the weather conditions that prevailed during the trip: "The flight from Natal, Brazil to Africa produced the worst weather we have experienced—heavy rain and dense cloud formations necessitated blind flying for ten of the thirteen hours we were in flight."[6]

For most of the long day over the south Atlantic, the Electra hung suspended in a world of gray murk as rain beat a staccato tattoo on the windshield. Earhart let the automatic pilot do the flying while she made notes for her book: "Have tried to get something on radio. No go. Rain, Static. Have never seen such rain. Props a blur in it."[7]

Unable to monitor their progress by landmarks or celestial observations, Noonan could do no more than give Earhart his best guess at a compass heading that would keep them more or less on track. Popular legend has Noonan confined to the navigator's station in the rear cabin and able to communicate with Earhart only by means of notes passed forward over the fuel tanks by means of a bamboo pole. In fact, Noonan spent much of his time in the cockpit with Earhart, clambering over the fuel tanks into the rear cabin only when he needed room to spread out a chart or use the lavatory.

Earhart and Noonan did, however, communicate primarily in writing. Even when sitting side by side, the din of the engines prohibited anything but shouted verbal exchanges. The Lockheed Model 10 had been designed with passenger, rather than pilot, comfort in mind. The propellers, the source of most of the noise in a propeller-driven aircraft, were placed well forward, directly opposite the cockpit. Consequently, the decibel level in the cockpit was truly punishing. In May, Dick Merrill and Jack Lambie had been rendered temporarily deaf during their round-trip flight to England in the other 10E Special. Aboard Earhart's Electra, pilot and navigator communicated mostly by passing scribbled notes back and forth.

After six and a half hours the weather began to improve. Earhart noted, "Clouds seem to be changing. Formation seems thinner. Rather bright in spots. Can hardly believe sun is north of us but so it is."[8] An hour later, Noonan was able to get a shot of the sun through the cockpit windows. He then climbed over the fuel tanks into the rear cabin and took another celestial observation through the glass panel in the cabin door. A few minutes later he passed a note forward to Earhart. "By a second observation crossed with the first taken in the cockpit, find we are north of course—have averaged 147 mph. Now we have a tail wind—alter course to 76° M[agnetic]."[9]

Noonan hoped that the new course would take them directly to Dakar but, as it turned out, he had overcorrected for the wind. When he next took an observation, he found the Electra to now be well south of course, so he had Earhart reduce the amount of correction. An hour later, another observation established the airplane's position about 50 miles from the African coast and almost 150 miles south of Dakar. Noonan passed Earhart another note ordering a turn to the left: "3:36 change to 36°. Estimate 79 miles to Dakar from . . ." and here the note was later altered by someone (the handwriting is entirely different) to read "3:36 p.m."[10] Matching the note to Noonan's map, the note probably originally read, "Estimate 79 miles to Dakar from landfall." Across the bottom of the note,

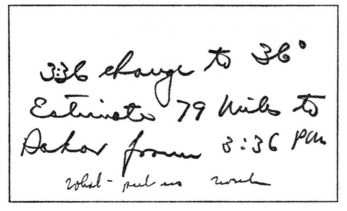

Photo 20.
Altered note by
Fred Noonan
Purdue University
Archives and Special
Collections

Earhart scribbled, "What put us north?" referring to the earlier need for a mid course correction.

When the flight came within sight of the coast, Earhart and Noonan encountered another problem. As Noonan wrote in his June 9 letter, "To add to our woes the African coast was enveloped in thick haze, rendering objects invisible at distances over a half mile, when we made the landfall. And our radio was out of order—it would be, in such a jam. However, with our usual good luck, if not good guidance, we barged through okay."[11]

Dakar sits on a peninsula extending out into the Atlantic. The Electra had made landfall south and east of the city. In heavy haze such as Noonan described, forward visibility while flying toward a setting sun is virtually zero. Turning back toward the ocean to try to find Dakar with no radio, dwindling fuel, and failing daylight was not an attractive proposition. Finding Saint-Louis was a simple matter of following the coastline northeastward to where the Senegal River meets the sea.

No one knows why Earhart so quickly put out a different story, but at least one good reason is apparent. The decision to bypass Dakar under the prevailing circumstances was operationally correct but bureaucratically risky. The world flight's path across Africa lay over French colonial possessions, and there had been a great deal of State Department correspondence with Paris discussing specific routes and the various restrictions that would apply to each. Once the French authorities had been told which of the approved routes Earhart would follow, they expected her to go where she said she would go. All of the approved routes across Africa began in Dakar. Failing to land there, if seen as willful disregard of the approved itinerary, might result in the airplane and crew being impounded and fined. If missing Dakar was represented as a navigational mistake, especially one for which the female pilot took the blame for not listening to her male navigator, the French authorities might be less likely to hold it against her. Whatever Earhart's motivations, French authorities accepted her version of events, and the next day the flight repositioned to Dakar without incident. Earhart's bogus account, cleverly expedient as it was, became a staple of the Earhart legend and has been used to justify endless speculation about Earhart's relationship with Noonan and whether and how she might have disregarded his instructions during the Lae-Howland flight.

The letter Fred Noonan sent from Dakar on June 9, 1937, was addressed to "Eugene Pallette, Hollywood Roosevelt Hotel, Hollywood, California, Etats-Unis." Pallette was a popular and prolific film actor, best remembered today for his role as the rotund and raspy-voiced Friar Tuck in the 1938

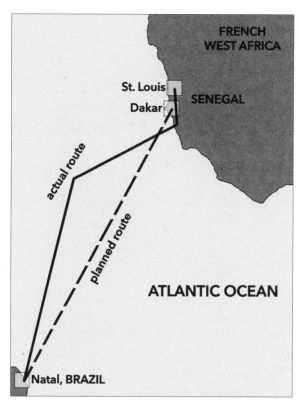

Map 2. Coast of Africa with routes

Warner Brothers film *The Adventures of Robin Hood*. It is clear from the letter that Noonan had promised to keep Pallette informed about the progress of the world flight via telegram. Noonan was running into difficulties meeting that obligation, and his letter, sent back across the south Atlantic via airmail, was apologetic: "Dear Gene, Having trouble sending messages such as I promised you— but I am doing the best that I can. Facilities are not always available, and therefore I am sending one message when possible, naming stop made since the previous message. Tried to get one off last night but some trouble developed at the cable station. As I had sent the cablegram to the cable office by messenger I have not yet ascertained the cause of the delay in transmission—but will do so later to-day."[12]

After describing the flight so far and the expected itinerary for the next few days, Noonan closed: "With kindest personal regards, and looking forward to a highball together in the not too distant future—I am, Sincerely, Fred Noonan."[13] Noonan's letter to Pallette ended up in the possession of Noonan's widow and eventually in a private collection of his correspondence. If there are other letters or telegrams from Noonan to Pallette, they have not been released. Just what Noonan and Pallette were up to is a matter for speculation, but Noonan's promise to feed Pallette information is not—Noonan's letter from Dakar is unequivocal—and the promised updates must have had a purpose that justified the considerable cost of sending international telegrams and airmail letters. It seems likely that they were hoping to interest Hollywood in a film featuring the famous navigator. Whatever the plan, it probably reflected Noonan's desire to capitalize on the expected success of the world flight.

12

Mad Scramble

JUNE 9–22, 1937

As Earhart and Noonan pursued their own agendas on the coast of Africa, Capt. Stanley V. Parker, commander of the Coast Guard's San Francisco Division, discovered that, like Richard Black in Hawaii, he had been blindsided by Earhart's surprise departure. On June 7 a message had arrived from Coast Guard commandant Admiral Waesche in Washington, asking, "Have arrangements been made to have vessel at Howland Island end of June cooperation Earhart flight?" Captain Parker replied, "Earhart negative. No official information of itinerary and schedule received but private information promised two weeks advance notice of time of expected arrival Howland Island."[1]

If that time was going to be late June, there was a problem. Parker explained to the commandant that all of the ships currently assigned to the Hawaiian Section were either laid up for maintenance or committed to other duties until the end of June. He added: "Please advise closest estimate expected arrival time Howland."[2] Admiral Waesche's response dumped the problem squarely back in Parker's lap: "Best estimate Earhart flight is depart from New Guinea June 20 for Howland. Advise action contemplated by you."[3]

The commandant had ordered him to pay Paul, so Captain Parker had no choice but to rob Peter. USCGC *Itasca* was in port near Los Angeles, having recently been reassigned to the Coast Guard's Southern Section for duty on the West Coast. He would have to send it back to the Hawaiian Section. Parker alerted the cutter's captain to "be prepared on short notice to proceed Howland Island via Honolulu."[4]

Meanwhile, the Department of the Interior was also trying to cope with the schedule change. On June 8, the day Earhart and Noonan crossed the south Atlantic, acting director Ruth Hampton received a letter from George Putnam saying that Earhart would probably be at Howland in the latter part of June or early July. Hampton immediately responded, cautioning him that Interior could not support a late June arrival because "the next regular quarterly expedition to Equatorial Islands cannot leave Honolulu before July 1st due to the nonavailability of appropriations before that date."[5] Hampton then cabled Black in Hawaii to bring him up to date on the situation and to suggest that he proceed with arrangements for the island reprovisioning and Earhart flight support expedition to leave Honolulu early on the morning of July 1.[6]

In San Francisco, Captain Parker, having been told to send a cutter to Howland in late June and not knowing that Interior was out of money until July 1, sent a message to the commander of the Hawaiian Section: "In view *Itasca*'s early departure for Honolulu and Howland Island, suggest possibility her performance routine line island cruise."[7] The Coast Guard commander in Honolulu ran the idea past Richard Black, who told him about the appropriations problem. Later that day, Black cabled Hampton with the news that the Coast Guard was sending *Itasca* to Honolulu and to offer a suggestion: "Since Putnam has been advised sailing date July 1st, please advise me whether combine cruise to aid flight and regular cruise visiting JBH [Jarvis, Baker, Howland], or special cruise immediately and regular cruise mid July. Commander Hawaiian Section leaves decision to us but respectfully suggests [a] conference [with the] Coast Guard [in] Washington would obviate necessity such early departure of *Itasca* from coast if cruises combined."[8]

Howland Island was nearly two thousand miles from Hawaii. Black and the Coast Guard commander could hardly believe that their superiors in Washington were contemplating two separate trips. The sensible course of action was to wait and do the island resupply and flight support as a combined cruise after July 1, but the decision rested with the Interior Department's division of territories and island possessions and its acting director, Ruth Hampton.

Faced with the prospect of his wife cooling her heels somewhere on the far side of the world until it was convenient for the Department of the Interior to resupply the Equatorial Islands' colonists, Putnam quickly wrote back to Hampton:

I hasten to reply to your letter of June 8th. . . . I have today received a letter from Admiral Waesche of the Coast Guard. He informs me that a cutter is at Honolulu and will depart for Howland when required. . . . From my understanding, as above set forth, it would appear that the departure for the Island of Mr. Black, even before July 1st, would not necessarily necessitate the expenditure of Department funds as transportation, and I assume sustenance, are supplied by the Coast Guard. . . . I have taken the liberty of assuming that Mr. Black would, so far as Howland Island is concerned, be in charge of the entire matter. I have had very pleasant and helpful exchanges of letters with him and am deeply grateful for his intelligent and efficient cooperation and his evident intention to follow the matter through thoroughly.[9]

Putnam's representations were disingenuous at best. The letter from Admiral Waesche did not say that "a cutter is at Honolulu and will depart for Howland when required." Waesche's letter said only, "I have notified our San Francisco representative to be prepared to have a vessel at Howland Island the latter part of June."[10] *Itasca*, at that moment, was still tied to a California pier.

Putnam's assumption that the Coast Guard was covering the cost of "sustenance" for the colonists was also in error. The Interior Department was responsible for provisioning the islands, and, as Hampton had told him in her letter, could not resupply the colonists until appropriations became available on July 1. Putnam's claim to have exchanged pleasant and helpful letters with Black is not supported by the historical record. All of the correspondence with Black to coordinate support for the first world flight attempt had been handled by the Bureau of Air Commerce liaison, William Miller. The only communication Black had ever received from Putnam was a telegram sent to him aboard *Shoshone* on the day of the Luke Field wreck, and that message merely relayed Earhart's apologies for breaking their "engagement for tonight."[11]

Putnam was right about one thing. With regard to government support of Earhart's second attempt to fly to Howland Island, Black was indeed in charge of the entire matter. Putnam was also correct in saying that it was Black's intention to follow the matter through thoroughly. But at that moment Richard Black was growing apprehensive at the lack of communication from George Putnam.

Nonetheless, Putnam's letter had the desired effect, and Hampton sent Black a cable authorizing two expeditions to Howland Island:

> Letter from Putnam just received indicates possible arrival Earhart at Howland before July 1st. . . . Putnam states all arrangements with Coast Guard and Navy have been made and cutter will leave Honolulu sufficiently in advance to permit several days at Howland to recondition runways and disperse bird population, also to establish radio contact with Earhart plane. . . . You are authorized to proceed with coordination all arrangements and if departure necessary before July 1st to make special trip to Howland, regular expedition to follow at such time as you may decide after 1938 appropriation becomes available. Please cooperate and assist in every way possible and keep this division closely informed as to developments.[12]

Black would do as he was told, but he needed information about the flight he was supposed to support. He replied, "Will proceed with coordination of arrangements as directed. . . . Please give me direct radio address Putnam or other direct contact flight."[13]

The Coast Guard's San Francisco Division also needed information. Captain Parker was upset that Putnam had failed to provide the promised two weeks' advance notice of Earhart's anticipated arrival at Howland. On June 10 he asked of the commandant that "Putnam be required to keep this Division advised daily of progress of Earhart flight." The reply from Washington was not encouraging: "Headquarters unable contact Putnam."[14]

Itasca was at sea, steaming for Honolulu. Its captain, Cdr. Warner K. Thompson, also needed instructions. On June 11 he queried Parker: "Please advise any radio schedules to be observed with Earhart plane and frequency guarded." Parker replied with what little information he had: "No plane schedules have been arranged with this Division. On previous trip plane was equipped with 50 watt transmitter for operation on 500, 3105 and 6210 kilocycles with receiver covering all frequencies and direction finder covering 200 to 1500 kilocycles. All transmissions were by key although the transmitter may be used for voice. Will advise all details possible to obtain when received from headquarters."[15]

The next day, Parker also passed along to *Itasca* a comment forwarded by the Coast Guard air station in Miami: "When Amelia Earhart took off from Miami she stated she would not try to communicate with any radio station but would broadcast her position every 15 and 45 minutes past each hour on 6210 kcs [kilocycles]. She also transmits on 3105 kcs. She stated that her receiver will be used most of the time taking radio bearings."[16] This was outdated information and hearsay, but Earhart's flight to Howland might be as little as eight days away, and there was still no word from Putnam about what support she wanted and how the Coast Guard and Navy ships were supposed to communicate with her.

As division commander, Parker also faced the prospect of ships from his Hawaiian Section making back-to-back trips to Howland. On June 12 he sent a strongly worded appeal to Admiral Waesche: "Failure to combine Earhart mission and routine Equator Island cruise so awkward and embarrassing in variety of aspect[s] it would seem higher authority could compel action on basis of emergency funds." Parker pointed out that if *Itasca* did not resupply the islands on this trip, that job would have to be done in July by the cutter *Roger B. Taney*. *Taney* would thus not be available for law enforcement duties for the entire month of July, Parker noted, and added, "Some adverse comment may flow from special detail of *Itasca* to flight cooperation alone."[17]

Admiral Waesche saw Parker's point. Rather than risk adverse comment, the Coast Guard would pay for the supplies. He notified Parker: "*Itasca* authorized to obtain and issue to Department Interior necessary stores for islands. Invoice Coast Guard supplies to Interior after June 30." Waesche then telephoned Interior, and the good news was wired to Black in Hawaii the same day. The flight support and the island resupply missions would be combined in a single voyage that would sail according to Earhart's schedule.[18]

But what was Earhart's schedule? And what radio protocols would she be using? On June 14 Black wired Hampton with a message for Putnam, which she included in a letter sent to his New York address: "The following radiogram for you from Mr. Richard B. Black: 'Request latest estimate arrival date Howland Island and frequent supplementary information via Coast Guard radio to reach me here or aboard *Itasca*. Please give me full instructions on radio contact with plane as verification of information Earhart gave at Miami regarding frequencies and times of transmission. We have two radios dated March 13 covering plan on first flight.'"[19]

The "radios" Black referred to were messages sent to the Coast Guard a few days before the first world flight attempt was scheduled to leave California. The navigator/radio operator for that flight, Harry Manning, and the Bureau of Air Commerce liaison, William Miller, had designed the plan based on the capabilities of the aircraft and crew at that time. The information was now dangerously obsolete. In his appeal to Putnam for information, Black also explained what arrangements had and had not been made to provide Earhart with weather predictions: "Lieutenant True, Aerologist, Fleet Air Base, will give forecast from Howland to Honolulu and suggest you arrange forecast New Guinea to Howland through weather facilities at Lae."[20]

Itasca arrived from California on the morning of June 15, mooring to Honolulu's pier twenty-seven at 11:55 a.m. Commander Thompson immediately went ashore to report for duty. At the Hawaiian Section offices Thompson met the section's deputy commander, Lt. Cdr. Frank T. Kenner, and the Interior Department's representative, Richard Black. Kenner had skippered *Itasca* on earlier trips to the islands, had been in charge of landing construction equipment from USCGC *Duane* to build the Howland runways, and had helped coordinate support in Honolulu for Earhart's March attempt. Because the mission to Howland was to be Thompson's first cruise to the equatorial Pacific,

Kenner was going along in an advisory capacity. His presence on this trip would provide a measure of continuity.

Itasca's mission would be "to act as Earhart plane guard at Howland and furnish weather." On completion of its work in connection with the Earhart flight, the ship was to "continue on regular Line Island cruise." Black was the designated "leader of the expedition and coordinator of government assistance to Earhart flight as regards Howland Island."[21] It was his job to match Earhart's needs to the services offered by the various agencies, and he could already see that competent, reliable radio communication was going to be critical to the success of the mission.

The transmitters operated by the colonists on Howland and Baker were low-powered ones that could send only code. It was the cutter's radio operators who would handle the preflight coordination, provide weather information, and send the signals on which Earhart would take bearings to guide her to Howland. *Itasca*, however, arrived in Hawaii with only one experienced chief radioman. He was assisted by three young men rated radioman third class, the lowest rating for operators. As leader of the expedition, Black felt justified in arranging to have the men replaced with experienced U.S. Navy personnel. Commander Thompson would have none of it. He later explained: "This arrangement was not acceptable to the Commanding Officer of the *Itasca* for the reason that the Coast Guard has sufficient radiomen to perform its work."[22]

Thwarted in his attempt to improve the level of radio expertise aboard the ship, Black did what he could to give the island better radio capability. During the preparations for the first world flight in March, Manning and Miller had suggested that a radio direction finder be set up on Howland Island "if practicable."[23] If Earhart was having trouble using the plane's direction finder to home in on signals sent from the ship, the receiver on the island could take bearings on the transmissions from the plane, and the operator could then radio her with instructions about what course to follow. The plan designed in March was for the plane to transmit signals on 500 kilocycles. Setting up a direction finder on Howland had been a good idea, but the request had not been made until the supply ship was already at sea. Richard Black revived the idea for the second world flight attempt, but the very limited information available about Earhart's intentions made no mention of the lower frequency and spoke only of Earhart transmitting on her two higher frequencies.

High-frequency direction finding was problematic, but Black conspired with Army Air Corps lieutenant Daniel A. Cooper, who would be in charge of servicing the Electra at Howland, to borrow an experimental unit from the Navy. Commander Thompson was not supportive of this idea either: "Mr. Black and Lieutenant Cooper of the Army had the Navy send a high frequency direction finder on board. The Coast Guard did not request the equipment and did not receipt for it." Thompson later explained his skepticism: "It was the impression of Coast Guard officers that limits of accuracy reasonably to be expected from this equipment in the circumstances which would obtain on Howland Island were decidedly not sufficiently close to warrant its use as a dependable navigational device to bring the plane safely on the island. It was considered desirable however to set the equipment up at Howland as a necessary precaution."[24]

Itasca had a direction finder, but it was not able to take bearings on high-frequency signals, and there was no expectation that it would be used. The plan, as Thompson understood it and as Earhart had implied when she left Miami, was for the Coast Guard to be the passive partner in the direction-finding procedure. *Itasca*, standing just off Howland Island, would send signals, and Earhart would use the direction finder aboard her Electra to home in on the ship.

If Black and Cooper insisted on setting up the Navy high-frequency direction finder on Howland, someone would have to man it. Thompson had already made it clear that Navy radio operators were not welcome aboard *Itasca*, but Black thought he might be able to find a top-notch Coast Guard radioman for the job. The cutter *Roger B. Taney* was in drydock, and its crew was temporarily unemployed. The first operator selected was found to be "medically unfit," and the job ultimately fell to Radioman 2nd Class Frank Cipriani, who reported aboard *Itasca* the next day.[25]

June 16, 1937, was also the day that George Putnam broke his silence. In telegrams sent to the Chief of Naval Operations, the commandant of the Coast Guard, and Ruth Hampton at Interior, he advised that Earhart had wired from Karachi, India, saying that she expected to arrive in Lae, New Guinea, one week hence. Putnam estimated that she would fly to Howland on June 24 or 25.[26] The telegrams said nothing about radio arrangements.

Two days later, on June 18, as *Itasca* was about to put to sea, Black was handed a cable from Ruth Hampton in Washington. The message relayed long-awaited radio information she had just received in a letter from Putnam: "Earhart will broadcast radio phone quarter after and quarter to hour. Her frequencies 6210 and 3105, former used daylight. Also has 500 but dubious usability. Advise what frequencies *Itasca* will use, ditto naval vessels, so she can listen. Suggest Coast Guard and Navy coordinate so that helpful weather data be broadcasted to her after Lae takeoff on the hour and half. Will confirm arrangement with her by wire at Lae. Can *Itasca* forward Howland weather forecast to Lae possibly via the *Ontario* prior takeoff?"[27]

Responding to Black's request of June 14, Putnam was verifying what Earhart had reportedly said before her departure from Miami. There was still nothing about her radio direction finder or how she planned to use it to find Howland Island, but Putnam's message did include new information. Putnam said that Earhart would broadcast using radiotelephone and that her 500 kilocycle frequency was of "dubious usability." In fact, the usability of that frequency was not dubious; it was virtually nonexistent.

In the absence of updated instructions, Black and the Coast Guard had been studying the old radio protocols set up by Manning and Miller. Those procedures specified the use of telegraphy for most communications with the plane. Putnam now indicated that Earhart would broadcast using radiophone, but he did not make it clear that the plane could no longer communicate using Morse code.

Putnam's letter reveals another problem as well. In his June 14 message to Putnam, Black had told him, "Lieutenant True, Aerologist, Fleet Air Base, will give forecast from Howland to Honolulu and suggest you arrange forecast New Guinea to Howland through weather facilities at Lae." Now Putnam was asking Black, "Can *Itasca* forward Howland weather forecast to Lae possibly via the *Ontario* prior takeoff?" (USS *Ontario* was the Navy ship positioned halfway between Lae and Howland to provide Earhart with a checkpoint.) And to Hampton he wrote, "As you will readily understand a matter of vital importance is for Miss Earhart to get the best possible weather data concerning the Howland region and that along the route to Howland from Lae prior to her takeoff."[28]

Black replied by wire to Hampton. He would arrange for U.S. stations in the central Pacific (Howland, Baker, Jarvis, Fanning, Christmas Island, and the Navy ships USS *Swan* and *Ontario*) to send their weather observations to the main U.S. Navy radio stations in Hawaii and Samoa. The Navy would be asked to forward the data to the weather bureau at Lae, New Guinea.[29] Black made it clear that Putnam would have to cover the cost of forwarding the weather data to Lae via commercial services.

Over the next several days, the various stations made their weather reports to the Navy. Radio Tutuila in American Samoa had difficulty transmitting the information onward, but some of the compiled weather observations did reach Lae. Ultimately, it was pointless anyway. There was no weather bureau in Lae to make use of the raw data.

The same day that George Putnam wrote his letter to Hampton, he sent a plea for help to J. M. Johnson, the assistant secretary of commerce: "I am venturing this note to inquire the present whereabouts of W. T. Miller. I have the impression that he is due shortly back from his trans-Pacific trip." Putnam reminded Johnson how helpful Miller had been before Earhart's previous attempt to fly to Howland Island. Earhart was expected to be ready to try again on June 24, he told Johnson, and Putnam would soon be flying from New York to Oakland to help coordinate with the Coast Guard for the difficult Pacific legs. "Perhaps [Miller] could put in a few days there with me. He is, of course, intimately familiar with the entire Pacific situation, knows the personnel involved, etc. . . . I will be grateful for word as to Miller's whereabouts and doubly grateful if it is possible for him to lend me a hand should he be returning in time." Johnson replied that Miller was due back in a few days, but "several very important matters are being held in abeyance awaiting his return here. I would be glad to have him consult with you there but he would not be able to spend any time out at Oakland."[30]

Meanwhile, in Hawaii, as *Itasca* was preparing to put to sea, Black and the Coast Guard at last had some current information about Earhart's radios, but questions were now being raised about the cutter's own equipment. San Francisco Division sent a message to the Hawaiian Section saying that *Itasca*'s transmitter was faulty and ordering the section to send someone to check it out. Warrant Officer Henry Anthony, the Hawaiian Section's radio technician, went down to the dock and performed some tests, but he could not find anything wrong. "Transmitter checked and operation excellent," he reported; "no defects noted."[31]

At four o'clock on the afternoon of June 18, 1937, the 250-foot cutter cast off from pier twelve. *Itasca* normally carried a complement of ninety-seven officers and men, but for this cruise there were eleven additional sailors borrowed from the cutters *Taney* and *Reliance*. There was also an extra officer aboard: the ship's previous captain, Lt. Cdr. Frank Kenner, who would act as adviser to Commander Thompson.

Richard Black had loaded the ship with forty drums of water and several tons of supplies for the islands, and nine Hawaiians were coming along to relieve the colonists. The Army sent Air Corps lieutenant Daniel Cooper and two enlisted men to service the Electra, an engineer captain and an enlisted assistant to examine the runways, and a photographer. The Navy contributed two airplane mechanics and its own photographer. There was also a doctor from the U.S. Public Health Service. The press was represented by two wire service reporters: Howard Hanzlick from the United Press and James Carey from the Associated Press. Rounding out the ship's company were three civilian "guests of the wardroom," a Mr. P. Fricks and a Mr. E. W. Walsh, the latter accompanied by his eleven-year-old son, Geoffrey. In all, there were about 133 souls aboard as *Itasca* "stood to sea shaping course for Howland Island."[32]

Photo 21. USCGC *Itasca*
TIGHAR Collection, courtesy Frank Stewart

The ship had barely cleared the harbor when there was more trouble about the radios. The San Francisco Division communications officer had monitored the previous day's radio traffic and insisted that *Itasca*'s transmitter was not working properly. Worse, one of the ship's radio operators had refused to cooperate when directed to make adjustments. The division commander demanded "name of radioman responsible for disregarding orders." The cutter's captain replied, providing the name of the offender but also disagreeing with headquarters and begging their indulgence. "Transmitter not, repeat not, faulty based on repeated checks. *Itasca* has difficult communication problem with inexperienced personnel and desires Division's cooperation."[33]

The next day, as *Itasca* steamed southward, Black sent a message to Ruth Hampton in Washington answering Putnam's question about what frequency the Coast Guard would use to send weather reports: "*Itasca* can give her almost any frequency desired." If Earhart was going to find Howland Island by homing in on signals sent by *Itasca*, however, Black needed more information, and he needed it from Earhart, not from Putnam. He asked Putnam to have Earhart contact him with "what frequency best suited her homing device. Also, have her designate time and type of our signal."[34]

Earhart had no way of communicating directly with Black. She was in southeast Asia, and he was on a boat in the middle of the Pacific. Black suggested that Putnam have her send a commercial wire to the governor of American Samoa. The governor's office would then pass the message to the local U.S. Navy radio station at Tutuila, which would in turn relay it to *Itasca*.[35] It was an awkward, time-consuming arrangement, but as far as Black knew, it was the only one available. Putnam responded that it was difficult for him to get in touch with Earhart but promised that she would contact Black via Samoa when she reached Darwin, Australia, and that she would confirm all arrangements before leaving Lae for Howland.[36]

Putnam was lying again. In fact, Earhart had been in daily telephone communication with the *Herald Tribune*'s New York office for more than a week, providing a series of exclusive first-person narratives of her travels. As she made her way down through South America and across the south Atlantic, she sent her daily travelogues as telegrams, and they appeared in the paper under a byline that read "By Amelia Earhart—via wireless." She filed no stories during her three-day trip across Africa, so the *Tribune* published Associated Press coverage of that part of the flight. Once she reached Khartoum in Anglo-Egyptian Sudan, she resumed sending her daily contributions, but now the byline appearing above her articles in the newspaper read, "By Amelia Earhart—via telephone."[37] Over the next nine days she phoned in stories from Massawa, Eritrea; Karachi, India; Calcutta, India; Akyab and Rangoon, Burma; Singapore; and Bandoeng, Java, in the Netherlands East Indies.

Late on the night of June 20, the same day he had sent a telegram to Ruth Hampton telling her "Difficult contact Earhart satisfactorily before arrival Darwin," George Putnam talked to his wife again on the phone. She had just landed at Bandoeng, Java, after an easy 630-mile hop from Singapore. For Earhart it was midmorning on June 21. As she reported in the story she phoned in to the *Herald Tribune* later that day, "The conversation mostly concerned arrangements being made for the two flights from Lae, New Guinea to Howland Island and thence to Honolulu. The United States Navy and Coast Guard are kindly co-operating to help make these rather longish jumps a bit easier. There were details to settle about radio frequencies, weather reports, and the like."[38] If any details were, in fact, settled during the phone call, Putnam did not pass them along to the Navy or the Coast Guard—or to Richard Black.

The Electra arrived in Bandoeng needing what Noonan called "some minor instrument adjustments."[39] Royal Netherlands East Indies Airlines operated American-made aircraft, and the shop at Bandoeng was well equipped to address the problem. Weather delays in Burma had put the world flight a day behind schedule, and Earhart hoped that the repairs could be completed in time for a morning departure the next day. That afternoon, while the technicians worked on the airplane, she and Noonan visited an active volcano. "Tonight we go to the home of one of the K.L.M. pilots, for international 'ground flying' is one of the few social events our recent lives have permitted," she informed her *Herald Tribune* readers. "We are staying tonight at a very good hotel. My room is filled with flowers and everything is as neat and clean as Dutch reputation prescribes. I wish we could stay longer, but we must push on as soon as the plane is in condition."[40]

Whether she really wanted it or not, Earhart got her wish. On checking with the airfield later that night, Earhart learned that the needed repairs were taking longer than anticipated and that it would be another day before the Electra was ready. There was time for more sightseeing. Noonan had friends living in Batavia (today's Jakarta), about eighty miles away. He telephoned them that night, and they invited him and Earhart to spend the following day, June 22, with them. In a letter to a young woman friend the next night, Noonan wrote, "The local Nash automobile representative placed a car and driver at our disposal—so we drove down this forenoon—had a fabulous lunch at the famous 'Des Indies' hotel with a charming group—toured the town by car—and flew back on the local airways."[41]

While she was in Batavia that afternoon, Earhart had phoned her husband to say that she expected to be able to leave Bandoeng in the morning and would be in Lae by June 24, but the next day, Wednesday, June 23, brought further frustration. Her story for the *Tribune*, written that afternoon, explained the situation: "My plans for leaving Bandoeng today cannot be carried out, as K. L. M. engineers and mechanics pleaded for two hours more to complete their work on my plane, so we now plan to hop off some time after midnight, trying to reach Darwin, Australia, by nightfall." She described the previous day's visit to Batavia and concluded with: "Bandoeng is a charming place. If I must delay I am glad of such surroundings."[42]

Her June 23 press release, however, did not reach the newspaper; nor did her husband receive a phone call from her that day. Trans-Pacific telegrams and phone calls went by radio, and it may be that atmospheric conditions were bad that day. For whatever reason, there was no word from Earhart. Wednesday's *Herald Tribune*, for the first time since her departure from Miami, carried no news about Amelia Earhart's trip around the world.

That same day, Putnam confessed his puzzlement in a letter answering Ruth Hampton's request for updated information about when Earhart might make the flight to Howland. He wrote that he had spoken with his wife at two o'clock in the morning on June 22, and that at that time she had hoped to leave Bandoeng "tomorrow." "However, we have no word from her whatsoever this morning so I just don't know. All I can report is that when I talked to her yesterday she expected to be in Lae by the 24th, ready to take off for Howland. . . . I expect to leave tonight for the coast."[43]

13

Where Is Amelia?

JUNE 23–28, 1937

E arhart had not checked in, and for once Putnam did not know where she was. Neither did Richard Black. As *Itasca* neared the end of its five-day voyage from Honolulu to Howland, Black apparently reasoned that because he had not yet received the promised communication from Darwin, she was probably still in Bandoeng, Java. To be safe, he sent telegrams to both Darwin and Bandoeng, giving her the radio capabilities of the three ships that would help guide her flight and asking her to "please confirm and designate signals desired from *Ontario, Itasca* and *Swan* within these ranges best suited to your homing device." The oceangoing tug USS *Ontario* was positioned halfway between Lae and Howland; USCGC *Itasca* was approaching the island; and the seaplane tender USS *Swan* (with no seaplane aboard) was on station halfway between Howland and Hawaii. He also cautioned her that any messages she might send from Lae via Samoa would take four hours to reach *Itasca*.[1]

A few hours after Black sent his telegrams, Commander Thompson sent two as well, one addressed to Earhart in Darwin (at the time called Port Darwin), Australia, and the other to Lae, New Guinea: "Request you advise this vessel 12 hours prior to your departure from New Guinea full information regarding your desires in matter of radio frequencies and communication schedule. We will conform to any frequencies desired. Important anticipate your departure as communication via Port Darwin very slow."[2] Earhart did not see Thompson's message until she reached Australia five days later.

Yet another message reached *Itasca* from San Francisco Division again insisting that the ship had a faulty transmitter. Heeding Commander Thompson's earlier plea for patience with the cutter's inexperienced radio operators, headquarters provided a detailed diagnosis of the problem (a faulty relay). By later that day the problem had finally been fixed.[3]

Midday on June 23 at Howland Island was evening in New York as George Putnam boarded a United Airlines Douglas DC-3 for the all-night trip to Oakland, California. If all was going according to plan, Earhart should be on her way from Darwin to Lae about now.

In Java it was the morning of June 24, and Earhart was not on her way to Lae. She was not even on her way to Darwin. Earhart was still stuck in Bandoeng. The maintenance problems were taking longer to fix than expected. The Electra spent all of June 23 in the hangar, and mechanical difficulties once again frustrated an early morning departure the next day. By the time the work was completed that afternoon, there was not enough daylight left to fly any farther than Surabaya, a major city just 355 miles away.

At 1:15 p.m. (1:45 a.m. in New York) on Thursday, June 24, Earhart succeeded in placing a phone call to the *Herald Tribune*'s office in New York. She gave the paper the previous day's press release and reported that she was still in Bandoeng but was ready to depart for Surabaya. She also needed to talk to her husband. It was important that he know about this most recent delay before he made press commitments for her arrival in Oakland. But Putnam, she learned, was at that moment on an airplane en route to California. He was scheduled to arrive in Oakland at nine o'clock in the morning (Pacific time), ready to start the business day. She needed to catch him before he got there.

The United flight was scheduled to land in Cheyenne, Wyoming, for a brief refueling stop at 2:33 a.m. (Mountain time), about three hours from the time Earhart called New York. The flight to Surabaya should take only about two and a half hours, but if there were delays or unexpected head-winds, she could easily miss him. If she played it safe and waited to make the call from Bandoeng, it would then be too late to fly to Surabaya before dark. Playing it safe was not Earhart's style. When the United DC-3 arrived at the terminal in Cheyenne, passenger Putnam was told that there was an international phone call waiting for him from Surabaya, Java. Earhart told him of the delay but assured him that she would be able to continue on to Australia in the morning. The three-minute call cost twenty-four dollars.[4]

While Earhart and Noonan were flying to Surabaya and Putnam was flying to Oakland, the Coast Guard cutter *Itasca* was completing its five-day voyage from Honolulu. At 8:56 p.m. on June 23, the ship "raised Howland Island, bearing 90 degrees true, distance 7 miles. Stopped, drifted to the westward of the island awaiting daybreak."[5] The first thing the next morning, Richard Black led a delegation ashore to check the airfield. He found the runways to be in good condition, time and some rain having served to settle and compact the coral surface. Air Corps lieutenant Cooper erected windsocks and marked the boundaries with red bunting.

The island's birds, however, presented a problem. Black thought their numbers had increased since March. Cooper considered them to be a "significant hazard" and estimated the population at "10,000 Frigates, 8,000 Booby and 14,000 Terns. The Frigates and Boobies are the size of large buzzards while the Terns are the size of young pigeons."[6] Sailors used blocks of TNT and riot guns in an attempt to frighten the birds away but succeeded only in shifting them from place to place around the island. The best they could hope to do was clear the birds away from the approach end of the runway Earhart was most likely to use.

Howland was ready, but where was Earhart? In his first report sent from *Itasca*, Associated Press correspondent Jim Carey described the preparations being made for the flight's arrival and ended with a query: "Earhart whereabouts? *Itasca* not informed." United Press reporter Howard Hanzlick also filed his first story, painting a picture of "minute preparations for every emergency" with "all personnel on toes."[7] Incredibly, the one emergency for which no preparations were made was the possibility Earhart would not show up. There was no search plan.

Late in the afternoon, *Itasca*'s radio operators picked up press reports that Earhart was still in Java and was expected to remain there for three days. It was Thursday, June 24. If Earhart was not going

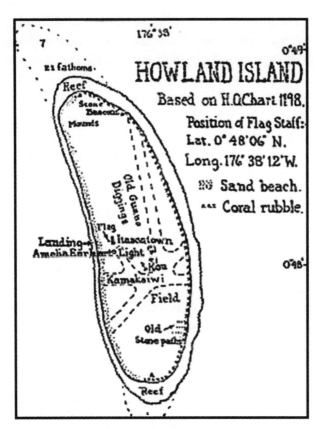

Photo 22. This 1942 map of Howland Island shows Kamakaiwi Field, the three crushed-coral runways built for Earhart's use. Amelia Earhart Light was a small commemorative lighthouse built in 1938. No aircraft ever used the airfield. American Polynesia and the Hawaiian Chain

to fly to Australia until Sunday, there was plenty of time to attend to other business. Black sent a message to Washington saying that *Itasca* would proceed to Baker Island and resupply the colonists there on Friday. "Please tell Putnam we would appreciate direct notification of all progress," he added.[8]

Earhart, in fact, was not making progress. During early morning preflight checks before leaving Surabaya for Darwin, she discovered that the Cambridge exhaust gas analyzer—vital for obtaining maximum fuel efficiency—that she thought had been repaired was again malfunctioning. Earhart and Noonan had no choice but to return to Bandoeng. In a press release filed from Bandoeng later that day, by wireless this time, Earhart expressed her frustration: "Today for the second time in a week I had to do what is unquestionably the most difficult thing I have ever done in aviation. It was necessary to return to Bandoeng this morning from Sourabaya [*sic*] for readjustment of certain long-distance flying instruments. . . . I do not know how long we shall have to be here, but it is probable that the trouble will be located today."[9]

Word of the reversal traveled fast. Within a few hours *Itasca*, unloading supplies at Baker Island, received a message from San Francisco Division: the Associated Press was reporting that Earhart had attempted to resume her trip yesterday but had gotten only as far as Surabaya, Java, before experiencing instrument problems. She was returning to Bandoeng, Java, and it was "uncertain when continuing flight."[10]

Later, another message from San Francisco Division brought word that Putnam, now in Oakland, had confirmed that Earhart was indeed back in Bandoeng, "departure indefinite." Putnam promised that once she got to Darwin, Earhart would cable the communication details for the

Lae-Howland flight directly to the Coast Guard in San Francisco, which would then convey them to *Itasca*. Putnam also tried to provide some of the radio information the Coast Guard had been clamoring for: "Communication from plane will be on 500, 3105 or 6210 kilocycles by voice." He repeated the previously given information that Earhart would broadcast her position at fifteen and forty-five minutes past the hour. *Itasca*, he said, should adjust its transmitter "for possible use 3105 kilocycles for voice."[11]

This was the first time the Coast Guard radio operators learned what frequency Earhart might want them to use when transmitting to her. It was an unusual request because, by federal regulation, only aircraft were allowed to transmit on 3105 kcs. Ground stations replied on a different frequency. In closing, Putnam added, "direction finder on plane covers range of about 200 to 1400 kilocycles."[12] That evening, *Itasca*, having completed its resupply of the Baker Island colonists, steamed the forty miles back to Howland.

In Bandoeng, it was the morning of June 26, and the Electra was once again in the Netherlands East Indies Airlines hangar. On her unscheduled return to Bandoeng, Earhart received a telegram that had arrived there after she left for Surabaya. The message was the one from Richard Black aboard the Coast Guard cutter *Itasca* informing her of the ship's radio capabilities and asking that she "designate signals desired from *Ontario*, *Itasca* and *Swan* within . . . ranges best suited to your homing device."[13]

While technicians worked on her airplane, Earhart drafted a response to Black's request and gave it to the local telegraph office. By midday the instrument problem seemed finally to be fixed, but once again there was time for only a few hours of flying before nightfall. Earhart and Noonan flew back to Surabaya while Earhart's telegram began its journey to Black.

That afternoon the Electra landed in Surabaya for the second time in as many days. Earhart did not file a *Tribune* story from Surabaya, and *Last Flight*, the book later compiled from her narratives, does not mention the second stop at that city. Apparently Earhart made another phone call to her husband later that night because the next morning—at 8:00 aboard *Itasca* and 11:30 in California— the Coast Guard's San Francisco Division sent a priority message to the cutter: "Repairs made and Earhart now at Surabaya. Expects leave dawn this date for Port Darwin and next day for Lae. Following information from Earhart this date; homing device covers from 200 to 1500 and 2400 to 4800 kilocycles. Any frequencies not repeat not near ends of bands suitable."[14] The admonition to avoid frequencies near the ends of the bands was to permit tuning the receiver slightly above and below the frequency, thus allowing for possible calibration discrepancies.

Just the day before, Putnam had said her homing device covered 200 to 1400 kcs. Earhart was now saying that it had much broader frequency limits, and she seemed to be asking the Coast Guard to designate which frequencies she should use for direction finding. San Francisco Division's commanding officer, Capt. Stanley Parker, was happy to oblige. In his message to *Itasca* he said: "We suggest using suitable frequencies having in mind uncertain characteristics of high frequencies. Use 333 kilocycles or frequency in that vicinity and try 545 kilocycles after tests with stations your locality to determine which is best." After several more suggestions and admonitions, he added: "Am advising Earhart that *Itasca* will voice radio her on 3105 on hour and half hour as she approaches Howland."[15]

San Francisco's suggestions were not welcome aboard *Itasca*. From the beginning, Black and Thompson had assumed that they were there to accommodate Earhart. It was up to her to tell them what she wanted. Black's June 23 telegram had asked Earhart to "designate signals desired from

Ontario, *Itasca* and *Swan* within these ranges best suited to your homing device," and Thompson had asked her for "full information regarding your desires in matter of radio frequencies and communication schedule. We will conform to any frequencies desired."[16] Now, not only was Parker pressing Commander Thompson to assume more responsibility for Earhart's flight by telling him to suggest what frequencies she should use, he was also taking it on himself to tell Thompson what to tell Earhart.

Not long after Parker's message reached *Itasca*, the U.S. Navy's main radio station in Hawaii, Radio Wailupe near Honolulu, contacted the cutter with a wire for Black from Earhart. Earhart's telegram from Bandoeng had taken more than sixteen hours to wend its way through the system. Her instructions were very specific. For the flight from Lae to Howland, she wanted *Ontario*, the Navy ship positioned halfway along the route, to be ready to transmit on 400 kcs. When she got close, she would call the ship, and it should then send the Morse code letter *N* (dash-dot) repeatedly for five minutes. At the end of each minute the ship should also send its call letters, NIDX, twice. By hearing the letter *N* and identifying the call letters, Earhart could be sure that she was listening to *Ontario*. She would then, presumably, use her direction finder to home in on the ship and make sure she was on course for Howland.

Her instructions for *Itasca* were somewhat different. Rather than wait for her to call, the cutter was to transmit the Morse code letter *A* (dot-dash), the ship's position, and its own call letters, NRUI, every hour on the half hour on a frequency of 7500 kcs. "Position ships and our leaving will determine broadcast times specifically. If frequencies mentioned unsuitable night work inform me Lae."[17]

The receipt of Earhart's detailed plan reinforced Commander Thompson's view that his job was to deliver the services the flier requested, not design a flight plan for her. He had now received a direct communication from Earhart via the Navy. The information being relayed through San Francisco Division was contradictory, and its commanding officer seemed to be trying to micromanage *Itasca*'s mission. Warner Thompson had had enough. A few hours after receiving Earhart's telegram, he fired off a strongly worded message to Parker: "Consider present relationship Division–*Itasca* communications unsatisfactory and potentially dangerous to Earhart contacts and other vital schedules. Urgently request *Itasca* be given complete communication independence. *Itasca* has reliable communications with Navy and routine traffic can be routed via that system. Recommend discontinuance all San Francisco Radio–*Itasca* schedules until Earhart flight reaches Hawaii."[18] Essentially, he was telling his boss to shut up and let him do his job as he saw fit. Parker acceded to Thompson's request; further messages from San Francisco were confined to Putnam's queries about press arrangements. Still, for Thompson, sorting out just what procedures Earhart desired was a bit of a challenge.

The day before, Putnam, via San Francisco, had informed *Itasca* that Earhart might want the ship to send voice on 3105 kcs. Earhart's telegrammed instructions contained no such request, but Parker had advised Earhart that *Itasca* would send voice on that frequency on the hour and half hour. Accordingly, Commander Thompson ordered the cutter's transmitter adjusted to enable voice transmissions on 3105 kcs.

Earhart's stated plan with regard to *Ontario* could have been more specific, but it was at least reasonable. She did not say what frequency she would use to call the ship, but presumably it would be either her daytime frequency of 6210 kcs or her nighttime 3105, depending on when she arrived in the area. Her request for signals on 400 kcs was within the stated limits of her direction finder. Her announced plan for finding Howland Island, however, was at odds with information received via San Francisco. Earhart was asking *Itasca* to send signals on 7500 kcs—signals useless to her direction finder, which, according to Putnam's message, covered a "range of about 200 to 1400 kilocycles," and according to San Francisco's latest message covered "from 200 to 1500 and 2400 to 4800 kilocycles."[19] Neither Richard Black nor Commander Thompson questioned Earhart's choice of frequencies, even though Thompson, at least, was well aware of the discrepancy. As he later wrote in his official report: "The above message [referring to Earhart's instructions] is the first contact that the *Itasca* has had with Earhart previous to the anticipated flight. The *Itasca* bases this message as the key message of the flight. It will be noted that the frequencies requested were high frequencies with the exception of *Ontario*. This is contradictory to the last message received from Commander San Francisco Division suggesting 333 and 545 kilocycles. It will also be noted that the requested 7.5 megacycles is beyond the frequency range, that at least to our knowing, of the plane direction finder."[20]

Thompson's implication that Earhart rejected San Francisco Division's suggestion that she use lower frequencies is misleading. The suggestion was made to Thompson, not Earhart. He and Black declined to pass the recommendation along to Earhart. Thompson's misrepresentation would later create the impression among senior Treasury Department officials that Earhart had disregarded instructions given to her by the Coast Guard.

The truth is more damning. Where Earhart got the idea that her direction finder could cover "from 200 to 1500 and 2400 to 4800 kilocycles" is not clear, but the signals she requested on 7500 kcs were far beyond even those limits.[21] She had laid out an unworkable plan for finding Howland with her direction finder. Thompson knew the plan was flawed, but he didn't question it.

The morning of Sunday, June 27, in Surabaya found the world flight ready to leave Java at last. The plan was to make the thirteen-hundred-mile flight to Darwin that day, but although the Electra was now cooperating, the winds were not. Earhart and Noonan spent the night in the town of Koepang on the island of Timor. As Fred explained in a letter to a friend:

> We arrived here about noon from Surabaya, Java, with intention of going on to Port Darwin, Australia, but upon arrival received a weather report indicating head winds of about forty miles per hour lay ahead of us. As Port Darwin time is two hours ahead of local time—that is—the sun sets there two hours earlier than it does here—we decided not to risk landing at a strange airport after darkness had fallen. So here we be—in a town without hotel accommodations—for the night. However, it is not as bad as it would appear at first sight. Throughout India, Burma, Siam, and Dutch East Indies the various governments have established what they call "Rest Houses"—comfortable habitations erected to take care of the infrequent travelers who drop in unexpectedly.[22]

Earhart wired a story to the *Tribune* with her impressions of the town "perched as it is on cliffs with winding paved roads" and the airport "surrounded by a stone fence a few feet high to keep out roaming wild pigs."[23]

Sunday night in Koepang was Sunday morning aboard *Itasca*. No further word was expected from Earhart until she reached Lae, so Black, the Hawaiian colonists, and the Army contingent used the time to build a small extension on the west end of the island's east-west runway. With a length of only 2,400 feet, it was the shortest of the three airstrips, but the prevailing easterly winds made it the

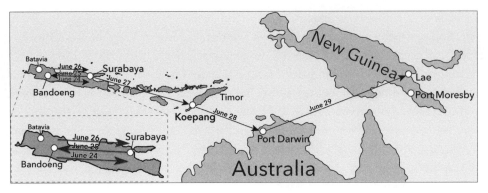

Map 3. Bandoeng to Lae

most likely to be used. "We found that with only a thin hand-placed layer of coral, it was better not to roll, as the rolling seemed to push the coral into the sand," Black reported.[24] The new area was to be marked unsafe for landing but could be used to extend the takeoff.

Earhart and Noonan arrived in Darwin on the afternoon of June 28, 1937. Asked why she had not answered the airport's radio calls, Earhart explained that her receiver was inoperative. In fact, the receiver had been dead since shortly after she left Miami. A local technician inspected the set, replaced a blown fuse, and conducted a successful ground test of the radio.[25] Earhart did not mention the incident in her Darwin press release, sent by wire to the *Tribune*; nor does it appear in *Last Flight*. The book, however, does include the passage: "At Darwin, by the way, we left the parachutes we had carried that far, to be shipped home. A parachute would not help over the Pacific."[26]

The correspondent for the Sydney, Australia, newspaper who was present for the Electra's arrival in Darwin told a different story: "The first thing she did after being officially welcomed was to inquire if parachutes, part of the emergency equipment for the Pacific crossing in front of her, had arrived from America. They reached here more than a week ago. . . . Fully tested and ready for immediate use, the parachutes were waiting in Mr. Collins's office."[27] (Alan Collins was the civil aviation officer for Darwin.) Earhart made no mention of the parachutes in her press release, but a photograph taken that day shows her and Noonan in front of the Electra's cabin door with what appears to be a pile of items about to be loaded aboard the airplane. Two parachutes are clearly visible. The parachute story is one of many discrepancies between the creatively edited posthumous book *Last Flight* and contemporaneous primary sources.

In Darwin that evening, Earhart sent information to Guinea Airways in Lae intending to arrange radio communications for her flight to New Guinea the next day. To make sure the message got through, she sent two cables via separate commercial services. Both telegrams expressed the desired radio frequency as wavelength in meters in accordance with the British system. One telegram said that she would be sending and receiving on a wavelength of thirty-six meters.[28] The second telegram had it that she would be "receiving and transmitting 36.6 meters D-F loop."[29] The message is ambiguous in that the "D-F loop" (the hoop-shaped radio direction finder antenna mounted on the cockpit roof) was a receiving antenna and could not be used for transmitting. Its mention in the telegram implies that Earhart intended to use her direction finder to home in on signals sent by Lae on 36.6 meters. Early the next morning, Tuesday, June 29, Earhart and Noonan left for New Guinea.

14

Personnel Unfitness

JUNE 29–30, 1937

Earhart and Noonan made the twelve-hundred-mile flight from Darwin to Lae without incident. Once more, though, there was radio trouble. After takeoff she was able to talk to Darwin for the first part of the journey, but as she approached New Guinea, she was unable to establish contact with the airfield at Lae. This time the problem was mathematical rather than mechanical. The airline manager at Lae later reported: "On arrival Miss Earhart pointed out that whereas these radios [the two telegrams she had sent from Darwin the night before] advised us of a wave length of 36 metres, in reality her wave length was 49 metres which explained why we failed to pick up any messages from her."[1]

Lae had not heard Earhart's transmissions because she had bungled the conversion from kilocycles to meters, and the Lae radio operator had been told to listen on the wrong frequency. But Earhart would not have heard Lae even if the conversion had been correctly computed. In her telegrams she had intended to advise Lae that she would be both transmitting *and* receiving on her daytime frequency of 6210 kcs. For her to receive on that frequency, Lae would, of course, have to be transmitting on that frequency. The radio station at Lae transmitted on 6522 kcs and, like most stations at that time, had neither the capability nor the legal latitude to alter its broadcast frequency. Because she did not receive any of Lae's transmissions, Earhart could not try to use her radio direction finder to navigate. If she had, it would not have worked. Lae's frequency was far higher than her direction finder's upper limit.

When Earhart landed at Lae, Black's reply to the message she had sent to him from Java was waiting for her. In outlining the radio procedures to be used on the flight to Howland, Earhart had asked Black to tell her if any of the frequencies she had requested were "unsuitable for night work."[2] The problem, of course, was not the time of day, but rather that her request for signals on 7500 kcs was at odds with her own description of the capabilities of her direction finder. Black's telegram did not point out the discrepancy, but simply assured her that *Itasca*'s transmitters were calibrated and ready to send her signals on 7500, 6210, 3105, 500, and 425 kcs.[3]

In the same message, Black advised Earhart that *Itasca*'s own direction finder had a frequency range of 270 to 550 kcs. The Electra could transmit only on 3105 and 6210 kcs. It was never in the plan for *Itasca* to take bearings on Earhart but, by stating the ship's frequency limitations, Black was reminding Earhart the cutter would be unable to take bearings on her signals. Like Commander Thompson, Richard Black had little confidence in Earhart and was eager to avoid blame in the event of disaster. His support of the flight would be passive rather than active, so he made no mention of the experimental high-frequency direction finder that had been set up on Howland Island. It was good to have as a back-up, but if she knew about it, she might rely on it. It was up to Earhart to find Howland, not up to him to guide her in.

Black did "request we be advised as to time of departure and zone time to be used on radio schedules."[4] The "zone time" was important. Earhart's twenty-five-hundred-mile flight from Lae to Howland would be crossing several time zones. *Itasca* normally kept its radio schedules on local time and, while at Howland Island, local time was Greenwich Time minus 11.5 hours. For the radio schedules to work, the ship and the plane would need to be in agreement about what time it was.

Black's telegram did clear up one issue. Earhart's earlier request that *Itasca* transmit the ship's position along with its call letters revealed that she was not sure exactly where the cutter would be. Black specified, "*Itasca* at Howland Island during flight."[5]

Early the next morning, Wednesday, June 30, in Lae, Earhart, apparently confused about who Black was and unaware that Coast Guard vessels are designated USCGC, not USS, sent off a reply to Richard Black via Samoa, addressing her cable to "Commander USS Itasca." "Plan midday takeoff here. Please have meteorologist send forecast Lae Howland soon as possible. If reaches me in time will try leave today. Otherwise July 1st. Report in English, not code, especially while flying. Will broadcast hourly quarter past hour GCT [Greenwich Civil Time; now Greenwich Mean Time, Universal Time, or Zulu Time]. Further information later; Earhart."[6]

Earhart had, as best she could, answered Black's query about when she would depart. She had also answered his question about what zone time to use for her radio schedules. The flight would use GCT, and she would transmit at quarter past each hour, not at quarter past *and* quarter to the hour, as specified in earlier messages. The decision to use GCT for radio schedules was a smart one because it avoided confusion over time zones. She also asked that messages sent to her, "especially while flying," be sent in "English, not code." Neither Earhart nor Noonan was adept at sending or reading Morse code. Both could "recognize an individual letter [only] if sent several times."[7]

Earhart next cabled her husband in Oakland: "Radio misunderstanding and personnel unfitness probably will hold one day. Have asked Black for forecast for tomorrow. You check meteorologist on job as [Fred Noonan] must have star sights. Arrange credit if *Tribune* wishes more story."[8] The message reveals a number of problems and misconceptions that were to plague preparations for the flight to Howland Island.

A few minutes earlier, she had sent a message to *Itasca* saying that she would depart at midday if the weather forecast reached her in time. Now she seemed resigned to delaying her departure until the next day, Thursday, July 1, due to "radio misunderstanding and personnel unfitness." What Earhart meant by "radio misunderstanding" is not hard to fathom. During the previous day's flight from Australia, confusion about frequencies had prevented her from establishing radio contact with Lae. The misunderstandings would have to be sorted out and the radios tested before she could undertake the long and difficult flight to Howland.

Her reference to "personnel unfitness" seems equally clear. Earhart's wire to her husband was sent at 6:30 a.m. local time in Lae. The previous day's eight-hour flight from Australia had capped a week of early mornings and frustrating delays. It is hardly surprising that Earhart and Noonan did not feel up to immediately setting off on a journey that was expected to take a minimum of eighteen hours. They were probably tired and stressed, but there is no indication in any of the contemporary accounts of their stay in New Guinea that either of them was in less than good health. Allegations that Earhart was ill and that Noonan was drinking heavily are based on stories told years later and are not supported by the historical record.

In her wire to her husband that morning, Earhart asked him to "check meteorologist on job as FN must have star sights." But there was no meteorologist on the job. Two weeks earlier, on June 14, Richard Black had advised Putnam that once Earhart reached Howland Island, Lt. Arnold E. True, the Navy meteorologist at Fleet Air Base, Pearl Harbor, would provide a forecast for the flight to Honolulu. Black suggested that Putnam arrange for a Lae-Howland route forecast through the weather facilities at Lae. Putnam's response, "Can *Itasca* forward Howland weather forecast to Lae?" suggests that he was confused on several points.[9]

When Earhart was ready to leave Lae, she would need more than a prediction of what the weather was likely to be when she got to Howland. She needed a forecast for the entire twenty-five-hundred-mile route. To provide such a forecast, a meteorologist needed observations and measurements from many points on and near the route over a period of several days. Lieutenant True could provide a forecast for Earhart's Howland to Honolulu flight because he had good weather data for that part of the northern Pacific. He did not, however, routinely receive weather observations from the southwestern Pacific because U.S. Navy operations in that region were very limited in 1937.

Except in the immediate vicinity of Howland Island, Earhart's route from Lae lay exclusively over the waters, territories, and colonial possessions of Great Britain. Black reasoned that the British/Australian administration in New Guinea would be better equipped to provide the weather services Earhart required—hence his suggestion that Putnam make arrangements with Lae. Doing what he could to assist the presumed meteorologist at Lae, Black set up a system intended to provide the weather bureau there with data from U.S. ships and islands in the central Pacific. It appears that neither Putnam nor Black inquired as to whether there was, in fact, a weather bureau or forecasting facility at Lae. There was not. In the end, Earhart arrived in New Guinea with no way to obtain a weather forecast for the longest and most dangerous leg of the world flight.

Fred Noonan would be using celestial navigation and dead reckoning to bring the flight close enough for Earhart to use radio direction finding to fine-tune the approach to Howland Island. Although his job was critical to the flight's success, it was performed autonomously aboard the airplane and required no particular coordination with external support services. Consequently, none of the messages sent to Black, the Coast Guard, or the Navy during the planning for the second world flight attempt and the preparations for the Lae-Howland trip included a reference to Noonan. Earhart mentioned Noonan regularly in her stories to the *Tribune*, but the men at sea did not see newspapers. The unintended effect was that no one aboard the ships that would be supporting the flight knew for certain that Noonan would be on the airplane.

Earhart's June 30 cable to her husband reveals yet another apparent information gap. Referring to the message she had addressed to "Commander USS Itasca," Earhart told Putnam that she had "asked Black for forecast for tomorrow."[10] It appears that Earhart was under the impression that Richard Black was the captain of *Itasca*. She and the Department of the Interior representative had never met. Earhart's first direct contact with Black was the telegram she had received from him while she was in Java. It was sent from "USCG *Itasca*" and signed simply "Black."[11]

The last line of Earhart's telegram to Putnam, "Arrange credit if *Tribune* wishes more story," refers to her precarious finances. The delays in Java and the consequent flurry of international phone calls were expensive, and she was running low on cash.

For Earhart and Noonan, Wednesday, June 30, was a day of recuperation and preparation. Fred Noonan helped the Guinea Airways maintenance staff service the Electra and address a number of minor problems. The mechanics were familiar with the aircraft type because the airline operated a Lockheed Electra of its own. Meanwhile, Eric Chater, the Guinea Airways general manager, did what he could to get weather information for Earhart. He sent a telegram to the chief wireless inspector in Rabaul, New Britain, saying: "Amelia Earhart would be grateful if you could obtain weather reports by about ten a.m. first July from Nauru or Ocean Island, Tarawa and Rabaul. Also, for your information, her plane KHAQQ will transmit on 6210 kcs quarter past each hour on her flight across to Howland Island."[12] Rabaul passed along the request, but the only response was from the radio operator on Nauru, an island about halfway along and just north of the route to Howland. The wind there was from the southeast at three knots, and the weather was "fine but cloudy."[13]

Sometime that day, Earhart phoned in a story to the *Tribune* describing the flight from Darwin and the airfield at Lae: "Everyone has been as helpful and cooperative as possible—food, hot baths, mechanical service, radio and weather reports, advice from veteran pilots here—all combine to make us wish we could stay. However, tomorrow about noon we hope to be rolling down the runway, bound for points east."[14]

Across the International Date Line in California, it was Tuesday afternoon, June 29, and George Putnam was trying to generate media interest in the imminent completion of Amelia Earhart's world flight. The only firm commitment he had was a guest spot on a popular radio program that aired on Monday nights, and he needed to know whether she would be back in time to do the show on July 5. The last information he had about his wife's whereabouts was an Associated Press report that she had left Darwin for Lae the previous afternoon, his time.[15] He had not yet received the telegram Earhart sent from Lae saying that she would "hold one day," nor was he aware of her phone call to the *Tribune*.[16] As far as Putnam knew, Earhart could already be on her way to Howland. A wire sent to Lae might miss her.

The Coast Guard's San Francisco Division, on the other hand, was in direct radio communication with *Itasca*. To be sure his message reached Earhart, Putnam had the Coast Guard send it to the cutter: "Following for Miss Earhart upon arrival Howland Island: Flight contingencies permitting, is Saturday arrival likely? Sunday latest? Either perfect. Confidential: Want you to know very important radio commitment Monday night. Nothing else whatever. Signed Putnam."[17] Putnam's message to his wife has been cited as an example of him pressuring her to make the flight to Howland before she was ready, but *Itasca* was not asked, and made no attempt, to forward the message to New Guinea. Earhart never saw it.

At noon in Lae, Earhart watched the airfield's radio operator, Harry Balfour, as he checked the aircraft's ability to receive "long-wave" (low frequency) signals of the sort most useful for radio direction finding. The test went well, and Balfour was able to receive signals sent by a nearby station on 500 kcs.

Although the radio receiver aboard the airplane seemed to be functioning well, other radio-related problems were threatening to delay the flight's departure. The accuracy of Fred Noonan's celestial navigation on the trip to Howland depended on the accuracy of his chronometer. To enable navigators to correctly set their timepieces, radio stations at selected locations around the world broadcast special signals at specified times each day. Lae, New Guinea, could usually receive the broadcasts from stations in Australia and French Indochina, but on this day local interference frustrated Balfour's attempts to get time signals for Noonan. The flight to Howland could not begin without a successful time check.

That afternoon—Wednesday, June 30, in Lae—Earhart sent another message to Black via Samoa announcing her latest departure plans and asking him to try to establish direct radio contact between *Itasca* and Lae: "Account local conditions plan start July 1st, 23:30 GCT, if weather okay. Will *Itasca* try contact Lae direct on 25 metres—Lae on 46 metres—so can get forecast in time? Particularly interested probable type percentage clouds near Howland. Now understand *Itasca* voicing 3105 on hour and half hour with long continuous signal on approach. Confirm and appoint time for operator here to stand watch for direct contact; Earhart."[18]

She wanted *Itasca* to call Lae on a frequency of 12000 kcs and listen for a reply on Lae's transmitting frequency of 6522 kcs. If the two could establish a direct radio link, it would eliminate the uncertainty, confusion, and hours of delay in routing messages through Samoa. Still unaware that there was no meteorologist aboard *Itasca*, Earhart hoped to have a forecast in hand in time for her planned departure at 9:30 a.m. local time the next morning, July 1.

That evening, nearly twelve hours after it was sent, Earhart's early morning message asking for the meteorologist's forecast finally reached *Itasca*. Commander Thompson immediately had a radio transmission sent to Fleet Air Base, Pearl Harbor, asking that Lieutenant True be contacted at his home. "Earhart appears to think *Itasca* has Navy aerologist aboard. Black requests you give at least an opinion."[19]

While Thompson and Black waited for True to respond, they sent a reply to Earhart via Samoa: "Reference your message. Have no aerologist aboard. Have requested forecast from Fleet Air Base, Pearl Harbor, for Howland to Lae though doubtful if obtainable. Will forward Honolulu Howland forecast as indicated."[20] This message does not appear to have reached Lae at all.

Late that night, Lieutenant True sent a message to Earhart, via Samoa, with his best attempt at a forecast for the Lae-Howland route. As weather forecasts go, it was largely meaningless. True's only sources of weather data for the area in question were USS *Ontario*, the Navy ship on station at roughly the halfway point along the route, and *Itasca* at Howland. *Ontario* was getting some rain squalls. The weather was good at Howland. Other than that, True's forecast was based on his knowledge of what was "generally average" for the region.[21] Even this minimal information does not appear to have reached Earhart.

Around nine o'clock that night, *Itasca* received Earhart's message requesting that the ship make direct radio contact with Lae. She had, however, neglected to provide Lae's call letters, so at ten o'clock another telegram was sent to her via Samoa: "Request *Itasca* be advised call letters of station to be contacted." In the same message, *Itasca* confirmed its understanding of the radio procedures to be used during the upcoming flight: "Will transmit letter 'A' with call letters repeated twice end every minute on half hour and hour on 7.5 megacycles. Will broadcast voice on 3105 kcs on request or start when within range."[22] Once again, the cumbersome system of relaying communications through Samoa appears to have failed. *Itasca* received no reply to its request for the station's call letters but seems to have made some attempt at direct communication anyway. The effort was not successful.[23]

15

Delay and Denial

JULY 1, 1937

The next morning was Thursday, July 1, in Lae. Earhart and Noonan were rested. The plane had been serviced and the radio receiver tested. A weather forecast from the meteorologist assumed to be aboard *Itasca* was expected shortly. Noonan still needed to set his chronometer, but everyone hoped that the necessary time signals would arrive in time for a midmorning departure. Rising terrain off the northwest end of Lae's three-thousand-foot turf runway dictated that Earhart would have to make the heavily overloaded takeoff to the southeast out over the Huon Gulf. The early morning offshore breeze was blowing the wrong way, but the wind direction typically reversed as the day progressed. At six o'clock Earhart sent a message to *Itasca*: "Plan leave by ten this morning New Guinea time."[1]

Before having the plane fueled for the flight to Howland, Earhart made a short test flight to confirm that everything was working. She was, at last, able to establish two-way voice communication with the ground, transmitting to Lae on her daytime frequency of 6210 kcs and receiving Balfour's reply on Lae's frequency of 6522 kcs. Balfour's assessment of the aircraft's transmitter was that the "carrier wave on 6210 kc was very rough and I advised Miss Earhart to pitch her voice higher to overcome distortion caused by rough carrier wave, otherwise transmitter seemed to be working satisfactorily."[2] Earhart then asked him to send a "long dash" while she attempted to take a bearing on the station, but this attempt to use her homing device was unsuccessful.

The airplane's radio direction finder was based on the principle that a circular antenna is most efficient when oriented edgewise to the incoming signal. When the loop antenna over the cockpit was rotated, the sound got louder or softer depending on the orientation of the antenna to the incoming signal. It was easier to tell when the signal was quietest, so the pilot turned the loop until a minimum signal was heard and from that could determine the direction from which the signal was coming.

During the test flight, Earhart found that she could receive Lae's signal, but the intensity of the sound did not change when she rotated the loop. In the terminology of the time, she could not "get a minimum" and so could not get a bearing on the sending station. Earhart decided that the test had failed because the airplane was too close to the station and the signal was too strong. In truth, the problem was that although the radio receiver could pick up the signal and she could hear the tone in her headphones, the direction-finding aspect of the system could not respond to such a high frequency.

It is not clear whether Balfour's previous ground test of the receiver included taking a bearing using the direction finder, but it is known that he carried out his test on a signal of 500 kcs, a frequency well within the Bendix loop antenna's 200 to 1500 kilocycle capability. In the flight test, Earhart tried to take a bearing on Lae's 6522 kilocycle signal but could not get a minimum. Balfour accepted Earhart's diagnosis of the problem, and so passed another opportunity to discover the flaw in her plan for finding Howland Island. In Balfour's defense, it must be said that the Bendix direction finder was new, and a wireless operator working in the wilds of New Guinea was unlikely to be familiar with it. Nor had Balfour been privy to earlier messages to the Coast Guard concerning the frequency limitations of Earhart's homing device. Earhart was under the erroneous impression the direction finder could respond to high frequencies, and Balfour had no reason to doubt her.

Earhart concluded her test flight shortly after seven o'clock, and the Guinea Airways ground crew began fueling the airplane for the long flight to Howland. There were still two unresolved problems: Earhart had not received a weather forecast for the route, and Noonan still needed to get a time check on his chronometer. The trip was expected to take at least eighteen hours. The arrival had to be in daylight, but Noonan's best celestial navigation required the stars. The approach to Howland, therefore, was best made in the hours immediately after sunup, and that meant a morning takeoff from Lae the previous day.

The departure window came and went with still no forecast and no time signals. Around eleven o'clock Earhart reluctantly postponed the flight. At noon, she sent a message to Richard Black aboard *Itasca*: "Due local conditions takeoff delayed until 21:30 GCT, July 2nd. Any forecast Lae/Howland before then appreciated. Notify Ontario change."[3] Earhart was saying that she now planned to depart from Lae at 7:30 the next morning.

Photo 23. July 1, 1937. This is the last known photograph of Amelia Earhart. The man beside her is Frank Howard, regional manager for Vacuum Oil. He had just supervised the fueling of the Electra for the next day's flight to Howland Island. TIGHAR Collection

Back in California, George Putnam, having learned that his wife had not left Lae on June 30 but not yet aware that the July 1 departure had also been canceled, was still trying to find out whether she would be home in time for the radio engagement Monday night. Knowing that *Itasca* was trying to establish direct contact with Lae and hoping to catch Earhart before the scheduled takeoff, he had the Coast Guard's San Francisco Division send an urgent message to the ship: "Please forward Earhart, Lae. Rush. Is there likelihood Oakland by Monday morning? Reply via *Itasca*. Important."[4] *Itasca* never established direct radio contact with Lae, and the message was not forwarded to Lae as a telegram.

Throughout the remainder of the day—Thursday, July 1—in Lae, Balfour continued his effort to receive time signals. Earhart and Noonan, as they had done during earlier enforced delays, used the time to do some local sightseeing. At some time during the day, a weather forecast for the Lae-Howland route came in from Lieutenant True at Fleet Air Base, Pearl Harbor. Guinea Airways manager Eric Chater, in a letter written three weeks later, recalled that the forecast had come in via Samoa at 7:30 that morning.[5] U.S. Navy records contradict Chater and show that True's forecast was not transmitted from Hawaii until more than an hour after that time, and that messages relayed through Samoa were taking a minimum of three and a half hours to reach Lae, if they got there at all. Whenever the forecast actually reached New Guinea, the picture it painted of the weather to be expected along the route was typical for the region:

Earhart, Lae. Forecast Thursday:
- Lae to *Ontario*: Partly clouded. Rain squalls 250 miles east Lae. Wind, east south east, 12 to 15.
- *Ontario* to longitude 175: Partly cloudy, cumulus clouds about ten thousand feet. [Visibility] mostly unlimited. Wind, east north east, 18.
- Thence to Howland: partly cloudy. Scattered heavy showers. Wind, east north east, 15.
- Avoid towering cumulus and squalls by detours as centers frequently dangerous.
  —Fleet Air Base, Pearl Harbor.[6]

When no storm systems are present, virtually every day in the central Pacific is partly cloudy with big, puffy cumulus clouds, often building to around ten thousand feet. Some get big enough to develop into localized squalls with heavy showers. Any pilot knows it is a good idea to stay out of such clouds. The forecast surface winds would be moderate quartering headwinds, as they would be almost any day in that part of the world. Winds at altitude might be quite different, but that information was not available.

The forecast was for "Thursday," but whose Thursday? True had sent the forecast at 12:20 Hawaiian time on Wednesday, June 30. Across the International Date Line in Lae, New Guinea, at that moment, it was 8:50 a.m. on Thursday, July 1. Was this a forecast for Earhart's today or for True's tomorrow? Unclear as the intended day may have been, the prognostication was so typical of the region that it did not much matter.

That evening, Earhart wrote another press release for the *Tribune*. She had received no reply to her suggestion that a charge account be arranged, so she sent her story as a telegram, collect. Echoing

Hamlet to express her frustration, she wrote: "'Denmark's a prison,' and Lae, attractive and unusual as it appears to two fliers, just as confining. Lockheed stands ready for longest hop weighted with gasoline and oil to capacity, however clouds and wind blowing wrong way conspired keep her on ground today. In addition FN has been unable, account radio difficulties, to set his chronometers. Lack knowledge their fastness or slowness. We shall try to get off tomorrow, though now we cannot be home by Fourth of July as hoped. Earhart."[7]

Finally, at nine o'clock that evening, the anxious listeners heard a marginal signal from Sydney, Australia, and at 10:30 the Adelaide time signal came through clearly. The time check indicated that Noonan's chronometer was three seconds slow. For a flight requiring the degree of precision needed to bring the plane as close as possible to such a small island, Noonan wanted another check.

The next morning—Friday, July 2, in Lae—the planned takeoff time of 7:30 a.m. came and went. Finally, at eight o'clock, another clear time signal came in, this time from Saigon, and the chronometer checked out the same as the night before. Chater later reported that "both Captain Noonan and Miss Earhart expressed their complete satisfaction and decided to leave at ten o-clock."[8] That hour happened to also be 00:00 Greenwich Civil Time. By happy coincidence, for a flight departing at that time, the Greenwich Civil Time throughout the trip would be the same as the flight's time aloft.

The Electra had been fueled for the trip following Earhart's test flight the previous morning. Although Earhart's press release described the aircraft as being "weighted with gasoline and oil to capacity," the plane was actually about fifty gallons shy of its maximum fuel load. The reason was simple and sensible. The Lockheed's engines performed best for takeoff on 100 octane aviation fuel, but the new high-test gasoline was not yet widely available. All but one of the Electra's twelve fuel tanks carried the standard 87 octane gas. An eighty-one-gallon tank in one wing had been filled with the 100 octane fuel at the last stop where it could be had, probably Bandoeng. Now that tank was about half empty, leaving an adequate forty gallons or so for the heavily overloaded takeoff; it could not be topped off with Lae's lower-grade fuel without diluting its contents.

Earhart's aircraft had a well-documented total fuel capacity of 1,151 U.S. gallons.[9] Accounts written shortly afterward by Eric Chater, Guinea Airway's manager, and James Collopy, the district superintendent for civil aviation, indicate that after fueling at Lae for the trip to Howland Island, the airplane had about 1,100 U.S. gallons of gasoline aboard.[10] Because the tanks were filled in the morning hours of the previous day, the loaded airplane necessarily sat through the heat of an entire New Guinea day, and it is reasonable to expect that some fuel was lost due to expansion and leakage through the fuel tank air vents. Such losses are common, fairly negligible, and quite apparent from the dribbling vents and wet patches on the ground. Although neither Chater nor Collopy mentioned it specifically, it is also reasonable to expect that, for such a fuel-critical flight, any such loss would have been replaced during the final inspection on the morning of the takeoff.

Given the controversy surrounding subsequent events, there has been a great deal of discussion and speculation about how long and how far the Electra could fly on 1,100 gallons of gas. The answer is, of course, it depends. According to "Lockheed Report No. 487—Range Study of Lockheed Electra Bimotor Airplane," an Electra carrying a fuel load of 1,100 gallons should be able to cover 3,680 miles in zero wind in twenty-four to twenty-seven hours, depending on a fairly narrow range of airspeed choices. Put another way, 1,100 gallons would give the Electra between twenty-four and twenty-seven hours of endurance at airspeeds between 135 and 150 mph. Headwinds or tailwinds would determine the actual distance covered. A flight equivalent to the distance from Lae, New Guinea, to Howland Island, in zero wind, could be expected to take between seventeen and nineteen hours, depending on the airspeed selected. If Earhart used the higher airspeed profile specified in the study, she could fly against an average headwind of 15 mph for the entire flight, arrive in the vicinity of Howland nineteen hours after takeoff, and still have at least a five-hour—26 percent—reserve.[11]

The long-range capabilities of the Model 10E Special were not merely theoretical. During the preparations for the world flight, Lockheed's Kelly Johnson had flown with Earhart in her Electra to gather further data and make sure Earhart understood how to implement the fuel management techniques and procedures he had worked out. In March, Earhart had departed Oakland, California, with 947 gallons of fuel aboard and landed in Honolulu, Hawaii, nearly sixteen hours and twenty-four-hundred miles later. According to Earhart, the tanks still held more than four hours' worth of fuel, a comfortable 25 percent reserve.[12]

As Earhart contemplated her impending ten o'clock departure from Lae on July 2, 1937, the only weather forecast to reach her had indicated that more or less average conditions existed along her entire route. She could expect moderate headwinds, and she might have to divert around occasional squalls, but if she could get the Electra airborne with the heaviest fuel load she had ever carried, she had every reason to expect that she could fly all that day, all night, and arrive in the Howland area around seven o'clock the next morning. If the island did not appear on schedule, she would have about five hours—until at least noon—to find it.

In the closing line of her press release to the *Tribune*, Earhart had written: "Not much more than a month ago I was on the other shore of the Pacific, looking westward. This evening, I looked eastward over the Pacific. In those fast-moving days which have intervened, the whole width of the world has passed behind us—except this broad ocean. I shall be glad when we have the hazards of its navigation behind us."[13]

The hazards of its navigation were even greater than she supposed and mostly of her own making. She and Noonan had flown two-thirds of the way around the world using only dead reckoning, landmarks, and, on rare occasions, celestial navigation. Now they were about to embark on a transoceanic flight that absolutely required navigational help from the radio direction finder—the radio direction finder she couldn't get to work during the test flight; the radio direction finder she had, in fact, never successfully used. And yet at the end of the test flight, she declared "everything about the aircraft was operating satisfactorily."[14] One can only conclude Earhart considered the Bendix radio direction finder to be nonessential and was confident Noonan could find Howland on his own. For his part, Noonan is known to have been skeptical of radio direction finding and had supreme, albeit occasionally misplaced, confidence in his own navigational skill. He told James Collopy he was "not a bit anxious about the flight to Howland Island and was quite confident that he would have little difficulty in locating it."[15]

Earhart's whistling-past-the-graveyard decision to proceed with the Howland flight was in keeping with the belief she expressed in a now-famous poem, written before she began her professional flying career:

Courage is the price that Life exacts for granting peace,

The soul that knows it not, knows no release
From little things;
Knows not the livid loneliness of fear
Nor mountain heights where bitter joy can hear
The sound of wings.

As a pilot, she had dealt with the livid loneliness of fear, not by mitigating danger with knowledge and training, but with what Elinor Smith called "gut courage that transcended the sanity of reason."[16] There is an old saying in aviation: "There are old pilots and bold pilots, but there are no old bold pilots."

At ten o'clock local time (0000 GCT), the die was cast. James Collopy witnessed the departure:

The takeoff was hair-raising as after taking every yard of the 1,000-yard runway from the north west end of the aerodrome towards the sea, the aircraft had not left the ground 50 yards from the end of the runway. When it did leave it sank away but was by this time over the sea. It continued to sink to about five or six feet above the water and had not climbed to more than 100 feet before it disappeared from sight. In spite of this however, it was obvious that the aircraft was well handled and pilots of Guinea Airways who have flown Lockheed aircraft were loud in their praise of the takeoff with such an overload.[17]

What no one noticed, but is clearly discernible in 16-millimeter film of Earhart's departure, was a mishap that deprived the Electra of its receiving antenna. The wire antenna was attached to the starboard-side pitot tube under the chin of the aircraft and ran along the belly supported by two masts, one roughly amidship and a final support under the cabin door. As the heavily loaded aircraft taxied out to begin its trek to the far end of the airfield, the aftmost mast can be clearly seen, barely clearing the turf. The plane goes out of sight, but when it comes back past the camera on its takeoff run, the mast and the antenna are gone. The most likely explanation is, in swinging the tail around in the over-run to get as much runway as possible, the aft mast hit a hummock and broke off. At such a heavy weight, nothing would be felt in the cockpit. The broken mast was dragged along the ground by the antenna wire during the takeoff run until it snagged on the ground and ripped the wire free. In the film of the takeoff run, a puff of dust can be seen to erupt under the plane, which may be the moment the mast snagged. It was later claimed that a length of antenna was found on the runway. Regardless of how it happened, the loss of the antenna is a simple matter of now you see it, now you don't. The aircraft could still transmit using the dorsal vee antenna but, unbeknownst to Earhart, could now receive signals only on the loop antenna.

Earhart had begun her final press release with a line from *Hamlet*, but it is a quote from *Macbeth* that speaks to her departure from Lae:

I'm for th' air; this night I'll spend
Unto a dismal and a fatal end:
Great business must be wrought ere noon.[18]

PART TWO

1937: THE FINAL FLIGHT, THE FAILED SEARCH, AND EARHART'S TRUE FATE

16

Everything Okay

0000–0719 GCT, JULY 2

Across the International Date Line, it was July 1, and the Howland Island airport was ready for its first customer. Just offshore, the men aboard the Coast Guard cutter *Itasca* were preparing to provide weather and navigational assistance and trying to find out if Earhart was finally on her way.

The cutter's communications capabilities were considerable, but they were not unlimited. Of *Itasca*'s four transmitters, two could send the high-frequency signals Earhart had requested. Only one of them could provide the Morse code letter *A*s on 7500 kcs that Earhart hoped to home in on. That radio, however, was also needed for communication with the outside world. The other high-frequency transmitter, if tuned somewhat beyond its normal limits, could handle Earhart's request that *Itasca* talk to her on 3105 kcs. *Itasca* had only one high-frequency transmitting antenna, so the two transmitters could not be used simultaneously. A switch mounted on the ceiling of the radio room selected which of the two units was connected to the antenna.

Situated on the top deck just behind the funnel, the radio room measured sixteen feet from side to side with a door at each end, and a scant nine feet front to back. Large metal cabinets that housed the ship's transmitters and receivers stood on the floor and hung from the walls, leaving just enough room for the desks of two operators. Each man had a clock, a telegraph key for sending Morse code, and a typewriter he used to keep a running log of incoming and outgoing transmissions. Normally, the operators listened over headphones, but incoming signals could also be broadcast over a loudspeaker mounted on the wall.

The principal players on this narrow stage were the cutter's radiomen. *Itasca*'s communications officer was Ens. W. L. Sutter, but apart from certifying the copies of the logs, he is virtually invisible in the official record. As in most small military detachments, the person running the show was the senior noncommissioned officer. In *Itasca*'s communications section, that was Chief Radioman Leo G. Bellarts. The thirty-year-old Bellarts had joined the Coast Guard as a teenager to follow his passion for radio.

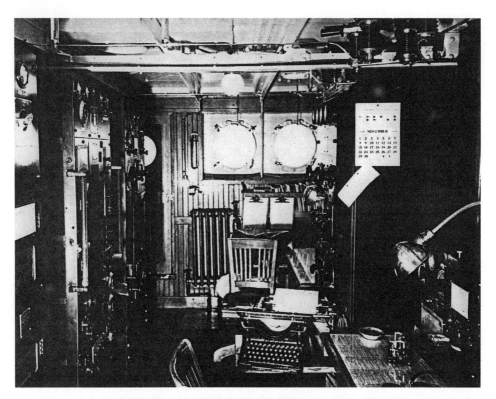

Photo 24. The radio room of USCGC *Tahoe*, seen here, was virtually identical to that of its sister ship *Itasca*. National Archives and Records Administration

Under Bellarts' supervision aboard *Itasca* were three young men who had not yet progressed beyond the Coast Guard's lowest rating for radio technicians. Many years later, Leo Bellarts remembered Radioman 3rd Class William Galten as his most trusted operator: "I could give Galten a job and Galten would go ahead and carry it through. He would do what I told him to and I was perfectly at ease because I knew Galten was a reliable man. He was a good man."[1]

Bellarts was less complimentary about Radioman 3rd Class George Thompson (no relation to the cutter's captain): "Thompson was a very peculiar individual. He was an ex-Army man— ex-Army operator—and you'd tell him to do something and he'd do it as long it fit with his idea." It was George Thompson who had disregarded orders from San Francisco Division during the dispute about *Itasca*'s transmitter. "Thompson was a good operator. Maybe better than Galten as [far as being an] operator is concerned. But as far as reliability, I'd put Galten ahead of Thompson."[2]

Radioman 3rd Class Thomas O'Hare was, in Bellarts' opinion, a "fast operator" in more ways than one. Everyone aboard *Itasca* knew that the Earhart flight was of great interest to the press and to the public. O'Hare seems to have been ready to take full advantage of the situation. Bellarts noted:

I started missing little papers that was [*sic*] around the shack—radio shack. . . . [S]omebody was picking souvenirs up. . . . I knew there was somebody in the radio shack that was doing it. Snitching that stuff. . . . O'Hare, I think was one of 'em because I never got a copy of his log. And I got a little bit disgusted so I passed the word—absolutely those things, when they get off a watch, they are to deliver [the logs] to me by hand only. Lt. Commander Baker, he was the exec and I told him about it and he said, take care of the logs. Keep all that stuff, he says. Don't let it out of your hands.[3]

Radioman 2nd Class Frank Cipriani, the fourth operator under Bellarts' supervision, was an outsider aboard *Itasca*. Normally assigned to the cutter *Roger B. Taney*, Cipriani had been brought aboard at the request of Richard Black specifically to man the high-frequency direction finder to be set up on Howland Island. "Temporary. He was a temporary man," Bellarts remembered. "And so he went over on the beach and it was just as good. . . . We didn't want him."[4]

George Thompson had the watch just after midnight on July 1 when a radiogram arrived for Black from U.S. Navy Radio in Tutuila, American Samoa. Earhart had sent the message from New Guinea the previous afternoon: "Due local conditions, take-off delayed until 21:30 GCT, July 2nd. Any forecast Lae/Howland before then appreciated."[5]

Earhart was saying that she intended to take off from Lae at 7:30 a.m. on Friday, July 2. That would be ten o'clock in the morning on Thursday, July 1, aboard *Itasca*. Richard Black had less than ten hours to get a new forecast to her. The only means of communication with her was by telegram via Samoa. That was taking a minimum of four hours, and often much longer. The forecast had to come from Lieutenant True, but it was now the middle of the night in Hawaii, and True was probably at home and asleep. *Itasca* immediately sent a message to Fleet Air Base, Pearl Harbor: "Request forecast Lae to Howland Island for Earhart. Anticipate early departure this date."[6] Seven and a half hours passed before Fleet Air Base transmitted a forecast to be forwarded to Earhart via Samoa. Once again, True cautioned that he really didn't have much information: "Accurate forecast difficult account lack of reports your vicinity. Conditions appear generally average over route. No major storm. Apparently partly cloudy with dangerous local rain squalls about 300 miles east of Lae and scattered heavy showers remainder of route. Winds east southeast about 25 knots to *Ontario* then east to east northeast about 20 knots to Howland; Fleet Base Pearl Harbor."[7] *Itasca* received the forecast, but Earhart did not. It arrived in Lae too late to catch her before she left.

Before her departure from Oakland for her first world flight attempt, Lockheed engineer Kelly Johnson had made fuel consumption test flights with Earhart in NR16020 and worked out a simple altitude and power management program designed to deliver maximum fuel efficiency. It was a profile familiar to any long-distance aviator: high power settings early in the flight to accommodate the overweight condition and the need to climb to an efficient altitude. As fuel and weight are burned off, power is progressively reduced until the engines' most efficient setting is reached and fuel consumption is stabilized at peak economy. In Earhart's case, the optimum profile was the following:[8]

Time	Altitude	Manifold Pressure	RPM	Gallons/Hour
1 hour	0–8,000 feet	28.5 inches mercury (Hg)	2,050	100
3 hours	8,000 feet	28.5 inches Hg	1,900	60
3 hours	8,000 feet	26.5 inches Hg	1,800	51
3 hours	8,000 feet	25 inches Hg	1,700	43
Rest	10,000 feet	24 inches Hg	1,600	38

Manifold pressure is set with the throttles. Revolutions per minute is set with the propeller controls. Johnson's predicted fuel burn assumed Earhart would set the air/fuel mixture according to the Cambridge exhaust gas analyzer. The guidelines would work just as well for the flight to Howland as they did for the trip to Hawaii.

Earhart had made arrangements to send progress reports back to Lae on her daytime frequency of 6210 kcs at eighteen minutes past each hour and receive weather updates. At dusk she would switch to her nighttime wavelength. It was a good plan, but local interference, or a propagation problem with the aircraft's transmitting antenna, prevented the Lae operator from hearing anything intelligible from Earhart until 2:18 p.m. local time, more than four hours after takeoff.[9] She gave her position, but reception was poor, and all the Lae operator could make out was, "height 7000 feet, speed 140 knots" and some remark concerning "Lae," then "everything okay."[10]

The seven-thousand-foot altitude generally matches Johnson's recommendations for this portion of the flight. The 140-knot speed is probably ground speed rather than airspeed. Earhart's Pioneer airspeed indicator read in miles per hour. Noonan worked in nautical miles and would report ground speed in knots. Earhart flight-planned the Electra at 150 mph (130 knots),[11] so a 140-knot ground speed suggests a 10-knot tailwind, as does the comment "everything okay."

The next message, received an hour later at 3:19 p.m., was erroneously transcribed. It was recorded as "height 10,000 feet position 150.7 east 7.3 south, cumulus clouds, everything okay."[12] More than five hours into the flight, the position is only 186 nautical miles from Lae, giving the plane an impossible average ground speed of only 37 knots. If accurate, everything was definitely not okay. Also, the position is over water and far from any landmark. Noonan needed multiple star shots to get a fix using celestial observations, but this was broad daylight. He would need a landmark to get a precise latitude/longitude.

The most likely explanation is that Earhart reported her position as 157 east, 7.3 south. That would put her 600 nautical miles from Lae on the coast of Choiseul Island in the Solomons, 130 nautical miles south of her planned course. Noonan could get the latitude/longitude by noting their position on the Choiseul coastline. The latest weather forecast had called for "dangerous local rain squalls about 300 miles east Lae." If such squalls were present and Earhart diverted southward to avoid them, it would put her on the coast of Choiseul five hours into the flight with an average ground speed of 115 knots since departure. The low average ground speed, despite a small tailwind, was probably due to low airspeed during the long, heavily loaded climb after takeoff and the diversion around the rain squalls. Nothing was heard at the next scheduled hour.

Aboard *Itasca*, the morning, noon, and afternoon passed with no word as to whether Earhart had left Lae. At 4:45 p.m. (0415 GCT), Thomas O'Hare, who was on duty in the radio room, asked U.S. Navy Radio in Tutuila to "give me flash if you find out. . . . We don't think she took off or we would know by now."[13] An hour later, just to be safe, O'Hare made his first attempt to pick up the plane: "Tuning for KHAQQ [Earhart's radio call sign] on 3105 kcs—Results negative."[14]

At 6:10 p.m. (0540 GCT), San Francisco Division sent word that United Press was reporting that Earhart had taken off at noon Lae time.[15] If true, it meant that she had been in the air for several hours. Commander Thompson considered the news reliable enough to order a special radio watch begun specifically to listen for the inbound aircraft. He also sent Frank Cipriani, the radioman borrowed from *Taney*, ashore to man the high-frequency direction finder that had been set up on the island.[16]

The Associated Press correspondent aboard *Itasca*, James Carey, filed a report that described the situation as it was understood aboard the cutter at that time: "Earhart arrival expected 10:30 morning. Estimate 20 hour plus flight. Easterly winds forecast Howland. Headwinds en route."[17]

In setting up the special radio watch to communicate with the Electra, *Itasca*'s chief radioman had to sort out Earhart's desired frequencies, schedules, and procedures from the fragmentary instructions received in the past weeks. The protocols Bellarts and his operators later used in trying to communicate with Earhart indicate that he was missing a key piece of the puzzle.

Bellarts does not seem to have been aware of instructions contained in a cable Earhart sent the morning after she arrived in Lae. Addressed to "Commander USS Itasca," it said, "Plan midday takeoff here. Please have meteorologist send forecast Lae Howland soon as possible."[18] The realization that Earhart was counting on the cutter to provide a weather forecast for the upcoming flight had prompted a frantic effort to contact Lieutenant True at home in Honolulu and get him to come up with some kind of prognostication. The information in the second half of Earhart's message was vital but required no immediate action: "Report in English, not code, especially while flying. Will broadcast hourly quarter past hour GCT."[19]

In 1937 virtually all marine and aviation long-distance communication was conducted in Morse code. Most ships did not use radiotelephone at all, and aircraft used voice radio only for short-range calls. Earhart's request that *Itasca* use exclusively "English, not code" was thus highly unusual. The idea that an aviation professional, especially a famous long-distance flier, would not be fluent in Morse code was almost inconceivable. It was for just that reason that Earhart had gone to some pains to explain to her hosts in New Guinea that both she and Noonan "entirely depended on radiotelephone reception as neither of them were able to read Morse at any speed but could recognize a single letter sent several times."[20] And it was also why she had warned *Itasca* to "report in English, not code." Bellarts never received the warning. The vast majority of the cutter's transmissions to the plane were sent in Morse code.

Equally important, and equally missed, was Earhart's stipulation that she intended to transmit only once each hour, at quarter past the hour, and that she would keep her radio schedule according to Greenwich Civil Time. In this respect, Earhart was very much up to date. Recognizing the need for standardized time coordination with aircraft that were crossing several time zones during a single flight, Pan American Airways used Greenwich Civil Time for all communications schedules.

Coast Guard captains—and, for that matter, the U.S. Navy—had no such need, and often operated according to a system of half-hour time zones while at sea. Throughout the time Earhart was in flight, *Itasca*'s radio operators used local time calculated as Greenwich minus eleven-and-one-half hours. In practice, being eleven hours out of synch was of little consequence, but the half-hour discrepancy was a problem. "On the hour" for Earhart was "on the half hour" for *Itasca*. When Earhart's watch read quarter past the hour, the clocks aboard *Itasca* were at quarter to the hour. As a result, the men aboard the cutter had the impression that Earhart was contradicting herself, when in fact she was doing exactly what she had said she would do.

How it happened that *Itasca*'s chief radioman had not seen this single crucial message is not known. One obvious explanation is that the radio room's copy of the message was one of those "little papers" that went missing as a souvenir and so was not available to Bellarts when he tried to piece together Earhart's instructions.

Bellarts took the first special watch himself and began listening for signals at 1900 (7:00) on the evening of July 1. At 1950 (7:50) he typed, "No sigs on [3105] during period 19:45–48."[21] Earhart was transmitting at that time, but Bellarts did not hear her because she was sixteen hundred miles away sending another position report to Lae on her other frequency. There are two reports of what she said. According to Guinea Airways manager Eric Chater, at 5:18 p.m. local time, the Lae operator heard, "Position 4.33 south, 159.7 east, height 8000 feet over cumulus clouds, wind 23 knots."[22]

The message puts the flight back on course at the recommended altitude. It would soon be dark. USS *Ontario* was waiting up ahead at the halfway point in their trip to act as a checkpoint, but Earhart and Noonan would have to be on the planned route to find her—hence the course correction.

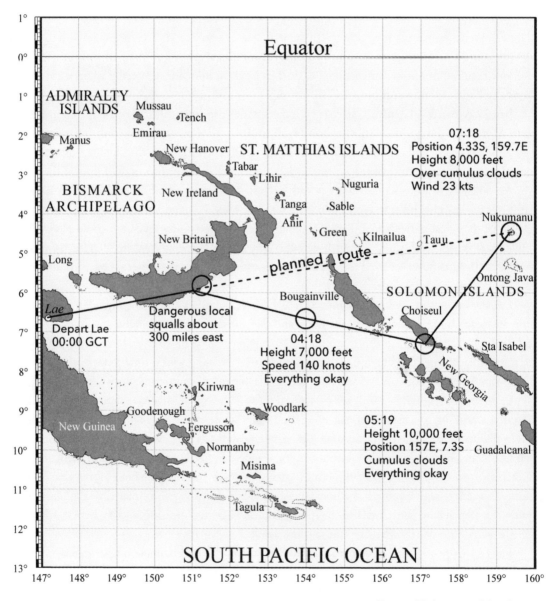

Map 4. Lae to Nukumanu Islands

The latitude/longitude puts them in the vicinity of the Nukumanu Islands, a landmark that would enable Noonan to get a latitude/longitude position in daylight. "Wind 23 knots" is the first and only time Earhart said anything about wind, but she did not specify whether it was a headwind, tailwind, or crosswind.

New Guinea District superintendent for civil aviation James Collopy was also there. In a letter dated August 28, 1937, he wrote, "The next and last message was to the effect that they were at 7,000 feet and making 150 knots, this message was received at approx. 5 p.m."[23] The altitude is different, and Chater's version does not mention what speed the plane was "making"—meaning ground speed. The Electra cruised at 150 mph (130 knots).[24] Ground speed came from Noonan and would be expressed in knots, so "making 150 knots" suggests a 20-knot tailwind, which could be due to help from the forecast 25-knot east-southeast winds as they flew north to get back on course after the southward diversion. It is also consistent with Chater's "wind 23 knots" if Earhart was describing a tailwind.

Lae was hearing Earhart, but she was not hearing them. The last weather forecast from Lieutenant True at Fleet Air Base Pearl Harbor reached Lae too late to catch her before she left. The Lae operator sent the weather forecast that she missed each time he heard from her, but he never received an acknowledgment. The plan was for Earhart to switch to her nighttime frequency, 3105 kcs, at dusk but because Lae was receiving her well on 6210 kcs, the operator urged her to remain on that frequency. He listened on both frequencies for another three hours and heard nothing.

All that can be said with certainty about the first section of the flight is that roughly seven hours after departure, the aircraft had covered a little more than eight hundred nautical miles and was on course and proceeding normally. For Earhart and Noonan, visual confirmation of their position at Choiseul and the Nukumanu Islands had provided reassuring waypoints in their progress across the trackless ocean, but now nightfall was upon them. Until the sun reappeared, any check on their position would have to come from radio or the stars.

17

Darkness and Silence

0720–1743 GCT, JULY 2

Four hundred nautical miles away, USS *Ontario* was on station at roughly the halfway point, 1,108 nautical miles from Lae and 1,115 nautical miles from Howland. The ship's mission was to provide weather and send signals so that Earhart could take a bearing with her direction finder. Earhart's instructions were for the ship to wait for her to call and then send the Morse code letter *N* (dash-dot) on 400 kcs. She and Noonan could "distinguish letters made individually,"[1] so the repeated *N*s were within her capability and would tell her she was hearing *Ontario*. The 400 kcs frequency was within the Bendix direction finder's 200 to 1500 kcs ability to respond but, once again, there was a fatal flaw in the plan.

Earhart had not said on what frequency she would call *Ontario*. Unless informed otherwise, they would expect a call on the standard 500 kcs calling frequency and to communicate in code. The Electra now had no meaningful ability to transmit on 500 kcs, and Earhart intended to make a radiotelephone call to the ship on her nighttime frequency of 3105 kcs. USS *Ontario* was an ancient seagoing tug. Her radios could not receive high frequencies, nor could she receive voice transmissions.

Back on June 23, Richard Black aboard *Itasca* had tried to get that information to Earhart. He didn't know where she was, so he had commercial telegrams sent to Darwin, Australia, and Bandoeng, Java, telling her *Ontario*'s frequency range was 195 to 600 kcs, that the ship could communicate only in code, and that there was "no high frequency equipment on board."[2] Earhart was in Bandoeng on June 23 and in Darwin five days later. Whether she ever saw the telegrams is unknown.

At about the time Earhart was reporting her position near the Nukumanu Islands, *Itasca* received word from Lae: "Urgent . . . Amelia Earhart left Lae at 10 a.m. local time July 2nd. Due Howland Island 18 hours' time."[3] This presented a new picture. The plane had left Lae two hours earlier than previously reported, and the eighteen-hour time en route estimate indicated *Itasca* should now expect the plane to arrive at around 6:30 a.m.

Eighty miles to the north of *Ontario*, the British radio operator on the island of Nauru had been monitoring Earhart's frequencies and hearing her hourly reports to Lae. If the Electra was at the position Earhart reported at 0718 GCT and making 150 knots, it should have covered the four hundred miles to *Ontario* in about two and a half hours, or by 0948 GCT. At 0915 GCT, the Nauru operator heard her trying in vain to reach *Ontario*. He tried to help, calling her in code, but to no avail.[4]

For Earhart, the time of the expected rendezvous with *Ontario* came and went with no answer to her calls and no *N*s in her earphones. Once again, radio had failed to be of help. Then at 1030 GCT the navigation lights of a ship appeared ahead on the dark ocean. Earhart transmitted, "Ship in sight ahead," but there was no response. Only the Nauru operator heard her.[5]

The phantom ship was SS *Myrtlebank*, a freighter out of Auckland, New Zealand, scheduled to arrive at Nauru the next morning. The vessel's estimated position at 1030 GCT was about a hundred miles south of the island and roughly in line with the Electra's route to Howland. Third Mate Syd Dowdeswell was on the eight o'clock to midnight (0830 to 1230 GCT) watch. At about ten o'clock (1030 GCT), he heard an aircraft overhead: "I told the skipper about it and he said I was going nutty, but next day the harbourmaster told us about the missing fliers."[6]

According to Dowdeswell, the night was "fine and clear." If Noonan was able to get a celestial fix, he knew the Electra had covered the 488 nautical miles since the Nukumanu Islands in three and a half hours and was making an average ground speed of 139 knots, suggesting a slight tailwind. If conditions held, with just over a thousand miles to go, they could expect to arrive at Howland in about seven and a half hours—1800 GCT.

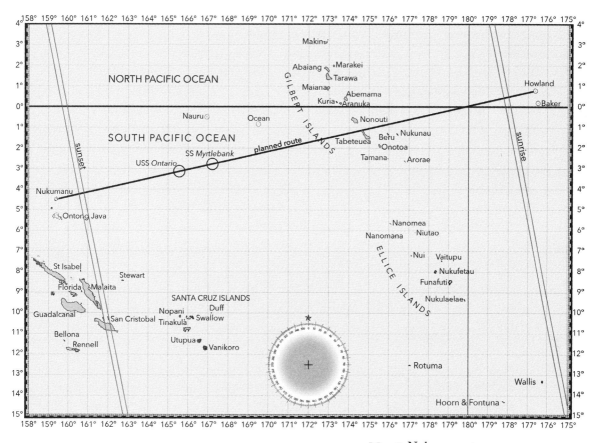

Map 5. Nukumanu to sunup

Aboard *Itasca*, Radioman George Thompson was manning the special Earhart watch and following Chief Bellarts' instructions. He listened for signals from Earhart on 3105 kcs, especially at quarter to and quarter past the hour. A few minutes before each hour and half hour, he sent the local weather in Morse code, followed on the hour and half hour by the Morse code letter *A* repeated for three minutes, all on 7500 kcs. On three occasions during his six-hour watch, he heard unreadable voice transmissions, but nothing he could identify as coming from the airplane.[7]

On Howland, Frank Cipriani set up the borrowed high-frequency direction finder and began listening for Earhart, but the log he kept can be misleading. He started listening at nine o'clock in the evening on July 1, but the radio log he kept indicates he began his watch at ten o'clock in the evening on July 2.[8] The log is one day and one hour ahead of the actual local time. When Cipriani went ashore on the evening of July 1, he was confused about what day it was (not at all unusual aboard a ship on a long voyage) and believed the date to be July 2. Consequently, events recorded in the Howland radio log as happening on July 3 actually occurred on July 2. July 4 is really July 3. By July 5 Cipriani had figured out his error, and the log is correct from then on.

The date discrepancy was an error, but the one-hour time difference was intentional. Cipriani, like the radio operators aboard the cutter, kept his radio log in local time. *Itasca* used actual local time as computed according to U.S. Navy conventions. On the island, the colonists used Honolulu time for the sake of convenience in coordinating radio schedules with Hawaii. In 1937 Hawaii was using Greenwich minus ten and a half hours. Local time in the Howland area, as used by *Itasca*, was Greenwich minus eleven and a half hours. (For the sake of clarity, events on Howland will be described in *Itasca* local time.) The net result was that local time on Howland was an hour later than local time aboard the ship standing just offshore. Over the years, the obvious errors and apparent contradictions in the various radio logs have prompted charges of negligence where there was in fact only a lack of information and allegations of conspiracy where there was merely confusion.

Aboard the cutter, as George Thompson stood the special Earhart radio watch, William Galten performed the ship's regular radio duties. When he was not handling routine administrative traffic, Galten, too, listened for Earhart at quarter to and quarter past each hour, noting in his log what he did and did not hear. Like Thompson, he heard nothing that he could be sure was the plane, but a few minutes before ten o'clock in the evening (0930 GCT), he heard a very weak Morse code transmission, "KHAQQ [the Electra's call sign] this is VK [Galten couldn't get the rest of the sender's call sign]. What is your position now?"[9] The station Galten heard was Nauru, call letters VKT, trying to contact the plane. All Galten knew was that someone, somewhere, was trying to call Earhart.

At two o'clock in the morning, Thomas O'Hare relieved Galten on the administrative watch, and Bellarts once more took the Earhart watch. Half an hour later, he spoke into the microphone for the first time: "*Itasca* to Earhart."[10] He reasoned that at this point, the plane should be within radio range, but the only sound in Bellarts' headphones was the familiar crackle of static. No word of the flight's progress had come in since the initial report of its departure from New Guinea. If Lae or anyone else had heard from Earhart since then, they had not told *Itasca*. The sleeping ship drifted on the dark ocean to the west of Howland. On the bridge, the officer of the deck ordered the engine ahead one-third to ease the ship to within five miles of the island.[11] In the radio room, Bellarts continued to send the weather and *A*s.

Two o'clock in the morning aboard *Itasca* was 1330 GCT aboard the Electra. Earhart and Noonan had now spent thirteen and a half hours in the deafening confines of the Electra, longer than at any time during the world flight. Earhart had put all her cards on Noonan's navigational skills and he had gotten her this far, but a new development was about to make his job much harder.

A layer of high clouds had moved in to hide the stars Noonan needed to check their progress and keep them on course. Without celestial fixes, he could use only dead reckoning to estimate their position based on the last available wind information and his best guess about how it might change. They had another four hours or so to go before sunrise—a long time to fly based on a guess when the target is a flyspeck like Howland. They thought they should be getting close enough to be within radio range, so Earhart resumed her quarter-past-the-hour transmissions.

In *Itasca*'s radio room Bellarts, thinking Earhart intended to transmit at quarter to and quarter past the hour, listened for her on 3105 kcs at quarter to three. For Earhart, the time was quarter past the hour (1415). Bellarts heard a voice. It was barely discernible against the background noise, but he was sure it was Earhart. The transmission lasted for three minutes, but he could not make out a word of what she was saying. He typed: "Heard Earhart plane but unreadable thru static" and notified the bridge that first contact had been made.[12]

Commander Thompson, in his official report, later claimed that at this time, "Bellarts caught Earhart's voice and it came in through loud speaker, very low monotone 'cloudy, overcast.' Mr. Carey, Associated Press representative, was present. Also Mr. Hanzlik [*sic*] of United Press, both gentlemen recognized voice from previous flights to and from Hawaii. There was no question as to hearing Earhart."[13]

An overcast would prevent Noonan from making celestial observations, his only way to establish the plane's position and keep the flight on course, but Thompson was not present in the radio room, and the ship's radio logs do not support his version of events. Asked about the discrepancy many years later, Bellarts vehemently denied that he had heard Earhart say "cloudy, overcast" and explained that at that time, the loudspeaker was not in use: "That static was something terrific, you know, just crashing in on your ears. And I'll guarantee you that Hanzlick and that other joker never heard that. Oh, I would definitely be on the phones. Absolutely. Not on a loudspeaker."[14]

Bellarts was wrong. That "other joker" was Associated Press reporter James Carey. Although no one knew it at the time, the next morning he made a handwritten note: "Friday, July 2. Up all last night following radio reports—scanty—no position from Amelia once—heard voice first time 2:48 a.m.—'sky overcast' all heard."[15] Bellarts, sure it was Earhart but unable to make out what she was saying, apparently passed his headphones to Carey, who happened to catch a break in the static long enough to hear the two words "sky overcast" and later passed the information to Thompson.

Exactly an hour after the first reception, Bellarts heard her again. This time the signal was a bit stronger, and he could make out that she "will listen on hour and half on 3105."[16] Normally, it would be illegal for *Itasca* to transmit on 3105 kcs. By international agreement, that frequency could only be used by U.S. registered aircraft calling a ground station,[17] but to make things as simple as possible for Earhart, Coast Guard San Francisco Division had taken the unprecedented step of clearing *Itasca* to talk to her on 3105 kcs, the same frequency she used for transmitting.[18]

While she was in Lae on June 30, Earhart had advised Richard Black, "Now understand *Itasca* voicing 3105 on hour and half hour with long continuous signal on approach."[19] In her instructions to *Itasca* sent from Java on June 26, she had said that her direction finder "covers from 200 to 1500 and 2400 to 4800 kilocycles."[20] A signal sent on 3105 kcs would fall within the 2400 to 4800 range, but Earhart was mistaken. Her Bendix direction finder did not cover that band. She would not be able to take a bearing on a "long continuous signal" sent on 3105 kcs.

Before she left Lae, Earhart still intended to find the island by homing in on *Itasca* using her radio direction finder. She was not able to get the device to work on the July 1 test flight, but she made excuses, saying she was probably too close to the station, and declared all systems on the plane to be working satisfactorily.

Commander Thompson's version of *Itasca's* 3:45 a.m. in-flight reception from Earhart, as related in his official report written after the search for Earhart had failed, is quite different from the entry that appears in the radio log. According to Thompson, Earhart said, "*Itasca* from Earhart . . . *Itasca* from Earhart . . . overcast . . . will listen on hour and half hour on 3105 . . . will listen on hour and half hour on 3105."[21] There is no "overcast" in the radio logs, nor does the word appear in the transcript filed by Army Air Corps lieutenant Daniel Cooper, who joined the group in the radio room at 3:40 a.m.[22] Cooper's version of the 3:45 reception matches Bellarts' log entry: "Will listen on hour and half hour on 3105—(very faint, S-1)."[23]

"S-1" means strength 1. The strength of received radio signals was rated on a subjective scale of one to five. According to accepted international standards in 1937, strength 1 was "hardly perceptible, unreadable"; strength 2 was "weak, readable now and then"; strength 3 was "fairly good, readable but with difficulty"; strength 4 was "good, readable"; and strength 5 was "very good, perfectly readable."[24] Cooper should have rated the 3:45 reception as S-2.

In the 3:45 a.m. (1515 GCT) transmission, Earhart said only that she would listen for messages on the hour and half hour, with no mention of *Itasca* sending a long continuous signal on approach. *Itasca* didn't know it yet, but Earhart had decided that, rather than struggle with a system she had never been able to make work, she would send a long continuous signal herself and let the Coast Guard do the radio direction finding.

Just before four in the morning *Itasca* time (1530 GCT), San Francisco Division sent a message asking *Itasca*, "Have you established contact with plane yet?" Radioman O'Hare replied, "Heard her but don't know if she hears us yet."[25]

In accordance with Earhart's request, Bellarts sent the current weather using voice on 3105 kcs. Two minutes later, he sent the weather again on the same frequency, this time using Morse code. At quarter past the hour he listened on 3105 for a transmission from Earhart but heard nothing. On the half hour, he broadcast the weather again by voice and in code. During this time, O'Hare, at the other radio position, was switching back and forth between keeping schedules with other stations and listening for Earhart on 3105. Radio Wailupe, the main U.S. Navy radio facility in Hawaii, asked, "Do you hear Earhart on 3105?" O'Hare replied, "Yes, but can't make her out."[26]

There should have been a transmission from Earhart at 4:45 a.m. (1615 aboard the Electra), but there wasn't. O'Hare listened for five minutes and logged: "Tuned to Earhart. No hear."[27] Bellarts was presumably listening as well, but his log contains no entry for that time.

What happened next can only be pieced together from the two radio logs. Although the logs were intended to provide a minute-by-minute record of what the operators heard and the messages they sent, the logs kept by the two operators do not always agree. Aboard *Itasca*, operators in the same room often recorded the same event in their respective logs as occurring at times that varied by as much as three minutes. When things got hectic, phrases were sometimes inserted and logged times changed after the fact to maintain an appearance of chronological discipline. Consequently, although the surviving *Itasca* radio logs are an invaluable record, they often reflect the chaotic nature of events in the ship's radio room on the morning of July 2.

At 1623 GCT Earhart surprised *Itasca* with an off-schedule transmission. At that moment, Bellarts, knowing what he was going to do at five o'clock (1630 GCT), typed in his log: "Sent weather/code/fone/3105 kcs." But before he got to the end of that line on the log sheet, Earhart's voice was suddenly in his headphones. On the same line he typed "heard Earhart (part cldy)" and entered the actual time: 4:53.[28]

Earhart's breach of protocol is not difficult to understand. She was reporting an important new development. For the past three hours, and probably more, an overcast had prevented Noonan from using his octant. Now the blanket of clouds was beginning to break up. If he could catch the right stars peeking through the gaps, he could get a celestial fix that would tell them whether they were still on schedule and on course for Howland.

Bellarts and O'Hare continued to listen, but Earhart's expected transmission times at 5:15 and 5:45 passed in silence. By six o'clock it had been more than an hour since the last transmission from the plane. So far, they had heard Earhart's voice three times, at 2:45, 3:45, and 4:53. Bellarts had logged portions of two receptions as intelligible phrases. O'Hare had not been able to understand anything she said.

The long night was coming to an end. All hands were up and breakfasted, and the ship was now standing just offshore of Howland Island. The eastern sky blushed with the promise of dawn as the cutter's boats headed shoreward carrying the various teams designated to support the aircraft's landing, greet the famous flier, and service the airplane.[29] Somewhere over the dark western horizon, the Electra was drawing closer with each passing minute.

There is no evidence the broken pattern of clouds revealed enough suitable heavenly bodies for Noonan to get a fix, but he knew one star was guaranteed to appear. The sun was about to break the horizon and would give him at least some information about their progress. The line between day and night, known as the terminator, moves from east to west across the face of the Earth at a predictable rate on a line ninety degrees to the rising sun. The higher you are above the surface of the Earth, the sooner you see the sunrise. Noting his altitude and the exact time the sun became visible, Noonan could consult his almanac, draw the terminator on his map, and know he was, at that moment, somewhere on what was known as a line of position. On the morning of July 2, 1937, the sun rose at 67 degrees, so the terminator was a line running 337 degrees one way and 157 degrees the other. Fortunately, for Noonan, that line was almost exactly perpendicular to their course to Howland. Drawing the 337/157 line on his map would tell him how far along they were, but not whether they were north of, exactly on, or south of their course.

As dawn broke, Noonan recorded the exact time with his chronometer, and drew the line of position on his map. He then drew a parallel 337 degree/157 degree line through Howland Island and measured the distance between the lines. With no evidence to the contrary, he apparently assumed they were on course and passed the information to Earhart that they were two hundred miles from Howland.

18

We Must Be On You

The radiomen aboard *Itasca* had heard nothing for the past hour when, at 6:14 a.m. (1744 GCT), Earhart was back on the air: "Wants bearing on 3105//on hour//will whistle in mic." She then announced that she was approximately two hundred miles out and started whistling.[1] They were dumbfounded. It was never the plan for the ship to take bearings on signals from the plane. While she was in Lae, Black had informed Earhart that *Itasca*'s direction finder was limited to frequencies from 270 to 550 kcs.[2] Now she was asking *Itasca* to take a bearing while she whistled into the microphone on 3105 kcs.

Bellarts later said that she did not actually whistle: "I put down 'whistle' because she said she was whistling. Actually it was an audible sound. . . . It was higher than a hum. A shrill note."[3] In Bellarts' opinion, Earhart was trying to mimic the steady, high-pitched tone of a telegraph key being held down. He felt that if *Itasca*'s direction finder had been able to respond to such a high frequency, "We could have handled it. But notice when she did that. One minute after she asked 'on the hour.'"[4] For Bellarts, "on the hour" was three-quarters of an hour away.

For Earhart, the time was not 6:15, it was 1745. She was asking *Itasca* to send the bearing at the ship's next regular transmission time at the top of the hour. Unaware of the misunderstanding, Bellarts saw an irrational woman who refused to answer his calls, changed her plans from one minute to the next, and was now asking him for help he could not provide. "And I was sitting there sweating blood because I couldn't do a darn thing about it."[5]

The only person who might be able to do something about it was Frank Cipriani, the radioman Commander Thompson sent ashore the previous evening to set up the high-frequency direction finder Black had borrowed from the Navy. As Earhart "whistled," O'Hare called Cipriani and told him to take bearings on the signal.[6] Cipriani could hear Earhart at strength 3 ("fairly good") using a long antenna rigged to the receiver, but when he switched to the smaller loop antenna on the direction finder, reception dropped to almost nothing. Then she stopped transmitting: "Bearing nil."[7]

In the radio room, the two operators kept trying to establish communication with the plane. At about this time O'Hare abandoned any attempt to maintain communication with San Francisco and Hawaii. For the rest of the morning, both radio positions were occupied exclusively with trying to reach out to Earhart, while Coast Guard headquarters, the Navy, George Putnam, and the press waited anxiously for news of the plane's arrival.

Half an hour later, at 6:45 a.m. (1815 GCT, her regular broadcast time), Earhart was back on, stronger now. Bellarts typed: "Please take bearing on us and report in half hour. I will make noise in mic" and added "about 100 miles out."[8] O'Hare's log records the event somewhat differently: "Earhart on now. Reception fairly clear now. . . . Want bearing and want report in ½ hour."[9]

Reviewing the log more than thirty-five years later, Leo Bellarts was still baffled by Earhart's request: "'Take bearing on us and report in half an hour.' Well, why do that? If you take a radio bearing you get the bearing back like that. You don't wait no thirty minutes to get it back to them."[10] Once again, the time discrepancy between ship and plane created a false impression that Earhart was being unreasonable. For Earhart, the time was quarter past the hour, and she was asking for the bearing to be sent in fifteen minutes at *Itasca*'s next scheduled broadcast time "*on* half hour," not "*in* half hour."

On Howland Island, Cipriani heard the transmission as well, although he was "using the direction finder and receiver sparingly due to heavy drainage on batteries."[11] The signal Cipriani heard was strong. He rated it strength 4 ("good, readable"), but it was too short and obscured by too much static for him to get a bearing.

Coming as it did only half an hour after both Bellarts and O'Hare heard her say she was two hundred miles out, Earhart's assertion that she was now one hundred miles away caused consternation. If true, it meant either that the aircraft was traveling at the unlikely speed of two hundred miles per hour or that her earlier distance estimate was significantly in error, but there is reason to question that she ever said she was one hundred miles out.

Three operators—Bellarts, O'Hare, and Cipriani—heard and separately logged the transmission. All three logs agree that Earhart asked for a bearing, and both Bellarts and O'Hare noted that she wanted the bearing sent to her "in [sic] half hour." O'Hare and Cipriani both mentioned that the signal was strong. Only the chief radioman's log includes a comment about the plane being one hundred miles out. A platen misalignment in Bellarts' original log reveals that the phrase was an afterthought inserted after the carriage return for the next line.

It may be that the notation "about 100 miles out" was Bellarts' estimate based on the strength of the signal and was misinterpreted as a quote from Earhart by those reading the log. Whether she said it or not, the estimate was attributed to Earhart and contributed to the growing impression among the ship's company that they were dealing with someone who did not know what she was doing. It is also possible the Electra was, indeed, making a ground speed of two hundred knots. The high speed would be reasonable if they had been at the ten-thousand-foot altitude recommended by Kelly Johnson and were now descending at cruise power to make up for time lost in the long, slow climb to altitude.

For the next half hour the two operators shared the single high-frequency antenna as O'Hare sent *A*s on 7500 and Bellarts tried to reach Earhart on 3105. If she made another report at quarter past the hour, it was blocked by a transmission that Bellarts was sending at that moment.[12]

At 7:18 a.m. (1848 GCT) Bellarts sent Earhart a voice message on 3105: "Cannot take bearing on 3105 very good. Please send on 500 or do you wish to take a bearing on us? Go ahead please."[13]

There was no reply. On the chance that Earhart would comply with his request that she send a signal on 500 kcs, Bellarts handed the special Earhart radio watch off to William Galten and went forward to the bridge to man the ship's own direction finder.[14]

The flight was now approaching its nineteenth hour aloft, and the growing strength of the plane's radio transmissions through the early morning hours meant that it was drawing steadily closer to *Itasca* and the island airfield. James Kamakaiwi, the leader of Howland Island's colonists and the man for whom the airport was named, described the morning and the mood in the island's daily log: "The sky was partly cloudy, mostly with high scattered cumulus drifting slowly past. The *Itasca* kept in close to the lee of the island, sending out huge clouds of smoke to aid Miss Earhart in finding the island. Rescue party were stationed on the runways and out in boats, while the official greeters waited anxiously at the reception spot. All eyes gazed fondly, proudly, and eagerly over the horizons."[15]

But for the radio operators, there was more frustration than fondness. As the sun and the temperature rose, so did their sense of foreboding. On the bridge, Bellarts had the ship's direction finder working but heard nothing on 500 kcs. He told George Thompson to keep trying while he returned to the radio room to see if there had been any further word from Earhart. All five of the Coast Guard radiomen were now engaged in trying to establish contact with the plane. On the island, Frank Cipriani listened on 3105, hoping to be able to get a bearing with the high-frequency direction finder if and when Earhart transmitted again. On *Itasca*'s bridge, George Thompson manned the ship's direction finder and monitored 500 kcs in case she sent a signal on that frequency. In the radio room, William Galten sent both voice and code on 3105 when Thomas O'Hare was not sending *A*s on 7500 kcs. The receiver that was set to listen on 3105 was plugged into the loudspeaker so that everyone in the room could listen. All the while, Chief Radioman Bellarts stood by, directing the effort.

At 7:30 a.m. (1900 GCT) Galten asked Earhart, "Please reply to our signals on key, please," and listened in vain for a reply.[16] Earhart heard nothing, but she wouldn't have been able to reply "on key" if she did; she had left her code-sending key in Miami. In nineteen hours of flying, she had heard nothing but static over her earphones. Noonan alone had brought the flight this far, and she had only his word that their destination now lay in the trackless ocean before her. It was daylight, and she was down below the scattered clouds, scanning the shadow-pocked ocean for an island, or a ship, or smoke—anything. Noonan's estimated time of arrival was upon them, but there was nothing but blue Pacific in sight.

From 7:35 to 7:40 (1905 to 1910 GCT), O'Hare sent *A*s on 7500. Then the antenna was switched to Galten, who sent more *A*s on 3105. At about this time a third transmitter, this one with low-frequency capability and its own antenna, was fired up so that O'Hare could send code on 500 kcs at the same time Galten was transmitting on 3105. As Bellarts recalled, "We have everything blasting on her. And it appeared to us that she just didn't—wasn't even trying to hear us."[17]

For the past five hours, Earhart had faithfully transmitted at her scheduled times, but there had been no reply from *Itasca*. To Earhart, the silence was worrisome but perhaps not surprising. Throughout the world flight, radio problems had been the rule rather than the exception. She had learned to rely on Noonan, but now his estimated time of arrival at Howland had come and gone with no sign of the island. She had left Lae with an estimated twenty-four hours of fuel for an expected nineteen-hour flight, giving her a five-hour reserve. Now she was in the middle of the

Pacific Ocean, unsure of her position, with no communication with anyone who might be able to help, and starting to burn into her fuel reserve. On the chance that *Itasca* might hear her, Earhart picked up the mic.

In the radio room, despite their frantic pleas, *Itasca's* operators had heard nothing from Earhart for the past hour when, suddenly, Earhart was back on again, very strong now. Galten's log records the message as "KHAQQ calling *Itasca*. We must be on you but cannot see you. But gas is running low. Been unable to reach you by radio. We are flying at 1000 feet."[18] The entry was logged at 7:42 (1912 GCT).

O'Hare logged: "Earhart on now. Says running out of gas. Only ½ hour left. Can't hear us at all." He then commented, "We hear her and are sending on 3105 and 500 same time constantly and listening for her frequently."[19] He had the time as 7:40.

None of the radio logs assigns a strength value to the transmission, but later reports have it at strength 5 ("very good, perfectly readable"). As Bellarts described it many years later: "I actually did go outside and stand right outside the radio shack and started listening like that—you know, thinking, well, I must hear a motor any second. Actually we had people out on deck. We thought she was going to be flying right down into our rigging the way—oh, man—she came in like a ton of bricks. I mean that."[20]

This was real trouble. Earhart had clearly reached the place where she expected her destination to be but could see neither the island nor the ship. Most puzzling to the men of *Itasca*, they were hearing her loud and clear and yet no airplane was visible or audible in the sky above and around them. The answer to the enigma would not be known until TIGHAR senior researcher Robert L. Brandenburg used twenty-first-century computer technology to model the propagation properties of the Electra's transmitting antenna.[21] The changes made to the aircraft's dorsal vee by Joe Gurr in California and Pan American in Florida had so degraded the antenna's performance that it was impossible for transmissions on 3105 kcs to be heard at strength 5 unless the aircraft was within line-of-sight distance—34 nautical miles from an altitude of 1,000 feet (which it clearly was not), or between about 150 and 260 nautical miles away. At that distance, the chances of hearing a signal at maximum strength was still only 50 percent.[22]

The significance of this discovery is difficult to overstate. With an understanding of the Electra's radio propagation pattern, the difference between what *Itasca* was hearing and what Earhart and the ship's crew were seeing—or rather, not seeing—makes perfect sense and places the aircraft in time and space when *Itasca* was hearing Earhart on the morning of July 2, 1937.

As Bellarts watched the sky for an airplane that must be overhead but wasn't, Earhart was two hundred nautical miles away looking for an island that must be there but wasn't. Mistaken assumptions added to the disconnect between the radiomen and the pilot they were trying to help. They now realized that Earhart had not heard their transmissions, she hadn't heard the weather sent in code, she hadn't heard the "A"s they were sending, and she hadn't heard any of the information they had given her by voice. As Bellarts later said: "And it appeared to us that she . . . wasn't even trying to hear us. . . . 'Gas is running low. Been unable to reach you by radio. We are flying at one thousand feet,' and bingo—she turns the thing off. Not saying nothing at all or go ahead, or this or that or the other thing. That's what made us, as operators, disgusted with her."[23]

She was down low, flying below the base of the clouds at one thousand feet. To Leo Bellarts, who had never flown, it didn't make sense: "They were puffy clouds, you know. Just billow . . . and there was plenty of blue in between them. Plenty of blue."[24] Lieutenant Cooper could have explained to Bellarts that even widely scattered clouds, when seen from above, merge to mask from view anything that is not directly below the airplane, but the Air Corps lieutenant was ashore preparing to meet the arriving flight.

Worst of all, Earhart was low on fuel—but how low? Galten heard her say that her gas was running low. O'Hare thought he heard her say she had only a half hour of gas left. Which version was correct? Lieutenant Cooper later wrote in his official report that the Electra's fuel supply was "estimated to last 24 hours with a possibility of lasting 30 hours." He also noted that "a 20% gas reserve is usually required."[25] Earhart's radio call was made just over nineteen hours into the flight, so she should still have a reasonable reserve, but if O'Hare's "only 1/2 hour gas left" was correct, the situation was inexplicably critical.

Years later, Bellarts' opinion of the discrepancy was unequivocal: "Well, don't go on O'Hare's log. . . . I wasn't even aware that O'Hare was putting that stuff down. . . . No, I mean that. . . . O'Hare shouldn't have been putting that down because it was not his responsibility. It was actually mine and Galten['s], you know. . . . It's in error . . . it should never have been in O'Hare's log. He's just adding confusion to it, and that's not correct."[26]

Itasca's commanding officer knew only that he had two different, but not necessarily contradictory, reports of Earhart's fuel situation. He had little choice but to accept the more pessimistic version. Commander Thompson was not present in the radio room and did not personally hear the call. In his official typed report, he quoted both versions accurately, but after O'Hare's "running out of gas, only ½ hour left," he added the parenthetical comment "(unverified as heard by other witnesses)." Sometime later, Thompson, or someone else, crossed out the "un" by hand.[27]

Galten immediately replied to Earhart's "We must be on you" call: "KHAQQ from *Itasca*. Your message okay. Please reply with voice."[28] Onshore, Cipriani heard Galten's transmissions, but his batteries were now so weak that he had not been able to hear Earhart's call, let alone take a bearing on her.[29]

Aboard NR16020, the question was, what to do now? Standard procedure for finding an island using a single line of position was for the navigator to not try to hit the island dead-on, but to intentionally offset the approach. Upon reaching the line, he would know which way to turn and could run down the line, sure of finding his destination. In Earhart's case, an offset would not be necessary. Radio direction finding would bring the flight directly to Howland. It was a system that worked well for Pan American and had worked for Harry Manning on the Oakland to Honolulu flight in March, but it wasn't working for Earhart. She had heard no reply to her requests that *Itasca* take a bearing on her.

Noonan was confident they were on the advanced line of position that ran through Howland but, with no offset, there was no way to know whether they were north or south of the island. Searching up and down along the line should bring them to Howland, but they only had about five hours of fuel. They would have to be judicious in deciding which direction to search first and how far to go before giving up and reversing course.

Baker Island lay on the 337 degree/157 degree line forty nautical miles south of Howland. If they were south and searched northward, they would come to Baker and know they were going in the right direction. If they were north of Howland and searched north, there was nothing but ocean for the next three thousand miles. The sensible thing to do was to first search northward. If they didn't see Baker within a reasonable period of time, they would turn around, retrace their steps to the starting point, and search southward.

Sixteen agonizing minutes passed while Earhart waited in vain for a reply from *Itasca*. Why were they not answering her? Was her receiver not working, or was she doing something wrong? At 1928 GCT (7:58 for *Itasca*) she picked up the mic and, for the first time, began her call with the plane's radio call sign: "KHAQQ calling *Itasca*. We are listening but cannot hear you. Go ahead on 7500 with a long count either now or on the scheduled time on half hour."[30] In desperation, she was returning to the original plan that called for *Itasca* to send a long signal upon which she would take a bearing using her loop antenna and Bendix direction finder.

Galten heard her, still at strength 5 and so loud there was some distortion. He recorded her words as: "KHAQQ calling *Itasca*. We are drifting but cannot hear you. Go ahead on 7500 with a long count either now or on the scheduled time on half hour."[31]

O'Hare did not log the message; nor did Cipriani. To Galten, Earhart was once again not making any sense. What could she mean by "we are drifting?" And *Itasca* could not give her a long count on 7500 kcs. A long count was a voice transmission, slowly counting from one to ten and back down to one, but *Itasca* could not send voice on 7500. Earhart's original instructions were for the ship to send Morse code *A*s on 7500, and that is what they had been doing faithfully for the past twelve hours. And why would she ask for the signal "either now or on the scheduled time on half hour?" That was over half an hour from now and, according to O'Hare's version of her previous message, she would be out of fuel before then.

Galten was uncomfortable with "drifting." After thinking about it, and possibly discussing it with the others in the room, he decided that she must have said she was "circling." He went back and erased "drifting" and typed "circling" over the erasure. The remnants of the word "drifting" are still apparent on the original log, and the overtyped word "circling" is misaligned with the rest of the line. All future versions of the transmission in various logs and reports accepted that Earhart said she was circling, leading to pointless speculation about why she was doing something she never said she was doing.

Although he could not send the long count Earhart requested, Galten immediately responded with a series of *A*s on 7500 kcs. Earhart, having turned on the Bendix direction finder and tuned her Western Electric receiver from 3105 kcs to 7500 kcs, heard the dit-dah, dit-dah, dit-dah through the static. Reaching above her head, she rotated the loop, trying to discern any change in the volume. If she could find the spot where the *A*s were least audible, a needle on an instrument in front of her would give her the bearing to where the signals were coming from but, try as she might, there was no change. Disappointing, frustrating, but hardly surprising; she had never been able to get the damn thing to work.

After two minutes of trying, at 1930 GCT (8:00) she switched off the Bendix and transmitted, "KHAQQ calling *Itasca*. We received your signals but unable to get a minimum. Please take bearing on us and answer 3105 with voice."[32]

Hoping against hope for a bearing from *Itasca*, Earhart keyed her mic to send long dashes on 3105 kcs while Galten tried to call Cipriani, the only operator who could take a bearing on a high-frequency signal, to alert him to the transmission, but it was no good. Cipriani was trying to conserve his weak batteries and heard only the tail end of Earhart's transmission.[33]

Bellarts instructed O'Hare to do nothing but concentrate on sending *A*s on 7500 whenever Galten was not using the antenna to call her on 3105. Meanwhile, Galten tried again to explain the problem to Earhart: "KHAQQ from *Itasca*. Your signals received okay. We are unable to hear you to take a bearing. It impractical to take a bearing on 3105 your voice. How do you get that? Go ahead."[34] The loudspeaker crackled with static, but there was no reply from Earhart. The antenna was switched over and O'Hare banged out a steady stream of *A*s on 7500.

Both the 1912 GCT (7:42) "We must be on you" and the 1930 GCT (8:00) "unable to get a minimum" transmissions from Earhart were heard at strength 5, indicating that, at those times, the aircraft was most likely on the line of position somewhere in the 50 percent probability envelope.

At 8:11, Galten tried again: "KHAQQ from *Itasca*. Did you get that on 7.5 megacycles? Go ahead on 500 kilocycles so that we may be able to take a bearing on you. Impossible to take a bearing on 3105. Please acknowledge this transmission with voice on 3105. Go ahead."[35] Nothing. Four minutes later, Galten again blocked any quarter-past-the-hour call from Earhart on 3105 with his own transmission on the same frequency: "KHAQQ from *Itasca*. Do you hear my signals on 7500 kilocycles or 3105 kilocycles? Please acknowledge with receipt on 3105 with voice. Go ahead."[36] There was no reply.

The temperature in the radio room climbed with the tropical sun, the heat generated by the constant use of the massive transmitters, and the tension of each passing minute. As Bellarts remembered, "Believe me, we [were] trying everything we knew. . . . We tried stuff that actually is not in the log. . . . Really, I mean it. We [were] frantic."[37]

The men on shore knew that the plane was overdue. As Richard Black wrote in his report, "After eight o'clock uneasiness was felt by the party ashore, but all stood by searching the sky in all directions."[38] Aboard *Itasca*, when the clock passed O'Hare's "one-half hour left" deadline with no sign of the aircraft, Commander Thompson decided the game was up. On the island, Black and the others received "a blinker message . . . from the ship stating that the plane was probably down at sea and recalling all hands to the ship as soon as possible. The parties were summoned from their stations and all ran at top speed for the beach where ferrying to the ship started at once."[39]

The word reached Frank Cipriani at 8:26 a.m.: "Received information that *Itasca* believe[s] Earhart down. Landing party recalled back to vessel."[40] The report Black wrote and the cruise report Commander Thompson filed both have the shore party being recalled to the ship after the receipt of a subsequent transmission from Earhart at 8:43 a.m. but Cipriani's log entry leaves no doubt that the recall order was issued earlier. Cipriani remained ashore with the colonists to keep operating the high-frequency direction finder.

In the ship's radio room, Galten continued his efforts to reach Earhart. At 8:27 he sent another voice message, this time calling her by name: "*Itasca* to Earhart. We [are] transmitting constantly on 7.5 megacycles. Do you hear us? Kindly confirm receipt on 3105. We are standing by."[41] No answer.

For the next fifteen minutes both operators repeatedly tried to contact the plane, but each time, the only reply was the empty hiss and pop of static on the loudspeaker. At 8:44, Galten entered in his log that he was listening on 3105 but heard "nil." He also noted that the chief radioman was tuning up for a transmission to San Francisco Division. It was time to let headquarters know about the crisis. Galten tried to raise Division, but there was no answer.[42] He logged the time as 8:45.

Aboard NR16020, an anxious hour had now passed since Howland failed to appear. The *As Itasca* sent in response to Earhart's request meant they must be hearing her, but her attempt to take a bearing on them had come to naught. She should at least tell *Itasca* what little she knew about where she was and let them know what she was doing so they would have some idea where to search if she was forced to ditch. Fighting back panic, she picked up the microphone.

Because he was wearing his headphones while trying to raise San Francisco, Galten missed Earhart's voice as it suddenly burst from the speaker, as Bellarts recalled, "so loud she couldn't hardly get any louder."[43] Galten typed her words as: "KHAQQ to *Itasca*. We are on the line 157 337. We will repeat message. We will repeat this on 6210 kilocycles. Wait."[44] He added the notation that the transmission had been heard on 3105 kcs in voice at strength 5. In the time column at the end of the line he entered "43," meaning the message was received at 8:43, but he had already logged entries at "44" and "45." To keep the log chronological, he went back and crossed out "44" and changed it to "41"; "45" became "42."

After "We are on the line 157 337" at 8:43, Galten logged that, from 8:44 to 8:46, he listened for the expected repeat of the message on 6210 and told Earhart, in code on 7500 kcs, that he was hearing her okay on 3105 kcs.[45] From the altered times in the raw log, it is apparent that Galten's transmission to Earhart was made after 8:45. Suddenly, Earhart was back on, still on 3105, saying, "We are running on line north and south." Rather than make a new entry, Galten went back and crammed the words into the same line with the 8:43 entry, setting them off in parentheses. The log is a mess and has caused endless confusion about exactly when *Itasca* heard the final in-flight transmission from Earhart. Neither O'Hare's nor Cipriani's log records the transmission. The actual time was not established until 2006 when TIGHAR discovered a note, written in the moment by Associated Press reporter James Carey, "Last on 08:55" (2025 GCT).[46]

The message confirms that Earhart and Noonan had been searching for the island by running up and down the 157/337 line of position and, like Earhart's two previous transmissions, this one was received at strength 5, suggesting the aircraft was still in the 50 percent probability envelope, between 150 and 260 nautical miles from Howland.

Later, the men who heard the transmission discussed the quality of Earhart's voice. Commander Thompson heard the call himself and, in his official report, described her message as "hurried, frantic, and apparently not complete."[47] Lt. Cdr. Frank Kenner was also present. In a letter to his wife a few weeks later, he wrote, "I heard her last broadcasts myself. She realized too late that she was in trouble, then she went to pieces, her voice clearly indicated that fact, by the desperate note in her transmissions."[48]

The anxiety in Earhart's voice was still fresh in Leo Bellarts' memory many years later: "I'm telling you, it sounded as if she would have broken out in a scream, it would have sounded normal. She was just about ready to break into tears and go into hysterics. That's exactly the way I'd describe her voice, now. I'll never forget it."

19

Salvation

T he sun was well up, and Earhart had said she was switching to her daylight frequency of 6210 kcs. Galten listened, but heard nothing. The *A*s sent on 7500 kcs were the only signal from *Itasca* that Earhart seemed to have heard, so he tried repeatedly to contact her in code on that frequency: "Heard you OK on 3105 kilocycles. Please stay on 3105 kilocycles. Do not hear you on 6210. Maintain sending on 3105. Your signals OK on 3105. Go ahead with position on 3105 or 500 kilocycles."[1] Nothing.

If Earhart switched to 6210 kcs, as she said she would, *Itasca* did not hear her because she was too close. When reporting her position to Lae on that frequency the day before, she could not be heard until more than four hours after takeoff, by which time she was nearly six hundred nautical miles away.

By 9:15 a.m., the shore party was back aboard and the boats hoisted.[2] *Itasca* was ready to begin searching for the lost plane, but the situation had changed. Earhart's most recent radio call meant that the airplane was not out of gas, even though her supposed "1/2 hour gas left" deadline had expired. She was transmitting on schedule and making a position report of sorts, not announcing fuel exhaustion. Earhart was clearly worried and upset, but she was just as obviously still in the air and trying to find the island.

Her statement that she was "on the line 157 337" was correctly presumed to be a reference to a line of position, but the line was meaningless without a reference point. She probably meant she was on a line of position that passed through Howland. "Running on line north and south" would make sense as a means of locating the island given the failure of radio direction finding.

Commander Thompson decided to sit tight. The plane was supposed to have at least twelve hours of endurance, enough gas to stay aloft until noon. *Itasca* would maintain its vigil at Howland until then. The Electra might appear overhead any minute, or the radio room might at last be able to establish communication with the plane, and there was still a chance that Cipriani might be able to get a bearing with the high-frequency direction finder. If so, and the plane had to land at sea, they would at least know in what direction to start searching.

With the shore party back aboard ship, the clouds of birds reclaimed their island. On the cutter's deck, every eye scanned the horizon for any speck or glint that might not be a booby or a frigate bird. Every ear strained through the squawking din to hear the rumble of distant engines. In the sweltering radio room, shirtless operators pounded out pleas in Morse code and listened in vain for a reply.

At 9:35, O'Hare called Cipriani on Howland and told him to "get the direction finder going at all cost." But it was no good. Half an hour earlier, Cipriani had logged: "All batteries on the island are discharged. Commenced to charge them." He did not hear O'Hare's directive and could not have done anything about it if he did.[3]

Earhart's scheduled broadcast time of fifteen minutes before the hour came and went, marking a full hour since her last anguished transmission. Ten o'clock, and another futile call to Cipriani on Howland to "get the D/F going at any cost."[4]

Three and a half hours had passed since *Itasca* cut off communication with the outside world to concentrate on Earhart. It was time to advise headquarters of the situation. At 10:15 a.m., the word went out: "Earhart contact 07:42 reported one half hour fuel and no landfall, position doubtful. Contact 06:46 reported approximately one hundred miles from *Itasca* but no relative bearing. 08:43 reported line of position 157–337 but no reference point; presume Howland. Estimate 12:00 for maximum time aloft and if non-arrival by that time will commence search northwest quadrant from Howland as most probable area. Sea smooth, visibility nine, ceiling unlimited. Understand she will float for limited time."[5]

Anticipating the worst, Commander Thompson also sent a request to the Coast Guard Hawaiian Section in Honolulu that they contact the Navy for a "seaplane search," noting that there was plenty of aviation fuel and oil available on Howland.[6] Then, having just advised his superiors that *Itasca* would remain at Howland until noon, Warner Thompson changed his mind and decided to leave. *Itasca* would abandon its plane guard station and initiate a search before the aircraft's estimated maximum time aloft had expired. At 10:40 a.m., having "definitely assumed that the plane was down,"[7] Commander Thompson gave the order for *Itasca* to get under way "at full speed" to begin searching "the area which at that time seemed most logical."[8]

It is difficult to fault Commander Thompson's decision. In dealing with the question of whether Earhart said "gas is running low" or "only 1/2 hour left," he had prudently acted on the more pessimistic possibility, recalling the shore party and beginning preparations for a search as soon as the half-hour deadline expired. When a subsequent transmission from Earhart made it apparent that the plane was still in the air, the captain amended his plan and kept the ship on station at Howland for a time.

When two hours had passed with no further word from the plane, Thompson felt he had to act. Should the flight make a belated arrival over Howland, *Itasca*'s presence was not required for the Electra to accomplish a safe landing on the island. On the other hand, if Earhart was already down, she was in urgent need of assistance, and minutes could mean the difference between life and death.

As the ship got under way, the officers and men tried to make sense of the confusing and frustrating events of the morning. Frank Kenner later described the consensus that prevailed:

> We all admired her nerve and pluck to attempt such a flight, but we cannot admire her good sense and judgment in her conduct of it. She was too sure of herself and too casual.

She devoted no effort to the details at all. When it was too late and she was going down, she hollered for our aid but that was too late. We did all we could. She never gave us any of her positions as we repeatedly requested her to do, she never answered or acknowledged any of our messages. She gave us no information as to her plans, what plans she had for communication she changed in the middle of the flight. All in all, it was a mess.[9]

It was, indeed, a mess, but rather a different mess from the one Kenner and his shipmates perceived. Their frustration with Earhart's fragmented preflight coordination with the Coast Guard was understandable, but it is also apparent that *Itasca* failed to keep track of all the fragments. During the flight, the airplane and the ship were following different communication protocols.

In his official report, Commander Thompson complained, "Earhart asked *Itasca* to take bearings on her. This was never planned."[10] The statement is true, but it is also true that Earhart was never informed that a high-frequency direction finder was installed on Howland. Thompson also noted, "The signals that Earhart acknowledged were transmitted on 7500 [kilocycles]. Her direction finder loop could not handle this frequency."[11] The criticism is legitimate, but the conflict between the described frequency limitations of Earhart's direction finder and her stated intention to try to find Howland by homing in on high-frequency signals was apparent from her earliest telegrams. In all of the many preflight coordination exchanges with Earhart, neither Richard Black nor Commander Thompson questioned her obviously unworkable plan.

The perception aboard *Itasca* that Earhart was acting irrationally colored the way events were interpreted. Earhart's failure to reply to radio calls was attributed to arrogance. Only later did Commander Thompson acknowledge that "Earhart probably had receiver trouble."[12] The impression that Earhart was thoroughly incompetent also made it easier to assume that she had grossly mismanaged her fuel and been forced to land in the ocean hours before her tanks should have been dry. If Earhart was following Kelly Johnson's recommended flight profile, the Electra still had about three and one-half hours of in-flight fuel left when Earhart was last heard from at 8:55 (2025 GCT).

That the aircraft ultimately landed at Gardner Island has been established beyond a reasonable doubt. Precisely how it got there is unknown and unknowable, but the known data provide constraints that suggest a plausible sequence.

1. Computer modeling of the Electra's propagation pattern on 3105 kcs suggests the aircraft arrived at the advanced 157/337 line of position roughly two hundred nautical miles south of Howland at 7:42 (1912 GCT).

2. Turning left to search northward along the line of position, the aircraft was still within the 50 percent strength 5 probability envelope at 8:00 (1930 GCT) when Earhart tried to take a bearing with her Bendix direction finder.

3. Earhart and Noonan continued their northward search for about half an hour until, at approximately 8:13 (1943 GCT), with still no island in sight, they concluded they had been searching in the wrong direction and reversed course to retrace their steps.

4. At 8:45 (2015 GCT) they were back at their origin point and about to begin their southward search, but the island that lay over the horizon ahead of them was not Howland; it was Gardner Island, an uninhabited coral atoll in the Phoenix Group.

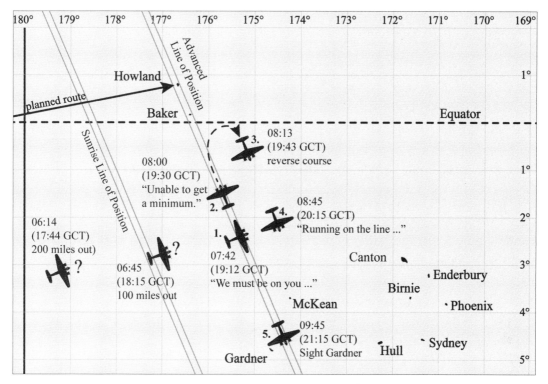

Map 6. LOP to Gardner

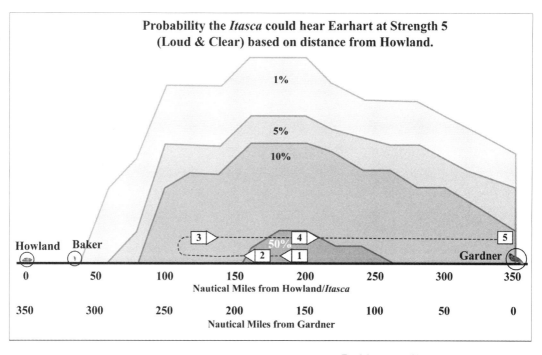

Map 7. Positions profile

5. The aircraft's arrival time at Gardner Island is constrained by the water level on the reef. The Electra could land safely in standing water up to an estimated depth of four inches. On the morning of July 2, 1937, the reef surface was dry until about 10:00 (2130 GCT), but the tide was coming in, and the water level on the reef surface would reach four inches at about 10:30 (2200 GCT). Assuming a cruising speed of 130 knots, the Electra probably sighted Gardner Island at roughly 9:45 (2115 GCT).

Exhausted and deaf after nearly a full day sitting between the roaring engines, Earhart and Noonan were functioning with the adrenaline-fueled concentration that comes with the prospect of imminent death. An agonizing hour had passed with no glimmer of hope when a turquoise smudge appeared on the relentlessly blue horizon and soon resolved to become a lagoon surrounded by a ribbon of trees, white beach, a dark fringing reef, and a line of surf. It wasn't Howland, but it was land.

At such a moment, tears would not be out of place, but there were decisions to make. Where were they? There were no islands north of Howland, so they must be south. They had turned around too soon, but with only two hours of fuel left, if they backtracked they would run out of fuel before they could continue a northward search. The only option was to land, but where? The island was an atoll that looked to be roughly four miles long and about a mile across the lagoon at its widest point. The land area was covered with trees and dense bush, and the beaches were steeply sloped, but they had caught the island at low tide, and the fringing reef was virtually dry in places. The reef surface along the outer edges looked surprisingly smooth, almost like a runway. With luck, they might be able to land, get the radio working, call for help, and have *Itasca* bring enough gas to let them take off and fly to Howland, where they could rest, refuel, and continue the world flight. Earhart had done it before. In her 1932 trans-Atlantic flight, her intended destination was Paris, but she strayed far off course and landed at the first land she came to without knowing where she was. It turned out to be northern Ireland. Welcomed by the local people, she got fuel, continued her journey, and was hailed as a hero.

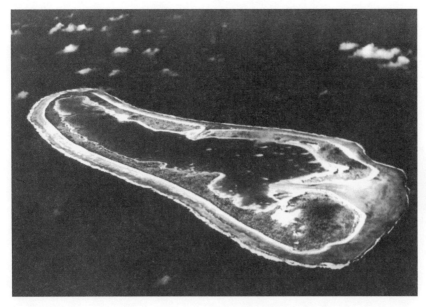

Photo 25. Gardner Island photographed during a U.S. Navy aerial survey, April 30, 1939
National Archives and Records Administration

This time there was no cow pasture to land in, nor was there any sign of a village. The only visible evidence of human presence was a ship aground on the reef at the western end of the island, rusty and abandoned, but the reef just north of the wreck looked dry and inviting. Earhart set up an approach coming in over the ship into the light northeasterly wind. She pulled back the throttles, lowered the wheels and flaps, and set the Electra down on the hard coral. The landing roll was a bit bumpy but no worse than some of the strips she had used in Africa, and the plane came to a stop undamaged. Earhart pulled the mixture levers to idle cutoff, and as the engines died she flipped the magneto and electrical switches to off. For the first time in nearly a full day, the props were still.

For a while the exhausted fliers probably just sat there, trying to absorb what had just happened. The hot engines tinkled as they cooled, seabirds chattered overhead, and a light surf pounded on the reef edge, but for the Electra's crew, the world was eerily silent. It would be some time before their hearing returned. The tide was coming in and, within an hour of their arrival, the airplane stood in six inches of water. How deep would it get? The Electra was not watertight. If the cabin flooded and the transmitter got wet, they would not be able to call for help. They had landed out near the reef edge where the coral was smoothest. It was about five hundred feet to the shore. What was the reef surface like farther in? Could they taxi across the reef and up onto the beach? The only way to know was to get out and go look.

They had been on the ground nearly an hour when, 350 miles to the northwest, Commander Thompson decided to search for the plane he was sure must be down at sea. At 10:40 (2210 GCT) a shudder ran through *Itasca* as the engine came to maximum revolutions, and within minutes the blue Pacific was hissing along the ship's sides. As the cutter steamed away from Howland, each passing minute of silence from the radio room seemed to validate the decision to begin a search. Exactly where Commander Thompson intended to look was still evolving. His initial message to headquarters indicated that he considered "the northwest quadrant" of a circle centered on Howland to be the most logical search area, but he offered no explanation of his reasoning at that time.

Photo 26. NR16020 plane on the reef at low tide
TIGHAR composite recreation by P. Thrasher

In the United States, the news that Earhart had not arrived at Howland and might be down at sea arrived like a thunderclap. It was 1:45 p.m. in San Francisco when Division received *Itasca's* message and immediately forwarded the word to all commands and agencies involved in supporting Earhart's flight. Major media outlets began to scramble for access, and the Coast Guard was quick to recognize the public relations benefits of a high-profile rescue. Within an hour and a half of *Itasca's* message, the commandant's office in Washington was advising San Francisco Division that "if plane is located, headquarters has no objection to commanding officer *Itasca* broadcasting for National Broadcasting Company or other broadcasting company if requested after official report is made by radio to headquarters. Don Thompson of National Broadcasting Company will contact you."[13]

San Francisco Division and the Hawaiian Section were more concerned about whether there was going to be a rescue than about which broadcasting network was going to cover it. Two hours after *Itasca's* first alert, they had still not received an update on the situation. No news was bad news. If the plane had not arrived by now, it was almost certainly out of gas. Another three-quarters of an hour passed, and still nothing more from the cutter. The Hawaiian Section finally sent *Itasca* a direct order: "Advise by dispatch full details concerning Earhart plane such as position reports, bearings, and all information Earhart flight that will be of value to naval search if plane dispatched from here. Recommend you broadcast data to all ships to be on lookout."[14]

In Oakland, George Putnam assumed the plane was down and sent a telegram to Adm. William D. Leahy, the Chief of Naval Operations, in Washington: "Technicians familiar with Miss Earhart's plane believe, with its large tanks, can float almost indefinitely. With retractable gear and smooth sea, safe landing should have been practicable. Respectfully request such assistance as is practicable from naval aircraft and surface craft stationed Honolulu. Apparently plane's position not far from Howland."[15]

Putnam need not have bothered. Leahy had already sent a wire to Hawaii addressed to the commandant of the Fourteenth Naval District, Rear Adm. Orin G. Murfin: "Use available naval facilities to conduct such search for Miss Earhart as, in your opinion, is practicable."[16] Contrary to legend, President Roosevelt had nothing to do with authorizing the search.

An hour and a quarter after the expiration of the noon fuel deadline, and three hours after Commander Thompson first reported Earhart's "non-arrival" at Howland, the Coast Guard's San Francisco Division received a terse message from *Itasca*: "Earhart unreported Howland at 12:00. Believe down shortly after 09:15 a.m. Searching probable area and will continue."[17]

Amelia Earhart was officially missing and presumed down. Thompson now believed that the plane had been in the water for four hours, but, again, he did not explain his reasoning. He seems to have taken the "one-half hour gas left" version of the 7:42 message and applied it to the 8:43 "We are on the line" message to arrive at his estimate that the plane had landed in the ocean shortly after 9:15.

A few minutes later, Thompson followed the recommendation from headquarters and broadcast an alert to "all ships, all stations": "Amelia Earhart plane en route Howland Island from Lae, New Guinea unreported since 20:45 GCT July 2 and apparently down at sea, position unknown. *Itasca* searching probable northwest sector off Howland Island. Request ships and stations listen on 500 kcs for any signals from plane. Commanding officer, U.S. Coast Guard cutter *Itasca*."[18]

From the very beginning of the search, Thompson recognized that the plane might send distress calls after it was down, but his "all ships" alert mentioned only one of the three wavelengths Earhart might use. Five hundred kilocycles was the international nautical distress frequency monitored by all ships at sea, but all of Earhart's in-flight calls heard by *Itasca* had been on 3105 kcs, and when last heard from, she had said she was switching to 6210 kcs. *Itasca's* "all ships" alert mentioned neither frequency. The "all ships" broadcast unwittingly set a trap for anyone who might send a hoax distress call. Earhart's decision not to reinstall the Electra's long trailing wire antenna after the accident in Hawaii meant that the plane had virtually no capability to transmit on 500 kcs. Any alleged signal from Earhart on that frequency would be, by definition, bogus. Although virtually every ship on the ocean had the ability to send and receive on 500 kcs, throughout the entire search no one claimed to hear Earhart on that frequency.

As *Itasca* steamed into the northwest quadrant, scouring the ocean for any sign of the downed plane, Commander Thompson and the other officers were still trying to figure out what had happened. Headquarters wanted "full details," but that was the problem: they didn't have any details.[19] What they did know was that the world's most famous woman aviator had gone missing on *Itasca's* watch. In their view, they had done everything they were supposed to do, and more, but her refusal to cooperate had defeated their best efforts. Now she was down at sea and, if not already drowned, might soon be. *Itasca* was the only means of rescue within hundreds of miles. The focus now had to be on figuring out where the plane had come down and getting there as quickly as possible.

At two o'clock in the afternoon, Thompson tried to explain in a message to San Francisco: "We have had no positions, speed, or courses from Earhart's plane except so called line of position at 08:43 which had no reference point. She gave us none of her bearings. Believe she passed to north and west of island about 0800 and missed it in the glare of rising sun though we were smoking heavily at that time. Judge she came down between 337° and 90° from Howland and within 100 miles. Have broadcast as indicated."[20]

Thompson's catalog of Earhart's shortcomings was somewhat disingenuous. The "so called line of position" was so called by *Itasca*, not Earhart; and Thompson's statement that "she gave us none of her bearings" implied that she had bearings to give, when, in fact, Earhart had made it quite clear that she was unable to use her homing device.

Commander Thompson now believed that Earhart "passed to the north and west" of Howland at about eight o'clock and continued to fly for another hour and a quarter before running out of fuel shortly after 9:15 "between 337° and 90° from Howland." He offered no rationale for his opinion that the plane had come down within one hundred miles of Howland. Just before two o'clock in the afternoon, having run northwestward from Howland for three hours, the captain ordered a cut back to the east.[21]

It was midafternoon in Honolulu when the Pan American Airways office received word that Earhart was down. At 3:30 p.m., the company's radio direction-finding station at nearby Mokapu Point began a constant radio watch on 3105 kcs and 6210 kcs.[22] The airline's capabilities were formidable. Pan Am had been offering scheduled passenger service across the northern Pacific for nearly a year using radio direction-finding facilities erected at Mokapu, Midway, and Wake Island to guide its flying boats across vast reaches of open ocean. Until recently, Fred Noonan had been one of their own. The Pan Am radio operators listened intently for any possible signal from the lost plane, but, like their counterparts aboard *Itasca*, they heard nothing but static.

Shortly after Pan Am began listening, another "all ships" alert went out, this time from the U.S. Navy Hydrographic Office radio station in San Francisco: "All ships, all stations. US Coast Guard ship *Itasca* believes Miss Amelia Earhart down between 337 and 90 degrees from Howland Island and within one hundred miles of island. Possibility plane may use radio on either 3105, 6210, or 500 kcs voice. Request any vessel that vicinity listen for calls and contact *Itasca*. Call NRUI [*Itasca*'s call sign] on 500 kcs."[23] This was the first request for all stations to listen on 3105 and 6210 kcs.

Later that afternoon, Commander Thompson received a message from San Francisco Division: "Possibility plane may attempt use of radio on water as radio supply was battery and antenna could be used on top of wing. Putnam and Lockheed state possibility of floating considerable time excellent and that emergency rubber boat and plenty of emergency rations carried on plane."[24] The message appeared to provide important new information. In fact, it was nothing more than wishful thinking. Technicians familiar with Earhart's Electra would later confirm that the plane could not send radio transmissions if it was afloat on the ocean. The news about a rubber boat and rations was speculation. No one in the United States, including Putnam, could possibly have known what emergency gear was aboard the aircraft on the Lae-Howland flight.

About an hour after San Francisco advised that the plane "may attempt use of radio on water," *Itasca* came back with: "Request frequencies Earhart emergency transmitter." Nobody had said anything about an emergency transmitter, but San Francisco replied, "Same as main transmitter. Possibility plane may be able receive *Itasca* 3105 voice." The message compounded *Itasca*'s misimpressions by seeming to confirm the presence of an emergency radio.[25]

The anxious afternoon wore on. *Itasca*'s deck rose and fell as the cutter rode the peaks and troughs of a heavy swell from the east, while every available pair of eyes scanned the ocean for some sign of a floating airplane or life raft. Visibility was unlimited; overhead, a few scattered clouds drifted on a light easterly breeze.[26] In the radio room, the operators kept a constant watch on 3105 but heard only the steady crash of static.

20

We Hear Her Now

For Earhart and Noonan, the situation had gone from hopeful to dire. If they were going to call for rescue, it would be good to know where they were. At noon, it would be possible for Noonan to shoot the sun and at least get their latitude—4°39.4′ south—but there was a problem. The available evidence strongly suggests they had flown some 127 nautical miles off the bottom of their chart. The exact chart Noonan used is unknown, but he appears to have had U.S. Navy Hydrographic Office chart number 5050. It was the best choice for navigating to Howland Island just north of the equator and from there northeastward toward Hawaii, but the southern edge of the chart is at 2°30′ south. At night, Noonan could get their full latitude/longitude position, but with no chart to plot it on, he had no way of knowing the name of the island he was on or what other islands might be nearby. In the several intelligible and credible radio distress calls heard over the next few days, Earhart tried to describe her location, including attempts to send her latitude and longitude, but she was never heard to say the name of the island.

Worse, both of them were hurt. Earhart was apparently suffering from a badly sprained ankle. Noonan's wound was more serious, but its exact nature is unknown. In addition to being stranded on an uninhabited island with no name, they were now facing a medical emergency. The injuries were most likely sustained while exploring the reef on foot to see if they could taxi the Electra to the safety of the beach. Crossing the reef is intimidating and best done at low tide. When the water is more than about a foot deep, dozens of sharks patrol for fish, their dorsal fins and gently swishing tail tips broadcasting a warning to anyone thinking of venturing out among them. But the greater danger is the reef itself. The coral surface where they landed near the reef edge is flat and smooth, but closer to the shore, it becomes jagged, deeply pitted, and extremely slippery. Walking is treacherous, and a fall on the coral means instant infection.

Getting word of their predicament to *Itasca* was more urgent than ever. There would be no taxiing to the beach, but the tide reached its highest at around two o'clock in the afternoon, and they were relieved to see the water was only about eighteen inches deep—no threat to the transmitter. Earhart knew the ship had heard them the night before on their nighttime frequency, 3105 kcs.

Once the sun was down, Earhart could try to reach them again, but she would have to be careful. The transmitter drew its power from the batteries, which were charged from a generator on the starboard engine. The same batteries were used to start the engine. If she ran down the batteries transmitting, she would not be able to start the engine to recharge them. The sensible thing to do was first start the engine, then transmit. She could afford to follow that procedure. They had landed with fuel enough for a couple hours of flight time at cruise power burning about thirty-eight gallons per hour, but to charge the batteries, she only needed to run the starboard engine at 900 RPM—not much more than idle power—burning a paltry six gallons per hour. Paul Mantz, asked by a newspaper reporter whether Earhart would have enough fuel to keep the batteries charged while sending distress calls, explained the procedure three days after the flight disappeared.[1]

The afternoon was probably spent in the sweltering cabin, nursing their injuries as best they could and getting some much-needed sleep. In Hawaii, Admiral Murfin was marshaling what few search resources he had. In 1937 Pearl Harbor was not yet the home of the Pacific Fleet, but at Fleet Air Base, Patrol Squadron Six (VP-6) was equipped with the new long-range PBY-1. In theory, one of these aircraft could make the sixteen-hundred-mile flight from Honolulu to Howland by flying all night and, on arrival in the morning, still have enough fuel to conduct aerial search operations all day. In the evening, the plane could land and refuel using the gasoline originally intended for Earhart. But such a flight would involve significant risks.

First of all, the Navy air crew would need to find Howland Island at the end of a very long overwater flight. In other words, they would have to do what Earhart and Noonan had just failed to do. If they did succeed in locating the island, they could not use the airfield. The PBY-1 was a flying boat; it would have to land offshore and refuel alongside *Itasca*. But flying boats were designed to land and take off in the protected waters of harbors and lagoons. Open-ocean operations in less than ideal sea conditions were extremely hazardous.

The aircraft commander, VP-6 squadron leader Lt. Warren Harvey, later described the situation in a letter to his mother:

> The flight never had much chance of success because of the distance involved, the total lack of facilities in that area, and total lack of information as to where to look. My prospects of cracking up were about 10 to 1 after searching for a little over 10 hours. I would have had to land down there by sundown in the open sea which had heavy swells with numerous white caps showing. There is no anchorage available either for a plane or a ship so the *Itasca* would have tried to take me in tow for several days until our small tender [USS *Swan*] could arrive to hoist me on board. Even the tender would have broken the plane's hull because the plane was bigger than the available space.[2]

Admiral Murfin ordered the mission to proceed, but he was careful to hedge his bet. As Lieutenant Harvey later told his mother: "[M]y orders on leaving here were not to hesitate to return if any adverse conditions were encountered."[3]

Sending the PBY was a gallant gesture, but what Murfin really needed was some way to put reliable aerial search capability on the scene for an extended period. The answer was, at that moment, moored to pier two in Honolulu. Just a day before, the battleship USS *Colorado* (BB 45) had put in to port. On its decks were three catapult-launched Vought O3U-3 Corsair floatplanes used for reconnaissance and spotting for the ship's eight sixteen-inch guns. Murfin sent a wire to the Chief of Naval Operations in Washington: "*Colorado* at present in Honolulu [on] ROTC [Reserve Officers Training Corps] cruise. If she can be made available for dispatch to Howland Island, her planes would be of great value."[4]

The battleship was at the midpoint of a month-long training cruise for the Naval ROTC and was host to 185 college students and four "distinguished guests of the Navy"—two university presidents, a dean, and a professor.[5] *Colorado* was scheduled to remain in port for five days over the Fourth of July holiday. On the afternoon of July 2, as Murfin was asking Washington for permission to hijack the ship, at Fleet Air Base, Patrol Plane 6-P-3 with four officers, four enlisted men, and a full fuel load taxied out into the waters of Pearl Harbor. Shortly after seven o'clock, as the sun settled into the western horizon, Lieutenant Harvey pushed the throttles forward. The prop blast from the flying boat's engines sent back a cloud of spray as the PBY began its takeoff run. At first there was more noise than progress, but soon the waves were rattling against the hull as the aircraft raced across the water and heaved into the air to begin a slow climb to the southwest.

A few minutes later at Fourteenth District headquarters, Admiral Murfin received a short message from Washington: "*Colorado* is made available." It was available, but hardly ready: the battleship needed refueling, and its three airplanes were in pieces on the hangar floor at Fleet Air Base. One of the pilots, Lt. (jg) William Short, described the situation in a letter to his father: "On the way in to Honolulu they sent us off and we went in to the air base at Pearl Harbor while the ship docked at Honolulu. That was last Thursday, the 1st [of July]. Friday morning, we 'turned to' on the planes as the primary object of sending us in to Pearl Harbor was to get some overhaul work done. We managed to get things pretty well torn apart Friday morning and the carburetors and such up to the shops—figuring on getting them back in shape for flying Monday."[6] Short was the only member of the ship's aviation section present at the air base that evening when word arrived that *Colorado* might be designated to search for the missing Earhart plane: "That kind of put me on the spot as you can well imagine—with the planes all out of commission and everybody scattered all over the place on liberty."[7]

As Short scrambled to round up *Colorado*'s aviation section and reassemble its airplanes, the battleship's commanding officer, Capt. Wilhelm L. Friedell, tried to come to grips with his new mission. Admiral Murfin had ordered *Colorado* to get under way "as soon as possible with planes to conduct search for Amelia Earhart," but the all-important question of where to search was left to the captain's discretion. To help evaluate the scant information available, Friedell "conferred with the Commanding Officer, Fleet Air Base, Captain Kenneth Whiting, U.S. Navy, and other officers of the District and Air Base relative to the probable path and location of the Earhart Plane in the event of a forced landing."[8]

It is not surprising that Friedell sought the advice of the Fleet Air Base commander. Kenneth Whiting, naval aviator number 16, had been taught to fly by Orville Wright in 1914. In 1918 he commanded the 1st Naval Air Unit in France and after the war became a major figure in the development of naval aviation. Ken Whiting was also acquainted with the subject of Friedell's search. Amelia

Earhart had been Whiting's house guest for several days in 1930 after her Lockheed Vega flipped over on landing at the Naval Air Station in Norfolk, Virginia. As the air station's commanding officer, Whiting had offered the hospitality of his home while Earhart recovered from a scalp laceration. Their paths crossed again in March 1937. Whiting by that time was commanding Fleet Air Base, Pearl Harbor, and was at Luke Field when Earhart's Electra crashed on takeoff. At the accident scene, Earhart greeted him with "Every time I see you I get in trouble," implying the whole mess was somehow his fault. Whiting was reportedly furious.[9]

In considering where *Colorado* should conduct its search, the officers had very little to go on. According to the information received thus far from *Itasca*, Earhart had said she was on a 157/337 degree line of position that presumably passed through Howland Island. If she was, in fact, on such a line, she was obviously either too far to the northwest or too far to the southeast to see the island. *Itasca*'s Commander Thompson had said that he believed the plane was "down between 337 and 90 degrees from Howland Island and within one hundred miles."[10]

Friedell, Whiting, and the other officers (almost certainly including meteorologist Lt. Arnold True) reached a different conclusion. They decided that the available information "seemed to indicate that the most probable reason for missing Howland Island would be that of stronger winds than normally expected in the region, and that the plane had probably been carried southeast of Howland, a greater distance than that from which Howland could be sighted."[11] Captain Friedell decided that *Colorado* would search for Earhart to the southeast of her intended destination. By later that evening the three floatplanes had been put back together and were "more or less ready," but the battleship still had to be moved from Honolulu to Pearl Harbor for fueling.[12]

Far to the south, evening had also come to the men on Howland Island and the crew of the cutter *Itasca*—and to Amelia Earhart, if she was still alive. Although the fading light hampered visual searching, the radiomen knew that their chances of picking up signals from the lost flier were better at night, when high-frequency radio waves were not inhibited by the sun's effect on the upper atmosphere.

Further to the south, Amelia Earhart was very much alive. The tide was out, the reef was dry, and she was about to make her first call for help. It is not difficult to imagine the scene. In the gathering dusk, she ran through the prestart checklist for the right engine, setting the switches, toggles, and levers to their ordained positions, being careful not to overprime. This was no time for an engine fire. As she pressed the starter button and the prop began to turn, she cracked the throttle and flipped on the magneto switch. The big Pratt & Whitney whined, coughed twice, and rumbled to life in a cloud of blue smoke. Setting the power to a gentle 900 RPM, she checked the ammeter to be sure the battery was charging, made sure the radio receiver was tuned to 3105 kcs, and flipped the transmitter toggle to "NITE 3105." With a deep breath, she put on her headphones, picked up the microphone, and started talking.

In *Itasca*'s radio room, George Thompson was on the special Earhart watch, listening intently on 3105 kcs but hearing only the usual scratch and hiss until, just on the hour of six o'clock, behind the static, there was a voice.[13] The signal was very weak. He could not make out any of the words, but it was a female voice, the same voice he had heard so many times earlier that day.

Thompson immediately sent a voice transmission: "KHAQQ, KHAQQ from *Itasca*. You are very weak. Repeat on 3105. Please go ahead." He repeated the message in code followed by a string of *As*.[14] Immediately afterward William Galten, at the other radio position, set his transmitter to 7500 kcs and tapped out, "KHAQQ this is NRUI. Go ahead on 3105 again please if you are on."[15]

Neither operator heard anything in reply, but this was still an exciting development. Fresh ears quickly manned the radio positions as Chief Bellarts took over from Thompson and Thomas O'Hare replaced Galten. At seven minutes past the hour, Bellarts sent a Morse code message asking Earhart to send "again please on 3105."[16] No reply. Five minutes later, he sent a voice message and tried something new: "KHAQQ, KHAQQ from *Itasca*. Please give long dashes if you hear us. Go ahead."[17] The signal was too weak to support intelligible voice, but long dashes would at least confirm she had heard their reply. But there was still no answer.

Just as the sun sank below the horizon, the voice was back. Bellarts missed the call, because at that moment he was sending a general broadcast asking all ships to contact *Itasca* if they had any information. But O'Hare heard and logged it: "We hear her on 3105 kcs now. Very weak and unreadable voice."[18]

The operators on Howland heard nothing because they were off the air, still recharging batteries, but at the same moment that O'Hare heard what he believed was a call from Earhart, the Pan American Airways station in Hawaii heard "steady carrier on 3105—no modulation, very weak."[19]

Pan Am Mokapu had been listening steadily for signals from the missing plane since midafternoon but, like *Itasca*, had heard nothing until evening brought improved reception conditions. When O'Hare was hearing an unintelligible voice transmission, Mokapu heard a minimal signal with only the basic "carrier" getting through. If the two stations were hearing the same signal, the sender was located closer to *Itasca* than to Hawaii. Although some ships and shore stations could communicate by Morse code on 3105 kcs, only U.S.-registered civilian aircraft—and by special arrangement, *Itasca*—were authorized to send voice transmissions on that frequency. If the signal was coming from an aircraft in Hawaii, Mokapu should have heard it loud and clear.

At 6:30 p.m., Bellarts tried again to get Earhart to send dashes. O'Hare logged the request as: "Phone very bad. If you hear us please give us a series of long dashes. Go ahead please."[20] This time the signal got through and, for the first time since leaving New Guinea, Earhart heard a human voice in her earphones. Why she could suddenly hear *Itasca* is unclear, but the aircraft's dorsal vee antenna could be used for both transmitting and receiving. If, after landing, Earhart and Noonan saw that the belly wire receiving antenna was missing, they might have attached the receiver to the intact dorsal vee or switched to listen via the loop antenna. However it was accomplished, *Itasca* was hearing her, and she was hearing them. Two-way communication was established at last, but the radio operator could not make out what she was saying. He wanted long dashes and, without a sending key, the only way she could send dashes was to key the microphone on and off.

A thousand miles to the southeast of Howland Island, the Royal Navy cruiser HMS *Achilles* was steaming en route from Samoa to Hawaii. Having heard the "all ships" request to listen for possible calls from Earhart, the warship was monitoring 3105. At the same moment Bellarts asked Earhart to send dashes, the radio operator aboard the cruiser heard an unidentified voice say: "Please give us a few dashes if you get us."[21]

Immediately after sending his request to Earhart, Bellarts heard on-again-off-again signals that he described in his log as "something like generator start and then stop on 3105." Two minutes later, the same sound was repeated. At one point he heard the word "Earhart."[22] *Achilles* heard the signals too and interpreted the intermittent transmissions as dashes: "A second transmitter was then heard to make dashes."[23]

In reply to the dashes, *Itasca* tried again to call Earhart, this time using Morse code. *Achilles* heard only the first part of the call: "First transmitter was then heard to make KHAQQ twice before fading out." The radio operator aboard *Achilles* did not know whom he had heard, but in reporting the reception to the U.S. Navy, the ship's commanding officer said, "The evidence exists that either transmitter was the airplane itself."[24] The radio operators aboard *Itasca*, unaware of what *Achilles* had heard, did not know what to make of the incident either. O'Hare's 6:37 p.m. radio log entry expressed cautious hope: "Signals on and off. Think it is plane?? Signals are unreadable [but] heard the word Earhart."[25]

Both ships had heard someone respond to *Itasca*'s request for Earhart to send dashes. The sound Bellarts described is particularly significant. Normally a radio operator transmits dashes by alternately holding down and releasing a sending key. The transmitter stays on and the key simply breaks the signal to create dots or dashes. The signals Bellarts heard were made by repeatedly turning the power supply to the transmitter on and off, as happens when a microphone is used.

Itasca again called the plane in both voice and code. This time, a man's voice answered, "still distorted and unreadable." Disappointed, O'Hare logged, "Guess it isn't her now."[26] The possibility that Earhart might have passed the mic to Noonan was never considered because they did not know there was a man aboard the plane. None of the messages sent to *Itasca* before Earhart's flight had mentioned Noonan, and all of the transmissions the *Itasca* operators had heard during the flight had been made by Earhart.

21

Hopes and Hoaxes

JULY 3

For the next twenty minutes Bellarts and O'Hare tried to figure out what was going on, but their efforts were complicated by interference on the frequency. Someone was sending code, trying unsuccessfully to raise other stations. During breaks in the interference, *Itasca*'s operators called the plane twice again and each time got an immediate response from the unintelligible man. For the past hour, the radiomen had been receiving unexplained intermittent voice transmissions on the plane's frequency in direct response to their calls to Earhart. The one word they had been able to understand was "Earhart," but when they decided the voice was male, the possibility that the signals were coming from the missing plane was discounted. Just before seven o'clock, they concluded, "Phone signals definitely not Earhart."[1]

Earhart had called *Itasca* for help; her plea had been heard, she had followed their instructions and sent dashes that were heard, and her navigator had also tried to get through. But *Itasca* lacked one key piece of information—that there was a man with her—and drew the wrong conclusion. Half an hour later, Commander Thompson sent a status report to headquarters: "*Itasca* Earhart search up to this time negative results. Broadcasting to steamers but few in this area."[2]

Thompson also provided his first detailed estimate of what had happened: "Earhart apparently handicapped through night by cloudy weather as portions of received messages indicated overcast and cloudy weather. Earhart direction finder apparently not functioning as well, as she could not get cut on *Itasca* on agreed frequencies. Earhart had barely sufficient fuel under the conditions to make Howland. Thought close to Howland at 07:58 when circling trying to pick up land and attempts [by] *Itasca* to give Earhart radio bearings failed after thorough tests both ways."[3] It was now an accepted fact aboard *Itasca* that "Earhart had barely sufficient fuel . . . to make Howland."[4]

Thompson continued his report, for the first time describing his reasons for searching to the north: "Belief, based on signal strength only, that at 07:58 Earhart passed close to and to northward of Howland as believed that she would have seen Baker Island if passing to southward."[5] In closing, Thompson said: "Have heard no signals from Earhart since 08:55 this morning when she gave *Itasca* a line of position believed to mean radio bearing and stated she was running north and south. *Itasca* using every resource to locate plane."[6] Thompson chose not to mention the strange dashes and unexplained voice transmissions recently heard on Earhart's frequency.

Up to this point, decisions about what had probably happened to Earhart and where *Itasca* should search for her had been the exclusive province of the cutter's commanding officer, but that was about to change. Ten minutes after Thompson sent his report to Coast Guard headquarters, Admiral Murfin ordered *Itasca* to "be at Howland Island at daylight tomorrow" to meet the PBY that was now en route. Once the flying boat was within five hundred miles of Howland, Thompson was to "keep the plane advised of your position, be prepared to provide radio bearings, and make smoke as requested."[7] The cutter was back on plane guard duty, this time for the Navy. By this time *Itasca* was nearly one hundred miles northeast of Howland. The ship would have to put about and steam back toward the island to be there by dawn—but not just yet; there was time for another couple of hours of searching.

In the radio room, Leo Bellarts was listening "on 3105 continuously but no signals heard."[8] Seven minutes later, the U.S. Army radio facility at Fort Shafter near Pearl Harbor heard dashes on that frequency.[9] No one else seems to have heard them. *Itasca*'s radio log does not say whether Bellarts was still listening at that time.

At eight o'clock, *Itasca* received a message sent out by the U.S. Navy radio station in Tutuila, Samoa, to all the stations involved in the search. *Achilles* had just informed Tutuila: "Unknown station heard to make 'please give us a few dashes if you get us' Heard good strength both on 3105 kcs. First station then made KHAQQ twice [then] disappeared. Nothing more heard of either at 06:20 GMT."[10] This secondhand account mentioned nothing about the dashes the cruiser had heard and misstated the 0600 GCT time of the incident. Not surprisingly, no one aboard *Itasca* saw the connection to events earlier in the evening, and as far as anyone else knew, the cutter had "heard no signals from Earhart since 08:55 this morning."[11]

For the next thirty minutes everything was quiet, but then, exactly on the half hour, government radio operators in Hawaii heard dashes and a weak voice signal, this time on Earhart's other frequency, 6210 kcs.[12] It is not clear whether Coast Guard operators at the Hawaiian Station or Army operators at Fort Shafter—or both—heard these signals. Dashes and voice heard together meant that, once again, the transmissions were being sent using a microphone rather than a sending key. *Itasca* did not hear the signals. The ship's radio operators were not listening on that frequency. Howland Island did not hear anything either. Cipriani was still recharging his batteries, but someone else heard a voice at that moment.

In Amarillo, Texas, thirty-one-year-old homemaker Mabel Larremore finally had some time to herself. Her husband and two sons had gone to bed, and Mabel, as she often did, stayed up to listen to overseas radio programs on the family's "very good shortwave set." At two o'clock in the morning, she was astonished to hear Amelia Earhart calling for help. The signal came in "very clear," and Mabel recognized Earhart's voice, having heard her interviewed on the radio and in newsreels. Earhart was sending the same message over and over. "She would complete one and start right in again," Larremore later reported.[13]

According to Larremore, the message stated that "the plane was down on an uncharted island. Small, uninhabited. The plane was partially on land, part in water. She gave the latitude and longitude of her location," but she never said the name of the island. Earhart also "gave two frequencies."[14]

Earhart also said that "her navigator Fred Noonan was seriously injured. Needed help immediately. She also had some injuries but not as serious as Mr. Noonan. . . . I listened to her for thirty to forty-five minutes after waking my family to also listen. . . . And I called our local paper to let them listen to her message also."[15] The *Amarillo Globe News* did not run a story.

Mabel only came forward with her story in 1990 when she was eighty-four years old. She died the next year. When interviewed, she said, "I'm sorry I can no longer remember the latitude and longitude of the island. With that, we had no trouble locating [the island] on a map the next day. I had it all written down but over the years, a lot of moves, a second marriage, it has been lost. I have tried to think of some way I could remember that important information [but] have not come up with the answer. Sorry."[16]

Mabel Larremore in Texas could hear a loud and clear voice message from Earhart on her home shortwave set. She was listening on a different frequency than radio operators thousands of miles closer to where the plane disappeared who were getting a signal that was too weak to understand. In tuning her shortwave set looking for a foreign broadcast, Mabel stumbled upon a harmonic of Earhart's frequencies. When Earhart's transmitter sent out a signal on one of her primary frequencies, it also broadcast a weaker signal on higher multiples of that frequency. These higher frequencies, or harmonics, although less powerful than the primary signal, are also less susceptible to degradation and can travel great distances. Under unusual and unpredictable propagation conditions, good reception can occur in places where nothing would ordinarily be heard. Earhart's "daytime" frequency of 6210 kcs was the second harmonic (double the frequency) of her "nighttime" frequency of 3105. Transmissions on 3105 might also be heard on the third, the fourth, or even the fifth harmonic (15525 kcs). Shortwave listeners often tuned for broadcasts in those frequency ranges. The higher the harmonic, the lower the power—but the greater the signal's ability to travel.[17]

Half an hour after the Coast Guard's Hawaiian Section reported "dashes and voice, weak" on 6210 kcs, and at the same time Mabel Larremore started hearing Earhart, Radioman George Thompson aboard *Itasca* noted in his log: "There is a weak signal on 3105 kilocycles, but cannot read it." After listening for two minutes, Thompson sent, "*Itasca* to Earhart plane: repeat message please again. Go ahead."[18] Mabel Larremore didn't hear him because harmonic reception is highly dependent upon the path between transmission location and reception location, and the path between Gardner Island and Amarillo was different from the path between *Itasca* and Amarillo.

While Thompson was calling Earhart, the radio operator aboard the PBY was informing Fleet Air Base that the flying boat had reached a point five hundred miles to the northeast of Howland. The patrol plane had received U.S. Navy Radio Tutuila's broadcast about what the British cruiser heard and was "setting watch on voice frequency 3105 kilocycles." The operator added that he would "attempt to establish communication."[19]

Aboard *Itasca*, George Thompson listened for two minutes and typed: "There are still weak voice signals on 3105 kilocycles." He listened for another three minutes, but he still could not make out the words. Earhart's signal was not strong enough to carry understandable voice, but it should be good enough for code, if only he could get her to send code. For the first time, it occurred to Thompson that Earhart might not have a sending key: "KHAQQ from *Itasca*. Cannot read your phone. Please go ahead on key. If no got key, make and break your antenna connection where it connects to transmitter and send us your position in code."[20]

George Thompson had correctly diagnosed the situation aboard the Electra and had told Earhart how to solve the problem. Reasoning that she might be having as much trouble understanding his words as he was having reading hers, he sent his instructions in a more reliable format: he sent them in Morse code, never imagining the world-famous flier did not know code.[21] If Earhart and Noonan received Thompson's transmission, they heard only an incomprehensible series of dots and dashes. Three minutes after asking Earhart to send her position in code, Thompson logged, "Still weak voice signals on 3105 kilocycles, but cannot read them."[22]

At about this time, according to one of the pilots, the radio operator aboard the PBY picked up dashes.[23] There is no corroboration for his claim in the official record, but the aircraft is known to have been maintaining a radio watch on Earhart's frequency.[24]

While the radio operator aboard *Itasca* was struggling to understand the garbled voice transmissions on 3105, a thousand miles to the west on the British island of Nauru, another operator was having the same problem with signals he was hearing on the second harmonic of that frequency—Earhart's "daytime" frequency of 6210 kcs. Like the radiomen aboard the Coast Guard cutter, the Nauru operator was familiar with Earhart's voice, having heard her position reports as the Electra passed south of the island the previous night.[25]

On three occasions, at twelve-minute intervals, during the period when *Itasca* was receiving unintelligible voice and Mabel Larremore was hearing Earhart repeatedly sending a distress message, the Nauru operator heard "fairly strong signals. Speech not interpreted owing bad modulation or speaker shouting into microphone. No hum of plane in background but voice similar to that emitted from plane in flight last night."[26] At cruise power, the engines of the 10E were deafening, but one engine turning at just above idle was much quieter. Shouting into the microphone? Back in New Guinea, the Lae operator, upon inspecting Earhart's radios, found "Transmitter carrier wave on 6210 kc was very rough and I advised Miss Earhart to pitch her voice higher to overcome distortion caused by rough carrier wave."[27]

Six minutes after the last transmission heard at Nauru, George Thompson aboard *Itasca* logged: "Still weak voice signals on 3105 kilocycles again." Two minutes later he tried once more: "KHAQQ, Earhart plane, from *Itasca*. Please go ahead again with position."[28] This time there was no response. The voice signals had stopped.

Aboard the cutter the time was 9:32 p.m. An hour later, the ship took up a course for Howland to keep its dawn rendezvous with the PBY. *Itasca*'s operators continued to listen for signals and periodically called the plane, but they heard nothing more that night. For Commander Thompson, it had been an anxious and frustrating day. He was convinced that Earhart had come down at sea and had devoted all of his ship's resources to looking for her. Now, under orders from the Navy, the cutter was on its way back to the one place he was sure she wasn't.

Itasca's visual search had turned up nothing. The results of the electronic search were more ambiguous. San Francisco Division had said that radio calls from the floating plane were possible. Thompson believed that Earhart might even be able to send distress calls from a rubber boat using an emergency transmitter. Starting just before sunset and continuing intermittently for three and one-half hours, *Itasca*'s operators had heard radiotelephone transmissions on 3105. The signals were weak and the voice was garbled, but on one occasion the word "Earhart" had been understood. Was it her?

Whoever had been transmitting on that first night of the search seemed to be responding directly to *Itasca*'s voice calls to Earhart. The sender also seemed to be located somewhere in the central Pacific. Other professional operators farther from the search area had heard some of the signals, but not as consistently or as clearly as *Itasca*. To the men aboard the cutter, unaware of Noonan's presence on the flight, there was one disqualifying observation: in at least some cases, the voice had been male.

Earhart's misconceptions about her radios and *Itasca*'s capabilities had crippled her ability to find Howland. Now *Itasca*'s misconceptions, compounded by assumptions and bad information, were making it impossible to accurately assess the clues that were staring the searchers in the face.

At about the time *Itasca* turned for Howland, San Francisco Division got the word that the radio operator at Nauru had heard a voice "similar to that emitted from plane in flight last night but with no hum of plane in background."[29] Wondering if Nauru might have overheard *Itasca* trying to call the plane, Division sent a message to the cutter asking, "Was *Itasca* on air from 0843 to 0854 GMT on 3105 kilocycles using voice?" Commander Thompson replied that the ship had not been transmitting but had heard weak voice signals during that time.[30] San Francisco passed along the Nauru report and relayed other news that had just come in: "Los Angeles men report hearing position report from KHAQQ [at] eleven thirty but as '1.6.179.'"[31]

There was much more to the story than San Francisco Division told *Itasca*. The spokesman for the Los Angeles men was an amateur radio enthusiast and Amelia Earhart fan by the name of Walter McMenamy. He first told the Associated Press that "he picked up weak signals on 6210 kilocycles at 6 p.m. and heard the letters 'L-A-T,' which he took to mean latitude. The letters were followed by undecipherable figures. The signals continued for some time."[32]

Over the next few days, McMenamy and his associates reported hearing more messages from Earhart. No one else picked up transmissions at the same times, but the Coast Guard passed along the information anyway. On July 11 San Francisco Division informed the Hawaiian Section that "further investigation this date of radio reports by amateurs at Los Angeles on night of July 3 [*sic*] confirmed by four separate stations and indicate credibility of receipt of distress call from Earhart plane."[33]

It happened that the "four separate stations" were all McMenamy's associates in the same amateur radio club, and they were apparently together at the same location at the time of the alleged reception. The four hoaxers would not be exposed until 1959, when Walter McMenamy made an audio tape in which he confessed, claiming that Naval Intelligence forced him and his friends to cooperate in a conspiracy. Earhart, it seems, landed safely but secretly at Howland Island after spying on the Japanese.[34]

By midmorning on July 3, another amateur had surfaced. Oakland ham Charles McGill telephoned the Coast Guard with a report that he had heard SOS calls at 6:55 a.m. on a frequency of 3480 kcs: "Twenty-five NNW Howland. Ask Putnam to fly kite."[35] The reported frequency, time, and location reveal the report to be another crude hoax. Over the following days, McGill would claim further receptions, but a Coast Guard investigation on July 6 "definitely determined report false. Verify [*sic*] and reputation of man making report extremely dubious after investigation."[36]

Across the country in Ashland, Kentucky, Nina Paxton, listening on her shortwave set, heard Amelia Earhart calling for help—or so she told the local newspaper almost a week later. According to the *Ashland Daily Independent*, at two o'clock on the afternoon of Saturday, July 3, she heard Earhart say she was

> "Down in ocean" either "on" or "near" "little island at a point near . . ." and then something about "directly northeast" although Mrs. Paxton was not sure about this part. "Our plane about out of gas. Water all around. Very dark." Then she said something about a storm and that the wind was blowing. "Will have to get out of here," she said. "We can't stay here long." This message was preceded by Miss Earhart's call letters, "KHAQQ calling, KHAQQ calling."[37]

Two o'clock in the afternoon in Ashland, Kentucky, was 7:30 a.m. aboard *Itasca*. At that time the cutter was busy trying to communicate with the PBY, but multiple other stations around the Pacific were monitoring both of Earhart's primary frequencies and hearing nothing. The entire radio propagation path between Paxton's location and the search area was in daylight, and the calculated probability that it was physically possible for her to have heard a transmission from the Earhart Electra, even on a harmonic, is less than one in ten million. There is nothing in Nina Paxton's claims that argues for her credibility.

Reports like McMenamy's and Paxton's were the only bright spots in an otherwise bleak picture. On the morning of Saturday, July 3, Earhart and Noonan had been missing for a full day, and the search for them was at a standstill.

22

All Possible Energy

JULY 3

Morning also came to the airplane parked on the reef. Reported credible receptions of calls and dashes stopped at midnight, suggesting Earhart and Noonan had shut down the engine because the tide was coming in and, in the dark, they couldn't be sure how high it was getting.[1] If the whirling prop tip hit the water, it would bend, and the propeller would be out of balance. The vibration would disable the engine.

Now, as the sun climbed, so did the temperature in the bare metal Lockheed. It is reasonable to assume Earhart and Noonan had left Lae with enough drinking water for the anticipated flight, not an extended stay on an uninhabited island. That was two days ago. Even with careful rationing, the water situation was becoming critical. The *Itasca* radio operator had said, "Phone very bad." How bad? How much of their message had gotten through? Rescue was surely on the way, but if help didn't arrive soon, they'd have to find water somehow.

A full day had passed since the flight went missing, and *Itasca* was still the only search asset on the scene. Its rescue efforts had been fruitless, and now the cutter was back at Howland, waiting for another plane that would never arrive. The PBY had run into severe weather three hundred miles to the north of Howland. After struggling unsuccessfully to find a way through, the pilot turned around and began the long trip back to Pearl Harbor.[2] USS *Swan*, the Navy seaplane tender that had been positioned halfway between Howland and Hawaii, was headed south but was days away.

In Hawaii, *Colorado* had rounded up its crew and was taking on fuel at Pearl Harbor for the coming voyage. The battleship's three airplanes were still being reassembled ashore.

At Fourteenth Naval District headquarters, Admiral Murfin responded to pressure from Washington to do more to find Earhart by raising the stakes: "If more extensive search operations are contemplated, dispatch of aircraft carrier most practicable, efficient method."[3]

At the Navy Department, it was late on Saturday afternoon, the day before the Fourth of July, and the CNO had a decision to make. On Friday he had told Admiral Murfin to "use available naval facilities to conduct such search for Miss Earhart as, in your opinion, is practicable."[4] Sending a PBY was marginally practicable, but that hadn't worked. It was now apparent that the only naval assets available that could be employed in the search were USS *Swan*, a small seaplane tender with no sea-plane, and USS *Colorado*, a commandeered battleship with three spotter planes.

If Washington wanted more of a search than that, Murfin needed an aircraft carrier. In 1937 the U.S. Navy had three: USS *Lexington* (CV 2), USS *Saratoga* (CV 3), and USS *Ranger* (CV 4). None was anywhere near the central Pacific. Just getting a carrier to the search area would take at least a week. By that time there was a good chance Earhart and Noonan would be either rescued or dead—if they weren't dead already. To buy some time before making a decision, the CNO sent a message to the commander-in-chief of the U.S. Fleet: "Request aircraft carrier be fueled and prepared for search Amelia Earhart, if so directed by Navy Department."[5]

Like everyone else, Earhart's husband had been encouraged by the news that a British cruiser had heard the plane's call letters. At his request, the Coast Guard's San Francisco Division sent a message to the Hawaiian Section: "Putnam asks that effort be made to confirm that HMS Achilles got call letters KHAQQ clearly and certainly."[6]

George Putnam also wanted to be sure the Navy had the latest information about radio recep-tions by amateurs. Shortly after noon, the commandant of Naval District 12 in California informed Admiral Murfin in Hawaii: "Putnam reports amateur operators vicinity of Los Angeles have inter-cepted position reports. Earhart plane one degree 36 minutes south latitude, 179 degrees east longi-tude. He believes possibility plane on land and sending intermittent signals."[7]

Earhart's husband was trying to reconcile the amateur reports with what he was hearing from Paul Mantz. As reported by the Associated Press in a story datelined Oakland, July 3:

> A theory that Amelia Earhart might have brought her plane down safely on a small coral atoll south of Howland Island was advanced today by her technical adviser, Paul Mantz, in a telephone conversation with George Palmer Putnam. Putnam, husband of the Aviatrix, said he conferred with Mantz at Burbank. "Several of the Phoenix Islands are large enough to allow a plane to land," Mantz was quoted by Putnam. "The undercarriage may have been damaged, but the flyers could have walked away from the plane uninjured."[8]

Paul Mantz, familiar as he was with the aircraft's layout, knew that the radios would be underwater if the plane was afloat. If signals were being sent from the plane, it had to be on land, but the islands of the Phoenix Group were hundreds of miles southeast of where *Itasca* was searching, and there was no land anywhere near 1°36′ S, 179° E.

Noon in California was morning in the central Pacific. At eight o'clock on July 3, *Itasca* arrived back at its plane guard station. For the past two hours it had been apparent that there would be no plane to guard, but the Navy had not released the cutter from its assigned duty. Commander Thompson complained to the Coast Guard's Hawaiian Section: "Drifting off Howland [in] com-pliance [with] commander 14th Naval District dispatch. . . . Plane apparently returning to base. Imperative continue search today. Time element vital." An hour later, he received Hawaiian Section's inane reply: "Navy plane reports returning Pearl Harbor due bad weather. *Itasca* resume search all possible speed. Advise if you concur."[9]

Commander Thompson probably rolled his eyes, and by 9:30 his ship was again headed north-ward toward the area where he believed the plane had come down. He hoped the Electra was still floating or that Earhart had managed to deploy the rubber boat she supposedly had with her, but he had little confidence that any of the radio signals received the night before were from the lost flier. Shortly after leaving Howland, he debunked the idea that *Achilles* had heard Earhart. The Hawaiian Section relayed the disappointing news to San Francisco: "*Itasca* advises that call received by HMS *Achilles* was sent by *Itasca*."[10]

Thompson was basing his judgment on the communication he received the night before from the U.S. Navy radio station in Tutuila, Samoa, but the information in that message was both inaccurate and incomplete. In relaying *Achilles*' report, the Navy operator got the time of the incident wrong and failed to mention that the cruiser had heard dashes. Without a full and accurate report, Thompson could not see the significance of the event. *Achilles* had heard *Itasca* ask Earhart to send dashes, and both ships had heard her reply with dashes. The cruiser was listening, not transmitting. When Bellarts heard the word "Earhart," it had to be coming from the person sending the dashes.

While *Itasca* steamed northward from Howland on a bright Pacific morning, Henry Morgenthau was working late on a Saturday evening in Washington. As secretary of the Treasury, Morgenthau was ultimately responsible for the actions of the Coast Guard, and on this Fourth of July weekend, one of his cutters was center stage in a drama that was playing out on the front pages of every newspaper in the country. Just before six o'clock on July 3, he had the Coast Guard commandant send a message to *Itasca*: "Secretary of Treasury Morgenthau requests latest information search of plane Amelia Earhart. Request information be sent Coast Guard headquarters immediately upon receipt of this message."[11]

Despite the request for an immediate response, it was an hour and a half before Commander Thompson sent a reply: "*Itasca* searched three thousand square miles [since] daylight yesterday. Guarded Navy plane during night and arrived Howland daybreak this morning under orders Commandant Fourteenth Naval District. Depart[ed] Howland 0900 today, plane having returned to base owing bad weather. Search being pressed with all possible energy and weather conditions favorable thereto. Area searched north of Howland on assumption most logical as no definite position from Earhart plane received at any time."[12]

The secretary was not satisfied with Warner Thompson's brief summary. The cutter's commanding officer had not addressed the question on everyone's mind: Was Earhart really out there calling for help? Before Morgenthau left for the night, he had another message sent to *Itasca*: "Secretary Morgenthau desires that you furnish the latest information available on Earhart plane at time of preparation of a dispatch which will reach headquarters not later than 0630 [Washington time] 4 July 1937. Advise if signals have been heard at any time and if so when they started and when they ceased."[13]

It was just after two o'clock in the afternoon aboard *Itasca* when Morgenthau's demand for a more complete report arrived. The deadline for sending the dispatch was midnight for *Itasca*, so there was ample time to compose the message. During the afternoon, Howard Hanzlick filed a report to the United Press that was long on drama and short on accuracy:

Men at stations tensely alert. Long wait capped by anxiety. Search felt deeply. Men working with grim efficiency. Great concern over why Amelia short of fuel in air only approximately twenty and half hours. Should have had several hours more fuel. Why Amelia never gave position? Her radio evidently not working properly. *Itasca* requested [in] each broadcast [that Amelia] give position. Never given. At 8:42 Amelia radioed "half hour fuel left. No landfall. Position doubtful." Last message 9:43 "Line of position 157–337. Am circling. Please give radio bearing." Her voice sounded very tired, anxious, almost breaking. Lack [of] information from Amelia making search difficult. Last night at 6:50 p.m. sailing east, investigated seeming light flash [on] horizon port beam. No result. Eleven thirty p.m. started back toward Howland. Several times excitement aroused. Stars low on horizon, seeming flares. Daybreak morning seeming smoke [on] horizon. Investigated. Futile. Searching full speed today area 150 miles northwest Howland, 100 miles north. Weather same [as] yesterday.[14]

Hanzlick's account grossly misquotes Earhart and illustrates the extent to which folklore had already replaced fact aboard *Itasca*. The men of the cutter were now wondering why Earhart had run out of fuel far too soon.

Just before nightfall, Commander Thompson sent his dispatch to Secretary Morgenthau: "No information Earhart plane since 08:43 2 July. Heard faint signals between 18:25 and 18:58 2 July which developed, as nearly as could be ascertained, into call Q85. Signals unreadable and, from call letters, definitely not Earhart. Unable contact Q85 after 18:58."[15]

Once again, Commander Thompson's description of the incident was at odds with the ship's radio logs. According to those records, the radiomen heard faint calls from an unknown station intermittently between 6:00 and 6:43 p.m. The signals included unintelligible voice transmissions and on-and-off signals sent in apparent direct response to *Itasca*'s request for Earhart to send dashes. At one point the word "Earhart" was heard. This was the exchange overheard by *Achilles*. Beginning at 6:43 and continuing until 6:58, further transmissions from the unknown station were partially blocked by Morse code transmissions from station QZ5 (not Q85) trying to raise stations KACA and KCWR. *Itasca* was never successful in establishing contact with QZ5. (Extensive research has failed to determine the identities of stations QZ5, KACA, and KCWR.)

In his message to the Treasury secretary, Thompson neglected to mention that weak voice signals, assumed by *Itasca*'s radio operators to be transmissions from the missing plane, began again at nine o'clock in the evening and continued for half an hour. During this second period of unexplained transmissions, the operator on Nauru heard "fairly strong signals. Speech not interpreted owing bad modulation or speaker shouting into microphone. No hum of plane in background but voice similar to that emitted from plane in flight last night."[16] *Itasca*'s captain either did not see or chose to disregard the corroboration. Because he said nothing about *Itasca*'s receptions during this period, no one else had a chance to connect the dots.

With an inaccurate impression of what had transpired in his ship's own radio room, Commander Thompson offered an explanation for the reports of calls from the missing flier: "We are calling Earhart frequently and consistently on 3105 kilocycles and, undoubtedly, amateur and other stations mistake us for Earhart plane. We are pushing search at top speed day and night in logical areas north of Howland and have thoroughly search 2000 square miles daylight today with negative results."[17] No one mistook *Itasca*'s calls for signals from Earhart. None of the ship's transmissions coincide with reported receptions on her frequencies, and credible calls from the missing plane were heard by the ship's own operators.

There was one amateur report that could be interpreted to fit Thompson's belief about where the plane might be. He had been told that "Los Angeles men" had heard Earhart give her position as "1.6 179."[18] If the numbers meant latitude 1.6°N, longitude 179°W, it put the plane in the ocean within the area Thompson believed was most logical. He was willing to check it out: "Amateur stations report unverified position from Earhart plane west of Howland which area we will search during daylight tomorrow. If party afloat on plane or raft they are drifting north and west at estimated maximum two miles per hour. Visibility and general search conditions excellent. Sea conditions to present time now favorable if plane or raft is afloat. Have auxiliary radio listening stations Howland and Baker Island and all reported commercial craft over large area familiar with situation and on the alert, both visual and radio."[19]

For Earhart and Noonan, the morning hours offered low tide and an opportunity to wade ashore and seek a solution to the water problem. The effort was apparently successful—thirst is not mentioned in any of the distress calls from the plane—but how they found water is unknown. The island has no naturally occurring fresh water. Afternoon rain squalls are not uncommon, but the island is porous, and the few puddles are soon contaminated with bird droppings. Wells produce only brackish, undrinkable water. One possible reservoir of potable water was a cache of provisions left on the island when the survivors of the shipwreck were rescued. In an abundance of compassion, the rescuers brought far more food and water than was needed. Paying the generosity forward, the captain of the stranded steamer left the excess supplies in the crude shelter he and his crew had erected while awaiting rescue, "but I sincerely hope that no-one will ever be so unfortunate as to need them."[20] High tide was at three o'clock in the afternoon, but two hours later, the water level on the reef was low enough to permit Earhart and Noonan to return to the Electra and prepare for another night of calling for help.

As sunset in the central Pacific marked the close of the second day of the Earhart search, *Itasca* was seventy-five miles north of Howland and steaming westward toward Thompson's interpretation of the position reported by the Los Angeles men. USS *Colorado*, fully fueled and with its airplanes aboard, was five hours out of Pearl Harbor on the four-day, sixteen-hundred-mile voyage to the search area. In California, the aircraft carrier USS *Lexington* and four destroyers were being readied in case the Navy Department decided to commit them to the effort to save the missing fliers.

Skeptical as *Itasca*'s captain may have been that legitimate distress calls had been heard, nightfall and the improved radio reception it brought were greeted with great anticipation in Honolulu and San Francisco. *Itasca* had been advised by headquarters to "not, repeat not, use 3105 or 6210 kilocycles next two nights to permit absolute check on authenticity of calls and to permit monitoring of above frequencies by use of directional antennae."[21]

As evening fell on Oahu, the Coast Guard's Hawaiian Section picked up on a suggestion Earhart's husband had made the night before: "Radio station KGU Honolulu offers to broadcast whatever desired on theory Earhart plane may be able to receive. Suggest use this means for aiding in search and sending encouragement to occupants of plane. Please contact Mr. Coll of KGU. Signed Putnam."[22]

Arrangements for a special broadcast to Earhart were made with NBC affiliate KGU and with Honolulu's other major commercial station, KGMB. Earhart was known to be familiar with both stations from her previous flights, and it was not unreasonable to suppose that she might be listening for news of efforts to come to her aid. Coast Guard and Navy stations would listen for any reply, while Pan American Airways' direction-finding receivers in Hawaii, Midway, and Wake Island, as well as the Coast Guard's own direction-finding radio facility in San Francisco, would try to determine where the signals were coming from. They were all in for a busy night.

23

Ship on Reef

JULY 3–4

The radio station on Howland Island, its batteries recharged, was back on the air. At sundown on July 3, *Itasca* sent instructions "for Howland and Baker [to] listen [on] 3105 kilocycles continuously" for any possible signals from Earhart's plane.[1] The cutter was not maintaining direct communication with Baker Island, so Howland would need to relay the message to the radio operator there.

On Howland, Coast Guard Radioman Frank Cipriani and the colony's radio operator, Yau Fai Lum, were using the island colony's radio to maintain schedules with *Itasca*, Hawaii, and the outposts on Baker and Jarvis islands. To listen for Earhart, they would need to use Cipriani's portable Coast Guard set. If Cipriani heard a good signal, he would try to get a bearing with the high-frequency direction finder Richard Black had borrowed from the Navy. The problem was that the portable Coast Guard receiver was not very sensitive. Yau Fai Lum replied to *Itasca*'s directive saying that Howland would be unable to comply with the orders to keep a continuous watch due to the portable's inability to receive weak signals.[2] He passed the instruction along to Baker Island's radio operator, Paul Yat Lum.

Aboard *Itasca*, Chief Radioman Leo Bellarts took the watch himself. Because he did not know Earhart's transmitter was crystal-controlled and therefore not susceptible to drifting off its designated frequency of 3105, Bellarts widened his search for signals that might be from the plane. At 7:15 p.m., on a frequency of 3110 kilocycles, he picked up something that sounded like a weak voice signal, but he could not make out the words. He kept listening, and eight minutes later, he heard the same sounds.[3]

While Bellarts was struggling with the off-frequency signal, Paul Yat Lum on Baker Island, listening on 3105 kilocycles, signaled Howland that he "heard Earhart plane, S4, R7."[4] The operator on Howland failed to grasp the significance of what Lum had heard and did not immediately pass the report to *Itasca*. According to the 1937 edition of the *Radio Amateur's Handbook*, an S4 signal (strength 4 on a scale of 1 to 5) was "good, readable." An R7 reception (readability 7 on a scale of 1 to 9) was a "good strong signal, such as copiable through interference."[5]

The signal received at Baker Island was markedly different from anything that had been heard so far. On the previous night, stations in and around the search area had reported dashes and faint, unintelligible voice signals in apparent response to *Itasca*'s calls to Earhart. Now a government radio operator in the search area had heard a clear and strong transmission he unequivocally identified as being from the missing plane.

Whom did Paul Lum hear? *Itasca*, under orders from headquarters, was no longer transmitting on Earhart's frequencies, so he did not overhear and misunderstand a call from the cutter. If Lum heard a strong signal at Baker, others in the region should have heard it too, if they were listening; but mostly they were not. Aboard *Itasca*, Bellarts was off frequency at the time. Howland Island was not listening at all. In Hawaii, the Pan American Airways station would not begin its radio watch on Earhart's frequency for another ten minutes. The only other station known to have been monitoring 3105 at that moment was the Coast Guard's Hawaiian Section in Honolulu. Operators there were hearing a weak carrier wave but no distinguishable voice.[6]

Itasca, meanwhile, was not aware that anyone was hearing anything. Unable to resolve the voice signals on 3110, Bellarts handed off the radio watch to George Thompson at 7:45 p.m. Thompson resumed listening for Earhart on 3105 but heard nothing.

An hour later, as the cutter settled into another night of searching and listening, wire service reporter Howard Hanzlick summarized the situation aboard *Itasca* in an update to the United Press: "Unresulting search covered over two thousand square miles north and northeast [of] Howland area [during] daytime today. Weather cloudy [with] afternoon rain squalls. Tonite heading southwest towards line of flight from Lae. Assumption Amelia fell short on course. Hope still expressed. Seas slightly choppy. Two searchlights constantly."[7]

Commander Thompson's new theory that the plane had never gotten as far as Howland was based on the position west of Howland the four hoaxers in Los Angeles had reported. Maybe Earhart was sending distress calls from the floating plane or from a life raft using a portable generator. Maybe the flight had come down at sea short of the island. Maybe not, but no trace of the plane had been found so far, and the position reported by the amateurs was the only lead he had.

Hanzlick's press release continued with some human interest: "Personnel [have] waited, thought, [and] talked [about] Amelia so long now, [that it is] like searching for close friend, though most have never seen her. Some heard her voice. Those who did have great admiration for [her] courage when she called in slow measured words 'half hour fuel left, no landfall.' Not until last message did [her] voice show emotion." He closed his report with: "Unverified here [that] Noonan [is] with Amelia. *Itasca* proceeding [to] investigate an amateur position rumor to westward."[8]

As arranged earlier in the evening, at ten o'clock in Honolulu (nine o'clock for *Itasca*), the NBC Radio affiliate KGU made a special broadcast on its regular frequency asking Earhart to reply on 500, 3105, or 6210 kcs if she heard the request. Immediately afterward, the Pan American Airways station at Mokapu heard "a faint carrier on 3105. Too weak to distinguish any words."[9] The Coast Guard Hawaiian Section also heard a weak carrier. *Itasca* was busy with administrative traffic and heard nothing. Howland was not listening, and if Lum on Baker heard anything, he didn't say so. Neither *Itasca* nor the radio operators on Howland and Baker had been told that commercial stations would be making broadcasts asking Earhart to respond.

When *Itasca* resumed monitoring 3105 twenty minutes later, Radioman George Thompson picked up the weak carrier. There was a voice, but he could not make out the words.[10] He continued to hear the signal sporadically for more than half an hour. Just after ten o'clock he logged an exchange with the operator on Howland:

Itasca:	K6GNW this is NRUI.
Howland:	Go ahead.
Itasca:	We have heard a weak carrier on 3105 kilocycles for the last 40 minutes. Do you hear it?
Howland:	No. The static is bad.
Itasca:	Roger. Try to get him and take a bearing. See you in half an hour.
Howland:	Roger. See you in half an hour.[11]

Thompson continued to hear the weak signal, although at times it almost faded away completely. At 10:30 p.m., the other powerful commercial station in Honolulu, KGMB, made a call on its broadcast frequency asking Earhart to respond on 3105. Pan American listened for a reply, but the static was especially heavy, and the operators heard no signals.[12]

Itasca was still hearing the faint carrier, and it was time to check back with the operator on Howland:

Itasca:	K6GNW this is NRUI.
Howland:	Go ahead.
Itasca:	Do you hear the carrier now?
Howland:	Yes, maybe the second harmonic from a broadcasting station.
Itasca:	No, it is impossible for a second harmonic to go 1000 miles. [Only the higher harmonics are capable of spanning great distances.] Did you get a bearing?
Howland:	No, will get one now.
Itasca:	Roger, see you in half hour.
Howland:	Roger.[13]

For the next thirty minutes *Itasca* continued to hear the weak carrier on Earhart's frequency. KGMB made another broadcast at midnight (eleven o'clock for *Itasca*) asking Earhart for signals. This time, three stations in the Honolulu area heard a reply. Pan American Airways at Mokapu heard a carrier but no voice on 3105; the static was too bad to try for a directional bearing. The Coast Guard's Hawaiian Section heard the signal a little bit better and was able to discern a weak voice, but could not understand what was being said. The U.S. Navy radio station at Wailupe also heard the voice and was able to pick out the number "thirty-one."[14] (The radio frequency 3105 is usually spoken as "thirty-one-oh-five.")

The Hawaiian Section now decided that *Itasca* should know about the KGMB broadcast and the response that had been heard. At 11:05 p.m. the cutter received a message: "Radio Oahu, PAA, [and] this office heard voice carrier [at] end [of] KGMB broadcast 3105. Continuing broadcast. Concentrating [on] 3105 for reply. Several dashes also heard."[15] Someone out there was sending voice on 3105, and everyone—*Itasca*, Howland Island, the Coast Guard's Hawaiian Section, the Navy, and Pan American—was hearing it, and Earhart was the only credible source.

Only U.S.-registered civilian aircraft were permitted to talk on that frequency. An aircraft operating in the territory of Hawaii was not a likely source. In 1937 the lack of lighted airfields in the islands limited civilian night flying. In any event, Hawaiian stations should have heard a local aircraft loud and clear. A call from an aircraft on the U.S. West Coast might be heard weakly in the distant Pacific under the right conditions, but the Coast Guard's monitoring station in California was listening on 3105 and heard nothing.

What direction were the signals coming from? *Itasca* immediately queried Cipriani on Howland:

Itasca:	K6GNW this is NRUI.
Howland:	Go ahead.
Itasca:	Did you get a bearing?
Howland:	No, the signals were very weak and when I shifted to the direction finding antenna the signal faded out completely.
Itasca:	Roger, well how about a schedule in one hour?
Howland:	How about some sleep?
Itasca:	Roger, will see you at 8 a.m. Honolulu standard time, that is 7 a.m. here.
Howland:	Roger, see you at 8 a.m., signing off.[16]

Howland was done for the night, but *Itasca* continued to hear an intermittent carrier on 3105.

An hour and a half later, the Coast Guard monitoring station in California informed *Itasca* that its operators had been hearing a "strong carrier on 6210 kcs being on about fifteen minutes. We have three receivers picking it up. . . . Signal is stronger from westerly direction."[17] In Honolulu it was 1:30 a.m., and the Hawaiian Section again heard a transmission on 3105: "One minute duration, speech identified as man's voice."[18] A few minutes later, the Pan American station on Wake Island heard an intermittent voice signal with "rather wobbly characteristics . . . male voice although unreadable through static."[19]

Another person claimed to have heard a man's voice during that time. Later that night, the U.S. Navy radio station at Wailupe described the incident in a message to *Itasca*, *Colorado*, and others.[20] A man named Donaldson, who lived in the town of Wahiawa, about twenty miles from Honolulu, had heard a man's voice make "three or four calls." Donaldson had been able to make out the figures "31.05" and "31.07," the word "help," and the call letters "KHAQQ."[21] The half-hour period during which Donaldson heard the calls coincided with the time that the Hawaiian Section and Pan Am Wake had heard an unintelligible man's voice on 3105 kilocycles.

The frequency Donaldson was listening on is not known, and the details of his story may also have suffered in translation. Wishing to report what he had heard, Donaldson phoned his local Mutual Wireless telegram office. Mutual sent a wire to the U.S. Navy radio station at Wailupe, which in turn forwarded the message "for what it may be worth" to the various search authorities. The Navy message seems to be the only surviving account of Donaldson's report.

The Donaldson incident is similar to the Baker Island reception earlier that same night. In each case, a listener heard an identifiable call from the missing plane at a time when other stations were hearing a much weaker signal. Baker Island was listening on Earhart's primary nighttime frequency. The strength of the signal received there was probably a function of Baker's geographical proximity to the sender. Donaldson, on the other hand, might have heard more than the Coast Guard station in Honolulu twenty miles away because he was listening on a harmonic. Both incidents are consistent with the sender being somewhere south of Howland.

Like Walter McMenamy, Donaldson could have been fabricating the whole thing. Unlike McMenamy's account, though, Donaldson's claim is synchronous with other reported receptions. At the time he made his call to the local telegram office, Donaldson could not have known that the Coast Guard's Hawaiian Section and the Pan Am station on Wake Island had both heard a man's voice during the time he said he heard a man calling from KHAQQ.

Earhart and Noonan had heard, and responded to, the commercial broadcasts. Their replies had been heard, but their signal was too weak for their words to be understood. The exchange resulted in no useful information for anyone, but it was nonetheless encouraging for everyone. On the reef, the tide had come in higher this time and was getting dangerously close to the prop. After four hours of intermittent receptions on Earhart's frequencies by multiple stations, the signals stopped.[22]

In Los Angeles, hoaxer Walter McMenamy announced more receptions from Earhart. A reporter for the *New York Herald Tribune* asked Paul Mantz what he thought of McMenamy's claims. Mantz said she could send radio messages only if her plane were on land. "She has no hand-crank aboard to generate power," Mantz said. The right engine, turning over at 900 R.P.M. creates about 50 amperes, burning almost six gallons of gas hourly. "To the best of my knowledge, Miss Earhart did not have much fuel when she was forced down. Yet, the signals appear to be sent regularly."[23] Mantz was skeptical of McMenamy's claims because he was having a hard time believing the plane could have enough fuel to support them, but he remained hopeful. "If I heard the voice, I could tell instantly if Amelia were sending. She speaks right into the microphone with her lips almost on the instrument. The resultant sound is calm, drawling, and sort of whispery."[24]

The cutter's radio operators, too, were familiar with Earhart's speaking style, but the voice that was being reported by the Hawaiian stations was male, and as Hanzlick had told the United Press earlier that night, no one on *Itasca* was certain that Noonan was with Amelia. They were also still operating under the assumption the plane had an emergency generator and could transmit distress calls if afloat on the ocean.[25]

As the cutter steamed southwestward, the airwaves on 3105 remained quiet. At two o'clock in the morning, searching slightly off frequency as he had done before, Bellarts found a familiar sound and typed, "Signal on about 3110. Sounded like QZ5."[26] An hour later, Pan American's facilities at both Midway and Wake heard a "wobbly" signal on 3105 that "sounded like a phone but was too weak to identify."[27] No one else heard it. A few minutes later, Midway heard "a very faint broad signal, apparently a phone," but was unable to take a bearing. Wake heard nothing, but according to the operator at Midway, the Pan American station at Mokapu in Hawaii "reported taking a bearing on it which might be 175 approximately."[28]

A bearing of 175 degrees goes into a part of the Pacific far beyond where the plane could possibly be and where there were no known sources for a signal. The directional estimate was so uncertain that the operator at Mokapu did not even mention it in his report, but he did confirm that three minutes later, he began hearing "rough, weak signals" that continued for the next quarter of an hour. During that time he was able to get a "doubtful bearing of 213 . . . maybe plus or minus ten degrees." The information was passed along to *Itasca* with the caution that it was "offered only as [a] possibility."[29]

In trying to take bearings on signals that, if they were legitimate calls from the Electra, had to be coming from the search area, Pan American was pushing the limits of its direction-finding system. The stations at Mokapu, Midway, and Wake were designed to guide the Pan Am Clippers as they island-hopped across the north Pacific. The refueling stops were roughly twelve hundred miles apart, so the island stations were never required to take bearings on a plane that was more than about six hundred miles away. The Earhart Electra had vanished somewhere in an area that was three times that distance from each of the three Pan Am stations, but the accuracy of a Pan Am bearing was related to the quality and duration of the signal, not the distance from the station. Quality was primarily affected by atmospherics. Duration was up to the sender. A transmission several minutes long from a distant station that happened to catch a quiet period could produce an accurate bearing.[30]

The "plus or minus ten degrees" margin of error for Mokapu's "doubtful bearing of 213" takes in Howland, Baker, and the Phoenix Group as potential locations for the source of the signal. Neither Howland, nor Baker, nor *Itasca* was transmitting on 3105 at that time. The islands of the Phoenix Group were uninhabited except for a small coconut plantation on Hull Island. The overseer there had a transmitter, but it had been out of service since June. In short, there was no known source for the signal heard by Mokapu, but the bearing passes closest to uninhabited Gardner Island in the southwestern part of the Phoenix Group.

By four o'clock in the morning, the tide had receded enough for Earhart to restart the engine and resume her calls. In describing her situation, she had been saying the plane was part on land, part in the water, on a small uninhabited island—but there might be many such islands. She did not know the name of her island. She needed a description more concise, easily understood, and something specific, something like the nearby shipwreck.

Aboard *Itasca*, the airwaves had been quiet for the past several hours. While the Pan Am station in Hawaii was taking a doubtful bearing on rough, weak signals, the cutter's radio operator was hearing nothing but heavy static. Five thousand miles away, yet another shortwave listener was hearing a call from the missing plane. A more unlikely witness in a more unlikely place is difficult to imagine.

Rock Springs is a precarious patch of green in the Red Desert of southwestern Wyoming. In 1937 New Deal programs had somewhat softened the impact of the Great Depression on the coal-mining town, and perhaps for that reason Cyrus Randolph was able to support his son Dana's hobby. Dana was sixteen years old, and for the past eight years he had been fascinated with radio. Under the tutelage of his uncle John Randolph, he had "studied and worked on the mechanics of radio" and "built his own sets." At eight o'clock on the morning of July 4, Dana was listening on a commercial set with a shortwave receiver using "a new antenna he had designed and just had erected." His father was in the kitchen when he heard Dana yell, "Hey, Paw! I got Miss Earhart!"[31] As the local *Rock Springs Rocket* reported, Dana had heard a woman say, "This is Amelia Earhart. Ship is on a reef south of the equator. Station KH9QQ [*sic*]." Then the signal died off.

The elder Randolph came running, and he and his son listened closely. Again the woman's voice came from the speaker, repeating her name, the call letters of her station, and fading away again as she began to give her location. The cycle continued for twenty-five minutes. Dana's uncle Victor Randolph, who lived next door, came in and was told about the reception of the call for help. "Everybody wants to know about that," he told his nephew. "Get downtown and report that." Cyrus and Victor Randolph immediately went to the police station to learn where the report should be made.

Rock Springs happened to be on an established Bureau of Air Commerce air route, so they were directed to the local Department of Commerce radio operator. After hearing the Randolphs' story, the operator notified Washington of their report, saying that the plea for help had come in on 16000 kilocycles. The three of them then dashed to the Randolph home to listen, but, despite constant vigilance at the radio, no more understandable messages came through. At times, Earhart's voice was heard, but her words were not clear enough to be understood.[32]

It was almost noon in the central Pacific before word of the incident reached *Itasca*. A message from San Francisco Division read: "Unconfirmed reports from Rock Springs, Wyoming, state Earhart plane heard 16000 kilocycles. Position on a reef southeast of Howland Island. This information may be authentic as signals from mid-Pacific and Orient often heard inland when not audible on coast. Verification follows."[33]

Verification did follow three hours later. "Following received from Rock Springs in response to inquiry. 'Investigation reveals signals heard near sixteen megacycles [are] thought to be from KHAQQ, signed KDN.'"[34] Station KDN was the Department of Commerce aeronautical radio facility in Rock Springs. The operator there believed that Dana Randolph had heard Amelia Earhart because he knew from personal experience that receptions like the one the boy reported were possible. He realized that the frequency Dana read from the dial of his commercial set was very close to 15525 kilocycles—the fifth harmonic of 3105.[35] In assessing the credibility of the story, the government investigator may have also been influenced by another consideration. The Randolph family was African American. In the Rock Springs of 1937, for these men to spread false information about a famous white woman would be, to say the least, unwise.[36]

There appears to be no bandwagon aspect to the Randolph family's claim. The local paper was published only every other day, and news of distress calls from the lost fliers had not yet reached Rock Springs. When Dana Randolph's story appeared in the July 6–7 edition of the *Rock Springs Rocket*, the headline read "First Radio Contact with Miss Earhart Made by Springs Boy."[37]

The call sign mentioned in the newspaper article, KH9QQ, is incorrect, but the Department of Commerce radio operator who investigated the report made no mention of the discrepancy. It seems likely that the newspaper reporter simply got it wrong.

The description of the plane's position and situation reported by the Randolph family was at odds with the prevailing assumption that Earhart was afloat on the ocean. According to the *Rocket*, Dana heard Earhart say, "Ship is on a reef south of the equator."[38] The position information given to the Coast Guard by the Department of Commerce investigator was more specific. According to his report, the reef was "southeast of Howland."[39] In 1937, a multiengine aircraft was commonly called a "ship," so everyone assumed the ship on the reef in Earhart's message was her airplane. No one considered the possibility that Earhart was describing a distinguishing feature of her location, the wrecked ship on the reef.

At the same time Dana Randolph was hearing Earhart, someone else was also hearing her. In Toronto, Ontario, Mrs. Gertrude Crabb had also stumbled upon a harmonic of 3105 kcs and was astonished to hear a man and a woman she believed were Amelia Earhart and Fred Noonan. Their words were muffled and indistinct, but she could make out: "Do you think they heard our SOS?" Then "Oh, oh, oh" by the woman. And finally, "Are you all right?"[40] Mrs. Crabb would not be the last to hear such an exchange.

24

Confusion and Chaos

JULY 4

As the tropical sun climbed in the sky on the morning of Earhart and Noonan's third day on the reef, the bare metal Electra became a veritable oven, but the tide was low, offering another shark-free opportunity to pick their way ashore. Escape to the shade of shoreline vegetation probably seemed worth the risk, and any sources of food and water were on the island, not the airplane.

In New York it was Sunday, the Fourth of July, and just as George Putnam had hoped, Earhart's name was on the front page of every newspaper in the country, but the headlines were not what he had planned: "Storm Turns Back Plane Sent to Find Miss Earhart; Several Radio Calls Heard";[1]"Storms Balk Navy Plane on Earhart Hunt"; "U.S. Battleship and Aircraft Carrier Sent to Join Search as Radio Signals Die Out."[2] The American public awoke to the news that Earhart was out there somewhere calling for help, but her pleas were fading. The Navy plane had been forced to turn back, and now a battleship and an aircraft carrier were rushing to her rescue. It was not drama. It was melodrama.

Truth be told, the press had jumped the gun. The Chief of Naval Operations had not yet committed to sending the aircraft carrier and its escort of destroyers. Reporters had found out that USS *Lexington* was ordered to "prepare for a south seas cruise that might last four weeks." Word had also leaked that the naval air station at North Island in San Diego was preparing to put six squadrons of aircraft aboard the carrier. There could be no doubt about the ship's projected mission.[3]

The leaks had made the decision for him and, at noon, the CNO did the only thing he could do. He issued the order to Admiral Hepburn, commander-in-chief, U.S. Fleet: "When *Lexington* Group [the aircraft carrier and three destroyers] is in all respects ready, proceed to assist in search for Earhart plane. Cooperate with Commandant Fourteenth Naval District, *Colorado*, and *Itasca*."[4]

The Navy Department now had a new reason for finding Earhart and Noonan as soon as possible. Critics of the Roosevelt administration were sure to protest the cost of sending an armada of warships thousands of miles to search for one lost private airplane. If the missing fliers could be rescued quickly, the ships could stand down.

On Friday, naval aviation officers in Hawaii had reasoned that strong winds had probably carried the plane southeast of Howland. On Saturday night, Pan American had taken a directional bearing on a radio signal that seemed to be coming from somewhere in the Phoenix Group southeast of Howland. On Sunday morning, an amateur report that was judged to be authentic put the plane on a reef southeast of Howland. Now the newspapers were quoting Paul Mantz as saying that the plane had to be on land to transmit. Mantz believed "Miss Earhart landed on one of the Phoenix Islands, a group southeast of Howland Island."[5]

What the Navy needed was for someone to search the Phoenix Islands as soon as possible. *Itasca* was the only ship actively searching, and it was concentrating on the ocean north and west of Howland. *Colorado* was still days away. What about that British warship that had heard possible signals from the plane? It was down there somewhere, on its way from Samoa to Hawaii, and British cruisers carried a catapult-launched seaplane. An hour after the CNO activated the *Lexington* group, the U.S. Navy radio station at Tutuila, American Samoa, sent a message to HMS *Achilles*: "What is your present position? The Navy Department requests this information in connection with Earhart search now in progress."[6] The cruiser replied with a position that put it some thirteen hundred miles east of the search area—almost exactly as far east as *Colorado* was to the north. There was no point in getting the British involved if they could not get there any faster than the American battleship. No request was made for *Achilles* to assist in the search.

As *Colorado* plowed southward, the battleship's commanding officer, Capt. Wilhelm Friedell, was monitoring the developing situation. In his official report of *Colorado*'s role in the search, he described his perception of how things stood on that morning of July 4: "On the night of 3 and 4 July no signals were heard on the plane frequency by the *Itasca* or *Colorado*, but reports were received from Wyoming, Honolulu, Los Angeles, Australia and other points that signals, and in some cases voice reports, had been received from the plane. . . . There was no doubt that many stations were calling the Earhart plane on the plane's frequency, some by voice and others by signals. All of these added to the confusion and doubtfulness of the authenticity of the reports."[7]

Friedell's impressions were almost completely in error. During the night, *Itasca* heard numerous signals on the plane's frequency. The battleship's commanding officer did not know it because nobody knew it. Information was flowing in to *Itasca* about what other stations were reporting, but the cutter was silent about what its own operators were hearing. Captain Friedell's assumption that "many stations were calling the Earhart plane on the plane's frequency" was also wrong. The Coast Guard's San Francisco Division had not told the Navy about the precautions taken to avoid misunderstood signals. The lack of communication was largely due to the absence of a centralized command structure for the search effort. Earhart and Noonan had been missing for forty-eight hours. The Coast Guard, the Navy, Pan American Airways, and commercial radio stations in Hawaii were all doing their best to help find the lost fliers, but no one was in charge of the overall effort.

As *Itasca* began its third day of searching, Commander Thompson was grudgingly investigating the position reported by McMenamy and his friends. As he explained in his later report: "In view of possibilities of the plane being able to transmit on the water as indicated in prior information, [*Itasca*] stood west to this latest reported position for the purpose of proving or disproving the reports which could not be consistently ignored."[8]

As daylight returned, the cutter's radio room resumed its calls to Earhart on the plane's frequency. Throughout the day, every thirty minutes, on the hour and half hour, the operator on duty would transmit a long count in voice on 3105 kcs: "*Itasca* calling Earhart 1–2–3–4–5–6–7–8–9–9–8–7–6–5–4–3–2–1. If you get me, come in please."[9] But the airwaves were as silent as the sea was empty. At one point during the day, *Itasca* received a position report from SS *Golden Bear*.[10] The Matson Line ship was about 350 miles northwest of Howland and almost exactly on the 157/337 line of position Earhart had said she was following. The ship had no voice radio capability and so was not a potential source of hoax messages.[11] *Golden Bear*'s only reason for contacting *Itasca* was to ask the cutter to relay its position to another of the company's passenger/cargo liners. *Itasca* complied with the request but made no attempt to enlist *Golden Bear*'s help in the search for the missing plane; nor did it advise Coast Guard headquarters or the Navy that there was a ship near the search area.

In an afternoon update to Treasury Secretary Morgenthau, Commander Thompson's tone was not optimistic:

Have searched area NW to NE of Howland [within] radius [of] 120 miles with negative results though visibility, weather, and sea conditions [have been] excellent. Extra and vigilant lookouts posted and continual use both high power searchlights during darkness. Am reasonably certain party is not afloat in area indicated. Commenced rectangular search this morning at daybreak [from] 180 Meridian to Howland Island between Latitude 0.20° North and 1.30° North. Estimate origin [of] this search [is] well to westward and leeward of plane position if plane down west of island.

Will have covered indicated area to Howland by Tuesday evening 6 July. Estimate searching three thousand square miles daylight visibility and one thousand five hundred square miles during night.[12]

The secretary of the Treasury was not the only one asking Commander Thompson for information. The newsmen aboard *Itasca* wanted to send their wire services more detail. Thompson contacted his superiors seeking permission to release the content of Earhart's communications: "Press requesting release exact text [of] Earhart messages. Aside from [necessity for] long transmission and regulations, have no reason not to permit release. Request permission to release."[13] Thompson appears to have been eager to provide the press with specifics about what had happened on Friday. He was increasingly doubtful that the search would end well, and the public needed to know that he, his ship, and the Coast Guard were blameless. The commandant's office approved the request, provided that the regulation prohibiting the sharing of private communications (such as commercial telegrams) was not violated and that the long transmission needed to send the text did not interfere with search operations.[14] Rather than give the two wire service reporters aboard *Itasca* access to the radio room logs, Thompson composed his own version of events and sent it to Washington. Coast Guard headquarters could then release the story to the press:

Following text [is] messages received by *Itasca* from Earhart [on the] morning [of] 2 July . . . forwarded for headquarters release to Associated and other presses.

All messages [were in] voice on 3105 kilocycles. Any press release should clearly indicate that *Itasca* was at Howland as homing vessel only and that this, with weather, was sole radio duty requested by Earhart.

Ship met all Earhart requests with [the] exception [of] inability to secure emergency radio bearings on 3105 kilocycles due [to] brief Earhart transmissions and [her] use of voice.

With [the] exception [of the] 08:03 message, no *Itasca* message or request [was] acknowledged by Earhart. Earhart apparently never received *Itasca* requests [to] transmit on 500 kilocycles in order [for] *Itasca* to cut her in with ship direction finder.[15]

Thompson then provided the requested "exact text" of the voice messages received from Earhart. He took all of the transmissions he quoted from the log for position two, the radio position dedicated to communicating with the plane. In nearly every case there are significant discrepancies between what the operators logged on the morning of July 2 and what Commander Thompson alleged two and a half days later. Thompson never claimed to have heard any of the transmissions himself:

"02:45: Recognized Earhart voice message. Not clear except 'cloudy weather cloudy.'"[16] Nobody heard "cloudy weather cloudy." Chief Radioman Leo Bellarts had the watch at that time. His radio log entry for 02:45–48 was: "Heard Earhart plane but unreadable through static."[17] Associated Press reporter Jim Carey heard "cloudy, overcast."

"03:45: *Itasca* from Earhart. *Itasca* broadcast on 3105 kilocycles on hour and half hour. Repeat broadcast on 3105 kilocycles on hour and half hour. Overcast."[18] Thompson's time and text agree with Bellarts' log entry except for the word "overcast."[19] Thompson was putting words in Earhart's mouth.

"04:53: Heard Earhart voice signals [but] unreadable with five [people] listening."[20] Five people could not have been listening at 04:53 because the signals were still only strength 1, not nearly strong enough to be put over the loudspeaker in the radio room. Only the two operators heard the transmission over their headphones. Bellarts logged, "Heard Earhart. Part cloudy." O'Hare, at the other position, was busy transmitting a message when "Earhart broke in on phone 3105." He logged the message as "unreadable."[21]

"05:12: Wants bearing on 3105 kilocycles on hour. Will whistle in microphone."[22] No signal was heard at 05:12. Bellarts logged the message Thompson quoted at 06:14.[23]

"05:15: About 200 miles out. Whistled briefly in microphone."[24] Again, Thompson was an hour off. Bellarts logged the message at 06:15.[25]

"05:45: Please take bearing on us and report in half hour. I will make noise in microphone. About 100 miles out."[26] The time should be 06:46.[27]

"07:30: We must be on you but cannot see you, but gas is running low. Have been unable reach you by radio. We are flying at 1000 feet."[28] Galten logged the transmission at 07:42, not 07:30. The difference is only twelve minutes in this case, but it is an important discrepancy. Earhart was transmitting at quarter past the hour Greenwich Time, just as she had said she would. A message at 07:30 would be off schedule. Despite having earlier reported to headquarters that Earhart said she had only a half hour of gas left, Thompson was now quoting the "gas is running low" version of the transmission.[29]

"07:57: We are circling but cannot see island. Cannot hear you. Go ahead on 7500 kilocycles with long count either now or on schedule time on half hour."[30] Once again, when faced with ambiguity, Commander Thompson clarified the situation by changing the facts. Galten's original 07:58 log entry was: "We are drifting but cannot hear you."[31] That didn't seem right, so he erased "drifting" and typed in "circling." "We are circling but cannot hear you" still didn't make much sense, so the captain changed it to something that did. "We are circling but cannot see island."

"08:03: Earhart calling *Itasca*. We received your signals but unable to get minimum. Please take bearings on us and answer on 3105 kilocycles." Earhart made long dashes for a brief period but the emergency high-frequency direction finder could not cut her in on 3105 kilocycles.[32] This is the only message that Thompson reported just as it appears in the radio log.[33]

At 8:44, Earhart called *Itasca*: "We are on the line of position 157 dash 337. Will repeat this message on 6210 kilocycles. We are now running north and south."[34] It is obvious from the actual log entry for 08:43 that Earhart's message took the operators by surprise. The message was received in two parts, and there was clearly some uncertainty about what she said.[35] None of that is reflected in Thompson's version. His account of events ends: "Nothing further [was] heard from Earhart on 6210 or other frequencies. High frequency direction finder on Howland was set up as an additional emergency caution without Earhart's request or knowledge."[36] This was a not-so-subtle slam at Richard Black, who had brought the Navy high-frequency direction finder along over Thompson's objections but had failed to mention it in his preflight messages to Earhart:

> *Itasca* had it [the high-frequency direction finder] manned throughout night but [was] never able to secure bearings due to Earhart [making] very brief transmissions and her use of voice. Earhart [was] advised [on] 28 June [that] *Itasca* direction finder frequency range [is] 550 to 270 kilocycles. *Itasca* ship direction finder [was] manned at 07:25 and Earhart [was] repeatedly requested to transmit on 500 kilocycles to enable ship to cut her in. She neither acknowledged nor complied, though our advice indicates her ability to transmit on 500 kilocycles. Communications [were] monitored throughout by Lieutenant Commander Baker, Lieutenant Commander Kenner, Ensign Sutter, and Lieutenant Cooper U.S. Army Air Corps.[37]

This was another inaccuracy. Baker and Cooper did not monitor the communications; both officers were ashore on Howland all that morning.[38]

The story Commander Thompson sent to Washington was a self-serving portrayal of a stubborn woman who would not allow herself to be helped. Earhart ran into bad weather and got lost. Low on fuel, she went around in circles while refusing to cooperate with the Coast Guard's best efforts to save her. When last heard from, she was flying along a north-south line. The Coast Guard released Thompson's account, the Associated Press picked it up, and major newspapers ran it verbatim on page one without comment.[39] The press and the public were less interested in who was to blame than in the possibility that the missing fliers might yet be rescued.

At Coast Guard headquarters in Hawaii, Sunday, July 4, was spent making plans for the coming night. The officers and operators had high hopes that darkness would bring more radio signals and that the plane's location would be discovered. Early in the day, Coast Guard Hawaiian Section told *Itasca*: "Beginning after darkness, contemplate repeating organized listening operations 3105 [and]

6210 kilocycles of nite [of] 3–4 July. Pan American Airways will follow same procedure with all stations concentration [*sic*] and endeavor [to] obtain bearings. Suggest Howland direction finder be on standby for bearing if practicable." And as an afterthought: "Suggest *Itasca* remain silent 3105 and 6210 during listening period again tonight."[40]

Commander Thompson responded: "Will contact Howland as soon as possible and proceed as indicated. We are about out of range and possibly no contact until evening."[41] His difficulty contacting Howland is puzzling. At that time, *Itasca* was about 200 nautical miles from Howland, and Thompson was communicating with Hawaii, 1,500 nautical miles away.

Thompson also thought it would be a good idea if *Itasca*, but only *Itasca*, were permitted to transmit on Earhart's frequencies from eight o'clock to nine o'clock in the evening: "Submit desirability *Itasca* operating 3105 kcs, 6210 kcs and 7500 kcs between 20:00 and 21:00 this evening. If Earhart afloat in this area we are most favorably situated for communication. Our contacts [with] Earhart indicate her best reception on 7500 kcs and best transmission on 3105 kcs. If you approve, submit desirability radio silence those frequencies during period indicated except for this unit. We are sweeping east from 180 [degrees longitude]. Visibility excellent, slight sea, moderate swell, wind east 15 knots."[42]

The Hawaiian Section had no problem with *Itasca's* request and sent permission to "proceed as you deem necessary."[43] Warner Thompson was taking no chances. He sent the same request to San Francisco Division, noting that the commander of the Hawaiian Section had already approved his plan. San Francisco approved but cautioned that if *Itasca* intended to transmit Morse code signals to Earhart, its operators should "send at speed not greater than ten words per minute [and] sign [*Itasca's*] call letters in order [to] avoid any possible chance [of] mistaken identity of signals."[44]

As the sun settled into the central Pacific for the third time since the Electra had gone missing, San Francisco Division also passed along to *Itasca*, and all the other Coast Guard and Navy stations involved in the search, some recently obtained information: "Reference Earhart transmitter. Due to design of transmitter, following frequencies are highly practicable. Odd harmonics of the 3105 crystals which the antennae will be resonant on without change of the dial settings 9315, 15525 and 21935. Other possible harmonic points 12420 and 18630."[45]

Commander Thompson for some reason understood that this message "again indicated that the Earhart plane can possibly transmit on water."[46] The news about the harmonics bolstered the credibility of civilians like Dana Randolph in Wyoming and Mr. Donaldson in Hawaii, but there is no indication that any of the government stations subsequently monitored the harmonic frequencies listed. As they had done on the first two nights, the Coast Guard, the Navy, and Pan American Airways listened on Earhart's primary wavelengths of 3105 and 6210 kcs.

The special broadcasts by commercial stations KGU and KGMB the night before had brought a promising response, and Putnam wanted to try again. San Francisco forwarded to the Hawaiian Section his request that "KGMB broadcast to Miss Earhart that help is on the way and that signals have been heard."[47] The Hawaiian Section contacted the commercial station, made the arrangements, and, just before sundown, sent a message to *Itasca*, *Swan*, and *Colorado* and to the two major U.S. Navy radio stations in the central Pacific, Radio Wailupe near Honolulu and Radio Tutuila in American Samoa:

At 06:30 GCT KGMB [will] broadcast [on] 1320 kcs "To Earhart plane. We [are] using every possible means [to] establish contact with you. If you hear this broadcast please come in on 3105 kcs. Use key if possible, otherwise [use] voice transmission. If you hear this broadcast, turn [your] carrier on for one minute so we can tune you in, then turn [the] carrier on and off four times, then listen for our acknowledgement at 06:45 GCT." Broadcast will be repeated at 07:00 and 07:30 GCT. Request *Colorado*, *Itasca*, *Swan*, Tutuila, and Radio Wailupe report results after each broadcast.[48]

The Pan American direction-finding facilities at Mokapu in Hawaii, Midway, and Wake Island were also alerted. As the hour of the first KGMB broadcast approached, everyone had been alerted except for the stations on Howland and Baker. All of *Itasca*'s communication with Baker was being relayed through Howland Island, but the cutter had been unable to contact the operators there.[49]

The searchers were as ready as they were ever going to be. Now it was up to Earhart, if she was out there.

25

Dashes

JULY 4–5

By late afternoon, low tide was again approaching at the island. If Earhart and/or Noonan was ashore, they could get back to the plane for another night of calling for help. Whether from the faded name on the bow or a battered lifeboat washed up on the beach, they had apparently learned that the stranded ship was *Norwich City*.

As dusk came to the central Pacific, Hawaiians who were not at a Fourth of July picnic or on their way to a fireworks display heard the KGMB radio announcer interrupt the station's regular programming to make a special announcement: "Calling Earhart plane. Every effort being made to locate you. This station will call at 06:30 GCT at which time please reply on 3105 kilocycles. Listen on 1320 as all communications originate here."[1] The preparatory call was made twice, once just before sundown at 6:30 p.m. and again an hour later.

At 0630 GCT, eight o'clock Honolulu time, the experiment began: "To Earhart plane. We are using every possible means to establish contact with you. If you hear this broadcast please come in on 3105 kcs. Use key if possible, otherwise use voice transmission. If you hear this broadcast, turn your carrier on for one minute so we can tune you in, then turn the carrier on and off four times, then listen for our acknowledgement at 06:45 GCT."[2] In Coast Guard and Navy radio rooms around the Pacific, operators pressed their headphones to their ears, closed their eyes, and listened for a response.

Mother Nature was providing her own fireworks display that evening, and electrical storms in some areas filled the airwaves with crashing static. *Itasca* heard nothing in reply to the KGMB broadcast; nor did *Swan* or *Colorado*. The Navy facilities at Wailupe and Tutuila did not hear a reply, but the Coast Guard's Hawaiian Section heard "answering signals, carrier broken."[3]

The best hope for pinning down Earhart's location rested on the Pan American Airways direction-finder stations at Mokapu near Honolulu, at Midway Atoll, and on Wake Island. Ten minutes before the KGMB broadcast, the operator in charge at Wake received a message from Mokapu advising him to "have men at DF and Receiver station, and one at hotel radio listening for KGMB broadcast." He complied, but Wake heard nothing in response to the commercial station's instructions for Earhart to send four dashes.[4]

Photo 27. SS *Norwich City* photographed from HMS *Wellington* in 1935 TIGHAR Collection

Pan Am Midway also received the instructions from Mokapu. The direction finder began monitoring 3105, but in Midway's case, no one actually listened to the KGMB broadcast. Consequently, when the operator heard "a strange wobbly tone" that "cut out, remaining on the air for only short durations of time," he did not understand that what he was hearing were the intermittent transmissions the broadcast had asked for. As he listened, "A man's voice was distinctly heard but not of sufficient modulation to be understood or identified. . . . [A] quick shot was taken which resulted in a [bearing] of approximately 201, although the signal was of such a short duration that it was impossible to narrow it down properly."[5]

The operator at Midway informed Mokapu immediately. The Hawaiian station too had heard dashes in reply to the commercial broadcast. The *Honolulu Star-Bulletin* captured the excitement: "KGMB's first broadcast at 8 last evening brought electrifying results when several listening stations heard the signals turned on and off in conformity with instructions given by the broadcaster. 'To Earhart plane, your signals have been heard,' the hopeful announcer said in the third of the broadcasts which were continued at intervals of about 15 minutes for many hours. 'Send two long dashes if on sea, three if on land.' The response to this message was too vague and weak to be deciphered, however, and hopes of quickly learning the plane's position were dashed."[6]

In their official reports, the Mokapu operators told a slightly different story. That evening, K. C. Ambler, the section supervisor, manned the direction finder aided by his visiting boss, G. W. Angus, communication superintendent for the airline's Pacific Division. Both men heard "four distinct dashes on 3105 immediately following [the KGMB] broadcast."[7] Angus later reported: "We immediately called KGMB by phone and asked them to repeat the test. This was done and immediately after the second test, we again heard the same signals except at this time, only two dashes were received and the second dash trailed off to a weak signal as though the power supply on the transmitter had failed. During the time these dashes were heard, it was possible to observe an approximate bearing of 213 degrees from Mokapu."[8]

Ambler's log provides more details but is also more circumspect: "Occasionally signal strength rises sufficiently to hear voice but still too weak to distinguish a single word. Once it seemed as though it was a woman's voice but may only have been our imagination. Carrier heard from direction finder close to 3105 but signals so weak that it was impossible to obtain even a fair check. Average seems to be around 215 degrees—very doubtful bearings."[9] Doubtful though the bearings might be, they were virtually identical with those taken on a similar transmission the night before. In both cases, a voice signal on 3105 seemed to be coming from the direction of the Phoenix Islands.

The men at Mokapu were sure that their receiver was correctly calibrated. As Angus explained, "We are certain of the frequency because the Coast Guard cutter, *Itasca*, had previously set their transmitter on this frequency in an effort to contact the plane. Shortly before, we had taken bearings on the *Itasca* on this frequency, obtaining an approximate bearing of 210 degrees."[10]

Mr. Angus was mistaken. Whatever station Mokapu took a bearing on, it was not *Itasca*. The cutter made its last call on 3105 at 5:00 pm Honolulu time. The Mokapu station did not start listening on 3105 until 7:30 p.m.[11] What did Angus and Ambler hear that made them think it was the cutter trying to contact the plane? Did Mokapu hear the plane responding to KGMB's 7:30 p.m. preparatory broadcast? The bearing they took passed nowhere near *Itasca*'s position. For the third time in two nights, Mokapu had taken a bearing on a signal coming from the direction of the Phoenix Group. The Coast Guard was concerned that partially heard calls to the plane might be misunderstood to be calls from the plane. It appears that the reverse may have happened.

As the KGMB broadcasts continued, reception conditions improved, and more stations began to hear the replies. After the 8:30 broadcast, the Navy radio station in Tutuila, Samoa, "heard four series of dashes." Fifteen minutes later they heard the same thing, as did the Coast Guard's Hawaiian Section.[12] *Itasca* was still hearing nothing, but in accordance with the agreed-upon plan, at 9:30 p.m. Honolulu time (eight o'clock aboard the cutter), *Itasca* began broadcasting to Earhart. Radioman George Thompson made the first call in code on 3105. Five minutes later he repeated the transmission. At 8:15 and again at 8:20, he tried code on 6210. Next, at 8:30 and 8:35, Thompson sent code on 7500. Each time the call was the same: "NRUI, NRUI calling Earhart. Please answer."[13] Each time the only response was the crackle of static.

Earhart was now being called every fifteen minutes or so by KGMB on 1320 kcs and by *Itasca* every five or ten minutes variously on 3105, 6210, and 7500 kcs. If there was ever a time when amateurs were likely to overhear and misunderstand calls to the plane as being distress calls sent from the plane, this would be it—and yet no amateur receptions were reported. The special Coast Guard monitoring station in San Francisco was also listening and heard *Itasca*'s initial Morse code call to the plane: "Shortly after that [a] carrier was heard on 3105. Carriers were heard [on] 3105 at approximately 15 to 20 minutes past each hour to 05:05 PST seemingly [on] a prearranged schedule."[14] San Francisco Division's impression was correct. There was a prearranged schedule. Their own Hawaiian Section had arranged for KGMB to make broadcasts to the plane "at intervals of about 15 minutes for many hours," asking for a reply on 3105.[15] The Hawaiian Section had not included San Francisco Division in its message alerting various ships and stations to the plan, so the San Francisco operators did not know about the KGMB broadcasts and did not understand the possible significance of what they were hearing.

If any of the responses to the KGMB broadcasts were hoaxes (and there is no evidence that any were), they did not originate in the mainland United States. Interference from two twenty-four-hour commercial stations operating on the same frequency as KGMB—KID in Idaho Falls, Idaho, and KGHF in Pueblo, Colorado—prevented listeners in the United States from hearing the Hawaiian station's calls to Earhart.[16]

At 8:45 p.m. aboard *Itasca*, George Thompson, for the first time that night, tried calling Earhart using voice on 3105.[17] He heard nothing in reply; nor did anyone else. Ten minutes later he tried again, but the result was the same. *Itasca's* agreed-upon hour of transmitting to Earhart was over, but KGMB continued its periodic calls. At 9:13 p.m. Thompson heard a weak carrier on 3105 that might be voice, but it was too faint for him to be sure.[18] Two minutes later he received a message from Hawaiian headquarters. They had heard the earlier responses to KGMB's broadcasts and, for the past hour, had heard the cutter calling the plane, but the replies seemed to have died out: "Unable to get response [to] last broadcast. Have you heard signals? Are you in communication with plane?"[19] Before Thompson had a chance to reply, there was another weak signal in his headphones near 3105, and a few minutes later there was a "noise as of [a] generator starting up." Leo Bellarts had heard that same sound two nights before at the time of the *Achilles* incident. This time the noise was followed by a "weak carrier varying in frequency" and a "man's voice," but Thompson could not make out what the man was saying.[20]

A few minutes later, Hawaiian headquarters advised *Itasca*: "Baker Island reports [that he] heard [the] following, 'NRUI from KHAQQ' [in] voice [a] short while ago. Howland heard weak voice."[21] Just as on the previous night, the operator on Baker Island had heard an understandable voice transmission from the plane on 3105 at the same moment that stations farther north were hearing a weak, unintelligible signal.

Freak receptions do occur. It is possible for a hoaxer in Hawaii, or even California, sending voice on 3105, to be heard clearly by a station in the middle of the Pacific but hardly at all by stations close to home. The probability of such an event is on the order of one in several tens of millions. The chance of the phenomenon occurring twice on successive nights approaches infinity. Whether genuine or bogus, the signals heard at Baker were sent from a location in the central Pacific that was closer to Baker than to Howland or *Itasca*. In other words, somewhere south of Baker Island there was a man sending voice signals on Earhart's frequency who was either Fred Noonan or an impostor.

Aboard the cutter, Radioman Thompson continued to hear the man's voice. Over the next few minutes the signal seemed to improve, but he still could not make out what the man was saying.[22] At ten o'clock Thompson called the operator on Howland. All that afternoon and evening *Itasca* had been trying to reestablish radio communication with the island. When the ship began its search for Earhart, Radioman Frank Cipriani had been left behind on Howland to operate the high-frequency direction finder. He also had a portable Coast Guard radio with him, but it proved to be too weak to be of much use. Communication between *Itasca* and Howland, such as it was, had been via Department of the Interior operator Yau Fai Lum's amateur set. With *Itasca* searching hundreds of miles to the west, contact had been lost. Now the ship was working its way back eastward, and this time there was a reply. The following exchanges were all in Morse code and, according to the ship's radio log, were conducted between Radioman George Thompson aboard *Itasca* and Yau Fai Lum on Howland.

Itasca:	Calling Howland Island, over.
Howland:	Go ahead.
Itasca:	Take bearings on any signals you hear on 3105 kilocycles and how about schedules . . . wait a minute. . . . Take bearing now.
Howland:	Roger.[23]

Eight minutes went by with no word from the island. Thompson called again, but there was no answer. Four minutes later he tried yet again.

Itasca: Calling Howland Island.
Howland: Go ahead.
Itasca: Did you get a bearing?
Howland: No, the antenna is being used to transmit.
Itasca: Roger, do you hear anyone on 3105 now? Waiting.[24]

Two minutes later: "Howland Island, calling *Itasca*: Yes, at 22:46 heard Earhart call *Itasca* and Baker heard Earhart plane strength 4, readability 7 last night at 8:20 P.M."[25] Lum's casual statement was remarkable. He was saying that he heard Earhart calling *Itasca* a half-hour ago and passing along news of Baker's clear reception the night before. A time check between the cutter and the island a few minutes later revealed the clock on Howland to be eight minutes slow, so the actual time of the call was 10:54. The cutter heard a man's voice for sixteen minutes, from 10:37 until 10:53. It would appear, therefore, that between 10:53 and 10:54, the voice on 3105 switched from male to female.[26]

Earlier in the evening, the Pan American operator at Midway distinctly heard a man's voice. Shortly afterward, the Mokapu operators thought they heard a woman. Later, Baker heard a voice claiming to be KHAQQ calling *Itasca*. No gender was mentioned, but at the same time the cutter was hearing an unintelligible man's voice. Still later, the Howland operator seems to have heard a woman's voice.[27]

Coast Guard and Navy authorities could not ponder such nuances because *Itasca* did not pass along the information. Even Commander Thompson's later report, "Radio Transcripts—Earhart Flight," contains no mention of *Itasca* hearing a man's voice, nor of the strong, understandable call heard by Baker Island the night before. Yau Fai Lum's notation, "Yes, at 22:46 heard Earhart call *Itasca*" was changed to "Howland reports hearing KHAQQ at 22:46."[28]

Asked about the report more than half a century later, Lum denied it completely: "I do not know anything about hearing signals from Earhart after she went down." He also had no recollection of Coast Guard Radioman Frank Cipriani being with him on the island and believed Cipriani's radio log to be a fabrication.[29] A second Chinese-American radio operator, Ah Kin Leong, supported Lum's recollection: "No idea who wrote the false log. I stand no radio watch on Howland Island. Cipriani, Henry Lau and me was on the Coast Guard Cutter *Itasca* when it left Howland Island looking for Earhart."[30]

Multiple primary source documents, including *Itasca*'s radio log, the ship's deck log, and diary entries by Richard Black and James Kamakaiwi, leave no doubt that Lum's and Leong's memories are incorrect. When *Itasca* departed Howland Island on July 2, ten men were left behind on the island. James "Jimmy" Kamakaiwi was in charge of five Hawaiian-American colonists (Albert Akana Jr., William Tavares, Joseph Anakalea, Carl Kahalewai, and Jacob Haili) plus three Chinese-American licensed amateur radio operators: Yau Fai Lum (K6GNW), Ah Kin Leong (K6ODC), and Henry Lau (K6GAS). Frank Cipriani also remained on the island to operate the Navy's direction-finding equipment.[31]

Recollections often change over time to fit accepted versions of events. When the 1937 search failed, it became received wisdom among most of the participants that Earhart had never called for help. When asked in a 1973 interview whether "the guys on Howland and Baker ever heard" Earhart, *Itasca*'s chief radioman, Leo Bellarts, replied, "No, they never heard her. They never heard her. We checked with them."[32] The contemporaneous records tell a different story.

As the night of July 4 wore on, *Itasca* received reports from Hawaii, Howland, and Baker. Commander Thompson and his executive officer, Lieutenant Commander Baker, were losing their skepticism about the radio calls and feeling the pressure from headquarters to find out where the signals were coming from. At 10:30, Howland Island received a stern message from the cutter: "This [is] very important. From Mr. Baker here. Honolulu [is] apparently getting Earhart signals. Want Howland [to] keep loop in use especially at night. Use Chinese operators under your control. Keep Baker [Island] also on alert [for] plane data and to report to *Itasca* through Howland. Keep log. Captain expects results." To be sure the signals he was hearing were not coming from Howland, Radioman Thompson then asked, "Have you been calling us 3105?" Howland responded, "No, we have been calling you on 24 [meters or 12,500 kilocycles]." Thompson said, "Well we have been hearing [a] carrier on 3105 [with] a man's voice from 21:37 to 21:53.33."[33]

To make sure that Lum understood the schedule and the urgency of the situation, and to make it clear that the Department of the Interior radio operators were to follow Coast Guard orders, Radioman Thompson closed his message with: "Next schedule at 1 A.M. your time here. Use Interior's batteries if necessary. Mr. Black says Cipriani is in control and to keep continuous watch on 3105 and take bearings. Use Chinese operators. If you have trouble having [them] stand watches Mr. Black says to tell Jimmy [Kamakaiwi]. Baker heard plane calling NRUI tonight. Get direction finder in operation. *Itasca* [will be] going south of island tomorrow. If [not] possible to contact *Itasca* give all important information to Honolulu immediately. See you at 1 A.M. your time. How do you copy?" Lum replied: "Roger."[34]

At about this time, Commander Thompson had the radio room reply to the query Hawaiian headquarters had sent nearly an hour and a half earlier asking, "Have you heard signals? Are you in communication with plane?" He answered with a single word, "Negative."[35]

Once again the Pacific went quiet. No one heard anything for the next quarter hour. Then, at 10:43 p.m., *Itasca* began hearing a "very weak rough carrier on 3105." The faint signal continued for the next fifteen minutes but was "impossible to make out." Just before the top of the hour, there was "another carrier now, smoother note on 3105. Slightly higher in frequency than [the] last one. Too weak to make out." Eighteen minutes later, "Still hear weak carrier on 3105 and now hear weak CW [Morse code] signals [a] little higher in frequency and about 20 words per minute but unread."[36] Earhart's 3105 kcs frequency was crystal-controlled and could not transmit at a higher frequency. Twenty words per minute is a respectable speed. Whoever was tapping out code on a frequency slightly higher than 3105, it was not Earhart or Noonan.

Another fifteen minutes passed. The Pan Am direction-finding station at Midway resumed listening, and immediately "a strong carrier was heard on 3105 KC and a shot taken on it . . . resulting in a bearing of 175 which proved to be some unidentified station probably in South America or Russia and was later definitely disregarded as a possibility."[37] *Itasca* was still hearing unreadable twenty-word-per-minute code. On Howland, Cipriani too heard a signal and logged: "Weak carrier on 3105. No call [letters] given. Unilateral bearing impossible due to night effect.[38] Using small packed [presumably 'pocket'] compass to determine relative direction. Bearing only approximate SSE or NNW."[39]

This was the first and only time during the entire search when two direction-finding stations were able to take simultaneous bearings. If Midway and Howland were hearing the same signal, if their respective bearings were reasonably accurate, and if the bearings crossed, there was a high probability that the signals were coming from that point—quite literally, a case of *X* marking the spot. The bearings do, in fact, cross near Gardner Island, but the other questions are more difficult to answer.

The operator at Midway heard a strong carrier on 3105. Cipriani on Howland heard a weak carrier on the same frequency. Neither reported hearing code or voice. Were they hearing the same signal? Without some distinguishing characteristic reported by both stations, it is not possible to know for certain. *Itasca*, at that moment, was hearing a weak carrier on 3105 and twenty-word-per-minute code on a slightly higher frequency. None of the other stations around the Pacific reported hearing anything at that time.[40]

Midway's statement that the signal "proved to be some unidentified station probably in South America or Russia" is a non sequitur. If the station remained unidentified, nothing was proved. A 175-degree bearing from Midway passes nowhere near South America. If the source of the signals was in the opposite direction, the station was in eastern Siberia.

The bearing taken by Cipriani on Howland is even more difficult to pin down. He rotated the direction finder's loop antenna until he got a minimum signal and then determined the loop's orientation using a pocket compass. That gave him a line, not a direction, and a fairly imprecise line at that. The best he could say was that the signal seemed to be coming generally from either the north-northwest or the south-southeast. Whether by coincidence or not, Cipriani's line agreed with the 157/337-degree line Earhart had described in her last in-flight transmission.

In the end, what can be said about the simultaneous bearings taken by Midway and Howland on the night of July 4 is that both signals were of unidentified origin, either or both could have been sent from the missing plane, and neither station considered its bearing to be precise.

As midnight approached, *Itasca* continued to hear a faint carrier on 3105. There were two, and sometimes three, other stations sending code on nearby frequencies, but none of it was clear enough to be understandable.[41] The reported receptions by other stations were nonetheless encouraging. Perhaps *Itasca* should again try to call the plane. At twenty-five minutes into the new day, the cutter advised Hawaiian headquarters: "In view [of] Howland and Baker reports, we will open up at 0030 for one hour as earlier in evening. Suggest PAA listen for response. Estimate 7500 [is the] frequency she is receiving, from past experience."[42] It was a reasonable guess. On Friday, as the flight seemed to be drawing closer and closer to its destination, the only time Earhart had acknowledged hearing *Itasca* was when the ship transmitted on 7500 kcs. If they tried again, and if she received the signal, maybe she could at least indicate whether she was north or south of Howland. In any case, if she replied at all, maybe Pan American could take a bearing on the signal.

At 12:30 a.m. Leo Bellarts tapped out a Morse code message on 7500: "NRUI calling KHAQQ. Indicate reception by four long dashes and then give bearing Howland, north or south. This is

NRUI."[43] The steady carrier on 3105 did not break in reply, but, on another receiver, a message came in from the U.S. Navy station in Tutuila, Samoa: "Following received from SS *Moorsby*, [call letters] GYSR, at 11:57 GCT, 'Hear continuous carrier wave 3105 kilocycles. Been going last couple of hours but no indication as to what it is. No way of getting in touch unless he can read Morse.'"[44]

Navy Radio Tutuila had the ship's name slightly wrong—it was actually SS *Moorby*—but the call letters were correct. Tutuila also relayed the British freighter's position as "4.5 on 185.28W."[45] The first number was clearly intended to be latitude, but was it 4.5 degrees south or north? The second number was nonsense. There is no longitude greater than 180 degrees. Despite the confusion, the message was more confirmation that some unknown station out there was transmitting continuously on 3105 kcs. *Itasca* was hearing it, Midway was hearing it, and now *Moorby* was hearing it.

Two minutes later, Wake resumed its listening watch on 3105 and the operator in charge, R. M. Hansen, soon heard "a very unsteady voice modulated carrier." The signal was strong, strength 5, an unreadable male voice just like the one he had heard the night before. The signals continued for thirteen minutes, gradually fading to strength 2 before stopping. In his official summary, written a few days later, Hansen reported that, during that time,

> I was able to get an approximate bearing of 144 degrees. In spite of the extreme eccentricity of this signal during the entire length of the transmission, the splits were definite and pretty fair. . . . At the time I believed this bearing to be reasonable [*sic*] accurate and I am still of that opinion. After I obtained the observed bearing, I advised Midway to listen for the signal (couldn't raise Hawaii). He apparently did not hear it. . . . The characteristics of this signal were identical with those of the signal mentioned as being heard the previous night . . . with the exception that . . . the complete periods of no signal occurred during shorter intervals. . . . While no identification call letters were distinguished in either case, I was positive at the time that this was KHAQQ. At this date, I am still of this opinion.[46]

Hansen's statement was by far the most confident assertion that a reasonably accurate bearing had been taken on a signal sent from the missing plane. A total of six bearings had now been taken: three by Pan Am Mokapu, one by Pan Am Wake, one by Pan Am Midway, and one by Howland Island. None could be considered definitive, but two were simultaneous and five of the six crossed the 157/337 line of position near Gardner Island.[47]

Hansen was sure he had taken a bearing on Earhart, but his boss, division communication superintendent G. W. Angus, did not share his opinion: "I do not believe the signals that Wake heard were from the Earhart plane inasmuch as they were unheard at Mokapu at this time. The signals heard at Wake were a continuous carrier for several minutes at a time and we [Angus and K. C. Ambler, the section supervisor for communications at Mokapu] were of the opinion that possibly these signals emanated from somewhere in Japan."[48]

Records show that no station in Japan was licensed to transmit voice on 3105, and that Angus misinterpreted Hansen's report. Hansen did not say the carrier was continuous for several minutes at a time. He said he heard a signal "identical" with the intermittent voice signal with "rather wobbly characteristics" he had heard the night before, except this time "the complete periods of no signal occurred during shorter intervals."[49]

According to Mokapu's report, the operator at Midway heard it too but was able only to get a "very poor bearing" of 201 degrees.[50] The Midway operator considered the bearing to be so poor that he did not mention it in his own report.

Angus and Ambler at Mokapu did not hear the transmissions, but just a few miles away at Radio Wailupe, three U.S. Navy operators had been puzzling over strange code messages for the past hour. When the signals stopped, they contacted Coast Guard headquarters in Honolulu, which passed the news to *Itasca*: "Following copied [by] Navy Radio Wailupe [from] 11:30 to 12:30 GCT, '281 north Howland call KHAQQ beyond north don't hold with us much longer above water shut off.' Keyed transmission [but] extremely poor keying behind carrier. Fragmentary phrases but copied by three operators."[51]

After three days of fruitless searching, Commander Thompson felt that he finally had a solid lead. Here was a message, verified by three Navy operators, that included Earhart's call letters and was clearly a cry for help. Most important, it contained information about the plane's position. Unfortunately, just how that information should be interpreted was not at all clear. *Itasca* received it via Coast Guard headquarters in Honolulu, not directly from the Navy. Apparently someone at Wailupe telephoned the Coast Guard with a description of what they had heard. Whoever took the call at Hawaiian Section wrote it down, and the radio operator passed the report along to *Itasca*. In such a transfer of information there was plenty of opportunity for error, and many questions remain unanswered. How did the fragments of the message break down? For example, was it "281 north . . . Howland call KHAQQ," or was it "281 north Howland . . . call KHAQQ"? The reception was reported to have spanned a one-hour period. Was each phrase heard only once, or were they parts of a message sent over and over again? And on what frequency were the fragments of code heard? Others were hearing something quite different on 3105 kcs at the same time.

If Commander Thompson was troubled by these questions, he didn't say so. The reported phrases could be interpreted to support his long-held belief that the plane was afloat somewhere north of Howland. As he had done before, Thompson resolved ambiguities by adjusting the facts. He assumed the signals were heard on one of Earhart's frequencies, and he was sure that the phrase "281 north Howland" meant 281 miles north of Howland. He immediately ordered the ship's course altered to head for that spot.[52] Just before three o'clock in the morning he had the radio room send a message to the Navy seaplane tender *Swan* still plodding southward toward the search area: "Official information indicates Earhart down 281 miles north of Howland. Suggest you search as indicated. *Itasca* proceeding."[53]

If Thompson's interpretation was correct, the plane had flown 281 miles beyond Howland to the north, landed in the ocean, and was now in imminent danger of sinking, but that position was nearly two hundred miles from *Itasca*'s present location. Even steaming at full speed, the cutter could not reach it before late in the day. Neither *Swan* nor *Colorado* could do better. At 3:14 a.m. Commander Thompson had the radio room make a general broadcast for "nearest vessel [to] search 281 miles north [of] Howland."[54] There was no response.

A few minutes later, Howland Island called with the first news of the bearing taken by Cipriani: "At 00:35 Hawaiian Standard Time [we] obtained [a] bearing on a continuous wave of unknown origin indicating south southeast or north northwest on magnetic compass. Unable to obtain unilateral bearing due to night effect. No call [letters] given. Frequency is slightly above 3105 kilo-cycles."[55] Thompson took the report as further confirmation that he had been right all along. Now it was a life-or-death race against time.

The radio room had succeeded in establishing direct contact with SS *Moorby* long enough to get the freighter's correct position.[56] It was about 250 miles northeast of the target area.[57] After several unsuccessful attempts to reestablish radio contact, Thompson asked the Navy stations at Wailupe and Tutuila to relay a message: "Following for GYSR, master SS *Moorby*: Earhart plane apparently down 281 miles north of Howland Island and you are closest vessel. If you can divert, suggest search that vicinity. *Itasca* proceeding and will arrive this afternoon. Commander *Itasca*."[58]

While waiting to learn whether *Moorby* was willing to help, *Itasca* continued to send Morse code requests for the plane to reply with dashes but heard no response. At times during the remainder of the night, there was weak code on 3105 but no voice. Howland, too, heard a few weak signals and once picked up "distinct Japanese music on 3105."[59]

On one occasion, the Coast Guard's San Francisco monitoring station heard the cutter call the plane: "Almost immediately 4 dashes of approximately 4 or 5 seconds duration, spaces same length, [were heard] on 3105 and shortly afterward a carrier and a man's voice, the only distinguishable English being [the] letter 'I.' This [was heard] at end of transmission. Duration [of] voice transmission [was] approximately 2 minutes. Dashes were heard by three radiomen and voice by two." San Francisco also mentioned that "local transport planes on 3105 were heard at various times." They were confident that the signals in question were coming from the central Pacific because the "monitors [were] using 6 receivers on 2 Honolulu diamond beam antennas."[60]

The picture was clear. The numerous government and civilian receptions of post-loss radio signals on Earhart's frequencies, her responses to requests for dashes, and the absence of credible alternative explanations left no doubt that Earhart was alive and calling for help.

26
Damsel in Distress

JULY 5

High tide on the reef had come at 4:30 on the morning of July 5 with the deepest water yet—almost three feet, enough to flood the fuselage from the cabin door rearward. If waves washing in and out across the reef were now strong enough to move the airplane around, it would be a terrifying feeling for Earhart and Noonan in the dark, not knowing how close they were getting to the reef edge.

Signals sent during the night indicate Noonan had been able to take his turn at the radio sending dashes and distress calls, but transmissions heard later that morning suggest the normally unflappable navigator was increasingly disoriented and susceptible to panic attacks, possibly due to septicemia after falling on the coral the first day. As the sun came up, the water was low enough to run the engine, so Earhart decided to keep calling for help and listening for any response.

Dawn of the fourth day since the Electra failed to arrive at Howland Island found *Itasca* steaming northward with renewed hope. Earhart's response to the KGMB broadcasts had been heard by multiple stations, and reports that Baker and Howland had heard the plane calling *Itasca* seemed to leave little doubt that the fliers were still alive. The fragmented message heard by the Navy and the bearing taken by Howland could be interpreted to support Commander Thompson's established opinion that the plane had come down north of the island. The indicated course of action seemed clear.

It was time to brief headquarters. As soon as the sun was up, Commander Thompson sent a cautiously hopeful update to Washington: "For Secretary Morgenthau: Intercepts of ragged transmission indicate possibility Earhart plane [is] still afloat two eighty one miles north [of] Howland. Bearings [by] radio direction finder on Howland confirmed approximate position. We will arrive indicated position this afternoon about 17:00 [5 p.m.]."[1] His report to San Francisco Division was equally positive: "Reported position Earhart plane 281 north Howland apparently confirmed by radio compass bearing from Howland during night. We should arrive by dark. Will open up late afternoon on short wave and endeavor [to] get radio bearing from ship."[2]

The wire service reporters aboard *Itasca* were also eager to relate the results of the long, eventful night. Correspondent James Carey's story for the Associated Press was a mixture of fact, scuttlebutt, and misconception: "Aboard USCG *Itasca* en route north Howland. Most definite news [in] search [for] missing Earhart [and] Noonan heard Monday [at] two A.M. Navy Radio Wailupe intercepted message '281 north Howland call KHAQQ beyond north won't hold with us much longer above water shut off.'"[3] Carey changed the reported phrase "don't hold with us much longer" to the more logical "won't hold with us much longer."

Carey continued: "At two a.m. *Itasca* [was] west [of] Howland approximately 300 miles from area [indicated in] Earhart message. [*Itasca*] immediately changed course [to] proceed there. Expect [to] arrive [at] five p.m. tonight."[4] Carey had the anticipated time of arrival correct but not the distance. *Itasca* expected to cover 180 nautical miles in fifteen hours at an average speed of twelve knots, not 300 miles at twenty knots. "At four A.M. [during] regular schedule [between] *Itasca* and Howland, latter reported bearing approximately north to north northwest."[5] Carey was echoing Commander Thompson's half-truth. The bearing from Howland might also be south-southeast.

No one aboard the cutter knew yet that Pan Am Wake had taken a bearing on a strong voice modulated carrier and an unintelligible man's voice on 3105 kcs during the time Navy Wailupe was hearing the "281 north" message in fragments of poorly sent code on an unspecified frequency. Both transmissions could not be from the same transmitter. The operator at Wake was "positive . . . that this was KHAQQ," and the bearing passed near Gardner Island, not the open sea 281 miles north of Howland.[6]

More to the point, *Itasca* did not have the crucial piece of information that made the ship's rush to the rescue a fool's errand. The officers and men aboard the cutter were still interpreting clues and making search decisions based on their mistaken belief that the signals could be coming from a floating plane.

There was good news for America that Monday morning. Headlines across the country shouted: "HEAR AMELIA'S FAINT CALLS";[7] "EARHART HEARD BY HONOLULU; DEFINITE SIGNALS REPORTED BY COAST GUARD; WORD IS OFFICIAL";[8] "NAVY RUSHES 60 PLANES TO EARHART SEARCH; HOPE FOR SAFETY OF TWO FLYERS REVIVED AS SIGNALS BY RADIO RECUR ALMOST HOURLY."[9] Amelia Earhart was alive, and the Navy was hurrying to her rescue. Many papers carried an Associated Press story in which Paul Mantz reiterated his earlier admonition that the plane could not transmit if afloat. Mantz now added his opinion that Earhart and Noonan "probably are sitting on an island."[10] The *Honolulu Star-Bulletin* noted that Pan American bearings during the night "placed the transmitter roughly in the direction of Gardner and McKean Islands in the Phoenix Group, the same locality as the 'squeal' when it was first heard on Saturday night."[11]

San Francisco Division looked at the available evidence and sent a telegram to Coast Guard headquarters in Washington: "Suggest consideration be given proposal that State Department obtain cooperation [of] British government in examination of the uninhabited portion of the islands of the Phoenix Group southeast of Howland Island. British cruiser *Achilles* recently in South Pacific nearby."[12] The suggestion came too late. The Navy had already considered and rejected the idea of asking *Achilles* to help.

On July 5 the Japanese embassy in Washington notified the U.S. State Department Division of Far Eastern Affairs that it had received an urgent telegram from Tokyo offering the Japanese government's assistance in the search "in view of the fact that Japan had radio stations and warships in the Marshall Islands."[13] Now George Putnam asked CNO Admiral Leahy what the Japanese were doing or might be willing to do. Leahy couldn't help him: "Replying to your dispatch: There is no information available here regarding any search being made by the Japanese. W. D. Leahy."[14]

Reports of receptions by amateurs continued to come in. Mrs. Thelma Dunham in Indianapolis said she had been listening on her shortwave set early Monday morning and heard a woman's voice say, "This is Amelia Earhart calling all stations. Sending equipment getting weak. Have landed on water. Don't know position. Navigator is trying to check longitude and latitude. Getting hungry but can survive for twenty-four hours." Mrs. Dunham said she heard the voice on a wavelength of "13 meters," or 23077 kilocycles.[15] That frequency is nowhere near a harmonic of 3105, and, of course, the plane could not have landed in the water and be sending signals. If Mrs. Dunham heard anyone, it wasn't Amelia Earhart.

A man named Ray Mahoney in Cincinnati told a seemingly more plausible tale. The Associated Press reported that Mahoney "heard Amelia Earhart broadcasting distress signals at ten minute intervals yesterday from a position which he interpreted to be within fifty-seven miles of Howland Island. 'The signals were weak,' he said. 'About all I could make out were the call letters of her plane, that apparently it had hit a reef or was near a reef.'"[16] The *New York Times* noted that Mahoney's report seemed to agree with the message Dana Randolph in Wyoming had heard the previous night in which Earhart gave the plane's call letters and said that she was on a reef.[17] If Mahoney gave specific times or a frequency for the transmissions, there was no mention of them in the press. There is no reef within fifty-seven miles of Howland.

While Coast Guard and Navy headquarters were becoming increasingly convinced that the plane was down on an island or reef in the Phoenix Group, *Itasca* was steaming at full speed in the opposite direction. To manage the Navy's search, Rear Adm. Orin G. Murfin and his staff at Pearl Harbor plotted the movements of the various ships and recorded essential information on the best chart available, Hydrographic Office chart number 5050. (The actual chart they used is now in the National Archives.) The 157/337 line Earhart had said she was running on was clearly a line of position, so they drew that in, running north and south through Howland. They also laid down the north-northwest/south-southeast bearing taken by Cipriani using the high-frequency direction finder on Howland. When they drew in the three most accurate bearings taken by Pan American, it became apparent that all five lines were converging. If the bearings were genuine distress calls sent from the missing plane, where the lines crossed should be its location. But there was a problem. The lines intersected somewhere beyond 2°30′ south latitude, the southern limit of the chart.

Their solution was expedient and simple. They cut a few inches off the top of the chart, turned the strip of paper over, and pasted it along the bottom edge. They then extended the lines of longitude and drew in more lines of latitude down to 7 degrees south by hand. They could now extend the bearing lines. Unlike Earhart and Noonan, Murfin's staff could consult other charts to see if any islands fell within the expanded area. There were two: McKean Island and Gardner Island in the Phoenix Group. They drew in the islands. The five lines crossed in the vicinity of Gardner.

At 9:30 a.m. aboard the cutter, Chief Radioman Bellarts was finally able to get through to the British freighter. The master of SS *Moorby* confirmed that he was "diverting and proceeding to 281 miles north of Howland."[18]

Photo 28. Rear Adm. Orin G. Murfin (*right*) traces Pan American radio bearings on H.O. chart number 5050. Note the extension pasted to the bottom of the chart. National Archives and Records Administration

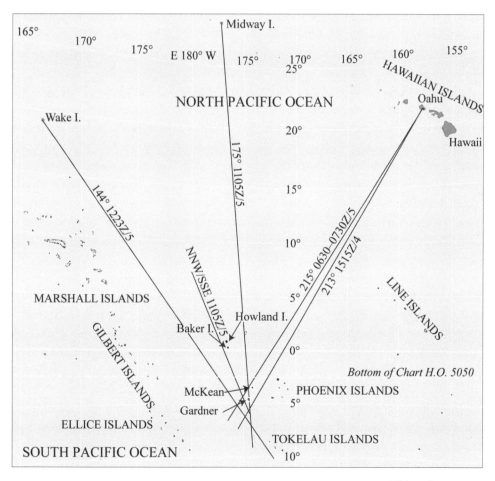

Map 8. All bearings

Although the sun was well up, Bellarts continued to monitor Earhart's frequency. Just before ten o'clock he began hearing something on 3105. The signal was a "little low in frequency," and he could not make out any content.[19] A half hour later he called Earhart on 3105 kcs in Morse code.

As the sun climbed in the tropical sky, so did the temperature in the cockpit of the Electra. Earhart had been calling all morning with no luck, and Noonan was becoming increasingly panicked and irrational. Suddenly, there was code in her headphones. The dots and dashes were just dots and dashes, but they were a sign that *Itasca* was again hearing her. To reassure her distraught companion, she held up her headphones so that he could hear the reassuring signals.

Over five thousand miles away, a fifteen-year-old girl in St. Petersburg, Florida, heard Amelia Earhart say, "Here, put your ear to it."[20] In the little house at 2027 Auburn Street South, it was late afternoon, and Betty Klenck had just settled down in front of the family radio. The Klencks were not wealthy, but Betty's father, through his job at the local power company, had been able to get a good deal on a top-of-the-line set. Kenneth Klenck was an amateur radio buff, and he had rigged a special antenna from the house to the garage and across the backyard to a utility pole at the rear of the property. The resulting reception was phenomenal, and Betty spent many hours in front of the large console listening to music. While she listened, she doodled pencil sketches of handsome men and glamorous ladies and jotted down the lyrics of her favorite songs in a notebook she kept by the set.

Cruising the shortwave bands, she would often hear foreign stations, but on this afternoon she stumbled upon a woman's voice, speaking in English and obviously frantic. Betty listened for a while and was startled to hear the woman say, "This is Amelia Earhart. This is Amelia Earhart. Help me!" This was not a radio play. There was no announcer, no music, no commercials. She later explained, "I was so floored at hearing 'This is Amelia Earhart' several times I didn't start writing right away until the numbers started being said."[21]

For the next one and three-quarter hours, Betty Klenck copied down, as best she could, the numbers and phrases that came through the speaker. The words came too fast for her to get everything, and often she got only a word or two of what was said. Sometimes the sound was distorted and the voice hard to understand. At other times the words seemed to make no sense at all. The signal faded in and out, often dying away completely for several minutes at a time before returning.

As Betty listened and wrote, the woman's pleas for help and attempts to give out information were often interrupted by verbal exchanges with a man who seemed to be in the same confined space. She knew Amelia Earhart had disappeared—it was all over the news—but she had not been following the world flight, and she didn't know the man's name. Whoever he was, he was out of control, and Betty had the impression he was delirious from a head injury. The woman who said she was Amelia Earhart was trying to deal with the man's erratic behavior while struggling to maintain her own composure enough to use the radio. It was clear to Betty that both individuals were under tremendous physical and emotional stress. She made what notes she could; if she didn't understand something, she wrote down the words she knew that were closest to the sound she heard. Betty's notebook reads like a modern 911 call on a bad phone line: desperate pleas for help and attempts to communicate location, interrupted by the caller dealing with an ongoing emergency. The phrases are fragmentary and occasionally garbled but, with a firsthand familiarity with the cramped Electra cockpit and personal experience on the same reef, it's possible to fill in the gaps with some informed guesses.

In the sweltering cockpit, Amelia wracked her brain. What if the code signals were not coming from *Itasca* but from some other station? There were radio operators at the airfield on Howland

Island. Maybe she should address her pleas to them, so she made a transmission calling Howland airport. Betty could make out only part of it and wrote down "W40K Howland port or WOJ Howland port." Or maybe one of the British stations in the south central Pacific was replying to her. Everyone in Australia and New Guinea had insisted on calling her Mrs. Putnam, so she broadcast, "This is Amelia Putnam. This is Amelia Putnam. SOS." Betty couldn't hear her clearly and thought her husband's name was Putman, so that's what she wrote down. Her next entries were: "stop— Amelia . . . speak . . . Uncle . . . Oh Klenck's . . . (crying now) . . . help . . . help us quick . . . I can feel it . . . your right." The notes imply an exchange that may have gone something like: "Stop Amelia, I want to speak to them." In struggling with him, she bumped or twisted her foot and exclaimed, "My ankle . . . oh, oh," and cried in pain as she continued to transmit, "Help. Help us quick." Turning to Noonan, she said, "I can feel it's a bad sprain," to which he replied, "I think you're right."

For the next hour the signal faded in and out, and Betty only caught snippets of the drama playing out on the other side of the world: "Come here just a moment. . . . Send us help. . . . I need air. . . . Amelia, things are . . . Here I come—oh. . . . Let me out of here." Several times Earhart broadcast *Norwich City*, the name of the ship on the reef that might help rescuers identify where they were. Betty thought she was saying New York City and wrote "N.Y. N.Y." in her notebook. At one point, Noonan grabbed the mic and probably shouted his wife's name, "Mary Bea, Mary Bea," which Betty heard as "Marie, Marie." There were more calls to Howland airport, more mentions of *Norwich City*, and more cries of Mary Bea.

While Amelia was focused on making distress calls, Noonan, determined to exit the plane, turned to crawl over the fuel tanks into the rear cabin. Betty heard Amelia say, "Where are you?" to which Noonan replied, "Water's knee deep—let me out." Amelia said, "Where are you going? We can't bail out." Possibly pointing to the sharks circling the plane, she said, "See?" Noonan got the point: "Yes." Betty heard and logged the exchange without understanding its meaning.

As she had in previous calls, Earhart broadcast their latitude and longitude coordinates, but the signal was poor, and Betty was unfamiliar with the terminology. As a result, the letters and numbers she wrote in her notebook are gibberish.

After three days and nights with no sign of rescue, Earhart recognized she might not get out of this alive. She had always had a fatalistic view of her flying career and often sent "popping off" letters to her mother and sister before a dangerous flight, reassuring them that the adventure was worth the risk. She accepted the possibility, even the likelihood, that her luck would someday run out. Dying young in exchange for immortal fame is a trade-off as old as Achilles. Now it was looking like the reckoning had come, and there was something that needed to be done to protect her legacy. Betty heard her say, "George, get the suitcase in my closet . . . California."

She had taken this precaution before. The day after Christmas 1934, Earhart and Putnam were aboard the Matson liner SS *Lurline* en route to Hawaii with Earhart's red Lockheed Vega lashed to the ship's deck. The plan was for Amelia to fly the twenty-four-hundred miles back to California, thus making the first flight from Hawaii to the U.S. mainland. As they were about to dock in Honolulu, Earhart wrote a letter to her mother, Amy, who was house-sitting at the Putnams' new home in North Hollywood, California. The letter was newsy and very matter-of-fact, but toward the end Amelia wrote: "I have taken possession of the stuff in the zipper compartment of my briefcase. Put it away until I turn up and if I don't—burn it. It consists of fragments that mean nothing to anybody but me."[22] Earhart had memorabilia that she wanted destroyed in the event of her death.

The material was now in a suitcase in her closet. Her husband knew about it. He would know what to do if the worst happened.

Over the next hour and three-quarters, the signal faded away and returned; the words were sometimes clear, sometimes garbled. Increasingly, Earhart's desperate calls for help were interrupted by Noonan's ravings and her efforts to control him: "Mary Bea, hey! . . . Will you help me . . . will you please. . . . All right! . . . What are you doing?"

Periodically, Earhart again tried to send position information, but the letters and numbers Betty copied don't make any sense. As the tide came in, the aircraft moved alarmingly as the running surf buffeted the tail. Noonan was panicked: "Quick, let me out." As he crawled over Earhart to climb out through the open cockpit hatch, she tried to restrain him: "Stop!" He struggled with her: "I can't make it!" In her fear and frustration, Earhart let loose with a string of profanity that fifteen-year-old Betty changed to "Darn." (Betty later recalled it was "Goddamn son of a bitch!"[23]) The water was getting high enough to threaten the prop and she would have to shut down, but not before one last description of the island's only unique feature, "Norwich City, Norwich City." The final entry in Betty's notebook is "N.Y. N.Y. or something that sounds like New York."[24]

Betty later explained, "I was home alone until Dad got home from work and heard the last part of her cries for help." Her father immediately ran next door to see if his neighbor Russell Rhodes could also pick up the signal. "Russ couldn't get it . . . although he had the same kind of set but hardly any aerial."[25] Convinced that the distress calls were genuine, Betty's father, Kenneth Klenck, drove to the St. Petersburg Coast Guard station to report what he and his daughter had heard. The duty officer assured him that the Coast Guard was on top of the situation. "Mom was in town with my sister," Betty later recalled, "and got home before Dad got back from the Coast Guard. She came in and I was still at the radio to see if any more would come on from Amelia. I told her what had happened and she was so excited, she called Jean in (my sister) who had stayed out to play. Then Russ and Virgie Rhodes came over, then Dad got home, upset at the Coast Guard because of the way they wouldn't listen to him and do something for A. E."[26]

On July 5 the Coast Guard was aware of, and had accepted, numerous reports of Earhart calling for help. There is no record of the St. Petersburg station passing Klenck's information up the chain of command. By July 5, based on the Pan American radio bearings, Gardner Island was already considered a prime suspect for the plane's location, but neither San Francisco Division, nor the Navy, nor, perhaps more important, George Putnam ever had an opportunity to evaluate the transcriptions in Betty's notebook.[27]

Shortly after the voices on Betty's shortwave faded away for the last time, Capt. Stanley Parker, commander of the Coast Guard's San Francisco Division, informed *Itasca*: "Opinion of technical aids here that Earhart plane will be found on original line of position which indicated position through Howland Island and Phoenix Group. Radio technicians familiar with radio equipment on plane all state that plane radio could not function now if in water and only if plane was on land and able to operate right motor for power. No fears felt for safety of plane on water provided tanks hold as Lockheed engineers calculate 5000 pound positive buoyancy with plane weight 8000 pounds."[28]

In other words, if the plane was down at sea, it could still be afloat, but if it was sending radio messages, it had to be on land and was probably on one of the islands of the Phoenix Group. Parker was trying to get through to Commander Thompson that his interpretation of the message fragment "281 north Howland" could not be correct. His warning fell on deaf ears.[29]

27

281 North

JULY 5

Warner Thompson pressed on. Throughout the morning and afternoon of Monday, July 5, *Itasca* steered a steady northward course at maximum speed. The radio room maintained its watch on Earhart's frequency, but the airwaves once again yielded only static. Nonetheless, anticipation aboard the cutter was running high. As evening approached, *Itasca* sent a message to the men on Howland Island: "Get everything in readiness for tonight as it will be a vital one in the search. We are nearly [at] Howland bearing and Navy position."[1]

Commander Thompson's interpretation of Cipriani's ambiguous north-northwest or south-southeast bearing and the fragments of code copied by Navy Radio Wailupe had become, in his mind, "the Howland bearing" and the "Navy position." Once again, speculation had solidified into accepted fact.

The press knew that *Itasca* was drawing close to "281 north," and the National Broadcasting Company (NBC) did not want to miss the story. An NBC executive sent an urgent message to Admiral Murfin in Hawaii: "Have talked to Chief of [Naval] Operations re Earhart and have been told [to] make request to you for permission to send Putnam, NBC man, and Paramount newsreel man from Honolulu to scene of Earhart rescue via navy patrol plane provided you can provide ship. Personnel involved would leave San Francisco [via] Pan American clipper Wednesday. Chief of Operations says if you relay our request they will approve. Please wire rush if you can supply such transportation. Chief of Operations requests [to] have copy [of] your answer to this wire."[2]

The CNO had to know the request was ridiculous, but he passed the ball to Murfin, who replied: "Sorry, do not consider it advisable to send patrol plane to Howland again. Plane to Howland must land in open sea and be serviced by such ship as may be available there. All available ships engaged in search and not available to tend plane. No anchorage for plane or servicing ship. Much danger involved except with fairly smooth sea. In spite these conditions, plane was dispatched last Saturday because life was at stake. Will not take another chance except under similar extreme urgency."[3]

At about the same time, *Itasca* was also fending off a media request. The Coast Guard Hawaiian Section had advised Commander Thompson: "National Broadcasting Company and KGU respectfully

199

request Earhart telephone statement for national release through RCA Kokohead if and when aboard *Itasca*." Thompson was tactful but noncommittal: "*Itasca* will be pleased cooperate as conditions permit. Entire matter problematical and no advance plans can be made. Radio now required exclusively to conduct search."[4]

As the sun set for the fourth time on *Itasca*'s hunt for the missing plane, San Francisco Division tried to lay out the situation in a message to Commander Thompson: "Pan American Airways . . . report radio bearing on plane signal morning [of] fifth as 144 degrees from Wake Island and are reasonably certain of bearing. Possibility intersection [of] position line given just before last plane transmission, and latitude line 281 miles north of Howland using Howland as reference point, may be plane's position. Bearing from Wake Island places plane near line of position and intersection of radio bearings from Wake and Honolulu give indications of position in Phoenix Group. Which further substantiated by technicians who feel planes radio could function only if on shore."[5]

Everything pointed to the plane being on an island in the Phoenix Group, but Division was willing to accommodate Thompson. They were saying the plane might also be afloat in the ocean near where Earhart's 157/337 degree line of position and the line of latitude 281 miles north of Howland (5°13′ N) cross. Even so, Thompson was headed for a point, not a line of latitude, 281 miles north of Howland. The location San Francisco was suggesting was more than one hundred miles west of where Thompson was headed.

As soon as the sun was down, *Itasca* started trying to contact the plane by voice on 3105. Chief Radioman Bellarts made the calls, asking Earhart to reply with four long dashes and her bearing north or south of Howland. There was no response. Howland heard *Itasca*'s calls, and from time to time both stations heard weak carriers on or near 3105. On one occasion, Bellarts could hear what he recognized as voice radio traffic from commercial aircraft on the U.S. West Coast, but there was nothing that sounded like it might be from the Earhart plane.[6]

Having reached the target area, Commander Thompson ordered the ship's speed reduced. Lookouts scanned the darkening ocean, while searchlights flashed on and off in the hope of attracting a response from the floating fliers.[7] SS *Moorby* and USS *Swan* also arrived in the general area and started searching, but none of the ships were within sight of the others.

At eight o'clock in the evening *Itasca* received yet another clarification from San Francisco Division: "Information just received from Lockheed Aircraft Company states positively Earhart plane's radio transmitter could not, repeat not, operate if plane was in water." Commander Thompson clung to his theory. "Dashes as received here obviously from different set. Reports indicate messages received a little above 3105 kcs. Earhart set [on] night of flight was right on 3105." The cutter's commanding officer was arguing that the signals *Itasca* had been hearing must be coming from Earhart's mythical "emergency set."[8]

He soon had reason to believe that vindication was imminent. Just before nine o'clock, two lookouts and the officer of the deck saw a "distinct flare" arc up into the night sky on a bearing of 75 degrees. Bellarts sent a voice message on 3105: "Earhart from *Itasca*. Did you send up a flare? Send up another for identification." As Commander Thompson wrote in his later report, "A few seconds later another green light appeared bearing 75 degrees (25 witnesses)."[9]

Bellarts made another voice transmission on 3105: "Earhart from *Itasca*. We see your flares and are proceeding toward you." Navy Radio Wailupe overheard Bellarts' transmission and forwarded the word to other commands. Coast Guard Hawaiian Section informed San Francisco Division: "*Itasca* sighted flares and proceeding toward them."[10] Newspaper reporters dogging Division were soon running to the phones.

At "281 north Howland," the drama continued. Minutes after assuring Earhart that help was on the way, Bellarts "heard Strength 3 phone right on 3105 but call [was] so short that no check could be made." He immediately asked, "What station [was] calling *Itasca* on 3105? What phone on 3105? Go ahead again." But there was no reply.[11]

The sky and the airwaves had again gone quiet. *Itasca* steamed at reduced speed across the dark water, sweeping and flashing its searchlights, every available hand lining the rail and the rigging, hoping for some sign of a floating plane or raft. The ship's deck log recorded a temperature of 84°F, a cloudless sky, unrestricted visibility, and a calm sea—a perfect night in the equatorial Pacific, except that what had to be there was not there.

At 9:45 p.m. there was more bad news. Another message from San Francisco Division shot down Thompson's theory about signals being sent from an emergency transmitter: "Plane carried no emergency radio equipment except one spare battery in cabin. Dynamotors all mounted under fuselage and would positively be submerged if plane was in water. In absence of positive identity of signals suggest every effort be made to obtain direction finder bearings having in mind reciprocals from Howland. Roughness in note of plane radio could be caused by vibration and although set [is] crystal controlled [it is] possible [for] some slight deviation due to poor adjustment or fractured crystal."[12]

Moorby had not seen the flares, and Commander Thompson now thought that "it was a mistake and the signals seen were probably heat lightning."[13] At the top of the hour, Bellarts checked in with the operator on Howland. Frank Cipriani had heard *Itasca*'s calls to the plane and also a man's weak voice in apparent reply, but he did not mention it to Bellarts. He did, however, have a comment about the flares: "Say, old man, we saw green flares on the east southeast horizon about 10 P.M. Honolulu Standard Time. . . . Did you see the flares?" Bellarts replied: "We think it was heat lightning."[14]

That pretty well clinched it. If the lights in the sky were visible on Howland, 281 miles away, they certainly were not flares fired from a floating plane or raft. Forty-five minutes later Thompson sent a message to the Hawaiian Section: "Objects sighted were apparently meteors as Howland reported same effect." He later wrote in his report, "The flares were undoubtedly a meteoric shower. The position, appearance and timing gave credence to flares."[15]

Unfortunate timing created another problem. Just one hour passed between the time San Francisco and the press found out that the cutter had sighted flares and the time *Itasca* sent notification that they were only shooting stars, but that was the hour that East Coast newspapers were being put to bed. The news that flares had been sighted arrived in time to make the morning papers. The word that the flares were only meteors did not.

The early edition of the *New York Herald Tribune* for Tuesday, July 6, carried the banner headline: "EARHART FLARES BELIEVED SIGHTED BY CUTTER RACING TO '281 NORTH HOWLAND' IN PACIFIC."[16] The *New York Times* headline was: "EARHART SEARCHERS ARRIVE AT POINT REPORTED GIVEN BY PLANE ON RADIO." The paper reported, "The *Itasca* sent out a radio message to Miss Earhart: 'We see your flares and are coming toward you.'"[17]

Other news outlets quickly picked up the story and jumped to conclusions. At nine o'clock in the morning in Washington, the Coast Guard commandant's office learned that radio news stations were reporting "Amelia Earhart's plane sighted by *Itasca*."[18] In the central Pacific, it was still the wee hours of the morning after an exhausting and crushingly disappointing night. As the ship continued to search the dark and barren sea, the radio room was suddenly deluged with requests. From the *New York Times*: "Commander Brown [*sic*] *Itasca*. . . . Greatly appreciate your wirelessing story Earhart rescue [to] *New York Times*."[19] From the *London Daily Mirror*: "Captain US Coast Guard cutter *Itasca*. . . . Grateful you send us two hundred words on finding Earhart at our expense. . . . Reply prepaid $109.20."[20] From Paramount Pictures: "Commander Coast Guard boat *Itasca*. . . . Advise if movie camera aboard. Anxious secure pictures search [and] rescue [of] Earhart."[21] From NBC: "National Broadcasting Company and KGU respectfully request Earhart telephone statement for national release through RCA Kokohead if and when aboard *Itasca*."[22] From Pathé News: "Desirous getting any movies made Earhart rescue. Please collect any made [of] their docking."[23]

The United Press urged Howard Hanzlick, its correspondent aboard *Itasca*, to be sure to "please effort obtain pictures event rescue."[24] The Associated Press wired its man, James Carey, "Please hold messages [to] twenty-five word maximum [pending] concrete developments. Also get all possible pictures. . . . Will pay crew well pictures Earhart rescue. Advise any obtain."[25]

In Washington, the commandant wanted to know what was going on: "Tropical Radio reports [they are] in communication with *Itasca* and steamer *Moorby*. Press services have been advised by Tropical Radio that Earhart plane located. Advise." Commander Thompson's one-word reply has the feeling of being sent through clenched teeth. "Negative." An hour later he sent a more informative message to Washington: "For Secretary Morgenthau: Searching area [of] reported position [of] Earhart plane since dusk yesterday. Results negative."[26]

Media requests continued to come in, sometimes through official channels. A message from Navy Radio Wailupe read: "Desire statement regarding Earhart search for Columbia Broadcasting System transcontinental broadcast at 08:45 HST KGMB Honolulu." Thompson was tactful but firm: "Regret radio traffic relative search precludes."[27]

As the fifth day of the Earhart search began, Carey tried to clear up the night's confusion in a message to the Associated Press' San Francisco office: "Reports seen flares last P.M. in error. Merely meteors. Howland and *Swan* corroborate seeing same. Must refuel [from] *Colorado* prior further movements. Have taken measures secure photos event rescue. Will advise developments [as] soon [as] possible. Coast Guard, Navy, myself, forward reliable information. Believe none other. Appears information plane afloat 281 north Howland inaccurate. *Moorby* proceeding next port. Carey."[28]

The night was also disappointing in terms of signals that might be from the plane. In marked contrast to the three previous nights, almost no signals were heard on 3105 by stations in the search area or in Hawaii, or by Pan American. The one exception occurred nineteen minutes after Bellarts sent his voice message, "Earhart from *Itasca*. We see your flares and are proceeding toward you." At 9:32 p.m. aboard *Itasca*, he heard a transmission, "Strength 3 right on 3105," that was too short to identify.[29] At that moment, two hams in California—one in Los Angeles and one in Whittier—heard an "intermittent carrier" on 3105.[30] Six minutes later on Howland, Cipriani logged "a man's voice, very weak."[31] At virtually the same moment, two licensed ham operators on Oahu and Maui heard "a rippling carrier right on 3105 kilocycles." According to Navy Radio Wailupe, "One of them goes so far as to say that it sounds like [a] motor generator driven rather than DC."[32] Multiple stations hearing the transmission, with the quality of reception being related to distance from the Phoenix Group, fit the pattern of the signals heard on the previous three nights.

In the United States, there was another flurry of amateur reports, but most were questionable at best. San Francisco Division advised the Hawaiian Section: "[We are] checking reports received at 05:55 PST on 3105 kilocycles, 3 July. Considerable belief in one report which stated woman's voice made four distress calls followed by 'KHAQQ' followed on key by '225 garbled off Howland, battery very weak, can't last long' other garbled indicated 'sand' or 'bank.' Only banks charted are south and east of Howland, however report may have been 225 NNW of Howland. Investigating further."[33]

With the battleship *Colorado* due to arrive in the search area the next day, San Francisco Division decided it would be best if *Itasca* were put under the Navy's control. A message to the commandant's office on Tuesday afternoon read: "Propose to have Hawaiian Section direct *Itasca* to report for duty to Commandant Fourteenth Naval District to assure coordination of effort with increasing force of naval units. Approval requested." San Francisco had a reply within the hour: "Authorized."[34]

It was just past midday aboard *Itasca* when orders arrived for Commander Thompson from the Coast Guard's Hawaiian Section: "Report to Commandant Fourteenth Naval District for assignment."[35] It was an ignominious end to the Coast Guard's leadership of the Earhart search. Clinging doggedly to his initial decision that the plane had come down at sea, Warner Thompson had spent four crucial days and nights scouring the ocean north of Howland despite mounting evidence that the Electra was elsewhere. Believing that the plane had an emergency transmitter, he dealt with the flood of reported distress calls by selecting and interpreting the ones that seemed to fit his theory and rejecting the others.

Thompson orchestrated the three-ship dash to 281 north at a time when San Francisco Division was becoming increasingly convinced that the plane was on land somewhere in the Phoenix Group. Word finally arrived that Earhart could not transmit if afloat just as his northern search was proving futile. The flare incident, although not Thompson's fault, turned the whole affair into a national embarrassment for the Coast Guard.

In his chagrin, Warner Thompson's reaction was to dismiss the possible authenticity of all of the distress calls rather than question his own interpretation of some of them. Although he spent days chasing first Walter McMenamy's "1.6 179" and then Navy Radio Wailupe's "281 North Howland," in his later report he went so far as to deny that he took any of the messages seriously: "The *Itasca* was never convinced that signals were received from Earhart or that the plane was transmitting."[36]

As the 281 north fiasco came to an end, San Francisco Division sent George Putnam's concisely worded summary of the situation to all of the ships and commands involved in the search:

Following from Putnam, "Please note, all radio bearings thus far obtained on Earhart plane approximately intersect in Phoenix Island region southeast of Howland Island. Further, line of position given by Noonan, if based on Howland which apparently [is a] reasonable assumption, also passes through [Phoenix] islands. Believe navigator, after obtaining such line, naturally would follow it to nearest indicated land. Additionally, if message stating position 281 miles north of Howland actually was 'south' instead of north, [the message] also indicates same region. Weather analysis indicates likelihood headwinds aloft [were] much stronger than Noonan reckoned, with probability [that the plane] never got 100 miles from Howland as they thought. Lockheed engineers state positively [that the] plane could not operate its radio unless on shore and no islands apparently exist north of Howland. Therefore, [it is] suggested that planes from *Colorado* investigate Phoenix area as promptly as practicable."[37]

Putnam was repeating what Paul Mantz had been saying for days. Earhart was probably down on one of the islands of the Phoenix Group. Pan Am direction-finding operators were more specific. Buried in the second page of the same July 6 *New York Herald Tribune* article headlined "Earhart Flares Believed Sighted Cutter" was "Pan American radio men estimated the Earhart ship might be in the vicinity of Gardner and McKean Islands in the Phoenix Group."

Everyone but Commander Thompson accepted that Earhart was sending distress calls. Pan Am stations in Hawaii, Midway, and Wake and the Coast Guard high-frequency direction finder on Howland had taken bearings on the signals. Admiral Murfin's extended chart showed the bearings crossing in the southwestern part of the Phoenix Group. Lockheed said the airplane must be on land to transmit, and the only land in that part of the ocean was Gardner and McKean Islands. Five days into the search, the answer to the riddle was coming into focus.

28

Colorado

JULY 6–7

Betty Klenck's was the last credible reception with intelligible content on July 5. The tides were getting higher, and shortly after noon, the water level on the reef was high enough to force Earhart to stop transmitting. By high tide at 4:30 p.m. the water was high enough to flood the aft cabin, but it did not reach the transmitter. It was after midnight before the water on the reef receded enough for Earhart to start the engine and resume transmitting.[1] Nobody heard her except Mrs. Crabb in Toronto, who again heard the man and woman: "The first words I actually got were 'San Francisco.' The woman's voice was high-pitched and she sounded as though she were excited. Her voice was pent-up with emotion. Both voices were very muffled and I could not get what they were saying. I am sure I heard billowing waves."[2]

The morning of July 6 brought low tide, but whether Earhart and/or Noonan ventured ashore is unknown. If so, it was for only a few hours. By early afternoon the incoming tide was high enough for the sharks to resume their patrols. High tide was at 5:30 p.m., and it was sunset before the water was low enough for Earhart to start the engine and begin transmitting.

The late-day edition of the *New York Herald Tribune* for Tuesday, July 6, brought the disappointing news: "Earhart Plane Not at '281 North Howland,' Cutter's Dash on Radio Clew Is Fruitless." The paper was openly critical of *Itasca*'s handling of the search: "Although Navy experts doubted that the message, which included the phrase '281 north Howland,' was intended to say that the Earhart plane was 281 miles north of the tiny island, the *Itasca* apparently accepted that interpretation."[3]

Expectations of an early rescue by the Coast Guard had flared and died with the falling meteors, and hopes that Earhart and Noonan would be found alive now rested on the U.S. Navy. For the first time, all of the U.S. government ships participating in the Earhart search were under the direction of a single commander, Rear Adm. Orin G. Murfin, commandant of the Fourteenth Naval District headquartered at Pearl Harbor. *Itasca*, now critically low on fuel, continued to steam at reduced speed far north of Howland, awaiting the arrival of USS *Colorado*, while the seaplane tender USS *Swan* cruised nearby.

In the northern Pacific, the aircraft carrier USS *Lexington* and its escort of three destroyers pounded westward from California. They were scheduled to refuel in Hawaii on Thursday before heading south. It would be the following Monday, July 12, ten days after the plane vanished, before they joined the search. Until then, all eyes were on *Colorado*, and Murfin delegated the prosecution of the search to the battleship's commanding officer, Capt. Wilhelm L. Friedell. In a priority message, he ordered Friedell to "take charge of Naval and Coast Guard units in search area and direct and coordinate Earhart search until arrival Lexington Group who will then be directed to take charge. Keep Commandant Fourteenth Naval District advised of progress. Will keep you advised any pertinent information received."[4]

Friedell replied: "Report[ing] for duty. Plan to fuel *Itasca* 7 July then, by plane, inspect Winslow Reef then each island Phoenix Islands including Carondelet reef."[5] Winslow Reef was reported to be roughly halfway between Baker Island and McKean, the first island of the Phoenix Group; Carondelet was an ocean reef south of Gardner. Friedell's plan was based in part on a message he had received the night before from the Coast Guard's San Francisco Division. "Held consultation this date with persons familiar with navigation methods of Noonan. . . . [I]f short of gas, it was stated, he probably would follow line of position to nearest land."[6]

In a later report, Captain Friedell outlined his reasoning:

The line of position 337°–157° was given in one of the last reports received from the plane. It was also stated in a report that the plane was short of gas.

Considering the question as to what Mr. Noonan did do, it must be considered which way he would turn on the line. To the northwest of Howland was [*sic*] wide stretches of ocean, to the southeast were spots of land. To a seaman in low visibility, the thing to do when in doubt of own position would be to head for the open sea. To the Air navigator with position in doubt and flying a land plane it is apparent that the thing to do would be to steer down the line toward the most probable land. To the Air Navigator, land would be a rescue, just as the sea would be to the seaman. Would and did Mr. Noonan do this or had he other reasons to do otherwise? The answer was, of course, unknown, but logical deduction pointed to the southeast quadrant.[7]

Friedell was correct that Noonan flew southeast on the line to find land, but it appears he was not proceeding to a known alternate destination. He was looking for Howland.

Soon after sunup on Tuesday, July 6, Captain Friedell reported the ship's position to Admiral Murfin and informed him, "Expect begin searching with planes tomorrow, Wednesday, southeast of Howland Island."[8] During the voyage southward, the men of *Colorado* tried to stay abreast of what was happening in the search. Every day, the ship's press yeoman put together a typed sheet of news reports received by the radio room. Copies were distributed around the ship as the *Radio Press News*. The edition for July 6 included a report about *Itasca's* disappointing search of "281 north," but it also carried more encouraging news: "WASHINGTON: The first authenticated reports from the Earhart Noonan plane were picked up at 5:15 EST at Howland Island. The radio distress signals were definitely identified as having come from Amelia Earhart and her navigator Capt. Fred

Noonan. Coast Guard officials in Washington maintained constant communication with the Cutter *Itasca* which is sweeping the waters in the vicinity of Howland Island. The *Itasca* also picked up the distress calls at the same time that the radio receiving station at Howland heard the flashes from Miss Earhart."[9]

Another story referenced the same event: "HONOLULU: The Coast Guard reported at 5:50 A.M. PST, that it had just received a radio message from Amelia Earhart. The Coast Guard said the message was picked up on a portable set at Howland Island. The message was also heard at Baker Island. The message was 'KHAQQ calling *Itasca*.' The Coast Guard said the *Itasca* now has a definite clew to the whereabouts of the missing plane."[10] The news items were somewhat misleading. Although they appeared in the July 6 issue, the events described occurred on the night of July 4–5.

Another article suggested that *Colorado*'s mission to help search for Earhart might be of little consequence:

HONOLULU T. H.: . . . The famous navy airplane carrier *Lexington* was heading at full speed toward the scene of action with 72 aircraft on her decks. She left her base at San Diego for the four thousand mile run to Howland. Her planes can be sent on ahead, however, since they have a flying radius of three thousand miles. The battleship *Colorado* which left Honolulu Saturday night for Howland Island also reported that she expects to catapult three planes into the air to help search the area in which the *Itasca* is searching. It has been reported that the *Colorado* is not expected to be of much assistance.[11]

The aircraft aboard *Lexington* actually numbered sixty-three, and the story did not mention the carrier's need to refuel in Hawaii before speeding toward the scene of action. The claim that the biplanes on its deck had a flying radius of three thousand miles was patently ridiculous.

These articles, interesting though they may have been to the crew members and Naval ROTC students aboard *Colorado*, did not merit front-page coverage in the ship's *Radio Press News*. Page one on July 6 was dedicated to news of more immediate interest. The battleship's course would soon take it across the equator. With so many passengers aboard (including a number of college presidents and very important people) who had never before crossed the line, the portents of that event were ominous:

Considerable excitement and enthusiasm was experienced today by the arrival on board of the following dispatch:

From: Neptune Rex, Ruler of Raging Main, on the Equator

To: U.S.S. *Colorado*

Captain Friedell; I have learned from good authority that your ship is heading for my domain with a cargo of eminent passengers. I am gratified to learn of their presence on board the *Colorado* and request that you advise if they are all loyal Shellbacks or if you have aboard some Pollywogs, in order that a proper and fitting reception may be given them upon their arrival in my domain upon the Equator.

The commanding Officer, Capt. W. L. Friedell, U.S. Navy, replied:

> From: U.S.S. *Colorado*
>
> To: Neptune Rex, Ruler of Raging Main, on the Equator
>
> I have your message and permission is requested to enter the eminent domain of Neptunus Rex of the Raging Main. It is regretted that there are on board the *Colorado* a large number of Pollywogs consisting of President Sieg, President Brittain, Dean Derleth, Dr. Bell, Commander Beary, members of ROTC units of the University of California and Washington, and members of the crew; but with the able assistance of the trusty Shellbacks as directed by your loyal subjects, I feel sure that they will be properly initiated into the mysteries of the deep; allowed to enter the realms of Neptunus Rex, Ruler of the Raging Main; and will in the future be welcome.
>
> Anticipating another visit with Your Royal Highness, I remain, Captain Friedell.[12]

Radio operators on all of the ships and islands involved in the search continued to listen for Earhart, but July 6 ended in silence. For the first time since the plane disappeared, a full twenty-four hours had passed without a single reception. Then, at 12:25 a.m., Yau Fai Lum on Howland Island heard two long dashes on 3105 kcs with "weak voice in the background." An hour later he again heard a weak voice signal on 3105 kcs.[13]

Yau couldn't make out what the person was saying but, more than seven thousand miles away in St. Stephen, New Brunswick, someone else understood her clearly. Thelma Lovelace heard an anxious woman's voice say, "Can you read me? Can you read me? This is Amelia Earhart. This is Amelia Earhart. Please come in."[14] Like Mabel Larremore and Dana Randolph on the first night, and Betty Klenck on the fourth day, Thelma was not listening for Earhart. She stumbled upon a harmonic of 3105 kcs while trying to tune in a favorite foreign station on the shortwave band of her DeForest Crosley radio. The message Thelma heard was more desperate than those heard by the others: "We have taken in water. My navigator is badly hurt. My navigator is badly hurt. We are in need of medical care and must have help. We can't hold on much longer."[15] As she had in other messages, Earhart sent her latitude and longitude but, as with the others, the information did not survive. Thelma wrote the coordinates on the flyleaf of a book that was later lost.

Mabel Larremore reported her experience to the Amarillo newspaper, but they ignored her. Dana Randolph reported what he heard to the government radio facility in Rock Springs and was taken seriously. Betty Klenck's father was rebuffed by the St. Petersburg Coast Guard station. Thelma Lovelace made her report to the customs and immigration office at the International Bridge in St. Stephen: "The officers almost laughed in my face."[16]

Thelma Lovelace was the last person to hear an intelligible message from Earhart. What happened next can only be surmised from clues discovered later. Just before dawn, four hours after Lovelace heard "We can't hold on much longer," it was high tide on the reef and the water reached its greatest level yet, three feet, enough to flood the transmitter on the floor of the cabin. There would be no more calls for help, and, much worse, the larger swells were now big enough to briefly pick up the aircraft, moving it perilously close to the reef edge.

For Earhart, abandoning the Electra was now imperative. If she had a badly sprained ankle, as suggested in Betty Klenck's transcription, her injury presented a problem. She seems to have swapped her flying shoes for her more comfortable sightseeing shoes, but her swollen foot made it impossible to wear one of them. Crossing the reef on a bare foot was out of the question, so she appears to have appropriated one of Noonan's shoes. By this time he may have been dead, but, if still alive, he was almost certainly in no condition to navigate the slippery, jagged inner reef. In such a circumstance, it would be all Earhart could do to salvage a few essentials, and she would have no choice but to abandon Noonan to his fate. Exactly when she hobbled ashore is impossible to know, but the best opportunity was during low tide at midday.

High tide returned that evening and, as the aircraft was repeatedly picked up and slammed down, at some point the side load was more than the struts could withstand. In a replay of the stresses generated in the ground loop in Hawaii only eighty days before, the landing gear folded, dumping the plane on its belly. Now the surging surf battered the wings and fuselage, driving the crippled wreck across the reef surface with each succeeding wave until it eventually washed over the edge into the pounding surf. Earhart's feelings as she watched from shore can only be imagined.

In the Hawaii accident, one of the main landing gear assemblies tore loose from the aircraft as it slid along the pavement and was left lying on the runway. This time, scraping along the surface of the reef had the same effect with the same result. The separated landing gear jammed in a reef crevice, where it would be unwittingly photographed months later.[17]

Photo 29. USS *Colorado* (BB 45) with its three catapult-launched float planes, July 7, 1937. Photographed from USCGC *Itasca*.
Photo by Associated Press reporter James Carey (used with permission)

Four hundred miles to the north, *Itasca* eased alongside *Colorado* to take on fuel oil and provisions. The transfer was completed in just under four hours, and by eleven o'clock the battleship was steaming southward again. Early in the afternoon she crossed the line into the southern hemisphere. The hazing of first-timers was an honored tradition, but King Neptune would have to wait. Back home, expectations were high. The *New York Times* headlines reported: "Earhart Search Shifting to Southeast of Howland after Fifth Fruitless Day. . . . *Colorado* Is Heading for Winslow Bank, 175 Miles South of Isle . . . to Release Planes Today. . . . Belief Grows That Flier and Her Navigator Are on an Island or Coral Reef."[18]

At 2:30 p.m. the battleship's three aircraft were launched to inspect the charted position of a "Reef and Sand Bank north of Winslow Reef."[19] The planes were Vought O3U-3 Corsairs, floatplanes capable of landing only on water. They were carried on the deck and placed on gunpowder catapults—one on the fantail and two on top of a gun turret—by means of a large crane. The ship maneuvered so that the catapults could be swung into the wind for the planes to be fired down a rail and into the air. Recovering the planes was more involved. When the pilots returned from their mission, the ship steered a sharp turning course that created a stretch of relatively calm water on the inside of the turn. Each pilot landed and gunned his engine, bounding across the sea to catch up with a net, known as a "sled," being towed by the ship. Once on the sled, the pilot reduced power so that a hook on the underside of the plane's central float caught the net. With the plane now being towed via the sled, the ship's crane was swung out. The plane's observer in the rear cockpit climbed up, caught the cable, and attached it to a harness on the top wing. The aircraft was then hoisted aboard. *Colorado*'s deck log records that the recovery procedure could be accomplished in as little as two minutes.[20] Battleships and cruisers carried floatplanes to spot and adjust fire for the ship's guns. Each of *Colorado*'s eight 16-inch guns could put a 2,700-pound projectile on a target more than twenty-two miles away. The planes' mission was to observe the fall of shot and radio corrections back to the ship. The crews received no training in search and rescue.

The mission flown on July 7 went smoothly but failed to achieve its objective. Not only did the pilots and observers not find the lost fliers, they did not even find the place they were supposed to search. The ship's senior aviator, Lt. John O. Lambrecht, wrote up the experience for the weekly newsletter of the Navy's Bureau of Aeronautics: "The exact locations of these reefs are not known and, indeed, there seems to be some doubt as to their existence. Several ships have, at various times, passed over the Latitude and Longitude of Winslow Reef without encountering any 'Rocks and Shoals' and without even seeing signs of anything but plain ocean. And that is exactly what the planes found."[21]

Lieutenant (jg) William Short was more descriptive in the diary of the voyage he was writing as a letter to his father: "We . . . launched the planes about 2:30 and went out to look at the northernmost reef. (We crossed the equator on this hop.) It was a good idea only we couldn't find the damn thing. We had a moderate run out, of about 85 miles, and I'm reasonably certain that our navigation was fair enough because we hit the ship 'on the nose' on our return. In addition, the visibility was excellent with moderate sea and swells. If there was a reef with breakers I don't see how we could have missed it."[22]

It was an inauspicious beginning to *Colorado*'s search for Earhart and Noonan. Lieutenant Short privately expressed his misgivings about the overall mission:

This whole business is certainly a royal pain in the neck—not but what I welcome this opportunity for a cruise down in this part of the world, mind you, but it's the principle of the thing. First place, I can't see it as anything but a publicity stunt. "Flying Laboratory" indeed! Even if she had been successful, what would have been proven thereby except that she was the first woman to fly around the world? As it stands now, she has only demonstrated once more that long flights over water in a land plane are foolishly dangerous. It is my own personal opinion that she should never have been permitted to attempt this flight, or having once started it, more elaborate measures for safeguarding it should have been established.[23]

In Washington, the Chief of Naval Operations was also uncomfortable with the battleship's participation in the search, but for different reasons. *Colorado* had been commandeered in the middle of its annual Naval ROTC training cruise. Not only would the ship's civilian guests be late getting home, but there were also many Naval Reserve officers aboard who, by law, could not be held on active sea duty more than six weeks from the date of embarkation.[24] The battleship had sailed from Seattle on June 15 and so was already halfway through its allotted maximum time. On Wednesday, July 7, the CNO informed Admiral Murfin: "In view *Colorado* schedule, desire release that vessel as soon as practicable. Recommendation requested." Murfin replied: "Expect to release *Colorado* and direct her proceed on previously assigned duties upon arrival *Lexington* Group in search area."[25]

That day, Wednesday, Admiral Murfin assured the gentlemen of the press that the answer to the question on everyone's mind would soon be answered: "Admiral Orin G. Murfin, directing the search, said today it should be known by mid-afternoon Monday whether the round-the-world flier and her navigator are still alive. . . . [T]he aircraft carrier *Lexington* should reach the search area Monday morning. If it used all its planes, it would be able to scout thoroughly 36,000 square miles about the Phoenix Islands in six hours."[26]

All of the evidence pointed toward the Phoenix Group. If the battleship didn't find Earhart and Noonan, the aircraft carrier would.

29

Death Warrant

JULY 8

The *New York Times* did not share Admiral Murfin's confidence. The next morning, Thursday, July 8, under the headline "Warship's Planes Start Search for Miss Earhart; No Definite Signals Heard," the paper told the public, "Weak carrier wave signals, possibly from the radio of Amelia Earhart's missing monoplane, were reported heard again by the Coast Guard just as hope for the safety of the foremost woman flier sank to its lowest point since she disappeared with her navigator in mid-Pacific last Friday."[1]

By that time it had been a full day since the weak carrier was heard, and no one knew of Mrs. Lovelace's simultaneous reception of an intelligible message. The silence was discouraging, but Paul Mantz knew it did not necessarily mean Earhart and Noonan were dead: "Friends of George Palmer Putnam, Miss Earhart's husband, expressed belief there would be grounds for continuing the search another two weeks, even if no further word came from the lost plane. . . . The five feverish nights of radio manifestations so convinced observers of Miss Earhart's safety that they said there would be justification for searching the southern island area over and over. . . . Mr. Putnam reiterated his theory that Miss Earhart was on solid footing somewhere in the Phoenix Islands area."[2]

While *Colorado*'s planes scouted in vain for the elusive reefs, two thousand miles to the north the four ships of the *Lexington* group arrived in Hawaii for refueling before heading south to join the search. The three destroyers proceeded directly to the fueling dock at the Navy base, but the aircraft carrier did not come into the harbor. In earlier radio exchanges with the ship and with the Navy Department in Washington, Admiral Murfin had noted that no *Lexington*-class carrier had ever entered Pearl Harbor and the narrow entrance channel might be hazardous, especially in high winds. On the other hand, he cautioned, fueling the carrier at an anchorage outside the harbor would be "a long process." The Chief of Naval Operations in Washington decided to play it safe. He ordered the ship to refuel in Lahaina Roads off Maui from the oiler USS *Ramapo*.[3]

On the day the Earhart flight disappeared, before sending *Colorado* south, Murfin had called a meeting of senior officers to review the available information and solicit opinions, but it was up to the ship's commanding officer to decide where and how to search. On *Lexington*'s anchoring at

Lahaina six days later, he again convened a conference. Whether *Lexington*'s sixty-three airplanes and escort of three destroyers were to spend six hours or two weeks searching for the lost Electra, there was general agreement that the Phoenix Group was the place to look, but as before, the commanding officer on the scene would call the shots.

On the afternoon of Thursday, July 8, a patrol plane from Fleet Air Base took *Lexington*'s commanding officer, Capt. Leigh Noyes, two officer assistants, and the officer in overall charge of the *Lexington* group, Capt. J. S. Dowell, to Fourteenth Naval District Headquarters, Pearl Harbor.[4] During the conference, "all available information and studies of the weather and probable location of the Earhart plane were made available to the *Lexington* Group."[5] The available information is described in Captain Dowell's six-page report, "Discussion as to the Best Area in Which to Conduct Search,"[6] but much of the data he used to formulate the *Lexington* group's search plan were inaccurate.

Dowell's analysis of Earhart's flight was based on information derived from Commander Thompson's contradictory and often distorted descriptions of Earhart's in-flight radio transmissions. For example, Dowell stated as fact that at "0742 Howland time (1912 GCT) Earhart reported '30 minutes gas remaining, no landfall, position doubtful.'"[7] The cutter's radio log shows that at 0742 *Itasca* time (not Howland time), the radio operator assigned to monitor Earhart heard her say, "We must be on you but cannot see you, but gas is running low. Have been unable reach you by radio. We are flying at 1000 feet."[8] The operator tasked with handling other radio traffic overheard the transmission and logged it as "Earhart on now. Says running out of gas. Only ½ hour left. Can't hear us at all."[9] Over an hour later, the plane was still aloft and transmitting.

Dowell's analysis of the flight was based on a list of "Assumptions." These included: "that [Noonan] was closest to Howland Island at 0758 (based on strength of radio signals received by *Itasca*) and that he may have been on any course at that time; that fifty-seven minutes later the fuel gave out and the plane was forced to land; and that the plane landed shortly after 0855 (on July 2) on the water within 120 miles of Howland Island, actual position unknown, but approximately on a line running through Howland Island in a direction 157–337 [degrees]."[10]

Dowell discussed other scenarios but concluded that only two were possible:

That the plane may have landed well to the north of its intended course. This is substantiated by several radio messages supposed to have been sent out by the plane. One message stated "281 north;" another "225 NNW." Broadcast experiment of KGMB indicated that the plane was north of Howland and on the water. [The KGMB broadcasts established only that someone was responding on Earhart's frequency with the requested dashes.]

That the plane may be well to the south of Howland. This is substantiated by dubious radio bearings supposed to have been taken on the plane two or three days after it landed. . . . The *Colorado*, *Itasca*, and *Swan* are investigating the area to the south and it need not be considered by the Lexington group.[11]

Dowell considered the radio messages suggesting the plane was north of Howland, including the infamous "281 north" message, to be credible. The five radio bearings that placed the plane in the Phoenix Group were somehow "dubious."

Dowell's report estimated how fast, how far, and in what direction a floating plane or rubber boat might drift in eleven days and concluded that the missing fliers "may be anywhere from the position at which the forced landing occurred to a position 528 miles to the leeward."[12] Dowell ended his analysis with: "DECISION: That this force will search the vicinity of Howland Island to a distance of 120 miles, using all available aircraft on the first day. Thereafter, extending the search to the westward up to and including the Gilbert Islands. Then should this search be negative, proceed to the point 290 miles north of Howland and conduct such search as remaining fuel will permit."[13]

Gone was Admiral Murfin's assurance that the aircraft carrier would use all of its planes to search the Phoenix Group. Dowell had embraced debunked falsehoods and taken the islands off the table. It would be up to *Colorado*, under pressure from the CNO to head for home "as soon as practicable," to cover the Phoenix Group. If Earhart and Noonan were still alive on one of the islands where all the genuine evidence pointed, and the battleship's hurried search did not produce immediate results, Dowell's decision would be a death warrant for the stranded fliers.

In the days and nights following Earhart's disappearance, her distress calls provide an intimate glimpse into conditions and emotions in the cockpit of the Electra. That window slammed shut when the plane went over the reef edge into the surf. What little is known, or can be deduced, about Earhart's time as a castaway on Gardner Island derives from historical photos, archival documents, archaeological discoveries, and a thorough firsthand understanding of the island environment.

On July 8, while the aircraft carrier was being refueled and its officers were deciding where to conduct their search, far over the horizon Earhart was coming to grips with her new reality. If the Electra went over the edge into the surf on July 7, as suggested by tidal data, Earhart had passed her first night on the island, perhaps building a fire to keep inquisitive rats and crabs at bay. Earhart had always been a private person. In a wedding day note to her husband she had warned him, "I may have to keep some place where I can go to be myself, now and then."[14] This was probably not the sort of place she had in mind.

With daylight she could see there was no sign of the Electra except a tire and strut far out near the reef edge where it had hung up when the plane went over the edge. The plane and her companion were gone, but rescue was still possible. She knew that some of her distress calls had been heard, and she was sure *Itasca* was trying to find her. Her best hope was for the cutter, or any ship, to appear on the horizon. To increase her chances of being seen, it would be logical for her to gather up driftwood and make piles on the beach that could be set alight to attract attention. She had no way of knowing ships with aircraft were on the way. As far as she knew, hers had been the only aircraft for thousands of miles, so she had no reason to create a message that could be seen from the air.

Throughout the day as *Colorado* steamed southward, the ship's aviators made three separate attempts to locate Winslow Reef or any other associated reefs or sandbanks, and each time they returned frustrated. Lieutenant Lambrecht wrote in his newsletter article: "Anyhow, the Senior Aviator wants to go on record as saying that the mariners (?) who saw and reported these reefs are probably the same ones who are constantly reporting having seen sea serpents!"[15]

As night fell on July 8, *Itasca*, now under orders from *Colorado*'s commanding officer, was crisscrossing the ocean immediately to the south of Howland and Baker islands. Richard Black, who had virtually disappeared from official message traffic from the time Earhart went missing, now reported in to his superiors at the Department of the Interior: "Searching as unit in Navy organization. . . . Hope remains that plane search in Phoenix might be successful; Black."[16]

Aboard *Colorado*, Lieutenant Short, still smarting from the embarrassment of not being able to find Winslow Reef, resumed his letter to his father:

> You can imagine what a nightmare it must be for the Captain in command of one of U.S. Navy's best battleboats charging around in waters where the latest charts and Sailing Directions provide such reliable information. Tomorrow we expect to look over the westernmost islands of the Phoenix Group, McKean I., Gardner I. and Carondelet Reef and possibly Hull I. We at least ought to be able to find the islands—I hope.
>
> The ship crossed the "Line" yesterday (Wednesday) afternoon but due to the search operations, his Majesty, King Neptune Ruler of the Raging Main postponed His arrival on board to greet His loyal subjects and to mete out just punishment to the lowly polywogs, until tomorrow morning. As the schedule calls for an early morning launching for us I will probably miss most of the fun. However, if I can only keep my date with Amelia it will be worth it![17]

At 6:56 a.m. on Friday, July 9, 1937, *Colorado*'s quarterdeck catapult hurled Plane 4–0–4 into a blue Pacific sky of light winds and a few scattered clouds. Senior aviator Lt. John Lambrecht was at the controls in the front cockpit; Seaman 1st Class J. L. Marks was riding as observer in the rear seat. Thirty seconds later, the high catapult launched Plane 4–0–6, flown by Lt. (jg) L. Orin Fox. In the rear cockpit was Radioman 3rd Class Williamson. He could communicate with the ship using Morse code, but the planes could not talk to each other. The pilots signaled to each other using hand gestures. Lieutenant Short's mount, Plane 4–0–5, left the quarterdeck catapult at exactly seven o'clock. Along for the ride as Short's observer was the ship's assistant first lieutenant, Lt. Charles F. Chillingworth.[18]

The three planes joined up in loose formation and set off on a heading calculated to bring them to the charted position of McKean Island, forty-five miles and about half an hour away. Lambrecht later wrote, "M'Kean Island was visited first and when first sighted was about a half point to port, bearing out the statement in Sailing Directions that the island's actual position is somewhat WNW of that shown on the chart. M'Kean did not require more than a perfunctory examination to ascertain that the missing plane had not landed here, and one circle of the island proved that it was uninhabited except for myriads of birds."[19]

The pilots also saw evidence that people had once lived on the island: "Signs of previous habitation remained and the walls of several old buildings apparently of some sort of adobe construction, were still standing."[20] Beginning in 1859 the Phoenix Guano Company began mining the accumulated bird dung in McKean's shallow lagoon as fertilizer. Thirty to forty Hawaiian laborers lived in crude huts made from piled slabs of coral. Working under horrific conditions of heat and filth, the "Kanakas" shoveled guano into bags that were stored until the next ship arrived to transport the valuable phosphate to markets in the United States and Europe. By the turn of the twentieth century, the Pacific guano trade had been abandoned, and McKean once again belonged exclusively to the birds.[21] Lambrecht described a desolate scene:

M'Kean is perfectly flat and no bigger than about one square mile. Its lagoon, like those of several of the smaller islands of the Phoenix Group, is very shallow and almost dry. This island had no vegetation whatsoever. As in all of these atoll formations coral extends out from the shoreline a distance of 100 to 150 yards and then drops precipitously into water many fathoms deep. There is no anchorage off any of these islands. As in the case of the subsequent search of the rest of the Phoenix Islands one circle at fifty feet around M'Kean aroused the birds to such an extent that further inspection had to be made from an altitude of at least 400 feet.[22]

The senior aviator's caution was justified. The wingspan of an adult lesser frigate bird often exceeds seven feet. A midair collision could bring down an O3U-3.

Lambrecht continued, "From M'Kean, the planes proceeded to Gardner Island (sighting the ship to starboard en route) and made an aerial search of this island which proved to be one of the biggest of the group."[23] The run from McKean down to Gardner was sixty miles, or about forty minutes for *Colorado*'s Corsairs. Allowing five minutes for the "perfunctory examination" of McKean, the planes arrived over Gardner at about 8:15 a.m. local time.

30

Signs of Habitation

JULY 9

Earhart may have been finishing a breakfast of water and hardtack biscuits at the *Norwich City* survivor's camp when there was the unmistakable, and equally unbelievable, rumble of aircraft engines overhead. McKean Island had taught the Navy pilots to stay above four hundred feet to avoid bird strikes. The one photograph taken during their search of Gardner was made from an altitude of about 1,500 feet.

Senior Aviator Lambrecht later described what he saw: "Gardner is a typical example of your south sea atoll . . . a narrow circular strip of land (about as wide as Coronado's silver strand) surrounding a large lagoon. Most of this island is covered with tropical vegetation with, here and there, a grove of coconut palms."[1]

The palm trees were no surprise. The limited information the pilots had about the islands of the Phoenix Group was that all of the atolls had active coconut plantations, but it was not true. The 111 coconut palms on Gardner were the last survivors of a failed planting. In 1892 twenty laborers employed by British entrepreneur John T. Arundel planted cocos on the west end of the atoll. Drought defeated the effort, and by 1894 the island was once again uninhabited.[2]

Lieutenant Short described his impression of the atoll in his letter to his father: "Gardner was very different [from McKean]—a ring of land surrounding a lagoon about 2½ miles long by about a mile wide. Almost completely covered with short bushy trees including two small groves of coconut palms."[3] Gardner's lagoon was actually three and a half miles long, and the "short bushy trees" were as much as sixty feet tall. With nothing on the ground of known dimensions to provide a sense of scale, it was difficult for the pilots to accurately assess size and distance. Objects such as people or an airplane would appear much smaller than the searchers expected.

Nonetheless, Lambrecht saw something that made him think someone might be down there: "Here signs of recent habitation were clearly visible but repeated circling and zooming failed to elicit any answering wave from possible inhabitants and it was finally taken for granted that none were there."[4] The most likely reason for the searchers' failure to see Earhart is the island's dense vegetation,

Photo 30. Gardner Island photographed from one of USS *Colorado'*s aircraft, July 9, 1937. Despite the handwritten N, the camera is looking west from the southeast end of the atoll. The tide is high, with heavy surf at the reef edge. Royal New Zealand Air Force Archive and Museum

which makes people on the ground impossible to see unless they are out in the open, and also makes getting to an open area difficult. If Earhart was any distance from the shoreline when the planes arrived, she probably did not make it to the beach before the searchers moved on to inspect another part of the island.

Later asked to elaborate on what he meant by "signs of recent habitation," Lambrecht said they looked like "markers of some kind." He didn't know Gardner had been uninhabited for nearly a half century and there would not have been signs of recent activity. The markers Lambrecht saw might have been piles of driftwood Earhart intended to set on fire should a ship appear.

The shipwreck on the reef was unexpected. Lambrecht saw it as confirmation of the poor reliability of available charts: "At the western end of the island a tramp steamer (of about 4000 tons) bore mute evidence of unlighted and poorly charted 'Rocks and Shoals.' She lay high and almost dry head onto the coral beach with her back broken in two places."[5]

Lieutenant Short's estimate of the ship's size was a little different: "There was the wreck of a fairly large steamer—of about 5000 tons hard up on the beach—her back broken in two places and covered with red rust, but otherwise fairly intact. Apparently it had been there less than ten years."[6] Short's guess was quite good. *Norwich City* was a ship of 5,587 tons and it had gone aground eight years earlier.

To Lambrecht, the lagoon looked like the best place for an emergency landing: "The lagoon at Gardner looked sufficiently deep and certainly large enough so that a seaplane or even an airboat could have landed or taken off in any direction with little if any difficulty. Given a chance, it is believed that Miss Earhart could have landed her plane in this lagoon and swam or waded ashore. In fact, on any of these islands it is not hard to believe that a forced landing could have been accomplished with no more damage than a good barrier crash or a good wetting."[7]

Lambrecht did not know there was a better place to land an Electra at Gardner Island. At low tide the reef is dry or covered by only a thin film of water. At such times, from the air, the island looks like it is surrounded by a giant parking lot. In many places, especially near the ocean's edge, the reef surface is smooth enough to ride a bicycle—or land an airplane. But on the morning of July 9, 1937, the tide was high, and the reef did not look inviting. The photograph of the shoreline taken from one of the search planes shows lines of surf running across the flat to the beach. Heavy breakers all along the reef's seaward edge hid the wreck of the Electra from view if the searchers thought to look for it there.

The planes took up a course for the next objective, and for Earhart the sound of fading engines must have been devastating. Her long-awaited rescuers had come to the right place, but they had not seen her. There was little reason to think they would be back. "From Gardner," Lambrecht reported, "the planes headed southeast for Carondelet Reef, sighting its occasional breakers a good ten miles away. No part of the reef is above water and, although it could be plainly seen from the air, the water over it must have been at least ten to twenty feet in depth. Finding nothing here the planes returned to the ship."[8]

The pilots were at least gratified that their navigational abilities had been vindicated. Lieutenant Short wrote that "we felt right good about finding [Carondelet Reef] at all under all these conditions after a run of 80 miles from Gardner Is. And this confirmed our conviction that Winslow and that other reef either don't exist or are a hell of a long way from their charted positions."[9]

Colorado's log shows that the ship changed course to begin receiving the returning flight at 10:20 a.m.[10] The planes had been gone three hours and twenty minutes and had covered 272 nautical miles at their cruising speed of ninety knots.[11] They thus spent a total of no more than twenty minutes over each of their three objectives. A reasonable estimate might be five minutes at McKean, ten minutes at Gardner, and five at Carondelet Reef. There was never a thought of putting a search party ashore. This was a rescue mission, and there were six more islands to search. Earhart and Noonan might be near death on the next island.

Upon being hoisted aboard, Lieutenant Short found that "all the pollywogs were converted to shellbacks this morning and now they are all going around sitting down as little as possible and that very gingerly. I can well sympathize with them as this constant exposure to a parachute for three hours at a clip has much the same effect."[12] Short's bottom would have little time to recover; the pilots were scheduled for another search mission after lunch.

At noon, the United Press correspondent aboard *Colorado* sent the disappointing word about the morning flight to his company's Honolulu office: "Planes unsuccessfully search Mclean [sic] Gardner [and] Carondelet and water between this morning, dropping low over islands [to] insure thoroughness. Unceasing search [of] radio waves continues. [Planes will] scout Hull [and] Sidney this afternoon, then upswing [for] rendezvous [with] Swan [at] Canton Island [on] Saturday [to] obtain plane gas. KGU [and] KGMB broadcast excellent signal."[13]

Admiral Murfin's reaction to the news was to affirm his exit strategy in a message to Captain Dowell, the commander of the *Lexington* group: "I intend to abandon the search when the area discussed in our conference has been searched if Earhart and Noonan have not been located by that time or in case something unexpected happens."[14]

The admiral was concerned that Dowell not bite off more than he could chew: "Referring to our conference about [the] area for systematic scouting, please bear in mind the likelihood of possible unfavorable weather. Because of this, area should be confined to what can be searched in seven days."[15] Dowell responded: "Extremely advantageous *Colorado* make such coverage Phoenix Islands that same may be eliminated from *Lexington* plans."[16] Captain Friedell aboard *Colorado* was not copied on Dowell's message to Murfin. He was still under the impression *Lexington* would re-search the Phoenix Group if *Colorado*'s search was negative, and he was under orders to conclude operations as soon as practicable due to the six-week restriction on Naval Reserve officers being at sea.

Aboard *Colorado*, Lieutenant Short settled his sore bottom into the cockpit of his airplane and went back to work:

> We catapulted again at 2:00 this afternoon and went out some 90 miles to Hull I. This is very similar to Gardner only it is slightly larger and is inhabited. The population consists of one white man and some 30 or 40 natives who tend the coconut groves—the principal export being copra [dried coconut meat]. Johnny Lambrecht (our Senior Aviator) landed in the lagoon and talked with the white overseer in hopes that he might have heard or seen the plane passing. He had not even heard about the flight in the first place—lucky fellow![17]

The lucky fellow was John William Jones, supervisor of the Burns Philp Company's copra-harvesting operations on Hull and Sydney Islands. As Lambrecht described him:

> He was a man of about medium height, deeply tanned, and dressed as may have been expected, in white duck trousers, white shirt and a straw hat, which he removed to wave at us. His appearance led one to believe that his nationality was German, due, no doubt, to his closely cropped hair and rotund face, but his accent proclaimed him British.
>
> We told him we were searching for a plane which we believed may have been forced down somewhere in the Phoenix Islands, that the plane had left Lae, New Guinea for Howland Island a week past and had not [been] heard of since, and we wondered whether he'd seen or heard of it. He replied that he hadn't and added that he possessed a radio receiver but heard nothing on it. He was ignorant of the flight but evinced quizzical surprise when told it was being made by Amelia Earhart. He then asked where we had come from and was considerably startled when we told him "Honolulu." We hastily explained, however, that our ship was some fifty or sixty miles to the westward, awaiting our return. After informing him that we expected to search the rest of the islands, we took off, rendezvoused with the other planes, and returned to the ship.[18]

Jones had the only known radio in, or anywhere near, the islands of the Phoenix Group. Was he a hoaxer? Was he able to transmit on 3105 kilocycles? Was he the source of the signals heard by

Itasca, Howland, Baker, Tutuila, and Hawaii? Were the bearings by Pan American Airways at Mokapu, Midway, and Wake Island, and by Cipriani on Howland, taken on transmissions sent by Jones? Were Mabel Larremore, Dana Randolph, Betty Klenck, and other amateurs victims of an elaborate hoax perpetrated by the overseer on Hull Island?

No. When Jones told Lambrecht that he had heard nothing on his radio receiver, he was telling the truth. Jones had been without a functioning radio since early June, and a new set was not delivered and installed until the end of August.[19] British colonial officer Eric Bevington later related the circumstances surrounding the loss of Jones' radio:

> The trouble started just before the total solar eclipse of 1937 [June 8]. One day the labour refused to turn out for work. So he told them that unless they turned out to cut copra . . . he would black out the sun at midday. This threat was met with the derision it apparently deserved. The natives did not turn out . . . so Captain Jones repeated his threat. Next day, Tuesday, he would black out the sun at midday.
>
> Tuesday morning came with a bright sun. . . . [A]nd how stupid the "Kaben" (Captain) looked. But as the morning wore on, to their horror and amazement, the Tokelaus noticed that the sun was losing its shape, it was darkening at one side, the whole world was darkening. Terror struck. They watched in utter disbelief; then suddenly one panicked, then all panicked. They rushed to the shack where the Kaben [Jones] was reporting the eclipse on his radio, all tried to get in at once to beg him to restore the sun, and in the melee, vital radio equipment was smashed and the station put out of action.[20]

Aboard *Colorado*, the senior aviator's adventuresome landing quickly became the talk of the ship, and his fellow officers proclaimed that, henceforth, the lagoon at Hull Island should be known as Lambrecht Lagoon.[21]

On Saturday morning, July 10, the battleship's planes continued their inspection of the Phoenix Group with a morning flight to Sydney Island. Lambrecht wrote: "Upon dropping down for an inspection of that island [we] could discover nothing which indicated that the missing flyers had landed there. The lagoon was sufficiently large to warrant a safe landing but several circles of the island disclosed no signs of life and a landing would have been useless."[22]

In relating what he saw on the ground at Sydney, Lambrecht used some of the same language he had used in his description of Gardner: "There were signs of recent habitation and small shacks could be seen among the groves of coconut palms, but repeated zooms failed to arouse any answering wave." At least in this context Lambrecht's "signs of recent of recent habitation" were something other than dwellings, which he mentioned separately. The small shacks on Sydney belonged to eleven of Hull Island's Tokelau laborers, who until recently had been on the island harvesting copra.[23]

According to a press release filed by a correspondent aboard *Colorado*, the pilots also saw "letters scooped in Sidney [*sic*] beach spelling dozens [of] Polynesian words including 'kele, fassau, molei' seen from air, but pilots said life [was] unsighted, discounting [the] possibility [that the words] were messages relating [to the] lost plane."[24] Kele is a common male name in Tokelauan. Fassau, if actually "faasau," is a Samoan female name. Molei is the Polynesianized form of "Murray."[25] Apparently the workers had written their names and the names of wives or girlfriends in the sand. Man-made marks in the beach sand, like piles of driftwood, soon obliterated by wind or waves, might well be taken as signs of recent habitation.

From Sydney Island the planes continued on to inspect Phoenix, Enderbury, and Birnie, small, barren islands that offered no clue to the lost fliers' fate. After lunch, the three Corsairs were launched for a search of Canton Island, the largest and northernmost atoll of the Phoenix Group. Lambrecht wrote, "It held the *Colorado*'s only remaining hopes of finding Miss Earhart and her missing navigator. Search here, however, proved as fruitless as that of the other islands and hopes of locating the unfortunate flyers were virtually abandoned."[26]

The eight islands of the Phoenix Group had been covered in four flights, two on Friday, July 9, and two on Saturday, July 10. Lieutenant Short finished his letter to his father, "Well, our part in the search has been completed and we are headed for the barn."[27]

That evening, Captain Friedell sent a message to Admiral Murfin: "With completion [of] flight this afternoon, all islands Phoenix Group have been located and carefully searched for any sign of Earhart plane or inhabitants with exception Winslow reef and reef and sandbank to the northward. The charted position of these places and for several miles in vicinity was covered twice without locating them."[28] *Colorado*'s search was over. The United Press correspondent aboard the battleship described the mood as "disappointed and search weary."[29]

Colorado's search of Gardner Island, which a week of evidence and analysis had determined was the most likely place, had amounted to about ten minutes. With Friedell's proclamation that the islands of the Phoenix Group had been carefully searched, Dowell had his justification for ignoring them, and Earhart's death warrant was signed.

A few hundred miles to the north, the pilots who were about to take up the torch were not optimistic about their own prospects for success. A representative for International News aboard the aircraft carrier *Lexington* reported that the some of the officers were even offering money on bets that they would find Earhart. There were "no takers" as plans for the search were completed.[30]

31

Lexington

JULY 10

By July 10 Amelia Earhart's Electra had been missing for eight days. The Navy had been in charge of the entire search for four days, and the *Lexington* group's strategy had been in place for two days, when Admiral Murfin decided it would be a good idea to get some basic information about the missing airplane. That morning, he sent a message to his counterpart at the Eleventh Naval District in California asking him to contact the Lockheed Aircraft Company in Burbank for the answers to four questions about the aircraft's capabilities: What was the plane's total fuel capacity? How far could it fly on eleven hundred gallons of gas? What was its economical cruising speed? And what was the maximum distance the plane could fly at an average fuel consumption of fifty-three gallons per hour? He explained that his inquiries were "based on established facts that Earhart plane took off with eleven hundred gallons fuel and remained in air about twenty and three quarter hours."[1]

Murfin based his certainty about the plane's fuel load on a July 5 message sent out by the Coast Guard's San Francisco Division: "Lae verified that Earhart took off with 1100 gallons gas. Estimated flight time 24 to 30 hours."[2] His "established fact" that the Electra remained in the air for only twenty and three-quarter hours was not a fact. It was speculation based on the assumption that the plane ran out of gas about half an hour after the last in-flight radio transmission heard by *Itasca*. The fifty-three-gallon-per-hour figure assumed that the plane burned through eleven hundred gallons of fuel in twenty and three-quarter hours.

Lockheed answered Murfin's questions promptly: "Earhart, to our best belief, in air twenty-four and half hours. Took off with 1100 gallons. Her average cruising speed should have been 150 miles per hour. Her maximum flight should have been about 3600 miles in still air. We figure her average economical fuel consumption at 45 gallons an hour. . . . Base all estimates on fact that plane would average forty-five gallons per hour fuel consumption and approximately 150 miles per hour ground speed still air."[3]

Lockheed's response was inconvenient. Forty-five gallons per hour and twenty-four and a half hours aloft fit well with the idea that the plane might have reached one of the islands in the Phoenix

Group, but the Navy's new search plan was based on the assumption "that the plane landed shortly after 0855 [on July 2] on the water within 120 miles of Howland Island."[4] Like Cdr. Warner Thompson before him, when confronted with information that did not agree with his own opinion, Rear Adm. Orin Murfin simply ignored it. On Sunday morning, July 11, three hours after he received Lockheed's comments, Murfin ordered Captain Dowell to "take charge [of] all units in search area. Search of Phoenix Group area considered completed."[5]

While Admiral Murfin was clinging to his preferred facts, Coast Guard San Francisco Division was coming up with some of its own. That night, in a message to the Coast Guard Hawaiian Section, with copies to Murfin and Dowell, San Francisco reported: "Further investigation this date of radio reports made by amateurs at Los Angeles on night of 3 July confirmed by four separate stations and indicate credibility of receipt of distress call from Earhart plane."[6] This was the fraudulent report by McMenamy and his friends alleging that they had heard Earhart say "179 and what sounded like 1 point 6."[7] Commander Thompson had interpreted the numbers to mean longitude 179°W, latitude 1.6°N, but his search of that area found nothing.[8] San Francisco Division now believed the message was supposed to mean longitude 176°E, latitude 1.6°S.[9] That would put the plane near the islands of the southern Gilberts:

> Conferred with wife of Noonan this date and she states characteristic of Noonan was to turn back when in doubt. This appears reasonable assumption in view of prevailing winds and apparent sufficient fuel for about three hours, computed from actual time in air of slightly over 20 hours to last radio contact, and established fact that fuel consumption was 42 gallons per hour at cruising speed of about 130 knots [150 miles per hour]. Technical advisor for Earhart states plane could operate at slow speed on 30 gallons per hour and positively states that radio could not be used in water. Above indicates possibility plane may be in Gilbert Group.[10]

Aboard *Lexington*, Captain Dowell considered this new information. The plane's performance described in the Coast Guard message—twenty-three hours aloft at forty-two gallons per hour, and possibly longer at reduced speed—was similar to the manufacturer's belief that the Electra had remained in the air for twenty-four and a half hours at forty-five gallons per hour. Nonetheless, Dowell's plan to confine the aerial search to areas of open ocean remained unchanged.

The Navy was not opposed to searching the Gilberts. The previous day, Secretary of State Cordell Hull had sent a "rush" telegram to Joseph Grew, the American ambassador in Tokyo:

> The authorities of the Navy Department and the relatives of Miss Earhart express the opinion that if Miss Earhart's plane was forced down on the ocean it may have drifted, because of the prevailing currents, in the general direction of the Gilbert islands. In view of the urgency of the time element involved, please endeavor to advise the appropriate authorities of the Japanese Government immediately of these facts and state to them that, because of the generous offer of assistance tendered by the Japanese government, and because of the continuing interest which the Japanese government has taken in the search for Miss

Earhart's plane, your government suggests that if any suitable vessels or airplanes of the Japanese Government are located in or near the Gilbert Islands they may be asked to be on the lookout for Miss Earhart's plane. Please telegraph such reply as may be made to you by the Japanese Government.[11]

The request was remarkable. The Gilbert Islands, as the State Department well knew, were not part of the Japanese Mandate. The archipelago was part of the British Empire, administered by the colonial office as part of the Gilbert and Ellice Islands Colony of the Western Pacific High Commission. Without consulting His Majesty's foreign office, Hull was telling Grew to ask the Japanese to send Imperial Navy assets into British territorial waters. The United States was growing increasingly suspicious of Japan's intentions in the Pacific. Hull's query may have been, at least in some respects, a ploy to find out whether the Japanese had warships or airfields in the Marshall Islands a few hundred miles north of the Gilberts. (In fact, construction of the first airfields and seaplane ramps in the Marshalls did not begin until 1940.[12])

A few hours later, Grew replied, "Contents of Department's telegram under reference communicated immediately to senior aide to the Navy Minister who stated that no Japanese aircraft in that area but survey ship *Koshu* has proceeded toward Marshall Islands and should now be there. Japanese radio stations have been ordered to be on continuous watch for Earhart signals and many Japanese fishing craft in and to east of Marshall Islands have been instructed to be on lookout. The senior aide expressed greatest willingness to cooperate. Grew."[13] In 1937 the Japanese were not about to poke the British. They would help look for Earhart, but only in their own back yard.

Shortly after receiving San Francisco's suggestion that the plane might have landed on one of the Gilbert Islands, Captain Dowell ordered *Itasca* to "proceed immediately at most economical speed laying course for Arorai [*sic*] Island, Gilbert Group."[14] The Earhart search had reached another turning point. For the first five days after the flight disappeared, the burden of trying to locate and rescue the missing fliers had fallen entirely on *Itasca*. The cutter's commanding officer, convinced that the plane had come down at sea, had scoured the ocean to the north and west of Howland without success. On July 6 the search entered a second phase with the arrival of the battleship *Colorado* and the transfer of all operational authority to the Navy. Based on general agreement among Coast Guard, Navy, and civilian authorities that legitimate distress calls had been received, the focus of the search shifted to the land areas near where the radio bearings crossed—the reefs and atolls of the Phoenix Group. When *Colorado* declared the islands carefully, but fruitlessly, searched, Admiral Murfin passed operational command to the arriving *Lexington* group and put a seven-day limit on the third and final phase of the search.

With the Phoenix Group eliminated, the consensus about where to search broke into two opposing camps. Admiral Murfin in Hawaii and Captain Dowell aboard *Lexington* returned to Commander Thompson's original belief that the plane had run short of fuel far earlier than expected and had come down at sea not very far from Howland. In California, the people at Lockheed, who had built the airplane and flown with Earhart to develop her long-range fuel management techniques, and Paul Mantz, the technical adviser who sat beside her on the flight to Hawaii, were sure the Navy was wrong. For their part, the Coast Guard's San Francisco Division remained convinced that at least some of the radio distress calls were genuine and that the plane must be on land. If it was not in the Phoenix Group, maybe it was in the Gilberts. The odds that the plane was down and unreported somewhere in the Gilberts were slim. The islands were densely inhabited. Overpopulation was such a problem, in fact, that British authorities were considering expanding the colony into the uninhabited Phoenix Group.

The curtain went up on act three of the Earhart search at dawn on Tuesday, July 13. On reaching a point roughly fifty miles northwest of Howland Island on Earhart's reported line of position, USS *Lexington* turned into the wind. At 6:36 a.m. the first of sixty planes roared down the flight deck and lifted into the Pacific sky. As the squadrons launched and assembled to begin their sweep, 450 miles to the southwest, *Itasca* was just arriving off Arorae to begin its search of the Gilberts.

Lexington's planes made two flights that day, two more the following day, and another two on July 15, working constantly westward into the area where the plane or life raft could conceivably have drifted. The pilots saw nothing of interest except "huge whales."[15]

Itasca and *Swan* made inquiries at several atolls in the southern Gilberts, but no one had any encouraging information. On the afternoon of July 15, as *Itasca* stood off Tarawa Atoll, Commander Thompson reported to Captain Dowell: "Senior District Officer in close contact with this group and Taritari reports negative for plane passage or wreckage. Island[s] all thickly inhabited and communication frequent. Do not believe further investigation this portion of Gilberts necessary and in view fuel situation request permission proceed Howland." Dowell agreed: "Permission granted to proceed Howland. Conserve fuel. Continue reports."[16]

Itasca's long search for Earhart and Noonan was over. That same day, the State Department sent an after-the-fact wire to the American embassy in London: "Developments of the search have led to the dispatch of the Coast Guard cutter *Itasca* and the Navy minesweeper [*sic*] *Swan* to the Gilbert Islands to make a careful search of the uninhabited islands and to establish contact with residents

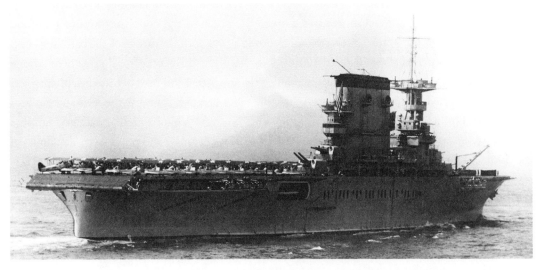

Photo 31. USS *Lexington* (CV 4) with six squadrons aboard: VT-2, VS-2, VS-3, VS-41, VS-42, and VB-4

National Archives and Records Administration

of inhabited islands. Inquire whether this action has the approval of the British government."[17] The British government granted permission two days later.[18]

Swan still had two more islands to visit in the southern Gilberts, but what hope remained for finding the lost fliers rested primarily on *Lexington's* ocean search. Based on their calculations of the effect of wind and currents on a floating plane or raft, Dowell's team made a prediction to the International News Service correspondent aboard the carrier: "'We will find Amelia tomorrow' [is the] belief [of] strategists on Lexington as planes returned [from] third unsuccessful day."[19]

That night, Admiral Murfin and Captain Dowell learned that George Putnam wanted the Navy to shift its search to an entirely new area. A message from the Coast Guard's San Francisco Division read: "For reasons which apparently possess plausibility, Putnam requests, if possible, you arrange immediate plane reconnaissance vicinity 170 degrees East longitude and about 9 minutes North latitude for drifting plane. Request [that you] advise results if flight made."[20]

San Francisco did not explain where Putnam got the coordinates or why he considered them plausible. The numbers do not appear in any of the reported radio distress calls, and the position they describe is in open ocean about two hundred miles west of the Gilberts—far beyond the designated search area. Murfin and Dowell ignored Putnam's request.

At dawn the next morning, Friday, July 16, *Lexington's* flight deck was a forest of wings and struts as dozens of biplanes were positioned for launch. Clouds of blue smoke whipped aft as forty-two engines coughed to life and the carrier came up to speed. According to the ship's Associated Press reporter, the pilots rolled up their sleeves and smeared their faces with grease against the tropical sun while laughing at news broadcasts that described their search as futile. "Confidence well based," the reporter agreed. "Success today or tomorrow if Amelia afloat since all data point [to] planes entering 'most probable area.'"[21] A local rain squall drenched the deck as the planes took off, formed up, and began their sweep.

In California, it was early afternoon, and no one had replied to Putnam's plea. San Francisco tried again: "Putnam requests *Itasca* search area if impracticable to use planes."[22]

Itasca was already on its way home via Howland. That evening, with still no response from Murfin or Dowell, George Putnam took his plea to Washington. In a telegram to CNO Adm. William Leahy, he wrote: "Deeply grateful if steps be taken to search area slightly north of intersection of longitude 170 east and equator contemporaneously with search of Gilbert Island[s]. Because [of] peculiar intimate nature [of the] alleged information, this is a confidential personal request to you. Most compelling unusual circumstances dictate, although sole obvious reasonableness lies in westward prevailing drift which might well [have] carried floating plane through Gilberts to designated area. Anyway cannot pass up this bet, forlorn as it may be."[23]

The search for Amelia Earhart had reached a new pinnacle of preposterousness. Since the day the plane went missing, Putnam had been bombarded with advice from clairvoyants and psychics. Not all of the visions were unsolicited. According to the Associated Press, he appealed to Earhart's "girlhood neighbor," the "internationally known psychic" Gene Dennis, for help. She worked with Putnam "in a series of long distance telephone conversations," and he sent her "a pair of Miss Earhart's stockings and a handkerchief of Miss Earhart's navigator, Fred Noonan, to aid her psychic efforts." The same day San Francisco transmitted Putnam's request to Murfin and Dowell, Gene

Dennis offered her reading that Earhart was "alive and safe on a South Seas island. The name 'Gelbert' has come to me." She predicted that "fishing boats or a fishing boat will discover the flyers . . . possibly this weekend."[24] Whether the location Putnam gave the Navy came from Gene Dennis or someone else, it seems apparent that the coordinates were given to him by someone who claimed to have received them from the beyond.

By late morning on July 17, Putnam had received no reply from Washington. The search for Earhart and Noonan was scheduled to end the next day. He sent another telegram to Admiral Leahy: "Appreciate, if possible, confirmation that request contained [in] my dayletter yesterday evening will be acted upon. To you alone I venture to say [that my] conviction they still live is vivid beyond my power to express, for intimate reasons one cannot rationalize or wisely make public. Please believe this is written by one [who is] essentially practical minded."[25]

An hour and a half later there was still no answer. Putnam asked San Francisco to try Murfin and Dowell again: "Following from Putnam 'Request you secure definite confirmation that region requested will be searched, also southern Gilberts, especially Beru and islands adjacent.'" An hour later Murfin responded with bad news: "Regret impracticable search area requested. All Gilbert Islands have been searched."[26]

Nearly five hours later, unaware of Admiral Murfin's reply to San Francisco, Admiral Leahy interceded on Putnam's behalf in a wire to Murfin: "Request that, if practicable before termination of search on eighteen or nineteen July, that search be extended to cover point 170 degrees East longitude and 0 degrees latitude and area slightly to northward of that point. Reply desired." Murfin's response to his superior was tactful but firm: "Search [of area] suggested [in] your despatch this date possible but impracticable. Would require abandoning remainder scheduled search plan and use most economical speed with possibility *Lexington* requiring some fuel at Pearl Harbor before proceeding San Diego. To search the area requested would require four days steaming to accomplish one days search. Will not search this area unless directed to do so by [Navy] Department."[27]

George Putnam had not become a successful businessman by taking no for an answer. He sent another telegram to Admiral Leahy: "Thanks for message and for all your great helpfulness. If humanly possible please have at least one plane examine area, the western edge of which is nine minutes north of equator at intersection of 170 longitude East. My last request, terribly urgent." Leahy tried to explain: "Commandant at Honolulu reports it is impracticable to send *Lexington* to 170 East longitude without abandoning remainder of scheduled search. All possible drift from vicinity anywhere near Howland Island will be covered by plan of present search."[28] Putnam persisted: "Thanks for message. Realize authorities on ground are doing everything possible. My suggestions was not for *Lexington* to proceed to area indicated but that, if possible, a couple of planes give it one quick reconnaissance which forever would put my mind at rest."

There was finality in Leahy's response: "Replying to your telegram. Firmly believe that, allowing for rate of drift, the area between Howland and the point mentioned has been thoroughly searched. Be assured that no possibility has been neglected."[29]

While Putnam pleaded, *Lexington*'s operations proceeded as planned. As the optimistic pilots began their search on July 16, Captain Dowell sent a message to Commander Thompson aboard *Itasca*: "Assuming that Earhart plane or rubber boat still afloat, please submit your estimate as of noon today most probable position first of plane, secondly of rubber boat." Thompson replied as ordered. His estimates of the plane's and rubber boat's present positions agreed with Dowell's calculations.[30] In justifying his estimates, Commander Thompson offered a new version of the events of July 2: "End of flight clear blue sky south and east of Howland. Heavy cloud banks approximately 50 miles north and west of Howland."[31] This was the first time Thompson mentioned the presence of the heavy cloud banks. According to the weather observations recorded in *Itasca's* deck log on July 2, there was "blue sky with detached clouds" throughout most of the day, including when the ship was searching north and west of Howland. The only time the sky was "mainly cloudy" was around one o'clock in the afternoon. At that time the ship was about twenty miles directly north of the island.[32] An observation taken at noon on Howland found cumulus clouds covering half of the sky with bases at 2,650 feet.[33]

Thompson also told Dowell that "*Itasca* had laid heavy smoke screen for two hours which had not disintegrated and clearly visible from south and east for 40 miles or more at altitude 1000."[34] At one thousand feet, in perfect visibility, the horizon is 41.6 statute miles away, but Thompson could not possibly know what could actually be seen from the air that day from forty miles away. According to the cutter's log, *Itasca* began making smoke at 6:14 a.m. There is no notation as to when the ship ceased making smoke, but it is difficult to explain how the procedure could have continued for more than about half an hour without risking severe damage to the ship's power plant.

"Doubtful if visible over 20 miles from north and west," Thompson added.[35] He offered no explanation for his opinion. Throughout the day on July 2, the cutter's deck log recorded the surface visibility at the maximum value, 9 (defined as "prominent objects visible above 20 miles").[36] "Signal strength and line of position would indicate Earhart reckoning correct as for distance, though she probably carried line of position east before circling and afterward probably flew north and south on this line."[37] *Itasca's* radio logs support Thompson's reasoning that Earhart reached a fairly accurate line of position drawn through Howland and then flew north and south along that line, but there is no support in the logs for his supposition that she continued eastward, and the notation about circling is clearly a later overtype of the partially erased word "drifting," which was itself a mishearing of "listening."

Later that evening, Captain Dowell reported the day's results to Admiral Murfin: "*Swan* searched Taputeuea [Tabiteuea] and Onutt [Onatoa] thus completing search of Gilbert[s] by surface craft. Results [of] aircraft search today negative."[38] The previous day's brave predictions of success now sounded like whistling past the graveyard. Looking for some good news to report, Dowell told Murfin about Commander Thompson's agreement with the *Lexington* group's calculations: "*Itasca* was asked by despatch at 0910 today to submit estimate [of] most probable position as of noon today, Friday—firstly [for] Earhart plane and secondly [for] Earhart rubber boat. Reply received gave area bounded by lines between following four points, 2° North, 179°30′ East; 5° North, 178°15′ East; 5° North, 175°45′ East; 2° North, 177° East. Consider this a very interesting coincidence since no previous communication with *Itasca* in this regard."[39] The coincidence was hardly remarkable. Starting from the same assumption about where the plane came down, both Dowell and Thompson had observed the same winds and currents and come up with similar projections.

The next morning, Saturday, July 17, Admiral Murfin advised the Chief of Naval Operations: "*Lexington* Group ordered discontinue search evening [of] 18th if flying conditions practicable [on] 17th and 18th. Otherwise discontinue evening [of] 19th."[40]

Aboard the aircraft carrier, flight operations got under way at dawn. Forty-one aircraft were launched, but two aborted. The remaining thirty-nine saw nothing but the blue Pacific and returned shortly after ten o'clock. During landing operations, one of the planes missed the arresting gear, hit the barrier, and ended up against one of the gun turrets. No one was injured, but the aircraft suffered major damage. The search planes were again sent out after lunch. By five o'clock, all were back aboard without incident, and without finding any sign of the lost fliers. This flight completed the coverage of the designated search area.

Flight operations on the next day were dedicated to "cleaning up rain holes" (areas previously skipped due to local squalls).[41] As the afternoon flight came up over the carrier to begin landing operations, Captain Dowell sent a message to Admiral Murfin: "Search today, Sunday, completed as scheduled."[42] At 4:58 p.m. on July 18, 1937, the last plane of the last squadron caught the wire and lurched to a stop. The Navy's search for Amelia Earhart and Fred Noonan was over. In Hawaii, Murfin passed the news to Admiral Leahy in Washington: "All search for Earhart terminated."[43]

32
Last Days

JULY 10–UNKNOWN

Gardner Island has changed little since 1937. The reef at the northwest end of the atoll near the shipwreck was ideal for landing, but from a survival perspective, the land area there was inhospitable. The beach was not sand but rough coral rubble, so sea turtles did not come ashore to lay their eggs. Inland, the handful of coconut palms provided no sustenance. Old nuts on the ground were impossible to open, and green nuts high in the trees might as well be on the moon. The towering buka trees provided shade but, sheltered from the prevailing easterly trade winds, the forest was dank and reeked of bird dung from the thousands of sooty terns and brown noddys nesting in the branches. Accessing the reef to look for fish trapped in tidal pools at low tide meant scrambling through dense beachfront vegetation. The lagoon was a source of giant clams the size of footballs, but the closest lagoon shore was more than half a mile away through the forest or over a mile via the beach. With the airplane gone, the only factor influencing Earhart to remain at the northwest end was the cache of water and provisions at the *Norwich City* survivors' camp, which, at some point, would be exhausted.

That she decamped from the northwest end and eventually settled at a more advantageous site near the southeast end of the atoll's northern arm where she ultimately died is beyond question.[1] How long it took her to find that spot and whether she tried other campsites on the way are unknown. The merits of the site she chose are many. The land is only one-tenth of a mile from ocean to lagoon. The ocean beach is sand and is frequented by sea turtles in season. Red-tailed tropic birds and red-footed boobys nest on the ground in the beachfront vegetation. There are no hills on the coral atolls, but there is a low ridge running through the middle of the site that catches the constant easterly wind. In 1937 the area was open kanawa forest, a hardwood tree suitable for climbing to watch for ships.

For Earhart, drinking water would be the primary concern, but a nearby buka forest appears to have provided an answer. The trees' large leaves fall and lay on the ground, in many cases concave side up, and the exposed roots often have large hollows that create natural catchments for rainwater. Archaeological evidence suggests Earhart collected water from the leaves and root bowls after a squall, using a small bottle made by Owens-Illinois in 1933 that once contained Campana Italian Balm, a popular skin lotion made in Batavia, Illinois.

Earhart also used giant clam shells to collect rainwater. Once the clams had been opened and the contents eaten, she laid out the empty shells concave side up. The collected water was then put in two vessels, a three-ounce green bottle made by Owens-Illinois that originally contained St. Joseph N and B (Nerve and Bone) Family Liniment, and a twelve-ounce amber American export-style beer bottle made in 1936. The bottles stood in a small fire, held upright with a length of heavy copper wire fashioned for that purpose. Once rendered safe by boiling, the water appears to have been transferred for storage into a bottle that once contained Benedictine liqueur.[2]

Bottles were important survival tools, and Earhart had several. How many she brought from the plane and how many, if any, were beachcombed are not known. The skin lotion and liniment were three-ounce "travel-size" bottles and were probably among other personal care items carried in a small bag or case. There were also a Zell Fifth Avenue compact with makeup and mirror and an ointment pot of Dr. Berry's Freckle Ointment. Freckles, considered at the time to be unsightly, tend to darken as the skin tans, a concern during a trip through the tropics. The ointment made freckles fade due to its high mercury content.

The beer and liqueur bottles were likely found objects. Earhart didn't drink alcohol. Noonan, famously, did, but the known weight-consciousness of the departure from Lae argue against him having a stash of booze aboard for the Howland flight. Bottles tossed overboard from ships at sea washed up on islands then, as they do now.

Earhart caught birds and small fish, possibly with spears whose points were the blades from a bone-handled Easy-Open double-bladed jack knife made by the Imperial Cutlery Company of Providence, Rhode Island, found at the site. She removed the blades by bashing the knife apart with a blunt object. The knife may or may not be the same "Bone Handle, double-blade Jack knife" inventoried aboard the Electra after the accident in Hawaii.[3]

Earhart caught an adult sea turtle and appears to have used a sharp fragment of glass from the broken ointment pot to slice meat from one of its limbs. An easy-to-hold piece of broken glass from the freckle cream jar was found with the turtle bone several meters from the other glass fragments, and a sharp edge shows signs of it being used as an expedient cutting tool.[4] There were also the remains of a juvenile sea turtle. Catching a turtle in the ocean or the lagoon would be impossible for a castaway, so Earhart probably killed a female that had come ashore to lay its eggs and caught at least one of the hatchlings.

What clothing Earhart wore is not known, but she didn't need much. Days were hot with temperatures routinely in the ninety-degree range and often over one hundred degrees Fahrenheit. Nights were warm, usually in the eighty-degree range. The occasional squalls would be a welcome relief and brought life-giving rain, but they could also bring a chilling wind and even hail. She had something that had buttons and something with a zipper, a Talon size 06 "Autolok" zipper manufactured in Meadville, Pennsylvania, between 1933 and 1936.[5] Shoe pieces found in 1940 suggest she wore one of her comfortable brown and white sightseeing shoes with a one-piece molded sole and heel[6] and one of Noonan's black oxford-style shoes,[7] but both were in poor condition. The island's coral rubble footing and frequent soaking in salt water are extremely hard on footwear.

It seems safe to say that by the time Earhart established her final camp, she had come to terms with the island wildlife. In the lagoon and surrounding ocean, the sharks are mostly black tip reef sharks averaging five feet in length. More curious than aggressive, they are analogous to feral dogs, not overtly hostile unless stirred into a frenzy. More dangerous bull sharks, pelagic whitetips, and tiger sharks are infrequent visitors.

On land, there is nothing life-threatening to a healthy human. There are no snakes or mosquitoes. The only mammal is the Polynesian rat. The size of a large mouse, they are usually shy but sometimes surprisingly bold and even willing to be hand-fed. At times when the island is stressed due to severe drought, the rats reportedly become extremely aggressive,[8] but rainfall in 1937 was normal.[9]

An abundance of birds, large and small, and two of the larger species, red-footed boobys and lesser frigate birds, made up a significant part of Earhart's diet. Boobys are ground-nesting and easy to catch, so it's not surprising that the bones of at least forty-one red-footed boobys were among the remains of meals she ate. The nineteen lesser frigate birds are more difficult to explain. Frigates nest high in the buka trees and spend little time on the ground, but juveniles are notoriously curious and will hover close behind a person walking along the beach and are known to bop people on the head with their beak. Earhart may have exploited that habit and developed a technique to snag inquisitive birds. However she got them, the birds were not particularly appetizing due to their diet of fish. Neither species is considered edible by Pacific Islanders.[10]

Small fish of a wide variety of species from the reef and lagoon made up a slightly larger portion of Earhart's diet with a total of at least eighty-five individual fish indicated by the 817 bones found among the meal remains. The fish ranged in size from 6 centimeters (2.3 inches) to 62 centimeters (24 inches) in length with an average size of 28.5 centimeters (11 inches). Members of the grouper family were the most common. Many of the bones were burned, suggesting she cooked the fish by tossing them directly onto the coals. Pacific Islanders don't do that. The distribution of the bones suggests she did not eat the heads, which indigenous people consider a delicacy.[11]

And then there were the crabs. Of the five species of crabs on Gardner Island, two would have a significant impact on the life of a castaway. The strawberry hermit is the color suggested by its name and lives in a borrowed shell about the size of a baseball. The scent of food brings them scuttling out of the bush and down out of the trees by the hundreds to swarm over any stationary source of nourishment, whether dead or sleeping. Their pincers, though tiny, are powerful and capable of tearing through human skin.

The island is also home to the coconut or robber crab, the world's largest land crab. Growing to as much as a meter across the back with claws as large as a big man's hands, they can climb a coconut palm, snip off a nut, climb down, and pull the husk off the nut. They grow for as long as they live, up to seventy-five years or more, periodically shedding their shell. Shy and primarily nocturnal, they shelter from the heat of the sun during the day in burrows, often dug under a fallen coconut tree log or in the hollowed-out roots of a buka tree. Their diet consists of coconut, other vegetation, and, like all crabs, carrion. They are known to occasionally carry off body parts of dead animals. Prized by Pacific Islanders as the most delicious of shellfish, their size and appearance are traditionally terrifying to Westerners seeing them for the first time. It is reasonable to expect Earhart saw them not as a food source but as monsters who stalked the night. No coconut crab shell was found among the remains at her meal sites.

How long Earhart survived as a castaway is difficult to estimate. The remains of meals at the site where her partial skeleton was found suggest her presence there for a few weeks, but whether she previously spent time at another undiscovered site or sites is unknown. The adult and juvenile turtle remains found at her final campsite may be an indication she was there until September, when sea turtles come ashore to lay their eggs.

Earhart's manner of death is also unknown but can be narrowed down to a few possibilities. When found in 1940, the Benedictine bottle near her remains was said to contain "fresh water for drinking," which argues against thirst or dehydration being the primary cause. The food she was eating, though high in protein, was low in fat, and she had no access to carbohydrates. Such a diet can lead to protein poisoning, a form of malnutrition causing nausea, fatigue, diarrhea, and ultimately death.[12] Her partial skeleton was found lying under a tree, some of the bones presumably having been carried off by coconut crabs. Whatever the cause, if she became so weak as to be incapacitated, one can only hope she died before the strawberry hermits found her.

Historical documents, archaeological discoveries, and the realities of the island environment make it possible to reconstruct the physical parameters of Amelia Earhart's last days, but in the absence of any surviving diary or journal, her thoughts, regrets, emotions, and reflections on her life can only be imagined. That she appears to have worked out ingenious solutions to many of the challenges presented by the island and survived for a considerable time speak volumes about her character and abilities. Had she employed the same level-headed professionalism she demonstrated as a castaway to the preparations she made for her world flight, there would have been no need for the heroism she displayed with only the birds for an audience.

PART THREE

CHANGING MYSTERY
TO HISTORY

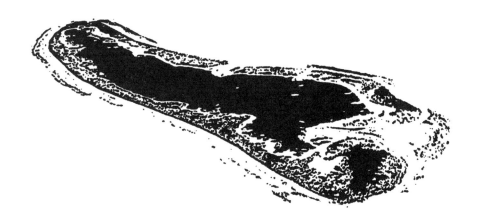

33

Blame the Victim

JULY 18–24, 1937

What the *New York Herald Tribune* called "the greatest rescue expedition in flying history" had failed.[1] The enticing clues, the carefully reasoned theories, and the confident assurances of imminent success had come to naught. No trace of the missing fliers had been found: no silver Lockheed parked on a reef or adrift at sea, no joyful survivors waving from a beach or rubber boat, no debris washed up on an island shore or afloat on the ocean—not so much as an oil slick.

In contrast to the utter dearth of physical evidence was the abundance of electronic clues. For three frantic nights after Earhart and Noonan went missing, professional operators and private citizens reported dozens of radio transmissions reputedly sent from the lost plane. Investigators discovered some reports from amateurs to be hoaxes but judged others to be genuine. Directional bearings taken by Pan American Airways radio installations and the Coast Guard pointed to the southeastern arm of the navigational line Earhart had said she was following. Confirmation from Paul Mantz and Lockheed that the plane carried no emergency radio set and had to be on land to transmit led to the Navy's decision to search the islands and reefs of the Phoenix Group. When *Colorado*'s captain reported the area thoroughly inspected, *Lexington*'s planes searched the open ocean west of Howland, while *Itasca* and *Swan* made inquiries in the Gilberts. Again, the results were negative. Sixteen days after Earhart and Noonan disappeared, the U.S. government abandoned all official efforts to find them.

As the ships steamed homeward, the specter of the radio distress calls hung over the failed search like Banquo's ghost. If even one of the nearly two hundred alleged transmissions from the plane was authentic, Earhart and Noonan had been alive and on land and might even now be standing on some island shore watching the horizon for a rescue that would never come.

As the commanders wrote their reports, each dealt with the body of radio evidence in his own way. Because his ship was released while the search was still under way, *Colorado*'s captain, Wilhelm Friedell, did not have to explain the distress calls. He needed only to show that they had not come from the area he searched.

"Resume Earhart Search by the U.S.S. *Colorado* (in Charge Search Group)" was completed July 13, 1937, as the battleship left the search area for Hawaii, San Francisco, and ultimately its home port, Tacoma, Washington. In the report, Friedell reviewed the rationale for the Phoenix Islands search and offered brief summaries of what the search planes saw at the various islands: "McKean Island showed unmistakable signs of having at one time been inhabited. . . . Carondelet Reef was under water but plainly could be seen from the plane at a distance of 10 miles." At Hull, "A European Resident Manager came out in a canoe to meet the plane."[2]

In describing the overflight of Gardner Island, Friedell mentioned the "four thousand ton tramp steamer," but he also stated that "no dwelling appeared at Gardner or any other signs of inhabitation." As if to reinforce the notion that there was nothing of interest on Gardner, he also wrote, "Sydney was the only island which showed any signs of recent habitation and, in appearance, was much the same as Gardner Island."[3]

Friedell concluded his report with a categorical affirmation that he had accomplished his assigned mission: "As this is written the *Lexington* Group is approaching the Search Area and will be able to conduct an extensive search over a large water area. The *Colorado* has, however, searched the land area within a radius of 450 miles of Howland Island and definitely ascertained that the Earhart Plane is not on land within the region unless on an unknown, uncharted and unsighted reef."[4]

Captain Friedell's confidence was misplaced. In 1937 the techniques and standards of aerial searching were in their infancy. According to present-day civil air patrol probability of detection tables, the chance of *Colorado*'s planes locating the aircraft in the course of a single inspection of an island was on the order of 10 to 20 percent.[5] The odds of spotting people on the ground who were not expecting an aerial search were worse, and seeing an aircraft hidden under the surf infinitesimal.

On July 16, as *Colorado* anchored off the entrance to Pearl Harbor, Lieutenant Lambrecht finished writing "Aircraft Search of Earhart Plane" for the weekly newsletter of the Navy's Bureau of Aeronautics. He subsequently submitted it to his commanding officer, Captain Friedell, who passed it up the chain of command when the ship reached its home port later that month. Lambrecht's description of the search largely agrees with Captain Friedell's version, with one glaring discrepancy. Friedell had said, "No dwelling appeared at Gardner or any other signs of inhabitation." But the man who had been there reported "signs of recent habitation were clearly visible."[6]

How did Friedell get it wrong? If Lambrecht gave his commanding officer written after-action reports following each search flight, they have not survived; nor is there any reference to such reports in the ship's records. It appears likely that the debriefings were verbal. The flight that inspected McKean, Gardner, and Carondelet Reef arrived back aboard the ship just as the pollywog initiation festivities were winding down. Lambrecht might not have mentioned the signs of recent habitation on Gardner, or Friedell might not have taken good notes.

In any event, both accounts of the search appear to have remained aboard *Colorado* until the ship reached the U.S. mainland. If in reviewing Lambrecht's article Friedell noticed that his own report was in error about what the senior aviator had seen on Gardner Island, he apparently did not think it was worth correcting. For Lambrecht's part, junior officers are seldom asked to proofread their commanders' reports, so he probably never had a chance to point out the mistake.

Captain Dowell's "Report on Earhart Search" for the *Lexington* group left the door open to the possibility that distress calls had been sent. His account, dated July 20, 1937, was written aboard

"U.S.S. *Lexington*, Flagship, Enroute Hawaiian Area." In his transmittal memo to Admiral Murfin, Dowell made a point of saying, "An effort has been made to confine the substance of this report to matters of fact rather than opinion."[7]

Dowell began with a ten-page section entitled "Estimate and Decisions" in which he reviewed the reasoning behind his conclusions concerning where the *Lexington* group should search. He took it as fact that at 7:42 a.m. Earhart had said, "One-half hour fuel and no landfall." He was also sure that the plane carried "a two man rubber life boat, life belts, flares, and emergency water and rations." The rubber boat "had a pair of oars and could be kept afloat by patching material and hand pump."[8] No one knew, and to this day no one knows, what emergency equipment was aboard the plane when it left Lae. An Army inventory taken of the Electra in Hawaii after the crash that ended the first attempt to fly to Howland included life preserver vests but not a boat.[9] Dowell acknowledged that the plane's "normal radio power supply was so located that it would not have been used with plane on the water." But he also stated as "known fact" that "the plane was equipped with an orange box kite to be flown as distress signal, and by means of which an emergency antenna might be carried to a moderate height."[10] No such kite was inventoried after the Hawaiian accident.

Despite his promise to confine the substance of his report to matters of fact rather than opinion, Dowell included a sixteen-item list of "Probabilities Arising from Rumor or Reasonable Assumptions." Among these was "that the plane was equipped with an emergency radio set that could be operated from battery power supply,"[11] even though as early as July 5, Paul Mantz had publicly stated the Electra was equipped with no such radio.[12] Dowell concluded that at about nine o'clock in the morning local time on July 2, the plane most probably "landed on the sea to the northwest of Howland Island, within 120 miles of the island." Implied, but unstated, was the possibility that distress calls had been sent from the floating plane or rubber boat, which sank before *Lexington* arrived on the scene.[13] Dowell followed the list of probabilities with a sixteen-page "Narrative of Earhart Search" recounting the daily operations of the ships and planes under his command and ending with the statement, "No sign nor any evidence of the Earhart plane was discovered."[14]

The report continued with four pages of "Aerological Data" describing weather conditions experienced during the search, followed by a nine-page "Report of Earhart Search Operations 3–18 July 1937" by *Lexington*'s commanding officer, Capt. Leigh Noyes. Noyes' report largely echoes the wildly inaccurate facts and baseless assumptions of his superior officer, but, unlike Dowell, he took an aggressive stand on the alleged radio distress calls: "Numerous radio messages were reported to have been received by various agencies, particularly amateur radio operators, which purported to give information received direct from the plane after it landed. Many of these messages were in conflict and many of them were unquestionably false. None could be positively verified. These messages were a serious handicap to the progress of the search, especially before the arrival of the *Lexington* Group."[15]

Captain Noyes ended his narrative with a pat on his own back: "Although unfortunately the fate of the missing flyers remains a mystery, it is considered that the search made was efficient and that the areas covered were the most probable ones, based on the facts and information available."[16]

On July 18 *Itasca* stopped briefly at Howland to pick up Frank Cipriani and the others who had been left on the island when the search began. That day, Warner Thompson received a request from headquarters that he submit "a written report of communications throughout the entire expedition with the Commanding Officer's recommendations for the information of the [San Francisco] Division office."[17] He began assembling the report the next day and finished the 106-page document on July 23, the day before the ship reached Hawaii. He was aware that Treasury Secretary Henry Morgenthau and his family were due to arrive in Honolulu aboard the Matson Line's SS *Lurline* the same day the cutter was scheduled to make port. Although Morgenthau was technically on vacation, the intense interest he had shown in the Earhart search made it likely that he would want a personal briefing from *Itasca*'s commanding officer.[18]

Although Warner Thompson titled the report "Radio Transcripts—Earhart Flight," it was much more than that. He described his intention in the opening paragraph.

> For purposes of clarity, this report will trace the Earhart flight from the communications angle from the time the *Itasca* was first ordered in connection with the flight on 9 June until the *Itasca* was released by Navy on 16 July, 1937. The report is divided into three sections, (a) Before Flight; (b) The Flight; (c) The Search. Comments are made directly as events occur. Summary of opinion is made at the end of each section and at the end of the report. This report has been made "confidential" due to the fact that it contains a large number of personal messages and that further it discusses, frankly, certain matters which might be considered as controversial. This has been done to present an accurate picture of *Itasca*['s] opinion.[19]

Thompson was well aware the Coast Guard might not want to make public what he had to say about Amelia Earhart, and regulations about maintaining the privacy of personal messages gave him an excuse to classify his report "confidential." "Radio Transcripts—Earhart Flight" was a chronological reproduction of 526 official communications sent and received by *Itasca* in the course of its involvement with the flight preparations, the flight from Lae, and the subsequent search. Interspersed among the messages are Thompson's comments, complaints, and explanations. Many of his representations are inaccurate. Twice in the report he asserted that Richard Black was designated by Putnam to be Earhart's representative aboard *Itasca*.[20] Black was not working for Putnam. He was a field representative employed by the Interior Department's Division of Territories and Island Possessions with orders to be the "leader of the expedition and coordinator of government assistance to Earhart flight as regards Howland Island."[21] Prior to the first world flight attempt, Putnam asked Black to be Earhart's press representative at Howland, and Black declined.[22] There is no record of the request being repeated for the second attempt.

Thompson complained about micromanagement during preflight preparations. Referring to an exchange of messages on June 21, 1937, he wrote: "We now have the following persons endeavoring to control the Earhart flight communications, Mr. Putnam; Mrs. Hampton in Washington; San Francisco division and Mr. Black on *Itasca*." He complained about Black's use of the ship's radio facilities: "Black's government messages were burdening a Navy–Coast Guard network with undue traffic which could readily be relieved by Coast Guard–Navy procedure. The commanding officer *Itasca* willingly stood ready to transmit any information Mr. Black deemed necessary to disseminate provided it be done in a Navy—Coast Guard manner."[23]

In one of his comments Thompson correctly identified the problem with Earhart's choice of frequencies in her message to Black on June 26: "It will be noted that the frequencies requested were high frequencies with the exception of *Ontario*. This is contradictory to the last message received from Commander San Francisco Division suggesting 333 and 545 kilocycles. It will also be noted that the requested 7.5 megacycles is beyond the frequency range, that at least to our knowledge, of the plane direction finder. . . . In view of the contradictory matter obtained in Earhart dispatch it was deemed necessary that the *Itasca* handle the situation."[24]

But *Itasca* did not handle the situation. The cutter never sent Earhart a message questioning her choice of frequencies. Referring to himself in the third person, Thompson explained why:

> The *Itasca's* technical opinion as to Earhart's radio desires was never consulted. The Commanding Officer only contacted Earhart once directly by radio as to the arrangements. This was done because the Commanding Officer fore-saw the chance of disaster and desired personal and special precautions on the Earhart departure and final radio plans. "Request you advise this vessel 12 hours prior to your departure from New Guinea full information regarding your desires in matter of radio frequencies and communication schedule. We will conform to any frequencies desired. Important anticipate your departure as communication via Port Darwin very slow."[25]

Thompson's assertion that Earhart never asked for *Itasca's* help in setting her radio protocols was untrue. In her message to *Itasca* on June 26 outlining her desired frequencies, she wrote, "If frequencies mentioned unsuitable night work inform me Lae."[26] Having admitted he knew Earhart's plan wouldn't work and that he "fore-saw the chance for disaster," Thompson, Pilate-like, washed his hands of responsibility and threw the blame on Richard Black: "The Coast Guard had no intention of navigating Earhart to Howland. The high frequency direction finder obtained from the Navy by Mr. Black was set up on Howland and manned by an *Itasca* radioman. This was in accordance with Mr. Black's request. Records show that Earhart was not advised by this vessel of the high-frequency direction finder's existence. Mr. Black states that he did not inform Earhart. This fact is very important as shown in Section (b)."[27] The "excerpts from *Itasca* radio log" he included in the report were embellished with his own additions and interpretations.[28]

Thompson was highly critical of Earhart's conduct. In various parts of the report he noted that:

- Earhart never answered *Itasca* questions and never gave a position.
- Earhart messages lacked any useful information and consisted of generalities.
- Earhart asked *Itasca* to take bearings on her. This was never planned.
- Earhart knew that *Itasca* could give her accurate bearings on 500 and yet never transmitted on 500 in order for *Itasca* to assist her.
- Earhart was on air very briefly and apparently over modulated. The attempts of the radioman on Howland to secure cut failed.[29]

In the picture Warner Thompson painted, his ship's valiant efforts to meet Earhart's unreasonable requests had been defeated by the flier's own incompetence.

In his discussion of the search, Thompson mounted an assault on the notion that radio calls had been sent from the plane after it was down: "Since 10:00 in the morning *Itasca* had been endeavoring to contact the Earhart plane by repeatedly calling the plane as the *Itasca* searched the immediate sector where it thought the plane was down. From this time on the *Itasca's* signal as picked up by other units are steadily reported as possible signals from other sources. A careful check of the *Itasca* radio logs shows that in most cases the signals were originated by *Itasca*."[30]

The statement is patently untrue. *Itasca's* radio logs show that not one of the purported receptions from the plane corresponds with a transmission by the cutter. In fact, *Itasca's* own radio operators logged more unexplained signals on Earhart's frequency—forty-four in all—than any other station.

Over the first several days of the search, information flowed in to *Itasca* about the suspected distress calls received by the Coast Guard Hawaiian Section, Navy Radio Wailupe, Pan American, and various amateurs, but the cutter shared no information about what its own radio operators were hearing. After the search, Thompson did not include the ship's complete radio logs as part of his report. The few excerpts in "Radio Transcripts—Earhart Flight" appear to be the only representations of the logs seen by anyone other than the ship's own officers and radiomen.

Radio logs were routinely "smoothed"—that is, retyped to correct errors, and the messy "raw" logs discarded. Fortunately, in this case, Chief Radioman Bellarts surreptitiously confiscated the invaluable raw logs for July 2, 1937. He kept them when he left the service and gave them to the National Archives before his death in 1974.

Thompson's report does not reveal that on the night of July 4, the radio operator on Howland unequivocally reported that he had recently "heard Earhart call *Itasca*." In the same message, the Howland operator passed along the information that "Baker [Island] heard Earhart plane QSA 4 [strength 4 of 5], R7 [readability 7 of 9] last nite at 8:20 P.M."[31]

Thompson, in fact, specifically denied that such receptions had been reported: "The *Itasca* was never convinced that signals were received from Earhart or that the plane was transmitting. The *Itasca* with two (2) operators, the *Swan*, Howland and Baker were closest to the signals. None of these units heard the apparently faked messages. Samoa, listening on 3105, did not hear them. Throughout, *Itasca* opinion was that if the plane was down some of these units would get the traffic."

Thompson went on to explain why he did not believe the plane was transmitting: "*Itasca* was of the opinion that the traffic would consist of some useful information and not just call signs and dashes. Both Earhart and Noonan could use code. Why should a plane in distress waste time on repeated calls or on making special signals. If the plane was using battery the carrier signals were out of all proportion to the length of time the battery could stand up."[32]

Again, falsehood and unwarranted assumptions reigned. Earhart had advised *Itasca* that neither she nor Noonan could use code, and all of the searchers had been advised that the plane must be on land, in which case it could replenish its battery by running the generator-equipped engine.

At the end of the report, Thompson offered a "Summary of Search" that included:

- Earhart plane went down after 0846, July 2, and apparently sent no distress message.
- Amateurs reported several messages, all probably criminally false.
- Pan American, Howland, and others took bearings on a carrier [wave signal] some place in the Pacific.

- *Itasca* signals calling Earhart, the March of Time program, and other signals were interpreted as from Earhart.
- If Earhart was down and sending messages, the guards maintained by *Itasca*, *Swan*, Samoa, Howland, *Colorado*, Baker, Plane 62c [the PBY], Wailupe, Pan American, San Francisco Radio, Honolulu Coast Guard Radio, and British stations in the Gilbert Islands should have intercepted legitimate Earhart traffic, whereas the only interceptions were by amateurs, with the exception of one Wailupe interception.
- All available land areas were searched; therefore Earhart plane was not on land. Was not in Gilberts.
- Extremely doubtful that Earhart ever sent signals after 0846, 2 July.
- Reports causing diversion of searching vessels should be, and were, carefully investigated. Once the searching vessel receives such a report it is required by public clamor to investigate.
- *Itasca*'s original estimate after three (3) weeks of search problem still appears correct, that plane went down to northwest of Howland.[33]

A more complete catalog of distortion and outright falsehood is difficult to imagine. As a hedge, Thompson also presented a disclaimer:

- The *Itasca* has been so close to the matter of the flight and search that it may be that this report lacks proper perspective and proportion.
- The failure of Earhart to reach Howland and the failure of the search efforts to find her was felt by every officer and man on the *Itasca*. The ship's company fully appreciates the responsibility of the ship to the Service and the public.
- In the course of time, opinions on the Earhart flight and its communications will definitely be formulated. Many of our opinions would probably be changed if Miss Earhart were able to give her side of the picture. It is with this in mind that the foregoing report has been frankly written and it is considered that on this date (July 23) it represents *Itasca*'s thought.[34]

Commander Thompson closed "Radio Transcripts—Earhart Flight" with a series of recommendations. Most of his suggestions concerned the need for better planning and preparation for Coast Guard support of future flights. Thompson expressed his opinion "that viewed from the fact that Miss Earhart's flight was largely dependent upon radio communication, her attitude towards arrangements was most casual to say the least." He also recommended "that immediate action be taken looking toward the suppression of amateur radio stations who repeatedly, upon occasions of this kind, spread rumors and originate false messages."[35]

At 11:10 a.m. on Saturday, July 24, *Itasca* moored at pier twenty-seven in Honolulu.[36] Commander Thompson met with Morgenthau and, given the tone of his recently completed report, gave the secretary an earful about Amelia Earhart's failings while, 2,500 miles away, she passed her fortieth birthday as a castaway on Gardner Island.

34

Cover-Up

JULY 20, 1937–JUNE 4, 1940

While Navy and Coast Guard officers made their case that all had been done that could be done, George Putnam was still trying to find his wife. On July 20 President Roosevelt's personal secretary, Marvin McIntyre, wrote the president a memo saying: "Gene Vidal has been in very close touch with the Earhart story, talking several times a day with her husband, Mr. Putnam. He has some very interesting sidelights and some speculations, which are probably true, as to what happened. You might find it interesting to spend 15 minutes with him." Roosevelt jotted a response on the bottom of the note, "Mac—I would like to see him for 5 or 10 minutes."[1]

Putnam was still convinced that the plane had reached an island. On July 23 he sent a telegram to the Secretary of the Navy: "Please accept my gratitude for Navies [*sic*] generous and efficient conduct of Amelia Earhart search. Respectfully request your good offices in obtaining cooperation of British and Japanese in continuing search, especially regarding Ellice, Gilbert and Marshall Island, Ocean Island and area north east of same. Also, if possible, request some examination of island northerly and north westerly of Pago Pago. Seek leave nothing undone. Looking toward securing information. What ever it may be possible to do will be sincerely appreciated."[2] The area northeast of Ocean Island was the mysteriously inspired location he had so desperately urged the Navy to search in the earlier series of telegrams to Admiral Leahy. The islands north of Pago Pago were the Tokelaus, far beyond the plane's expected range. Putnam was truly seeking to leave nothing undone.

The next day the Secretary of the Navy replied: "Navy Department has been informed that British and Japanese have given assurance their shipping operating in area concerned will maintain particular lookout for lost plane and fliers."[3] Merely keeping an eye out was not what Putnam had in mind.

The meeting between President Roosevelt and Gene Vidal took place on Friday, July 30. Vidal conveyed Putnam's strong belief that, despite the negative results of the inquiries by *Itasca* and *Swan* in the Gilberts, the plane may have landed there. Putnam wanted the State Department to ask the British to conduct a real search of the islands, and he was willing to back up his request with a reward. Roosevelt apparently agreed to the plan, because that same evening the secretary of state sent a message to Joseph Kennedy, the American ambassador in London:

Evidence, which to many sources seems positive, indicates that Amelia Earhart (Mrs. Putnam) was on land the two nights following her disappearance. In the circumstances, we should appreciate your getting in touch with the Colonial Office or other appropriate authority and telling them: (1) That if the authorities could send a boat from the Gilbert Islands to continue a thorough surface search in those islands, Mr. Putnam would be glad to defray the expenses involved, and (2) That word might be circulated that there is a reward of $2,000 offered for any evidence leading to a solution of her disappearance whether in the nature of wreckage or more positive indication of what happened.[4]

The next day Putnam wrote to thank McIntyre for the "friendly personal cooperation which you have extended all along in our present troubles." He also asked, "Is there any way of ascertaining what the Japanese are actually doing—especially as regards a real search of the eastern fringe of the Marshall Islands? That is one of the most fruitful possible locations for wreckage."[5]

On Sunday, Putnam had another favor to ask of the State Department. In a telegram to Sumner Welles, his principal contact at State, Earhart's husband wrote,

Supplementing action taken Friday following Gene Vidal conference requesting local British authorities Gilbert Island cooperation, now urgently request specific immediate search at my expense, if appropriate, [of] following position; 174°10' East longitude, 2°36' North latitude. This is only 85 miles from Tarawa. On making island, bearing thence 106° True. Have apparently authentic information from former commander copra vessel substantiated by reliable American that [an] uncharted reef exists [at] that point which [is] frequently visited for turtle eggs, etc., by older Gilbertese natives. Believe Captain I. Handley of Tarawa know[s] about it. Confidentially, this information astonishingly corroborates the position actually repeatedly given [to] me during [the] last ten days from other sources probably disclosed by Vidal which, [in] themselves, [are] interesting in their independent unanimity, if not necessarily convincing because of their nature. Grateful for word on outcome.[6]

In his desperation, Putnam was listening to psychics again. According to an article published in *Popular Aviation* two years later, Putnam had that morning received a telegram from Hamilton, Ontario, saying: "Amelia Earhart alive on coral shoal on one of Gilbert Islands, latitude 2 above equator 174 longitude. This messaged [*sic*] received by Mr. L____ New York Medium."[7]

After much back-and-forthing among Putnam, the State Department, and the British, Captain Handley eventually checked out the position of the supposed uncharted reef. On August 31 Putnam received a telegram with news of the result: "I regret to inform you that Foreign Office, London advises us that High Commissioner at Suva has telegraphed that Captain Handley has returned from the position you specified without finding any trace of reef or plane. Cordell Hull, Secretary of State."[8]

While Putnam grasped at straws, at the Coast Guard's San Francisco Division, Commander Thompson's scathing "Radio Transcripts—Earhart Flight" was causing second thoughts about the authenticity of the radio distress calls. On July 26 an Associated Press article in the *New York Times* quoted the division communications officer as saying that "aviators in the Eastern States probably were the senders of radio signals which were reported as possible distress calls from Amelia Earhart."[9]

If San Francisco Division now agreed with *Itasca*'s captain that none of the distress calls were legitimate, Pan American Airways felt otherwise. On August 26 the airline drafted a "Proposed Joint Rescue Procedure for Use in Aircraft Distress Cases in Vicinity of Honolulu" and sent it to the Coast Guard commandant's office in Washington. J. F. Farley, the Coast Guard's chief communications officer, studied the document, no copy of which seems to have survived. In a December 14, 1937, memorandum to the commandant, he wrote that while "some of the general or introductory statements contained on the first six pages of this report might be subject to controversy . . . this proposed communications plan appears to be based on sound practice and to be entirely practicable and, in general, is approved."[10]

As 1937 drew to a close, a new search for the missing fliers was taking shape, this time as a private venture. On December 23 the state of California recognized the "Amelia Earhart Foundation, a non-profit corporation." One of the organization's primary purposes was "to conduct an expedition to clear up the mystery surrounding the disappearance of Amelia Earhart, the lost aviatrix, and Frederick J. Noonan, her navigator, and to establish beyond a doubt whether or not they are still alive." The foundation had George Putnam's support and encouragement, but the board of directors was made up of Earhart's friends and business associates: Nellie G. Donohoe, G. Earle Whitten, Kenneth C. Gillis, James A. Maharry, and E. H. Dimity.[11]

In the foundation's charter, the organizers clearly articulated their reasons for continuing the search.

- At the time Miss Earhart's plane disappeared, the Navy Department came forward and offered its services and ships to conduct a search. It is well known that the Navy and Coast Guard made as thorough a search as was humanly possible under the hurried and unfavorable conditions prevailing at the time.

- In view of the well known aeronautical skill of Amelia Earhart and the navigating ability of Captain Frederick J. Noonan, it would seem more than reasonable that, after they had passed over numerous islands, fighting a head wind, with their gasoline supply low, they attempted to retrace their path. In this case, they may well have landed on one of the many islands they had previously sighted.

- From time to time, various amateur radio operators picked up messages, some of which were thought to be authentic. Although messages indicated that the fliers were down on land, they were so garbled that no definite information could be gleaned as to their whereabouts. A careful and lengthy analysis of messages and data obtained during and since the search, together with checking of American and British charts of the Pacific waters, has led the investigators to believe that some of the messages were authentic and that it is more than possible that the fliers came down on land. This belief has been further strengthened through checking information collected with a number of the oldest and best known Pacific Ship masters. A number of these, who have spent many years of their lives in sail and power in these Pacific island waters, believe a strong possibility exists that Miss Earhart and her navigator landed safely on some small island and may be still alive and awaiting rescue. One of them states: "I am firmly convinced that there is far more than an even chance of Miss Earhart and her navigator having landed on one of the hundreds of islands in that area, where any kind of a ship might not touch for a year or many years."

• In addition, there are instances where persons have been marooned on islands in this vicinity and have been able to sustain life for various lengthy periods.

To raise the money needed for the proposed expedition, the foundation formed a National Sponsor's Committee. Eleanor Roosevelt agreed to act as honorary chairman, and the list of committee members soon boasted names such as Mrs. Juan T. Trippe, wife of the founder of Pan American Airways; Earhart's old friend Louise Thaden, often described as America's second most famous female flier; Judge Florence E. Allen, the first woman ever appointed to a federal circuit court; and a virtual who's who of New York society. [12]

On January 6, 1938, the Coast Guard commandant formally approved Pan American's "Proposed Joint Rescue Procedure" and sent the plan to Capt. Stanley Parker, commander of the San Francisco Division. The commandant authorized Parker, at his discretion, to have the Hawaiian Section confer with Pan Am, the Navy, and the other organizations involved with a view toward adopting the plan.

Farley had been right about some statements in the Pan Am report being controversial. Stanley Parker was not happy. He waited until March 22 before sending the proposed plan to the commander of the Hawaiian Section. In his four-page transmittal memo he strenuously objected to Pan American's characterization of the events and circumstances surrounding the Earhart flight:

> The matters stated in paragraph 6 [of the Pan Am paper] are entirely in error. The statement that "The U.S. Coast Guard was officially charged with the safeguarding of the flight" had no basis in fact. The Coast Guard was not ordered or designated to safeguard the flight. Messrs. Miller and Black of the Department of the Interior had more information on the flight and were representing Mr. Putnam aboard the *Itasca*. The *Itasca* was ordered to Howland Island for the purpose of acting as a radio homing beacon and plane guard at Howland. [13]

Parker's objection was essentially correct in that Commander Thompson's orders had been "to act as Earhart plane guard at Howland and furnish weather." [14] But Black was not representing Putnam, and Miller was not even there: "It was very evident after the flight started that the entire flight was badly managed, and that Mr. Putnam, at San Francisco, was not aware of all facts, and that the information which he furnished was often at variance with that received from Miss Earhart." [15] Again, the record supports Parker's complaint: "Miss Earhart was specifically warned by the San Francisco Division against attempting to use the high frequencies for direction finding purposes." [16]

Parker was mistaken. No such warning appears in any of the messages sent to Earhart. The statement in paragraph 8, last sentence, is at absolute variance with the facts, and no basis exists for such a statement. Neither the Navy nor the Coast Guard was expected to arrange a search for the plane. There was no lack of coordination between any of the military forces. [17]

Parker's assertion that the Coast Guard was not expected to arrange a search is difficult to reconcile with his statement that *Itasca* was there as "plane guard." Then, and now, the job of a ship on plane guard duty is to go to the aid of aircraft forced to ditch in the ocean.

The commanding officer of San Francisco Division also vehemently rejected Pan American's premise that some of the distress calls had come from the missing plane: "*Not one* [emphasis in original] of the amateur reports received during the Earhart search was accurate, and all reports of receipt of such of signals from the Earhart plane were definitely known to be false, as the San Francisco Division had a continuous intercept watch at three separate locations guarding 3105 and 6210 kc. using beam receiving antennas, with better equipment than is available to amateurs, and no signals were heard other than those of the *Itasca* on 3105 kc."[18]

Parker seems to have forgotten the message his own experts sent to *Itasca* on July 4: "Unconfirmed reports from Rock Springs, Wyoming state Earhart plane heard 16,000 kilocycles. Position on a reef southeast of Howland Island. This information may be authentic as signals from mid-Pacific and Orient often heard inland when not audible on coast. Verification follows."[19] Parker went on to say: "However, no reports were discarded until after due investigation by either the Coast Guard or a representative of Mr. Putnam, on the chance that radio signals had actually been heard by the amateurs due to the vagaries of radio."[20] Captain Parker's memory seems to have failed him again. Some of the amateur reports were investigated; most were not. In some cases, hoaxes were exposed, but on other occasions government investigations judged amateur reports to be credible.

The Coast Guard's denial, as expressed in the *New York Times* article, that Earhart had ever sent radio distress calls did not sit well with Paul Mantz. He knew more about the Electra and Earhart's abilities than anyone, and he was convinced she had landed on an island and called for help. Mantz wanted facts, not categorical statements, but the Coast Guard turned down his request for a copy of *Itasca*'s confidential report, citing Treasury Department regulations. The report included radio traffic sent and received by the wire service reporters aboard during the cruise, and section 1601, paragraph (a) of communications instructions prohibited the public release of commercial messages.[21] Undaunted, in May 1938 Mantz wrote to Eleanor Roosevelt, asking her to intercede. Mrs. Roosevelt was sympathetic and forwarded the letter to Secretary of the Treasury Henry Morgenthau. During a staff meeting about WPA matters on May 13, he picked up the White House phone and asked for the first lady's personal secretary, Malvina "Tommy" Scheider. Everything said during a Treasury staff meeting was routinely transcribed, and the stenographer recorded Morgenthau's end of the conversation:

Hello, Tommy, How are you? This letter that Mrs. Roosevelt wrote me about trying to get the report on Amelia Earhart. Now, I've been given a verbal report. If we're going to release this, it's just going to smear the whole reputation of Amelia Earhart, and my . . . Yes, but I mean if we give it to this one man we've got to make it public; we can't let one man see it. And if we ever release the report of the *Itasca* on Amelia Earhart, any reputation she's got is gone, because—and I'd like to—I'd really like to return this to you. Now, I know what the Navy did, I know what the *Itasca* did, and I know how Amelia Earhart absolutely disregarded all orders, and if we ever release this thing, goodbye Amelia Earhart's reputation. Now, really—because if we give the access to one, we have to give it to all.

And my advice is that—and if the President ever heard that somebody questioned that the Navy hadn't made the proper search, after what those boys went through—I think they searched, as I remember it, 50,000 square miles, and every one of those planes was out, and the boys just burnt themselves out physically and every other way searching for her. And if—I mean I think he'd get terribly angry if somebody—because they just went the limit, and so did the Coast Guard. And we have the report of all those wireless messages and everything else, what that woman—happened to her the last few minutes. I hope I've just got to never make it public, I mean.—O.K.—Well, still if she wants it, I'll tell her—I mean what happened. It isn't a very nice story.—Well, yes. There isn't anything additional to something like that. You think up a good one,—Thank you.[22]

Morgenthau did not claim to have read the 106-page report himself, but he had been "verbally briefed" by Thompson in Hawaii. That Earhart had disregarded "orders" was a misconception created by Thompson. She had, quite pointedly, never received any orders from the Coast Guard. His concern was not only that release of the report would expose Earhart's incompetence but also that any suggestion the Navy had not conducted a proper search would make the president "terribly angry."

After the phone call, Tommy Scheider wrote a note to Mrs. Roosevelt: "Mr. Morgenthau says he can't give out any more information than was given to the papers at the time of the search of Amelia Earhart. It seems they have confidential information which would completely ruin the reputation of Amelia and which he will tell you personally some time when you wish to hear it. He suggests writing this man and telling him that the President is satisfied from his information, and you are too, that everything possible was done."[23]

The next day, Eleanor wrote Mantz: "My Dear Mr. Mantz, I have made inquiries about the search which was made for Amelia Earhart and both the President and I are satisfied from the information which we have received that everything possible was done. We're sure a very thorough search was made. Very sincerely yours, Eleanor Roosevelt."[24]

President and Mrs. Roosevelt might be satisfied, but Paul Mantz was not. He still wanted *Itasca*'s report. On June 21 he again wrote to Mrs. Roosevelt and she, once again, petitioned Morgenthau on his behalf. Stonewalling wasn't working, but the secretary hit upon a solution to the dilemma. The damning information was in Thompson's "Radio Transcripts—Earhart Flight." Maybe Mantz would be content with the ship's deck log detailing *Itasca*'s movements and transcripts of administrative messages sent and received during the search. On July 5 he wrote to the First Lady: "Dear Eleanor, We have found it possible to send to Mr. A. Paul Mantz a copy of the log of the *Itasca*, which I think will supply him with all the data he asked for in his letter of June 21st. Sincerely, Henry."[25] She replied: "Dear Henry, Thank you very much for your note, informing me that you found it possible to send a copy of the log of the *Itasca* to Mr. A. Paul Mantz, whose letter I had referred to you. Very sincerely yours, Eleanor."[26]

On July 21 Coast Guard Commandant Rear Admiral Waesche wrote to A. Paul Mantz, Burbank, California: "Sir: Your letter of June 21, 1938, addressed to Mrs. Eleanor Roosevelt, The White House, Washington, D.C., has been referred to this office for consideration. In reply, thereto, I am pleased to forward herewith, copies of the transcripts of the log of the Coast Guard Cutter *Itasca*, together with messages received and sent incident to this flight. Very truly yours, R. R. Waesche, Rear Admiral, U.S. Coast Guard Commandant."[27] The ploy worked. Deprived of the complete picture, Mantz gave up on his theory and accepted that the plane had probably gone down at sea. He wrote to Mrs. Roosevelt that Earhart and Noonan had one chance in ten thousand of making a successful water landing.[28]

It has often been alleged the U.S. Government tried to cover up the truth about the disappearance of Amelia Earhart. The allegations are true. The record shows that senior administration officials deliberately withheld information, but the cover-up was not to hide some covert relationship between Earhart and Washington. Amelia Earhart was a national hero whose friendship with the first lady and close ties to the Roosevelt administration were well known. President Roosevelt had taken considerable heat for the $4 million cost of the search (more than $83 million in current dollars) in the throes of the Great Depression. Release of an official government report on the eve of midterm elections revealing Amelia Earhart's disappearance to be due to her own incompetence, and the government effort to rescue her to be inept, was politically unacceptable. Eleanor Roosevelt understood politics and was complicit in the cover-up, but whether she ever received the private briefing offered by Secretary Morgenthau is not recorded.

Pan American's "Proposed Joint Rescue Procedure" appears to have died on the vine, as did the Amelia Earhart Foundation's plan to send an expedition to the Pacific. No dedicated private search was mounted but, in 1940 the foundation commissioned Capt. Irving Johnson, whose yacht *Yankee* was making an around-the-world tour, to make inquiries in the British Central Pacific. In May of that year, Johnson called at several islands in the Ellice and Gilbert Islands. A missionary on Beru told him of local reports that "the Earhart plane had flown eastward high up over the island of Taputeouea [Tabiteuea]."[29] The stories were probably true. The flight was, indeed, slightly south of course when it was five hundred miles from Howland.

Otherwise, the news was discouraging: "[N]ot a particle of a wrecked plane or any wreckage that could possibly be from airplane had been found on any of the islands although the natives often walk along the reefs to see what they can pick up in the way of drift, especially as their islands are so heavily populated that anything they can get is useful."[30]

Yankee also visited several islands in the Phoenix Group but, because he had no permission from British authorities, Johnson avoided the three atolls that had recently been colonized: Sydney, Hull, and Gardner.[31] Had he called at Gardner, he might have learned the island fishermen there were well aware of airplane wreckage on the reef.

35

Near-Misses

OCTOBER 13, 1937–DECEMBER 5, 1939

In July 1937, while Earhart scanned the sea and sky, hanging on to life for the rescue that she believed must surely come, the U.S. Coast Guard and Navy steamed away and wrote her off as having perished at sea. Her husband and friends, convinced she was alive on an island, strove to find some way to find her, but in the end, there was no further search, and there was no rescue. Amelia Earhart died in obscurity, and her fate passed into the realm of mystery and controversy.

In the next few months and years, ships and planes returned to Gardner Island, but not to search for Earhart. Ironically, it was international tension over commercial aviation that brought them to the remote atoll. The first ship to visit Gardner arrived on October 13, 1937, barely three and a half months after the Electra touched down on the reef. Royal Colony Ship (RCS) *Nimanoa* was a two-masted sailing ship of 120 tons, having completed a week-long six-hundred-mile voyage from the Gilbert Islands with two British colonial service officers, Lands Commissioner Harry Maude and Cadet Officer Eric Bevington, leading a delegation of sixteen Gilbertese elders. Their mission was to evaluate Gardner and the other islands of the Phoenix Group for possible settlement.

Great Britain had colonized the sixteen atolls of the Gilbert Islands in 1892. Putting an end to inter-atoll warfare brought Pax Britannica to the islands but also, within a few generations, brought severe overpopulation. Lands Commissioner Maude had long lobbied London for permission to explore the possibility of settling the uninhabited Phoenix Group but to no avail—too expensive. Then suddenly in early 1937, funding was approved for an exploratory expedition. What had changed was not a sudden compassionate concern in Whitehall for the well-being of Gilbert islanders but alarm over American claims to ownership of the Phoenix Group.

Pan American Airways, the "chosen instrument" of U.S. international expansion of air commerce, already had a monopoly on air service across the northern Pacific, refueling their flying boats at Midway and Wake, U.S. atolls with lagoons suitable for landing. To open the lucrative South Pacific routes to Australia and New Zealand required a stepping-stone between Hawaii and American Samoa, so the United States decided to challenge British ownership of the best ones.

On May 26, 1937, the Royal Navy cruiser HMS *Wellington* arrived at Canton Island, the largest atoll of the Phoenix Group, with a party of eight New Zealand scientists to observe a solar eclipse scheduled to occur on June 8. They were astonished to find an American warship occupying the only anchorage. Seaplane tender (minus seaplane) USS *Avocet* had come from Hawaii with a group of National Geographic Society astronomers to view the eclipse. The British government had not been told of the intended visit.

Wellington informed the interlopers that the atoll belonged to His Majesty King George VI and directed them to vacate the anchorage. *Avocet* refused to move. The Americans had been there since May 13 and had set up a twenty-tent encampment on the island. The New Zealanders went ashore, erected their tents, and raised the Union Jack, to which the Yanks replied by flying Old Glory. Raising the stakes, the Kiwis constructed a brick plinth and installed two hastily painted iron representations of their flag. Not to be outdone, the Americans built a concrete pyramid and embedded an enameled stainless steel Stars and Stripes they just happened to have with them. While the two groups played sophomoric one-upmanship, cables flew back and forth between diplomats in Washington and London. It was ultimately decided the scientists should just observe the eclipse and let real estate issues be negotiated by their respective governments. So ended the "Battle" of Canton Island.[1] Britain's immediate response was to put two radio operators on the island to report any future American incursions, but reliable sovereignty required permanent occupation—hence London's interest in finding out how many of the archipelago's seven other islands were suitable for settlement.

Canton was the intended first destination of Harry Maude's expedition, but contrary winds reduced *Nimanoa*'s speed to two knots, and the captain elected to alter course for Gardner. The ship reached the island at dawn on October 13, 1937. Upon seeing the atoll's forests of tall buka trees, the Gilbertese elders proclaimed the island to be "Nikumaroro," the mythical home of the powerful ancestor goddess Nei Manganibuka (politely translated as "the bitch of the buka trees"), who was said to reside on a beautiful atoll covered with buka trees somewhere to the southeast of the Gilberts.[2]

It was quickly apparent that the fringing reef dropped away too steeply to permit anchoring, and the violence of the surf along the reef edge would make getting people and equipment ashore extremely hazardous. It is a measure of the colonial service's lack of information about its uninhabited island possessions that the presence of the wrecked freighter was a surprise.[3] The 5,587-ton British steamer had been there since the stormy night of November 29, 1929. SS *Norwich City* was en-route from Melbourne, Australia, to Vancouver, British Columbia, to pick up a cargo of lumber. An overcast sky had prevented celestial observations, and *Norwich City*, like Earhart's Electra eight years later, strayed south of course. Running blind in heavy seas, the ship ground to a screeching halt a few minutes past eleven o'clock at night. Her master, thirty-eight-year-old Welshman Daniel Hamer, described the shock:

> I was on the bridge when the vessel struck what turned out to be the reef of a coral island, but one can well imagine the momentary consternation of those who were in their bunks on receiving orders to don lifejackets and prepare lifeboats. On deck nothing could be seen, the darkness was intense and it was raining heavily. Strong westerly wind and high seas were striking the ship and she was pounding heavily on the reef so that men coming along the deck were thrown in all directions. Lifeboats were provisioned and got ready for launching while the officers and myself sounded around the vessel to ascertain her exact position.[4]

In ballast only and riding high at the bow, the impact left the entire forward half of the hull perched on the coral. Hamer noted, "Having concluded that it was hopeless to attempt letting her off during the night, I decided to wait for daylight."[5]

Although the island in front of him was cloaked in darkness, a quick look at the charts told Hamer where he must be. In contrast to events on the same reef eight years later, the ship's radio operator tapped out a Morse code SOS that *Norwich City* was aground at Gardner Island. The message was received in Apia, Samoa, six hundred nautical miles to the south where two ships, SS *Trongate* and MV *Lincoln Ellsworth*, immediately made ready to go to the rescue.

A few hours later, Hamer's plan to have the thirty-five-man crew sit tight until daylight changed abruptly. Ships have a tremendous ability to weather high seas because the entire vessel moves as a unit, but with the forward half of the hull immobile and the stern half hanging off the reef and pounded by enormous waves, *Norwich City* was wagging her tail. The rivets holding her steel hull plates together began to fail, and she was taking water in two aft holds. Worse, the oil lines from the tanks to the boilers failed, and a layer of bunker fuel floated on the rising water: "Shortly after 4 a.m. smoke was seen issuing from the engine room and in less time than it takes to tell the engine room, stokeholds and number three hold burst into flames. Fanned by the strong wind it wasn't long before the vessel presented an alarming spectacle. Minor explosions were occurring at frequent intervals while the crew were engaged getting out lifeboats and lowering them to the rail. As dawn was not far off it was hoped that we could remain until then, but the situation developed too quickly and she was left about 5.15 a.m."[6]

Abandoning the exploding ship in the dark while being pummeled by heavy seas didn't go well. Only one of the three lifeboats was successfully launched but:

> When the lifeboat with all hands was leaving the ship it was drawn up into the tremendous surf and capsized, throwing most of the crew into the sea, eleven of them losing their lives. Four were imprisoned under the boat, one of them was found drowned when the bottom was cut out of the boat. The other three had managed to keep their heads above until help came.
>
> Most of the survivors in their efforts to reach safety had discarded as much of their clothing as possible, some were without boots, some without clothes and most of them were cut about the body by the sharp coral and rocks. All were in a very dejected state but thankful to have reached safety.[7]

Four bodies washed up and were buried. The other seven were presumably taken by sharks, as evidenced by the screams heard by their shipmates.

The ships *Trongate* and *Lincoln Ellsworth* arrived on the morning of December 3. By their fourth day as castaways, the twenty-four *Norwich City* survivors were in bad shape, sunburned and desperate for food and water. A surf boat from *Trongate*, crewed by skilled Pacific Islanders, made it to the beach laden with abundant provisions: "We assisted in getting the boat to the beach, took the water and provisions which Capt. Swindell of the *Trongate* had thoughtfully provided and made for camp, where I assure you they were made full use of."[8]

Rescue was still a problem. The violence of the surf made it impossible to get back out to the ship, so the boat was used to ferry the survivors across the lagoon to the southern lee side of the island where conditions were better. Only a portion of the generous supply of food and water had been used, so Captain Hamer made a humanitarian decision: "Before leaving camp all provisions etc., were placed in the shelter, but I sincerely hope that no-one will ever be so unfortunate as to need them."[9] Surf conditions on the southern shore were still severe, but after several harrowing trips, everyone was evacuated from the island.

Eight years later, faced with the problem of getting people and equipment ashore, albeit in calm seas, the crew of RCS Nimanoa made use of the shipwreck by tying off to the stern and landing their boats in the lee of the wreck. In keeping with tradition, when they reached the beach the Gilbertese all stooped and patted sand on their cheeks so that when the island's guardian spirit sniffed them (an action easily mistaken for a puff of breeze), she would say, "Ah, this is a man of the island. I will not molest him."[10]

Maude was having back trouble, so he remained at the northwest end to supervise the digging of wells and evaluation of the soil for coconut planting, while Cadet Bevington and a few Gilbertese undertook a circumnavigation of the atoll to see what it had to offer. The exploration party set out at nine o'clock in the morning. Believing the island to be about three miles around the edge, they did not bring water. They made their way down the southwestern arm of the atoll and by the time they rounded the far end they had traveled five miles and were only halfway around. It was two o'clock in the afternoon and, as Bevington put it in his journal, "The sun was bang overhead. . . . For the first time in my life I learned what thirst was; the temptation was terrific to drink the crystal clear lagoon water."[11] One of the Gilbertese did and soon regretted it.

The slog up the long northeastern shoreline took them past the area where Earhart's remains would later be found, but her campsite was several hundred feet inland behind dense beachfront vegetation, and they were out on the beach near the water where the sand is firm and walking is easiest. Earhart was almost certainly dead by then, but even if she was alive and shouting for help, the crashing surf would drown out her cries. Bevington completed his trip around the island at 3:30 p.m., a wiser man.

The expedition spent the next two days assessing the island for future settlement. The first wells produced only brackish water, but deeper excavations yielded water good enough for agriculture. For drinking water, a village would have to rely on rainwater collected in cisterns. The 111 coconut trees were healthy so it was reasonable to think the island would support future plantings. The British expected colonies to not only be self-sustaining but also to contribute to the wealth of the empire. Gardner was to be a coconut plantation producing copra (dried coconut meat) for making coconut oil used in the production of various products (Palmolive soap, for example). On balance, Gardner Island, thereafter Nikumaroro to the Gilbertese, was judged a prime candidate for development.

Early on the afternoon of October 15, the expedition boarded Nimanoa and set off for the next atoll to be inspected, Hull Island, some 160 miles to the east.[12] As the ship left Gardner, Bevington snapped a photo, one of dozens he took during the trip. Labeled in his scrapbook "Gardiner [sic] Island and the wreck," it shows the shipwreck in profile and part of the island's western shoreline. Unnoticed by Bevington, on the extreme left of the frame there is an object sticking up out of the water on the reef. In the wallet-size print in Bevington's scrapbook, the object is smaller than a grain of sand, but twenty-first-century forensic imaging reveals it to be the wreckage of a Lockheed Electra landing gear assembly.[13]

Photo 32. The western shoreline of Gardner Island, October 15, 1937. The object sticking up out of the water at the extreme left should not be there.
Photo by Eric R. Bevington
(used with permission)

In the end, Maude found four islands in the Phoenix Group—Canton, Gardner, Hull, and Sydney—to be suitable for settlement. In his November 1937 report to the government, he recommended Hull and Sydney Islands be colonized first.[14] They already had working coconut plantations serviced by eleven laborers from the Tokelau Islands and supervised by administrative officer John W. Jones under an agreement with Burns Philp South Sea Company, Ltd., based in Samoa. It was Jones to whom *Colorado* senior aviator John Lambrecht had spoken after landing in Hull's lagoon during the Earhart search. At Canton and Gardner, settlers would be starting from scratch.

It took more than a year but by December 2, 1938, Maude's plan had been officially approved. Dubbed the "Phoenix Islands Settlement Scheme," it was always referenced in correspondence with its full name or shortened to simply "Phoenix Scheme" rather than by its unfortunate acronym.[15]

The long-awaited colonization of the Phoenix Group was to get under way before the end of the year. To assist him on an expedition to recruit settlers for Hull and Sydney, select work parties for Canton and Gardner, and install them on the islands, Maude recruited a young cadet officer who would, unwittingly, become the first person to discover the fate of Amelia Earhart.

Gerald Bernard Gallagher was of Irish descent and Roman Catholic, unusual in the colonial service. Although nicknamed "Irish" by his brother officers, he was culturally as English as they were. His father, Gerald Hugh Gallagher, was a well-respected physician in the West African Medical Service, and his elder son and namesake had been expected to follow in the family tradition. After finishing four years at Cambridge, Gallagher started medical school at St. Bartholomew's Hospital in January 1935, but he lasted only one semester, dropping out in June. In a complete about-face, he moved to a farm in County Kilkenny, Ireland, in September to learn agriculture, but that lasted less than a year. At twenty-four, after two false starts and still in search of his place in the world, Gallagher took another sharp turn and applied for a position in the Colonial Administrative Service.[16]

On October 8, 1936, Gallagher was accepted and selected for probationary appointment as a cadet in the Fiji and Western Pacific Service, but first he would have to return to Cambridge for three university terms of specialized training: "Subject to his obtaining satisfactory reports, arrangements will be made for his departure to the Gilbert and Ellice Islands Colony."[17] He sailed on July 17, 1937, with fellow cadets Eric Bevington and David Wernham, bound for a life as far from England as he could possibly get.

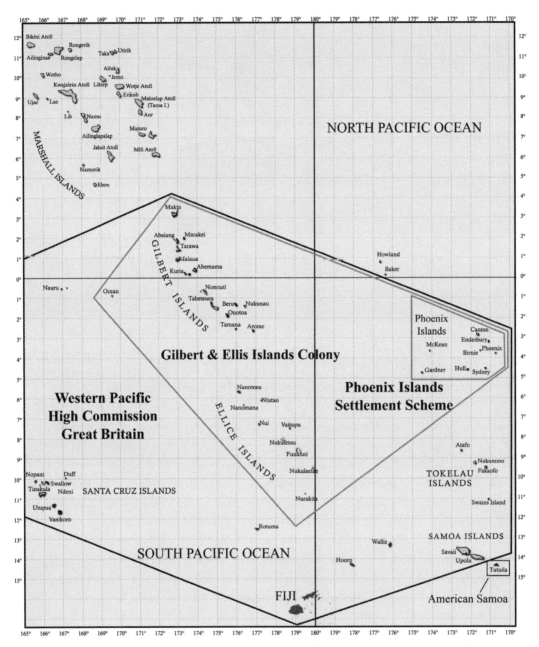

Map 9. The Western Pacific High Commission

The two-month voyage was a tour of the empire, dropping off and picking up colonial service personnel in Egypt, India, and Malaya before reaching the southwestern Pacific and the Ocean Island headquarters of the Gilbert and Ellice Islands Colony. Gallagher reported for duty to the colony's resident commissioner, Jack Barley, on September 14, 1937. Barley liked him and kept him on at headquarters while Wernham and Bevington got more exciting assignments in the colony's outer islands.

The following March, Gallagher sat for a required examination on regulations and passed with a mediocre 74.81 percent, but in April he failed the Gilbertese language test. The colonial authorities let it slide, and in May he was assigned acting administrative officer of the Ellice Islands District. In June he was commissioned as a deputy commissioner with duties as a customs officer and sanitary inspector. After a year in the South Pacific, his new career was turning out to be less than inspiring, so when Maude selected him to help launch the Phoenix Islands Settlement Scheme, he embraced the opportunity to at last do something meaningful.

While Maude and Gallagher were preparing to launch the last colonial expansion of the British Empire, another expedition was under way. Cementing British ownership of the Phoenix Group through colonization was an important step, but His Majesty's government had no clear idea whether any of the archipelago's atolls other than Canton had aviation development potential. The task of finding out was given to the Royal New Zealand Navy and Air Force. As Squadron Leader E. A. Gibson put it: "Although it had long been realised in New Zealand that ultimately an expedition would be required to investigate many islands in the British Pacific with a view to determining their value from an aviation viewpoint, any enthusiasm towards proceeding with this important work was confined to a few officials."[18] That changed with American construction of an airfield on Howland Island and the U.S. challenge to British ownership of Canton Island.

On December 1, 1938, the New Zealand Pacific Aviation Survey arrived at Gardner Island to assess its suitability for an airport and/or a seaplane base. The cruiser HMNZS *Leander* hove to off the west end and launched its Supermarine Walrus airplane to fly a photographic mapping survey of the atoll. One of the eighty-six aerial photos showed the area near the southeast tip where Earhart had lived and died as a castaway, but nothing unusual was apparent. (A contemporary forensic examination of the photo reveals what appear to be trails at this remote site on the uninhabited island.[19])

The same day, an eight-man survey team was put ashore at the northwest end of the atoll from a chartered vessel, MV *Yanawai*. Like Maude's expedition, they landed in the lee of the shipwreck, but the surf was high and it took ten days to get all their gear and supplies ashore: "The reef is excessively slippery—it is extremely difficult to walk on it unladen—and as a result of the frequent falls of the carrying party practically all the gear was landed wet and in some cases spoilt through the carriers slipping and falling into the reef pools."[20] The hazards that in all likelihood accounted for Fred Noonan's injury eighteen months earlier claimed the New Zealand expedition's leader, who fell, broke two ribs and punctured a lung, and had to be evacuated to Fiji aboard *Leander*.[21]

The New Zealanders found the island suffering from a prolonged drought, which had desiccated the vegetation. Due to the scarcity of water, the atoll's normally docile rat population was extremely aggressive: "We were sitting down to our first evening meal when we heard this strange noise coming from the direction of the water drums and on investigating we found the potatoes just swarming with rats. We killed dozens of them but as soon as we killed them they were set upon and eaten by the remainder. We lost all our potatoes that first night."[22]

On December 21, 1938, RCS *Nimanoa* arrived, bringing the first nine-man Gilbertese work party and their half-Portuguese, half-Tuvaluan supervisor, Jack Kima Petro. The laborers set about digging wells, building a cistern, and clearing land for a village while Maude and Gallagher continued on with seventy-six settlers bound for Hull and Sydney.

The two groups on Gardner had little interaction. The New Zealanders confined their activities to surveying the northwest end of the island, the only land area big enough to support an airfield, and taking soundings in the lagoon. By the time they left on February 5, 1939, having spent two months on the island, they had concluded Gardner did not hold "sufficient possibilities to recommend it either as a land or a sea alighting area."[23]

During their stay, they encountered the camp where the shipwreck survivors had awaited rescue ten years before. The captain of SS *Norwich City* had written, "Before leaving camp all provisions etc., were placed in the shelter, but I sincerely hope that no-one will ever be so unfortunate as to need them."[24] Apparently someone was. A photo of the camp shows only scattered empty containers.

The Anglo-American dispute over ownership of the Phoenix Group was settled on April 6, 1939, with an agreement for joint administration of the islands, and scarcely three weeks later, on the morning of April 30, U.S. Navy seaplane tender USS *Pelican* arrived at Gardner as part of the South Pacific Phoenix Island Aerial Survey conducted for the Navy Department Hydrographic Office. On its afterdeck was a Grumman J2F Duck amphibian, which was launched to perform a mapping survey of the atoll, duplicating for the United States the photo mission flown by HMNZS *Leander*'s Walrus five months before. The Duck was back aboard and *Pelican* was on its way to the next island by late that afternoon.

Aboard *Pelican* was Navy aviation mechanic Gerald V. Berger, the same Gerald Berger who had been the first on the scene of Earhart's crash in Hawaii two years earlier. According to Berger, he and other members of *Pelican*'s crew were keenly aware of the Phoenix Group's possible connection with Earhart's disappearance. "I remember that when we stopped at Hull Island about 20 men went ashore in the launch, spread out and did a search for her plane. Didn't find anything though."[25] Berger also remembered seeing a piece of aircraft aluminum about three feet by four feet sticking up out of the reef not far from the shipwreck at Gardner but, because of the rivet spacing, he dismissed it as being from Earhart's aircraft.[26]

Aerial photos were an essential first step, but an accurate map of the island required that they be reconciled with a detailed on-the-ground survey of the shoreline and depth soundings in the lagoon and coastal waters. It was seven months before the Navy survey ship USS *Bushnell* arrived to do that work. On November 28, 1939, surf boats landed a team of two officers, one hydrographic engineer, and twenty men with equipment to erect three eighty-foot steel towers along the atoll's northeastern shoreline. Surveyors with sextants would determine the latitude and longitude of numerous points along the ocean and lagoon shoreline and, where possible, triangulate their position with azimuth sightings to the towers. Meanwhile, men in flat-bottom skiffs took soundings in the lagoon, and the ship did the same in the deep water outside the reef. The entire process was completed in seven days and by December 5, 1939, *Bushnell* was on its way with the dismantled towers and all of the men and equipment back aboard—all except one piece of gear.[27]

The wooden box for the "Brandis Navy Surveying Sextant, serial number 3500, Naval Observatory number 1542," had somehow been left behind near one of the survey points along the lagoon shore at the southeast end of the atoll within two hundred feet of the remains of Amelia Earhart. How the box was lost and what happened to the sextant it presumably contained is not known, but the incident was to have far-reaching consequences.

36

The Castaway of Gardner Island

APRIL 1940–JANUARY 1941

While Gardner Island remained uninhabited, it was easy for Earhart's remains and the wreck of the Electra to go undiscovered. The three surveys of the island between October 1937 and November 1939 focused on the land areas at the northwest end of the atoll and the lagoon, so no one found Earhart's remains back in the trees at the southeast end or saw the wreckage of the airplane hidden beneath the surf just beyond the northwest reef edge. Once the island became home to an ever-increasing number of permanent residents engaged in clearing the land, building a village, and fishing, the discovery of both the dead body and the plane wreckage was inevitable.

The first nine-man work party of Gilbertese laborers had arrived in December 1938. By the end of 1939, the population had grown to fourteen laborers and their families supervised by native magistrate Buakee Koata. Lands Commissioner Maude had moved on to other projects, and in October 1939 Gerald Gallagher was appointed acting officer-in-charge of the scheme.

In his mission to create a new colony for the empire and a new life for the most destitute families of the overpopulated Gilbert Islands, Gallagher found his passion and threw himself into the work. Never of a particularly robust constitution, he neglected his health and labored long hours under primitive conditions. Dental problems, tropical sores, and abdominal maladies were constant companions.

Gallagher spent most of his first few months as officer-in-charge getting the settlement on Sydney Island up and running. The laborers on Gardner two hundred miles away were on their own. In his first quarter 1940 progress report, he wrote: "Although Gardner Island is, without any doubt, the most suitable island in the Phoenix Group for settlement by the Gilbertese, reports of progress on the island are always somewhat sketchy, since there is no European officer and no wireless on the island. Being, as yet, not ready for settlement, it has rather tended to become the Cinderella of the Phoenix Islands whereas, in point of fact, when settled, it will indeed be the pride of the Group."[1]

Gallagher visited the island briefly in January 1940, and things seemed to be going well: "Apart from an expert canoe builder and his family of four, there have been no additions to the population of Gardner since the last report was written. Two children have been born on the island. There have been no deaths and the health of the population has been excellent."[2] In addition to planting coconuts, the islanders were "clearing the bush, building houses, digging wells, building a water storage cistern and generally getting settled down. A certain amount of time has also to be spent each day supplementing the European rations provided with a supply of fresh fish and turtle meat."[3]

It was the latter activity that resulted in the Electra's discovery. Exactly when it was first noticed is not known, but by the time Gallagher visited the island in January 1940, it was common knowledge among the Gilbertese who fished along the reef edge that there was a wrecked airplane in the water north of the shipwreck.[4] Nobody mentioned it to the acting officer-in-charge because none of them spoke English, he knew little Gilbertese, he was there for only one day, and, besides, it wasn't important.

The newly arrived expert canoe builder soon learned about the plane when he too went fishing to supplement his family's diet. His name was Temou Samuela. He and his family came from the Ellice Islands, the second island group of the Gilbert and Ellice Islands Colony.[5] The people of the two archipelagos, although similar in appearance, belong to different ethnic groups. The people of the Gilbert Islands (the name of the present-day Republic of Kiribati, pronounced "Kiribas," is the local rendering of the English word "Gilberts") are Micronesian. Ellice Islanders (present-day Tuvalu) are Polynesian and were considered by the British colonial administrators to be more adept than the Gilbertese for training in skilled trades. Carpenters, policemen, medical practitioners, schoolteachers, translators, and radio operators on Gardner Island were invariably Ellice Islanders.

Temou's seventeen-year-old daughter Sengalo often went fishing with her father, but he would not let her go near the airplane debris visible on the reef edge at low tide. She saw it only from a distance, but the experience made a lasting impression.[6] Two years later she left to attend nursing school in Fiji. By then, the wreckage on the reef edge had been claimed by the sea, and only a few salvaged components survived in the village.

The discovery of Earhart's remains came about as a result of an interior decorating decision. In June 1940 Gallagher was on Beru Island in the Gilberts, preparing to establish his headquarters on Gardner. The elegant government rest house that would be his residence was being built from materials native to the island, and he thought it would be good for the furniture to be made with the attractive hardwood of local kanawa trees, but the only sawmill in the region was on Beru in the village of Rongorongo.

By then there was a wireless on Gardner and, on June 18, 1940, Gallagher sent a message to the labor overseer: "Please telegraph whether there are forty kanawa trees on Gardner good enough to send to Rongorongo to be sawn up into planks."[7] The reply was, "Kanawa trees over hundred on Gardner."[8] One of the work parties sent out to harvest the trees went to a kanawa grove at the remote southeast end of the atoll. As they began felling trees about two hundred feet inland from the lagoon shore, they came upon a human skull.

The laborers on Gardner were recruited from the southern Gilberts and, while nominally Catholic, retained many of the beliefs and rituals of pre-Christian Gilbertese culture. A person who died without the proper ceremonies and interment would return as a ghost and cause no end of trouble.[9] The skull, therefore, was duly buried where it was found, and no further work was done at the site. A bottle found near the skull was kept by Koata, the native magistrate.

Gallagher returned in mid-September 1940 to take up residence in the newly completed rest house as officer-in-charge of the Phoenix Islands Settlement Scheme, and it wasn't long before he heard about the skull and the bottle. Reasoning that there must be more, he went to the site.

On September 23 he reported what he found to the Gilbert and Ellice Islands Colony Resident Commissioner Jack Barley:

> Some months ago working party on Gardner discovered human skull—this was buried and I only recently heard about it. Thorough search has now produced more bones (including lower jaw) part of a shoe a bottle and a sextant box. It would appear that (a) Skeleton is possibly that of a woman, (b) Shoe was a womans and probably size 10, (c) Sextant box has two numbers on it 3500 (stenciled) and 1542—sextant being old fashioned and probably painted over with black enamel. Bones look more than four years old to me but there seems to be very slight chance that this may be remains of Amelia Earhardt [*sic*]. If United States authorities find that above evidence fits into general description, perhaps they could supply some dental information as many teeth are intact. Am holding latest finds for present but have not exhumed skull. There is no local indication that this discovery is related to wreck of the "Norwich City."[10]

Gallagher's "thorough search" had been wide enough to find the sextant box left behind the previous November by a *Bushnell* surveyor, and he quite naturally associated it with the bones and other objects. It was primarily the woman's shoe that made him think of Earhart. She was the only ethnically European woman missing in the entire central Pacific, but he apparently misremembered the year she disappeared. Nineteen thirty-seven was three years before, not four.

Photo 33. Gerald B. Gallagher, officer-in-charge, Phoenix Islands Settlement Scheme relaxes, at home in the newly completed government rest house in Gardner Island, 1940. Photo courtesy of relative of Gerard Gallagher

In his report Gallagher mentioned the bottle, but he hadn't seen it himself. Native Magistrate Koata, in need of medical treatment at the Central Hospital in Tarawa, had left on the same ship that brought Gallagher, and he took the souvenir with him. The same day he wired the resident commissioner, Gallagher fired off a telegram to his friend David Wernham, now acting administrative officer for the Central Gilbert Islands District in Tarawa: "Please obtain from Koata (Native Magistrate Gardner on way to Central Hospital) a certain bottle alleged to have been found near skull discovered on Gardner Island. Grateful you retain bottle in safe place for present and ask Koata not to talk about skull which is just possibly that of Amelia Earhardt [sic]."[11]

A week later, on September 30, Wernham replied, "Your telegram 23rd September. Koata has handed to me one Benedictine bottle."[12] Gallagher probably thought it was strange there had been no response from the resident commissioner. In fact, Jack Barley probably never saw his telegram. His twenty-eight-year career in the colonial service had been plagued by alcoholism, a not uncommon problem in the empire's remote Pacific outposts.[13] The day Gallagher's telegram arrived, Barley had left for six weeks of "interim vacation leave." Veteran administrator Francis Holland was named acting resident commissioner, but it was a week before he assumed his duties.[14] When Holland read Gallagher's report he immediately recognized this was something that should be passed up to the top.

The top was His Excellency Sir Harry Luke. Headquartered in Suva, Fiji, he was governor of the colony of Fiji and high commissioner of the Western Pacific High Commission (WPHC). Sir Harry had governing authority over Fiji, the Gilbert and Ellice Islands Colony (of which the Phoenix Islands Settlement Scheme was a part), the British Solomon Islands Protectorate, Tonga, and the New Hebrides—an area of some 2.5 million square miles, roughly the size of the continental United States west of the Mississippi. He answered only to Anthony Eden, secretary of state for war in London, and in October 1940, Eden had his hands full with the Battle of Britain and an expected Nazi invasion. Ten thousand miles away, High Commissioner Luke had what amounted to absolute power over his Pacific fiefdom.

On October 1, 1940, Holland notified the high commissioner: "Gallagher reports from Gardner Island the finding of a skeleton believed to be that of a woman. Near the skeleton was a box containing an old fashioned sextant. Box had number 3,500 stenciled on it and also bore the number 1,542. A woman's shoe was also found. Possibility of this being Mrs. Putnam is naturally remote but Your Excellency will probably wish to make enquiries concerning number of sextant box."[15]

Holland did not say Gallagher thought the dead woman might be Earhart. He didn't have to. Three years ago, USCGC *Itasca* and USS *Swan* had searched the Gilberts, and USS *Colorado* had searched the Phoenix Group on the suspicion the missing flier might have landed on one of the islands. The discovery of a female skeleton would naturally raise the possibility it was Earhart, but Holland did not want to appear gullible or naive so he was careful to echo Gallagher's caution and downplay the likelihood it was the famous American. Anticipating questions from His Excellency, Holland pumped Gallagher for more information:

Information has been passed on to the High Commissioner particularly with a view to identifying number of sextant box. Information on following points, where possible, would be of interest:

(a) How deep was skeleton buried when found,

(b) How far from shore,

(c) In your opinion does burial appear deliberate or could it be accounted for by encroachments of sand, etc.,

(d) Is site of an exposed one (i.e. if the body of Mrs. Putnam had lain there is it likely that it would have been spotted by aerial searchers)?

(e) In what state of preservation is shoe,

(f) If well preserved does it appears to be of modern style or old fashioned,

(g) Is there any indication as to contents of bottle. Do you know anything of wreck of "Norwich City"—e.g. when did it takes place, were any lives lost and how long were survivors marooned at Gardner Island?[16]

Gallagher replied to Holland three days later:

(a) Skeleton was not buried—skull was buried after discovery by natives (coconut crabs had scattered many bones),

(b) 100 feet from high water ordinary springs,

(c) Improbable,

(d) Only part of sole remains,

(e) Appears to have been stoutish walking shoe or heavy sandal,

(f) "Benedictine" bottle but no indication of contents, There are indications that person was alive when cast ashore—fire, birds killed, etc., "Norwich City" wrecked and caught fire 1930 or 1932. Number of crew sailed to Fiji in lifeboat, remainder picked up later at Gardner by "Ralum." Think Board of Enquiry held Suva—loss of life not known. This information derived from gossip only.[17]

Gallagher saw the skeleton's distance from the shore and the presence of a fire and dead birds as evidence that this was not a body that had washed up from the ocean. The woman was clearly alive when "cast ashore." Gallagher's "gossip" about *Norwich City* was way off, but the bit about some of the survivors sailing to Fiji in a lifeboat would turn up years later in an island story that had Gallagher himself sailing a lifeboat to Fiji.[18]

Holland passed the information to Sir Harry Luke, who added it to newly opened WPHC file number 4439, "Subject—Skeleton, Human: Finding of, on Gardner Island."[19] British files were manila folders containing all communications (telegrams, letters, memoranda, etc.) relevant to the subject. At the front of the file were pages for "Minutes," typed or handwritten notes of commentary. Only senior members of the high commissioner's staff had access to the "Skeleton, Human" file. One of them was the high commissioner's second in command, WPHC Secretary Henry Harrison Vaskess, O.B.E. In a minute written October 9, 1940, Vaskess made a suggestion:

His Excellency—A communication might be addressed to the U.S. Consul in Sydney, but, before doing so, I suggest that Mr. Gallagher should be asked by telegraph for full details including, e.g., any indications of age of skeleton, approximate height of woman, and anything that might be useful for identification, such as condition of teeth, etc. If Your Excellency concurs, Dr. Macpherson would no doubt advise as to points that might be put to Mr. Gallagher. It would perhaps be useful to know where the skeleton was found, e.g. if on the beach if might be an indication of whether the body was washed ashore. Mr. Gallagher should also be asked to state what has been done with the skeleton, as it may be desired to forward it for identification purposes?[20]

Gallagher had already provided some of the information Vaskess sought, but his minute shows the seriousness with which Gallagher's discovery was viewed in the upper echelon of the Western Pacific High Commission. Gallagher, Holland, and now Vaskess had suggested inquiries be made to American authorities to determine if the skeleton might be Earhart's, but in 1940 there was no American diplomatic presence in Fiji—hence Vaskess' suggestion the U.S. consul in Sydney, Australia, be contacted.

The Dr. Macpherson who he thought could best advise Gallagher was, by far, the most knowledgeable medical professional in Fiji. Duncan Campbell McEwen Macpherson, "Jock" to his friends, was a Scot who received his medical degree from the University of Glasgow in 1928 and became medical officer for the Gilbert and Ellice Islands Colony the next year. In 1933, under a fellowship awarded by the Rockefeller Foundation, Macpherson spent a year at the Johns Hopkins University in Baltimore, receiving his certificate in public health and diploma in tropical medicine in 1934. He returned to the Pacific to serve as pathologist for the colony of Fiji. By 1940 he was acting central medical authority for the entire western Pacific.[21]

Sir Harry replied to Vaskess, directing him to have Macpherson make the suggested inquiries and tell Resident Commissioner Holland and Gallagher to keep the matter secret.[22]

Sir Harry Luke had ratcheted up the level of concern and tightened his control. Vaskess consulted with Macpherson as directed and, on October 15, 1940, sent a telegram to Gallagher.

Confidential.
Please telegraph to me particulars of finding of skeleton in Gardner Island, including where found and state reason for believing it to be that of a woman and whether this belief based on anatomical characteristics. State dental condition and whether any evidence of dental work on jaw, length of skeleton from vertex of skull to arch of foot, approximate age and condition of bones and whether any hair found in the vicinity of skeleton.

What have you done with skeleton? It should be carefully cared for and placed in a suitable coffin and kept in secure custody pending further instructions.

Keep matter strictly secret for the present.

Secretary,

Western Pacific High Commission[23]

Vaskess also notified Resident Commissioner Holland and, perhaps to give the message greater authority, signed the telegram "high commissioner" and had it encrypted: "Confidential. I have telegraphed direct to Gallagher for particulars with a view to identification. Matter should be kept secret for the present."[24]

For a senior WPHC official to jump the chain of command and communicate directly with a low-level administrator rather than through the colony's resident commissioner was virtually unheard of. Receiving orders directly from the secretary told Gallagher he was at the center of an extremely serious matter.

In his response to Vaskess on October 17, Gallagher drew on his medical training:

Confidential. Complete skeleton not found only skull, lower jaw, one thoracic vertebra, half pelvis, part scapula, humerus, radius, two femurs, tibia and fibula. Skull discovered by working party six months ago—report reached me early September. Working party buried skull but made no further search.

Bones were found on South East corner of island about 100 feet above ordinary high water springs. Body had obviously been lying under a "ren" tree and remains of fire, turtle and dead birds appear to indicate life. All small bones have been removed by giant coconut crabs which have also damaged larger ones. Difficult to estimate age bones owing to activities of crabs but am quite certain they are not less than four years old and probably much older.

Only experienced man could state sex from available bones; my conclusion based on sole of shoe which is almost certainly a woman's.

Dental condition appears to have been good but only five teeth now remain. Evidence dental work on jaw not apparent.

We have searched carefully for rings, money and keys with no result. No clothing was found. Organized search of area for remaining bones would take several weeks as crabs move considerable distances and this part of island is not yet cleared.

Regret it is not possible to measure length of skeleton. No hair found.

Bones at present in locked chest in office pending construction coffin.[25]

On October 21, 1940, the high commissioner asked Dr. Macpherson for his opinion of Gallagher's report. Macpherson was noncommittal. In a typed entry to the minutes of file 4439, he wrote,

No positive evidence of identification was found, and I am afraid the data available does nothing to establish the skeleton as that of Mrs. Putnam. It is unfortunate that the complete pelvis is not available as this would have done much to establish remains as being those of a woman. It is unfortunate also that no evidence of dental work was found as this frequently affords a most valuable means of identification. Bones, per se, unless correlated with some known physical deformity or injury in the deceased (such as a healed fracture, etc.,) are of little value as regards identification, although of course sex and age can often be established.

I would suggest the bones be sent either to the Anatomical Department at the University of Sydney or to Fiji for farther examination, and that the search be continued with a view to discovering farther bones, personal trinkets, etc. Up till the present the number on the sextant case appears to afford the most hopeful means of identification. The instrument itself moreover, if a good one, should have engraved on it a number assigned either by the Bureau of Standards in the case of the United States, or the National Physical Laboratory in the case of the United Kingdom. This number indicates as a rule the result of tests for which compensation requires to be made in using the instrument. D. C. M. Macpherson, Acting Central Medical Authority.[26]

Secretary Vaskess liked Macpherson's suggestions. He wrote a note to minutes telling the high commissioner he would submit a draft of a telegram to Gallagher for His Excellency's approval, and suggesting the American consul be asked to obtain a description of the sextant carried by Mrs. Putnam and any number or distinguishing mark on it.

Sir Harry okayed the draft telegram but once again declined to approve saying anything to the Americans: "Better I think await the arrival of the remains etc. Thinnest rumours which may in the end prove unfounded are liable to be spread."[27]

The high commissioner's caution is understandable. It was a delicate time in British-American relations. Winston Churchill was desperately petitioning Roosevelt for help with Britain's fight against the Third Reich, but America was still officially neutral, isolationist sentiment was running high, and a presidential election was ten days away. An announcement that the remains of Amelia Earhart might have been found on a British island would bring a flood of press attention from American journalists and inquiries from Whitehall. If it turned out to be a false alarm, it would embarrass His Majesty's government and might be seen in the United States as a stunt to garner the favor of the American public. To Sir Harry, the prudent course of action was to keep the matter under his control as long as possible.

On October 26 Vaskess wired Gallagher: "Confidential: Organised search should be made in the vicinity and all bones and other finds, including box, sextant and shoe, should be forwarded to Suva by the first opportunity for examination."[28] The first opportunity would turn out to be months away. Gallagher went ahead with another more intensive search. The Gilbertese laborers enlisted to help knew the work was important to "Kela" (as they rendered his name) and apparently knew the bones might be those of a famous person named Amelia Earhart, but with no English and no source of outside news, they had no way of knowing why she was famous unless Gallagher told them, and he could not speak Gilbertese. If any of them connected the bones at the far end of the atoll with the airplane wreckage at the northwestern reef edge, they never spoke of it.

The new search turned up parts of a man's shoe and some corks attached to brass chains like the ones used as stoppers on "breakers," the small wooden water casks carried in lifeboats.[29] Gallagher exhumed the skull and, in a gesture sympathetic to family members should the castaway be identified, had the island carpenter Temou Samuela construct a finely crafted coffin with wood from a kanawa tree that stood on the lagoon shore not far from where the person died.[30]

The tropical storm season in the south central Pacific in 1940 was a bad one. Beginning in mid-November, Gardner was struck with "severe and almost continuous North-Westerly gales, which did considerable damage to houses, coconut trees and newly planted lands."[31] The northwestern and western end of the island took the brunt of the storm, and high seas probably tore apart and scattered the wreckage of the Electra.

The village had to be moved inland and, to make matters worse, in mid-December the island's wireless telegraph failed, leaving Gallagher "completely cut off from headquarters for some five weeks until communication could be restored on the 11th January, 1941."[32] While he waited for a ship from Fiji to bring a new radio, he wrote a letter to accompany the coffin and found objects when the ship returned to Suva. For the first time, he used the atoll's Gilbertese name in an official communication.

Nikumaroro (Gardner) Island,
Phoenix Islands District,
27th December, 1940.
Sir,

I have the honour to acknowledge the receipt of your confidential telegram No. 2 of the 26th. October, 1940, and to state that two packages are being handed to the Master, R.C.S. "Nimanoa," for eventual delivery to the High Commission Office in Suva. The larger of these packages is the coffin containing the remains of the unidentified individual found on the South Eastern shore of Gardner Island; the second package is the sextant box found in the immediate locality and contains all the other pieces of evidence which were found in the proximity of the body.

2. The fact that the skull has been buried in damp ground for nearly a year, whilst all the other bones have been lying above ground during the same period, was probably not apparent from previous correspondence, but may be helpful in determining the age of the bones. In spite of an intensive search, none of the smaller bones have been discovered and, in view of the presence of crabs and rats in this area, I consider that it is now unlikely that any further remains will be traced. A similar search for rings, coins, keys or other articles not so easily destroyed has also been unsuccessful, but it is possible that something may come to hand during the course of the next few months when the area in question will be again thoroughly examined during the course of planting operations, which will involve a certain amount of digging in the vicinity. If this should prove to be the case, I will inform you of the fact by telegraph.

3. Should any relatives be traced, it may prove of sentimental interest for them to know that the coffin in which the remains are contained is made from a local wood known as "kanawa" and the tree was, until a year ago, growing on the edge of the lagoon, not very far from the spot where the deceased was found.

I have the honour to be,
Sir,
Your obedient servant,
(Sgd) Gerald B. Gallagher.
Officer-in-Charge,
Phoenix Islands Settlement Scheme

In mid-January RCS *Nimanoa*, outfitted with a diesel engine since its first visit to Gardner in 1937, delivered Gallagher's new wireless and sailed for Suva with the coffin and found objects aboard. The possible significance of its strange cargo was hidden by the mandated veil of secrecy, and the coffin was listed on the ship's manifest as simply "Human Remains."[33] Three and a half years after landing on the reef and surviving for a time as a castaway before dying, Amelia Earhart was at last continuing her journey. Now she was about to be kidnapped.

37

Losing Amelia

FEBRUARY–SEPTEMBER 1941

allagher had done his duty. An organized search of the castaway's campsite and surrounding area had turned up a few more small items, and he had exhumed the skull. Confident he had found what there was to find, he put the bones in a custom-made kanawa wood coffin, packaged the other material, and sent everything off to Fiji under a veil of secrecy, where it was urgently awaited by the highest officials in the WPHC.

He was therefore no doubt alarmed on February 6, 1941, to receive a telegram from the newly appointed acting senior medical officer for the Gilbert and Ellice Islands Colony at district headquarters in Tarawa, where RCS *Nimanoa* was making a stop on the way to Suva: "I understand from the Master R.C.S. Nimanoa, that he has certain human remains on board consigned to Suva. As I am in charge of Medical and forensic investigation of such objects throughout the whole colony and have no knowledge of the matter, I preasume [*sic*] that the package was intended to be consigned to myself? Isaac."[1] Eric Bevington later described Dr. Lindsay Isaac as "a most difficult, self-opinionated man with an inordinate 'amour-propre' [self-love], and a complex that made him self-assertive."[2]

For Gallagher, it must have been a difficult moment. Isaac had the bones but not the secret transmittal letter. With no knowledge of the bones' possible significance, there was no telling what he might do with them, and yet Gallagher did not have the authority to "read him in." Fortunately, Isaac had sent a copy of his telegram to the resident commissioner, Francis Holland, on Ocean Island. Holland took Gallagher off the hook in a telegram the next day, February 7: "Senior Medical Officer repeated to me his telegram to you regarding human remains addressed to Suva on 'Nimanoa.' I am informing him of position and there is no need for you to take further action. Resident."[3]

February 7 was a Friday, and Holland took no action for the next two days, possibly because it was the weekend, but by Tuesday, February 11, the situation had gotten much worse. Isaac had quarantined the entire port of Tarawa. Holland felt compelled to alert the high commissioner:

> Confidential. Acting Senior Medical Officer has taken objection to presence on Government vessel of human remains consigned to Suva. Circumstances indicate that these are

those referred to in your correspondence ending with your telegram No. 500, 1940, Confidential. Acting Senior Medical Officer appears to be acting in unorthodox fashion and is detaining all ships calling at Tarawa (at present four) on health grounds on account of this incident. I am enquiring as to authority under which he presumes to do so but in the meantime should be grateful for definite instructions from Your Excellency to pass on to him. Resident.[4]

Meanwhile, Isaac had examined the bones and, with no information about the objects found with them or the context of their discovery, and with no training in forensic pathology, he pronounced his conclusions in a telegram to Gallagher: "Confidential: For your information remains taken from 'Nimanoa' part skeleton elderly male of Polynesian race and that indications are that bones have been in sheltered position for upwards of 20 years and possibly much longer. Isaac."[5]

Knowing only that the situation was no longer his problem, Gallagher composed a reply designed to mollify Isaac without divulging any classified information: "Confidential. Your confidential telegram 11th February. Many thanks—rather an anticlimax! Personal should be delighted if you keep box but matter has been mentioned in private letter to High Commissioner who is interested in timber used and may ask to see it. It would be fun to make you one for yourself or perhaps a little tea table—we have a little seasoned timber left. Please let me know whether you prefer box or table and if former give any particular inside measurements. Gallagher."[6] Then he had second thoughts. The resident commissioner had essentially told him to stay out of it. Before giving the telegram to the radio operator for transmission he crossed out all but "Your confidential telegram 11th February. Many thanks—rather an anticlimax!"[7]

Three days later, Sir Harry Luke told the resident commissioner to lay down the law to Isaac: "IMMEDIATE. Confidential. Instruct acting Senior Medical Officer that ships must not be detained without good reason and then only in accordance with Regulations or higher instructions. He should also be directed to report reasons for action taken referred to in your telegram and instructed that if human remains are those they are assumed to be he is not to detain shipping. High Commissioner."[8]

Holland wired Isaac as instructed. Isaac complied and opened the port, but in his reply he repeated the evaluation he had given Gallagher. Holland passed it on to Sir Harry on February 17: "Acting Senior Medical Officer has now apparently examined the remains. He states that they are part of skeleton of elderly male of Polynesian race, bones having been probably in sheltered position for upwards of 20 years, possibly much longer. He notes some disintegration of the bones in the course of transportation and suggests if they are considered of archaeological interest Your Excellency might wish him to strengthen them by a method with which he states Your Excellency knows he is specially familiar. Resident."[9]

By what process Isaac was offering to strengthen the bones is not recorded, but it was apparently not performed, and nobody in Fiji seems to have taken Isaac's assessment of the bones seriously. In a somewhat disjointed final telegram to Gallagher, Isaac confessed his befuddlement that what he had assumed would be a simple telegraphic exchange had been cut off and replaced with irate admonishments from headquarters: "Confidential. Matter became somewhat tense and complex after guillotine conversation between us. As I had (and still have) no information save presence of remains and therefore . . . quarantine from . . . no danger infaction [*sic*]. I am still wondering how wretched relics can be interesting. Isaac."[10]

The bones were no longer being held hostage in Tarawa, but there would be another delay before they reached Fiji. RCS *Nimanoa* was ordered to make a two-thousand-mile side trip to Christmas Island to pick up people and equipment, and it was March 24, 1941, before the ship made port in Suva.

The next day, the coffin and package of found objects were delivered to headquarters with Gallagher's letter of December 27, 1940. Given the potential importance of the castaway's identity and Sir Harry's resistance to seeking outside help, the examination of the bones should logically have been done by Dr. Duncan Macpherson, the central medical authority for the entire western Pacific and, by far, the most highly trained medical professional in Fiji, but that's not what happened.

Three days later, on March 28, Secretary Vaskess gave file 4439 to Assistant Secretary Patrick "Paddy" Macdonald with a three-word note, "For Immediate action."[11] Macdonald presumably knew what action was to be immediately taken, but the file is uncharacteristically silent on how he got that information. It must have been passed verbally from Sir Harry to Vaskess to Macdonald, but with no paper trail, there is no way to know what the instructions were.

On March 31, 1941, Assistant Secretary Macdonald sent a note to fellow Scotsman Macpherson: "We have spoken by telephone concerning this matter & I am sending you the file & the coffin to the Central Medical School to Dr. Hoodless. H.E. will be glad if the bones may be examined and a report submitted in due course. P.D. Macdonald Asst. Secy. W.P.H.C."[12] The note is remarkable in several respects. Macpherson was already familiar with the whole matter; why the phone call? The second part of the note does not specify who is to do the examination, but the coffin was being sent to Dr. Hoodless at the Central Medical School, and it was ultimately Hoodless who did the inspection and wrote the report. The avoidance of a paper trail that might explain why the task was given to Hoodless appears to have been intentional.

As principal of the Colony of Fiji Central Medical School, David W. Hoodless was primarily an administrator. Established in 1928, the school trained native medical practitioners, indigenous Pacific Islanders who provided basic medical services for the outer islands. Under Hoodless' direction, the native medical practitioners' program was credited with bringing vastly improved health and medical care to remote populations.

Although a superb manager, Hoodless had minimal experience as a practicing physician or pathologist. He did not hold the British equivalent of an American doctor of medicine. His medical certification was a licentiate of medicine and surgery of the Society of Apothecaries. The society was authorized to license doctors in Britain. It did not operate any medical schools; rather, it conducted exams. If the applicants passed the tests, they were licensed to practice medicine. Hoodless' medical training was acquired piecemeal at King's College Hospital and Charing Cross Hospital in England over a span of fifteen years from 1920 to 1935, interrupted by periods of service in Fiji and bouts of severe illness.[13]

Hoodless received file 4439 from Macpherson on March 31, 1941, and Macdonald delivered the bones a few days later. He performed his examination on April 4, 1941. It didn't take him long to reach his conclusions. He submitted his "Report on Portion of a Human Skeleton" the same day.

I have to-day examined a collection of bones forming part of a human skeleton. These bones were delivered to me in a closed wooden box by Mr. P. D. Macdonald of the Western Pacific High Commission.

2. The bones included:– (1) a skull with the right zygoma and malar bones broken off: (2) mandible with only four teeth in position: (3) part of the right scapula: (4) the first thoracic vertebra: (5) portion of a rib (? 2nd right rib): (6) left humerus: (7) right radius: (8) right innominate bone: (9) right femur: (10) left femur: (11) right tibia: (12) right fibula: and (13) the right scaphoid bone of the foot.

3. From this list it is seen that less than half of the total skeleton is available for examination.

4. All these bones are very weather-beaten and have been exposed to the open air for a considerable time. Except in one or two small areas all traces of muscular attachments and the various ridges and prominences have been obliterated.

5. By taking measurements of the length of the femur, tibia and the humerus I estimate that these bones belonged to a skeleton of total height of 5 feet 5 inches approximately.

6. From the half sub-pubic angle of the right innominate bone, the "set" of the two femora, and the ratio of the circumferences of the long bones to their individual lengths it may be definitely stated that the skeleton is that of a MALE.

7. Owing to the weather-beaten condition of all the bones it is impossible to be dogmatic in regard to the age of the person at the time of death, but I am of the opinion that he was not less than 45 years of age and that probably he was older: say between 45 and 55 years.

8. I am not prepared to give an opinion on the race or nationality of this skeleton, except to state that it is probably not that of a pure South Sea Islander—Micronesian or Polynesian. It could be that of a short, stocky, muscular European, or even a half-caste, or person of mixed European descent.

9. If further details are necessary I an [sic] prepared to take detailed and exact measurements of the principal bones in this collection, and to work out the various indices (e.g. the platymeric index for the femur or the cnemic index for the tibia) but if such a detailed report is required the obvious course to adopt would be to submit these bones to the Anthropological Dept of the Sydney University where Professor Elkin would be only too pleased to make a further report.

D. W. Hoodless, Principal, Central Medical School, Suva[14]

Noted forensic osteologist Dr. Karen Burns had this to say about Hoodless' report: "To a skeletal biologist, these read like the words of a person who never expects to be challenged. Forensic anthropologists will recognize this kind of statement as common in the analysis of skeletal remains by non osteologists. The victim is not going to contradict the opinion, and the people reading the report are concerned only with the bottom line, not the methodology. Snap judgments are made to satisfy those requesting the report, based on analysis that lacks methodological rigor."[15]

In fact, virtually all of the techniques Hoodless used to assess gender, age, stature, and ethnicity have since been shown to be unreliable. He included his handwritten notes detailing some of his measurements and calculations with the report. They document his errors but also permit a modern forensic assessment of the castaway's identity that "strongly supports the conclusion that the Nikumaroro bones belonged to Amelia Earhart."[16]

Hoodless' flawed conclusions had a profound effect on the WPHC investigation. Having presumably read the file delivered to him four days before he examined the bones, Hoodless was aware that the question of primary interest to the high commissioner was whether what he had before him were the remains of Amelia Earhart. His report stated the answer in all capitals, "It may be definitely stated that the skeleton is that of a MALE."[17]

The next day, Hoodless gave his report to Macpherson with a note: "My report on these bones is enclosed. I will take charge of these bones until it is decided what to do with them. DW Hoodless 5.4.41."[18] Two days later, Macpherson delivered the report to Secretary Vaskess at headquarters with a question: "My final report from Dr. Hoodless is enclosed. Do you wish to take the further action he mentions?"[19]

Hoodless had closed his report with his willingness to "submit these bones to the Anthropological Dept of the Sydney University."[20] Macpherson had made the same recommendation early in the investigation.[21] On April 11 Vaskess gave the report to Sir Harry Luke with his thoughts about further action:

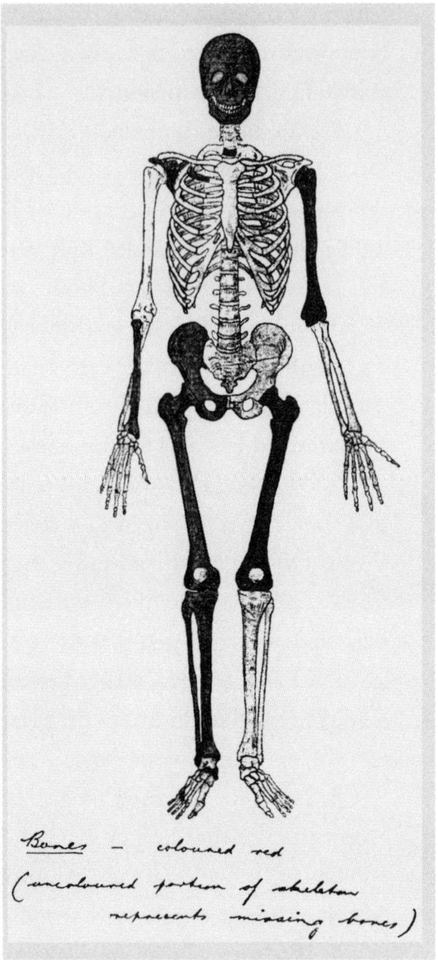

Photo 34. Sketch from the D. W. Hoodless report. The dark-colored bones represent those found by Gallagher. WPHC File 4439, "Skeleton, Human, Finding of, Gardner Island"

His Excellency, the report appears definitely to indicate that the skeleton cannot be that of the late Amelia Earhart, but Y. E. may wish action taken as suggested although it does not seem possible that any useful purpose will be served by proceeding farther.

2. The sextant box with its contents is now with me. Perhaps Captain Nasmyth might be will to examine this with a view to ascertaining the origin? [Commander G. B. Nasmyth was a naval officer and Fellow of the Royal Meteorological Society.] H. Vaskess 11.4.41.[22]

For Vaskess, the Amelia Earhart question was settled. The castaway was a male. Echoing the U.S. Coast Guard's confusion during the 1937 search, nobody in the WPHC knew Earhart had a man with her. Sir Harry Luke replied: "Secretary, Pl ask CMA to convey my thanks to Dr. Hoodless for his report and the trouble he has taken in this matter and to request him to retain the remains until further notice. 2. Pl ask Captain Nasmyth orally if he can throw any light on the origin of the sextant. Then to me again. HL 12/4/41."[23]

The high commissioner didn't express agreement that the skeleton was definitely not Earhart's, but he still wanted to keep the investigation within Fiji and under his control. As directed, Vaskess telephoned Nasmyth, who agreed to take a look at the sextant.

On April 12 Vaskess asked Macpherson to return file 4439, which he did six days later on April 18: "Secy. W.P.H.C. Returned to you. I have read Dr. Hoodless' report with interest and agree with his conclusions. D.M. Macpherson A.D.M.S. Fiji 18.4.41."[24] There is no record of Macpherson ever seeing the bones himself.

On June 6, as Vaskess prepared to send the sextant to Nasmyth, he discovered there was no sextant to send. The box contained only the objects Gallagher had found in his search of the area around the skeleton. Vaskess sent a hurried telegram to Gallagher: "Confidential. Your letter of 27th December remains and sextant box received but not the sextant. Did you forward sextant? Secretary, W.P.H.C."[25] The reply was immediate: "No sextant was found. Only part discovered was thrown away by finder but was probably part of an inverting eyepiece. Gallagher."[26] An inverting eyepiece is an attachment to a sextant usually stored in the box with the instrument. There may well have been an inverting eyepiece in the box left behind by the USS *Bushnell* surveyor in 1939 and, a year later, mistakenly associated with the castaway. Nonetheless, it seems odd that a laborer assisting Gallagher in his search would throw away something he found.

Vaskess advised His Excellency of the mistake and composed an embarrassed letter to Nasmyth for Luke's approval:

Dear Commander Nasmyth,

With reference to our telephone conversation relative to the identification of a sextant and box which I mentioned as having been found and which you were so good as to say you would examine, I regret to state that on further examination it was discovered that no sextant had actually been found but only a box thought to have contained a sextant.

I am forwarding the box to you with this letter and His Excellency would be grateful if you would examine it with a view to determining its use and origin if possible.

Yours sincerely,

(Signed) H. Vaskess Secretary to the High Commission[27]

The high commissioner approved the letter and ordered Vaskess to empty the sextant box and send it to Nasmyth. The contents of the box were to be carefully "parcelled."[28] On June 9 the box was sent to Nasmyth, and the parcel was put in Vaskess' office.[29]

Aside from the bones, the objects in the parcel were the best clues to the castaway's identity, and yet the only semblance of an investigation was done nearly a month later. On July 1 Dr. Kingsley Steenson, senior medical officer for the Gilbert and Ellice Islands Colony then on temporary duty in Suva,[30] stopped by Vaskess' office, took a look, and offered his opinion in a note to the file: "The Secretary. I have examined the contents of the parcel mentioned. Apart from stating that they appear to be parts of shoes worn by a male person and a female person, I have nothing further to say. Those corks on brass chains would appear to have belonged to a small cask. K.R.S. 1.7.41."[31]

Although maddeningly sparse, Steenson's comments provide important new information. This is the first and only mention of parts of a man's shoe being found in addition to the "part of sole" of a "stoutish walking shoe or sandal" from a woman's shoe, as described by Gallagher in his telegram of October 6, 1940.[32] The "corks on brass chains" are also new, but there is no mention of how many or what size except that they "appear to have belonged to a small cask."

There is nothing in the record to indicate how much Steenson was told about the context in which the objects were found or their possible significance, but the file is remarkable in that there is no discussion of the obvious questions the new information raised. The revelation that "parts of shoes worn by a male person and a female person" were found suggests two castaways, and yet only one skeleton was present. Hoodless said the castaway was definitely male, so where did the woman's shoe come from?

Neither Steenson nor Gallagher explained what made the fragment obviously female. One possible answer is color. Amelia's two-toned casual shoes had cream-colored rubber soles with a molded sandal-like heel. In 1940 a cream-colored sole was from a woman's shoe or sandal. The parts of a man's shoe were logically from Noonan's shoe, which Amelia was wearing because of her swollen ankle and foot. The corks with brass chains were probably from small water casks Amelia had taken from the *Norwich City* provisions cache.

Two days after Steenson made his dismissive comments, Gerald Gallagher, briefly in Suva on an administrative mission, had a chance to review the investigation his discoveries had set in motion and add his own comments to file 4439:

> The Secretary
> I have read the contents of this file with great interest. It does look as if the skeleton was that of some unfortunate native castaway and the sextant box and other curious articles found nearby the remains are quite possibly a few of his precious possessions which he managed to save. 2. There was no evidence of any attempt to dig a well and the wretched man presumably died of thirst. Less than two miles away there is a small grove of coconut trees which would have been sufficient to keep him alive if he had only found it. He was separated from those trees, however, by an almost inpenetrable [*sic*] belt of bush.
> GBG 3.7.41[33]

It had all come to naught. Gallagher was embarrassed that he had started the whole thing and was eager to distance himself from what now looked like a naive fantasy that the castaway might be the famous missing American.

On July 20 Gallagher left Fiji to return to the Phoenix Group, but it would be a month-long odyssey. On his way back to Gardner Island, Gallagher would supervise the installation of coast-watchers and radio equipment on several atolls in the Gilbert and Ellice islands. War had come to the Pacific in the form of German commerce raiders. On December 6, 1940, the Kriegsmarine auxiliary cruisers *Orion* and *Komet*, disguised as harmless Japanese cargo ships, had attacked the island of Nauru, sinking five unprotected British, Australian, and Norwegian merchant vessels with guns and torpedoes. *Komet* returned to Nauru on December 27 and shelled the harbor's loading terminal.[34]

Landing the coast-watchers and equipment on remote islands with no port facilities was dangerous work, which Gallagher insisted on supervising in person. Never of strong personal constitution and resistant to advice about medication and diet, his health went rapidly downhill.

Back in Fiji, the high commissioner was still interested in the sextant box. Famous Australian aerial navigator Harold Gatty happened to be visiting Suva and, on August 8, Sir Harry wrote a note to Vaskess: "Sec., H.C., I return the sextant box which I had retrieved from Captain Nasmyth in order to show it to Mr. Gatty who has expert knowledge of such matters. Mr. Gatty thinks that the box is an English one of some age and judges that it was used latterly merely as a receptacle. He does not consider that it could in any circumstance have been a sextant box used in modern trans-Pacific aviation. 2. What was Captain Nasmyth's opinion of it? HL 8.8.1941."[35]

Vaskess hadn't heard from Nasmyth, so he had his assistant Patrick Macdonald look into it. Three days later Macdonald wrote: "The Secretary. I have spoken to Captain Nasmyth who replied as follows:—'As the sextant box has no distinguishing marks, & since it was discovered that no sextant had been found, all I have been able to find out is that the make of the box—that is the dovetailing of the corners—makes it appear to be of French origin.' P.M. 11.8.41"[36]

So ends WPHC file 4439, "Skeleton Human, finding of, Gardner Island." The high commissioner was satisfied the castaway of Gardner Island was not Amelia Earhart. The last mention of the bones was in Sir Harry's April 12, 1941, instruction that Dr. Hoodless should be told to "retain the remains until further notice."[37] There was no further notice and what ultimately became of the bones, sextant box, shoe parts, and corks on brass chains is not recorded. File 4439 joined the hundreds, if not thousands, of inactive files in the records of the Western Pacific High Commission.

At His Excellency's insistence, American and Australian authorities were never contacted, and only a handful of people in Fiji ever saw the file. In later years, the few who knew what had happened never mentioned it to anyone, even close friends. The entire incident effectively ceased to exist.

The story that the bones of a famous American named Amelia Earhart had been found on Gardner Island survived only among the few Gilbertese laborers who had helped Gallagher in his 1940 search, but they knew nothing of the investigation that supposedly proved otherwise. Gallagher might have told them when he returned to Gardner in September, but he never had the chance.

On September 24, as the coast-watcher installation ship arrived at Gardner, Dr. Macpherson, who accompanied the expedition, wired Vaskess: "Regret inform you Gallagher has been very ill since Saturday 20th. Symptoms which are those of acute gastritis have not abated and are being much aggravated by sea conditions. Patient is also suffering from severe nervous exhaustion due to constant strain and worry present assignment of which he has not spared himself. . . . I consider he is quite unfit to undertake strenuous secretarial duties at present and should remain quietly at Gardner."[38]

Two days later, the patient was worse. Macpherson was worried he might have to operate, and Gardner Island was no place to perform surgery. This time his telegram went directly to the high commissioner: "Gallagher very weak owing incessant vomiting and severe distention upper half abdomen. Mental prostration very marked. Temperature and pulse within normal limits. Stomach and lower bowel washed out several times and are clear. Not retain[ing] anything swallowed but is not dehydrated. Am anxious to get him to Funafuti in case operative interference necessary for obstruction upper part alimentary tract although indications for this not present so far."[39]

Later that day, the situation changed: "Gallagher suddenly became much worse about noon today and symptoms of acute obstruction became apparent. Operation imperative and with his full consent I explored abdomen this afternoon. Early signs peritonitis apparent. . . . Prognosis very grave indeed."[40] And then: "Deeply regret inform you that Gallagher died at 12:06 a.m. 27th."[41]

In reporting Gallagher's death to the secretary of state in London, Sir Harry Luke wrote: "In him Gilbert and Ellice Islands Colony has lost one of its most devoted and zealous officers who never spared himself in bringing the Phoenix Islands Settlement Scheme to successful conclusion."[42] He was buried near the flagpole on the parade ground in front of the government rest house.

David Wernham who, with Eric Bevington, had come out to the Pacific with Gallagher as a cadet in 1937, was appointed acting officer-in-charge, Phoenix Islands Settlement Scheme, and designed a concrete monument that was erected over his friend's grave.[43] A bronze plaque read,

> In Affectionate Memory of Gerald Bernhard Gallagher, M.A., Officer in Charge of the Phoenix Islands Settlement Scheme, who died on Gardner Island, where he would have wished to die, on the 27th September, 1941, aged 29 years. His selfless devotion to duty and unsparing work on behalf of the natives of the Gilbert and Ellice Islands were an inspiration to all who knew him, and to his labours is largely due the successful colonization of the PHOENIX ISLANDS. R.I.P. Erected by his friends and brother officers.[44]

Many years later, Eric Bevington remembered Gerald Gallagher as "the most Christ-like man I ever knew."[45]

The tragic circumstances of his death upon arriving back on Gardner meant the Gilbertese laborers who had helped him recover the bones continued to think they were Amelia Earhart's, without understanding who she was or why she was famous. At the same time, the actions of the high commissioner meant the official record of the botched British investigation passed into oblivion.

38

Captured

1937–61

Once Gardner Island was inhabited, it was inevitable that Earhart's remains would be found; but when it happened, the opportunity to solve the puzzle of her fate foundered on the reef of bureaucratic self-interest. Ironically, the mysterious nature of Earhart's demise boosted her fame more than if she had successfully completed her world flight.

In October 1937, less than three months after the Coast Guard and Navy abandoned their search, George Putnam arranged with Harcourt Brace for *World Flight* to be published posthumously as *Last Flight*. The book was released just a month later, in time for the Christmas market. Compiled from Earhart's writings before and during the world flight, the book was touted as being entirely her work, "arranged" by George Palmer Putnam. How much of the content was actually written by Earhart is impossible to know, but the book's description of how she acquired the Electra and prepared for the world flight is largely whitewash. In transcribing Amelia's notes sent home during the world flight, Putnam, assisted by freelance journalist Janet Mabie, sometimes embellished Amelia's writing with more colorful language.[1]

In a handwritten note describing her departure from Caripito, Venezuela, Earhart wrote: "Rain clouds hung around us this morning as we left. We flew low over the jungle most of the way to the coast then played hide and seek with rain storms until I decided I better give up watching scenery and climb up on top of 8,000 feet topped all but highest. First big town Georgetown. Out at sea but could see neat fields along the coast . . . little clouds . . . white scrambled eggs."[2]

In *Last Flight*, the description reads: "Rain clouds hung thick about Caripito as we left on the morning of June third. We flew over jungles to the coast, and then played hide and seek with showers until I decided I had better forgo the scenery, such as it was, and climb up through the clouds into fair weather. An altitude of 8000 feet topped all but the highest wooly pinnacles."[3]

In some cases, Putnam and Mabie got the facts wrong, such as claiming parachutes were off-loaded in Darwin, Australia: "At Darwin, by the way, we left the parachutes we had carried that far, to be shipped home. A parachute would not help over the Pacific."[4] It is a complete fabrication. Parachutes were actually picked up in Darwin.[5]

In *World Flight*, Putnam presented Amelia as a meticulous and accomplished aviator, a persona he had carefully crafted and maintained throughout her career. The Roosevelt administration's decision to protect her reputation by not releasing Commander Thompson's damning report ensured Earhart's image remained unchallenged. Two years later, in 1939, Putnam further bolstered her legacy with a worshipful biography titled *Soaring Wings*. The book offered no solution to the mystery of her disappearance but, in its closing pages, Putnam related what she had told her friend, *Herald Tribune* reporter C. B. Allen: "A day or two before she took off she told Allen that the equatorial flight around the world would be her last great aerial adventure. 'I have a feeling,' she said, 'that there is just about one more good flight left in my system, and I hope this is it. Anyway, when I have finished this job, I mean to give up major long-distance flights.'"[6]

That Earhart's last great aerial adventure had ended in her mysterious disappearance seemed inexplicable. Events in the Pacific were about to suggest an explanation. The Japanese attack on Pearl Harbor inspired prolific screenwriter Horace McCoy to pen "Stand By to Die," a wholly fictional tale in which famous female aviator Toni Carter agrees to give the U.S. Navy an excuse to photograph Japanese installations in the Marshall Islands by becoming "lost" during a world flight with navigator Randy Britton in a Lockheed Electra. Carter is to secretly land on an island, but the plan is discovered, and Carter intentionally crashes the plane into the Pacific to preserve the Navy's need to search. Released by RKO Pictures in 1943 as *Flight for Freedom*, the film starred Rosalind Russell and Fred MacMurray as the ill-fated aviators.[7]

Publicity for the film included tag lines like "The story they couldn't tell before Pearl Harbor" and "Did woman flier strike first blow at Japs?" Putnam sued RKO and settled out of court for $2,500.[8] The film was popular with American troops serving in the Pacific, and their own experience told them the "Japs" were capable of anything. In the absence of accurate information, the notion that Earhart and Noonan had been "captured" seemed plausible. When U.S. forces invaded Saipan in June 1944, many soldiers and Marines were on the lookout for evidence and asked native Chamorros if they knew anything about the missing aviators. The grateful people did not disappoint their liberators.

A growing body of mythology shrouded Earhart's fate, but Gardner Island still held the answer, and clues continued to surface. After Gallagher's death on September 27, 1941, the Phoenix Scheme headquarters were relocated to Canton Island, now featuring air service to Hawaii and Fiji by Pan American's new Boeing flying boats. The next month the U.S. Army Corps of Engineers surveyed Canton for the construction of a major air base with a six-thousand-foot hard-surface runway. War with Japan now looked like a question of when, rather than if. The question was answered at Pearl Harbor barely two months later, and on December 9 Japanese troops landed on Tarawa. They captured the colonial service facilities there but did not advance farther southward into the Phoenix Group.

Canton quickly became a key refueling and maintenance stop for U.S. military aircraft en route to Australia and New Guinea, but the colonial settlements on Gardner, Hull, and Sydney languished until 1944 when the U.S. Coast Guard constructed the Long-Range Navigation (LORAN) Phoenix Chain as a navigational aid for ships in the region. Gardner was selected as the location for the master station, and a survey in June picked the atoll's southeastern tip as the best site. Construction began in September and, by November, Coast Guard Unit 92 was operational.[9]

The station's twenty-four men and one officer regularly received mail and perishables delivered by a PBY-5 from Patrol Aircraft Service Unit 2 based at Canton. Landing in the lagoon, the flying boat would be anchored and the cargo taken ashore. The load for January 10, 1945, was typical: 140 pounds of mail, 40 pounds of station supplies, 75 pounds of canteen supplies, 300 pounds of batteries. They dropped off seven passengers and picked up two.[10]

From December 1944 to March 1945, the resupply trips to Gardner were flown in PBY-5 Bu. No. 08456, piloted by Lt. (jg) John Mims.[11] The aircraft was met by outrigger canoes from the colonial village and, after off-loading the cargo, Mims and his navigator Eyvind Wahlgren would go ashore. On one occasion, one of the few villagers who spoke English proudly showed the Americans a large fish they had caught and dragged up onto the beach. To Mims it appeared to be a dolphinfish weighing at least a thousand pounds, but what caught his attention was the fishing tackle:

A large, crudely crafted aluminum hook was still in its mouth and this was tied to a leader which, upon inspection, was a control cable from an aircraft about the size of a twin-engine Beechcraft. [Mims had trained in an SNB, the Navy version of the Beech 18, an aircraft similar in size to a Lockheed Model 10.] It was much shorter than those of a PBY, and nothing other than a PBY could normally reach the island and return.

I asked the native about the hook and leader and he promptly informed me that it came from a wrecked airplane that was there when he arrived years earlier. He said the plane was much smaller than mine.[12]

The hook was roughly a six-inch circle with a sharpened end and a very small barb. The control cable used as a leader was very easily recognizable by all of us as a control cable, but obviously came from a smaller plane than any of ours.[13]

Mims estimated the length of the control cable to be about twenty-five feet (the exact length of an aileron control cable on the Lockheed Model 10). When Mims asked the fisherman where the wrecked plane was now, the man just shrugged.

When Mims returned to Canton he went to British lieutenant colonel F. W. Huggins, who served as the wartime district officer for the Phoenix Group and with whom he had become friends: "I asked him if the British had lost a plane there (at Gardner). He replied no British planes had been there, and neither had the Americans lost any planes there. I asked him if this could be a part of Amelia Earhart's plane, and he said it could well be, but he had little interest in a story of a lost pilot, since the war was in progress. Also, he joked, that the woman was American and that the 4th of July and Thanksgiving with the Americans was about all the American history he could take."[14] Lieutenant Colonel Huggins also "mentioned that bones had been found and that the natives were more interested in the shoes they found on the two dead European people. He did not say what happened to the bones."[15]

The story of the wrecked airplane, and the separate story about bones being found, had reached, in John Mims, a person who could connect the dots, but there was a war on. He was a junior officer posted to the middle of nowhere, and the only available British authority didn't care.

Like the coastguardsmen who staffed the LORAN station, Mims traded with the island villagers for local crafts such as hats woven from palm fronds, fans made from bird feathers, and shark-tooth swords. Among the most popular souvenirs were small, finely made boxes and model canoes carved from kanawa wood and decorated with inlaid aluminum hearts and diamond shapes. The same English-speaking islander who told him where the fishhook and control cable came from told him the inlaid decorations were metal from the crashed plane. LORAN technician Glen Geisinger served on Gardner from late 1945 through the closing of the station in May 1946. He also had souvenirs inlaid with metal that he was told came from "a downed plane" that had once been there.[16]

Around that same time, the island story about Amelia Earhart's bones reemerged. While walking along the shore near the wreck of SS *Norwich City*, coastguardsman Leslie Wiltshire came upon one of the ship's derelict lifeboats washed up in the beachfront vegetation. Nearby were two mounds that, although unmarked, he took to be graves. Wiltshire asked the English-speaking village magistrate and was told the mounds were the graves of a man and a woman whose remains had been found when the island was first settled. Leslie immediately thought of Earhart and Noonan but doubted the story. By the time the first settlers arrived, the bodies would surely have been reduced to skeletons. How could the islanders know they were a man and a woman?

Wiltshire casually mentioned the curious incident to his regular pinochle partner, Chief Petty Officer Floyd Kilts, who became intensely interested and set out to discover if any of the other islanders knew more.[17] He found someone who wanted to tell him the story but had very little English, so Kilts got an interpreter. What he was told was a wildly distorted, island-gossip version of actual events, but Floyd Kilts felt sure he had discovered what really happened to Amelia Earhart. It would be fourteen years before a newspaper article prompted him to come forward with his story.

George Palmer Putnam died of kidney failure at age sixty-three on January 4, 1950, and over the next decade, public interest in his wife's mysterious disappearance faded away. Then, in 1960, her name was back in the news. The May 27 edition of San Francisco Bay area newspaper the *San Mateo Times* carried the banner headline, "AMELIA EARHART SHOT BY JAPANESE: MATEAN—Former Saipan Resident Sure Flyer Executed."[18]

As an eleven-year-old girl on Saipan in the summer of 1937, Josephine Blanco Akiyama was taking lunch to her brother-in-law who worked in the Japanese military establishment when she saw "a large, silvery, twin-engined plane flying over the water and coming gradually down." After delivering the lunch she saw a crowd of people around an airplane on the beach. "About a hundred feet away were this man and woman. At first I did not know it was a woman, but the civilian workers were very excited. They kept saying, 'American lady pilot.'"[19] The two people were taken away by Japanese soldiers, and Josephine was later told they had been shot.

The times were ripe for a good real-life spy story. Ian Fleming's latest James Bond novels *From Russia With Love* (1957), *Dr. No* (1958), and *Goldfinger* (1959) were hugely popular. What's more, there was recent proof such things really happened. Just three weeks before Mrs. Akiyama's tale made headlines, Francis Gary Powers, an American U2 pilot on a spy mission for the U.S. government, had been shot down and captured.

The *San Mateo Times* story caught the attention of San Francisco KCBS news commentator Fred Goerner, who thought Mrs. Akiyama's story would be an unusual and entertaining piece for his afternoon radio show but, after interviewing her, Goerner was convinced he might be on to something big. He persuaded the radio station to sponsor an investigation, and twenty days later, he was on his way to Saipan.

In his 1966 book *The Search for Amelia Earhart*, Goerner said that his initial skepticism of Mrs. Akiyama's testimony was reversed in part because her attorney, William Penaluna, believed her. It seems Penaluna was representing the Akiyamas in a "war reparations case against Japan for damage done to their Saipan property during the war."[20] It was, in fact, the attorney who had arranged for the story to appear in the *San Mateo Times*. In his book, Goerner expresses no concern at this revelation nor at the Akiyamas' refusal to divulge the names of people on Saipan who could corroborate the story unless CBS paid all expenses, plus lost wages, for Josephine's husband Maximo (but not the witness herself) to accompany Goerner to Saipan to interview another eyewitness to the incident. Upon arrival, Fred learned that the corroborating witness was Mrs. Akiyama's own brother-in-law, Jose Matsumoto. It was he to whom she had been bringing lunch that day in 1937 when, as an eleven-year-old girl, she had seen the mysterious airplane and the two Americans. Rather than insist that they confront Matsumoto together, Goerner permitted Mr. Akiyama to first meet with Jose alone. When Fred arrived, "Maximo Akiyama was waiting for me and quite excited. 'Matsumoto remembers the incident. Matsumoto remembers the two American fliers.'"[21] But Matsumoto, it turned out, was not an eyewitness. He did not claim to have seen the fliers—only to have heard the story.

In the course of his investigation, Fred Goerner found other Saipanese to talk with. Of the two hundred people he interviewed, only thirteen said they remembered various versions of such an incident. Some claimed to have seen white people on the island before the war. Others, like Matsumoto, only recalled hearing a story. Nonetheless, Goerner decided to search the harbor bottom for Earhart's Electra and, on the second day, recovered assorted aircraft wreckage including a generator. At a press conference in San Francisco on July 1, 1960, Paul Mantz proclaimed the generator to be "exactly like the generator I put aboard AE's plane."[22] Then, on July 5 three U.S. Air Force captains announced they had "photographic evidence and affidavits from seventy-two eyewitnesses to the capture and execution" of Earhart and Noonan on Saipan.[23] The Air Force investigated and found that none of the three had gone to Saipan, and the "affidavits" were nothing more than names of people living on Guam and Saipan alleging to have information. The story was, according to one member of the investigating body, "a bunch of garbage."[24] The by-now-celebrated generator also became garbage when Bendix Aviation Corporation, which built the generators for the Earhart plane, completed an examination and reported that Goerner's artifact was a Japanese knock-off and "did not come from the airplane in which Amelia Earhart disappeared."[25]

Floyd Kilts, now sixty-eight, retired from the Coast Guard and living in San Diego, welcomed the news the Japanese capture theory had been debunked. He decided it was time to come forward with the truth about what happened to Amelia Earhart. His verbatim account, as told to reporter Lew Scarr, appeared in the July 21, 1960, issue of the *San Diego Tribune*: "SAN DIEGAN BARES CLUE TO EARHART FATE. Gardner Island is a five-mile hyphen of coral punctuating a million square miles of nothing in the Central Pacific. In the warm, blue water slapping the Gardner shore, Floyd Kilts says, Amelia Earhart's airplane, the Flying Laboratory, lies in a crust of shells."[26]

The tale Kilts related was his recollection of what he had been told fourteen years before:

A native tried to tell me about it, but I couldn't understand all of it so I got an interpreter. It seems that in the latter part of 1938 there were 23 island people, all men, and an Irish magistrate planting coconut trees on Gardner for the government of New Zealand.

They were about through and the native was walking along one end of the island. There in the brush about five feet from the shoreline he saw a skeleton. What attracted him to it was the shoes. Women's shoes, American kind. No native wears shoes. Couldn't if they wanted to—feet too spread out and flat. The shoes were size nine narrow. Beside the skeleton was a cognac bottle with fresh water in it for drinking.

The island doctor said the skeleton was that of a woman. And there were no native women on the island then. Farther down the beach he found a man's skull but nothing else.

The magistrate was a young Irishman who got excited when he saw the bones. He thought of Amelia Earhart right away. He put the bones in a gunnysack and with the native doctor, and three other natives in a 22-foot, four-oared boat started for Suva, Fiji, 887 nautical miles away.

The magistrate was anxious to get the news to the world. But on the way the Irishman came down with pneumonia. When only 24 hours out of Suva he died. The natives are superstitious as the devil and the next night after the young fellow died they threw the gunnysack full of bones overboard, scared of the spirits. And that was that.[27]

To *Tribune* city editor Leo Bowler, Kilts' bizarre tale seemed more credible than the idea Earhart had been a spy captured and executed by the Japanese. Before running the story, Bowler sent a letter on July 18, 1960, to the "British Colonial Secretary, British Embassy, Canton Island," the source he reasoned might best be able to confirm or deny Kilts' account:

Dear Sir,

The disappearance and apparent death of Amelia Earhart in 1937 is one of the great mysteries of modern times. It is of great importance to Americans everywhere. Amelia Earhart was a legend in her own time.

The mystery was stirred up recently with a report that an airplane part found near Saipan was from her airplane, the Flying Laboratory, and that it helped prove Miss Earhart was executed by Japanese on that island. This story was disproved but it has brought to us a new theory—one that you might help us with.

A skeleton was found on Gardner Island in the Phoenix group in 1938. The skeleton was that of a woman wearing size 9 narrow shoes. There were no women on the island at that time and certainly none wearing shoes. Beside the body was a cognac bottle containing drinking water.

The young magistrate on Gardner, thinking he indeed had found the remains of Amelia Earhart, hustled the bones into a sack and with natives set out for Suva. But the young magistrate contracted pneumonia on the way and, 24 hours out of Suva, he died.

The natives threw the sack of bones overboard.

Perhaps the natives related this story to your office. Perhaps you made a record of the report. Perhaps you still have these records. If you could look through your log or record book of 1938, or 1939 maybe you would find an account of the incident that would verify what I have recounted. If you could photostat a copy of the page of the log book or in some other way verify the story we would be indebted. We would, of course, repay you for any expense incurred. May I hear from you? Sincerely, Leo Bowler, City Editor[28]

There was no "British colonial secretary" or "British embassy" on Canton. Bowler's letter eventually landed in Tarawa where, on September 26, the information officer forwarded it to D. J. Knobbs, the district commissioner for the Phoenix Islands District on Canton: "The information requested is not available here. I should be very grateful if you would reply to this directly."[29] But Knobbs did not reply directly. The letter was addressed to the "British colonial secretary," so Knobbs apparently decided to play it safe and send the letter to the senior official it was addressed to, the WPHC secretary in Fiji.

File 4439, "Skeleton, Human, finding of, on Gardner Island" was buried and forgotten, and by 1960, there was no one left in Suva who had been privy to the matter. The request was sent back to Canton for Knobbs to deal with. Bowler's letter had rattled around the South Pacific for eight months before he received a reply dated April 6, 1961:

Sir,

I have the honour to inform you that I have just received via the Chief Secretary, Fiji a copy of your letter of 18th July 1960 concerning "The Story of Amelia Earhart."

I have searched through the early records of the Phoenix Islands District and can find no report of the discovery of a skeleton on Gardner Island in 1938. I am reliably informed that Te Tiriata, the first magistrate, committed suicide on Tarawa shortly after the end of the Second World War, so that the story of his death from pneumonia on the way to Suva is most suspect.

In addition, it would be most unusual for a ship to proceed direct from the Phoenix Islands to Suva direct and even more unusual for the magistrate to have obtained leave to go on this mission, which would involve him in many months delay before he could get back to Gardner Island.

I am sorry I cannot be more helpful.

I have the honour to be, Sir, Your obedient servant, DJ Knobbs, District Commissioner, Phoenix Islands District[30]

Bowler had not mentioned that the "young magistrate" in the story was an Irishman and Knobbs' records were incorrect in any event. The first native magistrate on Gardner was Buakee Koata. There is no Te Tiriata listed among the later magistrates.[31]

William Dorais, one of Fred Goerner's colleagues at KCBS, also tried to find corroboration of Kilts' story. According to Goerner: "Bill wrote to the Central Archives of Fiji and the Western Pacific High Commission for information, and the archivist, named Tuinceva, replied that 'No skeleton has ever been reported found on Gardner Island.' Bill finally decided (as did I) that Kilts' story was the result of a corruption of varied events, difficulty in translation, vivid imagination and the traditional exaggeration of the story over the years."[32]

As Kilts had said at the end of his story, "And that was that."

39

Backlash

1961–89

Kilts' story was overshadowed and largely forgotten as media coverage focused on Goerner's further discoveries on Saipan. More and more eyewitnesses came forward, but every time seemingly genuine evidence cropped up, it fell flat. A photo of Earhart found tacked to the wall of a Japanese officer's quarters showed a bedraggled-looking Amelia wearing what might be handcuffs. In the background was an Asian-looking man wearing an officer's cap.[1] (The photo proved to have been taken in Hawaii shortly after the March 1937 accident. The handcuffs were a bracelet, and the man was a taxicab driver.) With great fanfare, Goerner brought bones from a grave said to contain the remains of Earhart and Noonan back to the United States for identification, but they turned out to be the bones of four native Chamorros.[2]

After six years of investigation and four trips to Saipan, Fred Goerner presented his solution to the mystery in the book *The Search for Amelia Earhart*, published by Doubleday & Company in 1966. In brief: Earhart and Noonan were on a secret mission to observe a Japanese installation on Truk in the central Carolines before continuing on to Howland Island. To enable the Electra to complete the much longer flight, the airplane had been quietly modified with "Wasp Senior" engines. Their flight over Truk was detected, and Japanese authorities were alerted that their top-secret airspace had been violated. A tropical storm prevented Noonan from finding Howland, so they tried to return to the Gilbert Islands but miscalculated and reached Mili Atoll in the Marshall Islands, where they landed on the reef in shallow water. Earhart's failure to arrive at Howland made international news, and the Japanese now had no doubt who had spied on Truk. Amelia sent SOS calls on the plane's emergency radio and "the race was on to see which nation could find Amelia and Fred first." A Japanese fishing boat found them, picked them up, and transferred them to a ship that took them to Jaluit in the Marshall Islands and eventually to Japanese military headquarters on Saipan: "The kind of questioning and hardships they endured can be imagined. Death may have been a release they both desired."[3]

Although Goerner had found no documents, photos, artifacts, or remains to support his conclusions, the book was entertaining and sold well. In its closing pages, Goerner presented his best evidence, a verbal assurance from retired Fleet Adm. Chester Nimitz, with whom he had established a friendship: "I want to tell you Earhart and her navigator did go down in the Marshalls and were picked up by the Japanese."[4]

Fred Goerner kept looking for solid evidence that would corroborate Admiral Nimitz's assertion that Earhart and Noonan had come down in the Marshall Islands, but he was ultimately forced to discount his star witness:

> I truly believed the north of course theory when I wrote THE SEARCH FOR AE in 1966, and I picked Mili as the most logical landing place. Through the assistance of Dr. Dirk Ballendorf, who was Deputy Director of U.S. Peace Corps activities in the Pacific, I was able to disabuse myself of that conjecture by 1969. Dr. Ballendorf assigned a fine young American named Eric Sussman to assist me with the people of Mili Atoll. Mr. Sussman spent nearly two years in Mili as a Peace Corps Volunteer, and he interviewed every Marshallese who was old enough to remember anything about the pre-WWII years, especially 1937. A story existed about a woman pilot being picked up somewhere in or about the Marshalls in 1937, but Mr. Sussman satisfied himself and subsequently satisfied me that Mili HAD NOT BEEN [emphasis in the original] the landing place of the Earhart plane.[5]

Nimitz had apparently been expressing his opinion rather than revealing a highly classified secret, but *The Search for Amelia Earhart* was out there, and the bell couldn't be un-rung. The book unleashed a flood of amateur sleuths who flocked to the Marshalls and Saipan to find the proof that had eluded Goerner. More local people came forward with intriguing but conflicting memories about a white man and woman imprisoned or executed before the war. Dozens of American veterans of the Saipan invasion suddenly remembered finding evidence. Most of the servicemen's stories followed the same Alfred Hitchcockian template: An enlisted man finds something related to Earhart (a briefcase, a log book, a photo album, etc.). He brings what Hitchcock would call "the MacGuffin" to the attention of an officer, who takes possession and pledges the finder to secrecy. Nothing further is heard and, after many years, the informant decides he should reveal what happened, but there is never a receipt or photo, nor can the veteran remember the name of the officer.

Over time, the theories and the books got wilder and weirder. The Electra had been burned by the Marines.[6] A scrap of cloth was the blindfold snatched from Amelia's eyes before she was executed.[7] Earhart had been secretly repatriated to the United States after the war under a proto-witness protection scheme and was a now a New Jersey housewife named Irene Bolam.[8] (Bolam sued the publisher and settled out of court for a rumored $1 million. The book was pulled from further publication.)

Amidst all the hoopla, in 1970 Goerner learned of someone who claimed to have personally heard Amelia Earhart describe her plight in the days following her disappearance and had transcribed what she heard in a notebook. John Hathaway was friends with his neighbor Betty Klenck Brown in Hoopeston, Illinois. She knew the stories about Amelia being captured by the Japanese were wrong but was unwilling to fling herself into the controversy. She showed John Hathaway her notebook, and he agreed to see if he could find a responsible researcher who would agree to protect her privacy. He decided to write to Fred Goerner:

After being shown a copy of a radio transmission from Amelia Earhart I became interested in the topic. I am writing you concerning this message since your book was the most recent and best researched that came to my attention.

The message contains,

1. fact that plane is on water
2. possible location of landing
3. implication that Noonan was injured
4. and several other interesting and pertinent items

The story is that a certain lady, Mrs. B, as a girl, lived in Florida and was in the habit of listening to her father's short wave radio (with large outside aerial) daily. Imagine her surprise when she fired up the set one afternoon and found herself listening to distress calls from Earhart and Noonan. She copied down all one hour and forty-five minutes of what she heard. She and her father, who had also been listening, then took the message to the Coast Guard. The Coast Guard people checked out the map coordinates and informed the young lady and her father that ships were already searching that area. Nothing else was done. The message has been lying around till now.

I certainly hope you will take an interest in this Mr. Goerner. There is no doubt, in my mind at least, the message is factual. It has been lying around too long unappreciated. If you desire more information, please write to me and I will gladly act as a go between for you and Mrs. B since she desires no undue excitement.[9]

Goerner replied he would be pleased to hear more information with respect to the message the woman received in 1937. He understood her desire for anonymity and guaranteed not to use her name if she so preferred.[10]

Hathaway wrote back and included: "a somewhat laboriously scrawled copy of Mrs. Brown's radio message. Much of it is hard to understand without her verbal commentary. I did write in a few of her explanations with red ink however. According to Mrs. Brown the message is disjointed because the radio reception was garbled and faded at times. She wrote only what she heard, sensibly enough. She told me that Amelia sounded desperate and that she was having trouble with Fred who was hassling over the microphone and also occasionally trying to get out."[11]

Goerner replied: "Well, to tell you the truth Mr. Hathaway, I can't make anything out of the messages Mrs. Brown received. The figures do not seem at all relevant, especially the supposed position reports. It almost sounds as if several broadcasts were being received on the same frequency at the same time. . . . I do appreciate your having taken the time to communicate with me about the matter. I'm just afraid though that without a great deal more clarification of the messages it would be impossible to make any determination from them."[12]

Goerner, meanwhile, continued his research and, by 1982 found himself having to once again amend his conclusions. Inventor Frederick J. Hooven, a professor at Dartmouth University's Thayer School of Engineering, had a particular interest in the Earhart disappearance, having invented the Bendix radio compass he installed in the Electra in October 1936. Hooven was convinced Earhart would have found Howland if she had not later removed and replaced the device with a different, less user-friendly, radio direction finder.

On December 5, 1966, Hooven wrote to Fred Goerner: "I have just finished reading your book on Amelia Earhart. I started the book with a good deal of skepticism, but now that I have finished it I find that I share your conviction that this whole matter must be clarified and honor rendered to those to whom it is due."[13] Hooven offered his help as an expert in radio matters, and Goerner eagerly accepted. Over the next fifteen years Hooven dove into the available data on the electronic aspects of the Earhart tragedy and, in June 1982, published a twenty-three-page report titled "Amelia Earhart's Last Flight."

Hooven disagreed with the Navy's assertion that the plane had gone down at sea:

The plane's last message, "We are flying on a line of position of 157–337. We are flying north and south" showed they were going either toward Howland or away from it along a line that passes through the Phoenix group. Unless they were so misguided as to fly northward away from Howland, they must have been flying southward toward the Phoenix group. It is more reasonable to suppose that they reached the Phoenix group than to suppose they did not.

Finally, the official assertion that all the reports of radio reception from the downed plane are false is simply not credible. . . . Most undeniable, however, is the evidence of the radio direction finders. There were four of them, three Pan-American, on Oahu, Midway, and Wake, plus the instrument that had been supplied by the Navy to the Department of Commerce for installation on Howland Island. Five bearings were taken on the weak, wavering signal reported on the frequency used by the Earhart plane, and four of them, plus the 157–337 position line of the last message, all intersect in the general area of the Phoenix group.

This constitutes positive evidence of the presence of a transmitter in that area which could only be that of the downed plane. No hypothesis purporting to explain the events of the last flight can be credited that does not offer a plausible explanation of these signals, and why they originated along the plane's announced position line at the only location, except for Baker and Howland, where there was land.[14]

Hooven concluded, "The evidence strongly supports the hypothesis that has been presented here, that the flyers landed in the Phoenix area, probably on McKean or Gardner, that they transmitted signals from there during the next three days, that they were removed by the Japanese, who either removed or destroyed their plane, that they were taken to Saipan, where they died sometime before the end of 1937, that the U.S. Government knew about their fate, but for reasons of foreign relations and military secrecy were not able to make that knowledge public."[15] He was doing pretty well until he went beyond his area of expertise.

Goerner accepted Hooven's conclusion (to an extent): "McKean and Gardner are certainly possible (especially given Fred Hooven's extraordinary work)."[16] But wherever Earhart came down, he remained convinced she died on Saipan.

In 1987, to commemorate the fiftieth anniversary of the Earhart disappearance, the Republic of the Marshall Islands issued a series of four postage stamps depicting the Electra taking off from Lae, New Guinea, USCGC *Itasca* waiting at Howland Island, Earhart and Noonan crash-landing at Mili Atoll in the Marshalls, and the Electra being transported aboard a Japanese ship.

There was, of course, push-back to the notion that America's first lady of the air had been a spy. In 1971 airline pilot Elgen Long duplicated Earhart's approach to Howland Island during a record-setting pole to pole around-the-world flight in a small, twin-engine Piper Navajo. The experience convinced him the government's official verdict, that Earhart had crashed at sea near Howland, was correct. He set out to prove it with original-source documents, interviews with surviving players in the drama, and, ultimately, high-tech searches of the ocean floor.[17]

The late 1980s saw three major biographies of Earhart: *Amelia, My Courageous Sister* by Muriel Earhart Morrissey and Carol L. Osborne in 1987; *The Sound of Wings—The Life of Amelia Earhart* by Mary S. Lovell in 1989; and *Amelia Earhart—A Biography* by Doris L. Rich, also in 1989. All of the authors asserted that rumors of Earhart's demise at the hands of the Japanese were nonsense. The famous flier had gone down at sea.

As the decade came to a close, public opinion about the fate of Amelia Earhart was divided into two camps: "Crashed and Sank" or "Captured by the Japanese." The correct answer was still years away, but the journey had already begun.

◆

40

The Earhart Project

1988–91

L ike so many others, Lt. Col. Thomas Gannon, USAF (ret.), of Fort Walton Beach, Florida, and his friend Cdr. Thomas Willi, USN (ret.), were sure they knew what really happened to Amelia Earhart. They both had served as navigators during and after World War II using many of the same techniques employed by Fred Noonan. In studying Amelia Earhart's disappearance, they "had arrived at a conclusion as to the most probable position for the termination of the flight,"[1] but they were unable to raise $50,000 for an expedition.

On March 30, 1988, Gannon reached out to The International Group for Historic Aircraft Recovery, then headquartered in Wilmington, Delaware. The nonprofit aviation historical foundation, known by its acronym TIGHAR (pronounced "tiger"), had a reputation for conducting aviation archaeological field research in remote locations.

My wife, Pat Thrasher, and I had founded TIGHAR in 1985. Our flagship project, the search for the White Bird, the lost 1927 French trans-Atlantic aircraft of Charles Nungesser and François Coli, had received national media attention. We were also known for having performed a difficult archaeological survey of a rare World War II B-17E Flying Fortress in a Papua New Guinea swamp.

Gannon's letter was not the first one to have urged us to take on the Earhart disappearance, and our response had always been, "No thanks." The official "Crashed and Sank" verdict was the intuitive explanation—big ocean, tiny island, limited fuel—but the water around Howland is 18,000 feet deep, and the aircraft could be anywhere in an area encompassing thousands of square miles. A high-tech search for such a small target in such an immense expanse of ocean would be prohibitively expensive, but it sounded like Gannon and Willi had narrowed down the search area. The competing theory, "Captured by the Japanese," was based entirely upon anecdotal recollections and an alleged government cover-up for which there was no evidence. As with all conspiracy theories, its followers were passionate, vocal, and immune to facts that ran counter to their beliefs.

On April 11, 1988, Pat wrote to Gannon, "We are, of course, interested in the Earhart disappearance but we have yet to see any evidence that she is anywhere but at the bottom of the Pacific. I would guess that your evidence suggests the same thing. . . . [L]et's figure on getting together in early June to discuss evidence, ways, and means."[2] She added a note of caution about an expedition: "Without knowing what you have in mind, I can tell you it will cost probably in seven figures to do it."

In July, Gannon and Willi traveled to Delaware at their own expense to make their case. Spreading out maps and tables of minute-by-minute calculations, they explained that Earhart's last in-flight radio transmissions logged by *Itasca* make perfect sense to a navigator familiar with celestial aerial navigation. The 157/337 line she said she was running on was a line of position derived by Noonan from celestial observations of the rising sun. The line passed through Howland Island, nearby Baker Island, and, coincidentally, very close to McKean Island and Gardner Island. Earhart was searching for Howland by running north and south on the line. She obviously did not see Howland or Baker, but if she did what she said she was doing, she should have come upon McKean or Gardner—and nobody ever searched for her there.

Gannon and Willi were telling us nobody had ever looked for Amelia Earhart in the most likely place. What they were saying was not based on tales of the South Pacific but upon a quantifiable interpretation of a primary source document: the real-time *Itasca* radio log.

It was an intriguing possibility, but we were a long way from talking about an expedition. We had only a passing acquaintance with the facts of the Earhart case, and to evaluate their hypothesis we would need much more data. In the pre-Internet era, that meant spending money we didn't have on trips to libraries and archives, some of them overseas. But against our better judgment, we launched the Earhart Project in September 1988. TIGHAR members quickly stepped forward with contributions that made the research possible. We were surprised by what we found.

Gannon and Willi were wrong in one respect. It was not true that no one had ever looked for Earhart on McKean or Gardner. The now-declassified U.S. government after-action reports from the 1937 search we found at the National Archives in Washington, DC, revealed Gannon and Willi's new theory was, in fact, the oldest Earhart theory. Using exactly the same navigational logic, the U.S. Navy reached an identical conclusion during a conference at Pearl Harbor the same day she went missing. Their thinking was subsequently reinforced by Earhart's radio distress calls and the directional bearings taken by the Coast Guard and Pan American. The possibility that the missing fliers had landed on one of the islands of the Phoenix Group was abandoned only after *Colorado*'s aerial search failed to find an airplane.

A visit to the Smithsonian Institution's National Air and Space Museum library produced more evidence pointing to McKean and Gardner. Inventor and radio propagation expert Fred Hooven had written a twenty-three-page report titled "Amelia Earhart's Last Flight" for a 1982 Smithsonian symposium on the Earhart disappearance. His paper offered a knowledgeable analysis of the radio direction finder bearings taken on Earhart's distress calls and, despite being an advocate of the Japanese capture theory, he concluded: "The evidence strongly supports the hypothesis that has been presented here, that the flyers landed in the Phoenix area, probably on McKean or Gardner, that they transmitted signals from there during the next three days," but went on to claim, without evidence, the Japanese came and abducted them.[3]

Seeking detailed information about Lockheed Electras and Earhart's 10E Special in particular, we contacted Lockheed Corporation's director of corporate communications in Calabasas, California. It had been fifty years since the company built the Model 10, and no engineering drawings were available. We did learn that Roy Blay, editor of the company's internal magazine, Lockheed *Horizons*, had published a fourteen-page article in the May 1988 issue imaginatively titled "Amelia Earhart's Last Flight." Drawing from the *Itasca* radio log and from legendary Lockheed engineer Clarence "Kelly" Johnson's writings, Blay analyzed the aircraft performance aspects of the July 2, 1937, flight and argued there was no way the plane could have reached any of the Japanese-held islands. Earhart said she was on the 157/337 line, running north and south:

> One obvious contingency plan would be to continue flying south on the 157–337 line of position in the hope of still locating Howland Island or Baker Island. . . . While ditching at sea has to be considered a possibility, it would seem to be far more likely that Amelia and Fred crash-landed on some uninhabited island or reef in this [the Phoenix Islands] area of the Pacific, in such a manner that the aircraft wreckage was not easily discoverable from the air. That this wreckage should remain undiscovered for fifty years stretches the imagination, but perhaps it has been discovered and simply not recognized. To most people it would be just another World War II–vintage wreck.[4]

In retrospect, Blay's speculation was uncannily accurate, but all we knew at the time was that a Lockheed insider had looked at the question and saw a landing in the Phoenix Group as the most likely answer. It seemed like every time we turned over a stone, it said "Phoenix Islands" on the bottom.

At the Public Records Office in London we found official reports detailing the Phoenix Islands Settlement Scheme. Uninhabited at the time of Earhart's disappearance, Gardner was evaluated for colonization by Maude and Bevington in October 1937. A work party began clearing land for a village and coconut plantation in late December 1938. Gallagher took up residence as the island's first and only British administrator in September 1940 but died a year later and was buried on the island. Most of the atoll was never developed. The U.S. National Archives provided records of a U.S. Coast Guard LORAN station at the southeastern tip that operated from 1944 to 1946. A severe drought forced the evacuation of the atoll in 1963. No one had been there since.

And then there was the question of what to make of the crazy story about Amelia Earhart's bones and shoes being found on Gardner. Our research had turned up the July 1960 *San Diego Union* article with Floyd Kilts' verbatim rendition of the tale. On the surface, it was no different from many of the anecdotal recollections of the Japanese capture theory: an American World War II veteran describing what he had been told by Pacific Islanders decades before. Kilts' story was fantastical and lacked any shred of supporting evidence, and yet some details sounded like highly distorted, or perhaps badly translated, versions of documented events. There was never a young Irishman in charge of coconut planting, but Gallagher's nickname was "Irish." He certainly never tried to voyage to Fiji in a "22-foot four-oared boat," nor did he die of pneumonia twenty-four hours out of Suva, but he did die of peritonitis within twenty-four hours of arriving from Suva. On the other hand, the discovery of bones and shoes thought to be Amelia Earhart's should be mentioned in Gallagher's quarterly progress reports, but it isn't. None of it made sense, but once again, research had turned up mention of Gardner Island.

Floyd Kilts' strange tale aside, there was a good argument to be made for Gardner being where Earhart landed the Electra and called for help. But why wasn't it seen by *Colorado*'s search planes or later discovered after the island was settled? Roy Blay had wondered if it ended up someplace where it was hard to see from the air. The few aerial photos of Gardner we could find showed one possibility: an open flat area marginally long enough to land an Electra, bordered by dense vegetation. If Amelia tried to land there but overshot, the plane could have ended up buried in the undergrowth and as Blay suggested, if later found, might be dismissed as a wartime wreck. A search of the foliage around the possible landing area seemed justified and doable.

An expedition to the Phoenix Group would require diplomatic clearance from the Republic of Kiribati, the independent nation born in 1979 of the Gilbert Islands part of the Gilbert and Ellice Islands Colony. The Ellice Islands became the nation of Tuvalu. The Kiribati government in Tarawa approved our request, requiring only that we bring along a customs and immigration officer to stamp our passports, but getting to the Phoenix Group presented a challenge.

We needed an open-ocean ship capable of supporting a fifteen-person team for three weeks on site with no opportunity for resupply of fuel, food, or water. After much ship shopping, the closest place with a suitable vessel available for charter was Fiji, a thousand miles and five days from our destination. Three weeks on site meant a month-long expedition and a price tag of $165,000—not as bad as our initial seven-figure guess, but nonetheless daunting.

It was a far greater sum than we had ever raised, and the logistics for the expedition were much more complex than anything we had ever attempted, but by September 1989 we were ready to head for the Phoenix Group to see if Amelia's airplane, or whatever was left of it, was lurking in the bushes on Gardner Island. While we were in the neighborhood, we would also pay a call on McKean Island. This would be a one-shot deal. Either the plane was on one of those two islands or it wasn't.

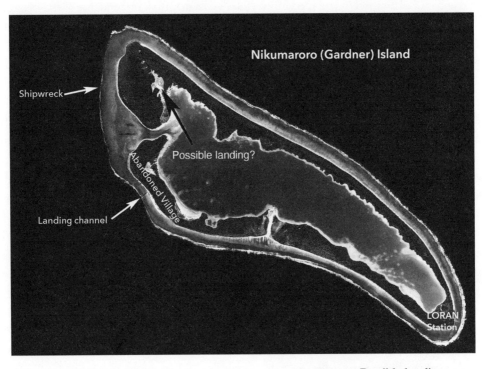

Map 10. Possible landing

Upon arriving at Gardner/Nikumaroro, we found it to be a picture-book tropical atoll: a densely jungled ribbon of land with white coral beaches and coconut palms gracing the shore of a beautiful turquoise lagoon. The rusting wreck of SS *Norwich City* was a stark reminder to stay well clear of the relentless surf pounding the edge of the fringing reef. The steepness of the drop-off made anchoring impossible, and the two lagoon passages were too shallow to permit a ship to enter, so the only relatively safe way ashore was by skiff through a five-hundred-foot long, thirty-foot wide channel blasted from ocean to beach when the colony was abandoned in 1963. Nikumaroro is a room with one door.

The hypothetical landing area we had identified in aerial photographs looked less inviting in person. It was a tidal mud flat, pockmarked with innumerable crab burrows. The surrounding nearly impenetrable tangle of undergrowth, officially known as *Scaevola frutescens*, soon acquired more colorful appellations. After a week of machete work in 110-degree heat, it was obvious there was no airplane there. Exploring the perimeter of the atoll, we found the oceanside beaches to be either too narrow or too soft and sloped for landing an airplane. There were no other possible landing areas on the island. We had disproved our hypothesis, and yet all the information that had led us here was still valid. Stumped, we decided to take a break and go have a look at McKean Island.

McKean is a roughly circular disk of coral about half a mile in diameter, devoid of vegetation other than some low scrub. You can see it from a few miles away, but when you get closer, you can hear it and smell it. Most of the surface is a giant shallow puddle of guano, droppings from the over one million seabirds who nest around the edges. The ruins of barracks constructed of piled coral blocks and a narrow trail of iron rails bear testament to horrific nineteenth-century forced-labor phosphate mining. Pacific Islanders abducted by "blackbirders" filled bags of guano for shipment to the United States and Britain for fertilizer.

After a day exploring the island in a steady rain of bird dung, McKean was easy to eliminate as Earhart's landing place. Returning to Gardner/Nikumaroro, we did a survey of the abandoned colonial village, mapping the location of features mentioned in the official record. In the process, we came upon pieces of aircraft wreckage that had been repurposed for local use, typically small rectangles of aluminum sheet used as fishing lures or fashioned into combs. Where did the people who lived here get this stuff? Was it World War II debris? Maybe, but no aircraft had ever crashed on the island since it was settled in 1938. The metal had to have been brought from another island or, just possibly, salvaged from an aircraft that was wrecked here before the first settlers arrived.

During our time on the island, as the tide waxed and waned in regular fashion, we noticed the water level on the fringing reef flat varied from about a meter to virtually dry. In several areas around the perimeter of the atoll, the surface of the reef flat was exceptionally level and smooth, especially near the outer edge. What if Earhart and Noonan had arrived overhead at low tide? The reef made an attractive runway, and a relatively safe gear-down landing might be possible, permitting the transmission of radio distress calls. After several days, rising tides and surf might wash the plane over the edge into the ocean, explaining why *Colorado*'s aerial searchers saw no airplane.

On the morning of the day we left to begin the voyage back to Fiji, two team members doing a last-minute "wildcatting" exploration came upon a small grave far from the settled area. We had seen several graves at house sites in the abandoned village marked with coral slabs as headstones. This one was similarly constructed and oriented facing east in accordance with Gilbertese custom and yet was far from the village. Could this be where the bones in the Floyd Kilts story were buried? There was no time to investigate, and we'd need permission to exhume remains.

The 1989 expedition had tested and disproved two hypotheses. The Electra was not hiding in the undergrowth on Nikumaroro, and it was not on McKean. In-person observations suggested new, more informed hypotheses to be tested. So much for a one-shot deal. We had to go back.

We returned to Nikumaroro in 1991 equipped to test three new hypotheses. The government of Kiribati had granted us permission to open the small grave to determine if it contained the bones of Amelia Earhart, and we had contracted with Oceaneering International to do a side-scan sonar survey of the waters adjacent to the fringing reef to see if the Electra had been washed into the ocean. Our third objective was to find what might be the place Earhart's skeleton was allegedly found.

In August 1990 we had received a letter from Coast Guard veteran Richard Evans, who wrote in response to a recent Associated Press article about artifacts we had found during our 1989 expedition. Evans had served in Unit 92, and his letter described the layout of the LORAN station and the Gilbertese village:

> If you found things on the East side of the island, you can be pretty sure it had nothing to do with the base. To my knowledge there were only three occasions when anyone went over there. With one exception we found nothing but turtles, one of which we ate and another we gave to the natives, which they ate.
>
> The exception was a small structure we found designed to collect rain water. We assumed the natives built it and we ignored it. But when we mentioned it to them a few months later they didn't know anything about it. . . . On the boat from Hawaii we were told that our destination was Gardner and were also told that it was the island where they really expected to find Earhart and Putnam [sic], so I have always been fascinated with the story.[5]

We had not found anything on the east side of the island and were eager to learn more about the mysterious water-collecting structure and exactly where he had seen it. Evans explained he and two companions had gone for a walk, exploring the eastern coastline. The beach along that shore is bordered by dense underbrush, but after about half an hour they came to a place where there was an opening, so they ventured inland. The structure they found was a rectangular metal tank with wooden poles erected at each corner to support a heavy cloth tarp fashioned in such a way as to direct rainwater into the tank. A sketch he made for us bore a remarkable resemblance to the aluminum fuel tanks in the fuselage of NR16020. His eight-foot-by-three-foot estimate of the size of the tarp matched the dimensions of Grenfell Cloth engine covers inventoried aboard the Electra after the accident in Hawaii.

One of the men who was with Evans was dead, but Herb Moffitt remembered the incident. The tank was fifty to seventy-five yards in from the beach. There were piles of bird bones and a rusty five-gallon can with the top cut out and a home-made wire handle, sitting on charcoal from a small fire.[6] We reasoned that the metal tank should still be there.

The 1991 trip, like the initial 1989 expedition, was both disappointing and encouraging. Upon arrival, we were surprised to see the west end of the island had recently been hit by enormous seas. Beach sand had been stripped away, and at least a hundred feet of beachfront vegetation had been

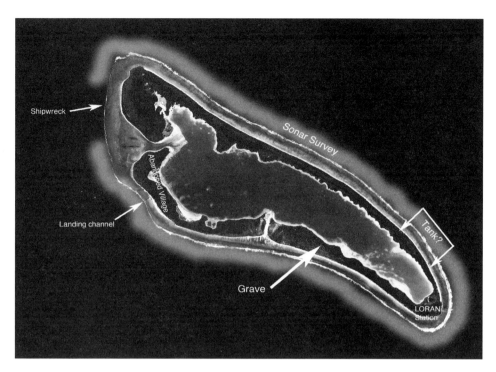

Map 11. 1991 expedition

ripped out and washed inland, collapsing the "Gardner Co-Op Store" frame building that had stood intact when we were last here. The compromise of potentially rich areas for archaeology turned out to be the least of our troubles.

The grave contained the bones of an infant, possibly stillborn; the side-scan sonar survey found nothing; and we were unable to locate the tank. The expedition was looking like a complete bust except that, near the baby grave, we stumbled upon the heel of a shoe labeled "Cat's Paw Rubber Co. USA" and the fragmented remains of a rubber shoe sole. Another heel nearby had no inscription, and metal detecting turned up one shoelace eyelet. Were these the "Women's shoes, American kind"[7] in the Floyd Kilts story?

The day before we left, we took one last look around the village and discovered an eighteen-by-twenty-four-inch piece of torn aluminum sheet in the wash-up from the storm. Rivet holes in a distinctive pattern and one intact rivet made it clear this was a piece of external skin from a wrecked aircraft—an aircraft that should be identifiable based on the materials and rivet pattern.

Initial research on the shoe suggested it was consistent with Earhart's, and the aircraft skin appeared to match the Electra. Both would eventually prove to be unrelated to the Earhart disappearance but, over the next thirty years of research and ten more trips to Nikumaroro, our knowledge, skills, and capabilities grew. It was always two steps forward, one step back. The steps back usually involved archaeological finds that looked good—until they didn't. The steps forward were documents, photographs, and forensic analyses that revealed what really happened.

41

Good Data and
Good Luck

1992–2010

Prior to TIGHAR's investigation, Earhart's writings as presented in *Last Flight*, the official 1937 Coast Guard and Navy reports submitted after the failed government search, and later recollections by involved individuals were taken to be the facts of the case. We quickly discovered those sources were unreliable, and much of the information they contained was simply not true. To know what really happened, we needed to find credible documentation of events written, as closely as possible, to when they occurred.

In some cases, good contemporaneous written sources were readily available and had been used by biographers, but few had acknowledged the less-than-flattering aspects of the story they told. Dozens of letters and telegrams in Purdue University Library's Amelia Earhart Special Collections chronicle the way George Putnam misled and manipulated university officials to get his wife an airplane for a world flight. Similarly, the Doris Rich papers in the Smithsonian Air and Space Archive at the Udvar-Hazy Center contain extensive correspondence between George Putnam and Paul Mantz detailing their disingenuous negotiations with Lockheed and the hare-brained plans they considered for getting Earhart across the Pacific.

Getting accurate information about the U.S. government's role in the tragedy was more difficult. In 1993 Dr. Randall Jacobson became affiliated with TIGHAR's investigation. As a scientist with the Office of Naval Research, he knew the importance of having accurate data and the danger of working from after-action reports. Jacobson's job took him to numerous government facilities and universities with archived records, and everywhere he went he sought out letters, logs, messages, and memoranda related to the Earhart mystery. He had a particular advantage when conducting archival research in that he held a high-level security clearance. Had he encountered still-classified documents, he would not be able to divulge their contents, but he could tell us that classified files existed. He didn't, and they don't.

By 1998, after five years of collecting, organizing, and data entry, Jacobson had built a searchable database of more than two thousand primary source documents that tell the story of the U.S. government's interaction with Earhart and its actions relating to her flight and disappearance, as they happened, day by day and often minute by minute. The Jacobson database exposed the official 1937 Coast Guard and Navy reports as rife with factual error and self-serving distortion and, for the first time, documented the debacle of Earhart's attempted flight to Howland and the search that failed to find her.[1]

Getting the facts often took more than good detective work; it also took luck. To boost our chances of getting lucky, we actively encouraged media coverage of our work, knowing that public awareness of our investigation sometimes prompted people to come forward with potentially important information. Throughout the project, many mysteries were solved that way.

One of the most maddening riddles we faced early in the project was the disappearance of a crucial report detailing what happened in Lae during the days (June 29–July 2) Earhart and Noonan were there before taking off for Howland. The stories Earhart filed with the *Herald Tribune* were newsy but short on detail about her flight preparations. We were not the first to want more information. Copies of telegrams in the Smithsonian National Air and Space Museum (NASM) library showed that William Miller at the Bureau of Air Commerce, who had been instrumental in planning Earhart's first world flight attempt, immediately tried to get specifics about what happened in Lae. The U.S government had no contacts in New Guinea, but Miller knew a Canadian gold mining company, Placer Management Limited, used the airfield in Lae to support its operations.

On July 21, three days after the search officially ended, Miller sent a telegram to M. E. "Frank" Griffin at Placer's San Francisco office:

> If convenient it will be appreciated by this bureau if you could obtain the following information from New Guinea relative to Miss Earhart's departure from Lae. Time of her departure from Lae/amount of gasoline aboard on takeoff/condition of motors and radio equipment/ weather conditions/length of takeoff/did Miss Earhart contact ground station by radio/if so content of messages and any other additional knowledge or information of interest relative Miss Earharts visit and flight. This is for government official record purposes. The above information if available could be air mailed to W T Miller Bureau of Air Commerce Department of Commerce Washington DC stop any courtesies or suggestions extended will be greatly appreciated. W T Miller Bureau of Air Commerce.[2]

The NASM file contained a July 27 telegram from Frank Griffin in reply: "Have following wire from New Guinea begins Miss Earhart departed Lae ten AM local time July 2nd eleven hundred US gallons gasoline seventy five gallons oil aboard motors perfect condition length take off run 850 yards Lae ground station received radiophone messages from machine until five eighteen PM local time July 2. full report posted via Sydney and kind regards Frank Griffin."[3]

To which Miller replied: "Received your telegram including information from Lae we appreciate very much your interest and courtesies extended. We shall be interested in receiving the full report if a copy can be made available to the Bureau of Air Commerce. WT Miller."[4]

And that's where the file ended. Griffin's telegram contained important information, but it also raised crucial new questions. In a July 1 telegram from Lae, Earhart had written, "Lockheed stands ready for longest hop weighted with gasoline and oil to capacity."[5] The airplane's fuel tanks would hold 1,151 gallons, yet Griffin's telegram said Amelia left Lae with only 1,100 gallons. Why would she take off fifty-one gallons short? And what did she say in the messages received after she left? Most important, what happened to the full report? It had apparently been sent, but it wasn't at NASM, nor was there any such report in the National Archives.

On December 16, 1991, my phone rang, and the answers arrived out of the blue. The caller introduced himself as Hugh Leggatt and said he had a letter that might be of interest to us. Leggatt explained that, as manager of corporate communications at Placer Dome, Inc., in Vancouver, British Columbia, he was responsible for publishing the company magazine *Prospect*. In rummaging through old files, looking for material for a story about Placer's early gold mining operations in New Guinea, he came upon a file labeled "Amelia Earhart." The file contained an eight-page letter dated July 25, 1937, from Guinea Airways General Manager Eric Chater in Lae, New Guinea, to Placer manager Frank Griffin in San Francisco describing Earhart's activities in Lae prior to her departure for Howland Island. Also in the file were copies of telegrams relating to the letter. Leggatt remembered reading newspaper articles about TIGHAR's investigation of the Earhart disappearance and thought his discovery might be of help.

I sat there with the phone to my ear, thinking, "My God, he has the lost New Guinea report." Hugh offered to send us copies of the entire file plus an original "flimsy" (carbon copy) of the letter. He would keep the original for the company's files. When the documents arrived, the associated telegrams revealed why the eight-page letter never made it to the Bureau of Air Commerce.

Miller had told Griffin that if information from New Guinea was available, a full report could be airmailed directly to him in Washington. Frank Griffin then sent a telegram to Eric Chater, general manager of Guinea Airways in Lae: "Chaeter [*sic*] United States Government requests following time Miss Earharts departure from Lae amount gasoline aboard at take off condition motors and radio equipment weather conditions length of take off did she contact ground station by radio if so contents of message any other information relative her visit and flight stop please air mail reply."[6]

Chater wrote up a detailed report, but Griffin's wire had said only that the information had been requested by "United States Government" with no mention of Miller or his desire for the full report to be airmailed to the Bureau of Air Commerce in Washington. Consequently, the "full report posted via Sydney" was sent to the only address Chater had, "Mr. M. E. Griffin, c/o Placer Management Limited, 2310 Russ Building, San Francisco, California,"[7] and that's where it stayed, to be discovered by accident more than half a century later.

Chater's letter provided key details that helped explain Earhart's disappearance, such as her decision to proceed with the flight to Howland despite her inability to get the Bendix direction finder to work on a previously unknown July 1 test flight.

With Chater's letter in hand, the mystery of the reduced fuel load was also solved:

July 1st—after the machine was tested the Vacuum Oil Co.'s representatives filled all tanks in the machine with 87 octane fuel with the exception of one 81 gallon tank which already contained 100 octane for taking off purposes. This tank was approximately half full and it can be safely estimated that on leaving Lae the tank [contained] at least 40 gallons of 100 octane fuel—(100 octane fuel is not obtainable in Lae). A total of 654 imperial gallons was filled into the tanks of the Lockheed after the test flight was completed. This would indicate that 1,100 US gallons was carried by the machine when it took off for Howland Island.[8]

It took more than luck to discover how close Earhart really came to Howland Island and why *Itasca* stopped hearing her. Lt. Cdr. Robert L. Brandenburg, USN (ret.), joined TIGHAR in 1999. He held master of science degrees in mathematics and operations research, commanded a destroyer during the Vietnam war, developed and taught antisubmarine warfare tactics, published papers in the *Proceedings* of the U.S. Naval Institute, and served on the staff of the Chief of Naval Operations. After retiring from active duty, he was a senior operations research analyst at the Naval Electronics Laboratory.

In 2006, through computer modeling and signal analysis, using programs developed by the Department of Commerce Institute for Telecommunications Science, Brandenburg discovered an anomaly in the Electra's antenna propagation pattern. *Itasca* would be unable to hear Earhart's transmission if the plane was closer than eighty nautical miles. When the Coast Guard heard her at strength 5 (maximum) on 3105 kHz, she was at least 150 and possibly as much as 250 nautical miles away, putting her much nearer to Gardner on the 157/337 line of position than anyone knew. Brandenburg had solved the mystery of Earhart's silence: "*Itasca* heard no signals from Earhart after 2013 GMT because: (a) she did not transmit on 6210 kHz following her 2013 GMT signal; (b) she was too far from the *Itasca* at 2115 GMT for her signal to be heard on 3105 kHz; and (c) she was too far from the *Itasca* at 2215 GMT for her signal to be heard on either frequency."[9]

Brandenburg also did an in-depth technical study of the Pan American Airways radio direction-finding facilities on Oahu, Midway, and Wake, and the Coast Guard high-frequency direction finder on Howland to assess the credibility of the bearings they took:

> The attempt to obtain DF bearings on possible signals from Earhart was undertaken in extremely difficult conditions and yielded a total of 8 bearings. The Pan Am Adcock DF sites, which obtained 7 of the bearings, were searching for signals with Signal to Noise Ratios far lower than those for which the DF system was designed. The DF system at Howland Island, an experimental Navy portable unit of doubtful reliability, obtained the eighth bearing. . . . The evidence associated with Bearings 2, 3, and 7 strongly supports the TIGHAR hypothesis that Earhart landed at Gardner Island and transmitted radio signals from there. The evidence associated with Bearings 1, 4, and 6 moderately supports the hypothesis, and the evidence associated with bearings 5 and 8 is inconclusive.
>
> In sum, the weight of available evidence strongly supports the TIGHAR hypothesis.[10]

Vigilance and curiosity often turned up important new information. In 2006 TIGHAR researcher Arthur Rypinski spotted a copy of "Amelia Earhart's Flight Plan" for sale on eBay. Rypinski knew there was no such animal and wondered what the seller really had. He bought the item and, when the document arrived, it appeared to be a diary kept by Associated Press reporter James Carey aboard USCGC *Itasca* during the Earhart search. The ship's radio logs included the wire service stories Carey had filed, but the nineteen typed pages of his personal diary were a detailed and often revealing description of the personalities, attitudes, and events aboard the cutter from June 24, the day *Itasca* arrived at Howland, to July 23, the day before the ship made port in Honolulu after the search.

The diary provided new insights into what was going on behind the scenes, but the document was unsigned. We had to be sure it was genuine. James Carey died in 1988, but his son lived in the Washington, DC, area and had saved his father's papers. When we visited him, he showed us the original handwritten diary, notes, and a number of photographs his father had taken during the search. One small, scrawled note cleared up an old discrepancy.

Itasca's radio log indicated Chief Radioman Bellarts first heard Earhart for three minutes from 0245 to 0248 in the wee hours of July 2: "Heard Earhart plane/but unreadable thru static."[11] According to Commander Thompson's official report, Earhart's voice "came in through the loud speaker, very low monotone 'cloudy, overcast.'"[12] Cloud cover would prevent Noonan from getting star sightings to keep the plane on course, but Thompson had not been in the radio room, and Bellarts was listening on headphones, not the loudspeaker.

Jim Carey's note read, "Friday, July 2—Up all last night following radio reports—scanty—no position from Amelia once—heard voice first time 2:48 a.m.—'sky overcast' all heard."[13] Bellarts may have passed the headphones to Carey just as the static cleared up enough to make out the words. Carey's notes also helped clear up conflicting reports of when Earhart's last in-flight message, "running on line north and south," was heard. The correct time was 0855, not 0843.[14]

Carey had transcribed his handwritten journal in 1986 and sent the typed version to the *Honolulu Star-Bulletin* in the hope of getting it published for the fiftieth anniversary of the Earhart disappearance. It wasn't accepted, and he died the next year. Twenty years later, the document turned up for sale on eBay as "Amelia Earhart's Flight Plan."[15]

From early in our investigation, Floyd Kilts' story about Earhart's bones and shoes being found on Gardner presented a conundrum. Kilts was dead, but Coast Guard records confirmed he had been in charge of dismantling the LORAN station after the war. Elements of his tale tracked with the island's known history, and yet there was no mention of such an incident in Gallagher's quarterly reports or any of the other known records. Colonial service officers Harry Maude and Eric Bevington were still alive, and they were more than skeptical.

In a May 1990 letter, Maude found Kilts' story to be "such stuff as dreams are made on." He was close friends with Dr. Macpherson and visited with him frequently during the war: "I find it difficult to understand why he never once, in our interminable reminiscences, spoke of Gallagher's 'Bones.'"[16] Eric Bevington also found the tale ludicrous. In January 1992 he told me, "If anything like that had happened it would be the talk of the [Gilberts and Ellice Islands Colony]."[17]

On June 27, 1997, I received an email from Pete McQuarrie, an author living in New Zealand who wrote books about World War II in the South Pacific. Peter and I had corresponded about TIGHAR's investigation, but it had been a while since I heard from him. He was writing to tell me he was back in Christchurch after a research trip to Tuvalu and Kiribati. At the end of his email, as a by-the-way, he mentioned: "In Kiribati I had a good look at the Government Archives and found the file on the remains found at Nikumaroro by Gallagher. It turned out they were the remains of a Polynesian man more than 60 years old when he died and the remains had been exposed to the atmosphere for at least 20 years. the sole of the shoe was a woman's alright. Stay in touch. Regards, Peter McQ."[18]

It was true: Gallagher did find bones, and there was even a woman's shoe. McQuarrie's email said nothing about Gallagher suspecting the remains of being Earhart's and he hadn't made a copy of the file, but this had to be the origin of the Floyd Kilts story. We had to see that file, but getting a copy would be no easy task. In a time before Kiribati had Internet or email, and a phone call was only possible by prior arrangement, it meant finding someone in Tarawa willing to go to the archives, find the file, and fax us copies of whatever it contained. We made it happen and soon had sixteen telegrams to and from Gallagher.

There it was. In a September 23, 1940, telegram to his colleague David Wernham, Gallagher wrote, "Please obtain from Koata a certain bottle alleged to have been found near skull discovered on Gardner Island. Grateful you retain bottle in safe place for present and ask Koata not to talk about skull which is just possibly that of Amelia Earhardt [sic]."[19] The other telegrams were correspondence relating to the bones, from Gallagher's first notice to the resident commissioner on September 23, 1940, to his telegram to Secretary Vaskess on April 28, 1941, explaining that no sextant had been found, only the box. These were obviously Gallagher's copies of telegrams that must have been taken to Suva after he died and sent to Tarawa after Kiribati became independent.

The correspondence ended when the remains arrived in Suva. What happened then? There must be more, and the place to look would be the archives of the Western Pacific High Commission, but those files were no longer in Fiji. Where were they?

TIGHAR researcher Kenton Spading succeeded in tracking the WPHC files to the British Foreign and Commonwealth Office Library and Records Department collocated with Her Majesty's Government Communications Centre in Hanslope Park, sixty miles north of London. The communications center was a secure facility where the UK's Secret Intelligence Service (also known as MI6) monitored terrorist traffic, but there was nothing secret about the archived WPHC files. They were there simply because the facility had room for them. Spading queried whether the records included a file on Amelia Earhart. They did, but when the archivist faxed him a copy, it turned out to be correspondence related to Putnam's 1937 request for someone to check out an island where a psychic said his wife had landed. The British sent an expedition that confirmed the island didn't exist, and there was no mention of bones.

We were stumped. There had to be a WPHC file with copies of Gallagher's telegrams and records of whatever else happened. Maybe we were asking the wrong question. I suggested Spading ask the archivist to search the finding aids for a file with the word "skeleton" in the title. Bingo: WPHC file 4439 was "Skeleton, Human—Finding of, on Gardner Island."

We soon had faxed copies that included Dr. Hoodless' report concluding that the castaway of Gardner Island was a short, stocky European or mixed-race male. Forensic anthropologists Dr. Karen Burns and Dr. Richard Jantz plugged Hoodless' cranial measurements into FORDISC 2.0, an interactive computer program developed by Jantz for the classification of adult crania according to race and sex: "Comparing the skull measurements to European, Polynesian and Micronesian populations, it is most similar to Norse females. [If the castaway was European] the individual represented was most likely female."[20]

It was beginning to look like the British had found Amelia Earhart in 1940 but had misidentified the body. To understand how that could have happened and the whole affair remain secret for fifty-seven years, we needed the entire file and a thorough understanding of the personalities and politics involved. We couldn't do that by fax; Kenton Spading and I would have to go to England.

Getting permission for two American researchers to waltz past the razor wire onto the home turf of MI6 wasn't easy, but in November 1998 we were able to get three days at the Foreign and Commonwealth Office Library. Upon arriving, we checked the finding aids and saw there were dozens of boxes of records we wanted to examine, but the archivist explained we would only be permitted to look at one box at a time: fill out a request card, wait for the box to be retrieved (usually at least half an hour), examine the documents, make copies of anything relevant to our investigation, return the box, request the next one. We could see there was no way were going to be able to get all the records we wanted in three days.

We asked to meet the senior librarian to see if we might be able to get the one-box-at-a-time rule waived. I knew her name was Mrs. MacPherson, and I came prepared in case we needed a special favor. When we were introduced, she looked at my necktie and said, "Do y'ken what tartan that is?" "Aye, it's MacPherson. I'm a Gillespie." (Clan MacPherson was founded by Gillespies in the thirteenth century.) I was suddenly family, and waiving the rule was no longer a problem. We got as many boxes as we wanted and came away with over three hundred copies of documents detailing not only the "Skeleton, Human" file but four volumes of files on Gerald Gallagher, service histories for all of the players in the drama, administrative files, ship schedules, and so forth.

On December 5, 1998, we released a paper at the annual American Anthropological Association convention in Philadelphia authored by Dr. Burns, Dr. Jantz, TIGHAR archaeologist Dr. Tom King, and me titled "Amelia Earhart's Bones and Shoes—Current Anthropological Perspectives on an Historical Mystery." The paper reviewed our research and concluded that Hoodless had neither the tools nor the training to evaluate the skeleton: "[T]he morphology of the recovered bones, insofar as we can tell by applying contemporary forensic methods to measurements taken at the time, appears consistent with a female of Earhart's height and ethnic origin."[21]

In 2015 an Australian archaeologist and a graduate student in England published a paper challenging TIGHAR's analysis, arguing that Hoodless, who had the bones in front of him, was more likely to be correct than Burns and Jantz, who had only measurements.[22] Karen Burns had died unexpectedly in 2012, but Richard Jantz picked up the gauntlet. Forensic techniques and technologies had advanced since 1998, and it might be possible to do a more thorough comparison of the bones to Amelia Earhart.

It was time to call in TIGHAR forensic imaging expert Jeff Glickman, a computer scientist who specializes in forensic imaging (the application of digital programs to extract information from photographs) and holds numerous patents in image processing and pattern recognition software. Much of his work has been done for the Department of Defense. Glickman was able to extract data from historical photos that enabled Jantz to compare Earhart's arm and leg bone dimensions and ratios with the castaway bone measurements taken by Hoodless. They were virtually identical. Analysis of examples of Earhart's clothing in Purdue's special collections showed her general body build to be consistent with that of the castaway.

In a fifteen-page peer-reviewed paper published in the February 2018 edition of the academic journal *Forensic Anthropology*, Jantz laid out his methodology and findings. His conclusion: "This analysis reveals that Earhart is more similar to the Nikumaroro bones than 99% of individuals in a large reference sample. This strongly supports the conclusion that the Nikumaroro bones belonged to Amelia Earhart. . . . Until definitive evidence is presented that the remains are not those of Amelia Earhart, the most convincing argument is that they are hers."[23]

In 2017 Coast Guard veteran Leslie Wiltshire, then ninety-nine, got in touch with us, and we soon had the backstory that explained why Floyd Kilts was asking islanders about Amelia Earhart. The convoluted trail that began with a pinochle game in 1946 had led us to a major body of evidence lost to history for more than half a century and a 99 percent certainty that Amelia Earhart died on Gardner Island.

WPHC file 4439 also took us to the spot where it happened. In 1991 we were unable to find the metal rainwater collector that might have been an Electra fuel tank. In 1995 Glickman examined a series of low-level aerial photos of Gardner taken in June 1941 when six PBYs visited the island as part of a Navy survey. One of the pictures showed an opening in the vegetation on the eastern shoreline where Coast Guard veteran Richard Evans said he saw the tank. When Glickman examined the image, he spotted a specular (metal) reflection back in the bush.

With a specific location to check, we hastily put together a special 1996 expedition. We found the tank buried in a hopeless tangle of scaevola, but it was a steel cistern similar to others we had seen in the abandoned village. Lying beside it were rotted wooden poles like the ones the Coast Guard veteran described. Nearby was a large depression that looked like someone had tried to dig a well. There were a few pieces of trash, green copper screening and shards of asbestos sheet, identical to material we had seen in the village. We also found a rusted food can and a button, but nothing that spoke of Amelia Earhart. Glickman's expertise had enabled us to find the tank, but it appeared to be a dead end.

Two years later, with the "Skeleton, Human" file in hand, we were trying to figure out where the discovery occurred, but Gallagher's description was frustratingly vague. His October 17, 1940, telegram to Secretary Vaskess said, "Bones were found on South East corner of island about 100 feet above ordinary high water springs. Body had obviously been lying under a 'ren' tree and remains of fire, turtle and dead birds appear to indicate life."[24] "South East corner" covers a lot of territory, and "100 feet above ordinary high water springs" means only that the bones were inland one hundred feet above the highest high tide line.

There was one further clue in Gallagher's December 27, 1940, letter that accompanied the bones to Fiji: "Should any relatives be traced, it may prove of sentimental interest for them to know that the coffin in which the remains are contained is made from a local wood known as 'kanawa' and the tree was, until a year ago, growing on the edge of the lagoon, not very far from the spot where the deceased was found."[25]

If the bones were one hundred feet above the oceanside high tide line, and the kanawa tree was "growing on the edge of the lagoon, not very far from the spot where the deceased was found," the site was somewhere at the southeast end where the ribbon of land was very narrow. That sounded like the spot where we found the tank in 1996. The tank was from the village, but what if it was brought there to provide water for the organized search Gallagher was ordered to make? What if that depression in the ground is where he dug up the skull?

Under the supervision of TIGHAR archaeologist Dr. Thomas F. King, we performed excavations of the site in 2001, 2007, and 2010, establishing that it was, indeed, where Gallagher found the bones. The tank was related not to Gallagher's search but to a later failed coconut planting, and the site had been used during the war when Coasties brought crockery from the mess hall and burned-

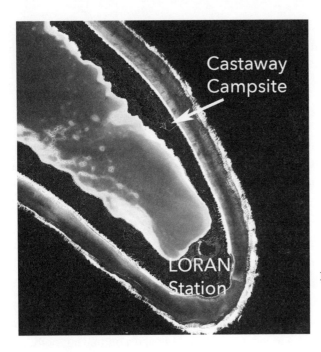

Map 12. Campsite location

out vacuum tubes from the LORAN for target practice with their .30 caliber M1 carbines. Mixed in among the archaeological "noise" from later activity, we found artifacts that spoke of an American woman of the mid-1930s, among them:

- a broken travel-size three-ounce bottle that once contained Campana Italian Balm, an American hand lotion popular with women in the 1930s[26]
- the broken mirror and fragments of rouge from an American 1930s-vintage compact[27]
- a small broken jar that once contained "Dr. Berry's Freckle Ointment," a skin-lightening product popular with American women in the 1930s[28]
- the pull tab and slider from a Talon "Autolok" size 06 American civilian zipper manufactured between 1933 and 1936
- a broken bone-handled, double-bladed "Easy Open" jackknife manufactured by the Imperial Cutlery Company of Providence, Rhode Island, between 1930 and 1945.

The knife had been beaten apart with a blunt object. The blades were not present, probably extracted for use as spear points. A "Bone handle, double blade Jack Knife, large Blade No. 22309" was inventoried aboard Earhart's Electra after the wreck in Hawaii.[29]

The depression in the ground proved to be a small skull-sized hole within a bigger hole, apparently created when Gallagher exhumed the skull. Numerous excavations for surviving bones found nothing except a finger bone too degraded to yield sequenceable DNA; however, forensic dogs did confirm that a person had died under what was left of a "ren" tree, as Gallagher had described. Attempts to find contact DNA on artifacts were unsuccessful. We had the right place, but after more than eighty years lying unburied in the brutal Nikumaroro environment, any bones missed by Gallagher were gone.

42

Red Herrings and
Wild Geese

1991–2019

Decades of hard work and a healthy dose of serendipity have unearthed the facts that solve the Earhart mystery, but for every success, there were dozens of false starts, dead ends, and frustrations.

In 1991 we recovered a cut-apart aluminum box found in the abandoned colonial village. It was clearly an aircraft component complete with stamped part number 28F 4023. Research quickly identified it as a bookcase designed to hold the navigator's almanacs and sight reduction tables in a Consolidated Model 28, known to the U.S. Navy as the PBY Catalina. But studying photos of the bookcase installed in the aircraft, it looked like the mounting holes on the back of the artifact were wrong. Might this navigator's bookcase have been used in another type of aircraft to hold the books needed by a navigator named Fred Noonan?

To test the hypothesis we first needed to confirm the apparent discrepancy, and that meant examining a bookcase in a surviving PBY. To be sure we were looking at an original installation, we had to find an aircraft that had not been restored—a perennial problem in identifying aviation artifacts. The New England Air Museum in Windsor Locks, Connecticut, had a PBY that had been scheduled for restoration until it was wrecked in a tornado, but the bookcase was still on the bulkhead of the navigator's station. Sure enough, the mounting holes on the artifact were all wrong for a PBY.

Consolidated delivered the first squadron of Catalinas to the Navy in early 1937 around the same time the Electra's cabin was being outfitted by Harry Manning, who held a reserve commission in the Navy. There were no good photos of the Electra's cabin interior, but a picture of Earhart and Noonan standing beside the open door in Darwin, Australia, provided a peek inside. There was a dark shape that just might be a bookcase.

It looked like we were really on to something, until a year later. I was going through photos of World War II aircraft at the National Archives looking for something else when I stumbled across a picture of the navigator's station in a Consolidated Model 32, the B-24 Liberator. On the wall was a bookcase that looked very much like our artifact and that was installed in a way that matched its mounting holes. The parts list confirmed that dozens of the interior furnishings in the Model 32 were Model 28 parts, including "28F-4023—Box—Furn.—Navig.—Books & Paper Stow."[1] I had found a home for our box, but it wasn't in NR16020.

Another artifact collected in 1991 might actually be from the Electra. It's a largely intact rectangular metal assembly. An aluminum sheet .032 inches thick and 16¾ inches long by 6.5 inches wide is reinforced along the top and bottom with riveted strips. Clearly an internal aircraft component, it was a freestanding "fence" not attached to the aircraft other than by nails (not rivets or screws) through a ninety-degree aluminum flange along the bottom edge. One side of the assembly was originally covered with glued-on quarter-inch kapok insulation with woven blue cloth on the exterior surface. Unlike World War II aircraft parts, the assembly has no stamped part number. The ends of the assembly appear to be designed to attach to other assemblies and, in 2003, we found two similar structures nearby in much poorer condition.

These assemblies may be heat shields associated with the Electra's fuselage tanks. The Model 10 had heating ducts that ran along the base of the cabin wall to keep the passengers warm, but the airplane was not designed to have fuel tanks and lines in the cabin. If fuel lines get too warm, vapor lock can disrupt or stop fuel flow.

During World War II, Lockheed Electra NC14915 was owned by Morrison-Knudsen Engineering Corporation and transported employees between Boise, Idaho, and Ketchikan, Alaska. To give the aircraft the necessary range, an auxiliary fuel tank was installed in the left forward cabin. On January 5, 1943, the aircraft crashed in what is now the Misty Fjords National Monument, a remote wilderness area forty miles northeast of Ketchikan. When a TIGHAR team surveyed the wreck in 2004, they discovered the cabin tank was insulated from the heater duct with a heavy mat of asbestos to prevent vapor lock. With only one auxiliary tank, the weight penalty was not excessive.

Earhart's 10E Special had six tanks in the cabin. They were removed and reinstalled shortly after delivery. It seems likely the problem was vapor lock. That much asbestos matting would be too heavy. Artifacts found more than half a century later suggest Lockheed solved the problem by installing a fence of aluminum and kapok insulating panels nailed to the plywood floor between the heating ducts and the tanks and lines. Unfortunately, there is no record of the nature of the problem that caused the tanks to be removed or how it was remedied.

Even when an artifact can be objectively identified as to what it is, figuring out how it got to where it was found requires interpretation, and interpretation is, by definition, subjective. The demon is coincidence.

At the time Gallagher found the castaway's skeleton, the only known human activity at that location was the work party that found and buried the skull. He therefore assumed the objects found in the area—the Benedictine bottle, the woman's shoe sole, the parts of a man's shoe, the corks with brass chains, the remains of a fire, the dead birds and turtle, the sextant box—were all associated with the castaway. So did we.

The sextant box seemed the most promising target for research. According to Gallagher, it was a box for an "old fashioned" sextant, probably painted with black enamel, and most importantly, it had numbers on it: "3500" (stenciled) and "1542." Before long, we had it figured out. The box was for a Brandis & Sons, New York, Navy surveying sextant. The 3500 was the sequential "maker's number," and the 1542 was the number assigned by the Naval Observatory when the instrument was checked for accuracy.

Maybe Noonan had a Brandis Navy surveying sextant with him on the world flight and Earhart, as a castaway, had used its box to carry things. But was that hypothesis plausible?

Brandis sextants were manufactured under a government contract let in early 1918 as part of a wartime expansion of the U.S. Navy, but the Great War unexpectedly ended that November and new ship construction was canceled. The Navy had more sextants than it needed, and many sextants were sold as war surplus. It was certainly conceivable that Noonan owned one, but Brandis Navy surveying sextants were not designed for taking celestial observations from an airplane. In fact, when Noonan joined Earhart's team a few days before her first world flight attempt, he insisted that Harry Manning borrow a Pioneer bubble octant from the Navy. Why would he have a nautical sextant aboard the Electra?

In 1935 Fred Noonan wrote a letter to Philip Van Horn Weems, the world's leading expert on aeronautical navigation, describing the equipment and techniques he used on the historic Pan American China Clipper flight to Hawaii. We found one sentence particularly interesting: "Two sextants were carried—a pioneer bubble octant, and a mariner's sextant. The former was used for all sights; the latter carried as a 'preventer' [a nautical term for a back-up or safeguard]."[2]

What kind of mariner's sextant did Noonan use as a preventer? A photograph of Noonan's navigation room aboard Pan Am's Martin M-130 China Clipper showed two sextant boxes on the shelf above the navigator's table: a box for a Pioneer bubble octant, and the distinctive box for a Brandis Navy surveying sextant. There was no doubt about it. The box Gallagher found was for the same kind of sextant Noonan probably had aboard the Electra but, without records linking an object to a particular source, archaeological evidence is always circumstantial. Was it possible to find documentation that proved the box was Noonan's?

By 2012 we had cataloged thirty-two surviving Brandis & Sons Navy surveying sextants and purchased several examples, but we were having no luck finding records that tied 3500/1542 to Fred Noonan. One of TIGHAR's most powerful research tools was the online Amelia Earhart search forum, where interested individuals could ask questions, make comments, debate theories, and post their own ideas, hypotheses, and research results. Appropriately enough, on Halloween, October 31, 2012, John Kada offered a new idea:

> Here's another possibility to think about; perhaps the sextant box found by Gallagher wasn't a surplus U.S. Navy item, but instead the box of a sextant still in use by the USN?
>
> In late 1939 the USS *Bushnell* mapped Gardner Island and its lagoon. One kind of instrument that I believe was typically used in doing this work was a surveying sextant. We know that surveying sextants were assigned Naval Observatory numbers . . . so this leads me to offer the hypothesis that a surveying sextant box was lost by a member of the *Bushnell* surveying team in the vicinity of the castaway's remains. One can imagine, for instance, a *Bushnell* sailor taking a break from Gardner's heat and sun in the shade of the forest, going off with his sextant, leaving the box behind to pick up later, but then being unable to find the box when he comes back for it.
>
> So then a few months pass by and the colonists find the skull. Some six months more pass and then Gallagher and helpers make a thorough search of the area looking for more of

the castaway's remains, but can find only about half of the castaway's bones. In the process of trying to find all those missing bones the sextant box is found (not by Gallagher, by the way, but by another searcher). Gallagher assumes the sextant box belonged to the castaway, and we naturally assume he was right. After all, wasn't the sextant box found right next to the skeletal remains of the castaway? That's how I've always pictured it, but when I go back and read the correspondence between Gallagher and his superiors in Research Document #12, The Bones Chronology, I see nothing precise about the proximity of the sextant box to the castaway's remains. All Gallagher says (in a July 3, 1941 communication) is that the sextant box was found "nearby the remains." So our *Bushnell* guy didn't necessarily sit himself down next to a partial skeleton, stare at it while reflecting on the meaning of life, and then go away, leaving his U.S. Navy sextant box behind for Gallagher to discover. Our *Bushnell* guy merely had to be somewhere close enough to the castaway's remains to be within Gallagher's search radius.

One thing this hypothesis has going for it is that it explains why no sextant was found in the castaway's sextant box. It also of course nicely explains how a sextant box with a USNO number and a Brandis number ended up on Gardner (I also acknowledge, of course, that the possibility that the box was Noonan's is also a good explanation.) But what intrigues me about this hypothesis is that maybe, just maybe, it can be verified. Perhaps somewhere in the surviving records of the *Bushnell* we can learn the Naval Observatory numbers of the sextants it carried. That to me is very interesting.[3]

I initially thought Kada's hypothesis was thoroughly bizarre. The coincidence of a sextant box for the same type of sextant Noonan used as a "preventer" being left on Gardner Island a stone's throw from Earhart's remains beggared the imagination, but that's exactly what happened.

It took John Kada six years, numerous trips to the National Archives, and many dead ends, but in August 2018 he found the proof. In a November 15, 1938, memo to the superintendent of the Naval Observatory in Washington, DC, the commanding officer of USS *Bushnell* included "a list of surveying instruments for which repairs are requested as outline."[4] Item 12 on the list was "Sextant, Brandis, N.O. 1542 General Overhaul." A handwritten notation confirmed it was returned to *Bushnell* on January 17, 1939.[5] The survey of Gardner was the following November. Were any of the other artifacts found in the area by Gallagher, or TIGHAR for that matter, left behind by the forgetful sailor? Not unless he wore women's shoes, carried a compact, and used hand lotion and freckle cream.

The coincidence demon struck again with a section of aluminum aircraft skin we found on Nikumaroro in 1991. The type of aluminum, the thickness of the sheet, and the type and size of the rivet holes and one surviving rivet were right for a Lockheed Model 10, but the unusual rivet pattern on the artifact did not quite match anywhere on surviving Electras. On the other hand, the belly of Earhart's airplane had been extensively repaired following the wreck in Hawaii. We wondered if that might be why the rivet patten was slightly different, or perhaps it came from a World War II wreck.

There was no record of any airplane ever crashing or even being damaged at Nikumaroro. We had found scraps of aluminum from aircraft skin brought to Nikumaroro, probably from the big wartime base at Canton Island, to be cut up for local use, but this piece was intact. We had found it in the wash-up from a storm, and there was coral growth on its surface indicating the metal had spent a long time in shallow water.

In 2014 we asked the National Museum of the United States Air Force to help us see if the rivet pattern was a better match to any of the World War II aircraft types known to have been lost within an eight-hundred-mile radius of Nikumaroro. On March 28 a nine-person TIGHAR team worked with the museum restoration supervisor to inspect aircraft in the Air Force collection. There was no match, but the restoration staff did disabuse us of the notion the rivet pattern on a repaired area would be different from the original. Unless there was a supplemental type certificate, the repair would have to follow the original design. We were stuck. The artifact didn't fit an Electra, but it didn't fit anything else either.

Then one of our researchers had an idea. There was one place on the aluminum skin of NR16020 that was unlike any other Electra or, for that matter, any other aircraft. When Earhart's aircraft was in Miami in May 1937 before departing on her second world flight attempt, a special navigator's window installed in the aft starboard side of the cabin was removed and replaced with a plain aluminum patch. Nobody knows why. The change is not mentioned in government records, private correspondence, or press reports, but it's obvious in numerous photos.

If the size and rivet pattern of the artifact matched the patch, it would be proof we had a piece of the Earhart Electra. Initial research, including physical comparison to two existing Electras, confirmed the size was right, and TIGHAR forensic imaging expert Jeff Glickman's examination of the available photos of the patch revealed details of the rivet pattern that suggested a match. To make a conclusive comparison, Glickman needed better imagery.

In 2017 Tom Palshaw, a volunteer in the New England Air Museum restoration shop, noticed a similarity to the rivet pattern on the artifact to a place on the upper surface of a Douglas C-47 wing in the museum's collection and brought his observation to my attention. We knew that a C-47 crashed and burned on Sydney Island in the Phoenix Group in 1943. After the war, a few families from Sydney relocated to Nikumaroro.

We did not have access to the upper wing surface of the C-47 at the Air Force museum three years before so, on July 16, 2017, TIGHAR video producer Mark Smith and I went to the New England Air Museum and took a close look at the wing. The rivet pattern in the area Palshaw pointed out was indeed quite similar to the artifact, but some of the rivet sizes were too big and, in checking an Army Air Forces technical manual, the skin thickness was wrong.

Meanwhile, our search for better pictures of the patch continued, and by 2021 we had found and acquired (at great expense) excellent previously unknown imagery, including photos of the airplane taken in Miami soon after the patch was installed and 16-millimeter movie film of NR16020 in Lae, New Guinea, on July 1, 1937. Glickman used every trick in the book, including artificial intelligence, to pull sufficient detail from the imagery and found there were features present on the artifact that did not appear to be present on the patch.

He decided to reinvestigate the C-47 as a possible source, and on August 18 and 19, 2022, he visited the New England Air Museum and performed an intensive forensic examination of the C-47 wing. The section Smith and I had inspected in 2017 was indeed not a match, but Glickman found a spot where the rivet sizes and pattern were perfect. Exactly how a torn section of skin from that particular part of a C-47 wing got to Nikumaroro and ended up looking the way it did will never be known but, after thirty-one years of research, I reluctantly concluded we had at last discovered its true identity. That a piece of wreckage from the one place on the one aircraft that is nearly identical to the patch on Earhart's aircraft should end up on the island where she landed is a coincidence of mind-boggling proportions, but it happened.

The sextant box and airplane skin demonstrate the frailty of archaeological evidence. What other crazy coincidences might lurk behind the artifacts that appeared to be associated with Earhart? We know a great deal about the island's history, but it would be foolish to suppose we know everything that happened there. Our 2007 expedition had found artifacts and features that reliably established we had found the site where Gallagher discovered the partial skeleton. But how to prove the castaway was Amelia Earhart? An expanded excavation of the site was bound to turn up more artifacts and, ideally, bones Gallagher had missed. Maybe DNA was the answer. We assumed that it would be a simple matter of comparing DNA that might be Earhart's with DNA that is known to be Earhart's—and we were right. The hard part is getting DNA to compare.

There are basically two kinds of DNA. Nuclear DNA is the kind that is specific to a particular individual—the kind used to convict a criminal or absolutely identify a bone as being Amelia Earhart's—but there is no way to get a sample of her nuclear DNA. Mitochondrial DNA (mtDNA) is inherited from the mother and is, therefore, a great way to check ancestry in the female line. A person's mtDNA is normally about 87 percent identical to their mother's and back throughout the matriarchic line. Siblings all have similar mtDNA. The same is true for a sister's children but not for a brother's, who will have their mother's mtDNA.

Although not as certain as nuclear DNA for specific identification of an individual, mitochondrial DNA is a lot easier to find simply because there's a whole lot more of it in any given cell. Getting nuclear DNA from a current crime scene is usually not a problem, but when we're talking about "ancient DNA" in decades-old material, it's a different story. DNA strands are the building blocks of life, but when the life is over, the blocks begin to crumble—ashes to ashes, dust to dust.

Any DNA we were likely to get from the castaway site would be mtDNA, and we were able to persuade a relative in Earhart's female line to give the scientists we were working with a cheek swab from which they could extract mtDNA. Now we had to find something to compare it to.

Finding bones would be iffy, but more artifacts were almost certain to turn up. Law enforcement routinely gets "contact DNA" from something the victim or perpetrator has touched. Might the castaway's mtDNA survive on an object they had handled? Some DNA experts thought it was worth a shot.

With high hopes, our 2010 expedition recovered artifacts under sterile conditions—no mean feat in the 110-degree Fahrenheit heat. To prevent contamination, objects of interest were collected by an archaeologist outfitted in protective gear who put them in specially sealed evidence bags, but in the end, none of them yielded DNA. Other experts later said we would have a better chance finding a unicorn than recovering ancient contact DNA from the Nikumaroro environment.

The one human bone recovered (a finger bone) yielded mtDNA, but after several tries, the lab was unable to get a complete sequence for comparison. The process is destructive, and when only a sliver of bone was left, we stopped trying; one more attempt would consume the last remaining piece. If, by chance, it was successful, there would be no way for a second independent lab to replicate the result.

Expeditions in 2017 and 2019 used forensic dogs to search for more bones and, although the canines confirmed someone had died at the site, excavations found nothing but coral rubble that had been impregnated with human cadaverine, an organic compound formed in the decay of animal protein. Bones that were undiscovered in 1940 were, in all likelihood, eventually consumed by crabs and rats for their calcium content.

Did the bones that Gallagher sent to Fiji still exist? An April 4, 1941, note from Sir Harry Luke to Secretary Vaskess in the WPHC file reads: "Pl ask CMA to convey my thanks to Dr. Hoodless for his report and the trouble he has taken in this matter and to request him to retain the remains until further notice."[6] The file contains no further notice.

Three research trips to Fiji failed to find any mention of the bones in burial records or credible recollections by individuals. A 2011 search of the Colonial War Memorial Hospital in Suva turned up a box of old bones, some of which looked like they might be the ones we were looking for. With Fijian and U.S. Customs approval, the TIGHAR team leader, Gary Quigg, brought them to the United States for analysis. Once again, our hopes were dashed when the bones turned out to be from several ethnic Polynesians.

Might the bones have been sent to Kiribati? In 2001 TIGHAR researcher Col. Van T. Hunn, USAF (Ret.), and I looked at bones in the Umwanibong Cultural Centre and Museum in Tarawa. Some were of known provenance, having been used in Gilbertese cultural ceremonies. Others, including a skull, were badly damaged and had been repaired with plaster or some similar material, possibly for use in an anatomy class. The skull Hoodless measured was intact except for a broken cheek bone. Nothing looked promising—another dead end.

In 2019 a National Geographic team with an archaeologist and a forensic anthropologist went to Tarawa and, in the same museum, found a fragmented skull. They brought it back and reassembled what they judged to be a female skull that appeared to match the right eye orbit (socket) dimensions measured by Hoodless, raising hopes that physical proof of Earhart's fate might be at hand.

In published photos, I recognized the skull as the one Van and I had dismissed in 2001. Dr. Richard Jantz looked at the photos and pointed out that the glabella (brow ridge) on the skull, the feature commonly used to differentiate sex, had very clearly been reconstructed with a plaster-like material. The skull may or may not be female. He also noticed the right eye socket had been reassembled using a dowel, so the dimensions of the orbit that appeared to match Hoodless' measurement were, in fact, a function of the length of the dowel. A hole in the maxilla (upper jaw) speculated to be from the type of sinus operation Earhart is known to have had looked more like it was caused by a severe tooth abscess, common among Pacific Islanders with no access to dental care. Attempts to identify the skull with DNA were inconclusive, but the sequence included markers typical in Polynesian populations. There was no reason to think the skull was the one Gallagher found.

When last mentioned in the WPHC file, the bones were believed to be of no importance. The skeleton was incomplete and in poor condition due to exposure and crabs, so it would logically be of little use in an anatomy class, but hopes persisted that the bones were still out there waiting to be discovered. Everyone wanted DNA to provide a "smoking gun" solution to the Earhart mystery, but the most dedicated quest is a wild goose chase if the prize no longer exists.

43

Chasing the Plane

1990–2012

onventional wisdom said solving the Earhart mystery meant finding her airplane or at least a conclusively identifiable piece of wreckage. From the beginning, we recognized the Pan American and Coast Guard directional bearings taken on Earhart's radio distress calls were compelling evidence that the Electra did not go down at sea. For the transmitter to work, the airplane had to be on land. The bearings crossed near Gardner, but the Navy's aerial search didn't see a plane. By 1990 it was clear the plane was not hiding on the island. Where did it go? At low tide, many places on the fringing reef flat were dry and smooth enough to permit a safe landing. A boy in Wyoming even said he heard Earhart say, "Ship is on a reef south of the equator."[1] The only plausible answer was that she had landed on the reef flat and the airplane had been washed into the ocean before the Navy got there.

The prospect of a largely intact Electra sitting on the ocean floor waiting to be discovered was enticing, but the side-scan sonar survey we did in 1991 found nothing. Did the plane float away to sink far from the island, or was it beaten apart by the surf and sank too close to the reef edge to be detected by the sonar search? If so, debris might have later washed up on the beach—but which beach?

In 1995 we were contacted by Dr. John Mims, a retired physician in Tuscumbia, Alabama, who related his story of being a PBY pilot during World War II and seeing salvaged aircraft components being used as fishing tackle by locals on Gardner. They told him it came from a wrecked airplane that had been there when they first arrived.[2] Mims had carved wood souvenirs from Gardner with small inlaid aluminum decorations he was told were made of metal from the crashed plane. He let us remove one of them for testing. Scanning electron microscopy performed by the National Transportation Safety Board lab found it to be 24S-T Alclad, the same type of aluminum used in Earhart's Electra—as well as every American aircraft used in World War II—but no aircraft had been lost or damaged at Gardner.[3] The Gilbertese settlers on Gardner could not salvage an airplane on the ocean bottom far from shore. If the story was true, the plane or debris from the wreck must have been where they could get at it.

Later that same year we got our hands on a mapping survey of the atoll flown in 1953. Excellent low-altitude black-and-white aerial photos covered every part of the shoreline, so we asked forensic imaging expert Jeff Glickman to see if he could find anything in the photos that might be airplane wreckage. There was nothing on the beaches, but in shallow water on the reef flat near the main lagoon passage, Glickman noticed four small, light-colored objects that were present in two overlapping images, proving they were not flaws in the film. One of them was exhibiting a specular reflection, indicating it was metal. There is plenty of metal on the reef flat distributed southwestward from the shipwreck toward the lagoon passage, but SS *Norwich City* wreckage is rusted iron and steel. None of it is light-colored. If these were pieces of aluminum aircraft debris, they were probably washed southwestward from somewhere near the shipwreck and may have eventually been washed through the passage and into the lagoon. It was our first clue to where the plane landed.

We scheduled our fourth expedition to Nikumaroro for February and March 1997, not realizing we were rolling the weather dice. We had done a short trip the year before around the same time with no problem, but November through April is storm season in the southwest Pacific. In the Atlantic the storms are called hurricanes, in the northwest Pacific, typhoons, and in the southwest Pacific, tropical cyclones. They're all the same animal and, by any name, they're no fun.

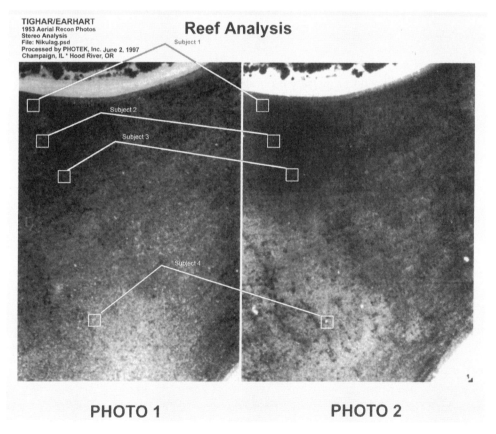

Photo 35. Light-colored metal debris on the reef flat near the main lagoon passage is present in 1953 aerial mapping photos. Courtesy Jeff Glickman, Photek

For this expedition we chartered *Nai'a*, a 120-foot motorsailer out of Lautoka, Fiji. The ship was popular for live-aboard scuba cruises in local Fijian waters, but she had the chops for open ocean work and proved to be ideally suited to TIGHAR's needs. The thousand-mile voyage to Nikumaroro was rough, and when we arrived we found high seas hitting the landing channel at an angle that sent geysers of foam thirty feet in the air. Getting back and forth to the ship was harrowing, and carrying out our research objectives on the island was a challenge. The violence of the surf prohibited an examination of the reef flat north of the shipwreck where we now thought the plane may have landed, but we succeeded in searching the suspect areas of the lagoon with an electromagnetic sensor—and found nothing. We were out of ideas, and, to make matters worse, on the voyage back to Fiji our ship ran smack into tropical cyclone Hina. Forty-foot seas and hurricane-force winds forced the captain to divert to the sheltered water of the lagoon at Funafuti in Tuvalu. While stranded there for six days, we discovered a local woman who had lived on Nikumaroro in the 1950s and remembered seeing airplane wreckage on the beach and "a piece of a wing"[4] on the reef flat in the same area where Jeff Glickman had spotted light-colored metal debris in the 1953 photos. There was nothing there now, but we reasoned there might be airplane debris deep in the dense beachfront scaevola along that shoreline.

In 1999 we mounted an expedition to test that hypothesis. Hacking our way into the bush at intervals close enough to see the ground between transects, we examined the coastline and found nothing but the usual jetsam: fishnet floats, flip-flops, and, incredibly, unbroken fluorescent light tubes tossed overboard from fishing vessels, but no airplane debris.

The *Norwich City* debris on the reef flat was distributed southwestward from the wreck. Airplane debris would follow the same pattern but, because it was lighter, probably came from somewhere beyond (that is, north of) the shipwreck.

While we whacked the bushes on Nikumaroro, a TIGHAR team in Fiji was following up on what we had learned from the recently discovered WPHC files in the hope the bones recovered in 1940 might still exist. The castaway's remains had been transported to Fiji in a purpose-built kanawa wood coffin fashioned by the island carpenter, Temou Samuela, an Ellice Islander who had arrived on Gardner in January 1940. With him was his seventeen-year-old daughter Sengalo who, we discovered, was seventy-six and living in Suva under her married name, Emily Sikuli. Interviewed by TIGHAR archaeologist Tom King and researchers Kristin Tague and Barbara Norris, Emily remembered her father making the coffin. She said, through an interpreter: "The bones were found in the sea on Nikumaroro. There was a boat that was wrecked, but that boat belonged to New Zealand and that part of the island was named for New Zealand. Where the boat was on the reef, not too far from there, is where the plane came down."[5]

She was clearly confused about the details, but no one had said anything about an airplane. Asked to elaborate, she described wreckage she had seen on the reef flat that her father told her was from an airplane. A few days later, when the expedition returned from Nikumaroro, I did a videotaped interview with Mrs. Sikuli in which I handed her a pen and asked her to indicate on a map the place where she saw the airplane wreckage. Without hesitation, she put a mark on the reef edge north of the shipwreck just where we had reasoned the plane probably landed.

The next year, we had another major breakthrough. John Hathaway in Hoopeston, Illinois, contacted us after seeing a newspaper article about our work. Hathaway said his neighbor Betty

Klenck Brown had transcribed a lengthy distress call she had heard from Amelia Earhart on her family radio as a girl in Florida. She had tried many times to get someone to take her seriously, and Hathaway himself had written to Fred Goerner on her behalf, but to no avail. She was pretty disgusted, and he wasn't sure she would talk to us, but he felt we should know about her.

He needn't have worried. Pat and I were soon sitting with Mrs. Brown in her living room as she went over each entry in her notebook. An in-depth investigation showed the physical notebook and its other entries to be of the correct vintage, and some of what she transcribed is "occult"—accurate information she could not have possibly known, including repeated apparent references to *Norwich City* transcribed by fifteen-year-old Betty Klenck as "N.Y., N.Y. (or something that sounded like New York City)."[6]

Betty's Notebook, as it has come to be known, is a transcription of a genuine distress call from Earhart and Noonan. The events and conditions it depicts provide an almost-too-intimate window into the anxiety that reigned in the Electra's cockpit as the plane was being washed inexorably toward the reef edge.

We were finding more and more support for our hypothesis of what happened to the plane, but there were two tests that had to be performed before we could say with confidence that we were correct. Our research had found over a hundred alleged receptions of distress calls sent from the Earhart plane in the days and nights following her disappearance. TIGHAR radio propagation expert Robert L. Brandenburg cataloged and analyzed each of them, drawing on his many years of experience as an analyst with the Naval Electronics Laboratory. Bob used two computer models, the Ionospheric Communications Enhanced Profile Analysis and Circuit prediction program developed by the Department of Commerce Institute for Telecommunications Science, and the Ionospheric Communications Analysis and Prediction Program, a recognized world standard for analysis of high-frequency radio signal propagation, to assess the probability that a reported signal, if sent from NR16020 at Gardner, would be heard at the receiver site.

By 2006 Brandenburg had determined fifty-seven of the reported signals to be credible. They were received almost exclusively during hours of darkness on Gardner and spanned nearly a week, but for Earhart to be able to send distress calls over such an extended period, she would have to recharge the two batteries that powered the transmitter. The only way to do that was by running the aircraft's generator-equipped starboard engine, and starting the engine required power from those same batteries. If she ran down the batteries sending radio calls, it would be impossible to start the engine to recharge them. The only sensible thing to do was to send signals only when the engine was running, but to run the engine, the water level on the reef had to be low enough for the propeller to clear. For the hypothesis to survive, the credible receptions must coincide with periods when an engine could be run.

Brandenburg could hindcast the tides to determine highs and lows, but to calculate the hour-by-hour water level on the reef flat north of the shipwreck, he had to know the height of the surface above sea level. To get that information, we conducted a survey of the reef in 2007. After measuring the rise and fall of the tide at the landing channel, we compared the height of the coral surface there with the height at the shipwreck a mile and a quarter away using a Total Station surveying system. From there we could measure the reef height in the area of interest. When Brandenburg compiled the data and calculated the water levels, the credible signals occurred only when the water was low enough for the prop to clear—night after night after night.

The other question that had to be answered was whether there was enough fuel. As best we could figure, the plane had arrived at Gardner with about two hours of in-flight fuel remaining. At Kelly Johnson's predicted thirty-eight gallons per hour, that would be about seventy-six gallons, but Earhart would not have to run the engine at cruise power to charge the batteries. Three days after she disappeared, Paul Mantz, commenting on whether Earhart could send distress calls, told a *New York Herald Tribune* reporter, "The right engine, turning over at 900 R.P.M. creates about 50 amperes. This burns almost six gallons of gas hourly. To the best of my knowledge, Miss Earhart did not have much fuel when she was forced down. Yet, the signals appear to be sent regularly."[7] If true, she would have enough fuel to send the credible signals—but was Mantz correct? With the cooperation of Covington Aircraft Engines in Okmulgee, Oklahoma, we mounted a Pratt & Whitney R1340 engine like Earhart's, equipped with the same kind of generator, on a test stand and got the same results Mantz had described. Our hypothesis was good. It could have happened just the way the evidence suggested.

The clincher came in another bizarre twist of fate. In October 1991 David North, the American correspondent for *Pacific Islands Monthly* magazine, published in Fiji, had written an article about that year's TIGHAR expedition titled "Back to Nikumaroro." Paul Barber, a British expat living in Tuvalu, read the article and sent a copy to his friend Eric Bevington—then eighty years old, long retired from the colonial service, and living in the south of England. Bevington wrote back to Barber expressing his skepticism of TIGHAR's findings. Barber sent a copy of Bevington's letter to David North, who wrote a follow-up piece for the magazine summarizing the many letters the magazine had received in response to the first article. "PIM Readers Help in Earhart Search" included Barber's correspondence with "Eric Bennington [*sic*] who served in the Pacific from 1937 to 1963, and who now lives in Great Britain."[8]

On January 1, 1992, before publishing the piece, North faxed me a copy for fact-checking. I immediately realized Eric Bennington must be Eric Bevington and was astonished to see that he was still alive. Three weeks later Pat and I were visiting with him in his retirement cottage in the New Forest, discussing his 1937 expedition to Gardner to evaluate the uninhabited island for future colonization.

Distinguished, charming, and witty, Bevington was the embodiment of Kipling's benevolent vision of British colonialism. He was still dedicated to the people he had served as a district officer in the Gilbert and Ellice Islands Colony and was packing for a visit to Tarawa to see how they were getting on as an independent nation. Sitting in a pub with Bevington comparing our experiences on Nikumaroro, I complained, "One thing that bothers me is that my feet are always wet from getting ashore or crossing the lagoon passage." His solution was from another era: "No Ric, you're doing it wrong. Have the boys carry you."

Bevington gave us his book, *The Things We Do for England—If Only England Knew*, and a copy of the private journal he had kept during his 1937 trip. He also happily allowed Pat to take photocopies of the dozens of pictures in a photo album of the expedition.

Eighteen years later, we were planning an exhaustive archaeological excavation of the castaway site for our 2010 expedition and, as part of the pre-expedition research, Jeff Glickman was reviewing the many historical photos of Gardner we had collected over the decades in case there was something we should check out. Although his primary focus was the aerial photos, he noticed something in a photocopy Pat had made when we visited Bevington in 1992. A picture he had taken of Gardner's western shoreline in October 1937, as RCS *Nimanoa* was leaving the island, showed a profile view of *Norwich City* and was labeled "Gardiner [*sic*] Island and the wreck." On the extreme left of the frame, unnoticed by Bevington at the time or by me in the many years we'd had the photo, there was something sticking up out of the water on the reef. There should be nothing sticking up out of the water on an uninhabited island. The original print was wallet-sized and the resolution of the photocopy was poor, but Glickman suspected it might be a man-made object, and its location was very close to where we thought the Electra had gone over the reef edge. We needed to get a better look at that photo.

By then, Bevington was dead and his photo album was in the Rhodes House Library at Oxford University. At our request, the library made us a six-hundred-dots-per-inch scan of the original print from which Glickman was able to pull sufficient detail to confirm not only that the object was man-made, but also that its component features matched the shapes, hues, and sizes of wreckage from a Lockheed Electra main landing gear assembly. The tire, strut, and worm gear retraction mechanism had come apart in the same way shown in photos of the right main gear of NR16020 that separated from the aircraft during the Hawaii accident.

A photo of wreckage from Earhart's aircraft on the reef at Gardner Island taken three months after her disappearance and in precisely the place we had concluded the airplane was washed into the

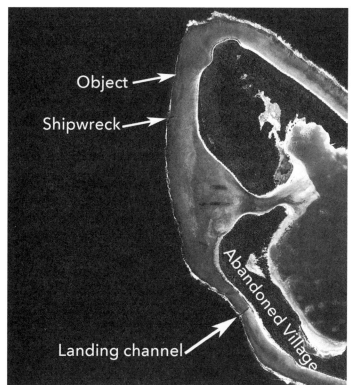

Map 13. Northwest end of Gardner Island

ocean was almost too good to be true. We needed a second opinion from experts who didn't have a dog in the fight, and before long, the perfect opportunity arose.

In June 2011 TIGHAR researcher and attorney Bill Carter and I were in Tarawa doing research at the Kiribati National Archives and negotiating the terms of an antiquities management agreement. The evidence that the Earhart/Noonan flight ended at Nikumaroro was so strong that the island needed to be protected to prevent looting. To ensure that any searching or excavation followed accepted archaeological protocols and recognized Kiribati's ownership of anything found, under the proposed agreement TIGHAR would have the exclusive right to govern Earhart-related research within the nation's borders.

TIGHAR member Richard Pruett, deputy chief of mission at the American embassy in Fiji, had tipped us off to a scheduled diplomatic visit to Tarawa by Dr. Kurt Campbell, assistant secretary of state for East Asia and Pacific affairs. He would only be there for a few hours but Pruett thought he

Photo 36. Analysis of photographed object by forensic imaging expert Jeff Glickman. The object in Bevington's photo is the wreckage of a Lockheed Electra main landing gear assembly. Courtesy Jeff Glickman, Photek

Photo 37. March 20, 1937. The right main landing gear was torn loose and left behind as the aircraft slid on the runway.
Photo by Gerald Berger (used with permission)

might be able to arrange a quick meet-and-greet with Campbell at the airport before he left. We had adjusted our travel plans accordingly. We got way more than we bargained for.

Campbell and his entourage arrived as scheduled, and, on the drive from the airport to meetings with Kiribati officials, Pruett started to brief him on local customs and protocols: "Oh, and by the way. There are a couple of American researchers here working on the Amelia Earhart mystery. They seem to have it pretty well solved." Campbell's reaction was not what Richard expected: "You've gotta be shitting me!"

Assistant Secretary Campbell turned out to be a big Amelia Earhart fan, and Pruett had a hard time finishing the briefing. TIGHAR's work was all his boss wanted to hear about. I met Campbell at the airport as planned, and we chatted for about two minutes before he turned to his chief of staff, deputy assistant secretary James Loi, and said, "I want a full briefing from these guys in Washington as soon as they get home."

Carter and I made our presentation to Campbell and his staff at the State Department on July 28, 2011. When we finished, Campbell said to let him know if there was anything he could do to help. We explained our need for an independent analysis of the Bevington photo, and Campbell said he would see what he could do. On August 2 James Loi wrote, "Making progress on having one of our relevant agencies do some analysis on the photo. They're asking for the file or photo. Can you send?"[9] On August 10 I sent him the high-resolution scan and a summary of what Glickman had been able to discern: "We refer to the mystery object as 'Nessie' with tongue firmly in cheek."[10]

We heard nothing more for two months until I was called to Washington for a briefing. On November 15 I met with the chief of the State Department's Bureau of Intelligence and Research, a senior analyst, and two junior analysts. The senior analyst explained he had a twenty-year career in photo analysis with the U.S. Air Force before coming to work at the State Department and was experienced in finding aircraft wrecks through photo analysis: "My colleagues and I have spent time with this photo and have also done some background research. We feel that what you have here may well be what you think it is—the landing gear of a Lockheed Electra."[11] They saw the same things in the photo Glickman saw: the strut, the mud flap, the worm gear, possibly the tire. What puzzled them was that the assembly seemed to be not only damaged but upside down: "The gear cannot still be attached to the airplane or we'd see more of the plane."

He said, "In this business we have three levels of certainty: possible, probable, confirmed. That this photo shows the landing gear of a Lockheed Electra is somewhere between possible and probable." The principal reason he was that cautious had nothing to do with the photo but the fact that we did not have the original negative: "What are the chances that the print you photographed was made from a negative that had been doctored sometime between the time the photo was taken in 1937 and when you photographed the print in 1992?"

The analyst need not have been concerned. The photo was one of many in Bevington's photo album and was of no special interest to him. The negative was lost along with Bevington's other personal effects and papers when the Japanese took Tarawa in 1941. He escaped with the clothes on his back. The prints and the journal of his trip to Gardner in 1937 survived only because he had sent them home to his father in England.

The analyst told us, "You have a strong circumstantial case. You're not trying to sell anybody a bill of goods. You're doing good work but you've chosen a tough mission." His only criticism of TIGHAR was that we called the anomaly Nessie. "You're selling yourself short. Nessie was a fraud."[12]

When I asked if they would be giving us a written report, he said, "No, and you can't talk about it publicly. We did this as a favor to Assistant Secretary Campbell. The people we really work for would not be pleased to learn we were spending time on something like this. What we've given you is our opinion as private individuals. The U.S. Government does not offer opinions on things like this."[13] I later learned they were actually from the National Geospatial-Intelligence Agency, an arm of the CIA. At that time, even the name of the unit was classified.

We couldn't talk about the analysis publicly, but on February 17, 2012, I emailed a confidential summary to Jim Loi and asked him to pass it along to Campbell. Half an hour later, Loi emailed, "Thanks. I passed to Kurt. What's the next step?"[14] I said there were three steps:

- We need to get the agreement with Kiribati signed making TIGHAR their exclusive agent for Earhart-related matters.
- With the agreement in hand, we can then establish that the plane, or whatever is left of it, belongs to Kiribati. It's important to get that done BEFORE the airplane is found. Otherwise there will be a festival of piracy and litigation by would-be treasure hunters seeking to obtain and exhibit the wreckage for profit.
- Raise the money for a high-tech search of the reef slope for plane wreckage in the summer of 2013.[15]

That same night, Loi asked: "What are the chances your expedition would take place this year? Is this a function of $$ or even if you had it the crew/ship isn't available until summer 2013?"[16] I replied: "If we had the money we might conceivably be able to put together a search this year, but finding the plane before we have the agreement with Kiribati in place and ownership of the wreckage settled would be irresponsible."[17] Loi wrote, "What's the anticipated cost of the expedition? I'll see Kiribati govt officials in the coming weeks out in Hawaii and then in Tokyo. If we can be helpful let me know."[18] The next morning I responded,

Three million, maybe less depending on the particular ship and technology contractor. Anything you can do to encourage Kiribati to sign the Antiquities Management Agreement would be extremely helpful. For Kiribati, the connection with Earhart is a valuable cultural resource that can be of great benefit to them if managed correctly. TIGHAR has been the trusted steward of that connection for over twenty years. Secretary of Foreign Affairs Tessie Lambourne knows that and is in favor of the agreement. So is Tukabu Teroroko, the Director of the Phoenix Islands Protected Area (PIPA). As far as we know, no one in the government is opposed. Getting it signed is a matter of bureaucratic procedure and priorities which, as I'm sure you know, can be a challenge in Micronesia. Your interest and offer of help is greatly appreciated.[19]

The next day from Loi: "Thanks. I'll be discussing with Kurt options on fund raising. I'll see Pacific reps the week of Feb 27 in Honolulu for South Pacific Tuna Treaty negotiations."[20]

I sent copies of the email thread to Bill Carter with a note: "This is crazy. I'm not sure how we ended up having the State Dept. working for TIGHAR—but I'm not knocking it."[21]

Things were about to get a whole lot crazier.

44

Missing the Plane

2012–19

A few days later Jim Loi emailed me to say Assistant Secretary Campbell would like me to come down to Washington for a meeting. When I arrived at the State Department, I went to the East Asia and Pacific affairs division and was ushered into a private room where Campbell was waiting: "Ric, I'll get right to the point. We think you have this nailed and we want to help you do your expedition, but it needs to happen this year. My secretary is excited and thinks we should help you make the announcement."

I responded, "That's fine but we hadn't planned on . . . wait a minute, what secretary are you talking about?" Campbell's answer: "The one I work for. Secretary [of State Hillary] Clinton wants to hold an event in the Benjamin Franklin Room here at the State Department and make the announcement herself, then you'll describe the plan for the expedition, and we'll also invite some other speakers. We can't give you funding but this should get you plenty of attention and I know how to raise money."

Things had gone from crazy to surreal. How do you refuse an offer like that? We had planned the expedition for 2013 because the technology we wanted to use, the University of Hawaii's manned submersibles, would not be available until then, but this was an awfully big bird in the hand. There was no guarantee we'd be able to raise the money for the subs, and Campbell said he had sponsorship commitments from several large corporations. We could proceed with confidence. What we didn't know was that Clinton was planning to resign after the election in November whether or not President Barack Obama was reelected. For her to be perceived as having a role in the discovery of Amelia Earhart's airplane, it had to happen before then—hence the pressure to go this year.

March 20 was chosen as the date for the State Department event, and for the next month I commuted to planning meetings with Campbell's staff—bright, friendly, hardworking professionals who jokingly referred to me as the deputy assistant secretary for Earhart affairs. On the dais with me, Kurt Campbell, and Hillary Clinton would be Secretary of Transportation Ray LaHood; discoverer of the *Titanic*, Dr. Robert Ballard; and Kiribati permanent secretary for foreign affairs, Tessie Lambourne. Mrs. Lambourne would come from Tarawa at TIGHAR's expense and, while she was in Washington, execute the antiquities management agreement with TIGHAR.

We landed a deal with the Discovery Channel for exclusive coverage of the expedition and signed a contract with the University of Hawaii to charter its 223-foot oceanographic research vessel R/V *Ka'imikai-O-Kanaloa* (aka *KOK*) for a twenty-six-day expedition to depart from Honolulu on July 2, 2012, the seventy-fifth anniversary of the Earhart disappearance. With the university's manned submersibles down for inspection and upgrading, we went for what we thought would be the next-best technology. Maryland-based Phoenix International would use a side-scan–equipped autonomous underwater vehicle (AUV). The robot torpedo would be turned loose in the evening to swim programmed transects up and down the reef, recording sonar imagery that would be downloaded and interpreted when the device was hoisted back aboard *KOK* at the end of an all-night run. The location of sonar returns that might be man-made objects would be given to subcontractor Submersible Systems Incorporated, which would investigate the targets with a tethered remote operated vehicle (ROV) outfitted with high-definition video cameras and a claw for collecting artifacts.

I would lead the expedition, and TIGHAR underwater archaeologist Megan Lickliter-Mundon would advise on archaeological matters. Megan and I would take turns in the darkened shipping container outfitted as an ROV command center, sitting in the cockpit beside the ROV pilot, watching real-time video monitors. Unlike previous TIGHAR expeditions, this would be a purely nautical expedition, and the work would be carried out entirely by contractors. The price tag came in at $2 million.

On the appointed day, under the crystal chandeliers of the State Department Benjamin Franklin Room, I joined the dignitaries in front of about three hundred invited guests and media. I gave my speech, and the secretary of state, the assistant secretary for East Asia and Pacific affairs, the secretary of transportation, the Kiribati foreign affairs secretary, and Dr. Ballard all said nice things about me and TIGHAR. Afterward I was predictably inundated with interview requests, and for the next few days it was hard to read a newspaper, turn on a radio, or watch a morning talk show without hearing about our planned expedition—but you can't take media coverage to the bank. The promised funding from major corporations did not materialize, and suddenly Assistant Secretary Campbell was overseas and out of touch.

Sponsors came forward, including Lockheed Martin, which made a significant cash donation. The Discovery Channel kicked in beyond the contracted rights fee, and FedEx donated the shipment of the technology to and from Hawaii, constituting a huge savings; but as the July 2 departure date approached, we were still short. Phoenix International insisted on getting paid up front, but the University of Hawaii School of Ocean and Earth Science and Technology generously agreed to a payment plan for the *KOK* charter.

We conducted the expedition on faith, hoping that the search would be successful, but our faith turned out to be misplaced. The ROV was delivered with a mismatched camera system, and it was only through TIGHAR video producer Mark Smith's ingenuity and haunting of Honolulu Radio Shack stores that we sailed with ROV video capability at all. Some of the technology worked well. Upon arriving at Nikumaroro, *KOK*'s hull-mounted multi-beam sonar operated by the university's underwater research laboratory mapped the ocean bottom around the entire atoll out to a depth of nearly 15,000 feet, giving us more information about Nikumaroro's underwater topography than anyone had ever had. Initial tests of the submersible systems' ROV went without a hitch, but the limitations of the AUV became immediately apparent.

The AUV was great for surveying a level seabed, but it had never been used to search a steep, rugged reef slope like Nikumaroro's. A collision with the coral damaged its nose and triggered an automatic return to the surface. Upon being hoisted onto the deck, it was discovered the impact had cracked one of the lithium battery housings, allowing water to enter the battery. The damaged battery was smoking heavily and had to be removed, but, as with removing ruby slippers, these things must be done delicately. A lithium spill and fire could sink *KOK.*

Twice the AUV got hung up and had to be found and rescued with the ROV. In one case it got stuck in a cave at a depth of 716 meters (2,349 feet), near the maximum length of the ROV's umbilical. From my notes at the time:

> Rescue mission successful—but it was a real cliff-hanger. Operating literally at the end of our tether, we searched for over an hour in nightmare terrain. Vertical cliff face pockmarked with caves and covered with fern-like marine growth. Finally came across the AUV wedged cross-wise (parallel parked) in a narrow cave. Flew in and used the claw to gently grab a handle near the stern of the fish, then pulled the AUV out of the cave and well clear of the cliff face before releasing it to float to the surface. Hard throttle usage keeping the ship in position during the AUV rescue caused a propulsion system control failure that will take 6 to 7 hours to repair. We just lost the afternoon.[1]

Our confidence in the sonar's ability to image man-made objects was shaken when the AUV flew directly over, but failed to see, massive *Norwich City* wreckage that we had seen with the ROV at a depth of almost a thousand feet. Every time we checked a target identified by the AUV as a possible man-made object, it turned out to be a lump of coral. In the end, the search area was covered without finding any trace of airplane wreckage, and we ended the expedition $400,000 in the hole. It was only through the emergency philanthropy of one of our board members that we were able to retire the debt.

When we got home we began reviewing the reams of data collected during the expedition. Something was wrong; the plane should have been there. We published sonar imagery from the expedition in our quarterly journal *TIGHAR Tracks*, and in May 2013 a TIGHAR member called our attention to an anomaly. At a depth of 187 meters (613 feet), about 250 meters (820 feet) from the edge of the reef near the spot where Bevington's 1937 photo shows wreckage of Electra landing gear, there was a shape the length and width of the airplane's fuselage. Nothing like it was apparent anywhere else. It was not among the targets identified by Phoenix, and, checking the mapped ROV dives, we had never been close to that spot. Could it be that the fuselage of NR16020 was sitting right where it should be after being washed off the reef flat and Phoenix just missed it? We knew they had missed shipwreck debris that was bigger than whatever this was. Independent sonar interpretation experts reviewed the anomaly but could find nothing to prove it was not what we hoped it was.

The only way to test the hypothesis was to go back and have a look, and it wouldn't take a $2 million expedition to do it. We found a contractor with an ROV that could go to the required depth and was small enough to be deployed from our old friend *Nai'a.* The plane may have left debris on its way down, so our divers would also do a detailed search of the shallow water near the reef edge.

On shore, a land team could test another hypothesis. Virtually all of the credible post-loss transmissions had been sent during hours of darkness. High-frequency radio wave propagation is best at night and, during the day, the bare metal airplane parked in the tropical sun was an oven. Earhart and Noonan might have come ashore to escape the heat and set up some kind of campsite like the one at the southeast end where Earhart died. A search of the northwest shoreline might find evidence of a small fire or useful objects brought from the plane, maybe even the sextant. One of the team members labeled the hypothetical site Camp Zero.

Raising the money for the twenty-four-day expedition scheduled for June 2015 was difficult after the disappointing results of the much-hyped 2012 effort, but by late May we had the budget covered—until we didn't. At the last minute, FedEx notified us their giving guidelines had changed, and TIGHAR would no longer get free shipping. We suddenly couldn't afford the cost of shipping an eight-hundred-pound box with a back-up ROV and spare parts to Fiji. Long experience had taught us Nikumaroro eats technology, but the contractor assured us his primary unit was in excellent condition and he could fix anything that broke. Our options were to go without system redundancy or to stay home.

When we got to Nikumaroro, the land team began a systematic search for Camp Zero with eyeballs and metal detectors. The area to be examined extended well inland from the beach at the northwest end, and just getting there meant a mile-and-a-half hike from the landing channel. In the end, the only thing we found was ample evidence that if there had ever been a campsite, it was now buried under tons of coral rubble tossed up from the storms that routinely impact the northwest part of the island.

The dive team had their own frustrations. The only interesting artifact they discovered was a small metal structure twenty-three inches long by six inches wide in twenty-five feet of water. It was too far north to be shipwreck debris and not far from the Bevington photo landing gear location. Scratching with a knife revealed a shiny surface that almost immediately turned black, suggesting it might be cast aluminum. Unable to dislodge it, the divers took photos and videos to show us at the evening team meeting. We decided they should try to collect it, but the thing was next to impossible to distinguish from the surrounding coral, of which it had become a part. When the divers went back the next day, they couldn't find it.

Early in the expedition, the motherboard of the contractor's ROV malfunctioned, and despite heroic efforts by the contractor and two skilled TIGHAR assistants, field repair proved to be impossible. In desperation, we cobbled together and lowered down a crude but functional camera system— dubbed the Hail Mary Device—and succeeded in getting 170 high-definition photos of the bottom in the area where the anomaly should be. They revealed nothing of interest except a photo-bombing grouper.

We went home deeply frustrated but also confused. The anomaly was big—roughly the size of a Lockheed 10 fuselage—and yet the photos showed only coral (and fish). Did we have the location wrong, or was there something else going on? Digging further into the sonar imagery delivered by Phoenix, a TIGHAR member with experience in sonar interpretation discovered that the mosaic of separate images in which the anomaly appeared was a selective, condensed summary. There were more sonar images of that part of the reef than were shown in the mosaic. We dug out the raw data, and by September 2015 we had the answer.

The anomaly was not an anomaly at all. The AUV had imaged at least four similar features in that area. Unless a squadron of Lockheed Electras came to grief on the reef, we were looking at natural coral ridges. The Hail Mary Device had shown us what was there: coral. There was no intact

Electra in the immediate vicinity of the reef, but might it have floated away to eventually sink in deep water far from the island? The day the Electra disappeared, George Putnam had wired the Chief of Naval Operations: "Technicians familiar with Miss Earhart's Plane believe with its large tanks can float almost indefinitely STOP With retractable gear and smooth sea safe landing should have been practicable STOP."[2]

But we weren't talking about a safe landing on a smooth sea. The Electra's buoyancy depended upon the watertight integrity of its fuel tanks, and the landing gear wreckage left behind at the reef edge was proof the airplane had sustained damage to its underside. Each fuel tank was vented at the top and had a strainer-drain at the bottom to check for water or sediment in the fuel and permit emergency dumping. The strainer-drains for the six fuselage and two wing-locker tanks were on the belly and were likely to have been torn off when the plane scraped along the reef flat, as at least some of them were when the gear collapsed and the aircraft slid along the runway in the Luke Field ground loop (hence the puddle of fuel).

Brandenburg did an analysis of how long the aircraft would remain afloat in a variety of scenarios. After first calculating the component-by-component weight of the Electra from Lockheed documents and estimating the weight of the equipment aboard, he concluded that NR16020's net buoyancy with empty fuel tanks was 2,062 pounds. To be conservative, he assumed only the 102-gallon tanks located in the wing roots immediately behind the landing gear would be compromised when the gear collapsed: "A buoyancy of 2062 pounds corresponds to a volume of 241 gallons, at 8.56 pounds of seawater displaced per gallon of tank capacity. So if both 102 gallon tanks are ruptured, a total of 1746 pounds buoyancy will be lost. That leaves a net buoyancy of 316 pounds, corresponding to 37 gallons of tank capacity. So, in terms of sheer weight, we would need more than 316 pounds of additional stuff in the cabin to sink the plane."[3]

Even a minimal amount of personal gear, spare parts, and tools could easily exceed that limit. In other words, the answer to how long the plane would float under the best reasonable scenario was "not very long."

Brandenburg continued, "On the other hand, if either engine got jolted—while the plane was on its belly being shoved around on the reef—and the fuel line was dislodged, the associated 98 gallons of tankage [in the main wing tanks] would be compromised, 839 pounds of buoyancy would be lost, and the plane would sink. So it looks plausible for the plane to sink immediately after leaving the reef, provided the engine fuel line connection could fail."[4] If the strainer-drain for one or more of the six fuselage tanks was ripped off, it wouldn't matter whether a fuel line was dislodged. The trip to Davy Jones' locker would be almost instantaneous. Did the airplane float away? The math said: no.

That Earhart landed on the reef north of the shipwreck and sent distress calls for nearly a week before the plane was washed over the edge had been established beyond a reasonable doubt. We even had a photo of a wrecked landing gear assembly that showed exactly where it happened. During World War II, a credible witness had seen a control cable used as fishing tackle that was attributed to a wrecked airplane that was said to be present when the first settlers arrived. Aerial mapping photos corroborated anecdotal accounts of airplane debris on the reef flat in the 1950s, and the one small piece of metal we had found in the water that might be Electra wreckage was in shallow water near the reef edge, embedded in the coral.

Figuring out what happened to the airplane meant following the evidence wherever it led, even if it took us someplace we didn't want to go. We dearly wanted an airplane, or at least a large identifiable piece of wreckage, but everything pointed to an airplane that had sunk within minutes and lay hidden under the surf for years, battered and scattered by periodic storms. Whether shredded, grown over by coral, or buried by underwater landslides, more than three-quarters of a century later, there was nothing left to find.

Not everyone agreed. In December 2018 an old friend, previously in charge of documentaries at the Discovery Channel and now a senior vice president at National Geographic Studios, called to tell me National Geographic was going to fund an expedition to Nikumaroro by Robert Ballard and his research vessel *Nautilus* to search for the Earhart Electra. She wanted my help as a consultant and on-screen personality in a two-hour show about the expedition. I was happy to help and offered to go along, but the show's producer felt sure Dr. Ballard would not be interested. He had reviewed our evidence and was confident the airplane could be found with his ship's advanced technology and his own personal expertise:

> I have always been intrigued by the story of Amelia Earhart because she shocked the world doing what everyone thought was impossible, much like what I have attempted to do in my entire career as a deep-sea explorer. Also, like Amelia, I was born in Kansas, so it is only appropriate that a Kansan solves this riddle. I would say we have a real shot at rewriting history by solving one of the greatest mysteries of our time.[5] . . . I've been looking at the data and I've finally convinced myself. It's not the Loch Ness monster, it's not Bigfoot, that plane exists which means I'm going to find it.[6]

A second simultaneous expedition with its own ship, a National Geographic archaeologist, a few veteran TIGHARs, and two forensic dogs would once again comb the castaway site for bones, but I would stay home. National Geographic needed me to help the producer with the backstory, and they would want to license some video from TIGHAR expeditions.

I was personally skeptical that either effort—land or sea—would find anything, but I welcomed the endorsement of TIGHAR's research and the opportunity to present our answer to the Earhart riddle in a National Geographic special. Regardless of the outcome, it would be a win for TIGHAR. If Ballard found the plane, or the National Geographic archaeologist found a bone and got a DNA match, it would be seen as the proverbial "smoking gun" proof that we were right. If they came up dry, it would be their failure, not ours, and all the historical, photographic, and analytical evidence TIGHAR had assembled would still be valid.

The expeditions took place in August 2019. *Nautilus* conducted a thorough, well-executed search and found a few artifacts, including a sonar fish Oceaneering International had lost during TIGHAR's 1991 survey, but Ballard and his team found no aircraft or aircraft debris. Similarly, the search for bones at the castaway site was unsuccessful. Nonetheless, the two-hour special *Expedition Amelia* aired on October 20, 2019, and was well received. Chasing after Earhart's aircraft and bones will probably continue, but the available evidence strongly suggests they are the wildest of wild geese.

45

Changing Mystery
to History

The 1937 search failed to find Earhart and Noonan, but their fate need not have remained a mystery. In lieu of conducting an investigation into the loss of NR16020, the Bureau of Air Commerce accepted the U.S. Navy's error-filled *Report of Earhart Search* filed two days after the operation was called off.

Other accidents received the attention mandated in the bureau's charter. On January 11, 1938, six months after Earhart and Noonan disappeared, Pan American Airways chief pilot Ed Musick and a crew of six died when Sikorsky S-42B Samoan Clipper was lost during an approach to Pago Pago, American Samoa. The Bureau of Air Commerce immediately convened an investigation, and following a thorough review of crew qualifications, aircraft condition and capability, weather, radio transmissions, and witness reports, the investigating board issued a thirteen-page report on April 1, 1938. The board found "the probable cause of this accident was fire and explosion associated with the dumping of fuel, the precise cause of ignition being undeterminable."[1]

The Bureau of Air Commerce convened no investigating board to examine the loss of the Electra. The Navy's hasty after-action report stated that among the "Most Probable Actions of Plane" was that it "landed on the sea to the northwest of Howland Island, within about 120 miles of the Island."[2] That was good enough for the Bureau of Air Commerce and, on May 5, 1938, Jesse W. Lankford, chief of the bureau's accident analysis section, wrote a memo to the registration section, "Subject: NR16020—Lockheed Electra 10-E": "The subject airplane was presumably washed out in an accident in the Pacific Ocean near Howland Island, on July 2, 1937, while being piloted by Amelia Earhart, owner. Inasmuch as it is presumed that Miss Earhart was fatally injured in the above accident, no further action is being taken by this section."[3] And that was the end of it. There was no attempt to determine the cause of the accident or reexamine the Navy's conclusion.

TIGHAR's Earhart Project is the investigation that was not done in 1937. The immediate cause of Earhart's inability to find Howland Island was her failure to use the aircraft's radio and radio navigation equipment properly. The transmitter, receiver, and radio direction finder appear to have been fully functional, but they could not do what they were never designed to do.

The proximate, or underlying, cause of the accident was Earhart's resolve to press on despite disqualifying setbacks. She knew radio direction finding would be essential for finding Howland Island, but she made excuses for the failed test of the Bendix direction finder on July 1. After departing New Guinea the next day, Earhart was unable to hear the scheduled hourly weather updates from Lae, probably due to the loss of a receiving antenna. Unable to establish even basic two-way radio communication, she chose to continue the flight rather than return to Lae.

When Howland Island did not appear on schedule, Earhart and Noonan searched north and south along the 157/337 line of position. It was a reasonable course of action that might have succeeded had Noonan not grossly underestimated how far off course the plane had strayed during the night and abandoned the northward search too soon.

Ironically, Earhart's fame and the special treatment it brought were her undoing. Before her first world flight attempt, the Bureau of Air Commerce repeatedly reminded Earhart that she would need an instrument rating to get approval for the trip. Knowing she could not pass the radio navigation portion of the test, Earhart used a bogus excuse to request a waiver. Robert Reining, chief of the Bureau of Air Commerce registration section, allowed her to skip the written exam and radio navigation flight test, thus permitting the famous aviator to undertake a flight for which she was manifestly unqualified.

When Harry Manning quit after the wreck in Hawaii, Earhart disposed of the radio equipment that only he knew how to use rather than replace him or learn how to use it herself. Compounding the error, her preflight coordination with the Coast Guard for the second world flight attempt was virtually nonexistent until the eleventh hour and then often haphazard and contradictory.

Earhart's failure to find Howland was entirely due to pilot error. *Itasca* had its own shortcomings but, because she never heard any of the radio operators' transmissions on 3105 kcs during the flight, the errors had no bearing on Earhart's inability to find Howland. Their only effect was to create unnecessary confusion aboard the cutter. The Coast Guard's greatest sin was one of omission. Before the flight, no one alerted her to the obvious discrepancy between her own description of her radio's capabilities and her instructions to *Itasca*.

Piecing together what went wrong on Earhart's final flight, and why, was a matter of finding and compiling the contemporaneous records, letters, telegrams, and messages, and the real-time radio logs, that tell the story. Determining what happened to the flight after the last in-flight message heard by *Itasca* was more difficult.

From the beginning, TIGHAR saw Earhart's statement that the plane was running north and south on the 157/337 line, and the Pan American radio direction finder bearings that cross near Nikumaroro, as strong clues that the flight ended there. TIGHAR conducted a dozen expeditions to the island at great cost in effort and dollars, hoping to find the aircraft, identifiable pieces of the aircraft, artifacts that could be conclusively linked to Earhart or Noonan, or human remains for DNA matching. Unfortunately, as often occurs in cold-case inquiries, the passage of time has destroyed most of the physical evidence. The archaeological work, while producing compelling circumstantial evidence, found nothing that could be incontrovertibly linked to Earhart.

But smoking guns come in many calibers. As archaeological teams combed the island and surrounding waters, TIGHAR scientists analyzed historical records using forensic technologies undreamt of in the 1930s and, as with any jigsaw puzzle, the clearer the picture became, the more the pieces fell into place.

In 2006 Brandenburg used radio propagation software developed by the U.S. Department of Commerce Institute for Telecommunication Sciences to calculate the probability that reported radio distress calls from Earhart could have been heard at the point of reception if the aircraft was transmitting from Nikumaroro. The data showed many alleged receptions were impossible, but more than fifty were credible, i.e. lacking any reasonable alternative source. Even one genuine reception meant the aircraft was on land, and the only land in the region, other than Howland and Baker, is the Phoenix Islands.

The calculated probability of reception was greatest at stations closest to Nikumaroro. Between July 2 and July 5, twenty-three transmissions on 3105 kcs with reception probabilities greater than 84 percent were heard by USCGC *Itasca*, HMNZS *Achilles*, Navy Radio Tutuila (American Samoa), Howland Island, and Baker Island. For twelve of the twenty-three reported receptions, the probability that the signal came from Nikumaroro was greater than 90 percent. Seven were greater than 95 percent. The first transmission heard by *Itasca* after the aircraft could no longer be in flight was heard as the sun went down on July 2. The operator recognized Earhart's voice but couldn't make out what she was saying.[4] The calculated probability that he could receive a signal from Nikumaroro is 99.12 percent.[5]

The most striking reception was at 0650 GCT on July 4. The government radio operator on Baker Island (the radio station closest to Nikumaroro) heard KHAQQ (Earhart's call sign) calling *Itasca*. He rated the signal strength 4 (out of 5) and readability 7 (out of 10)—a strong, intelligible message.[6] Brandenburg calculated the probability of a transmission from Nikumaroro at that time being heard at Baker as 95.67 percent. There was no reasonable alternative source for these signals.[7] A radio signal, reliably documented in a primary source document, heard on a particular frequency, at a known location at a particular date and time, is as real as a smoking Smith and Wesson.

Between July 4 and July 6, 1937, Pan American and Coast Guard radio direction finder stations took eight bearings on signals suspected of coming from Earhart. In an exhaustive study published in 2006,[8] Brandenburg found that six of the eight support the hypothesis that the signals were coming from Earhart on Nikumaroro, not because the bearings pass close to Nikumaroro (that would be circular reasoning), but based on the content, duration, and lack of possible alternative sources for the transmissions.

Light-colored metal on the reef in a 1953 aerial mapping photo, anecdotal accounts of aircraft wreckage seen on the reef, and the known distribution pattern of *Norwich City* debris suggest the Electra landed and sent distress calls from the reef north of the shipwreck. If the radio calls came from there, it had to be possible for them to be sent. Earhart's transmitter relied upon the plane's batteries for power, and the batteries were recharged by a generator on the starboard engine. Transmitting drains battery power, and the batteries were also used to start the engine. For transmissions to continue night after night, the engine would have to be running when the signals were being sent to keep the batteries charged, but the engine could only be run when the water level on the reef was low enough for the propeller to clear.

If we had the right place, the credible distress calls should occur only when the water was low enough to run the engine. In 2007 TIGHAR measured the tidal flow at Nikumaroro and surveyed the height of the reef surface in the subject area north of the shipwreck. With that data, Brandenburg was able to hindcast the tides and chart the hour-by-hour water level on the reef in July 1937.[9] The correlation was virtually perfect. All but one of the dozens of credible transmissions were sent when the water level was low enough to permit the engine to be run.

The other limiting factor was the maximum water depth. Over the course of five days, the water on the reef at high tide got progressively deeper. If the water reached the plane's transmitter in the cabin, the device would be disabled. The last credible signals from the Electra were heard at low tide in the wee hours of July 7. High tide arrived just before sunup and, for the first time, was high enough to reach the plane's transmitter. No further calls were heard.[10] Pure coincidence, or more gunsmoke?

In 2010 Glickman spotted an object on the reef in a photo taken by Eric Bevington in 1937 which, through forensic processing, he was able to identify as the wreckage of Lockheed Electra landing gear. The object in the black-and-white photo has four distinct visible components that match the known shape, grayscale value, and size of the oleo strut/fork, worm gear, tire, and fender of Lockheed landing gear assembly 40650. Three photo analysts from the National Geospatial-Intelligence Agency examined the photo and agreed with Glickman's assessment. The probability of an object other than the wreckage of Lockheed Electra landing gear with these shapes and dimensions being on the reef at uninhabited Nikumaroro in 1937 is as close to zero as it gets.

In 2017 forensic anthropologist Dr. Richard Jantz at the University of Tennessee, Knoxville worked with Glickman to determine Amelia Earhart's arm and leg bone dimensions from historical photos. Jantz compared the data to the measurements made by British doctor David Hoodless when he examined the bones found on Nikumaroro in 1940. From a database of skeletal measurements of 2,777 individuals, Jantz found that Earhart's bones were more like the Nikumaroro bones than 2,758 (97.28 percent) of the cataloged skeletons. In other words, if the Nikumaroro bones were found on an island where 2,777 people were known to have died and their skeletal measurements recorded, 18 individuals (0.65 percent) could be expected to be more like the Nikumaroro bones than Earhart. That is better than a DNA match. Had we been able to get mtDNA from a bone, the best probability we could expect to get by comparing it to the mtDNA of a relative would be on the order of 87 percent.

The actual probability that the bones were Earhart's is much higher. The only people known to have died at Nikumaroro before the bones were discovered are the eight unaccounted-for *Norwich City* crewmen presumed to have drowned or been taken by sharks. Three are known to have been too short or too tall to be the castaway whose bones were found. Therefore, the number of known candidates is not 2,777 as in Jantz's study. It is a population of 5 individuals, one of whom could have reached the shore but was somehow unable to rejoin his shipmates and was left behind when the others were rescued five days later. To be the castaway whose bones were found in 1940, he would have to have a man's shoe and another shoe that Gallagher could mistake for a woman's shoe. More to the point, he would have to be physically (pardon the expression) a dead ringer for Amelia Earhart.

Jantz had previously determined from the skull measurements taken by Hoodless that the castaway was almost certainly female. The known population of women who died on Nikumaroro before the bones were discovered is zero.

Jantz's peer-reviewed findings were published in a highly respected academic journal in February 2018.[11] In his paper, Jantz noted that his conclusions were drawn solely from the osteological data without regard to other evidence. As Jantz explained, the "posterior probability"—the overall likeli-hood that Earhart was on Nikumaroro—depends upon "prior probability"—that is, other evidence. Regardless of how high the probability for the bone evidence, if the prior probability is zero (for example, if the remains had been found on Grand Bahama Island instead of Gardner Island) the posterior probability would be zero. If the prior probability is other than zero, the posterior prob-ability can be converted to posterior odds by multiplying by the prior odds. In this case, multiple lines of non-osteological evidence have a greater than 99% probability. The posterior probability that Earhart landed and died on Nikumaroro is as close to 100% as it is possible to get. As Dr. Jantz said, "We will probably never convince the deniers, but anyone capable of processing evidence should consider the matter closed."[12]

With the mystery of her disappearance solved, I have pulled all the threads together to weave the full narrative of the Amelia Earhart tragedy. My object is not to dethrone an American icon, but to provide a verifiable account of what really happened so as to permit an accurate assessment of her place in history.

Amelia Earhart may not have been the aviation pioneer of legend, but throughout her flying career she used her celebrity to campaign for equal opportunity for women in aviation and other fields. She was well aware her record-setting flights were publicity stunts, but they served her larger agenda. "My flights haven't meant anything toward the scientific advancement of aviation, but they proved that a woman can fly."[13]

Over the decades, the Amelia Earhart of legend has become a beacon of inspiration, best expressed by a twelve-year-old girl who, when asked what she admires most about Amelia Earhart, replied, "I admire the courage she had to say that I'm a woman and I can do the same things that men can."[14]

In that sense, every female airline pilot, corporate pilot, military pilot, and astronaut is the granddaughter of Amelia Earhart. She couldn't have hoped for a finer legacy.

Notes

Notes are reproduced on the TIGHAR website (tighar.org) with links to images of primary source material and TIGHAR studies.

Abbreviations
Archives, Libraries, and Collections

FAA	Federal Aviation Administration Records, Oklahoma City, OK
FDR	Franklin D. Roosevelt Library, Hyde Park, NY
KNA	Kiribati National Archives, Tarawa, Republic of Kiribati
NARA	National Archives and Records Administration, Washington, DC; College Park, MD; San Bruno, CA
NASM	Smithsonian National Air and Space Museum Archives, Udvar-Hazy Center, Chantilly, VA
NHHC	Naval History and Heritage Command, Navy Yard, Washington, DC
NZAM	Royal New Zealand Air Force Museum and Archive, Christchurch, New Zealand
PRO	Public Records Office, Kew, London, UK
PURDUE	Purdue University Archives and Special Collections, West Lafayette, IN
TIGHAR	The International Group for Historic Aircraft Recovery, Oxford, PA
WPA	Western Pacific Archives, University of Auckland, Auckland, New Zealand

U.S. government radio messages

CINCUS	Commander-in-chief, U.S. Fleet
CNO	Chief of Naval Operations
COM11	Commandant, 11th Naval District
COM12	Commandant, 12th Naval District
COM14	Commandant, 14th Naval District
COMDESRON2	Commander Destroyer Squadron 2 (*Lexington* Group)
COMDT CG	Commandant Coast Guard
COMFRANDIV	Commander Coast Guard San Francisco Division
COMHAWSEC	Commander Coast Guard Hawaiian Section
COMSOSEC	Commander Coast Guard Southern Section
FAB PH	Fleet Air Base, Pearl Harbor
NAVSTA	NAVSTA Naval Station
RDO CGFS	Coast Guard Radio, San Francisco
RDO Tutuila	U.S. Navy Radio Tutuila, American Samoa
RDO Wailupe	U.S. Navy Radio Wailupe, Hawaii

RLP1 and RLP2   *USCGC Itasca* Radio Position 1 and Radio Position 2

(Itasca maintained two simultaneous radio watches during the Earhart flight and search. Each operator kept his own log. The operator at position 1 was tasked with handling administrative traffic and maintaining schedules with other stations. The operator at position 2 was dedicated solely to communicating with Earhart during the flight.)

SECNAV   Secretary of the Navy

Chapter 1. Plane Crazy

1. Barbara H. Schultz, *Pancho: The Biography of Florence Lowe Barnes* (Lancaster, CA: Little Buttes Publishing Co., 1996), 114.
2. Keith O'Brien, *Fly Girls: How Five Daring Women Defied All Odds and Made Aviation History* (New York: Mariner Books, 2018), xiii.
3. Robert Wohl, *A Passion for Wings: Aviation and the Western Imagination, 1908–1918* (New Haven and London: Yale University Press, 1994), 2.
4. Charles A. Lindbergh, *The Spirit of St. Louis* (New York: Charles Scribner's Sons, 1953), 130.
5. Vernon Dalhart, "Lindbergh, The Eagle of the USA," Columbia Records, 1927.
6. Janet Mabie, *Lady in the High Wind*, unpublished biography of Amelia Earhart, cited in Susan Butler, *East to the Dawn: The Life of Amelia Earhart* (Reading, MA: Addison-Wesley, 1997), 157.
7. Butler, 168.
8. O'Brien, 52.
9. *New York Times*, September 1, 1928, 1.
10. Elinor Smith, *Aviatrix* (New York: Harcourt Brace Jovanovich, 1981), 93–94.
11. René Françillon, *Lockheed Aircraft Since 1913* (Annapolis, MD: Naval Institute Press, 1987), 72.
12. Amelia Earhart, *Last Flight* (New York: Harcourt Brace, 1937), 14.
13. Butler, 230.
14. O'Brien, 88.
15. O'Brien, 85.
16. O'Brien, 101.
17. Smith, 132–33.
18. George Palmer Putnam, *Soaring Wings* (New York: Harcourt Brace, 1939), 76.

Chapter 2. Fame and More Fame

1. O'Brien, 132.
2. Amelia Earhart, *The Fun of It* (New York: Brewer, Warren, and Putnam, 1932), 214.
3. Doris L. Rich, *Amelia Earhart: A Biography* (Washington, DC: Smithsonian Institution Scholarly Press, 1996), 197.
4. Smith, 73.
5. "Paper Avers Venture Has Sinister Aim," *Bakersfield Californian*, January 4, 1935, 1.
6. Butler, 325.
7. O'Brien, 224.
8. Earhart, *Last Flight*, 4.
9. Earhart, 49.
10. Putnam, 272.
11. Letter from Elliott to Earhart, May 18, 1935, scrapbook 12, Purdue.
12. Speech in Fort Wayne, Indiana, March 21, 1935, Doris Rich papers, National Air and Space Museum (NASM).
13. "Amelia Earhart Purdue Professor," *Ames Daily Tribune*, June 3, 1936.
14. "Major Al Williams Rips Earhart Flight as Stunt," *Cleveland Press*, March 27, 1937.
15. *Newsweek*, January 19, 1935.
16. Letter from Earhart to her mother, May 22, 1936, in Jean Backus, *Letters from Amelia* (Boston: Beacon Press, 1982), 197.
17. Letter from Putnam to Mantz, January 7, 1936, Doris Rich papers, NASM.
18. George Palmer Putnam, memorandum, "The Amelia Earhart Project," 1935, PURDUE.
19. Putnam, "Earhart Project."
20. Putnam, "Earhart Project."
21. Putnam, "Earhart Project."
22. Putnam, "Earhart Project."
23. Putnam, "Earhart Project."
24. Thomas M. Emmert and William T. Larkins, "Lockheed's Model 10 Electra," *Journal of the American Aviation Historical Society*, Summer 1978.

25. Letter from Elliott to Putnam, November 11, 1935, Purdue.
26. Ruth W. Freehafer, *R. B. Stewart and Purdue University* (West Lafayette, IN: Purdue University Press, 1983), 59.
27. Letter from Elliott to Putnam, December 7, 1935, Purdue.
28. Letter from Putnam to Elliott, December 9, 1935, Purdue.
29. Putnam to Elliott, December 9, 1936.

Chapter 3. Bait and Switch
1. Undated telegram from Putnam to Mantz, Doris Rich papers, NASM.
2. Françillon, 129.
3. Undated Western Union message from Putnam to Mantz, Doris Rich papers, NASM.
4. Letter from Putnam to Elliott, January 2, 1936, Purdue.
5. Putnam to Elliott, January 2, 1936.
6. Putnam to Elliott; copy of letter to LaGorce included with Putnam to Elliott, January 2, 1936, Purdue.
7. Letter from Elliott to Putnam, January 2, 1936, Purdue.
8. Letter from Putnam to Elliott, January 4, 1936, Purdue.
9. Putnam to Elliott, January 4, 1936.
10. Letter from Putnam to Mantz, January 4, 1936, Doris Rich papers, NASM.
11. Putnam to Mantz.
12. Françillon, 122.
13. Letter from Elliott to Putnam, January 6, 1936, Purdue.
14. Letter from Putnam to Elliott, January 6, 1936, Purdue.
15. Copy of letter to LaGorce included with Putnam to Elliott, January 6, 1936, Purdue.
16. Telegram quoted in Putnam letter to Mantz, January 7, 1936, Doris Rich papers, NASM.
17. Putnam to Mantz.
18. Putnam to Mantz.
19. Putnam to Mantz.
20. Putnam to Mantz.
21. Putnam to Mantz.
22. Putnam to Mantz.
23. Putnam to Mantz.
24. Putnam to Mantz.
25. Putnam to Mantz.
26. Putnam to Mantz.
27. Letter from Putnam to Elliott, January 8, 1936, Purdue.
28. Telegram from Putnam to Elliott, January 10, 1936, Purdue.
29. Letter from Meikle to Elliott, January 23, 1936, Purdue.
30. Meikle notes included in letter to Elliott, January 23, 1936, Purdue.
31. Meikle notes.
32. Meikle notes.
33. Meikle notes.
34. Meikle notes.
35. Meikle notes.
36. Meikle notes.
37. Meikle notes.
38. Meikle notes.
39. Letter from Elliott to Putnam, February 10, 1936, Purdue.
40. Letter from Putnam to Mantz, January 7, 1936, Doris Rich papers, NASM.
41. Letter from Putnam to Elliott, February 12, 1936, Purdue.
42. Putnam to Elliott.
43. Letter from Putnam to Elliott, February 15, 1936, Purdue.
44. "General Notes Pertaining to the A. E. World Flight," February 14, 1936, Purdue.
45. "General Notes."
46. Putnam, "Earhart Project."
47. "Tentative Proposal," February 14, 1936, Purdue.

48. "Tentative Proposal."
49. "Tentative Proposal."
50. "General Notes."
51. "General Notes."

Chapter 4. The Realization of a Dream

1. Letter from Putnam to Elliott, March 2, 1936, referenced in letter from Meikle to Elliott, March 11, 1936, Purdue.
2. *TIME* magazine, March 29, 1937.
3. Letter from Putnam to Elliott, March 2, 1936, Purdue.
4. Putnam to Elliott.
5. Putnam to Elliott.
6. Putnam to Elliott.
7. Putnam to Elliott.
8. Letter from Stuart to Meikle, March 11, 1936, Purdue.
9. Letter from Elliott to Putnam, March 14, 1936, Purdue.
10. Cost estimate, February 27, 1936, Purdue.
11. Telegram from Putnam to Gross, March 16, 1936, Purdue.
12. Letter from Elliott to Putnam, March 25, 1936, Purdue.
13. Emmert and Larkins, 141.
14. Letter from Putnam to Lockheed, March 20, 1936, partially reproduced in Muriel Earhart Morrissey and Carol Osborne, *Amelia, My Courageous Sister* (Santa Clara, CA: Osborne Publishers, Inc., 1987), 177.
15. Lockheed interdepartmental communication, March 20, 1936, reproduced in Morrissey, 176.
16. Letter from Mantz to Putnam, March 24, 1936, Doris Rich papers, NASM.
17. Mantz to Putnam.
18. Mantz to Putnam.
19. Letter from Earhart to "Rufus," April 1, 1936, Doris Rich papers, NASM.
20. Letter from Putnam to Meikle, April 6, 1936, Purdue.
21. Telegram from Meikle to Putnam, April 9, 1936, Purdue.
22. Letter from Meikle to Elliott, April 11, 1936, Purdue.
23. Meikle to Elliott.
24. Press release, April 19, 1936, Purdue.
25. *Salt Lake Tribune*, April 19, 1936, 2.
26. *Berkeley Daily Gazette*, April 20, 1936, 3.
27. Lockheed Report 487, "Range Study of Lockheed Electra Bimotor Airplane," The International Group for Historic Aircraft Recovery (TIGHAR).
28. Lockheed Report 487.
29. Lockheed Report 487.
30. Lockheed memo, weight statement for serial number 1055, June 2, 1936, TIGHAR.
31. Bureau of Air Commerce aircraft inspection report, X16020, July 19, 1936, Federal Aviation Administration (FAA).
32. Bureau of Air Commerce aircraft inspection report, license application X16020, July 19, 1936, FAA.
33. Elmer McLeod, pilot log, July–August 1936, TIGHAR.
34. Letter, Putnam to Meikle, July 20, 1936, Purdue.
35. Second letter, Putnam to Meikle, July 20, 1936, Purdue.
36. Second letter, Putnam to Meikle.
37. UCLA Film/TV Archives.
38. *Los Angeles Times*, July 2, 1936, A1.
39. Elmer McLeod, pilot log, July 21, 1936, TIGHAR.
40. *Los Angeles Times, July 2, 1936.*
41. Letter from Earhart to Lockheed, July 21, 1936, Purdue.
42. Bill of sale, X16020, July 24, 1936, Purdue.
43. Bureau of Air Commerce license application, R16020, July 27, 1936, FAA.

Chapter 5. Teething Troubles

1. McLeod, pilot log, July–August 1936.
2. "Amelia Earhart in Test Flight Here," *Oakland Tribune*, August 3, 1936, 1.
3. "Heat Shields: Detective Story," TIGHAR bulletin 51, July 12, 2007.
4. Bureau of Air Commerce inspection report and license application, R16020, August 7, 1936, FAA.
5. "Purdue Head Arrives to View Earhart Plane," *Los Angeles Times*, August 21, 1936.
6. "To Enter Air Race," *Salt Lake Tribune*, August 15, 1936.
7. O'Brien, 176.
8. O'Brien, 176.
9. O'Brien, 186.
10. O'Brien, 204.
11. O'Brien, 186.
12. *Sedalia Democrat*, August 30, 1936, 1.
13. Second letter, Putnam to Meikle, July 20, 1936, Purdue.
14. Putnam, quoted by *Christian Science Monitor* writer Janet Mabie, Doris Rich papers, NASM.
15. Second letter, Putnam to Meikle.
16. "Amelia Earhart Putnam Is 'Nearly Sold' on World Flight," *Syracuse Herald*, September 16, 1936.
17. *Arizona Republic*, September 20, 1936.
18. *New Castle News*, September 23, 1936; Berkshire *Evening Eagle*, September 24, 1936; Associated Press, September 27, 1936.
19. Letter from Putnam to Mantz, September 30, 1936, Doris Rich papers, NASM.
20. Putnam to Mantz.
21. Director, Fleet Maintenance Division to Director, Central Division, November 10, 1936, Naval History and Heritage Center (NHHC).
22. Putnam to Mantz.

Chapter 6. Delay, Desperation, and Deliverance

1. Letter from Putnam to Swanson, October 16, 1936, NHHC.
2. Bureau of Air Commerce Aircraft license dated August 18, 1936, FAA.
3. Letter from Putnam to Cone, October 24, 1936, FAA.
4. Letter from Cone to Putnam, November 3, 1936, FAA.
5. Letter from Chief of Bureau of Aeronautics to CNO, October 27, 1936, NHHC.
6. Chief of Bureau of Aeronautics to CNO.
7. Letter from CNO to Putnam, October 30, 1936, NHHC.
8. Letter from Putnam to Mantz, November 9, 1936, Doris Rich papers, NASM.
9. Letter from Mantz to Putnam, November 12, 1936, Doris Rich papers, NASM.
10. Letter from Earhart to Franklin D. Roosevelt, November 10, 1936, Purdue.
11. Navy Department memorandum from Paul Bastedo to CNO, NHHC.
12. Navy Department memorandum from Paul Bastedo to Missy LeHand, NHHC.
13. Letter from CNO to Putnam, November 19, 1936, NHHC.
14. Letter from Putnam to CNO, November 20, 1936, NHHC.
15. Letter from Putnam to Mantz, November 14, 1936, Doris Rich papers, NASM.
16. Putnam to Mantz.
17. Letter from King to Leahy, November 29, 1936, NHHC.
18. King to Leahy.
19. Message from CNO to CINCUS, December 4, 1936.
20. Telegram from Hampton to Black, November 16, 1936, NARA.
21. Telegram from Vidal to Miller, November 17, 1936, NARA.
22. Telegram from Miller to Earhart, November 17, 1936, NARA.
23. Elgen Long and Marie Long, *Amelia Earhart: The Mystery Solved* (New York: Simon and Schuster, 1999), 60.
24. Telegram to Earhart from Cone, September 21, 1936, FAA.
25. Bureau of Air Commerce inspection report, NR16020, November 27, 1936, FAA.
26. Bureau of Air Commerce license application, NR16020, November 27, 1936, FAA.

27. Unsigned State Department memorandum, December 4, 1936, NARA.
28. "Woman Fliers Seeking Excitement-Knowledge," *Daily Times*, Wichita Falls, TX, December 6, 1936.
29. "Wright Field Workmen Busy with Amelia Earhart's Plane," *Dayton Daily News*, December 8, 1936.
30. Second letter, Putnam to Meikle, July 20, 1936, Purdue.

Chapter 7. House of Cards

1. "Flames Threaten New Earhart Plane," *Santa Rosa Press Democrat*, January 5, 1937; "Fire Damages Earhart Plane," *Oakland Tribune*, January 4, 1937; "Amelia Earhart's Plane Threatened," *Chico Enterprise*, January 5, 1937; "Earhart Plane Catches Fire," *Napa Daily Journal,* January 5, 1937.
2. Message from J. S. Wynne, chief, airports section, to R. L. Campbell, December 12, 1936, NARA.
3. Message from Campbell to Wynne, January 5, 1937, NARA.
4. Message from Campbell to Wynne, January 7, 1937, NARA.
5. Telegram from Earhart to President Roosevelt, January 7, 1937, NARA.
6. "$36,000 Grant from WPA to Finance Work," *Honolulu Star-Bulletin*, January 14, 1937.
7. Letter from George Putnam to Bureau of Air Commerce, October 15, 1936, FAA.
8. Wire from Bureau of Air Commerce to Amelia Earhart, September 21, 1936, FAA.
9. Morrissey and Osborne, 208.
10. "Earhart Planning Round World Hop," *Bakersfield Californian*, January 25, 1937.
11. "Amelia Earhart's Flying Plans," *Boston Globe*, January 27, 1937.
12. "Events of Interest in Shipping World," *New York Times*, January 31, 1937.
13. Bureau of Air Commerce license authorization, NR16020, expiring June 5, 1937, FAA.
14. Don Dwiggins, *Hollywood Pilot: The Biography of Paul Mantz* (New York: Doubleday, 1967), 99.
15. "Amelia Earhart Spends Night Here on Flight East," *Albuquerque Journal*, February 10, 1937.
16. Associated Press, dateline St. Louis, February 11, 1937.
17. "Amelia Earhart to Circle Globe in Her 'Flying Laboratory' Plane," *New York Times*, February 12, 1937.
18. International Radiotelegraph Conference, Madrid, 1932.
19. Telegram from Earhart to Mantz, February 14, 1937, Doris Rich papers, NASM.
20. Telegram from Mantz to Earhart, February 16, 1937, Doris Rich papers, NASM.
21. *The Evening Star*, dateline Cleveland, February 18, 1937.
22. Long and Long, 60.
23. Associated Press, dateline Blackwell, OK, February 20, 1937.
24. Letter from Joseph Gurr to Fred Goerner, May 3, 1982, TIGHAR.
25. "Miss Earhart Sets Take-Off Time," *Miami* (OK) *News Record*, February 26, 1937.
26. Putnam memorandum, "Earhart Project."

Chapter 8. The Weakest Link

1. "Navigator Arrives Here," *Oakland Tribune*, March 2, 1937.
2. Letter from George Putnam to William Miller, March 1, 1937, NARA.
3. "Work on Lockheed Electra Plane in Final Stages," *Oakland Tribune*, March 2, 1937.
4. Long and Long, 64, and newsreel film footage, UCLA collection.
5. Telegram from C. Johnson to Amelia Earhart, March 11, 1937, TIGHAR.
6. Long and Long, 65.
7. Letter from Robert R. Reining, chief, Bureau of Air Commerce registration section, to W. T. Miller, March 11, 1937, NARA.
8. Bureau of Air Commerce aircraft inspection report, NR16020, May 19, 1937, FAA.
9. Message from R. D. Bedinger, chief, Bureau of Air Commerce general inspection services, to Robert R. Reining, chief, Bureau of Air Commerce registration section, March 11, 1937, NARA.
10. "Amelia to Fly Pacific," *Oakland Tribune*, March 12, 1937.
11. "Noonan's Addition Made Suddenly," *Oakland Tribune*, March 13, 1937.
12. "Amelia Plans Take-off Today," *Los Angeles Times*, March 14, 1937.
13. "Amelia Plans Take-off Today."
14. Message from R. D. Bedinger to Robert R. Reining, March 13, 1937, NARA.
15. "Amelia Plans to Takeoff," *Oakland Tribune*, March 14, 1937.

16. Message from Fred D. Fagg, director, Bureau of Air Commerce, to R. D. Bedinger, chief, Bureau of Air Commerce general inspection services, March 14, 1937, NARA.
17. Message from Naval Station San Diego to Secretary of the Navy, March 15, 1937, NARA.
18. Message from Naval Station San Diego to Naval Reserve Air Base Oakland, March 16, 1937, NARA.
19. Dwiggins, 99.
20. Dwiggins, 102.
21. "Amelia Sets Record," *Oakland Tribune*, March 18, 1937.
22. Luke Field crash report, exhibit A, statement by the engineering officer, Wheeler Field, NARA.
23. Luke Field crash report, exhibit E, statement by the engineering officer, Hawaiian Air Depot, NARA.
24. Luke Field crash report, exhibit E.
25. Luke Field crash report, exhibit D, statement by operations officer, Luke Field, NARA.
26. Gerald V. Berger, interview with Ric Gillespie, April 30, 2000, TIGHAR.
27. Earhart, *Last Flight*, 72.
28. "Amelia Crashes in Honolulu Takeoff," *Berkeley Daily Gazette*, March 20, 1937.
29. Berger interview.
30. Berger interview.
31. Facebook post, South Carolina Law Enforcement Officers Hall of Fame, January 7, 2022.
32. "Amelia Crashes in Honolulu Takeoff."
33. Harry Manning, interview with Fred Goerner, 1972, TIGHAR.
34. "Amelia Sets May 1 for New Take-off Here," *Oakland Tribune*, March 28, 1937.

Chapter 9. Aftermath

1. Telegram from Fred Noonan to Beatrice Martinelli, March 19, 1937, Elgen Long personal collection.
2. "Earhart Navigator Marries," United Press, March 29, 1937.
3. "Bride of Plane Navigator Hurt in Fresno Crash," *The Fresno Bee*, April 5, 1937.
4. "Mourning Becomes Electra," *TIME*, March 29, 1937.
5. "Maj. Al Williams Rips Earhart Flight as Stunt," *Cleveland Press*, March 31, 1937.
6. Telegram from Putnam to Roper, March 20, 1937, NARA.
7. Telegram from Roper to Putnam, March 22, 1937, NARA.
8. Adjutant General Conley to General Drum, April 22, 1937, NARA.
9. Secretary of the Navy to Miller, March 25, 1937, NARA.
10. Message from Earhart to Rear Admiral Waesche, April 27, 1937, NARA.
11. Message from Rear Admiral Waesche to Earhart, April 27, 1937, NARA.
12. Message from CNO to NAVSTA Tutuila, April 27, 1937, NARA.
13. Letter from Gruening to Richard Black, April 29, 1937, NARA.
14. Message from Coast Guard commander, Hawaiian section, to COMHAWSEC, April 21, 1937, NARA.
15. Message from Ruth Hampton to Richard Black, April 2, 1937, NARA.
16. Encrypted message from Ruth Hampton to Richard Black, April 23, 1937, NARA.
17. Message from Richard Black to Ruth Hampton, April 24, 1937, NARA.
18. Jon E. Krupnick, *Pan American's Pacific Pioneers* (Missoula, MT: Pictorial Histories Publishing Co., 2000), 235.
19. "Clipper Service to South Pacific Planned," *Atlanta Constitution*, April 11, 1937.
20. "Amelia Earhart Expected to Take Off Again," *Oakland Tribune*, April 11, 1937.
21. Earhart, *Last Flight*, 56.
22. Krupnick, 14.
23. Krupnick, 149.
24. Pan American memo, April 19, 1935, to operations manager, Pacific Division, Alameda, CA, from navigator, Pan American clipper operations. Subject, Hawaiian flight of NR 823-M, April 16–17 and 22–23, 1935, TIGHAR.
25. Pan American memo.
26. Letter from William Van Dusen to Ed Rollman, January 14, 1974, TIGHAR.
27. Harry Canaday, interview with Peter Leslie, January 1975, TIGHAR.

28. Letter from Josephine Sullivan Noonan to the grandmother of Teri Noland-Schildgren, read to Ric Gillespie by William Schildgren, TIGHAR.
29. Letter from Russell D. Brines to "Richard," August 3, 1937, TIGHAR.
30. Unpublished autobiography, Hugo Leuteritz, TIGHAR.
31. William S. Grooch, *From Crate to Clipper* (New York: Longman, Green, and Co., 1939), 213–14.

Chapter 10. Formula for Failure
1. Letter from George Putnam to Stanley Meikle, April 12, 1937, Purdue.
2. "U.S. Proposes Curb on Freak Ocean Flights," *Washington Post*, May 11, 1937.
3. Earhart, *Last Flight*, 79.
4. Letter from Putnam to Southgate, May 5, 1937, NARA.
5. Letter from Putnam to Admiral Leahy, May 8, 1937, NHHC.
6. Putnam to Leahy.
7. Putnam to Leahy.
8. Letter from Southgate to Putnam, May 8, 1937, NARA.
9. Letter from J. M. Johnson to Secretary of State, May 14, 1937, NARA.
10. "Noted Woman Flier Drops In on Miami," *Miami Herald*, May 24, 1937, 2.
11. C. B. Allen, unpublished draft manuscript, "The True Earhart Story," undated, C. B. Allen papers, NASM.
12. Ruckins D. McKneely, conversation with Ric Gillespie, 1990, TIGHAR.
13. C. B. Allen, "Earhart Plane Ready to Start Today on Globe-Circling Trip," *New York Herald Tribune*, June 1, 1937.
14. Message from COMFRANDIV to COMHAWSEC, June 12, 1937, NARA.
15. "To Circle Globe Just for Fun," *Danville Bee*, May 24, 1937, Danville, VA.
16. Dwiggins, 105.
17. Message from Poindexter to Hampton, June 1, 1937, NARA.
18. Message from Hampton to Poindexter, June 2, 1937, NARA.

Chapter 11. Barging Through
1. Earhart, *Last Flight*, 100.
2. Earhart, *Last Flight*.
3. Letter from Noonan to Helen Day, June 5, 1937, TIGHAR.
4. "Miss Earhart Flies Ocean to Africa in 13-Hour Hop," *New York Herald Tribune*, June 8, 1937, 1.
5. Sailing chart of south Atlantic, Earhart Collection, Purdue.
6. Letter from Fred Noonan to Eugene Pallette, June 9, 1937, TIGHAR.
7. Earhart notes made during south Atlantic crossing, June 7, 1937, Purdue.
8. Earhart notes.
9. Noonan, note given to Earhart during south Atlantic crossing, June 7, 1937, Purdue.
10. Noonan, note.
11. Noonan to Pallette.
12. Noonan to Pallette.
13. Noonan to Pallette.

Chapter 12. Mad Scramble
1. Message, COMDT CG to COMFRANDIV, June 7, 1937, NARA; message, COMFRANDIV to COMDT CG, June 7, 1937, NARA.
2. Message, COMFRANDIV to COMDT CG, June 7, 1937, NARA.
3. Message, COMDT CG to COMFRANDIV, June 8, 1937, NARA.
4. Message, COMFRANDIV to COMSOSEC, June 9, 1937, NARA.
5. Letter from Putnam to Hampton, June 4, 1937, NARA; letter from Hampton to Putnam, June 8, NARA.
6. Message, Hampton to Black, June 8, 1937, NARA.
7. Message, COMFRANDIV to COMHAWSEC, June 10, 1937, NARA.
8. Message, Black to Hampton, June 9, 1937, NARA.

9. Letter from Putnam to Hampton, June 9, 1937, NARA.
10. Letter from Admiral Waesche to Putnam, June 7, 1937, NHHC.
11. Telegram from Putnam to Black, March 20, 1937, NARA.
12. Message, Hampton to Black, June 10, 1937, NARA.
13. Message, Black to Hampton, June 10, 1937, NARA.
14. Message, COMFRANDIV to COMDT CG, June 10, 1937, NARA; COMDT CG to COMFRAN-DIV, June 11, 1937, NARA.
15. Message, *Itasca* to COMFRANDIV, June 11, 1937, NARA; COMFRANDIV to *Itasca*, June 11, 1937, NARA.
16. Message, COMFRANDIV to *Itasca*, June 12, 1937, NARA.
17. Message, COMFRANDIV to COMDT CG, June 12, 1937, NARA.
18. Message, COMDT CG to COMFRANDIV, June 15, 1937, NARA; message, West to Black, June 15, 1937, NARA.
19. Letter from Hampton to Putnam, June 16, 1937, NARA.
20. Message, Black (via Poindexter) to Hampton, June 14, 1937, NARA.
21. Message, COMHAWSEC to COMFRANDIV, June 18, 1937, NARA; Black, report, "Tenth Cruise to the American Equatorial Islands," 1, NARA.
22. Warner Thompson, U.S. Treasury Department report, "Radio Transcripts—Earhart Flight," July 19, 1937, 5, NARA.
23. Message, COMFRANDIV to *Shoshone*, March 13, 1937, NARA.
24. Thompson, 5.
25. Message, Black to Hampton, June 16, 1937, NARA.
26. Message, Putnam to CNO, COMFRANDIV, and Hampton, June 16, 1937, NARA.
27. Message, Hampton to Black, June 18, 1937, NARA.
28. Message, Black (via Poindexter) to Hampton, June 15, 1937, NARA; message, Hampton to Black, June 18, 1937, NARA; letter from Putnam to Hampton, June 17, 1937, NARA.
29. Message, Black to Hampton, June 19, 1937, NARA.
30. Letter from Putnam to Johnson, June 17, 1937, NARA; letter from Johnson to Putnam, June 18, 1937, NARA.
31. Message, COMFRANDIV to COMHAWSEC, June 18, 1937, NARA; message, COMHAWSEC to COMFRANDIV, June 18, 1937, NARA.
32. Warner Thompson, U.S. Treasury Department Report, "Cruise Report 4 June to 24 July, 1937—Embracing Earhart Flight and Equatorial Island Cruise," 3, NARA.
33. Message, COMFRANDIV to *Itasca*, June 18, 1937, NARA; message, *Itasca* to COMFRANDIV, June 18, 1937, NARA.
34. Message, Black (via Hampton) to Putnam, June 19, 1937, NARA.
35. Black (via Hampton) to Putnam.
36. Message, Putnam (via Hampton) to Black, June 20, 1937, NARA.
37. *New York Herald Tribune*, June 1–9, June 10–12, June 13–21, 1937.
38. "Amelia Earhart Has Java to N.Y. Chat on Phone," *New York Herald Tribune*, June 22, 1937, 1.
39. Letter from Noonan to Helen Day, June 22, 1937, TIGHAR.
40. "Amelia Earhart Has Java to N.Y. Chat on Phone," 11.
41. Noonan to Day.
42. "Miss Earhart Waits in Java as Dutch Work on Her Plane," *New York Herald Tribune*, June 24, 1937, 1.
43. Letter from Putnam to Hampton, June 23, 1937, NARA.

Chapter 13. Where Is Amelia?

1. Message, Black (via Samoa) to Earhart, June 23, 1937, NARA.
2. Message, *Itasca* (via Samoa) to Earhart, June 23, 1937, NARA.
3. Message, COMFRANDIV to *Itasca*, June 23, 1937, NARA; message, *Itasca* to COMFRANDIV, June 23, 1937, NARA.
4. "Putnam and Amelia Chat by Phone from Cheyenne to Java at Cost of $24," *Wyoming Tribune Eagle*, June 25, 1937, 1.

5. Thompson, "Cruise Report 4 June to 24 July 1937," 3.
6. Daniel Cooper, U.S. Army report, "Expedition to the American Equatorial Islands in Connection with Amelia Earhart Flight," July 27, 1937, 3, NARA.
7. Message, Carey to Associated Press, June 24, 1937; message, Hanzlick to United Press, June 24, 1937, NARA.
8. Message, *Itasca* to *Swan*, June 24, 1937, NARA; message, Black to Hampton, June 24, 1937, NARA.
9. "Miss Earhart Back in Bandoeng to Have Instruments Repaired," *New York Herald Tribune*, June 25, 1937, 1.
10. Message, COMFRANDIV to *Itasca*, June 25, 1937, NARA.
11. COMFRANDIV to *Itasca*.
12. COMFRANDIV to *Itasca*.
13. Black (via Samoa) to Earhart.
14. Message, COMFRANDIV to *Itasca*, June 26, 1937, NARA.
15. COMFRANDIV to *Itasca*.
16. Black (via Samoa) to Earhart; *Itasca* (via Samoa) to Earhart.
17. Message, Earhart to Black, June 26, 1937, NARA.
18. Message, *Itasca* to COMFRANDIV, June 26, 1937, NARA.
19. Message, COMFRANDIV to *Itasca*, June 25, 1937, NARA; message, COMFRANDIV to *Itasca*, June 26, 1937, NARA.
20. Thompson, "Radio Transcripts Earhart Flight," 22, NARA.
21. Message, COMFRANDIV to *Itasca*, June 26, 1937, NARA.
22. Letter, Noonan to Day, June 27, 1937, TIGHAR.
23. "Amelia Earhart Flies Timor Sea to Port Darwin," *New York Herald Tribune*, June 28, 1937, 1.
24. Black, "Tenth Cruise to the Equatorial Islands," 6, NARA.
25. Letter from C. L. A. Abbott to Albert M. Doyle, American Consul, Sydney, Australia, August 3, 1937, NARA.
26. Earhart, *Last Flight*, 128.
27. "Mrs. Putnam at Darwin," Sydney, Australia, newspaper (name unknown), June 28, 1937, TIGHAR.
28. Message, Amalgamated Wireless to Lae, June 28, 1937, NARA.
29. Message, Vacuum to Lae, June 28, 1937, NARA.

Chapter 14. Personnel Unfitness

1. Letter from Eric Chater to Frank Griffin, July 25, 1937, TIGHAR.
2. Message, Earhart to Black, June 26, 1937, NARA.
3. Message, Black (via governor of Samoa) to Earhart, June 28, 1937, NARA.
4. Black (via governor) to Earhart.
5. Black (via governor) to Earhart.
6. Message, Earhart to *Itasca*, June 30, 1937, NARA.
7. Chater to Griffin.
8. Telegram from Earhart to Putnam, June 30, 1937, Purdue.
9. Message, Hampton to Black, June 18, 1937, NARA.
10. Earhart to *Itasca*; Earhart to Putnam.
11. Message, Black to Earhart, June 23, 1937, NARA.
12. Chater to Griffin.
13. Chater to Griffin.
14. Earhart, "Amelia Earhart Ready to Fly to Howland Island," *New York Herald Tribune*, June 30, 1937, 1.
15. "Amelia Earhart Quits Australia for New Guinea," *New York Herald Tribune*, June 29, 1937, 1.
16. Earhart to Putnam.
17. Message, Putnam to Earhart, June 29, 1937, NARA.
18. Earhart to *Itasca*.
19. Message, *Itasca* to FAB PH, June 29, 1937, NARA.
20. Message, *Itasca* to Earhart, June 29, 1937, NARA.
21. Message, FAB PH to Earhart, June 29, 1937, NARA.

22. *Itasca* to Earhart.
23· Message, *Itasca* to COMFRANDIV, June 30, 1937, NARA.

Chapter 15. Delay and Denial
1. Message, Earhart to Black, June 30, 1937, NARA.
2. Letter from Eric Chater to Frank Griffin, July 25, 1937, TIGHAR.
3. Message, Earhart to Black, July 1, 1937, NARA.
4. COMFRANDIV/Putnam to Earhart, June 30, 1937, NARA.
5. Chater to Griffin.
6. Fleet Air Base to Earhart, June 30, 1937, NARA.
7. Earhart to *New York Herald Tribune*, July 1, 1937.
8. Chater to Griffin.
9. Bureau of Air Commerce, aircraft inspection report, May 19, 1937, FAA.
10. Chater to Griffin; James Collopy, letter to the secretary, Civil Aviation Board, August 28, 1937, Purdue.
11. C. L. Johnson and W. C. Nelson, "Lockheed Report No. 487—Range Study of Lockheed Electra Bimotor Airplane," June 4, 1936, 6, TIGHAR.
12. Earhart, *Last Flight*, 35.
13. Earhart to *New York Herald Tribune*.
14. Chater to Griffin.
15. Collopy to Civil Aviation Board.
16. Smith, *Aviatrix*, 133.
17. Collopy to Civil Aviation Board.
18. William Shakespeare, *Macbeth*, act 3, scene 5.

Chapter 16. Everything Okay
1. Leo G. Bellarts, transcript of interview, April 11, 1973, 36, TIGHAR.
2. Bellarts interview.
3. Bellarts interview.
4. Bellarts interview, 2.
5. Message, Earhart to Black, July 1, 1937, NARA.
6. *Itasca* to FAB PH, July 1, 1937, NARA.
7. FAB PH to Earhart, July 1, 1937, NARA.
8. Telegram, C. L. Johnson to Earhart, March 11, 1937, TIGHAR.
9. There is evidence that transmissions from NR16020 on 6210 kcs could not be heard by stations closer than about four hundred nautical miles away. Four hours after takeoff, the Electra should have been at least that far away. The next morning, when Earhart was within two hundred nautical miles of Howland, she was unable to hear *Itasca* on 3105 kcs, so she said she would repeat the message on 6210 kcs. *Itasca* had been hearing her clearly on 3105 kcs, but then heard nothing further. *Itasca* radio log, 0843, July 2, 1937, NARA.
10. Chater to Griffin.
11. Lockheed Report 487.
12. Chater to Griffin.
13. *Itasca* radio log, RLP1, 1645, July 1, 1937, NARA.
14. *Itasca* radio log, RLP1, 1750, July 1, 1937, NARA.
15. Message, COMFRANDIV to *Itasca*, July 1, 1937, NARA.
16. *Itasca* deck log, July 1, 1937, NARA.
17. Message, Carey to Associated Press, July 1, 1937, NARA.
18. Message, Earhart to *Itasca*, June 30, 1937, NARA.
19. Earhart to *Itasca*.
20. Chater to Griffin.
21. *Itasca* radio log, RLP2, July 1, 1937, NARA.
22. Chater to Griffin.
23. Collopy to Civil Aviation Board.
24. Lockheed Report 487.

Chapter 17. Darkness and Silence

1. Message, Black (via governor of Samoa) to Earhart, June 23, 1937, NARA.
2. Black to Earhart.
3. Thompson, "Radio Transcripts," 36.
4. *Itasca* radio log, RLP1, 2151, July 1, 1937, NARA.
5. Message, U.S. Embassy Sydney, Australia, to Department of State, Washington, DC, 1145 GCT, July 3, 1937, NARA.
6. Correspondence between Syd Dowdeswell and Richard Gillespie and Dr. Randy Jacobson, September 1990, TIGHAR.
7. *Itasca* radio log, RLP2, 0001–0600, July 2, 1937, NARA.
8. Howland radio log, 2200, July 2, 1937, NARA.
9. *Itasca* radio log, RLP1, 2151, July 1, 1937, NARA.
10. *Itasca* radio log, RLP2, 0236, July 2, 1937. NARA.
11. *Itasca* deck log, July 1, 1937, NARA.
12. *Itasca* radio log, RLP2, 0245–0248, July 2, 1937, NARA.
13. Thompson, "Radio Transcripts," 39.
14. Bellarts interview.
15. Carey diary, 4.
16. *Itasca* radio log, RLP2, 0345, July 2, 1937, NARA.
17. Robert Brandenburg and Richard Gillespie, "Catalog and Analysis of Radio Signals During the Search for Amelia Earhart in July 1937," September 2011, TIGHAR.
18. Message, COMFRANDIV to *Itasca*, June 26, 1937, NARA.
19. Message, Earhart to Black, June 30, 1937, NARA.
20. Message, COMFRANDIV to *Itasca*, June 26, 1937, NARA.
21. Thompson, "Radio Transcripts," 40.
22. Thompson, "Radio Transcripts."
23. 1st Lt. Daniel Cooper, U.S. Army Air Corps, report, "Expedition to the American Equatorial Islands," 5, NARA.
24. International Radiotelegraph Conference, Madrid, 1932, *Report to the Secretary of State by the Chairman of the American Delegation, with Appended Documents* (Washington, DC: Government Printing Office, 1934).
25. *Itasca* radio log, RLP1, 0358, July 2, 1937, NARA.
26. *Itasca* radio log, RLP1, 0440, July 2, 1937, NARA.
27. *Itasca* radio log, RLP1, 0445–0450, July 2, 1937, NARA.
28. *Itasca* radio log, RLP2, raw version, 0453, July 2, 1937, NARA.
29. *Itasca* deck log, July 2, 1937, NARA.

Chapter 18. We Must Be On You

1. *Itasca* radio log, RLP2, raw version, 0453, July 2, 1937, NARA.
2. *Itasca* (via Samoa) to Earhart, June 28, 1937, NARA.
3. Bellarts interview, 72.
4. Bellarts interview, 73.
5. Bellarts interview, 74.
6. *Itasca* radio log, RLP1, 0620, July 2, 1937, NARA.
7. Howland radio log, 0717, July 3, 1937, 1, NARA.
8. *Itasca* radio log, RLP2, raw version, 0645, July 2, 1937, NARA.
9. *Itasca* radio log, RLP1, July 2, 1937, NARA.
10. Bellarts interview, 76.
11. Howland radio log, 0747, July 3, 1937, 1, NARA.
12. *Itasca* radio log, RLP2, raw version, 0715, July 2, 1937, NARA.
13. *Itasca* radio log, RLP2, raw version, 0718, July 2, 1937, NARA.
14. *Itasca* radio log, RLP2, raw version, 0718.
15. James C. Kamakaiwi, daily log for Howland Island, March 21–July 18, July 2, 1937, NARA.
16. *Itasca* radio log, RLP2, raw version, 0730, July 2, 1937, NARA.

17. *Itasca* radio log, RLP2, raw version, 0735–0741, July 2, 1937, NARA; *Itasca* radio log, RLP1, 0740, July 2, 1937, NARA; Bellarts interview, 81.
18. *Itasca* radio log, RLP2, raw version, 0742, July 2, 1937, NARA.
19. *Itasca* radio log, RLP1, 0740, July 2, 1937, NARA.
20. Bellarts interview, 24.
21. Robert Brandenburg, "The Post-Loss Radio Signals: Technical Analysis," October 2000, TIGHAR.
22. Robert Brandenburg, email exchange with Richard Gillespie, June 6–7, 2019, TIGHAR.
23. Bellarts interview, 22.
24. Bellarts interview, 23.
25. Cooper, "Expedition to the American Equatorial Islands," 7, 8.
26. Bellarts interview, 22, 35.
27. Thompson, "Radio Transcripts," 42.
28. *Itasca* radio log, RLP2, raw version, 0749–0750–0757, July 2, 1937, NARA.
29. Howland radio log, 0845, July 3, 1937, NARA.
30. *Itasca* radio log, RLP2, raw version, 0758, July 2, 1937, NARA.
31. *Itasca* radio log, RLP2, raw version, 0758.
32. *Itasca* radio log, RLP2R, 0800–0803, July 2, 1937, NARA.
33. Howland radio log, 0859, July 3, 1937, NARA.
34. *Itasca* radio log, RLP2, raw version, 0805, July 2, 1937, NARA.
35. *Itasca* radio log, RLP2, raw version, 0811, July 2, 1937.
36. *Itasca* radio log, RLP2, raw version, 0815, July 2, 1937.
37. Bellarts interview, 84.
38. Black, "Tenth Cruise to the American Equatorial Islands," 1, NARA.
39. Black.
40. Howland radio log, 0926, July 3, 1937, NARA.
41. *Itasca* radio log, RLP2, raw version, 0827, July 2, 1937, NARA.
42. *Itasca* radio log, RLP2, raw version, 0845, later changed to 0843, NARA.
43. Bellarts interview, 56.
44. *Itasca* radio log, RLP2, raw version, 0843, July 2, 1937, NARA.
45. *Itasca* radio log, RLP2, raw version, 0843.
46. Handwritten note by Associated Press reporter James Carey, July 2, 1937, TIGHAR.
47. Thompson, "Radio Transcripts," 47.
48. Frank Kenner, letter to Eve Kenner, August 10, 1937, TIGHAR.

Chapter 19. Salvation

1. *Itasca* radio log, RLP2, raw version, 0844–0846, 0847, and 0854–0907, July 2, 1937, NARA.
2. *Itasca* deck log, July 2, 1937, NARA.
3. *Itasca* radio log, RLP1, 0935, July 2, 1937, NARA; Howland radio log, 1000, July 3, 1937, NARA.
4. *Itasca* radio log, RLP1, 1005, July 2, 1937, NARA.
5. Message, *Itasca* to COMFRANDIV, 2145Z, July 2, 1937, NARA.
6. Message, *Itasca* to COMHAWSEC, 2148Z, July 2, 1937, NARA.
7. *Itasca* to COMHAWSEC.
8. Thompson, "Radio Transcripts," 47.
9. Kenner to Kenner.
10. Thompson, 47.
11. Thompson.
12. Thompson.
13. Message, COM CG to COMFRANDIV, 2315Z, July 2, 1937, NARA.
14. Message, COMHAWSEC to *Itasca*, 0031Z, July 3, 1937, NARA.
15. Message, Putnam to CNO, 0042Z, July 3, 1937, NARA.
16. Message, CNO to COM14, 0040Z, July 3, 1937, NARA.
17. Message, *Itasca* to COMFRANDIV, 0045Z, July 3, 1937, NARA.
18. Message, *Itasca* to all ships, 0103Z, July 3, 1937, NARA.

19. Message, COMHAWSEC to *Itasca*, 0031Z, July 3, 1937, NARA.
20. Message, *Itasca* to COMFRANDIV et al., 0132Z, July 3, 1937, NARA.
21. *Itasca* to COMFRANDIV et al., 0132Z, NARA; *Itasca* deck log, July 2, 1937, NARA.
22. Memorandum from K. C. Ambler, PAA section supervisor, communications, Honolulu, to division superintendent, communications, Alameda, July 10, 1937, TIGHAR.
23. Message, U.S. Navy Hydrographic Office, San Francisco, to all ships, 0245Z, July 3, 1937, NARA.
24. Message, COMFRANDIV to *Itasca*, 0310Z, July 3, 1937, NARA.
25. Message, *Itasca* to COMFRANDIV, 0403Z, July 3, 1937, NARA; message, COMFRANDIV to *Itasca*, 0410Z, July 3, 1937, NARA.
26. *Itasca* deck log, July 2, 1937.

Chapter 20. We Hear Her Now

1. "Plane's Letters Heard on Radio at Los Angeles," *New York Herald Tribune*, July 5, 1937, 2.
2. Letter from Warren Harvey to Mrs. S. D. Harvey, July 24, 1937, TIGHAR.
3. Harvey to Harvey.
4. COM14 to CNO, 0330Z, July 3, 1937, NARA.
5. Wilhelm Friedell, "Resume Earhart Search by the USS *Colorado*," July 13, 1937, 1, NARA.
6. Letter from Lt. (jg) William Short to his father, July 22, 1937, TIGHAR.
7. Short to father.
8. Message, COM14 to *Colorado*, 0745Z, July 3, 1937, NARA; Friedell, 3.
9. Adm. Kenneth Whiting's daughter Edna Nisewaner, telephone interview with Richard Gillespie, February 24, 1989, TIGHAR.
10. Message, *Itasca* to COMFRANDIV et al., 0132Z July 3, 1937, NARA.
11. Friedell, 3.
12. Short to father.
13. *Itasca* radio log, RLP2, 1800, July 2, 1937, NARA.
14. *Itasca* radio log, RLP2, 1801, July 2, 1937, NARA.
15. *Itasca* radio log, RLP1, 1800 and 1801.
16. *Itasca* radio log, RLP1, 1800 and 1801.
17. *Itasca* radio log, RLP2, 1812, July 2, 1937, NARA.
18. *Itasca* radio log, RLP2, 1824, July 2, 1937, NARA; *Itasca* radio log, RLP1, 1825, July 2, 1937, NARA.
19. Ambler to division superintendent, communications.
20. *Itasca* radio log, RLP1, 1830, July 2, 1937, NARA.
21. Message, Radio Tutuila to *Itasca*, 0730Z, July 3, 1937, NARA.
22. *Itasca* radio log, RLP2, 1834 and 1836, July 2, 1937, NARA; *Itasca* radio log, RLP1, 1830, July 2, 1937, NARA.
23. Radio Tutuila to *Itasca*, 0730Z.
24. Message, HMNZS *Achilles* to Radio Tutuila, 22xxZ, July 3, 1937, NARA.
25. *Itasca* radio log, RLP1, 1837, July 2, 1937, NARA.
26. *Itasca* radio log, RLP2, 1840 and 1841, July 2, 1937, NARA.

Chapter 21. Hopes and Hoaxes

1. *Itasca* radio log, RLP1, 1856, July 2, 1937, NARA.
2. Message, *Itasca* to COMFRANDIV, 0710Z, July 3, 1937, NARA.
3. *Itasca* to COMFRANDIV.
4. *Itasca* to COMFRANDIV.
5. *Itasca* to COMFRANDIV.
6. *Itasca* to COMFRANDIV.
7. Message, COM14 to *Itasca*, 0720Z, July 3, 1937, NARA.
8. *Itasca* radio log, RLP2, 1950, July 2, 1937, NARA.
9. Message, COMHAWSEC to *Itasca*, 0802Z, July 3, 1937, NARA.
10. Message, Radio Tutuila to *Itasca*, 0730Z, July 3, 1937, NARA.
11. *Itasca* to COMFRANDIV.

12. Message, COMHAWSEC to *Itasca*, 0810Z, July 3, 1937, NARA.
13. Mabel Larremore Duncklee, interview with Richard Gillespie, October 2, 1990, TIGHAR.
14. Letter from Mabel Duncklee to TIGHAR, October 2, 1990; Duncklee interview.
15. Duncklee interview.
16. Duncklee interview.
17. For a technical discussion of harmonics and how they apply to reports of signals heard from the Earhart plane, see "Harmony and Power: Could Betty Have Heard Earhart on a Harmonic?" TIGHAR.
18. COMHAWSEC to *Itasca*; *Itasca* radio log, RLP2, 2103 and 2105, July 2, 1937, NARA.
19. Message, PBY to FAB PH, 0835Z, July 3, 1937, NARA.
20. *Itasca* radio log, RLP2, 2107, July 2, 1937, NARA.
21. *Itasca* radio log, RLP2, 2110, July 2, 1937, NARA.
22. *Itasca* radio log, RLP2, 2113, July 2, 1937, NARA.
23. Page W. Smith, interview with Richard Gillespie, August 6, 1993, TIGHAR.
24. PBY to FAB PH.
25. Message, U.S. Consul, Sydney, Australia, to U.S. State Department, 1200Z, July 3, 1937, NARA.
26. Consul to State Department.
27. Chater to Griffin.
28. *Itasca* radio log, RLP2, 2130 and 2132, July 2, 1937, NARA.
29. Message, KPH to RDO CGFS, 101xZ, July 3, 1937, NARA.
30. Message, COMFRANDIV to *Itasca*, 1020Z, July 3, 1937, NARA; message, *Itasca* to COMFRANDIV, 1140Z, July 3, 1937, NARA.
31. Message, COMFRANDIV to *Itasca*, 1145Z, July 3, 1937, NARA.
32. "Miss Earhart Forced Down at Sea," *New York Times*, July 3, 1937, 1.
33. Message, COMFRANDIV to COMHAWSEC, 0640Z, July 12, 1937, NARA.
34. Walter McMenamy audio tape, 1959, summary by Richard Gillespie, January 12, 2004, TIGHAR.
35. Message, COMFRANDIV to *Itasca*, 1840Z, July 3, 1937, NARA.
36. Message, COMFRANDIV to *Itasca*, 2240Z, July 6, 1937, NARA.
37. "Ashland Lady Hears Earhart," *Ashland Daily Independent*, July 9, 1937.

Chapter 22. All Possible Energy

1. Brandenburg and Gillespie.
2. Smith interview.
3. Message, COM14 to CNO, 2028Z, July 3, 1937, NARA.
4. Message, CNO to COM14, 0040Z, July 3, 1937, NARA.
5. Message, CNO to CINCUS, 2145Z, July 3, 1937, NARA.
6. Message, COMFRANDIV to COMHAWSEC, 1830Z, July 3, 1937, NARA.
7. Message, COM12 to COM14, 2015Z, July 3, 1937, NARA.
8. "2 Aids Believe Earhart Plane Safe on Pacific Atoll," *New York Herald Tribune*, July 4, 1937, 1.
9. Message, *Itasca* to COMHAWSEC, 1930Z, July 3, 1937, NARA; message, COMHAWSEC to *Itasca*, 2026Z, July 3, 1937, NARA.
10. Message, COMHAWSEC to COMFRANDIV, 2135Z, July 3, 1937, NARA.
11. Message, COMDT CG to *Itasca*, 2256Z, July 3, 1937, NARA.
12. Message, *Itasca* to COMDT CG, 0020Z, July 4, 1937, NARA.
13. Message, COMDT CG to *Itasca*, 0140Z, July 4, 1937, NARA.
14. Message, *Itasca* to United Press, 0215Z, July 4, 1937, NARA.
15. Message, *Itasca* to COMDT CG, 0450Z, July 4, 1937, NARA.
16. Consul to State Department.
17. Message, *Itasca* to COMDT CG, 0450Z.
18. Message, COMFRANDIV to *Itasca*, 1145Z, July 3, 1937, NARA.
19. Message, *Itasca* to COMFRANDIV, 1140Z, July 3, 1937, NARA.
20. Daniel Hamer, "Stranding and Subsequent Rescue of the Survivors of the *Norwich City*," December 1929, TIGHAR.
21. Message, COMFRANDIV to *Itasca*, 0120Z, July 4, 1937, NARA.
22. Message, COMFRANDIV to COMHAWSEC, 0420Z, July 3, 1937, NARA.

Chapter 23. Ship on Reef

1. *Itasca* radio log, RLP2, 1806, July 3, 1937, NARA.
2. *Itasca* radio log, RLP2, 1806.
3. *Itasca* radio log, RLP2, 1915 and 1923, July 3, 1937, NARA.
4. *Itasca* radio log, RLP2, 2216, July 4, 1937, NARA.
5. A. Frederick Collins, *The Radio Amateur's Handbook*, 14th ed. (West Hartford, CT: American Radio Relay League, 1937), 364.
6. Message, COMHAWSEC to *Itasca*, 0846Z, July 4, 1937, NARA.
7. Message, *Itasca* to United Press, 0815Z, July 4, 1937, NARA.
8. *Itasca* to United Press, 0815Z.
9. Ambler memorandum.
10. *Itasca* radio log, RLP2, 2120, July 3, 1937, NARA.
11. *Itasca* radio log, RLP2, 2205, July 3, 1937, NARA.
12. Ambler memorandum.
13. *Itasca*, radio log, RLP2, 2233, July 3, 1937, NARA.
14. Ambler memorandum; message, COMHAWSEC to *Itasca*, 1035Z, July 4, 1937, NARA.
15. COMHAWSEC to *Itasca*, 1035Z.
16. Message, *Itasca* to Howland Island, RLP2, 2306, July 3, 1937, NARA.
17. Message, COMFRANDIV to *Itasca*, 1200Z, July 4, 1937, NARA.
18. Message, COMHAWSEC to *Itasca*, 1340Z, July 4, 1937, NARA.
19. Memorandum from R. M. Hansen, PAA operator in charge, communications, Wake Island, to communications superintendent, Alameda, July 10, 1937, TIGHAR.
20. Message, RDO Wailupe to *Itasca* and *Colorado*, 1415, July 4, 1937, NARA.
21. RDO Wailupe to *Itasca* and *Colorado*.
22. "Plane's Letters Heard on Radio at Los Angeles," *New York Herald Tribune*, July 5, 1937, 2.
23. "Plane's Letters Heard."
24. "Plane's Letters Heard."
25. Message, *Itasca* to United Press, 0815Z, July 4, 1937, NARA.
26. *Itasca* radio log, RLP2, 0200, July 4, 1937, NARA.
27. Memorandum from G. H. Miller, PAA operator in charge, communications, Midway Island to division communications superintendent, Alameda, July 11, 1937, TIGHAR.
28. Miller memorandum.
29. Message, COMHAWSEC to *Itasca*, 1610Z, July 4, 1937, NARA.
30. Robert L. Brandenburg, "Analysis of Radio Direction Finder Bearings in the Search for Amelia Earhart," August 2006, TIGHAR.
31. "First Radio Contact with Miss Earhart Made by Springs Boy," *Rock Springs Rocket*, July 6–7, 1937, 1.
32. "First Radio Contact."
33. Message, COMFRANDIV to *Itasca*, 2310Z, July 4, 1937, NARA.
34. Message, COMFRANDIV to *Itasca*, 0057Z, July 5, 1937, NARA.
35. Robert Brandenburg, "Post-loss Radio Probability Analysis," TIGHAR.
36. "First Radio Contact," 1.
37. "First Radio Contact."
38. "First Radio Contact."
39. COMFRANDIV to *Itasca*, 2310Z.
40. "Amelia's Frantic SOS Heard Here at 1 P.M.," *Toronto Star*, July 5, 1937, 1.

Chapter 24. Confusion and Chaos

1. "Storm Turns Back Plane Sent to Find Miss Earhart; Several Radio Calls Heard," *New York Times*, July 4, 1937, 1.
2. "Storms Balk Navy Plane on Earhart Hunt," *New York Herald Tribune*, July 4, 1937, 1.
3. "Storms Balk Navy Plane."
4. Message, CNO to CINCUS, 1700Z, July 4, 1937, NARA.
5. "Storms Balk Navy Plane," 1.

6. Message, RDO Tutuila to *HMNZS Achilles*, 1800Z, July 4, 1937, NARA.
7. Friedell, "Resume Earhart Search," 4.
8. Thompson, "Cruise Report 4 June to 24 July, 1937," 6.
9. *Itasca* radio log, RLP2, 0930–1600, July 4, 1937, NARA.
10. Message, *Golden Bear* to *Itasca*, time unknown, July 4, 1937, NARA.
11. Bureau of International Telecommunication Union, *List of Coast Stations and Ship Stations* (Berne, Switzerland, 1937), 332.
12. Message, *Itasca* to COMDT CG, 0245Z, July 5, 1937, NARA.
13. Message, *Itasca* to COMDT CG, 2205Z, July 4, 1937, NARA.
14. Message, COMDT CG to *Itasca*, 2355Z, July 4, 1937, NARA.
15. Message, *Itasca* to COMDT CG, 0630Z, July 5, 1937, NARA.
16. *Itasca* to COMDT CG, 0630Z.
17. *Itasca* radio log, RLP2, 0245–0248, July 2, 1937, NARA.
18. *Itasca* to COMDT CG, 0630Z.
19. *Itasca* radio log, RLP2, 0345, July 2, 1937, NARA.
20. Message, *Itasca* to COMDT CG, 0630Z, July 5, 1937, NARA.
21. *Itasca* radio log, RLP2, 0453, July 2, 1937, NARA; *Itasca* radio log, RLP1, 0455, July 2, 1937, NARA.
22. *Itasca* to COMDT CG, 0630Z.
23. *Itasca* radio log, RLP2, 0514, July 2, 1937, NARA.
24. *Itasca* to COMDT CG, 0630Z.
25. *Itasca* radio log, RLP2, 0615, July 2, 1937, NARA.
26. *Itasca* to COMDT CG, 0630Z.
27. *Itasca* radio log, RLP2, 0646, July 2, 1937, NARA.
28. *Itasca* to COMDT CG, 0630Z.
29. Message, *Itasca* to COMFRANDIV, 2145Z, July 2, 1937, NARA.
30. *Itasca* to COMDT CG, 0630Z.
31. *Itasca* radio log, RLP2, 0758, July 2, 1937, NARA.
32. *Itasca* to COMDT CG, 0630Z.
33. *Itasca* radio log, RLP2R, 0803, July 2, 1937, NARA.
34. *Itasca* to COMDT CG, 0630Z.
35. *Itasca* radio log, RLP2R, 0843, July 2, 1937, NARA.
36. *Itasca* to COMDT CG, 0630Z.
37. *Itasca* to COMDT CG, 0630Z.
38. Black, "Report of Tenth Cruise to American Equatorial Islands," 13.
39. "Earhart Flares Believed Sighted by Cutter Racing to '281 North Howland' in Pacific," *New York Herald Tribune*, July 6, 1937, 1.
40. Message, COMHAWSEC to *Itasca*, 2025Z, July 4, 1937, NARA.
41. Message, *Itasca* to COMHAWSEC, 2140Z, July 4, 1937, NARA.
42. *Itasca* to COMHAWSEC, 2140Z.
43. Message, COMHAWSEC to *Itasca*, 0225Z, July 5, 1937. NARA.
44. Message, *Itasca* to COMFRANDIV, 0535Z, July 5, 1937, NARA; message, COMFRANDIV to *Itasca*, 0605Z, July 5, 1937, NARA.
45. Message, COMFRANDIV to *Itasca*, 0555Z, July 5, 1937, NARA.
46. Thompson, report, "Radio Transcripts," 68.
47. Message, COMFRANDIV to COMHAWSEC, 0326Z, July 5, 1937, NARA.
48. Message, COMHAWSEC to *Itasca* et al., 0445Z, July 5, 1937, NARA.
49. *Itasca* radio log, RLP2, 1810, July 4, 1937, NARA.

Chapter 25. Dashes

1. "*Itasca* Combing Howland Area," *Honolulu Star-Bulletin*, July 5, 1937, 1.
2. Message, COMHAWSEC to *Itasca* et al., 0445Z, July 5, 1937, NARA.
3. Message, COMHAWSEC to *Colorado*, *Swan*, RDO Tutuila, *Itasca*, 0730Z, July 5, 1937, NARA.
4. Memorandum from R. M. Hansen, PAA operator in charge, communications, Wake Island, to communications superintendent, Alameda, July 10, 1937, TIGHAR.

5. Memorandum from G. H. Miller, PAA operator in charge, communications, Midway Island, to division communications superintendent, Alameda, July 11, 1937, TIGHAR.

6. "*Itasca* Combing Howland Area," 1.

7. Memorandum from K. C. Ambler, PAA section supervisor, communications, Honolulu, to division superintendent, communications, Alameda, July 10, 1937. TIGHAR.

8. Memorandum from G. W. Angus, PAA division communication superintendent, Pacific Division, Alameda, to chief communication engineer, communications, New York, July 10, 1937, TIGHAR.

9. Ambler memorandum.

10. Angus memorandum.

11. *Itasca* radio log, RLP2, 1600, July 4, 1937, NARA; Ambler memorandum.

12. Message, RDO Tutuila to COMHAWSEC, 0745Z, July 5, 1937, NARA; message, COMHAWSEC to *Itasca*, 0845Z, July 5, 1937, NARA.

13. *Itasca*, radio log, RLP2, 2000, 2005, 2015, 2020, July 4, 1937, NARA.

14. Message, COMFRANDIV to *Itasca*, 1930Z, July 5, 1937, NARA.

15. "*Itasca* Combing Howland Area," 1.

16. Brandenburg, "Analysis of Radio Direction Finder Bearings," 21.

17. *Itasca* radio log, RLP2, 2045, July 5, 1937, NARA.

18. *Itasca* radio log, RLP2, 2113, July 5, 1937, NARA.

19. Message, COMHAWSEC to *Itasca*, 0845Z, July 5.

20. *Itasca* radio log, RLP2, 2128, 2137, July 4, 1937, NARA; *Itasca* radio log, RLP2, 1834, July 2 1937, NARA; *Itasca* radio log, RLP2, 2141, July 5, 1937, NARA.

21. Message, COMHAWSEC to *Itasca*, 0910Z, July 5, 1937, NARA.

22. *Itasca* radio log, RLP2, 2141–2149, July 5, 1937, NARA.

23. *Itasca* radio log, RLP2, 2202, July 5, 1937, NARA.

24. *Itasca* radio log, RLP2, 2210, 2214, July 5, 1937, NARA.

25. *Itasca* radio log, RLP2, 2216, July 5, 1937, NARA.

26. *Itasca* radio log, RLP2, 2233, July 5, 1937, NARA.

27. Miller memorandum; Ambler memorandum; message, COMHAWSEC to *Itasca*, 0910Z, July 5; *Itasca* radio log, RLP2, 2233, July 5.

28. *Itasca* radio log, RLP2, 2216, NARA; Thompson, "Radio Transcripts—Earhart Flight," 69, NARA.

29. Yau Fai Lum, letter to Thomas F. Gannon, January 10, 1989, TIGHAR; John P. Riley, "The Earhart Tragedy: Old Mystery, New Hypothesis," *Naval History* 14, no. 2 (August 2000): 22–28.

30. Riley, "The Earhart Tragedy," 26.

31. Black, "Tenth Cruise to the Equatorial Islands," 13.

32. Bellarts interview, 49.

33. *Itasca* radio log, RLP2, 2232, July 5, 1937, NARA.

34. *Itasca* radio log, RLP2, 2240, July 5, 1937, NARA.

35. Message, COMHAWSEC to *Itasca*, 0845Z, July 5, 1937, NARA; message, *Itasca* to COMHAWSEC, 1008Z, July 5, 1937, NARA.

36. *Itasca* radio log, RLP2, 2243, 2258, 2259, 2317, July 5, 1937, NARA.

37. Miller memorandum.

38. For an explanation of "night effect," see Brandenburg, "Analysis of Radio Direction Finder Bearings."

39. Howland radio log, 0035, July 5, 1937, NARA.

40. Howland radio log; *Itasca* radio log, RLP2, 2335, July 5, 1937, NARA.

41. *Itasca* radio log, RLP2.

42. Message, *Itasca* to COMHAWSEC, 1155Z, July 5, 1937, NARA.

43. *Itasca* radio log RLP2, 0030–0035, July 5, 1937, NARA.

44. Message, RDO Tutuila to *Itasca*, 1210Z, July 5, 1937, NARA.

45. RDO Tutuila to *Itasca*.

46. Hansen memorandum.

47. Brandenburg, "Analysis of Radio Direction Finder Bearings."

48. Angus memorandum.

49. Hansen memorandum.

50. Angus memorandum.
51. Message, COMHAWSEC to *Itasca*, 1312Z, July 5, 1937, NARA.
52. *Itasca* deck log, July 5, 1937, NARA.
53. Message, *Itasca* to *Swan*, 1425Z, July 5, 1937, NARA.
54. *Itasca* radio log, RLP2 0314, July 5, 1937, NARA.
55. *Itasca* radio log, RLP2 0035, July 5, 1937, NARA.
56. *Itasca* radio log, RLP2 0307, July 5, 1937, NARA.
57. *Moorby*'s position as recorded in *Itasca*'s radio log—latitude 5°59′N, longitude 163°41′W—is some eight hundred miles from the target area and cannot be correct based on where the ship was known to be a few hours later. The correct position was almost certainly latitude 5°59′N, longitude 173°41′W.
58. Message, *Itasca* to RDO Wailupe and RDO Tutuila, 1449Z, July 5, 1937, NARA.
59. Howland radio log, 0518, July 5, 1937, NARA.
60. Message, COMFRANDIV to *Itasca*, 1930Z, July 5, 1937, NARA.

Chapter 26. Damsel in Distress

1. Message, *Itasca* to COMDT CG, 1810Z, July 5, 1937, NARA.
2. Message, *Itasca* to COMFRANDIV, 1955Z, July 5, 1937, NARA.
3. Message, Carey to Associated, 2030Z, July 5, 1937, NARA.
4. Carey to Associated.
5. Carey to Associated.
6. Hansen memorandum.
7. "Hear Amelia's Faint Calls," *Oakland Tribune*, July 5, 1937, 1.
8. "Wyoming and Ohio Listeners Believed She Was Trying to Give Position Near Howland," *New York Times*, July 5, 1937, 1.
9. "Mantz Believes Fliers Are 'Sitting on an Island,'" *New York Herald Tribune*, July 5, 1937, 1.
10. "Mantz Believes Fliers Are 'Sitting on an Island,'" 2.
11. "Officials Pin New Hopes on Radio Signals," *Honolulu Star-Bulletin*, July 5, 1937, 4.
12. Message, COMFRANDIV to COM CG, 1845Z, July 5, 1937, NARA.
13. Memorandum, U.S. State Department, "Search for Plane of Amelia Earhart," July 5, 1937, NARA.
14. Message, Putnam to CNO, 1659Z, July 8, 1937, NARA; message, CNO to Putnam, 18xx, July 8, 1937, NARA.
15. "Woman Asserts She Got Communication by Voice," *New York Herald Tribune*, July 6, 1937, 2.
16. "Wyoming and Ohio Listeners," 1.
17. "Wyoming and Ohio Listeners"; "First Radio Contact with Miss Earhart Made by Springs Boy," *Rock Springs Rocket*, July 6–7, 1937.
18. Message, *Moorby* to *Itasca*, 2100Z, July 5, 1937, NARA.
19. *Itasca* radio log, RLP2, 0957, July 5, 1937, NARA.
20. Betty Klenck, transcription of transmission from Amelia Earhart, July 5, 1937, TIGHAR.
21. Klenck transcription.
22. Letter from Amelia Earhart to her mother, December 26, 1934, Schlesinger Library, Radcliffe College.
23. Betty Klenck Brown, conversation with Richard Gillespie, November 5, 2000, TIGHAR.
24. Klenck transcription.
25. Betty Klenck Brown, email to Richard Gillespie, September 28, 2000, TIGHAR.
26. Brown email.
27. "Officials Pin New Hopes on Radio Signals," 1.
28. Message, COMFRANDIV to *Itasca*, 2325Z, July 5, 1937, NARA.
29. COMFRANDIV to *Itasca*.

Chapter 27. 281 North

1. *Itasca* radio log, RLP2, 0407Z, July 6, 1937, NARA.
2. Message, NBC to COM14, 0316Z, July 6, 1937, NARA.
3. Message, COM14 to NBC, 0521Z, July 6, 1937, NARA.
4. Message, COMHAWSEC to *Itasca*, 0036Z, July 6, 1937, NARA; message, *Itasca* to COMHAWSEC, 0455Z, July 6, 1937, NARA.

5. Message, COMFRANDIV to *Itasca*, 0535Z, July 6, 1937, NARA.
6. *Itasca* radio log, RLP2, 1840, 2010, July 5, 1937, NARA.
7. *Itasca* deck log, July 5, 1937, NARA.
8. Message, COMFRANDIV to *Itasca*, 0730Z, July 6, 1937, NARA; message, *Itasca* to COMFRANDIV, 0740Z, July 6, 1937, NARA.
9. *Itasca* deck log, July 5; Thompson, "Radio Transcripts," 75, 76; *Itasca* radio log, RLP2, 2105, July 5, 1937, NARA.
10. *Itasca* radio log, RLP2, 2113, July 5, 1937, NARA; message, RDO Wailupe to several COMM offices, 0845Z, July 6, 1937, NARA; message, COMHAWSEC to COMFRANDIV, 0913Z, July 6, 1937, NARA.
11. *Itasca* radio log, RLP2, 2132, 2133, July 5, 1937, NARA.
12. Message, COMFRANDIV to *Itasca*, 0915Z, July 6, 1937, NARA.
13. Thompson, "Radio Transcripts," 76.
14. *Itasca* radio log, RLP2 2200, July 5, 1937, NARA.
15. Message, *Itasca* to COMHAWSEC, 1015Z, July 6, 1937, NARA; Thompson, "Radio Transcripts," 76.
16. "Earhart Flares Believed Sighted by Cutter Racing to '281 North Howland' in Pacific," *New York Herald Tribune*, July 6, 1937, 1.
17. "Earhart Searchers Arrive at Point Reported by Plane on Radio," *New York Times*, July 6, 1937, 1.
18. Message, Jacksonville Beach to COM CG, 14xxZ, July 6, 1937, NARA.
19. Message, *New York Times* to *Itasca*, 15xxZ, July 6, 1937, NARA.
20. Message, *London Daily Mirror* to *Itasca*, 15xxZ, July 6, 1937, NARA.
21. Message, Paramount Pictures to *Itasca*, 15xxZ, July 6, 1937, NARA.
22. Message, Honolulu (Thurston) to *Itasca*, 15xxZ, July 6, 1937, NARA.
23. Message, New York Pathé News to *Itasca*, 15xxZ, July 6, 1937, NARA.
24. Message, United Press to Hanzlick, 15xx, July 6, 1937, NARA.
25. Message, Honolulu Press/Associated to Carey, 15xx, July 6, 1937, NARA.
26. Message, COM CG to *Itasca*, 1658Z, July 6, 1937, NARA; *Itasca* to COM CG, 1754Z, 1850Z, July 6, 1937, NARA.
27. Message, RDO Wailupe to *Itasca*, 1900Z, July 6, 1937; message, *Itasca* to RDO Wailupe, 1914Z, July 6, 1937, NARA.
28. Message, Carey to Associated, 2030Z, July 6, 1937, NARA.
29. *Itasca* radio log, RLP2, 2113, 2132, July 5, 1937, NARA.
30. Message, RDO Wailupe to COM14, 1005Z, July 7, 1937, NARA.
31. Howland radio log, 2238, NARA.
32. Message, RDO Wailupe to COM14, 1005Z.
33. Message, COMFRANDIV to COMHAWSEC et al., 1040Z, July 6, 1937, NARA.
34. Message, COMFRANDIV to COM CG, 2038Z, July 6, 1937, NARA; message, COM CG to COMFRANDIV, 2133Z, July 6, 1937, NARA.
35. Message, COMHAWSEC to *Itasca*, 0001Z, July 7, 1937, NARA.
36. Thompson, "Radio Transcripts," 75.
37. Message, COMFRANDIV to COMHAWSEC et al., 1010Z, July 6, 1937, NARA.

Chapter 28. *Colorado*

1. Robert L. Brandenburg and Richard Gillespie, "Post-loss Radio Signals Catalog and Analysis 2.0," *TIGHAR Tracks* 34, no. 2 (August 2018).
2. "Toronto Woman Sure She Heard Amelia Earhart Calling for Aid," *Toronto Daily Star* (2nd Edition), July 5, 1937, 1.
3. "Earhart Flares Believed Sighted," *New York Herald Tribune*, July 6, 1937, 1.
4. Message, COM14 to *Colorado*, 0135Z, July 7, 1937, NARA.
5. Message, *Colorado* to COM14, 0225Z, July 7, 1937, NARA.
6. Message, COMFRANDIV to *Itasca* and *Colorado*, 0752Z, July 7, 1937, NARA.
7. Friedell, "Resume Earhart Search," 8.
8. Message, *Colorado* to CNO, 1615Z, July 6, 1937, NARA.

9. USS *Colorado, Radio Press News*, July 6, 1937, 5, TIGHAR.
10. USS *Colorado, Radio Press News*.
11. USS *Colorado, Radio Press News*.
12. USS *Colorado, Radio Press News*, 1.
13. Howland log, July 7, 1937, 01:50, NARA.
14. Letter from Thelma Lovelace to TIGHAR, March 21, 1991, TIGHAR.
15. Lovelace to TIGHAR.
16. Lovelace to TIGHAR.
17. "The Object Formerly Known as Nessie," *TIGHAR Tracks* 29, no. 1 (March 2013).
18. "Earhart Search Shifting to Southeast of Howland after Fifth Fruitless Day," *New York Times*, July 7, 1937, 1.
19. Friedell, "Resume Earhart Search."
20. *Colorado* deck log, July 8, 1937, NARA.
21. Lt. John O. Lambrecht, "Aircraft Search for Earhart Plane," *Bureau of Aeronautics Weekly Newsletter*, July 16, 1937, 2, NARA.
22. Letter from Lt. (jg) William Short to his father, July 22, 1937, TIGHAR.
23. Short to father.
24. Message, CNO to COM14, 2021Z, July 9, 1937, NARA.
25. Message, CNO to COM14, 2112Z, July 7, 1937, NARA; message, COM14 to CNO, 0130Z, July 8, 1937, NARA.
26. "Warship's Planes Start Search for Miss Earhart; No Definite Signals Heard," *New York Times*, July 8, 1937, 1.

Chapter 29. Death Warrant

1. "Warship's Planes Start Search for Miss Earhart; No Definite Signals Heard," *New York Times*, July 8, 1937, 1.
2. "Warship's Planes Join Earhart Hunt" and "Putnam Keeps Up Hope," *New York Times*, July 8, 1937, 12.
3. Message, COM14 to COMDESRON2, 0319Z, July 6, 1937, NARA; message, CNO to *Ramapo*, 1445Z, July 6, 1937, NARA.
4. Capt. J. S. Dowell, report, "Narrative of Earhart Search," July 1937, 1, NARA.
5. Rear Adm. Orin G. Murfin, "Report of Earhart Search, 2–18 July, 1937," 5, NARA.
6. Capt. Leigh Noyes, report, "Discussion as to the Best Area in Which to Conduct Search," July 1937, NARA.
7. Noyes report.
8. *Itasca* radio log, RLP2, raw version, 0742, July 2, 1937, NARA.
9. *Itasca* radio log, RLP1, 0740, July 2, 1937, NARA.
10. Noyes report, ii.
11. Noyes report, iii.
12. Noyes report, v.
13. Noyes report, vii.
14. Putnam, *Soaring Wings*, 76.
15. Lt. John Lambrecht, newsletter article, "Aircraft Search for Earhart Plane," NARA.
16. Message, Black to Gruening, 1145Z, July 9, 1937, NARA.
17. Short to father.
18. *Colorado* deck log, July 9, 1937, NARA.
19. Lambrecht; Eric Clapp, Smithsonian Institution, "SIC #19 Preliminary Report, McKean Island, 13–15 July 1968." A 1968 survey by ornithologists found McKean Island to be home to the world's largest known colony of lesser frigate birds, an estimated 85,000 individuals, plus more than 150,000 seabirds of other types.
20. Lambrecht.
21. Jimmy M. Skaggs, *The Great Guano Rush: Entrepreneurs and American Overseas Expansion* (New York: St. Martin's Press, 1995), 80–81.
22. Lambrecht.
23. Lambrecht.

Chapter 30. Signs of Habitation

1. Lambrecht.
2. H. E. Maude, "Colonization of the Phoenix Islands by the Surplus Population of the Gilbert and Ellice Islands," 7, PRO.
3. Short to father.
4. Lambrecht.
5. Lambrecht.
6. Short to father.
7. Lambrecht.
8. Lambrecht.
9. Short to father.
10. *Colorado* deck log, July 9, 1937, NARA.
11. Letter from John Lambrecht to Fred Goerner, undated, TIGHAR.
12. Short to father.
13. Message, *Colorado* to United Press, 2304Z, July 9, 1937, NARA.
14. Message, COM14 to COMDESRON2, 2331Z, July 9, 1937, NARA.
15. Message, COM14 to COMDESRON2.
16. Message, COMDESRON2 to COM14, 2040Z, July 10, 1937, NARA.
17. Short to father.
18. Lambrecht.
19. Captain, HMS *Leith*, "Report of Proceedings: Island Cruise—Second Part," September 18, 1937, PRO.
20. Eric R. Bevington, *The Things We Do for England—If Only England Knew!* (Hampshire, UK: Acorn Bookwork, 1990), 25.
21. Lambrecht to Goerner.
22. Lambrecht to Goerner.
23. Maude, 71–75.
24. Message, *Colorado* to Associated Press, 0825Z, July 11, 1937, NARA.
25. Foua Tofinga, letter to Dr. Thomas F. King, October 5, 1999, TIGHAR.
26. Lambrecht to Goerner.
27. Short to father.
28. Message, *Colorado* to COM14, 0600Z, July 11, 1937, NARA.
29. Message, *Colorado* to United Press, 0425Z, July 11, 1937, NARA.
30. Message, Brooks to International, 0100Z, July 11, 1937, NARA.

Chapter 31. *Lexington*

1. Message, COM14 to COM11, 2215Z, July 10, 1937, NARA.
2. Message, COMFRANDIV to *Itasca* et al., 2219Z, July 5, 1937, NARA.
3. Message, COM11 to COM14, 1705Z, July 11, 1937, NARA.
4. Noyes report, iii.
5. Message, COM14 to *Colorado* and COMDESRON2, 2015Z, July 11, 1937, NARA.
6. Message, COMFRANDIV to COMHAWSEC et al., 0640Z, July 12, 1937, NARA.
7. "Noonan Sends SOS from Earhart Plane," *Oakland Tribune*, July 3, 1937, 1.
8. Message, *Itasca* to COMFRANDIV, 1145Z, July 3, 1937, NARA.
9. Message, COMFRANDIV to COMDESRON2, 1200Z, July 12, 1937, NARA.
10. Message, COMFRANDIV to COMHAWSEC et al., 0640Z, July 12, 1937, NARA.
11. Message, State Department to American Embassy, Tokyo, 1900Z, July 10, 1937, NARA.
12. Thomas Wilds, "How Japan Fortified the Mandated Islands," U.S. Naval Institute *Proceedings* 81, no. 4 (April 1955): 2.
13. Message, U.S. Embassy Tokyo to State Department, 0200Z, July 11, 1937, NARA.
14. Message, COMDESRON2 to *Itasca*, 0920Z, July 12, 1937, NARA.
15. Message, Welty to Associated, 2323Z, July 15, 1937, NARA.
16. Message, *Itasca* to COM14 and COMDESRON2, 0230Z, July 16, 1937, NARA; message, COMDESRON2 to *Itasca*, 0444Z, July 16, 1937, NARA.
17. Message, U.S. State Department to American Embassy, London, 2200, July 15, 1937, NARA.

18. Letter from Department of State to Claude A. Swanson, Secretary of the Navy, July 17, 1937, NARA.
19. Message, Brooks to International, 0845Z, July 16, 1937, NARA.
20. Message, COMFRANDIV to COM14 and COMDESRON2, 0735Z, July 16, 1937, NARA.
21. Message, Welty to Associated Press, 2009Z, July 16, 1937, NARA.
22. Message, COMFRANDIV to COM14 and COMDESRON2, 2120Z, July 16, 1937, NARA.
23. Message, George Putnam to CNO, 0220Z, July 17, 1937, NARA.
24. "Woman Psychic Asserts Amelia Earhart Is Safe," *New York Herald Tribune*, July 16, 1937, 11.
25. Message, Putnam to CNO, 1908Z, July 17, 1937, NARA.
26. Message, COMFRANDIV to COM14 and COMDESRON2, 2035Z, July 17, 1937, NARA; message, COM14 to COMFRANDIV, 2130Z, July 17, 1937, NARA.
27. Message, CNO to COM14, 0212Z, July 18, 1937, NARA; message, COM14 to CNO, 0845Z, July 18, 1937, NARA.
28. Message, Putnam to CNO, 1910Z, July 18, 1937, NARA; message, CNO to Putnam, 1920Z, July 18, 1937, NARA.
29. Message, Putnam to CNO, 2053Z, July 18, 1937, NARA; message, CNO to Putnam, 23xxZ, July 18, 1937, NARA.
30. Message, COMDESRON2 to *Itasca*, 2040Z, July 16, 1937, NARA; message, *Itasca* to COMDES-RON2, 2330Z, July 16, 1937, NARA.
31. Message, *Itasca* to COMDESRON2.
32. *Itasca* deck log, July 2, 1937, NARA.
33. Message, Black to Miller, 0840Z, July 22, 1937, NARA.
34. *Itasca* to COMDESRON2.
35. *Itasca* to COMDESRON2.
36. *Itasca* deck log, July 2, 1937.
37. Message, *Itasca* to COMDESRON2, 2330Z, July 16, 1937.
38. Message, COMDESRON2 to COM14, 0730Z, July 17, 1937, NARA.
39. COMDESRON2 to COM14.
40. Message, COM14 to CNO, 2025Z, July 17, 1937, NARA.
41. Message, COM14 to CNO, 1950Z, July 18, 1937, NARA.
42. Message, COMDESRON2 to COM14, 0321Z, July 19, 1937, NARA.
43. Message, COM14 to CNO, 0520Z, July 19, 1937, NARA.

Chapter 32. Last Days

1. Richard L. Jantz, "Amelia Earhart and the Nikumaroro Bones: A 1941 Analysis versus Modern Quantitative Techniques," *Forensic Anthropology* 1, no. 2 (February 2018): 1–16.
2. "San Diegan Bares Clue to Earhart Fate," A-4.
3. Inventory item 24, receipt, "Proceedings of a Board of Officers appointed to investigate the crash of Amelia Earhart at Luke Field, March 1937," U.S. Army, Headquarters Hawaiian Department, April 16, 1937, NARA.
4. Geoffrey Cunnar, "Examining Evidence for Secondary Use on Historic Glass Associated with the Possible Landing Site of Amelia Earhart and Fred Noonan on Nikumaroro Island," January 2011, specimen 2-9-S-1b, TIGHAR.
5. Letter from Thomas Allison to Richard Gillespie, analysis of zipper "slider" artifact, March 26, 2008, TIGHAR.
6. "Shoe Fetish, Part III," Earhart Project Research Bulletin, February 2, 2004, TIGHAR.
7. Minute in WPHC File M.P. 4439, Steenson to Vaskess, July 1, 1941, WPA.
8. M. H. Hay journal, New Zealand Pacific Aviation Survey, undated, NZAM.
9. Maude.
10. Sharyn Jones, "Report on Zooarchaeological Remains from the Seven Site, Nikumaroro, Phoenix Islands," TIGHAR.
11. Jones.
12. Natalie Olsen, "What is Protein Poisoning?" Healthline, updated September 17, 2018, https://www.healthline.com/health/protein-poisoning#:~:text=Protein%20poisoning%20is%20when%20the,rabbit%2C%20without%20consuming%20other%20nutrients.

Chapter 33. Blame the Victim

1. "Greatest Rescue Force in History of Aviation," *New York Herald Tribune*, July 5, 1937, 1.
2. Friedell, 11.
3. Friedell, 10, 11.
4. Friedell, 13.
5. Civil Air Patrol, *Mission Aircraft Reference Text*, chapter 9, "Search Planning and Coverage," section 9.2.1, "Probability of Detection Table."
6. Friedell, 10; Lambrecht.
7. Memorandum, J. S. Dowell, commander, *Lexington* Group to commandant, Fourteenth Naval District, July 20, 1937, NARA.
8. Dowell memorandum.
9. Lt. D. M. Tites, USAAC, "Inventory NR16020," March 26, 1937, sheet 3, item 53, in U.S. Army Proceedings, "Investigation of Earhart Crash, Luke Field, March 20, 1937," NARA.
10. Capt. J. S. Dowell, report, "Narrative of Earhart Search," Estimate and Decisions, Annex A, 1, July 1937, NARA.
11. Capt. J. S. Dowell, report, "Narrative of Earhart Search," Estimate and Decisions, Annex B, 3, July 1937, NARA.
12. "Plane's Letters Heard on Radio at Los Angeles," *New York Herald Tribune*, July 5, 1937, 2.
13. "Plane's Letters Heard on Radio at Los Angeles," 3, 5, 8.
14. Dowell report, Annex B, 16.
15. Capt. J. S. Dowell, report, "Narrative of Earhart Search," Estimate and Decisions, Annex D, "Report of Earhart Search Operations 3–18 July 1937," 4, NARA.
16. Dowell report, Annex D, 9.
17. Thompson, 105.
18. Thompson, 105; Message, CNO to COM14, 2020Z, July 16, 1937, NARA.
19. Thompson, 1.
20. Thompson, 7, 34.
21. Black, 1.
22. Black to Miller, 0333Z, March 5, 1937, NARA.
23. Thompson, 12, 15–16.
24. Thompson, 22.
25. Thompson, 34; message, *Itasca* (via Samoa) to Earhart, June 23, 1937, NARA.
26. Message, Earhart to Black, 0720Z, 2216, June 26, 1937, NARA.
27. Thompson, 34.
28. Thompson, 1, 40.
29. Thompson, 46, 47.
30. Thompson, 52.
31. *Itasca* radio log, RLP2, 2216, July 4, 1937, NARA.
32. Thompson, 75.
33. Thompson, 105.
34. Thompson.
35. Thompson, 106.
36. Thompson, 9.

Chapter 34. Cover-Up

1. Marvin McIntyre, memorandum for the president, July 20, 1937, NARA.
2. Message, Putnam to SECNAV, 1645Z, July 23, 1937, NARA.
3. Message, SECNAV to Putnam, 1810Z, July 24, 1937, NARA.
4. Message, State to Embassy London, 0000Z, July 31, 1937, NARA.
5. Letter, Putnam to Marvin McIntyre, July 31, 1937, NARA.
6. Putnam to U.S. State Department, unknown time, August 1, 1937, NARA.
7. Dean S. Jennings, "Is Amelia Earhart Still Alive?" *Popular Aviation* (December 1939): 76.
8. Message, State to Putnam, 2133Z, August 31, 1937, NARA.

9. "Says Calls Were Not Earhart's," *New York Times*, July 26, 1937, 17.
10. Memorandum, J. F. Farley to commandant, December 14, 1937, NARA.
11. Articles of Incorporation, Amelia Earhart Foundation, article IIb, Purdue.
12. Charter of the Amelia Earhart Foundation, "An Unsolved Mystery," December 23, 1937. Purdue.
13. Memorandum from commander, San Francisco Division to commander, Hawaiian Section, March 22, 1938, 2, NARA.
14. Message, COMHAWSEC to COMFRANDIV, 1210, June 18, 1937, NARA.
15. Commander, San Francisco Division to commander, Hawaiian Section, 1.
16. Commander, San Francisco Division to commander, Hawaiian Section, 2.
17. Commander, San Francisco Division to commander, Hawaiian Section, 3.
18. Commander, San Francisco Division to commander, Hawaiian Section, 4.
19. Message, COMFRANDIV to *Itasca*, 2310Z, July 4, 1937, NARA.
20. Commander, San Francisco Division to commander, Hawaiian Section, 4.
21. Treasury Department communications instructions for the United States Coast Guard, 1930, NARA.
22. Transcription of Treasury Department staff meeting, May 13, 1938, FDR.
23. Undated note from Malvina "Tommy" Scheider on White House note paper, FDR.
24. Dwiggins, 127.
25. Undated note from Henry Morgenthau to Eleanor Roosevelt, FDR.
26. Undated note from Eleanor Roosevelt to Henry Morgenthau, FDR.
27. Letter from R. R. Waesche to A. Paul Mantz, July 21, 1938, NARA.
28. Dwiggins, 127.
29. Letter from Capt. Irving Johnson to Bessie Young, June 4, 1940, Earhart Collection, Purdue.
30. Johnson to Young.
31. Johnson to Young.

Chapter 35. Near-Misses

1. Stephen Luscombe, "Canton and Enderbury Islands," The British Empire, https://www.britishempire.co.uk/maproom/canton.htm.
2. Journal of Eric Bevington, Phoenix Islands Expedition 1937, TIGHAR.
3. Bevington journal.
4. Records of the Board of Trade Naval Court Apia, Samoa, December 9, 1929, TIGHAR.
5. Board of Trade Naval Court records.
6. Board of Trade Naval Court records.
7. Board of Trade Naval Court records.
8. Board of Trade Naval Court records.
9. Board of Trade Naval Court records.
10. Bevington journal.
11. Bevington journal.
12. Bevington journal.
13. "The Object Formerly Known as Nessie," 31.
14. H. E. Maude, administrative officer and native lands commissioner, "Colonization of the Phoenix Islands by the Surplus Population of the Gilbert and Ellice Islands," November 19, 1937, PRO.
15. H. E. Maude, officer-in-charge, Phoenix Islands Settlement Scheme, "Preliminary Progress Report," PRO.
16. Service record, Gerald Bernard Gallagher, WPA.
17. Letter from W. Gore, Colonial Administrative Service, to Sir Arthur Richards, High Commissioner, Western Pacific High Commission, July 5, 1937, WPA.
18. Squadron leader E. A. Gibson, Royal New Zealand Air Force, New Zealand Pacific Aviation Survey Expedition, "General Report on Activities and Results," February 29, 1939, NZAM.
19. "Not-So-Happy Trails," *TIGHAR Tracks* 16, no. 4 (December 2000): 2.
20. P. W. D. Wellington, "Pacific Islands Survey Expedition, Gardner Island," March 28, 1939, NZAM.
21. M. H. Hay, "Journal of the Pacific Islands Survey Expedition," undated, NZAM.
22. Hay.
23. Wellington.
24. Statement by Daniel Hamer, Master, SS *Norwich City*, December 9, 1937, TIGHAR.

25. Gerald V. Berger, conversation with Richard Gillespie, March 2000, TIGHAR.
26. Gerald V. Berger, conversation with Ron Bright, 2002, TIGHAR.
27. Progress Report, 16 November to 17 December 1939, commanding officer, USS *Bushnell*, to hydrographer, December 19, 1939, NHHC.

Chapter 36. The Castaway of Gardner Island

1. Gerald Gallagher, "Phoenix Islands Settlement Scheme, Quarterly Progress Report," January–March 1940, PRO.
2. Gallagher, "Phoenix Islands Settlement Scheme."
3. Gallagher, "Phoenix Islands Settlement Scheme."
4. John P. Mims, recollections during conversation with Richard Gillespie, transcribed by Mims' daughter Rosemary Fisk, March 2000, TIGHAR.
5. Emily Sikuli (through interpreter Foua Tofinga), interview with Tom King, Kristin Tague, and Barbara Norris, July 15, 1999, TIGHAR.
6. Sikuli interview.
7. Telegram from officer-in-charge, Phoenix Scheme, Beru Island, to labor overseer, Phoenix Scheme, Gardner Island, June 18, 1940, WPA.
8. Telegram from labor overseer, Phoenix Scheme, Gardner Island, to officer-in-charge, Phoenix Scheme, Beru Island, June 19, 1940, WPA.
9. Arthur Grimble, *Tungaru Traditions* (Honolulu: University of Hawaii Press, 1989), 77.
10. Telegram from officer-in-charge, Phoenix Scheme, Gardner Island, to resident commissioner, Ocean Island, September 23, 1940, Kiribati National Archives (KNA).
11. Telegram from officer-in-charge, Phoenix Scheme, Gardner Island, to administrative officer C.G.I.D. Tarawa, September 23, 1940, KNA.
12. Telegram from administrative officer C.G.I.D. Tarawa, to officer-in-charge, Phoenix Scheme, Gardner Island, September 30, 1940, KNA.
13. Eric Bevington, conversation with Richard Gillespie, January 1992, TIGHAR.
14. Western Pacific High Commission, service records for Barley and Holland, 1940, WPA.
15. Telegram from acting resident commissioner, Gilbert and Ellice Islands Colony (G&EIC), to high commissioner, October 1, 1940, WPA.
16. Telegram from resident commissioner, G&EIC Ocean Island, to officer-in-charge, Phoenix Scheme, Gardner Island, October 1, 1940, WPA.
17. Telegram from officer-in-charge, Phoenix Scheme, Gardner Island, to resident commissioner, G&EIC Ocean Island, October 6, 1940, WPA.
18. "San Diegan Bares Clue to Earhart Fate," A-4.
19. WPHC file M. P. no. 4439 (G. & E.) 1940, Subject—Skeleton, Human: Finding of, on Gardner Island, October 9, 1940, WPA.
20. Minute to WPHC file M. P. no. 4439 (G. & E.).
21. WPHC Service History, Duncan Campbell McEwen Macpherson, obituary in *British Medical Journal*, August 14, 1943, WPA.
22. Minute to WPHC file M. P. no. 4439 (G. & E.).
23. Telegram from Vaskess to Gallagher, October 15, 1940, WPA.
24. Telegram from Vaskess to resident commissioner, October 15, 1940, WPA.
25. Telegram from Gallagher to Vaskess, October 17, 1940, WPA.
26. Minute to WPHC File 4439 from D. C. M. Macpherson, October 23, 1940, WPA.
27. Minute to WPHC File 4439 from high commissioner, October 26, 1940, WPA.
28. Telegram from Vaskess to Gallagher, October 26, 1940, WPA.
29. Note in WPHC File 4439 from Dr. Kingsley Steenson to Secretary Vaskess, July 1, 1941, WPA.
30. Letter from Gallagher to Vaskess, December 27, 1940, WPA.
31. Gallagher, "Ninth Quarterly Progress Report."
32. Gallagher.
33. Telegram from Lindsay Isaac, medical officer, Tarawa Island, to the officer-in-charge, Phoenix Islands, February 6, 1941, WPA.

Chapter 37. Losing Amelia

1. Telegram from medical officer, Tarawa Island, to the officer-in-charge, Phoenix Scheme, Gardner Island, February 6, 1941, KNA.
2. Letter from Eric Bevington to Richard Gillespie, July 29, 1997, TIGHAR.
3. Telegram from resident commissioner, Ocean Island, to officer-in-charge, Phoenix Scheme, Gardner Island, February 7, 1941, WPA.
4. Telegram from resident commissioner, G&EIC, to high commissioner, February 11, 1941, WPA.
5. Telegram from senior medical officer, Central Hospital, Tarawa, to officer-in-charge, Phoenix Islands Scheme, Gardner Island, February 11, 1941, KNA.
6. Telegram from officer-in-charge, Phoenix Islands Scheme, Gardner Island, to senior medical officer, Central Hospital, Tarawa, February 11, 1941, KNA.
7. Officer-in-charge to senior medical officer.
8. Telegram from high commissioner to resident commissioner, G&EIC, February 14, 1941, WPA.
9. Telegram from resident commissioner, G&EIC, to high commissioner, February 17, 1941, WPA.
10. Telegram from senior medical officer, Central Hospital, Tarawa, to officer-in-charge, Phoenix Islands Scheme, Gardner Island, February 14, 1941, KNA.
11. Minute in WPHC File 4439 from HV to assistant secretary, March 28, 1941, WPA.
12. Note in WPHC File 4439 from assistant secretary to central medical authority, March 31, 1941, WPA.
13. Margaret W. Guthrie, *Misi Utu: Dr. D. W. Hoodless and the Development of Medical Education in the South Pacific* (Suva, Fiji: Institute of Pacific Studies, 1979), 31–40.
14. D. W. Hoodless, "Report on Portion of a Human Skeleton," WPHC File 4439, April 4, 1941, WPA.
15. Karen Ramey Burns, "Amelia Earhart's Bones and Shoes," report to the American Anthropological Association, December 5, 1998, TIGHAR.
16. Richard L. Jantz, "Amelia Earhart and the Nikumaroro Bones: A 1941 Analysis versus Modern Quantitative Techniques," *Forensic Anthropology* 1, no. 2 (Spring 2018): 1–16.
17. Hoodless report.
18. Note to WPHC File 4439 from D. W. Hoodless to Dr. Macpherson, April 5, 1941, WPA.
19. Note to WPHC File 4439 from Dr. Macpherson to Mr. Secretary, April 7, 1941, WPA.
20. Hoodless report.
21. Minute to WPHC File 4439 from D. C. M. Macpherson, October 23, 1940, WPA.
22. Note to WPHC File 4439 from Secretary Vaskess to Sir Harry Luke, April 11, 1941, WPA.
23. Note to WPHC File 4439 from Sir Harry Luke to Secretary Vaskess, April 12, 1941, WPA.
24. Note to WPHC File 4439 from D. C. M. Macpherson to Secretary Vaskess, April 18, 1941, WPA.
25. Telegram from secretary, WPHC, to officer-in-charge, Phoenix Scheme, Gardner Island, April 28, 1941, WPA.
26. Telegram from officer-in-charge, Phoenix Scheme, Gardner Island, to secretary, WPHC, April 28, 1941, WPA.
27. Note in WPHC File 4439 from Secretary Vaskess to Commander Nasmyth, June 6, 1941, WPA.
28. Note in WPHC File 4439 from Sir Harry Luke to Secretary Vaskess, WPA.
29. Note in WPHC File 4439, June 9, 1941, WPA.
30. WPHC service history, Kingsley Rupert Steenson, MB ChB, WPA.
31. Note in WPHC File 4439 from Dr. Kingsley Steenson to Secretary Vaskess, July 1, 1941, WPA.
32. Telegram from officer-in-charge, Phoenix Scheme, Gardner Island, to resident commissioner, G&EIC Ocean Island, October 6, 1940, WPA.
33. Note to WPHC File 4439 by Gerald Gallagher, July 3, 1941, WPA.
34. "The Battle of Nauru," Military History Now, January 24, 2014 https://militaryhistorynow.com/2014/01/24/the-battle-of-nauru-nazi-germanys-forgotten-foray-into-the-pacific/.
35. Note from high commissioner to secretary, August 8, 1941, WPA.
36. Note from P. D. Macdonald to secretary, August 11, 1941, WPA.
37. Note to WPHC File 4439 from Sir Harry Luke to Secretary Vaskess, April 12, 1941, WPA.
38. Telegram from Dr. D. C. M. Macpherson, Gardner Island, to secretary, Western Pacific High Commission, September 24, 1941, WPA.
39. Telegram from Dr. D. C. M. Macpherson, Gardner Island, to high commissioner, September 26, 1941, WPA.
40. Macpherson to high commissioner.
41. Telegram from Dr. D. C. M. Macpherson, Gardner Island, to high commissioner, September 27, 1941, WPA.

42. Telegram from high commissioner to secretary of state, September 27, 1941, WPA.
43. Letter and sketch from D. W. Wernham, acting officer-in-charge, Phoenix Islands Settlement Scheme, to the secretary, Western Pacific High Commission, June 17, 1942, WPA.
44. Telegram to high commissioner, Suva, from resident commissioner, Tarawa, March 25, 1949, WPA.
45. Eric Bevington, conversation with Richard Gillespie, January 1992, TIGHAR.

Chapter 38. Captured

1. Mary S. Lovell, *The Sound of Wings: The Life of Amelia Earhart* (New York: St. Martin's Press, 1989), 302.
2. Undated handwritten note, Purdue.
3. Earhart, *Last Flight*, 108.
4. Earhart, *Last Flight*, 217.
5. "Mrs. Putnam at Darwin," Sydney, Australia, newspaper (name unknown), June 28, 1937, Purdue.
6. Putnam, *Soaring Wings*, 290.
7. *Flight for Freedom* (1943), IMDb, https://www.imdb.com/title/tt0035888/.
8. Lovell, 321.
9. "LORAN Unit 92, Gardner Island," https://www.loran-history.info/Gardner_Island/gardner.htm.
10. U.S. Naval Air Facility, Canton Island, flight plan for PATSU 2-2 Aircraft, January 10, 1945, TIGHAR.
11. U.S. Naval Air Facility.
12. Letter to TIGHAR from Dr. John Mims, March 1995, TIGHAR.
13. Letter to Richard Gillespie from Dr. John Mims, April 29, 1995, TIGHAR.
14. Mims recollections.
15. Mims recollections.
16. Glen Geisinger, telephone interview by Richard Gillespie, August 23, 2001, TIGHAR.
17. Leslie Wiltshire, interview by Richard Gillespie, April 14, 2017, TIGHAR.
18. "Amelia Earhart Shot by Japanese: Matean," *San Mateo Times*, May 27, 1960, 1.
19. "Amelia Earhart Shot by Japanese."
20. Fred Goerner, *The Search for Amelia Earhart* (New York: Doubleday and Company, 1966), 2.
21. Goerner, 45.
22. Goerner, 67.
23. Goerner, 68.
24. Goerner, 68.
25. Goerner, 70.
26. "San Diegan Bares Clue to Earhart Fate," A-4.
27. "San Diegan Bares Clue."
28. Letter from Leo Bowler to British colonial secretary, Canton Island, July 18, 1960, KNA.
29. Letter from information officer, Bairiki, Tarawa, to district commissioner, Canton Island, September 26, 1960, KNA.
30. Letter from D. J. Knobbs, district commissioner, to Leo Bowler, city editor, *San Diego Tribune*, KNA.
31. "The Colonization of the Phoenix Islands," *The Journal of the Polynesian Society* 61, no. 1/2 (March and June 1952), 62–89.
32. Letter from Fred Goerner to Richard Gillespie, March 1, 1990, TIGHAR.

Chapter 39. Backlash

1. Goerner, 175.
2. Goerner, 284.
3. Goerner, 330.
4. Goerner, 315.
5. Letter from Fred Goerner to Rob Gerth, April 13, 1989, TIGHAR.
6. Thomas E. Devine, *Eyewitness: The Amelia Earhart Incident* (Berkeley, CA: Renaissance House, 1987), 41.
7. T. C. "Buddy" Brennan, *Witness to the Execution: The Odyssey of Amelia Earhart* (Berkeley, CA: Renaissance House, 1988), 154.
8. Joe Klaas, *Amelia Earhart Lives: A Trip Through Intrigue to Find America's First Lady of Mystery* (New York: McGraw-Hill Book Co., 1970), 169.

9. Handwritten copy of letter from John Hathaway to Fred Goerner, July 1970, TIGHAR.
10. Letter from Fred Goerner to John Hathaway, August 21, 1970, TIGHAR.
11. Handwritten copy of letter from John Hathaway to Fred Goerner, September 1, 1970, TIGHAR.
12. Letter from Fred Goerner to John Hathaway, September 4, 1970, TIGHAR.
13. Letter from Frederick Hooven to Fred Goerner, December 5, 1966, TIGHAR.
14. Frederick J. Hooven, "Amelia Earhart's Last Flight," June 1982, NASM.
15. Hooven.
16. Goerner to Gerth, April 13, 1989.
17. Elgen Long, "Crash and Sank Theory," https://www.elgenlong.com/earhart/crash-and-sank.html.

Chapter 40. The Earhart Project

1. Letter from Thomas Gannon to TIGHAR, April 1988.
2. Letter from Pat Thrasher to Thomas Gannon, April 1988, TIGHAR.
3. Hooven.
4. Roy Blay, "Amelia Earhart's Last Flight," Lockheed *Horizons*, May 1988.
5. Letter from Richard Evans to Pat Thrasher, August 25, 1990, TIGHAR.
6. Interviews with Herb Moffitt, November 7, 1990, and February 10, 1991, TIGHAR.
7. "San Diegan Bares Clue," A-4.

Chapter 41. Good Data and Good Luck

1. Jacobson database, TIGHAR.
2. Telegram from W. T. Miller to Frank Griffin, July 21, 1937, NARA.
3. Telegram from W. T. Miller to Frank Griffin, July 27, 1937, NARA.
4. Telegram from W. T. Miller to Frank Griffin, July 22, 1937, NARA.
5. Telegram from Earhart to *New York Herald Tribune*, July 1, 1937, Purdue.
6. Telegram from Frank Griffin to Eric Chater, July 22, 1937, TIGHAR.
7. Letter from Eric Chater to Frank Griffin, July 25, 1937, TIGHAR.
8. Chater to Griffin.
9. Robert L. Brandenburg, "The Radio Riddle," 2006, TIGHAR.
10. Brandenburg, "Analysis of Radio Direction Finder Bearings."
11. *Itasca* radio log, 0245–0248, July 2, 1937, NARA.
12. Thompson report, 39.
13. Handwritten note by James Carey, July 2, 1937, TIGHAR.
14. Richard Gillespie, "Last Words," April 2007, TIGHAR.
15. Carey diary, TIGHAR.
16. Letter from Harry Maude to Richard Gillespie, May 4, 1990, TIGHAR.
17. Eric Bevington, conversation with Richard Gillespie, January 1992, TIGHAR.
18. Email from Peter McQuarrie to Richard Gillespie, June 27, 1997, TIGHAR.
19. Telegram from officer-in-charge, Phoenix Scheme, to ag. administrative officer, CGID, September 23, 1940, KNA.
20. Karen R. Burns, Richard L. Jantz, Thomas F. King, and Richard E. Gillespie, "Amelia Earhart's Bones and Shoes: Current Anthropological Perspectives on an Historical Mystery," December 5, 1998, TIGHAR.
21. Burns et al.
22. Richard E. Wright and Pamela Cross, "The Nikumaroro Bones Controversy," *Journal of Archaeological Science*, May 2015.
23. Jantz, "Amelia Earhart and the Nikumaroro Bones."
24. Telegram from officer-in-charge, Phoenix Scheme, to secretary, WPHC, October 17, 1940, WPA.
25. Letter from Gerald B. Gallagher, officer-in-charge, Phoenix Scheme, to WPHC, December 27, 1940, WPA.
26. Joseph Cerniglia, "A Notion of a Lotion: Artifact 2-8-S2a," February 13, 2013, TIGHAR.
27. "Archaeological Update," *TIGHAR Tracks* 24, no. 4 (October 2008).
28. Joseph Cerniglia, "A Freckle in Time," September 2013, TIGHAR.
29. Item 24, Electra inventory, March 26, 1937, Luke Field, Hawaii, NARA.

Chapter 42. Red Herrings and Wild Geese

1. T.O. No. 01-5-7 AAF Interchangeable Parts List, B-24 D & J. NARA.
2. Letter from Fred Noonan to P. V. H. Weems, May 11, 1935, published in *Popular Aviation*, May 1938.
3. Amelia Earhart Search Forum/Join the Search/"Re: Who did the USN give its surplus sextants to after WWI?" Reply 11, October 31, 2012, TIGHAR.
4. Memo from commanding officer, USS *Bushnell*, to superintendent, Naval Observatory, November 15, 1938, NARA.
5. Commanding officer memo.
6. Note from Sir Harry Luke to Secretary Vaskess, minutes of WPHC File 4439, April 4, 1941, WPA.

Chapter 43. Chasing the Plane

1. "First Radio Contact with Miss Earhart Made by Springs Boy," *Rock Springs Rocket*, July 6–7, 1937, 1.
2. Letter to TIGHAR from Dr. John Mims, March 1995, TIGHAR.
3. National Transportation Safety Board senior metallurgist Joseph Epperson, consultation with Richard Gillespie, June 1995, TIGHAR.
4. Tapania Taeke, interview with Richard Gillespie and Kenton Spading, Funafuti, Tuvalu, March 1997, TIGHAR.
5. Emily Sikuli (through interpreter Foua Tofinga), interview with Tom King, Kristin Tague, and Barbara Norris, July 15, 1999, TIGHAR.
6. Betty's Notebook, TIGHAR.
7. "Plane's Letters Heard on Radio at Los Angeles," *New York Herald Tribune*, July 5, 1937, 2.
8. "PIM Readers Help in Earhart Search," *Pacific Islands Monthly*, December 1991.
9. Email from James Loi to Richard Gillespie, August 2, 2011, TIGHAR.
10. Email from Richard Gillespie to James Loi, August 10, 2011, TIGHAR.
11. Verbal briefing at State Department, November 15, 2011, as described in Richard Gillespie, email to Kurt Campbell, February 17, 2012, TIGHAR.
12. State Department briefing.
13. State Department briefing.
14. Email from James Loi to Richard Gillespie, February 17, 2012, TIGHAR.
15. Email from Richard Gillespie to James Loi, February 17, 2012, TIGHAR.
16. Loi to Gillespie.
17. Gillespie to Loi.
18. Loi to Gillespie.
19. Email from Richard Gillespie to James Loi, February 18, 2012, TIGHAR.
20. Email from James Loi to Richard Gillespie, February 19, 2012, TIGHAR.
21. Email from Richard Gillespie to Bill Carter, February 19, 2012, TIGHAR.

Chapter 44. Missing the Plane

1. Richard Gillespie, field notes, July 17, 2012, TIGHAR.
2. Message, Putnam to CNO, 0042Z, July 3, 1937, NARA.
3. Email from Robert L. Brandenburg to Richard Gillespie, February 1, 2013, TIGHAR.
4. Brandenburg to Gillespie.
5. "Ballard Out to Solve Earhart Puzzle." Divernet, August 2, 2019, https://divernet.com/scuba-news/ballard-out-to-solve-earhart-puzzle/.
6. Reilly-McGreen, Marybeth. "The Explorer and the Aviator," University of Rhode Island, https://www.uri.edu/features/the-explorer-and-the-aviator/.

Chapter 45. Changing Mystery to History

1. "Report of the Investigating Board, Sikorsky S-42B 'Samoan Clipper,'" Bureau of Air Commerce, April 1, 1938, NARA.
2. "Report of Earhart Search," commander, *Lexington* group, July 20, 1937, 8, NARA.
3. Memorandum to registration section, Jesse W. Langford, chief, accident analysis section, Bureau of Air Commerce, May 5, 1938, FAA.

4. *Itasca* radio log, RLP2, 1824, July 2, 1937, NARA.
5. Brandenburg, "Post-Loss Signals Statistics."
6. *Itasca* radio log, RLP2, 2216, July 4, 1937, NARA.
7. Brandenburg, "Post-Loss Signals Statistics."
8. Brandenburg, "Analysis of Radio Direction Finder Bearings."
9. Gillespie and Brandenburg, "Post-Loss Radio Signals Catalog and Analysis 2.0," 8.
10. Gillespie and Brandenburg.
11. Jantz, "Amelia Earhart and the Nikumaroro Bones."
12. Richard Jantz, email to Richard Gillespie, November 16, 2022, TIGHAR.
13. Amelia Earhart, speech in Fort Wayne, Indiana, March 21, 1935, Doris Rich papers, NASM.
14. Conversation with Richard Gillespie, August 14, 2021, TIGHAR.

Selected Bibliography

Books

Backus, Jean. *Letters from Amelia*. Boston: Beacon Press, 1982.

Berne List. *List of Coast Stations and Ship Stations*. Berne, Switzerland: Bureau of International Telecommunication Union, 1937.

Bevington, Eric R. *The Things We Do for England—If Only England Knew!* Hampshire, UK: Acorn Bookworks, 1990.

Brennan, T. C. "Buddy." *Witness to the Execution: The Odyssey of Amelia Earhart*. Berkeley, CA: Renaissance House, 1988.

Bryan, Edwin H., Jr. *American Polynesia and the Hawaiian Chain*. Honolulu, HI: Tongg Publishing Co., 1942.

Butler, Susan. *East to the Dawn: The Life of Amelia Earhart*. Reading, MA: Addison-Wesley, 1997.

Collins, A. Frederick. *The Radio Amateur's Handbook*, 14th ed. West Hartford, CT: American Radio Relay Leagues, 1937.

Devine, Thomas E. *Eyewitness: The Amelia Earhart Incident*. Berkeley, CA: Renaissance House, 1987.

Dwiggins, Don. *Hollywood Pilot: The Biography of Paul Mantz*. New York: Doubleday, 1967.

Earhart, Amelia. *The Fun of It*. New York: Brewer, Warren, and Putnam, 1932.

———. *Last Flight*. New York: Harcourt Brace, 1937.

Françillon, René. *Lockheed Aircraft Since 1913*. Annapolis, MD: Naval Institute Press, 1987.

Freehafer, Ruth W. *R. B. Stewart and Purdue University*. Lafayette, IN: Purdue University Press, 1983.

Gillespie, Ric. *Finding Amelia*. Annapolis, MD: Naval Institute Press, 2006.

Goerner, Fred. *The Search for Amelia Earhart*. New York: Doubleday and Company, 1966.

Grimble, Arthur. *Tungaru Traditions*. Honolulu: University of Hawaii Press, 1989.

Grooch, William S. *From Crate to Clipper*. New York: Longman, Green, and Co., 1939.

Guthrie, Margaret W. *Misi Utu: Dr. D. W. Hoodless and the Development of Medical Education in the South Pacific*. Suva, Fiji: Institute of Pacific Studies, 1979.

Klaas, Joe. *Amelia Earhart Lives: A Trip Through Intrigue to Find America's First Lady of Mystery*. New York: McGraw-Hill Book Co., 1970.

Krupnick, Jon E. *Pan American's Pacific Pioneers*. Missoula, MT: Pictorial Histories Publishing Co., 2000.

Leuteritz, Hugo. Unpublished autobiography. Miami: Pan American Historical Foundation, undated.

Lindbergh, Charles. *The Spirit of St. Louis*. New York: Charles Scribner's Sons, 1953.

Long, Elgen, and Long, Marie. *Amelia Earhart: The Mystery Solved*. New York: Simon and Schuster, 1999.

Lovell, Mary S. *The Sound of Wings*. New York: St. Martin's Press, 1989.

Morrissey, Muriel Earhart, and Carol Osborne. *Amelia, My Courageous Sister*. Santa Clara, CA: Osborne Publishers, Inc., 1987.

O'Brien, Keith. *Fly Girls: How Five Daring Women Defied All Odds and Made Aviation History*. New York: Mariner Books, 2018.

Putnam, George Palmer. *Soaring Wings*. New York: Harcourt Brace, 1939.

Rich, Doris L. *Amelia Earhart: A Biography*. Washington, DC: Smithsonian Institution Scholarly Press, 1966.

Schultz, Barbara H. *Pancho: The Biography of Florence Lowe Barnes*. Lancaster, CA: Little Buttes Publishing Co., 1996.

Skaggs, Jimmy M. *The Great Guano Rush: Entrepreneurs and American Overseas Expansion.* New York: St. Martin's Press, 1994.

Smith, Elinor. *Aviatrix.* New York: Harcourt Brace Jovanovich, 1981.

Wohl, Robert. *A Passion for Wings: Aviation and the Western Imagination, 1908–1918.* New Haven and London: Yale University Press, 1994.

Journals and Magazines

Blay, Roy. "Amelia Earhart's Last Flight." *Lockheed Horizons,* May 1988.

Brandenburg, Robert L. "Post-loss Radio Signals Catalog and Analysis 2.0." *TIGHAR Tracks* 34, no. 2 (August 2018).

Cross, Pamela, and Richard E. Wright. "The Nikumaroro Bones Controversy." *Journal of Archaeological Science* 3 (September 2015).

Dye, Ira. "Liberty Lost Pursuing a Legend." *Naval History* 11, no. 3 (May–June 1997).

"Earhart: First Woman to Fly 2,408 Miles Over the Pacific." *Newsweek Magazine,* January 1935.

Emmert, Thomas M., and William T. Larkins. "Lockheed's Model 10 Electra." *Journal of the American Aviation Historical Society,* Summer 1978.

Jantz. Richard L. "Amelia Earhart and the Nikumaroro Bones: A 1941 Analysis versus Modern Quantitative Techniques." *Forensic Anthropology* 1, no. 2 (February 2018).

Jennings, Dean S. "Is Amelia Earhart Still Alive?" *Popular Aviation,* December 1, 1939.

Maude, H. E. "Colonization of the Phoenix Islands." *Journal of the Polynesian Society* 61 (March and June 1952).

"Mourning Becomes Electra." *Time* magazine, March 29, 1937.

North, David. "Back to Nikumaroro." *Pacific Islands Monthly* 61, no. 12 (December 1991).

Riley, John P. "The Earhart Tragedy: Old Mystery, New Hypothesis." *Naval History* 14, no. 2 (August 2000).

Wilds, Thomas. "How Japan Fortified the Mandated Islands." U.S. Naval Institute *Proceedings* 81, no. 4 (April 1955).

Newspapers

Albuquerque Journal, Albuquerque, NM

Ames Daily Tribune, Ames, IA

Ashland Daily Independent, Ashland, KY

Atlanta Constitution, Atlanta, GA

Bakersfield Californian, Bakersfield, CA

Berkeley Daily Gazette, Berkeley, CA

Berkshire Evening Eagle, Pittsfield, MA

Boston Globe, Boston, MA

Cleveland Press, Cleveland, OH

Danville Bee, Danville, VA

Evening Star, Cleveland, OH

Fresno Bee, Fresno, CA

Honolulu Star-Bulletin, Honolulu, HI

Los Angeles Times, Los Angeles, CA

Miami Herald, Miami, FL

Miami News, Miami, OK

Napa Daily Journal, Napa, CA

New Castle News, New Castle, PA

New York Herald Tribune, New York, NY

New York Times, New York, NY

Oakland Tribune, Oakland, CA

Rock Springs Rocket, Rock Springs, WY

Salt Lake Tribune, Salt Lake City, UT

San Diego Tribune, San Diego, CA

San Mateo Times, San Mateo, CA

Sedalia Democrat, Sedalia, MO
Syracuse Herald, Syracuse, NY
Toronto Daily Star, Toronto, ON
Vernon Daily Record, Vernon, TX
Washington Post, Washington, DC
Wyoming Tribune Eagle, Cheyenne, WY

Websites

"Ballard Out to Solve Earhart Puzzle." Divernet, August 2, 2019, https://divernet.com/scuba-news/ballard-out -to-solve-earhart-puzzle/.

"The Battle of Nauru." Military History Now, https://militaryhistorynow.com/2014/01/24/the-battle-of-na uru-nazi-germanys-forgotten-foray-into-the-pacific/.

"The Earhart Project." TIGHAR: The International Group for Historic Aircraft Recovery, https://tighar.org /Projects/Earhart/AEdescr.html. Historical documents, reports, analyses of artifacts, correspondence, and memos from 1936 and 1937; ships' logs and radio logs from the search; database of government radio messages concerning Earhart between January 1, 1937, and May 9, 1938; reports on field work and research.

"Elmer C. McLeod Photograph and Logbook Collection." Davis-Monthan Aviation Field Register, Tucson, AZ, https://dmairfield.org/people/mcleod_ed/index.html.

Long, Elgen. "Crash and Sank Theory." Elgen Long website, https://www.elgenlong.com/earhart/crash-and -sank.html.

"LORAN Unit 92, Gardner Island." Loran History, https://www.loran-history.info/Gardner_Island/gardner.htm.

Luscombe, Stephen. "Canton and Enderbury Islands." The British Empire, https://www.britishempire.co.uk /maproom/canton.htm.

Olsen, Natalie. "What is Protein Poisoning?" Healthline, updated September 17, 2018, https://www.health line.com/health/protein-poisoning#:~:text=Protein%20poisoning%20is%20when%20the,rabbit %2C%20without%20consuming%20other%20nutrients."https://www.healthline.com/health/protein -poisoning#:~:text=Protein%20poisoning%20is%20when%20the,rabbit%2C%20without%20con suming%20other%20nutrients

Reilly-McGreen, Marybeth. "The Explorer and the Aviator," University of Rhode Island, https://www.uri.edu /features/the-explorer-and-the-aviator/.

"SAR Results Worksheet." Civil Air Patrol: U.S. Air Force Auxiliary, last updated August 2009, https://www .gocivilairpatrol.com/media/cms/F104a_9C28EC8852937.pdf.

Archival Resources

Doris Rich Papers, National Air and Space Museum Archive, Washington, DC
Federal Aviation Administration records, Oklahoma City, OK
Franklin D. Roosevelt Library, Hyde Park, NY
Kiribati National Archives, Tarawa, Republic of Kiribati
National Archives and Records Administration, Washington, DC, and San Bruno, CA
Naval History and Heritage Command, https://www.history.navy.mil
Pan American Historical Foundation, Alameda, CA
Public Records Office, Kew, London, UK
Purdue University Archives and E-Archives, holding extensive correspondence between George Palmer Putnam and the University, and a collection of his papers
Royal New Zealand Air Force Museum, Christchurch, NZ
Schlesinger Library, Radcliffe College, Cambridge, MA
University of California Los Angeles Film and Video Collections
University of Wyoming American Heritage Center
Western Pacific High Commission Archives, University of Auckland, NZ

The TIGHAR Literary Guild

This book would not have been possible without the support of the individual TIGHAR members listed here who, over a period of ten years, made financial contributions to cover the thousands of hours it took to pull together the many threads of research and weave from them the narrative that tells the true story of the Amelia Earhart tragedy.

Guido Almekinders
Clifford T. Argue
John Balderston
Dag Henry Bering
Robert Bouchard
Grant Bruckmeier
Jason Byrd
Troy Carmichael
Camila Carter
Joseph Cerniglia
Robert H. Clinton
Mike Cord
Harbert W. Davenport
Daniel DiCenso
Barry and Cindy Dreher
James Dyson
Robert Evans
James Fischer
Garry C. Francis
Craig Fuller
Richard B. Gifford
Robert E. Gillespie
Stephen Gunderson
Vernon L. Hammersley
Linda Hasert

Dean Andrea
John F. Atwill
Douglass D. Benson
Margaret Betchart
Daniel R. Brown
David R. Bunting
Renato Cachina
Douglas M. Carson
Quinn Carter
Jack Chastain
Carolea C. Clothier
Garry Cratt
Richard E. Davis
James Dietterich
Bruce Drewett
Scott Elmore
Ron M. Feder
Thomas Flood
Kenneth Frankel
Steve Gardetto
Garred Giles
Tim Gilmartin
Harold Hahn
Robert Hanrahan
D. J. Henry

Rick Apostol
Jack Balch
Bob Benway
Peter Boor
Kathleen Brown
Tarn Burton
Carlos C. Campino
Bill Carter
Robert Castro
John Clauss
Robert Conner
Amy Damon
Dianne DeCamp
Barbara Ditman
Jeanne Durrer
Barbara Erb
Kittie Fenlason
Christopher C. Foltz
Clyde H. Freeman
Teri Hamilton Garrett
Richard T. Gillespie
Jonathan L. Greenberg
Jerry Hamilton
Brian Harrison
Heather A. Heusser

Craig A. Hoehne

Catherine Holloway

Randy Jacobson

David Jeane

Dawn Johnson

Robert L. Johnson III

Alan R. Kahn

Stephen R. Kelly

Stephen Klein

Andrew Kurman

Ernie LeRoy

Dr. Tommy L. Love

Ayn Maddox

Jeffrey Martin

Lydia A. McCallister

Dennis O. McGee

D. Scott McKenzie

Jane M. Morse

Aaron Olding

Matt Packard

Paul E. Penwell

Robert C. Phillips

John Pratt

John F. Rippinger

Mark Rodney

Robert Runge

Frank Sauerwald

Lonnie Schorer

Jeffrey D. Shaffer

Vic Skirmants

Adam Snyder

Laurie Stapleton

Ralph Symington

James Thompson

Curtis Tomlinson

Stephen Vadas Ph.D., P.E.

Charles Walker

Barry Weisman

C. Bart and Diane Whitehouse

Alexander J. Williams

David Work

Axel Hoewt

Karen Hoy

Frans Janson

Lynn Jencon

Robert I. Johnson

Ricker Jones

George Kastner

Karyn King

Richard Klingenberger

Gene Kuzminski

James Linder

Darleen and Phil Lunde

Roger Maier

Phil Martin

Andrew McComas

Christopher McGraw

David Meunier

Norris Noe

Hilary C. Olson

Ted Parsons

Reinaldo Perez

Michael S. Potts

John Quint

Stephen Roberts

Jonathan Romig

Arthur Rypinski

Thomas E. Sayers

Hilary Schweiso

Morley Shamblen

Timothy A. Smith

Kenton Spading

André Stern

Dave Tateosian

William T. Thursby

William G. Torgerson

Joseph Van Blargan

Col. Patricia Webb

Walter Weiss

Ed Whitson

Jean D. Wirth

James Zanella

Barry Hogrefe

Philip Ingraham

Richard L. Jantz

Kurt Johansen

Eugene Johnson

William Jones

James N. Kellen

Thomas F. King

Dutch Kluge

Renato V. LaRocca

Richard A. Lindsey

Ian MacKay

William M. Mangus

Don Mayborn

Thomas M. McCulloch

Andrew M. McKenna

Samuel Miller

Craig O'Mara

Gary Pace

Lee Paynter

Mihai Petrescu

Chris Powell

William A. and Carolin S. Renz

Patrick N. Robinson

Laurie Rubin

Leonid Sagalovsky

Jeffrey Schlader

Thomas Seiler

Capt. S. Martin Shelton

Bob Smith

Doug Stalnaker

Jim Swanik

Jack Thompson

Bryan Tolin

Lauren Travis

Marc Vepraskas

Curt Weil

John West

Joshua Whitson

Sheldon Wong

Kimberly Zimmerman

Index

Italicized page references indicate photos or maps.

About the Author

The son of a decorated World War II pilot, **Richard E. Gillespie** learned to fly while he was still in high school. After graduating from the State University of New York at Oswego with a BA in history, he flew professionally until going on active duty with the U.S. Army in 1970. Gillespie completed infantry officer candidate school and attended the Army's advanced radio systems school before being assigned to the First Cavalry Division, where he served as communications officer for an aviation battalion. Following his military service, he embarked on a career as an aviation risk manager and accident investigator for the aviation insurance industry. Servicing his clients throughout the northeastern United States, he logged many thousands of hours in single and twin-engined light aircraft, often with minimal avionics, in all kinds of weather. As Ric says, "It was a pretty good simulation of 1930s flying." In 1985 he left the insurance business and, with his wife Patricia Thrasher, founded The International Group for Historic Aircraft Recovery. Known by its acronym TIGHAR (pronounced *tiger*), the nonprofit foundation has an international membership of several hundred scholars, scientists, and enthusiasts whose volunteer expertise and financial contributions support the organization's mission to change aviation mysteries to history through applied science. Since launching TIGHAR's investigation of the Earhart disappearance in 1988, Ric has led twelve expeditions to the Phoenix Islands and multiple archival research trips to the United Kingdom, New Zealand, and Kiribati. Ric Gillespie's writings on the Earhart disappearance have appeared in the organization's journal *TIGHAR Tracks* and in the U.S. Naval Institute's *Proceedings* and *Naval History* magazines. His book, *Finding Amelia: The True Story of the Earhart Disappearance*, was published by the Naval Institute Press in 2006.

For TIGHAR's extensive archive of Earhart source material, information about other TIGHAR investigations, and the benefits of TIGHAR membership, visit the TIGHAR website at tighar.org.